SULLIVAN

Adobe
Illustrator 10

A STEP-BY-STEP APPROACH

Morton Publishing Company
925 W. Kenyon Avenue, Unit 12
Englewood, CO 80110
http://www.morton-pub.com

Joanne Saliger

Ginny McDonald

About the Authors

Joanne Saliger began working as a typesetter in 1963 and has owned a graphics/typesetting business since 1978, producing college textbooks, brochures, catalogs, and other printed materials. She began using Adobe Illustrator 88 on the Macintosh platform in 1988. She is the author of *QuarkXPress 4.0: A Step-by-Step Approach*.

Ginny McDonald graduated from Moore College of Art & Design, Philadelphia, PA, with a BFA degree in Illustration. She has been a designer and illustrator for the past 30 years and proficient in Adobe Illustrator since Version 88 was released in 1988. She has won awards for her illustration and design from the Rocky Mountain Chapter of the Society for Technical Communication and the Business Marketing Association in Denver, CO. Her work has appeared in *Adobe Acrobat 5.0 Classroom in a Book*.

Cover design by Kevin Kertz, Kertz Design Studio, Parker, CO (www.kertzdesign.com)

The illustration of the Mink in Practice Activity 5-1 is copyrighted by Michael Schenk and it cannot be used or reproduced without first obtaining written permission.

PANTONE® and PANTONE MATCHING SYSTEM® are the property of Pantone, Inc.

Trumatch®, Trumatch Swatching System®, and Trumatch System® are trademarks of TRUMATCH, Inc.

All other trademarks or registered trademarks are the properties of their respective owners.

First Edition
Copyright © 2003 by Morton Publishing Company

ISBN 0-89582-561-9

Printed in the United States of America

10   9   8   7   6   5   4   3   2   1

Preface

Adobe® Illustrator® 10 is the most powerful computer-based art production tool you can use. It's rapidly becoming the industry standard. Using its precision tools, you can obtain professional-quality results when creating printed materials, multimedia projects, and online graphics for Web pages.

The key to learning is doing. The secret to mastering Adobe Illustrator is practice and experimentation. The activities within the text and the exercises at the end of the chapters will give you a minimum of practice reinforcing each concept. Students may not remember how to do all the procedures to create their artwork, but they will remember that they did it in class so they can do it again.

Teaching students how to create artwork in Illustrator 10 is the purpose of this book. It is not the purpose of this book to teach students to be artists. Most activities within the chapters don't actually create anything. I don't want students to be so worried about creating an identifiable object that they miss the purpose of the lesson — which is simply to demonstrate how a tool or command works.

Activities are designed to demonstrate use of the tools or commands discussed in the chapter. If students have trouble with completing an activity, they should be encouraged to repeat it until they understand the tools and commands demonstrated in that activity. In most cases artwork will not be completed in the in-chapter activities. That's done in the Practice Activities and Exercises at the end of the chapters.

The Adobe Illustrator interface functions almost the same on both the Macintosh and the Windows platforms. The appearance of dialog boxes, palettes, and menus is slightly different, though. To keep the text from becoming cumbersome, in most cases I used screen shots from the Macintosh platform for the visuals in this book. Keyboard shortcuts are given for the most frequently used commands.

A legend is provided on page 2, explaining the icons for each modifier command. For example, ⌘ refers to the *Ctrl* key on Windows computers, but it's the Command key on the Macintosh platform. The ⌥ key is *Alt* on Windows, and it's *Option* on the Macintosh.

timesaver
Information that will speed up completion of the task being discussed.

fyi Presents *additional information of particular interest.*

read this!
Important information about the topic.

Features

- Step-by-step instructions that anyone can follow

- Applications broken down into small increments for easy understanding

- Activities to match the increasing skill level of the student

- Review questions to reinforce learning included on the CD-ROM that accompanies the book.

- Teaches basic concepts first, then progresses to more difficult procedures. For example, drawing shapes with the Shape tools before learning to draw shapes with the Pen tool.

- Activities and exercises keystroke-tested for accuracy by beginners who are unfamiliar with the program

- Quick-reference glossary included

Acknowledgments

We would like to express our sincere gratitude to the following people for their generous assistance to us in creating this book:

- Keystroke checkers Patricia Govro, Elaine McFarlane, Vikki Granger, Wayne Granger, John Hollberg, Loretta Burkholder, and Caryn Berg

- Jon Eriksson Youngblut and P. David Adams for their contribution of photographs used in this text

- Larry Prado for writing the Web graphics information and Appendix A, *Output: Printing and Exporting Files*

- Kevin Kertz for designing our beautiful cover

- George Hazelwood for contributing some of the illustrations using filters and effects

- And especially to Carolyn Acheson for correcting our grammar. We now know when to use the word *farther* instead of *further*.

Contents

CONTENTS

CONTENTS

CONTENTS

xiii

CONTENTS

CONTENTS

xvi

CONTENTS

xviii

LIST OF ACTIVITIES AND EXERCISES

Review Questions for each chapter can be found in a folder named *Review Questions* on the CD-ROM that accompanies this book.

Getting Started

Chapter Outline

- Before You Begin
- System Requirements
- Understand the Basics
- Terminology
- Menus
- Artwork Window
- Dialog Boxes
- Palettes

- Keyboard Commands
- Launch an Application
- Create a New Document
- Save a Document to a File
- Close a Document
- Open an Existing Document
- Exit a Program

Before You Begin

This book assumes that you are familiar with the function of your computer and its operating system. For example, you should be familiar with the use of the mouse — clicking, clicking and dragging, and so on. You should know how to launch the program, access menus and palettes, and know how dialog boxes function. You should also be familiar with the standard commands, such as New, Save, Save As, Open, Close, and Quit. This chapter is a brief refresher.

The Adobe Illustrator 10 interface works almost the same on both the Macintosh and the Windows platforms. The appearance of dialog boxes, palettes, and menus is slightly different, though, depending upon the platform and the operating system of your computer. To keep this text from becoming cumbersome, screen shots from the Macintosh platform, using Mac OS 9.2.1, are used in most cases for the visuals in this book. Any screen shots shown from the Windows platform are Windows XP. Even though dialog boxes, palettes, menus, and the like look different in Adobe Illustrator 10 for Windows than in the Macintosh version, functions are the same.

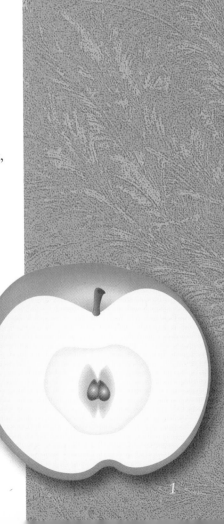

Printer

Make sure your printer is connected properly so you're able to print to it. Because some inkjet printers don't render EPS images accurately, Adobe Systems recommends that you use a PostScript® printer. If you have to use a non-PostScript printer, be aware that the images may not look as smooth as they should.

System Requirements

Minimum Requirements

Adobe Illustrator 10 requires the following hardware and software (minimum):

- At least 180 Mb of free space on your hard drive. If you work with large image files, you'll need additional free space.

LEGEND

The following legends tell you what the keyboard command icons used in this book mean on the Macintosh and Windows platforms.

Macintosh

▶   Indicates a submenu is present. To display the submenu, pause the cursor over the line to highlight it or click on the line. Move to the appropriate option on the submenu and click.

...   Indicates a dialog box will appear when clicked, with options you need to choose.

⌘   *Command* key; located on the keyboard on both sides of the spacebar.

⌥   *Option* key; located on both sides of ⌘ on an extended keyboard. A smaller keyboard may have the Option key on only one side of ⌘, usually the left side.

⇧   *Shift* key.

⌃   *Control* key (not available in *Windows*).

✓   Checkmark; indicates that a function has been performed or a feature has been turned on.

Windows

▶   Indicates a submenu is present. Pause the cursor over the line to highlight it or click on the line and the submenu will display. Move to the appropriate option and click.

...   Indicates a dialog box will appear when clicked, with options to be chosen.

⌘   *Ctrl* key; located at the bottom on the far left and on the far right of the keyboard.

⌥   *Alt* key; located on both sides of the spacebar.

⇧   *Shift* key.

⌃   This key (and its function) is not available in *Windows*.

✓   Checkmark; indicates that a function has been performed or a feature has been turned on.

Macintosh Users:

To determine which Mac OS System is resident on your computer:

1. Click on the background screen, or use the Application menu (upper right corner of screen) to highlight Finder.

2. Display the Apple menu (upper left corner of your screen) by clicking and holding on its icon (🍎).

3. Click on (or drag to highlight) About this Computer. An information box displays, telling you which System is resident, how much RAM is resident, how many applications are open currently, and how much memory each application is using.

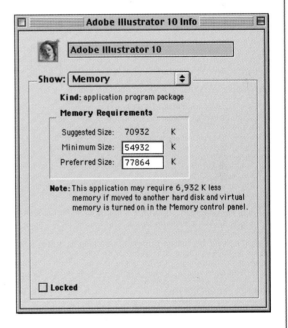

To increase the amount of RAM allocated to a program:

1. Make sure the program is not launched.

2. Find the application file. It's usually in the Adobe Illustrator 10 folder on your hard drive.

3. Click on it once to highlight it (you don't want to open it).

4. Choose **File** ➪ **Get Info** ➪ **Memory**

   or

   Press ⌘ i to display the program Info box, then choose **Memory** from the Show pop-up menu.

5. Locate the Memory Requirements section: Suggested Size, Minimum Size, and Preferred Size fields.

6. Highlight, then change the numbers in the Preferred Size field to the amount of RAM you want to allocate to the program. Remember to leave enough RAM free for the computer to run the System.

7. Click the close box to close the Info box.

- 128 Mb of RAM (random-access memory).
- If you are printing to a PostScript printer, the printer must be PostScript Level 2 or PostScript Level 3.

Macintosh

- Power PC: G3, G4, or G4 dual.
- Mac OS version 9.1, 9.2, or Mac OS X version 10.1.

Adobe Systems also recommends that you reduce the size of the disk cache, turn off the RAM disk, and verify that Virtual Memory is off. These controls can be found in the Memory dialog box in the Control Panels (**Control Panels ⇨ Memory**).

Windows

- Intel® Pentium® II, III, or 4, processor.
- Microsoft® Windows 98, Windows 98 Special Edition, Windows Millennium Edition, Windows 2000 with service pack 2, or Windows XP.

The requirements listed here are the minimum necessary to run Adobe Illustrator 10. The more RAM you have, the faster your CPU, and the larger the capacity of your hard drive, the better the program performs. For example, Macintosh users should, if possible, allocate more than 128 Mb of RAM to Adobe Illustrator 10.

Understand the Basics

If you are familiar with the basic operation of your computer and its operating system, you can skip the rest of this chapter, and go to Step 2, *Introducing Adobe Illustrator 10*. The remainder of this chapter is devoted to a brief explanation of basic functions for students new to using a computer.

Terminology

Click Press and release the mouse button quickly.

Click and drag Press the mouse button and, without releasing it, move the mouse. Release the mouse when the move is complete.

Double-click Press and release the mouse button rapidly two times.

Drag Press the mouse button and move the mouse, releasing when the move is complete (the click is implied).

Toggle Click on an option once to turn it on; click again to turn it off. Click once again to turn it back on, and so forth.

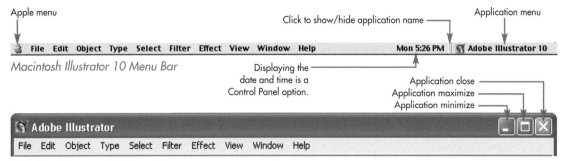

Macintosh Illustrator 10 Menu Bar

Windows Illustrator 10 Menu Bar

FIGURE 1.1 Menu bar that displays at the top of your screen when Adobe Illustrator 10 is active.

Menus

Menus contain an application's primary functions and make these functions easily accessible. The title of the menu usually tells you what functions the options on that menu perform. Many of the commands in the menus are self-explanatory.

A menu bar at the top of the screen (Figure 1.1) displays the menus available for the program that's currently open. Ten menus are on the Adobe Illustrator 10 menu bar: File, Edit, Object, Type, Select, Filter, Effect, View, Window, and Help. Each menu contains groups of related commands separated by gray rules. Some menu items are context-sensitive and change or become gray depending upon which object is active or which tool is selected.

When you click on a menu title on the menu bar at the top of the screen, that menu will display below its name. Once a menu has been displayed, you can display the other menus by passing the cursor over their titles in the menu bar. Each menu will remain visible until you pass the cursor over another menu title or until you click the mouse.

When a menu is visible, scroll to the line you want to use (it will highlight), and click on it. The line item will flicker a few times, then perform its function or open a dialog box. If the line of text in a menu is gray, it indicates that the option is not available for use.

Artwork Window

When you create a new document, a blank Artwork Window displays on your screen. The components of the Illustrator 10 Artwork Window are shown in Figure 1.2 (Macintosh) and Figure 1.3 (Windows). Take note of the name at the top of the window. This is the Title bar, where the name of your file, as well as other information, will always appear. If you don't name your document when you create it, it will be named consecutively by number (Untitled-1, Untitled-2, and so on).

On the Macintosh platform, when you have more than one window open on the screen, the active window has stripes across the top of the window (on both sides of the name). These stripes are not visible on artwork windows that are not active. On the Windows platform, the Title bar of an active document is solid blue. It turns light blue or gray when a document is not active.

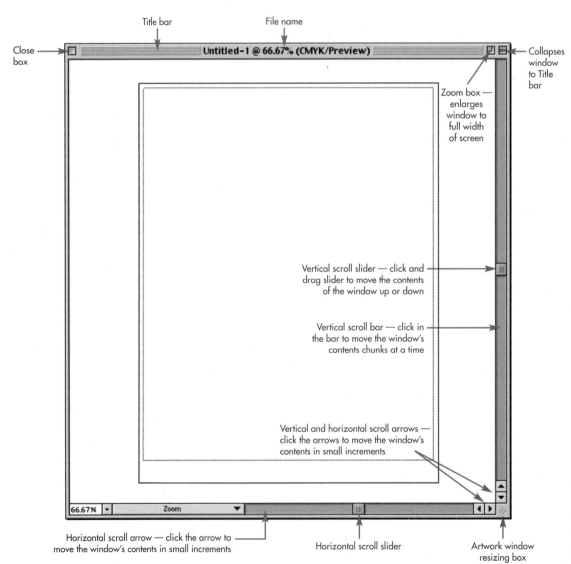

FIGURE 1.2 Macintosh artwork window (without palettes) that displays when a new document is created.

Moving Your Artwork Window Around on the Screen

You can move the artwork window around on your screen by clicking in the Title bar, holding, and dragging to reposition it on the screen. Mac OS 9 has a thin gray bar around the sides and bottom of the artwork window that you can click on to drag the window to reposition it. On the Windows platform, dragging this bar changes the size of the artwork window.

Macintosh: Move artwork window; Windows: resize artwork window

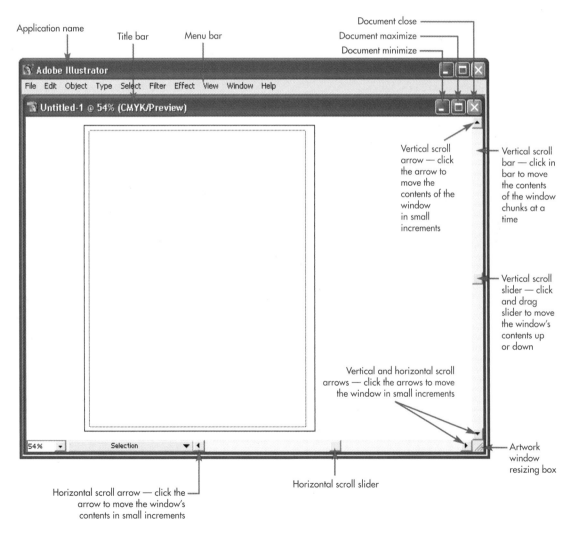

FIGURE 1.3 Windows artwork window (without palettes) that displays when a new document is created.

Changing the Size of the Artwork Window

You can change how much room the artwork window takes up on your screen by clicking and dragging the resizing icon at the bottom right side of the artwork window. You can move the resizing box (a) straight up to shorten the window, (b) to the left or right to make it narrower or wider, or (c) diagonally to change both the side and the bottom proportionally at one time. On the Windows platform, click and drag on the bar surrounding the artwork window.

Artwork window
resizing box

Moving Contents Around in the Artwork Window

You can move the *contents* of the artwork window around within the artwork window in a couple of different ways.

1. Use the scroll bars located on the right side of the artwork window and across the bottom.

   - Click in the middle of the scroll bar to move chunks at a time.

   - Position the cursor over one of the scroll arrows at the bottom and top of the document window and click to move the window in small increments. Click on the arrows and hold to scroll the document window up, down, or sideways continuously.

2. Click-and-hold on the slider in the vertical or horizontal scroll bar. Drag it up and down (in vertical scroll bar) or left and right (in horizontal scroll bar).

Artwork window
scroll arrows

Artwork window
scroll arrows

Artwork
window
scroll
slider

Dialog Boxes

A dialog box is a form that displays on the screen in response to (a) a menu selection that ends with an ellipsis (...) or (b) a keyboard command. The options you select or the info you enter in dialog box fields determines the appearance of your document.

Dialog boxes contain some or all of the following options:

- **Fill-in boxes** (792 pt) require numerical information to be typed in: (a) double-click in the field to highlight it, then type the correct information, (b) highlight, then delete the information that's there and type the new information, or (c) click in the field and drag the cursor across the field to highlight the information, then type in the new information.

- **Submenu arrows** (▶, ▼, or ↕) indicate that another menu containing more options is present. Pressing the arrow(s) displays the submenu.

timesaver

Any button with a darker border around it (usually a Save, Open, or OK button) is an indication that you can press return (Windows: enter) to activate it as well as clicking on that button with the mouse.

- **Checkboxes** (☑) toggle on and off. Pretend there's a question mark after the title. It's like answering yes or no; a check in the box means *yes* and an empty box means *no*.

  - Many Illustrator 10 dialog boxes have a Preview checkbox. Clicking in the box applies your changes while leaving the dialog box open. This allows you to see the effects of your changes as you make them so you can continue to change them until you're satisfied with the results.

- **Radio button** (◉) usually offers a choice between one or more items in a group. A black center indicates the function is turned on. A clear center means it is turned off.

- **Cancel button** (Cancel) allows you to quit the dialog box without any changes being applied. You can also press *esc* on the keyboard to exit without applying changes.

- **OK button** (OK) closes the dialog box and applies the changes you made.

Unfortunately, most dialog boxes are large and, if you have a small monitor, they take up a large portion of the screen. Sorry, you can't do anything about that.

Move between the fields in a dialog box without taking your hands off the keyboard by hitting the tab key to highlight the next field. Do not press return between tabs. To highlight the previous field, press ⇧-tab. When you get to the last field, tab again to start over at the first field.

Palettes

Palettes are small windows that contain settings, such as colors or fonts. In Illustrator, many of the controls you use to create or modify your artwork are contained on movable palettes. Each palette can be displayed using the appropriate Window menu command, or it can be hidden by clicking in its close box. A palette can be placed anywhere on your screen by clicking and dragging its Title bar at the top of the palette.

Many of the palettes have a submenu arrow (▶) on them. Click and hold on this triangle to display a menu with options available for that palette.

Keyboard Commands

There are keyboard shortcuts for many functions you'll perform. Using keyboard commands is more efficient than taking your hands off the keyboard to grab the mouse and use a pull-down menu. Some keyboard shortcuts use keys available only on an extended keyboard (*F1–F12* keys across the top). If you don't have one, these shortcuts aren't available.

If you've used other graphics applications on either the Macintosh or Windows platform, you'll recognize some of the keyboard shortcuts. Commands such as Save, Cut, Copy, Paste, and so on, are common to most graphics applications.

Keyboard commands are listed on the righthand side of pull-down menus. All keyboard command characters are to be struck in lower case unless ⇧ (*Shift*) is part of the command sequence. Striking commands in upper case (unless specified for ⇧) will likely give you a result other than what you wanted.

When using keyboard commands, hold the function key(s) (⌘, ⌥, ⇧, ⌃) down, then press the letter accompanying it. It isn't necessary to press all the keys at exactly the same time.

Launch an Application

An application can be launched in the following ways:

1. Double-click on the program file in the program's folder (usually located on the hard drive).

2. *Macintosh:* Pull down the Apple menu and click on the program's alias (if you've stored an alias in the Apple Menu Items folder within the System folder).

   Windows:
   a. Click the Start button (at the bottom of the screen).

   b. Choose All Programs from the menu that displays and click on the desired application name.

3. *Windows:* Double-click the Shortcut icon displayed on the screen (if one is available).

4. Double-click an existing file created in the program to launch the program and open the file in one action.

5. *Macintosh:* Store an alias in the Launcher Items folder in the System folder to launch Illustrator every time you start or restart the computer.

Create a New Document

You can create a new document in two ways:

- Choose **File** ⇨ **New** from the menu bar at the top of the screen.

or

- Press ⌘n

More complete information about creating a new Illustrator 10 document can be found in Step 2, *Introducing Adobe Illustrator 10.*

Save a Document to a File

Save Command

Use the Save command (choose **File** ➪ **Save** or press ⌘s) to save your document frequently. If you don't save often, hours of work may be lost if the power goes out or the computer "freezes."

The Save command overwrites a previously saved file with the same name, the same format, and in the same location. If you want to save your file under a different name, in a different format, or in a different location, use the Save As command.

Save As

The first time you try to save a new document, the Save As dialog box displays so you can name the document, choose a format, and specify the location on the computer where you want to store the file (its destination). Thereafter, use the Save As command only when you want to create a copy of the file (give it a different name) or when you want to save it in a new location. In that instance, the last-saved version of the file will remain where it is and, by specifying a new destination in the Save As dialog box, you will save a new copy of the file in a different location.

Where is Your File Going?

The first thing you should do is decide the location on your computer where you want your file to be saved. A mistake many beginners make is forgetting to pay attention to where their file is going. Then they can't find it when they want to open it again.

Macintosh

1. The field (⬭ Macintosh HD ⬍) at the top of the Save or Save As dialog box shows you the current destination of the file you're saving. Press the pop-up arrows (⬍) on the right side of the field to display a submenu that shows the hierarchy of your file placement. In the example in Figure 1.4, the file will be saved in the Lifetime folder that's on the hard disk (Macintosh HD) that's on the desktop. This is called *nesting* and you can have as many levels of folders as you want (a folder in a folder, in a folder, and so on), but simpler is better if you ever expect to find anything.

   - The icons to the left of the names in the window indicate whether the listing is the desktop (▦), a disk (⬭), or a folder (▮). Disk icons can have a different appearance, depending on the type of disk it is.

2. **To store your file on the desktop,** click the Save button at the desktop level. (I don't like storing files on the desktop, except temporarily, because the screen soon becomes cluttered.)

3. **To store your file on a disk,** highlight the disk name in the pop-up menu.

    ■ All the folders and files stored on the selected disk will be displayed alphabetically (by default) in the dialog scroll window.

        · To display the names according to the latest files modified, click the Date Modified button at the top of the window.

        · To display the names alphabetically in reverse order (displaying those files beginning with the letter z at the top), press the arrow next to the Date Modified button (⬆).

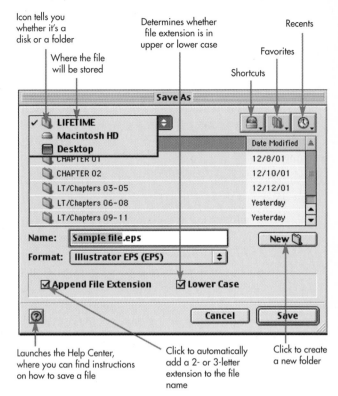

Icon tells you whether it's a disk or a folder

Where the file will be stored

Determines whether file extension is in upper or lower case

Recents

Favorites

Shortcuts

Launches the Help Center, where you can find instructions on how to save a file

Click to automatically add a 2- or 3-letter extension to the file name

Click to create a new folder

FIGURE 1.4 Macintosh Illustrator 10 Save As dialog box.

4. **To create a new folder into which you will store your new file:**

    ■ Click the New Folder button (New) on the righthand side of the dialog box to display the New Folder dialog box.

    ■ Type in the name of your new folder.

    ■ Click Create.

        ■ A new folder is stored on the disk you selected (or on the desktop) and is automatically opened. The name in the destination field will change to the name of your new folder.

New Folder dialog box

5. Type the name of your file in the Name field. Highlight the field, if necessary, by double-clicking in the box or clicking in the field and dragging across.

6. Choose a format from the Format pop-up menu. This option will be discussed in Step 2, *Introducing Adobe Illustrator 10.*

Windows

1. Click the **Desktop** button ( ) to list in the window all the disks and folders stored on the desktop. See Figure 1.5.

   ■ Use the slider on the right to scroll through the list if the items don't all fit in the window.

2. **To store your file on the desktop** (before you highlight anything in the window), click the **Save** button. (I don't like storing files on the desktop, except temporarily, because it quickly becomes cluttered.)

3. **To store your file in a desktop folder**, double-click the folder name in the window or highlight the folder name and click **Open**.

   ■ All the folders and files stored in the selected folder will be displayed in the dialog box window.

4. **To store your file on a disk**, double-click My Computer to see a list in the window of the disks currently available on your computer.

   ■ To see details of the listings in the dialog box window, click the View menu button ( ) at the top of the Save dialog box and choose Details from the drop-down menu.

5. **To create a new folder** in which to store your new file:

   ■ Click the **Create New Folder** button ( ).

   ■ A new folder (named New Folder) appears in the dialog window. It's highlighted when created so you can type a new name for the folder.

   · To rename an existing folder, make sure the folder name is highlighted and type a new name.

   ■ Click Open to open the new folder so you can store the file in it.

6. Type the name of your file in the **File name** field. Highlight the field, if necessary, by double-clicking in the box or clicking in the field and dragging across.

Create new folder

Folder name

Up one level — View menu

Folder icon —

Click to list recently opened files and folders

Go to Last Folder Visited

Click to list the files, folders, etc., located on the desktop

Click to save file into this default Windows XP folder

Click to list the disk drives and hardware connected to this computer

Click to list shortcuts to web sites, network computers and FTP sites

FIGURE 1.5 Windows Illustrator 10 Save As dialog box.

Thumbnails
Tiles
Icons
List
● Details

Submenu that displays when you click the View menu button

13

7. The Save as type pop-up menu allows you choose different formats in which to save your file. This feature will be discussed in Step 2, *Introducing Adobe Illustrator 10.*

8. Click the Save button to exit the Save dialog box.

Can't Find a File?

If you didn't pay attention to the file destination when you saved it, you may find it listed in the Open Recent Files option in the File menu. Click on the file name to open the file, then resave it to a new location using the Save As option. Doing that, of course, gives you two copies of the file. If you want to make sure you have only one copy of the file, delete the copy that's in the incorrect location.

Macintosh users also can find a file using the Sherlock utility or the Find utility located in the Apple menu to search all the drives on the computer. When you find it, click on the file to display its location in the bottom box. Navigate the folders until you find it, then drag it to the new location. You can open the file from the dialog box by double-clicking on the file name.

Windows users can click the Search button in the Start menu to find files and folders, pictures, and so on, and follow the prompts. In earlier versions of Windows, such as Windows 98, enter the name of the file in the Named field. Then, in the Look In field, specify which disk to look in, then click the Find Now button to start the search.

Close a Document

To close a document that's open on your screen:

- Click in the Close box:

Macintosh   ;   *Windows*

or

- Choose **File** ⇨ **Close** from the Menu bar.

or

- Press ⌘w

or

- Press the ⌥ key and choose **File** ⇨ **Close** to close all documents open on the screen at the same time.

If you don't save your document before clicking in the Close box or pressing ⌘w, an alert message will display on the screen. Click the appropriate button. The document will automatically close after it is saved.

Alert message that displays when closing a document to which changes have been made

14

Open an Existing Document

To open an existing document:

1. Display the Illustrator 10 Open dialog box (*Macintosh*, Figure 1.6; *Windows*, Figure 1.7):

   - Choose **File** ➪ **Open**

   or

   - Press ⌘ o

   - Do you remember where you stored the file you want to open?

     - *Windows:* Click the Desktop button (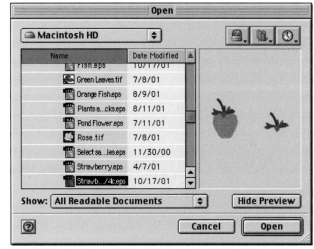) to show which disks are available on your computer.

     - Double-click a disk in the selection window to display the folders available on that disk.

     - Double-click a folder in the selection window to show the folders and files stored in that folder.

   - Choose the format of the file you want to find by displaying the Show (*Macintosh*) or Files of type (*Windows*) pop-up submenu and selecting the desired file format by scrolling to it and highlighting it. If you're not certain what format the file you're looking for was saved as or if you don't mind looking through all files, leave All Readable Documents (*Macintosh*) or All Formats (*Windows*) as the selection in that field.

   - Navigate through the files listed until you locate the file you want to open.

FIGURE 1.6 Macintosh Illustrator 10 Open dialog box.

FIGURE 1.7 Windows Illustrator 10 Open dialog box.

15

- Double-click the file name to open it, or highlight it and click the Open button.
- The document will display on your screen.

2. Double-click an existing Illustrator document file name. If the Illustrator 10 application has not been launched, double-clicking will both launch the application and open the file.

Exit a Program

When you are finished using a program, quit the application.

- Choose **File** ⇨ **Quit** (*Windows:* **File** ⇨ **Exit**) from the File menu.

or

- Press ⌘ q

Windows: You can also press ⇧ ⌥ *F4* or click the Close button (☒) at the top right area of the application window.

PRACTICE ACTIVITY 1-1

Practice using the mouse until you become proficient with its movements and review the commands for the following functions until you know them well:

- New
- Open
- Save
- Close
- Quit

There are no exercises for this chapter.

Introducing Adobe Illustrator 10

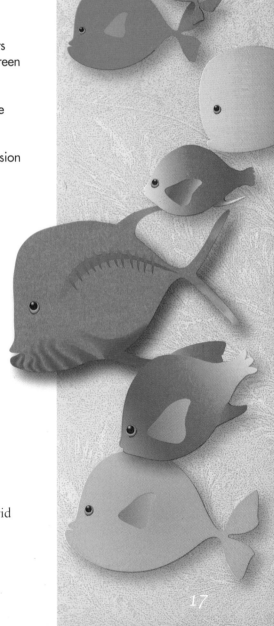

Chapter Outline

- Raster versus Vector Images
- Raster (Bitmap) Images
- Vector (or Object-Oriented) Images
- Illustrator Work Environment
- Help Menu
- An Illustrator Document
- Illustrator Artwork Window
- The Toolbox
- Palettes

- Restore Program Defaults
- View Artwork on the Screen
- Navigator Palette
- Multiple Windows
- Move Around Within the Artwork Window
- Save an Artwork File
- Revert to Last-Saved Version
- Print a Document

Raster versus Vector Images

There are two types of computer graphics formats: raster and vector. It's important to know the difference between them because some filters in Illustrator work only on raster (bitmap) images.

Raster (Bitmap) Images

A bitmap image has four basic characteristics: resolution, dimensions, bit depth, and color model. Each of these characteristics affects file size, which affects the time it takes to print the file and the amount of space you need on your computer to store it.

Resolution

The pixels in bitmapped images are arranged in a matrix or grid (like the small squares on graph paper) (see Figure 2.1). The number of pixels in a given distance is the *resolution* of the bitmapped image. The physical size of these pixels changes according to how many fit in a given space. You'll hear the term dpi (dots per inch) or ppi (pixels per inch) when referring to the resolution of a bitmapped image. The higher the number, the smaller is the size of each pixel because more will fit in a given space.

If you *enlarge* a photograph or line art, you can see the individual pixels, because the resolution is reduced. When you *reduce* its size, resolution increases because more pixels fit in the same amount of space. For instance, if you enlarge a 300 ppi photograph to 200% (double) in a page layout application such as QuarkXPress, its resolution, when printed, is half of its original resolution, or 150 ppi. Conversely, if you reduce the same photograph to half its original size, the new resolution is doubled, or 600 ppi.

A bitmap black-and-white image with low resolution looks jagged because the pixels are too big. A low-resolution grayscale or color image is said to be pixelated because you can see the individual pixels instead of a blend of gray or tones of color.

Dimensions

The dimensions of a bitmapped image can be stated in inches, picas, centimeters, and so on. You also might find dimensions stated in pixels, such as 1193 pixels × 2348 pixels. To get the physical size, in inches, of an image whose dimensions are stated in pixels, divide the number of pixels by the resolution of the image.

For instance, if the resolution of the image whose dimensions are given above (1193 pixels wide × 2348 pixels high) is 300 ppi, its size in inches would be 3.977 × 7.827 inches. If you change the resolution to 150 ppi, the physical size of the image would be 7.953 × 15.653 inches. The number of pixels didn't change, but now they're four times as big (double the height and double the width).

Bit Depth

Bit depth is a term you'll hear frequently in a conversation about photographs and other bitmap images. Each pixel in a bitmap image is composed of bits (*binary digits*) that describe the pixel. Bit depth tells you how many tones or colors each pixel in a bitmapped image can have. For instance, a 1-bit image has only black and white pixels. If the bit is on (1), the

Individual pixels are visible when bitmap image is enlarged too much

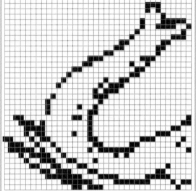

Enlarged view of raster image pixel matrix

72 ppi raster image (file size 12k)

1000 ppi (file size 412k)

FIGURE 2.1 An example of the difference between an image scanned at 72 ppi and 1000 ppi. The pixels are distinct in the 72 ppi sample but are smoothed out in the 1000 ppi image.

pixel is black. If the bit is off (0), the pixel is white. This type of image also is called a *bilevel image*.

When more than 1 bit is used to describe each pixel in a grayscale image, a range of gray tones is placed between the black bit and the white bit. An image with a bit depth of 4 means it takes four bits to describe each pixel and it can produce up to 16 shades of gray with each bit either on or off.

If most of the bits are off, the pixel is grayer; if more bits in the pixel are on, the pixel is darker. Most grayscale bitmap images have a bit depth of 8 bits per pixel, which produces 256 shades of gray ($2 \times 2 = 4 \times 2 = 8 \times 2 = 16 \times 2 = 32 \times 2 = 64 \times 2 = 128 \times 2 = 256$). This usually is sufficient to give a smooth gradation from white to black without displaying unwanted banding. Color images scanned at 24 bits per pixel can give millions of color possibilities.

Color Model

Bit depth in color models, such as RGB or CMYK, are calculated based on information required to describe the bits for each color channel.

- RGB images have three channels (red, green, and blue) and normally have a bit depth of 24 (3×8). Monitors and television screens display images using the RGB color model.

- CMYK has four channels (cyan, magenta, yellow, and black) for a bit depth of 32 (4×8). When each channel is described by 8 bits, 256 levels of color per channel are possible. The CMYK color model is used for printed material containing color photographs or when more than three colors are desired.

Color will be discussed in more depth in Step 7, *Add Color to Artwork*.

Vector (or Object-Oriented) Images

A *vector* image uses mathematical information to describe an image. This type of image is called object-oriented. It uses X and Y coordinates (distance and direction) instead of pixels to describe an image. Vector images are created and edited in programs such as Adobe Illustrator (see Figure 2.2).

A mathematical vector has three parts: a starting point (anchor point), an angle or direction, and a length (segment). Because a computer knows what shapes are (square, circle, line, and so on), they can be defined by specifying a starting point, its direction, and its length.

For this reason, an object-oriented image, including type, can be enlarged or reduced when printed or

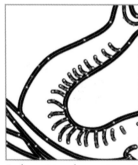

Anchor points and segments created when elephant was drawn are not visible in the printed artwork.

FIGURE 2.2 Vector image created in Adobe Illustrator 10 (file size 176k).

displayed on a monitor without affecting its appearance. The mathematical formula simply changes to reflect its new size.

In the Illustrator program, both vector and bitmap images are shown as pixels on the screen because computer monitors represent images by displaying them on a grid. If you enlarge the View of a line drawn in Illustrator, you can see the jagged edges as though it were created in pixels. The printed image, however, is not displayed in pixels and the line is smooth.

Illustrator Work Environment

When you launch Illustrator 10 for the first time, the Menu bar, the Toolbox, and four floating palette groups display. An artwork page doesn't display until you create a new document.

Menu Bar

The Illustrator 10 Menu bar has 10 menus that give you access to submenus, commands, and dialog boxes for creating objects in Illustrator: File, Edit, Object, Type, Select, Filter, Effect, View, Window, and Help.

Toolbox Palette

On the left-hand side of the screen is the Toolbox palette, which contains the tools you will use to create and edit paths in Illustrator. At the bottom of the Toolbox are color controls and screen view mode buttons.

Floating Palettes

Illustrator 10 has a large number of movable palettes and, in addition to the Toolbox, four palette groups containing 15 different palettes display on the screen when you launch Illustrator for the first time. The palettes are gray until you create a new document or open an existing document. They're joined into groups to avoid covering the screen with individual palettes. Folder tabs just below the Title bar of the palette display the names of the palettes contained in that group.

You can move the palettes, take them out of their group and make them individual palettes, create your own groups of palettes, or remove one or more palettes from the screen. See the section entitled Palettes later in this chapter.

Toolbox palette

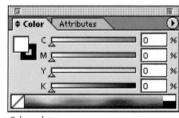

Color palette

Context-Sensitive Menus

A context-sensitive menu is a temporary menu that contains commonly-used options pertaining to the document or to what is currently selected in the document. Options in a context-sensitive menu change, depending upon the object or tool that's selected. See Figure 2.3. To display a context-sensitive menu:

- **Macintosh:** ⌃-click on the page. The upper left corner of the menu is positioned at the point of the click.

- **Windows:** Right-click on the page. The upper left corner of the menu is positioned at the point of the click.

Help		Help		Help	
Undo		Undo Rectangle		Undo Typing	
Redo		Redo		Redo	
Zoom In		Group		Font ▶	
Zoom Out		Join		Size ▶	
Show Rulers		Average…		Create Outlines	
Show Grid		Make Clipping Mask		Transform ▶	
Hide Guides		Make Compound Path		Arrange ▶	
✓ Lock Guides		Make Guides		Select ▶	
Select ▶		Transform ▶			
Outline		Arrange ▶			
		Select ▶			

Nothing selected
Single object in document selected
Type selected

FIGURE 2.3 Examples of context-sensitive menus.

Help Menu

The Adobe Illustrator 10 menu bar contains a Help menu that, for the most part, repeats what's in the Adobe Illustrator 10 User Guide that comes in the box with the program.

Balloons *(Macintosh only)* ✳

Balloons are graphics that display on your screen when you point to an item that has a balloon attached to it. The balloons contain information about the item. They're helpful when learning a new program, but can become annoying as you become more familiar with a program's functions. Turn them on by displaying the Help menu and clicking Show Balloons. It's a toggle — if the menu says Show Balloons, the balloons are off; if the menu says Hide Balloons, the balloons will display.

Help
- About Balloon Help…
- Show Balloons
- Illustrator Help…
- Top Issues…
- Downloadables…
- Corporate News…
- Registration…
- Adobe Links ▶
- Adobe Online…
- System Info…

Macintosh Help menu

Illustrator Help

To display information using Illustrator Help, you must have Microsoft Internet Explorer 4.0 (or later) or Netscape Communicator 4.0 (or later) installed on your computer and Java Script must be active. When you click this option, the window for the Internet browser displays with the available topics listed on the left. You do not, however, have to be connected to the Internet to use Internet Help. The files are retrieved from the Help folder that's loaded onto the hard drive when Illustrator is installed.

Help
- Illustrator Help…   F1
- About Illustrator…
- About Plug-ins…
- Top Issues…
- Downloadables…
- Corporate News…
- Registration…
- Adobe Links ▶
- Adobe Online…
- System Info…

Windows Help menu

Click a topic listed on the left side of the window to display the information in the window on the right. Text includes information that can be found in the Adobe Illustrator 10 User Guide. These pages can also be printed.

Miscellaneous Options

- **Top Issues** — View the latest articles or documents concerning Adobe Illustrator 10.
- **Downloadables** — Download information or products from Adobe's website.
- **Corporate News** — View news items about Adobe.
- **Registration** — Register your copy of Adobe Illustrator 10 by choosing this option when you're connected to the Internet.

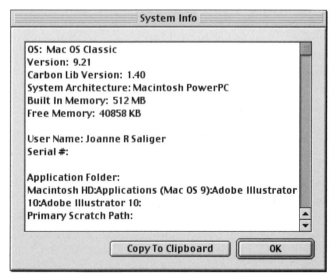

Help screen for Adobe Illustrator 10

Adobe Online

If you are connected to the Internet you can use the Adobe Online option to connect to the Adobe Systems home page on the World Wide Web. At that website, you can find information about Adobe Illustrator 10, including the latest Technical Support solutions.

System Info

When you choose System Info, a window displays that lists information about your computer and the Illustrator 10 program on your machine. Information such as the type of computer, the operating system it uses, the amount of memory installed, and the serial number of the Illustrator application is shown. In addition, all the plug-ins being used by the Illustrator program are listed.

System Info window for Joanne Saliger's Macintosh computer

An Illustrator Document

After you launch the Illustrator program, you must (a) create a new document, (b) open an existing document that's been stored on your computer, or (c) open an existing document that's on a removable disk that's mounted with its icon visible on the Desktop.

Create a New Document

To create a new document (or artwork file), display the New Document dialog box:

1. From the Menu bar, choose **File** ⇨ **New**

   or

   Press ⌘n

2. Type a name for your new artwork file in the Name field. If you don't give it a name, it's named Untitled and numbered according to how many new documents you've created since the program was launched.

New Document dialog box

3. Make choices in the Artboard Setup section to specify options for the work environment.

   ■ **Size** — The default size, as shown in the Size pop-up menu, is Letter, which is a U.S. standard 8½" × 11" sheet of paper. This is the size most commonly used in desktop printers. The other standard pre-set sizes that are available are:

   ▪ **Legal:** 8½" wide × 14" high. This is also a standard size sheet of paper in the U.S.

   ▪ **Tabloid:** 11" wide × 17" high. This size is a standard size sheet of paper in the U.S., frequently used for newsletters when two 8½" × 11" pages are side-by-side, folded in half.

   ▪ **A4:** 8.268" wide × 11.693" high — standard size sheet of paper in Europe.

   ▪ **A3:** 11.69" wide × 16.54" high — standard size sheet of paper in Europe.

   ▪ **B5:** 6.929" wide × 9.843" high — standard size sheet of paper in Europe.

   ▪ **B4:** 10.12" wide × 14.33" high — standard size sheet of paper in Europe.

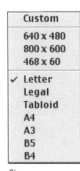

Size pop-up menu

- **Custom:** The pop-up menu displays this option when changes are entered in the Height and Width field to specify the size of the artboard.

  - Even though the default unit of measurement is points, you can enter a different unit of measurement (that is, type " (quotes) or *in* after the numbers) and Illustrator converts the values to the current unit of measurement, as shown in the Units pop-up menu.
  - **640 x 480, 800 x 600, 468 x 60:** Use one of these options to specify the size of the artboard when creating artwork for display on the Web.

- **Units** — The default unit of measurement for Illustrator 10 is Points. That means all measurements in fields in dialog boxes are displayed in Points. You can change it here by choosing a different unit of measurement from the pop-up menu that displays when you click on the pop-up menu. Unless I'm creating a lot of type in my artwork, I usually work in Inches rather than Points. If creating a lot of type, I work in Picas. Choose the unit of measurement that's easiest for you to control the size or position of objects as you create them.

  - Activities and exercises in this book use inches as the unit of measurement. Refer to Step 6, *Rulers, Grids, & Guides for more information about units of measurement.*

- **Orientation** — You can choose to display the artwork page so that it's taller than it is wide (portrait), which is the way a laser printer normally prints a page. Or you can display it wider than it is tall (landscape).

Points
Picas
✓ Inches
Millimeters
Centimeters
Pixels

Units of measurement available in pop-up menu

Portrait icon   *Landscape icon*

4. Choose either CMYK Color or RGB Color in the Color Mode section by clicking on the appropriate radio button.

   - If you're creating artwork that is to be printed — on paper or other material — choose CMYK Color.

   - If you're creating artwork that will be displayed only on a monitor, such as a web page, choose RGB Color.

   - Color Mode can be changed after a document is created by choosing **File** ➪ **Document Color Mode** and changing the selection in the pop-up menu.

5. Click OK or press *return/enter* to exit the dialog box and display an artwork page on the screen.

Illustrator 10 remembers the choices you make, so the next time you create a new document, the same specifications are used. If you use the keyboard shortcut for creating a new document (⌘ n), though, default page size and orientation are used, regardless of the size and orientation of the last page you created.

Open an Existing Document

To open an existing document (artwork file):

1. Choose **File** ⇨ **Open Recent Files** and highlight the name of the file you want to open from the menu that displays.

or

2. Display the Open dialog box.

   ■ Choose **File** ⇨ **Open** from the Menu bar

   or

   ■ Press ⌘ o

3. Locate the file you want to open, and highlight it.

   ■ Choose the disk the file is stored on, then the folder where it's stored by displaying the pop-up submenu at the top of the dialog box.

   ■ If you want to lessen the number of files you have to search through, choose the file format of the file you're looking for in the Show (*Macintosh*) or Files of type (*Windows*) submenu.

   ■ *Macintosh:* The Show Preview/Hide Preview button allows you to choose whether to display a thumbnail representation of the selected file in the Preview section of the dialog box. If no preview is available for a selected file, a message (No preview available) displays in the Preview area.

   ■ *Windows:* A preview of the contents of the file is shown below the files list window.

4. Click Open or press *return/enter* to display the artwork page on the screen.

Open dialog box

Missing Fonts If, for any reason, you have disabled some of your fonts and they are not available when you attempt to open an existing document, an alert will display. Make the appropriate response, according to the document specifications. A more complete discussion about fonts can be found in Step 5, *Add Type to Artwork*.

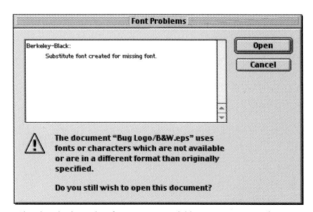

Alert that displays when fonts are not available on your computer for an Illustrator file you are opening

Illustrator Artwork Window

When you create a new document, the Illustrator artwork window displays on your screen. Inside the artwork window are the boundary lines for the page size you specified when you created the new document. Components of the artwork window are shown in Figure 2.4.

Title Bar

The Title bar on the window displays the current name of the file, the percentage at which it is being displayed, and the color mode that Illustrator uses to define any colors you use in the document.

Status Bar

At the bottom of the window, to the left of the scroll bar is a status bar that displays information about the document. The pop-up submenu allows you to choose the type of information you want displayed as you work. Click the pop-up submenu arrow and drag to select the option you want.

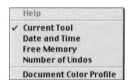

- **Current Tool:** The field changes according to the title of the tool selected in the Toolbox.

- **Date and Time:** Displays the date and time.

- **Free Memory:** Displays the amount of free RAM memory (*Macintosh*) or virtual memory (*Windows*) available for your open file.

- **Number of Undos:** The number of Undos and Redos available. The numbers change as you perform functions such as creating or editing paths. The number of Redos changes as you perform Undo functions.

In addition, if you hold down the ⌥ key as you click the status bar pop-up submenu, you can choose from a list of other things to display in the Status bar field.

View Percent Field

To the left of the status bar is an editable field that displays the percentage at which the page is being displayed on the screen — the same number is shown in the Title bar. To change the magnification of the view, highlight the field and type in a new percentage — from 3.13 to 6400. See *View Artwork on the Screen* later in this chapter for more information about the View Percent field.

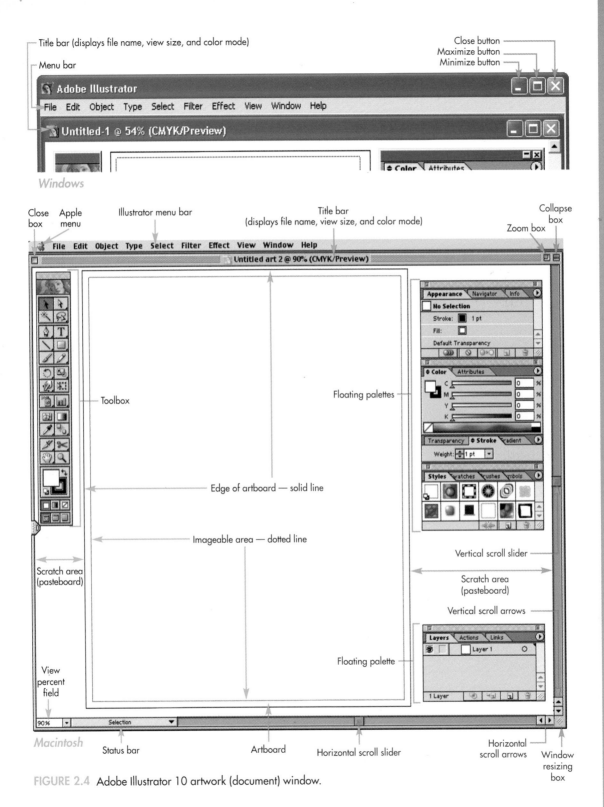

FIGURE 2.4 Adobe Illustrator 10 artwork (document) window.

Scratch Area (Pasteboard)

The scratch area of the window (see Figure 2.4) is the blank area on both sides of the artboard. This scratch area, also called the pasteboard, extends to a total of 227" with the artboard in its center. Use the scratch area to create, edit, or store elements of your artwork. Objects in the scratch area print if any part of them falls within the boundaries of the size of the paper you're printing on.

Artboard

The artboard is the section of the artwork window on which you draw your illustration. Its boundaries define the maximum printable area of your document and can be as large as 227" × 227". The default artboard size is 8½" × 11" (standard letter size). When you enter values in the Height and Width fields in the New Document dialog box, you're defining the size of the artboard.

That doesn't mean everything on your artboard can be printed, though. Page Size and Imageable Area is defined by your printer and determines how much of your artboard will print. See Figure 2.5. You can draw objects on the pasteboard, but they won't print. Only those objects or portions of objects that are inside the Imageable area (dotted lines) will print on the currently selected printer.

You can't move the artboard within the artwork window; it stays in the center of the pasteboard; for example, you can't move the artboard to one side so you have a larger scratch area on one side. You can, however, move the document page around in the artboard. This procedure is discussed in Step 6, *Rulers, Grids, & Guides*.

Hide the Artboard You can hide the boundary lines of the artboard, page area, and imageable area by choosing Hide Artboard in the View menu (**View ⇨ Hide Artboard**). This is a toggle command, so when the artboard isn't visible on the screen, the command reads Show Artboard. Just select the command (**View ⇨ Show Artboard**) to make it visible again.

You can change the size of the artboard as well as change the units by which it's measured after the document has been created. The procedure for doing this is discussed in Step 6, *Rulers, Grids, & Guides*.

Page Size The size of the printable page is determined by information taken from the PostScript Printer Description (PPD) file of the printer your computer is currently using. The boundaries of the artboard

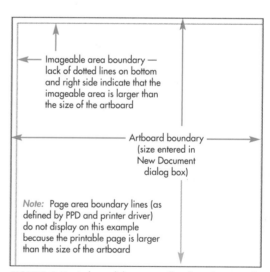

FIGURE 2.5 Artboard that is smaller than the size of the page. Notice that not all of the page (size of the paper specified in the Print Setup dialog box) fits on the artboard.

display on the screen as a solid line. The page boundaries (size of paper in the printer) display as a dotted line unless the artboard is the same size as the paper in the printer. The imageable area of the artboard display as a non-printing dotted line inside the page boundary.

Imageable Area The imageable area is shown by a non-printing dotted line inside the page boundary line. This imageable area is determined by information from the PPD file of your printer. Because most printers cannot print to the edge of the sheet of paper, you need to be aware how much of the page will print when creating artwork so you "stay in the lines." See Figure 2.6. Imagesetters, however, are an exception because most imagesetters can print to the edge of the page and beyond (bleed).

Because most desktop printers in the U.S. default to the standard 8½" wide × 11" high paper (612 × 792 points), the artboard in your artwork window probably looks similar to the artboard in Figure 2.4. Until you progress further in the book, that's the size of artboard you'll use for the Activities.

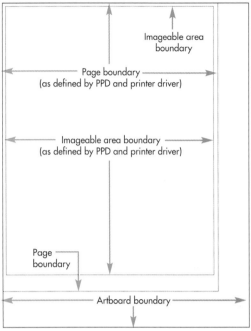

FIGURE 2.6 Artboard that is larger than the size of the page. All of the page fits on the artboard.

The Toolbox

Tools in the Toolbox palette are organized according to their functions. Select tools in the Toolbox by clicking on them. In most cases the mouse pointer (▶) changes to match the icon of the tool you have selected when it's in the artwork window. For example, if you click on the pencil tool (✏), the pointer changes to a pencil (✏).

You can remove the Toolbox from the screen by selecting the Tools option in the Window menu. When the checkmark is missing, the Toolbox is not displayed. To redisplay the Toolbox, choose Tools in the Window menu (a checkmark displays in the menu to the left of the option name).

Using the Hidden Tools

Many of the tools in the Toolbox have additional tools hidden under them, indicated by a small triangle (◣) on the lower right corner of the tool button. You can access hidden tools in two ways:

1. Click the tool and hold until the hidden tools pop out. Then drag to select the desired tool.

The Toolbox Palette

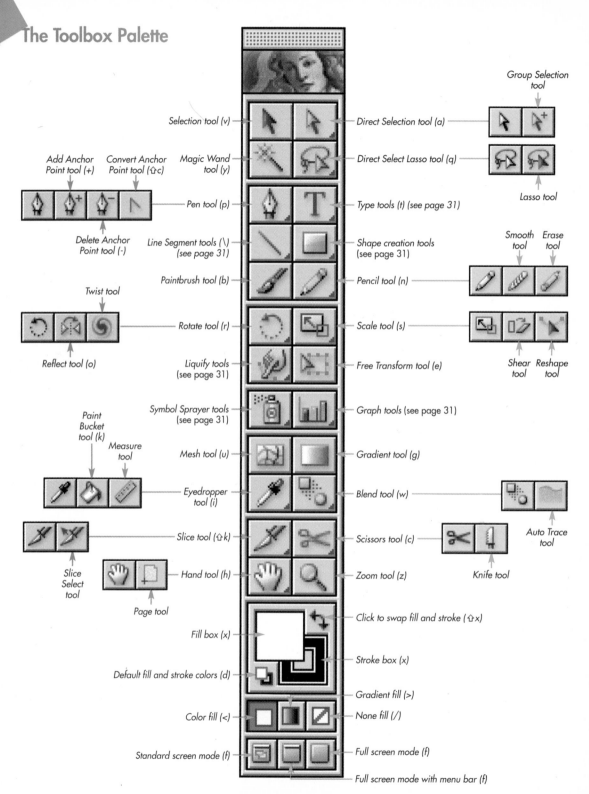

Group Selection tool

Selection tool (v)

Direct Selection tool (a)

Add Anchor Point tool (+)

Convert Anchor Point tool (⇧c)

Magic Wand tool (y)

Direct Select Lasso tool (q)

Lasso tool

Pen tool (p)

Delete Anchor Point tool (-)

Type tools (t) (see page 31)

Line Segment tools (\) (see page 31)

Shape creation tools (see page 31)

Smooth tool

Erase tool

Paintbrush tool (b)

Pencil tool (n)

Twist tool

Rotate tool (r)

Scale tool (s)

Reflect tool (o)

Liquify tools (see page 31)

Free Transform tool (e)

Shear tool

Reshape tool

Symbol Sprayer tools (see page 31)

Graph tools (see page 31)

Paint Bucket tool (k)

Measure tool

Mesh tool (u)

Gradient tool (g)

Eyedropper tool (i)

Blend tool (w)

Auto Trace tool

Slice tool (⇧k)

Scissors tool (c)

Knife tool

Slice Select tool

Hand tool (h)

Zoom tool (z)

Page tool

Click to swap fill and stroke (⇧x)

Fill box (x)

Stroke box (x)

Default fill and stroke colors (d)

Gradient fill (>)

Color fill (<)

None fill (/)

Standard screen mode (f)

Full screen mode (f)

Full screen mode with menu bar (f)

Shape Creation tools

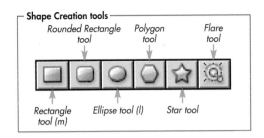

Rounded Rectangle tool — Polygon tool — Flare tool

Rectangle tool (m) — Ellipse tool (l) — Star tool

Graph tools

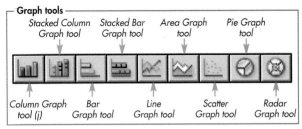

Stacked Column Graph tool — Stacked Bar Graph tool — Area Graph tool — Pie Graph tool

Column Graph tool (j) — Bar Graph tool — Line Graph tool — Scatter Graph tool — Radar Graph tool

Liquify tools

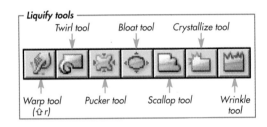

Twirl tool — Bloat tool — Crystallize tool

Warp tool (⇧ r) — Pucker tool — Scallop tool — Wrinkle tool

Symbol Sprayer tools

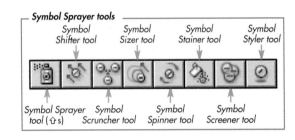

Symbol Shifter tool — Symbol Sizer tool — Symbol Stainer tool — Symbol Styler tool

Symbol Sprayer tool (⇧ s) — Symbol Scruncher tool — Symbol Spinner tool — Symbol Screener tool

Type tools

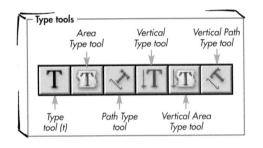

Area Type tool — Vertical Type tool — Vertical Path Type tool

Type tool (t) — Path Type tool — Vertical Area Type tool

Line Segment tools

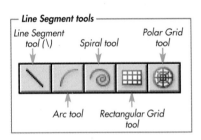

Line Segment tool (\) — Spiral tool — Polar Grid tool

Arc tool — Rectangular Grid tool

2. ⍂-click the tool. Each click selects the next tool in the hidden tool bar and displays it in the main Toolbox in place of the original tool. Continue ⍂-clicking until the desired tool is displayed.

If you use a tool frequently, you can tear off the hidden toolbar to keep those tools visible on the screen.

1. Press and hold the tool button that has hidden tools.

2. When the hidden tools display, drag to the tearoff (▯) at the right end of the toolbar and release the mouse.

The toolbar detaches from the Toolbox and displays on the screen. Move the new toolbar the same way you move any other palette — click and hold on the Title bar and drag to reposition it. To reattach the tools to the Toolbox so they are hidden, click the Close box in the Title bar of the detached tools.

Example of hidden tools with tearoff

Changing the Mouse Pointer to a Crosshair

If you're working with small, detailed artwork, you can change any of the drawing or editing tool pointers to a crosshair (✕) pointer, then position the center of the crosshair pointer precisely where you want to click. To change a selected tool to the crosshair pointer, press Caps Lock on the keyboard. As long as the pointer is in the artwork window, it will display as a crosshair pointer. To change it back to the tool icon, press Caps Lock again.

If you find you prefer working with the crosshair pointer all the time, you can make it permanent by changing that option in the General Preferences dialog box:

1. Display the General Preferences dialog box in the Edit Menu (**Edit** ⇨ **Preferences** ⇨ **General**) (see Figure 2.7):

   ■ Click on Edit in the Menu bar. Move the cursor over the Preferences option so that the submenu displays and click General.

   or

   ■ Press ⌘k

2. Click the Use Precise Cursors checkbox.

3. Click OK or press *return/enter* to exit the dialog box.

Other options available in the General Preferences dialog box will be covered in this text as the subject matter is discussed.

Using the Keyboard to Select a Tool

You can choose a tool without clicking on its icon in the Toolbox by pressing its keyboard equivalent shortcut. If a tool has a keyboard shortcut, it's shown in parentheses after its name when the cursor is paused over a tool long enough to display the tool name. For example, press the letter *p* to select the Pen tool (🖋). To deselect the tool, click another tool in the Toolbox or press another keyboard equivalent to select a different tool.

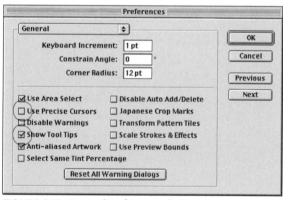

FIGURE 2.7 General Preferences dialog box.

Turning Off Tool Tips

You can turn off the option that allows the names of the tools to display when you hold the cursor over the tool. You probably won't want to do this, though, until you're more familiar with the program.

1. Display the General Preferences dialog box (Figure 2.7).

   ■ Choose **Edit** ⇨ **Preferences** ⇨ **General** or press ⌘k

2. Click on Show Tool Tips to deselect it.

3. Click OK or press *return/enter* to exit the dialog box.

Type Tool (T)

Example of a tool tip

activity 2.1

1. If Adobe Illustrator 10 is not launched, launch it now.

2. Create a new document: Letter size, CMYK color mode.

3. Locate the elements of the document window that were called out in Figure 2.4.
   - Title bar
   - Toolbox
   - Close box
   - Floating palettes
   - Status bar
   - Scratch area
   - View percent field
   - The artboard, including the imageable area defined by dotted lines

4. If you're new to computer use, practice using the scroll bars, scroll arrows, scroll sliders, and the resizing box.

5. Move the mouse pointer over the Pencil tool (✐) in the Toolbox until the Tool Tip displays.

6. Click the Pencil tool (✐) to select it.
   - The mouse pointer (▸) changes to the pencil icon (✐) when it's moved over the artboard.

7. Press the Caps Lock key on the keyboard.
   - The pencil icon changes to the crosshair icon (✕).

8. Press-and-hold the Pencil tool (✐) in the Toolbox until its hidden tools display.

9. Drag to the end of the bar to the tearoff (▯) and release the mouse.
   - The hidden tools create a new palette.

10. Click on the Title bar of the tool mini-palette you just created and reposition it on the screen.

11. Click in its Close box to put it back into the main Toolbox.

12. ⌥-click the Pencil tool.
    - The tool next in line in the hidden tool bar (✐) displays in place of the Pencil tool.

13. Keep ⌥-clicking until the original Pencil tool displays.

14. Change the cursor icon back to the Pencil tool pointer.
    - Press Caps Lock.

15. Don't save or close this document.

Palettes

Palettes in Illustrator 10 are contained in groups to keep your screen from being filled up with palettes. In addition to the Toolbox, four palette groups are displayed on the screen the first time you launch Illustrator 10. Figure 2.8 is an example of a floating palette.

Palettes can be opened or closed using the Window menu in the Menu bar. They're all listed there in alphabetical order and operate as toggle options. Select a palette name to change its display. If a checkmark displays to the left of the palette name, the palette is visible on the screen. Click on the palette name to remove the checkmark and remove the palette from the screen. Click again to add a checkmark and display the palette.

Manipulating Palette Groups

There are a number of ways to organize the palettes on your screen. You can take a palette out of its default group and make it an individual palette or you can move a palette to another group. You can make most palettes larger or smaller or collapse them to just their Title bar. In addition, you can "hook" palettes together, called *docking*.

- To make a palette in a group display in the palette window:
  - Click on its folder tab at the top of the palette.

- To take a palette out of its group:
  - Click-and-drag its folder tab at the top of the palette to a new position on the screen.

- To move a palette from one group to another:
  - Click on the selected folder tab at the top of its palette window.
  - Drag it over another palette window until a thick black line (**Windows:** a thick gray line) borders the new group window.
  - Release the mouse to drop the palette into the new group. It's folder tab and title appear in the new palette window.

- To dock two palettes together:
  - Click and drag the Title bar of a palette to the bottom of another palette.
  - Release the mouse when it snaps into place.

- To dock two palettes together so they move as one palette:
  - Click and drag the folder tab of a palette to the bottom of another palette. Move the palette up until you see a black line (**Windows:** a gray line) appears at the bottom of the palette you're docking to. Don't move so far that a black border appears in the first palette because the palette is put into that palette group instead of attaching to the bottom.

 Can't see your artwork because there are so many palettes on your screen? You can hide them temporarily by pressing the Tab key. Press the Tab key again to show them again. If you want to hide them all except the Toolbox, hold the Shift key down when you press the Tab key. You don't have to press the Shift key to show them again, though, but it doesn't hurt anything if you do.

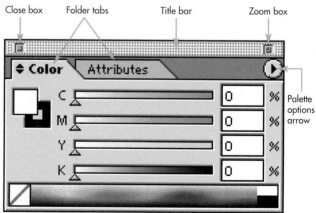

FIGURE 2.8 The Macintosh floating palette window.

- Release the mouse. The palettes are docked but the one you moved no longer has a Title bar and moves when you move the other palette.

■ To undock a palette:

- Click and drag its folder tab or Title bar (if it has one) to a new position.

■ To collapse a palette to display only its Title bar and folder tabs:

- Double-click a folder tab in the palette group. If a palette has several sections, you may have to click several times because sections collapse one at a time.

   or

   Macintosh: Click the palette's Zoom box.

   Windows: Click the palette's Minimize/Maximize box.

Zoom box (Macintosh)

Minimize/Maximize box (Windows)

■ To enlarge a palette group, click and drag the Resize box in the lower right corner of the palette window. If the palette doesn't have a Resize box in the lower right corner, it cannot be resized.

■ In many cases, the palette that displays on the screen when you first launch Illustrator is not all of the options available in that palette. To display the full palette:

- Click the small arrows in the folder tab to the left of the folder tab name (⬍). If no arrows are visible in the folder tab, no additional information is hidden.

or

■ Double-click the palette's folder tab in the palette group.

- You can cycle through the palette's size options by continuing to click or double-click. It'll go from it's folder tab to the full palette display, to the basic default information, and back to only the folder tabs.

Resize box (Macintosh)

Resize box (Windows)

■ To remove a palette from the screen:

- Click its Close box.

or

- Choose **Window** ⇨ [name of the palette].

■ To display a hidden palette, choose **Window** ⇨ [name of the palette].

- The palette displays on the screen where it was before it was removed, with the same palette information visible.

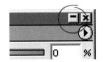

Close box (Macintosh)

Close box (Windows)

Changing Palette Menu Options

Most palettes have options for items in the palette. Click the palette Options arrow (▶) at the top right side of the palette window to display the menu. When the options menu displays, drag to the option you want to use and release the mouse. After you make a selection in the menu, the menu disappears. If you don't make a selection but you want the menu to disappear, click on the palette Options arrow again (▶) or click outside the menu area.)

1. The document you worked with in Activity 2.1 should still be open on the screen. If not, create a new document: Letter size, CMYK color mode.

2. Click in the Title bar of the Color/Attributes palette and drag it to the center of the screen.

3. Click on the Stroke folder tab and drag it down until it becomes its own palette.

4. Click on the Brushes folder tab in the Styles/Swatches/Brushes/Symbols palette to display that palette in the window.

5. Drag the Resize box to enlarge the palette window so all the available brushes display.

   - You may have to move the palette window up to be able to see all the brushes.

6. Dock, but don't connect, the Stroke palette under the Color/Attributes palette.

7. Collapse the Brushes palette to display only the Title bar and folder tabs and dock it under the Stroke palette.

   - You have to double-click on the folder tab twice. The first time collapses the palette window to its original size. The second time collapses the palette window to just the folder tabs.

8. Click and drag the Gradient folder tab and put it in the Styles/Swatches/Brushes/Symbols palette.

   - You don't need to expand the palette to put the new palette into it. The palette compresses the folder tabs so they all fit in the palette.

9. Dock the Stroke palette to the bottom of the Color/Attributes palette group, under Transparency, so that it moves with the Color/Attributes/Transparency palette group.

10. Click on the palette Options arrow on a palette to display its menu options.

11. Click on the palette Options arrow again to hide the menu.

    - When you make a selection from the menu, the menu disappears.

12. Click in the Close box of the Color/Attributes palette.

13. Open it again by choosing Color in the Window menu.

    - Notice that it displayed on the screen in the same position it was when you closed it.

14. Close this document without saving it to a file.

Restore Program Defaults

Changes you make to the position or groupings of palettes are permanent changes. The next time you launch Illustrator 10, the palettes are in the same configuration they were when you last quit the program.

To restore the menus to the program default:

1. Before launching Adobe Illustrator 10, locate its Preferences file:

   - *Macintosh OS 9.x: Adobe Illustrator 10.0 Prefs* can be found in the Preferences folder in the System folder (**System folder** ⇨ **Preferences** ⇨ **Adobe Illustrator 10 folder**).

   - *Macintosh OS 10: Adobe Illustrator 10.0 Prefs* can be found in the Preferences folder in the Mac OS X folder (**Max OS X** ⇨ **Users** ⇨ **Home** ⇨ **Library** ⇨ **Preferences** ⇨ **Adobe Illustrator 10 folder**).

   - *Windows 98 and ME: AIPrefs* can be found in the Adobe Illustrator 10 folder on your hard drive (Windows folder ⇨ Application Data ⇨ Adobe ⇨ Adobe Illustrator 10 folder).

   - *Windows NT: AIPrefs* can be found in the Adobe Illustrator 10 folder on your hard drive (WinNT folder ⇨ Profiles ⇨ *[user name]* ⇨ Application Data ⇨ Adobe Illustrator 10 folder).

   - *Windows 2000 and XP: AIPrefs* can be found in the Illustrator 10 folder on your hard drive (My Computer ⇨ Local Disk (c:) ⇨ Documents and Settings ⇨ *[user name]* ⇨ Application Data ⇨ Adobe ⇨ Adobe Illustrator 10 folder).

     - By default, the AIPrefs file is hidden. Be sure the option to display hidden files is on or you won't be able to see the file.

2. Delete the Preferences file.

   - *Macintosh:* Drag the *Adobe Illustrator 10.0 Prefs* file to the trash and empty the trash.

   - *Windows:* Delete the *AIPrefs* file by clicking on the file with the right mouse button. Select Delete from the menu that displays. You are asked if you're sure you want to send *AIPrefs* to the Recycle Bin. Click Yes, then empty the Recycle Bin.

3. Launch Adobe Illustrator 10. A new Preferences file is created with the program default settings. Just remember, any other changes you have made to settings and controls in Illustrator 10 are changed back to their default settings, too.

activity 2.3

Restore your program to its default status:

Macintosh:

1. Quit the Illustrator program (⌘ q or File ➪ Quit).

2. Find and open the System folder on your hard drive.

3. Locate the Preferences folder in the System folder and open it.

4. Open the Adobe Illustrator 10 folder.

5. Find the Adobe Illustrator 10.0 Prefs file and drag it to the trash.

6. Empty the trash.

7. Relaunch Illustrator 10.

Windows:

1. Quit the Illustrator program (⌘ q or File ➪ Exit).

2. Determine the location of the AI Prefs file by following the instructions for the operating system that's on your computer.

3. Locate the AI Prefs file and right-click it to display the context-sensitive menu.

4. Choose Delete from the menu and click Yes when the dialog box displays asking if you're sure you want to send the file to the Recycle Bin.

5. Delete the file from the Recycle Bin.

6. Relaunch Illustrator 10.

View Artwork on the Screen

Your artwork can be displayed on your screen in different ways. You can display all or only a part of your artwork, and you can create additional windows to show your artwork at different magnifications at the same time. One window can display the entire page and another can be magnified very large for close detail work.

Screen Modes for the Artwork Window

Illustrator 10 has three ways you can configure your screen. Click the corresponding button at the bottom of the Toolbox to change the screen mode.

1. **Standard Screen Mode** (▦) — (the lefthand button in the Toolbox) displays the standard default screen with the Menu bar at the top, the Title bar at the top of the artwork window, and scroll bars on the right side and along the bottom.

2. **Full Screen Mode with Menu Bar** (▦) — (the middle button in the Toolbox) displays a Menu bar but no Title bar or scroll bars.

3. **Full Screen Mode** (▦) — (the righthand button in the Toolbox) displays only the artwork window. The Menu bar, Title bar, and scroll bars are not visible.

To change the screen mode, click the appropriate button at the bottom of the Toolbox or press *f* on the keyboard to toggle between the screen modes.

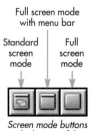

Full screen mode with menu bar

Standard screen mode

Full screen mode

Screen mode buttons at the bottom of the Toolbox

View Format Options

Preview The default View format when you launch Illustrator 10 for the first time is Preview mode. This View mode allows you to view your artwork on the screen with as many colors and shades, and as much detail as your monitor is capable of displaying.

Outline You can also view only the paths in your artwork, with all color attributes hidden. If you're working with complex artwork, the screen updates faster in Outline than in Preview. Changing from Preview to Outline can be accomplished by choosing the Preview/Outline toggle command in the View menu or by pressing ⌘y.

Overprint Preview Choosing Overprint Preview in the View menu allows you to see on your screen, as closely as possible, what your artwork will look like in color-separated output. It approximates how the overprinting, blending, and transparency of colors will appear when printed. The Overprint Preview option is explained in more detail in Step 7, *Add Color to Artwork*.

Pixel Preview If you're creating artwork for display only on a monitor (it won't be printed to paper), such as in a Web page, you can see what it will look like after it's been converted to a raster file (bitmap) and displayed in a Web browser. Viewing artwork as pixels is explained in more detail in Step 7, *Add Color to Artwork*.

View format options in the View menu

Preview mode   Outline mode

Magnification

The current size of the View is shown (a) in the Title bar to the right of the file name, (b) in the View Percent field at the bottom left corner of the window, and (c) in the lower left corner of the Navigator palette. The size of the artwork as viewed on the screen does not affect its size when it is output.

There are several ways to enlarge or reduce the size of your artwork as viewed on the screen: (1) choose an option in the View menu, (2) use the Zoom tool or the Zoom keyboard commands, (3) change the value in the View Percent field, or (4) use the Navigator palette.

Using the View Menu The View menu offers four options for displaying your artwork on the screen.

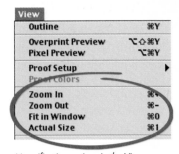

Magnification options in the View menu

- Choose Zoom In (⌘+) (enlarge) or Zoom Out (⌘- [hyphen]) (shrink) to change the view in preset increments. When the maximum or minimum view is reached, the command becomes gray (unavailable).
    - When using the keyboard commands, position the mouse pointer (or crosshair) over the part of the object you want to enlarge or shrink. Continue pressing the keyboard command until the view is enlarged to its maximum of 6400% or its minimum of 3.13%.
    - With nothing in the document selected, display the context-sensitive menu (*Macintosh:* ⌒-click; *Windows:* right-click) and click on the Zoom In or Zoom Out command.
- Choose the Fit in Window (⌘0 [zero]) command to size the window so the whole artboard is visible on your screen.
- Actual Size (⌘1) changes your view of artwork in the window to 100%.

Using the Zoom Tool Select the Zoom tool in the Toolbox:

1. Click the Zoom tool in the Toolbox.
2. Press the Zoom tool's keyboard shortcut (z).

When the Zoom tool () is selected, the mouse pointer changes to the Zoom In icon (⊕). Click in the area on your screen you want to magnify. Each time you click, the screen enlarges in preset increments to a maximum of 6400%. When the screen is enlarged to the maximum of 6400%, the magnifying glass becomes blank (Q).

To shrink the view, select the Zoom tool in the Toolbox, hold down the ⌥ key and click in the document window. The Zoom tool icon now has a minus sign in it to indicate that the view will shrink (⊖). The view of the document window shrinks in preset increments until the minimum of 3.13% is reached.

To set the View to 100% or Actual Size quickly, double-click the Zoom tool () in the Toolbox.

Zoom by Dragging You can zoom in on a selected portion of the document window by selecting the Zoom tool (), clicking in the area you want to zoom, and dragging before you release the mouse. A dotted rectangular box, called a marquee, is visible on the screen until you release the mouse.

Zoom tool icon in the Toolbox palette

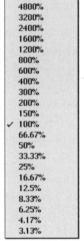

Preset increments for the Zoom tools or Zoom commands

fyi On some computers, the smallest view you can attain with a keyboard command is 4.17%. If that's the case with your computer, you can reach a view of 3.13% by clicking the submenu arrow in the View Percent field and choosing that value from the preset increments listed in the menu. Or you can type it in the View Percent field.

The smaller you make the marquee before releasing the mouse, the higher the magnification (the more the view is enlarged). The larger you draw the marquee, the lower the magnification (the less the view is enlarged). Continue clicking and dragging until the desired View is reached.

To zoom out on a selected portion of the document window, select the Zoom tool, and hold down the ⌥ key while you click and drag.

If you discovered you didn't position the marquee in the exact place on your artwork that you wanted, you can move the marquee to another position. Before you release the mouse, hold down the spacebar, and move the mouse to drag the marquee to a new area. Release the spacebar when it's in position, then release the mouse to zoom.

timesaver
While you're using another tool, you can Zoom In by pressing ⌘-spacebar-click and Zoom Out by pressing ⌥⌘-spacebar-click. The tool you were using remains selected.

Using the View Percent Field You can change the view size by highlighting the View Percent field at the bottom left corner of the document window, typing the desired percentage, then pressing *return/enter*.

To zoom by the preset increments, click the View Percent field submenu arrow to display the pop-up menu. Scroll to the view you want from the choices available, and click it.

View Percent field

Submenu arrow

Creating Your Own Custom View

If you don't want to use the preset Views in Illustrator 10, you can create your own view percentages.

1. Zoom to a magnification percentage (or enter a percentage in the View Percent field) that is different from any of the preset values.

2. Choose **View** ➪ **New View** to display the New View dialog box.

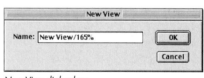

New View dialog box

3. Type a name for your new view in the Name field.

4. Click OK or press *return/enter*.

   ■ The View you just created appears at the bottom of the View menu.

   ■ You can create and store up to 25 custom views for each document.

New custom views displayed in the View menu

Editing Your Custom View To rename or delete a custom View:

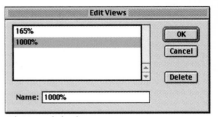

Edit Views dialog box

1. Choose **View** ➪ **Edit Views** to display the Edit Views dialog box.

2. Click on the name of a custom View in the window.

3. To rename it, type a new name in the Name field.

4. To delete it, click the Delete button.

5. Click OK or press *return/enter* to exit the dialog box.

Using Your Custom View To use your custom View, display the View menu, scroll to the bottom, and select the custom View you want.

activity 2.4

1. Locate the file named Strawberry/4c.eps in the Student Files folder on the CD-ROM attached to the back of this text. Double-click on it to open it.

2. Change the screen mode to the Full screen mode with Menu bar.

3. Change to the Full screen mode.

4. Change the screen mode back to the Standard screen mode.

5. Using the keyboard, execute the Fit in Window command (⌘0 [zero]).

6. Select the Zoom tool, then click and drag slightly (marquee) to enlarge the contents of the document window to the maximum magnification.

7. Click submenu arrow in the View Percent field and select 25% from the preset options.

8. Create a custom view of 500% and name it "My View."

9. Rename the view "500%."

10. Change the View percentage to 75%.

11. Change the View format to Outline.

12. Change it back to Preview.

13. Change the View to Actual Size (100%) using the keyboard command (⌘1).

14. Change the magnification to your new 500% view.

15. Do not save or close the document.

Navigator Palette

You can use the Navigator palette (Figure 2.9) to position your artwork in the document window and to change the View percentage. Display or remove the Navigator palette by clicking the **Navigator** option in the View menu. If the Appearance/ Navigator/Info palette is visible on the screen, click the Navigator folder tab to display the Navigator palette in the window.

Positioning Your Artwork

The entire document, including the scratch area, is displayed in thumbnail size in the Navigator palette window, showing the artboard edges and the page border. A red box also is displayed — the View box — showing the portion of the document that is displayed in the artwork window you see on your screen. As you resize your artwork window, the red View box resizes in the Navigator palette to reflect the change.

Sometimes when you zoom out or zoom in, your artwork gets lost. To easily position your artwork back into the center of your document window:

1. Click and hold in the View box in the Navigator palette.

   ■ The hand icon (🖑) displays when the mouse pointer is moved over the View box.

2. Click and drag the View box to a new position and release the mouse.

   ■ The contents of the artwork window move to the new position.

or

1. Move the mouse pointer over the Navigator palette to a spot outside the View box.

   ■ A hand icon with a pointing finger displays (☝).

2. Click.

   ■ The center of the View box in the Navigator palette moves to the spot of the click.

   ■ The contents of the document window move to the new position.

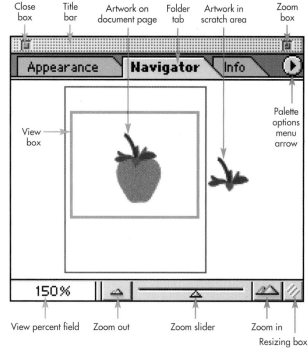

FIGURE 2.9 The Navigator palette (Macintosh).

Changing the Size of the View

There are several controls in the Navigator palette you can use to change the size of the contents of your document window.

- Click the Zoom in button (⌃) or Zoom out button (⌄) at the bottom of the palette. Continue clicking the button until the desired percentage is achieved.

- Click and drag the Zoom slider (▭) at the bottom of the palette — to the left to reduce the view, to the right to enlarge the view.

- Double-click or click-and-drag in the View Percent field (150%) at the bottom left side of the palette to highlight it. Enter the percentage for magnification you want. Press *return/enter.*

Showing Only Objects on the Artboard

If you want to see in the Navigator palette the objects you placed in the scratch area of the artboard:

1. Press the palette Options arrow (▶) at the top right side of the palette to display the menu options.

2. Choose View Artboard Only to uncheck it. The default is checked. This option is a toggle. Select it once to turn it on (a checkmark displays to the left of the option), then select it again to turn it off.

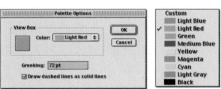

Navigator palette Options menu

Changing the Color of the View Box

You can change the default color (red) of the View box in the Navigator palette:

1. Click the palette Options arrow (▶) at the top right side of the palette to display the Navigator palette Options menu.

2. Click Palette Options to display a dialog box with options to change the appearance of items in the Navigator palette.

3. To use a pre-set color, click on the pop-up menu in the Color field to display the color choices and choose a different color.

    - Click OK or press *return/enter.*

Navigator palette Options dialog box   Pre-set colors

4. To specify a custom color:

    - Choose Custom in the pop-up menu, or double-click the colored box in the View box section of the dialog box. The Color Picker dialog box displays.

    - Position the crosshair in the color wheel over the color you want. Click.

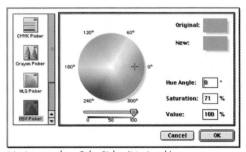

Navigator palette Color Picker (Macintosh)

- Your new color displays in the New field in the Color Picker dialog box.

■ To change the color that displays in the color wheel, change the values in the Hue Angle, Saturation, and Value fields or move the slider under the color wheel.

- *Windows:* The Color Picker dialog box looks different (square instead of a wheel), but the procedure is the same. And you have the option of changing the values in Red, Green, and Blue fields.

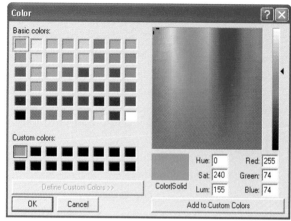

Navigator palette Color Picker (Windows)

■ Click OK or press *return/enter* to return to the palette Options dialog box.

- The color you selected displays in the View box in the upper left corner of the dialog box.

■ The Greeking and Draw dashed lines as solid lines checkboxes, when checked, enable faster screen redraw. *Greeking* means that type below the point size specified in the field displays on the screen as a gray bar rather than individual characters. Type is not affected when printed, just how it appears on-screen. The Draw dashed lines as solid lines checkbox determines how dashed lines display on the screen. Dashed lines print as dashed lines regardless how they appear on the screen.

■ Click OK or press *return/enter* to return to the Navigator palette.

 *activity 2.5*

1. With the Strawberry/4c.eps file still visible on the screen, verify that the Appearance/Navigator/Info palette group is visible on the screen. If it isn't, display the Window menu and select Navigator.

2. Click the View box and move it around, then watch what happens to the contents of the artwork window.

3. Watch the View box in the Navigator palette while you resize the artwork window.

4. Move the View box in the Navigator palette until the object on the artboard is centered on your screen.

5. Using the Navigator palette, enlarge the magnification using the Zoom slider.

6. Reduce the magnification by clicking the Zoom Out button in the Navigator palette.

7. Display the palette Options menu and choose View Artboard Only to turn off View Artboard Only.

   ■ Now you're able to see the artwork that's in the scratch area of the document.

8. Turn on the View Artboard Only option.

9. Change the color of the View box in the Navigator palette.

10. Don't save or close the document.

Multiple Windows

Illustrator has a feature that allows you to create additional document windows that are exact copies of the original. Changes you make to artwork in one window automatically change that artwork in the other windows. Each window can have different magnifications and viewing formats, though. By creating a smaller window with a lower magnification and positioning it so you can see it as you work, you can see what the overall result is of work you're doing at a large magnification in the first window. For example, one window can be in Preview mode and the other in Outline mode.

To create a new window:

1. Choose **Window** ⇨ **New Window**.

   ■ A copy of the document window is created and placed over the original window.

   ■ The new window is numbered consecutively from the first window, depending upon what its file name is. The original window becomes #1, whether it's actually part of the name or not. For example, if the original window is named Strawberry 4c.eps, its name now becomes Strawberry 4c.eps:1 and the new window is named Strawberry 4c.eps:2.

2. Adjust the size, position, and view mode of the new window so you can see your artwork in both windows.

3. After setting up the new window, click back to the original window to make it active, and continue to work.

   ■ As you make changes to artwork in the original window, those same changes are made automatically in any duplicate windows.

Arranging Document Windows *(Windows Only)*

You can arrange document windows on your screen using one of the three options available in the Window menu:

1. **Window** ⇨ **Cascade:** Arranges the document windows in a stack, then offsets them a little (cascading) from the top left to the bottom right of the screen.

2. **Window** ⇨ **Tile:** Arranges the document windows horizontally edge to edge across the screen.

3. **Window** ⇨ **Arrange Icons:** Arranges minimized document windows across the bottom of the screen in an orderly fashion.

activity 2.6

1. With Strawberry 4c.eps still open on your screen, create a second window.

2. Resize the new window and position the strawberry artwork so that very little blank area shows around it.

4. Change the mode of the original window to Outline.

5. Do not close the windows.

3. Move the new window to the upper right portion of your screen.

   - You may have to move palettes around or close some palette windows so you can see both windows.

Move Around Within the Artwork Window

In addition to the standard scroll tools on the righthand side and bottom of the document window, you can use the Hand tool to move the contents of the artwork window. This tool moves the entire artboard, not just the objects you've drawn.

Hand tool icon in the Toolbox palette

timesaver

To switch to the Hand tool temporarily *while you're using another tool, press and hold the spacebar, then drag with the mouse.*

1. Click the Hand tool () in the Toolbox

   or

   Press *h* on the keyboard

2. Click in the artwork window and drag to move the contents to a new position.

activity 2.7

1. With both Strawberry/4c.eps windows still open on your screen and window #1 active, select the Hand tool by pressing the letter *h* on the keyboard.

2. Click and drag the mouse to move the strawberry around in the artwork window.

   - Notice that the View box around the strawberry in the Navigator palette moved when you moved the strawberry within the artwork window.

   - Notice that the artwork in the second window doesn't move; only the artwork in the window that's active is moved.

3. Close the second window you created, but leave the first window open.

Save an Artwork File

The most important thing to remember about saving is "Save early, save often!" It's a good idea to save a file as soon as you create it and then save frequently while working on your artwork to avoid losing your work if the power goes out suddenly or the computer "freezes." I save every few minutes and always before I switch to another program, before I get up from my desk, and before I answer the phone.

When you create a new Illustrator 10 document, you have the opportunity to name it. If you don't enter a name, your file is named automatically as Untitled-1 (or 2, or 3, and so on, depending on how many new documents you've created since Illustrator 10 was launched for the current work session). It's not really necessary, though, to name the file (to something other than Untitled) until you save it for the first time.

The first time you save a file to disk, the program automatically displays the Save As dialog box. In this dialog box, you must specify its format and its destination. You can also choose **File** ⇨ **Save As** or press ⇧ ⌘ s) to display the Save As dialog box. Use the Save As command when you want to save an alternative copy of the file — a different name, a different location, or a different format.

In the Save As dialog box:

1. Pay attention to where the file is being saved. It'll be saved on the disk or in the folder that displays in the dialog box. Verify that it's going on the disk or in the correct folder. In Figure 2.10, the file will be saved in the Lifetime folder in the Macintosh hard drive.

2. Specify the format in which you want the file saved. Click the Format (*Macintosh*) or Save as type (*Windows*) pop-up menu and scroll to select a file format. The activities and exercises in this book will be saved in Illustrator EPS.

   - **Adobe Illustrator® document** — This is the native Illustrator format. Saving a file in this format creates a smaller file size, but it has no Preview and can be opened and edited only in Illustrator or

fyi Macintosh: If you attempt to save your file before you've created any artwork, the Save As box doesn't display and the file isn't actually saved.

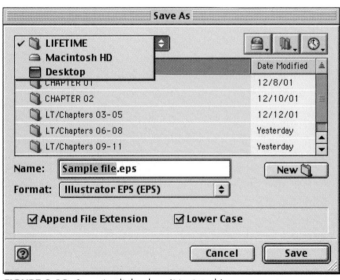

FIGURE 2.10 Save As dialog box (Macintosh).

Photoshop. If you're going to print the file only from Illustrator, you can use this format.

Format options for saving artwork file

- **Adobe PDF (PDF)** — (Portable Document Format) This option should be used if the document is to be displayed on the World Wide Web or imported into a page layout, word-processing, or graphic application that accepts PDF files. In addition, some commercial printers prefer to receive files from their clients in the PDF format. Check with your print service provider.

- **Illustrator EPS (EPS)** — (Encapsulated PostScript) Choose this option if you are going to import the file into a page layout program, a word processing program, or any other drawing applications that don't support native Illustrator files. Even though the file size is larger than a native Illustrator file, this is the file format you'll probably use most often.

- **SVG (SVG)** — (Scalable Vector Graphics) Choose this option to save files for use as Web graphics. It creates high-quality Web graphics without sacrificing quality. Unlike traditional image formats — GIF, JPEG, and PNG — files can be enlarged on-screen without sacrificing sharpness.

- **SVG Compressed (SVGZ)** — Saves the file as a compressed SVG file, which reduces the file size, but the file cannot be edited using a text editor.

3. *Macintosh only:* I suggest that you check the Append File Extension to add a file extension to the end of the file name. It immediately identifies the format in which the file was saved and the file can be opened on the Windows platform. Check the Lower Case checkbox to make the file extension appear in lower case rather than caps.

   - Extensions are automatically added to file names on the Windows platform, so this option is not on the dialog box.

4. Click OK or press *return/enter* to exit the dialog box and bring up another dialog box containing options for the file format you chose.

read this!

Adobe Illustrator doesn't support the PDF Writer format. Printing errors may occur if you attempt to print using PDF Writer.

read this!

Adding an extension to a file name does not make the file become that format. On the Windows platform, changing the extension of an existing file may make the file unusable. A 3-letter extension is not required on the Macintosh platform, and the file is not affected by any extension you add to the file name.

timesaver

You can close all of the Illustrator document windows that are open on your screen at one time by pressing the ⬉ key before you choose File ⇨ Close. This option doesn't work with the keyboard command (⌘ w).

Step 2 — INTRODUCING ADOBE ILLUSTRATOR 10

49

Saving Documents in Native Adobe Illustrator Format

When you choose Adobe Illustrator® document as the file format, the Illustrator Native Format Options dialog box displays when you click the Save button. Select the desired options then click OK or press *return/enter*.

Compatibility Click the submenu arrow to display the options and scroll to select the version with which you want the file to be compatible.

- Some features available in Illustrator 10 may not be supported when you save a file in an earlier version. A warning appears alerting you that some features may be disabled when the file is opened.

- If you save your file in a version earlier than Version 6 and you want to use the Japanese File Format, click the Use Japanese File Format box.

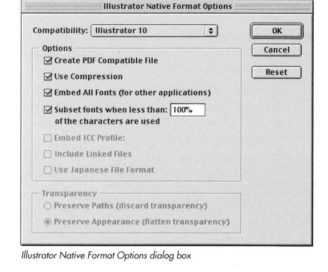

Illustrator Native Format Options dialog box

Options

- **Create PDF Compatible File** — Check this option if you want the file to be compatible with other Adobe applications, such as Photoshop. A PDF representation of the document is saved with the Illustrator file.

- **Use Compression** — This option is available only when Create PDF Compatible File is checked. When checked, PDF data in the file is compressed. The time it takes to save a file may be substantially increased.

- **Embed All Fonts (for other applications)** is, by default, checked and indicates that font information is included with the file when placed into a layout program, such as InDesign™. QuarkXPress does

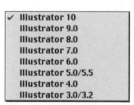

Choices available in the Compatibility pop-up menu

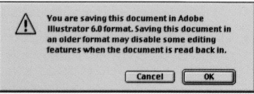

Warning that displays when a document is saved in an earlier version of Illustrator

not support the Native Illustrator file format, so a file saved in this format cannot be imported into a QuarkXPress file. You must still have the fonts installed on any computer on which you want to edit the Illustrator file.

- **Subset fonts when less than:** `100%` — Only information for the characters actually used in the document will be saved with the file. If you uncheck this box, all characters in the font will be saved with the document whether or not they are used in the document, making the file size larger unnecessarily.

  - Changing the percentage in the box tells Illustrator not to subset the characters if the percentage of characters exceeds that number. For instance, if you enter 35% and fewer than 35% of the characters in a font are used in the PDF file, only those characters will be embedded. If more than 35% of a font's characters are used, the entire font will be embedded.

  - This option is used to keep the file size as small as possible. If you use only one character of a font and file size is important, reduce the percentage in the field.

- **Include Linked Files** — If you've used a linked file in your Illustrator document, check this box to save it with the document. Information about linked files can be found in Step 8, *Layers & Links*.

- **Use Japanese File Format** — When checked, the document is saved as a Japanese language file that's compatible only with Illustrator versions 3, 4, or 5. Later versions of Illustrator are not compatible.

Transparency The options in this section determine what happens to objects that have transparency effects applied when the document is saved in a version earlier than Illustrator 9. Transparency effects are not available in earlier versions of Illustrator. The Transparency feature is covered in Step 12, *Meshes, Masks, Blends, & Transparency*.

- **Preserve Paths (discard transparency)** — When selected, transparency effects are removed and artwork is reset to 100 percent opacity.

- **Preserve Appearance (flatten transparency)** — When selected, the *appearance* of transparency is simulated by flattening transparent sections in the artwork.

Saving a Document as an EPS File

This is the most versatile of the file format options and is the one you'll probably use most frequently. An EPS file can be imported into almost all other graphics programs and it can be edited in Illustrator the same as the native file format.

When you choose this format and click Save to exit the Save dialog box, the EPS Format Options dialog box displays. Select the desired options then click OK or press *return/enter.*

Compatibility Choose the Illustrator version in which to save the file — they're the same as the Native Illustrator format. Earlier versions do not preserve some of the newer functions of Illustrator 10 and your artwork may be altered when opened. The earlier the version, the more features that will be affected. The warning box will display.

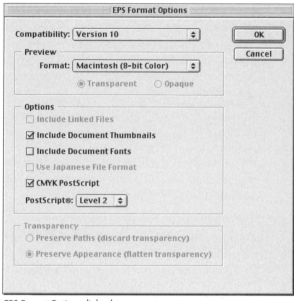

EPS Format Options dialog box

- If you save your file in a version earlier than Version 6 and you want to use the Japanese File Format, click the **Use Japanese File Format** box.

Preview These options determine how the screen preview attached to the Illustrator EPS file displays. Your choice doesn't affect the actual information in the file, only how it appears on the screen. It prints correctly, even if there's no preview.

Preview options in the Format pop-up menu

- The options are self-explanatory, except that Macintosh (Black & White) and Macintosh (8-bit Color) are created in PICT format, which is not compatible with Windows. If your file will be viewed on a Windows machine, use one of the TIFF formats, which are also okay for Macintosh applications.

- If you select the TIFF (8-bit Color) option, you have the option of saving the file with a transparent or an opaque (solid) background by clicking the appropriate radio button. Choose Opaque to use the file in a Microsoft Office application.

Options

- **Include Linked Files** — If you've used a linked file in your Illustrator document, check this box to embed it in the document. Information about linked files can be found in Step 8, *Layers & Links*.

- **Include Document Thumbnails** — Leave this box checked if you want to preview the contents of the document in the Preview section of the Open dialog box of graphic applications, including Illustrator 10.

- **Include Document Fonts** — When this box is checked, the fonts are saved with the document so you don't have to worry whether the fonts are installed if you import the document into a page layout program, such as QuarkXPress. The characters display on the screen and print correctly without having them installed. You do need the fonts installed, however, to edit the Illustrator file.

- **Use Japanese File Format** — When checked, the document is saved as a Japanese language file that's compatible only with Illustrator versions 3, 4, or 5. Later versions of Illustrator are not compatible.

- **CMYK PostScript** — When this option is checked, Illustrator automatically converts RGB colors used in the document to their CMYK equivalents, so they can be output from programs that use only CMYK color. RGB colors are retained when reopened in Illustrator.

- **PostScript®** — Three levels of PostScript are available. Level 3 is the latest, greatest, and can handle all the new features of Illustrator 10. This option should be used whenever possible, but some printers can't handle it. Level 2 is less sophisticated than Level 3 and all features of Illustrator 10 are not supported. Don't choose Level 1. It's the least desirable choice and shouldn't be used unless your output provider specifically tells you to use it. Check with your output provider to determine the correct level of PostScript for the output device that will be used to output the file.

Transparency The options in this section determine what happens to objects that have transparency effects applied when the document is saved in a version earlier than Illustrator 9. Transparency effects are not available in earlier versions of Illustrator. The Transparency feature is covered in Step 12, *Meshes, Masks, Blends, & Transparency*.

- **Preserve Paths** (**discard transparency**) — When selected, transparency effects are removed and artwork is reset to 100% opacity.

- **Preserve Appearance** (**flatten transparency**) — When selected, the *appearance* of transparency is simulated by flattening transparent sections in the artwork.

Saving a Document as a PDF File

Use of PDF files is becoming more widespread every day. Most applications can create them and the files can be read using a free program called Acrobat Reader, which is downloadable from the Adobe website. Many output providers prefer to have print jobs supplied to them in PDF format. Save your documents as PDF files when they're going to be viewed on the Web. You can keep all the Illustrator data intact by checking the Preserve Illustrator Editing Capabilities option so the PDF files can be opened and edited as Illustrator files.

When you choose to save your file in the Adobe PDF format and exit the Save dialog box, the Adobe PDF Format Options dialog box displays.

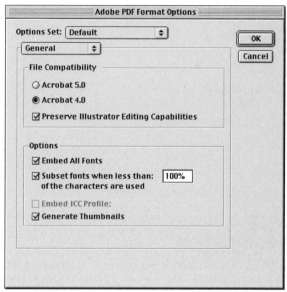

Adobe PDF Format Options dialog box

Options Set

- **Default** — Choose this option when the file is to be printed from the PDF file. All fonts are automatically embedded and maximum image quality is achieved. The file size is larger than if it was saved as Screen Optimized.

- **Screen Optimized** — Choose this option if the document is to be posted on the Web. The only changes from the default option is that Preserve Illustrator Editing Capabilities and Generate Thumbnails are unchecked. If a document was created in CMYK color mode and Screen Optimized is selected, a message displays at the bottom of the dialog box informing you that the document's color mode will be changed to RGB.

- **Custom** — Displays when any changes are made to the default values.

Choices available in the Options Set pop-up menu

General
These choices are displayed when the dialog box opens:

- **File Compatibility** — Choose either Acrobat 5.0 or 4.0 as the version of Acrobat Reader required to read the file. Uncheck Preserve Illustrator Editing Capabilities if you don't want anyone to change your artwork — but that means you can't open the file in Illustrator and edit it, either.

- **Options**
  - The Embed All Fonts feature is the same as saving a document as an Illustrator EPS. All characters of a font set are saved with the file, which means its appearance is retained even when fonts used in the document are not loaded on the computer when it's opened.

- Enter a smaller value in the Subset fonts field if you used only one or two characters of a font, which keeps the file size smaller.

- If an ICC color profile has been used in the document, the Embed ICC profile box will be available. When checked, the profile is applied to the document when it's reopened in Illustrator.

- Leave General Thumbnails checked so you are able to see the contents of a document on the screen or in the Preview area of an application's Open dialog box.

Compression To show Compression settings, press the arrow on the General button. This dialog box contains three sections providing options for compressing and resampling the different types of bitmap images in your artwork. Before you change default settings, be sure you understand what you're doing.

- **Average Downsampling at ☐ ppi** — Check this box and specify the resolution value in the field at which you want the file downsampled. *Downsampling* is the method by which Illustrator compresses a file. The average color of the pixels in an area of the image is determined by Illustrator, and those pixels are replaced by a larger single pixel of the average color.

- **Compression** — This pop-up menu offers three choices for color and grayscale images:

  - **ZIP** (the default) — Choose this option when the document contains color images with large areas of single colors or contains repeating patterns or black-and-white images with repeating patterns.

  - **Automatic** — Illustrator applies the best compression automatically. This option works well for most files and is the one you should select unless your output provider instructs otherwise.

  - **JPEG** — This method of compression removes image data to compress files. Smaller files are created but image quality is reduced.

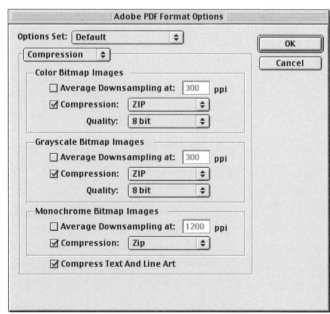

Compression options in the Adobe PDF Format Options dialog box

- **Monochrome Bitmap Images** — There are four choices in this pop-up menu. CCITT (Consultative Committee on International Telegraphy and Telephony) compression doesn't lose information during compression. Group 4 works well and Group 3 is used by most fax machines and compresses this type of image one row at a time. The Run Length option should be used when an image of this type has large sections of black or white.

  - **Quality** — When the ZIP compression method is selected, there are two choices in this pop-up menu. Choose the 4-bit option for 4-bit images and the 8-bit option for both 8-bit and 4-bit images. If you use the 4-bit option for an 8-bit image, however, it causes loss of data, which reduces quality.

    If you choose the Automatic or the JPEG compression method, there are five options from which to choose: Minimum, Low, Medium, High, and Maximum.

- **Compress Text And Line Art** — This box should be checked to apply the selected compression method to text and line art.

Quality options available when JPEG or Automatic compression is selected

Saving Documents in SVG or SVGZ Format

The SVG file format (Scalable Vector Graphics) saves your Illustrator file as vector graphics but some features in your artwork, such as mesh objects, are rasterized. Imported images containing no alpha channel are converted to the JPEG format and images with an alpha channel are converted to the PNG format. Creating Web graphics for saving in SVG format is discussed in Step 14, *Web Graphics*.

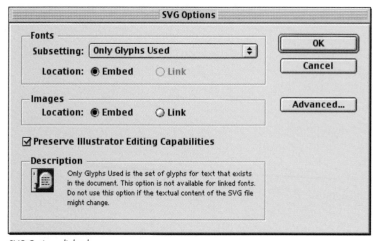

SVG Options dialog box

Fonts   Options in this section control how fonts are treated in the saved file.

- **Subsetting** — Determines which fonts in the exported SVG file are embedded or linked. Click the submenu arrow to display the options.

  - **None (use System fonts)** — No embedded or linked fonts are included with the file. The required fonts must be installed on the end-user's system.

  - **Only Glyphs Used** — Includes only those glyphs that are used in the artwork. Fonts must be embedded when this option is selected.

  - **Common English** — Standard English language characters.

  - **Common English & Glyphs Used**

  - **Common Roman**

  - **Common Roman & Glyphs Used**

  - **All Glyphs** — All glyphs are used whether or not they appear in the text.

- **Location** — You can choose to embed the subset fonts into the file or to link them to the exported fonts from the original Illustrator file.

  - **Embed** — Font data is included in the SVG file, ensuring that the correct fonts are used when the page is displayed. This option results in a larger file size.

  - **Link** — Links to the exported fonts from the original Illustrator file. If you have several SVG documents using the same fonts, you may want to link the fonts for each document to keep the file sizes smaller.

Images   Choose whether images are included in the file or linked to exported images.

- **Embed** — Data for rasterized images are included in the SVG file, ensuring that they will always display. This option results in a larger file size.

- **Link** — Links rasterized images to the exported JPEG or PNG images from the original Illustrator file. This option keeps the file size smaller and may be an efficient method if several pages use the same images.

Preserve Illustrator Editing Capabilities   When checked, the saved file can be reopened and edited in Illustrator. If you don't want anyone, including you, to change the file in any way, uncheck this option.

> None (Use System Fonts)
> ✓ Only Glyphs Used
> Common English
> Common English & Glyphs Used
> Common Roman
> Common Roman & Glyphs Used
> All Glyphs

Options available in the Fonts Subsetting pop-up menu

Save Command

After the first time you save your file, you can simply press ⌘s or choose the menu command **File ➪ Save**. The Save command overwrites the previously saved file with the same name and in the same location. If you want to change the file name, its format, or where its located on the disk, choose Save As (**File ➪ Save As** or press ⇧⌘s).

Save a Copy Command

The Save a Copy command (choose **File ➪ Save a Copy** or press ⌥⌘s) saves an exact copy of your file with the word *copy* added to the end of the file name. The original file stays open on the screen. This option is useful when you're making changes to artwork that you're not certain you want to keep. You can save the file you're working on and know that if, in the end, you don't like what you did, you can go back to the original file.

Save for Web Command

The Save for Web command (choose **File ➪ Save for Web** or press ⇧⌥⌘s) gives you easy-to-use controls for exporting your artwork in a standard Web bitmap format: JPEG, GIF, PNG-8, or PNG-24. These settings allow you to look at your artwork in different formats before saving it to a file so you can make sure you export the best-looking Web graphics possible. You can also check the download and display speed of your graphics. More information about saving files as Web graphics can be found in Step 14, *Web Graphics*.

fyi **Macintosh:**
If you have Extensis Suitcase 8.2 installed on your machine, pressing ⌥⌘s may display the Suitcase Sets dialog box rather than the Illustrator Save a Copy dialog box. To prevent this from occurring:

1. Launch Suitcase.
2. Choose Edit ➪ Preferences.
3. Uncheck the Hot-Key to open Suitcase application checkbox.
4. Click OK or press return.

Revert to Last-Saved Version

If you have made changes to a document that you decide you don't want, choose the Revert command in the File menu (File ➪ Revert) or press the *F12* shortcut key. Be sure you want to discard the changes, because you can't get them back once you've performed this action.

To restore the active document to the most recently saved version, choose **File ➪ Revert**. An alert will display on the screen asking you to verify that you want to revert to the last version saved. Click Revert.

If you think you may want to see your changes later, use the Save As feature to save your file with a different name instead of discarding them. Then open the original file and start over with making changes.

Alert box that displays when you use the Revert command

 **activity 2.8**

1. Save your file from Activity 2.7 in a new folder on your hard drive named Practice files. Store all the files you create in this folder when you complete the activities in this book.

   ■ Use the New Folder button in the Save As dialog box to create the new folder.

2. Name the file from Activity 2.7 My Strawberry and save it as a native Adobe Illustrator document.

3. Append a file extension in lower case. Save it as an Illustrator 10.0 file and use program defaults for the Embed All Fonts and the Subset Fonts options.

4. Do not close the document window.

Print a Document

Printing a document from Illustrator can be a complex process if you want to specify such things as color separations, crop marks and trim marks, negative, positive, and so on. For the purposes of these lessons, however, we'll use the basic Print command and print simple composite files.

You may be printing to a black-and-white PostScript printer, such as an Apple LaserWriter, or you may be printing to an inkjet color printer, such as the Epson Stylus Color 600. Whichever brand and type of printer you use, you should be familiar with its Page Setup dialog box and print options.

Printing a File *(Macintosh)*

1. Display the Apple menu and drag to select the Chooser.
2. Verify that your printer is available and that it is the chosen printer.
3. Click in the Close box to exit.

Page Setup

1. Choose **File ⇨ Page Setup** or press ⇧ ⌘ p to display the Page Setup dialog box (see Figure 2.11). Make the appropriate selections for the printer that's currently available.

   ■ **Format for** — Choose the printer that's currently selected in the Chooser.

   ■ **Paper** — Choose the size of paper that's loaded into the printer. If the paper size currently in the printer is not shown in the Paper field, click the submenu arrows to display the pop-up menu and make the appropriate selection.

   ■ **Orientation** — Highlight Portrait (▯) or Landscape (▭) to choose how to place the document on the paper:

      ▪ **Portrait** (▯) — normal orientation.

 *fyi* You cannot print a blank Illustrator page. If there's nothing on the page, the Print command line in the File menu is gray, therefore unavailable. If you press ⌘ p, nothing happens.

- **Landscape** (📭) — prints the page sideways.

■ **Scale** — To print at a size other than the size at which you created the document (100%), enter the appropriate number in the Scale field.

2. Click the Page Attributes submenu and choose PostScript™ Options to display the PostScript™ Options dialog box (Figure 2.12). Make the appropriate selections for the document you're printing.

■ If you're printing to a PostScript printer, all options can usually be unchecked.

3. Click OK or press *return/enter*.

Print

1. Choose **File** ⇨ **Print** or press ⌘ p to display the Print dialog box (Figure 2.13).

■ **Copies** — Enter the number of copies of the page you want to print (if different than 1).

■ **Collate** — I always leave this option checked.

■ **Pages** — Click the appropriate radio button to select the pages you want to print.

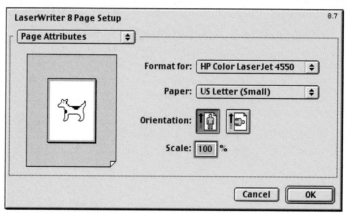

FIGURE 2.11 Macintosh LaserWriter 8 Page Setup dialog box.

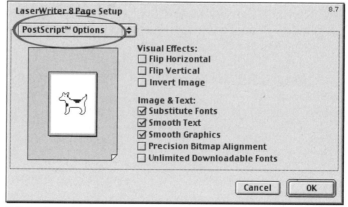

FIGURE 2.12 Macintosh LaserWriter 8 Page Attributes dialog box.

FIGURE 2.13 Macintosh LaserWriter 8 Print dialog box.

- **All** — Prints all pages in the document.
- **From/To** — Click this radio button and enter the page numbers of the pages you want to print in the fields. The number of pages that can be printed is determined by the selection made in the Document Setup dialog box (**File ⇨ Document Setup** or press ⌥ ⌘ p). By default, that setting is Single Full Page. More information about creating multiple pages can be found in Step 6, *Rulers, Grids, & Guides*.

■ **Paper Source** — These options are supplied by the printer driver. Follow the instructions for your specific printer.

2. To display a dialog box offering more options, click the General submenu arrow and select Adobe Illustrator 10 (Figure 2.14). Make the appropriate selections for the document you're printing.

■ **Output:** Composite. Select the other option, Separate, when you want to print color separations of your artwork, that is, a separate page for each color used in the document.

■ **Ignore Overprinting in Composite Output** — When checked, the printer ignores Fill and Stroke overprint settings you made in the Attributes palette in the document. See Step 7, *Add Color to Artwork*, for more information about this feature.

■ **PostScript®** — Click the submenu arrows to display the two options: Level 2 or Level 3. Choose the highest level supported by your printer to take advantage of all the features in Illustrator 10.

■ **Data** — Choose Binary to speed up the printing of bitmap images, if any. Choosing ASCII makes bitmap data usable on more printers, but it takes longer to print.

■ **Selection Only** — When checked, only objects in the document that are selected are printed.

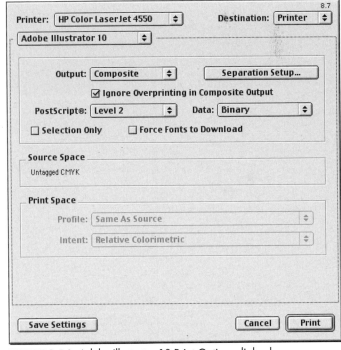

FIGURE 2.14 Adobe Illustrator 10 Print Options dialog box.

■ **Force Fonts to Download** — When checked, fonts are temporarily downloaded from the computer to the printer. Print quality is reduced. For best print quality, install the fonts in the printer.

3. Click Print or press *return/enter* to print the document.

Printing a File *(Windows)*

Print Setup

1. Choose **File** ⇨ **Print Setup** or press ⇧ ⌘ p to display the Print Setup dialog box (Figure 2.15). Make the appropriate selections for the printer that you're printing to and for the type of document you're printing.

   ■ **Printer** — Options in this section relate to the printer device that's connected to the computer.

     ▪ **Name** — If the correct printer driver for the printer isn't displayed in the Name field, click on the submenu arrow to display the list of printers and scroll to select the correct printer driver.

     ▪ **Status** — This option should read "Ready," indicating the printer is connected properly and is ready to receive data.

     ▪ **Type** — Indicates the kind of print device to which you're printing.

     ▪ **Where** — Indicates which printer port is being used.

   ■ **Paper** — Options in this section relate to the paper onto which the document will be printed.

     ▪ **Size** — If the paper size currently in the printer is not shown in the Paper field, click the submenu arrows to display the pop-up submenu and make the appropriate selection.

     ▪ **Source** — These options are supplied by the printer driver. Follow the instructions for your specific printer.

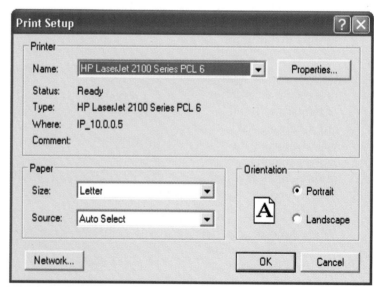

FIGURE 2.15 Windows Print Setup dialog box.

- **Orientation** — Highlight Portrait (image) or Landscape (image) to choose how to place the document on the paper:
  - **Portrait** (image) — normal orientation.
  - **Landscape** (image) — prints the page sideways.

2. Click the Properties button, change any options that are appropriate for your printer, and click OK or press *enter* to return to the Print Setup dialog box.

3. Click OK or press *enter* to exit the dialog box.

Print

1. Choose **File ⇨ Print** or press ⌘p to display the Print dialog box (Figure 2.16). Make the appropriate selections for the document you're printing.

   - **Properties** — Clicking the Properties button in the Print dialog box usually gives you the same options as those found in the Print Setup dialog box, although this may not hold true for all printers and printer drivers.

   - **Print Range** — Choose the pages of the document that you want to print.
     - **All** — Prints all pages in the document.
     - **Pages: From/To** — Click this radio button and enter the page numbers of the pages you want to print in the fields. The number of pages that can be printed is determined by the selection made in the Document Setup dialog box (**File ⇨ Document Setup**). By default, that setting is Single Page. More information about creating multiple pages can be found in Step 6, *Rulers, Grids, & Guides*.
     - **Selection** — When checked, only objects in the document that are selected are printed.

   - **Copies** — In the Number of Copies field enter the number times you want the document to print. Or, click the arrows on the left side of the field to change the value.

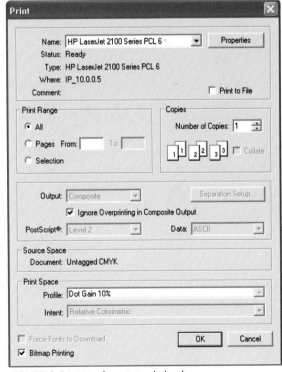

FIGURE 2.16 Windows Print dialog box.

- **Output:** Composite. Select the other option, Separate, when you want to print color separations of your artwork, that is, a separate page for each color used in the document.

- **Ignore Overprinting in Composite Output** — When checked, the printer ignores Fill and Stroke overprint settings you made in the Attributes palette in the document. See Step 7, *Add Color to Artwork*, for more information about this feature.

- **PostScript®** — Click the submenu arrows to display the two options: Level 2 or Level 3. Choose the highest level supported by your printer to take advantage of all the features in Illustrator 10.

- **Data** — Choose Binary to speed up the printing of bitmap images, if any. Choosing ASCII makes bitmap data usable on more printers, but it takes longer to print.

- **Force Fonts to Download** — When checked, fonts are temporarily downloaded from the computer to the printer. Print quality is reduced. For best print quality, install the fonts in the printer.

- **Bitmap Printing** — This option is for non-PostScript printers and can be used when printing documents containing complex objects, such as gradients, on low-resolution printers. Printing time may be increased, but fewer printing problems occur.

2. Click Print or press *return/enter* to print the document.

3. Click OK or press *return/enter* to print your document.

 *activity 2.9*

1. Print the document named My Strawberry.ai that you still have open on the screen.

2. Close My Strawberry.ai without saving changes.

3. Quit Illustrator 10.

There are no practice activities or exercises for this chapter.

Basic Shapes

Chapter Outline

- Components of a Path
- Undo/Redo
- Path Selection
- Select All
- Hide Edges
- Deselect Objects
- Select Multiple Objects
- Draw New Paths
- Draw Predefined Shapes
- Rectangle Tool and Ellipse Tool
- Polygon Tool
- Star Tool
- Line Segment Tool
- Arc Tool
- Spiral Tool
- The Grid Tools
- Move or Modify the Shape of a Path
- Add Color to Your Artwork
- Stroke Weight

Components of a Path

Adobe Illustrator 10 is a drawing program in which you create vector art. A vector object, or path, has a starting point and an ending point, and the shape of the object is determined by how you define those two elements.

All paths in Illustrator are created using Bézier (pronounced bay-zee-ay) curves and segments, named after the man who developed the mathematical formula for creating graphics in this manner — Pierre Bézier. A path can be open or closed and must have at least one segment.

- A shape that is continuous (has no beginning or end) is a *closed path*. Circles and rectangles are examples of closed paths.

- A path with loose ends, such as a single straight line or a half-circle, is an *open path*.

- A *segment* is a straight or curved line between two points.

- An *endpoint* is an anchor point that is placed at the ends of all open paths.

Anchor Points

An *anchor point* is the nonprinting point on the path that defines where each segment begins and ends. Once an anchor is established, it doesn't move unless you drag it to a new position. There are two kinds of anchor points: corner points and smooth points. If you discover that you've created the wrong kind of point for the path you want to create, you can change it.

Corner Points *Corner points* connect straight segments (Figure 3.1). They also are placed at the end of a noncontinuous curved path and at the point where a path abruptly changes direction. By default, when you make the first click to create a path, it's a corner point.

Smooth Points A *smooth point* connects two curved segments to form a smooth, continuous curve, such as a wavy line (see Figure 3.2).

Direction Lines and Direction Points

The anchor point of a curved segment has a nonprinting *direction line* attached to it with a nonprinting *direction point* at the end of the direction line (Figure 3.2).

- A smooth point has a direction line extending out from both sides of the point.
- A corner point between a curved segment and a straight segment has a direction line extending only from the curved segment side of the anchor point.
- Corner points on straight segments don't have direction lines or direction points.

The angle of the direction line determines the shape of the curve. The length of the direction line determines the height of the curve. To reshape a curved segment, change the length or angle of the direction line by dragging its direction point.

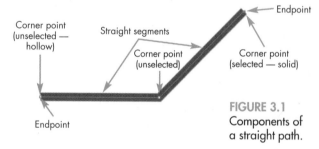

FIGURE 3.1
Components of a straight path.

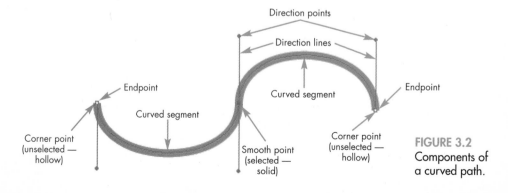

FIGURE 3.2
Components of a curved path.

66

When you change the angle or length of a direction line on a smooth point, the curved segments on both sides of the point are adjusted simultaneously. Changing the angle or length of a direction line on a corner point changes only the curved segment on the side of the point that has the direction line.

Undo / Redo

Undo

Before you begin drawing paths and creating illustrations, there's one editing function you should become acquainted with: Undo. Using the Undo command ($\mathcal{H}$ z), you can reverse your actions as though they never happened. Commit the keyboard command for this function to memory. You will use it often.

The Undo command is common in graphics programs, but Illustrator goes farther than most in making this function invaluable. You can undo as many actions as the amount of RAM allocated to the program allows, which means an unlimited number of times if you have sufficient RAM.

You can control the minimum number of Undos available by entering a higher value in the Minimum Undo Levels field of the Units & Undo Preferences dialog box (**Edit** ⇨ **Preferences** ⇨ **Units & Undo**). The default value is 5 and I can't think of a reason you'd want to increase the number because the program will allow as many as you have enough memory for. If you're working on a complex illustration, however, and an alert message asks you to reduce the number of undo levels because of insufficient memory, you may have to lower the number to make more memory available for the illustration.

Apply the Undo command in one of the following ways:

- Press $\mathcal{H}$ z
- Display the context-sensitive menu and choose Undo.
  - *Macintosh:* ⌥-click.
  - *Windows:* Right-click.
- Choose **Edit** ⇨ **Undo** [tool you have selected] (in this example, the Ellipse tool).

Continue pressing $\mathcal{H}$ z or clicking on the menu option until you've reversed as many actions as you need to.

Redo

The Redo command (**Edit** ⇨ **Redo**) works the same way as the Undo command except it restores the action you just undid. For instance, if you decided that what you just undid was not a mistake and you want it back or if you undid too many actions, press the Redo command (⇧ $\mathcal{H}$ z). Continue pressing ⇧ $\mathcal{H}$ z until you have reversed all the Undo actions you want.

Like the Undo command, you can continue to use the Redo command even after you've saved a file, but not if you've closed it and reopened it.

fyi You can Undo an action after you've saved a file, but not if you've closed the file and reopened it.

The Undo command in the Edit menu

Path Selection

Before you can modify, move, delete, or copy a path, you must identify the specific path or part of a path you want to work with and make it active. There are six selection tools at the top of the Toolbox (Figure 3.3) and one of them must be selected when you click on a specific path(s) or part of a path to make it active.

- **Selection tool** — selects entire objects
- **Direct Selection tool** — selects anchor points and segments
- **Group Selection tool** — selects paths in a group (Groups are discussed in Step 4, *The Pen & Pencil Tools.*)
- **Direct Select Lasso tool** — selects parts of a path
- **Lasso tool** — selects an entire path
- **Magic Wand** — selects objects having similar attributes (The Magic Wand is discussed in Step 7, *Add Color to Artwork.*)

Selection Tool

If you want to select an entire path, that is, all of its anchor points, use the Selection tool. Its keyboard equivalent is the letter *v*, so you can select the tool by pressing the letter *v* on the keyboard.

The placement of the cursor on a path changes the cursor icon:

- When the Selection tool cursor is over an unselected path, a small, solid black box appears with the cursor arrow (▸■).
- When the Selection tool cursor is over an active object or path, the cursor changes to an arrowhead (▸).
- When you position the Selection tool cursor over an anchor point in an unselected path, a small open box appears with the cursor (▸□).

To select an entire path and make it active:

1. Click on a segment of an unselected path (▸■).
   - The cursor changes to an arrowhead (▸) because the path is now active.

or

2. Click on an anchor point of an unselected path (▸□).

or

3. *Marquee* part or all of the path.
   - Click in a blank space outside the path and drag over the path. A dotted box displays momentarily until you release the mouse.

or

68

FIGURE 3.3 The selection tools.

Selection tool icon in the Toolbox palette

timesaver
You can temporarily choose the Selection tool when another tool is being used by pressing the ⌘ key and clicking on a path to select it.

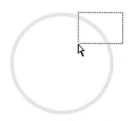

Marquee to select a path

4. You can select a path that has a fill color applied to it by clicking in the filled area if (a) you're working in Preview mode, *and* (b) the Use Area Select option is checked in the General Preferences dialog box (**Edit** ⇨ **Preferences** ⇨ **General**).

Refer to *Add Color to Your Artwork* later in this chapter for more information about filling paths with color.

Bounding Box A path or object selected with the Selection tool displays a rectangular box around the object with handles in its corners and in the middle of each side. This box is called the *bounding box*. You can use the handles on the bounding box to move, reshape, copy, or rotate the selected object.

The program default is to always show the bounding box when you select a path with the Selection tool. But you can hide it by choosing the Hide Bounding Box command in the View menu (**View** ⇨ **Hide Bounding Box**) or by pressing ⇧⌘b. You cannot reshape, rotate, and so on, using the Selection tool unless the bounding box is visible. When you want to show it again, choose Show Bounding Box or press ⇧⌘b again.

Direct Selection Tool

To select individual anchor points or a single segment of a path, use the Direct Selection tool. The keyboard equivalent for this tool is the letter *a*. When you select an object with the Direct Selection tool, anchor points, direction lines, and direction points become visible, but no bounding box displays.

■ When the Direct Selection tool cursor is over an inactive path, it changes to an open arrow with a small, solid black box at the bottom and to the right of the cursor arrow (▯).

■ When you position the Direct Selection tool cursor over an anchor point (on an active or inactive path), a small open box appears at the bottom right side of the cursor (▯).

When you click on the path line with the Direct Selection tool, all anchor points, direction lines, and direction points display. If an anchor point *is not* selected, it's a hollow square; if the anchor point *is* selected, it's a solid square. When you click on a hollow anchor point, it changes to a solid anchor point, which you can then manipulate.

If the Use Area Select option is checked in the General Preferences dialog box (**Edit** ⇨ **Preferences** ⇨ **General**) and you click inside a shape that's filled with a color (even white), all anchor points in the shape are selected (solid).

There are two ways to select only part of a path when the Direct Selection tool is the active tool:

1. Click within 2 pixels (very close) of the edge of the segment you want to make active.

2. Click and drag to marquee the portion of the path you want to select.

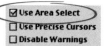

Check Use Area Select in the General Preferences dialog box to enable you to select objects filled with a color by clicking in them

The bounding box displays when a path is selected with the Selection tool

Direct Selection tool icon in the Toolbox palette

When you marquee to select a path with the Direct Selection tool active, any anchor points covered by the marquee "box" are also selected, so they become solid and, therefore, active.

Lasso Tool

When the Lasso tool is selected, you can select an entire path by dragging around any part of it — similar to the way the Selection tool works, except no bounding box displays. The trick is to create an arc when you drag through a segment or around a point. Select an object containing several paths by dragging around at least a portion of each separate path. There is no keyboard command for this tool.

- All anchor points in the path are selected.
- You cannot move, copy, reshape, or rotate a path with the Lasso tool selected. This tool is strictly for selecting paths or points.

Direct Select Lasso Tool

The Direct Select Lasso tool (letter *q*) allows you to select individual anchor points or segments by dragging around or across the parts of the path you want to select. Direction lines and direction points display on the selected path. An anchor point selected by dragging around it is solid, making it active. The other anchor points are hollow because they're not selected.

- You cannot move, copy, reshape, or rotate a path with the Direct Select Lasso tool selected.

Select All

You can select all the paths in a document with one command, regardless of which tool is active: press ⌘a or choose **Select ➪ All** from the menu bar.

Hide Edges

When creating complex artwork, path lines and anchor points that are visible while drawing or selecting a path in Preview mode can be distracting. You can make them invisible by choosing Hide Edges in the View menu or by pressing ⌘h. The selection can still be moved, painted, reshaped, and so on, as though the path lines and anchor points were visible.

This command is a toggle so if path lines and anchor points of selected paths are visible on the screen, Hide Edges is the option in the View menu. Conversely, if path lines and anchor points of selected paths are invisible, Show Edges is the option. Pressing ⌘h once hides edges; pressing ⌘h again shows edges.

Lasso tool icon in the Toolbox palette

Drag in an arc to select paths with the Lasso tool or Direct Select Lasso tool

Direct Select Lasso tool icon in the Toolbox palette

timesaver

The keyboard command for Select All is a universal command and is the same for nearly all computer programs. You should make an effort to commit it to memory. Many of the other editing keyboard commands — cut (⌘x), copy (⌘c), paste (⌘v) — are also universal commands and you should memorize them, too.

Deselect Objects

You can deselect one path at a time, several paths at a time, or all the paths in your illustration at one time. Once you deselect a path, you can't edit it until you reselect it. With the Selection tool in the Toolbox active, do the following:

1. To deselect only part of an illustration:

   ■ Hold the *Shift* key down and click a selected path to deselect it.

   or

   ■ Hold the *Shift* key down and drag a marquee over the path or segment you want to deselect.

2. To deselect everything on your page:

   ■ With a selection tool active, click somewhere on the page that is at least 2 pixels away from any object.

   or

   ■ Press ⇧ ⌘ a (any tool active).

   or

   ■ Choose **Select** ⇨ **Deselect** (any tool active).

Select Multiple Objects

There are several ways to select more than one path at a time. With one of the selection tools active in the Toolbox, do one of the following:

1. Drag a marquee over the paths you want to make active.

2. If one or more paths are already selected:

   ■ Hold the *Shift* key down and draw a marquee over additional paths you want to select.

   or

   ■ Hold the *Shift* key down and click on the paths you want to select.

3. To select all *unlocked* paths in a file (see *Lock/Unlock Objects* in Step 4, *The Pen & Pencil Tools*):

   ■ Press ⌘ a.

   or

   ■ Choose **Select** ⇨ **All**.

4. To select all unselected paths in the artwork window, choose **Select** ⇨ **Inverse**.

   ■ Using this option *deselects* selected paths and *selects* unselected paths in the entire artwork window. In other words, what was on is now off and what was off is now on.

activity 3.1

To be certain that all tools used in the activities in this chapter function properly, restore the preferences to program defaults before starting the activities. Refer to page 37, Restore Program Defaults, for instructions.

1. If Illustrator is not launched, launch it now.

2. Open the file named Strawberry.eps in the Student Files folder on the CD-ROM attached to the back of this book.

3. Zoom in as far as you can and still see the entire shape on your screen.

4. Click on the Selection tool (▶) in the Toolbox to make it the active tool.

5. Move the cursor over the path that created the right side of the strawberry.
   - Notice that the small black square next to the arrow pointer (▶▪) displays to indicate that it is not an active path.

6. Move the cursor along the bottom of the object until the pointer displays an open box (▶▫), indicating that you are over an anchor point.

7. Click on a segment on the right side of the strawberry.
   - The bounding box displays and the anchor points become visible.
   - The bounding box displays only around the object created by the path you selected. The stem of the strawberry is a separate path, so the bounding box doesn't enclose it.

8. Click on a segment of the path that created the stem of the strawberry to see its bounding box.

9. Click inside one of the leaves.
   - Note that the cursor changes to an arrowhead, indicating that it is an active path.
   - The leaf has a fill of white, so you don't have to click on the segment, just somewhere inside the leaf.

10. Position the pointer over an anchor point of the selected leaf.
    - The small open box next to the arrowhead indicates that it is an active anchor point.

11. Click in a blank spot (not inside one of the "seeds") inside the strawberry. The path of the strawberry isn't selected because the strawberry is not filled with a color.

12. Select the Direct Selection tool (▶) by pressing the letter *a* on your keyboard.
    - Note that the Direct Selection tool in the Toolbox is now highlighted.

13. Click on the outline of the strawberry to make it the active path.
    - Unless you inadvertently clicked on an anchor point, all anchor points in the active path are hollow, indicating that they are not selected. Only the segment you clicked on is active.

14. Click on an inactive anchor point to select it.
    - It becomes solid, indicating it is now active.
    - Direction lines and direction points are visible on the segment that was selected.

15. Click the right-most anchor point on the bottom of the strawberry to make it active and display its direction lines and points.

16. With the Direct Selection tool selected, marquee a "seed" of the strawberry.

17. Enlarge the View to 1600% and notice that the anchor points on the seed are selected.

18. With the Direct Select Lasso tool selected, draw a partial circle around the top end of a seed.
    - Notice that the path of the seed displays with the top anchor point solid, meaning it's selected. The direction lines and direction points associated with both anchor points are visible.

19. Select the Direct Selection tool by pressing *a* on the keyboard.

Continued

20. Using the keyboard command (⌘1), reduce the View to 100%.

21. Switch to the Selection tool and marquee to select the entire strawberry so that every path and segment is selected and displays its bounding box.

22. Enlarge the View to 300%, even if you can't see the entire illustration.

23. Press ⌘h to hide the path lines and anchor points.

24. Press ⌘h again to make them visible.

25. With the Selection tool active, hold the *Shift* key down and click on three of the seeds in the strawberry to deselect them.

26. *Shift*-click-and-drag to marquee two more seeds that are active to deselect them.

27. Switch to the Direct Selection tool and *Shift*-click on a couple more seeds.

   ■ Notice that the seeds you selected with the Direct Selection tool display direction lines and direction points and the anchor points are hollow.

28. With the Direct Selection tool active, *Shift*-click on the bottom anchor point of another seed.

   ■ Notice that only the anchor point you clicked on displays its direction lines and is hollow.

29. Deselect all paths in the illustration.

30. Close the document without saving it to a file.

Draw New Paths

In Adobe Illustrator 10, there are fourteen path creation tools, plus six type creation tools. The type creation tools are discussed in Step 5, *Add Type to Artwork*. The Illustrator path creation tools are:

■ **Rectangle tool** (▢) — Draws squares and rectangles with square corners.

■ **Rounded Rectangle tool** (▢) — Draws squares and rectangles with rounded corners.

■ **Ellipse tool** (◯) — Draws circles and ovals.

■ **Polygon tool** (◯) — Draws shapes having straight sides of equal length, with each side the same distance from the center of the object; you can specify its size and the number of sides the shape has.

■ **Star tool** (☆) — Draws star-shaped objects; you can specify its size and how many points the object has.

■ **Line Segment tool** (◣) — Draws single straight segments.

■ **Arc tool** (◜) — Draws single curved segments.

■ **Spiral tool** (◎) — Draws spiral-shaped paths; you can specify its size and the number of times it winds around the starting point.

■ **Rectangular Grid tool** (▦) — Creates a rectangular or square grid with straight segments; you can specify its size and the number of dividers it contains.

■ **Polar Grid tool** (◉) — Creates a grid consisting of concentric circles; you can specify its size and the number of dividers it contains.

- **Pen tool** (⬚) — Draws shapes with straight or curved lines. The Pen tool is the most versatile of the drawing tools and it's the one you'll likely use most often.
- **Pencil tool** (⬚) — Creates freehand shapes, as if you were drawing with a pencil on paper.
- **Flare tool** (⬚) — Creates objects having an effect similar to a lens flare in a photograph. This tool is discussed in Step 7, *Add Color to Artwork*.
- **Paintbrush tool** (⬚) — Creates paths with a brushstroke. This tool is discussed in Step 10, *Brushes, Patterns, & Symbols*.

Draw Predefined Shapes

Many basic graphic shapes, such as rectangles, squares, ovals, and circles are created using the tools in the Toolbox. Other tools in the Toolbox that draw predefined shapes are the Polygon, Star, Line Segment, Arc, Spiral, Rectangular Grid, and the Polar Grid tools.

Draw a Predefined Shape by Dragging an Edge

By default all predefined shape tools are created from a corner. The exceptions are the Polygon, Star, and Spiral tools. These shapes, by default, are drawn from the center. To draw a shape with one of the shape creation tools:

1. Click the tool in the Toolbox that corresponds to the shape you want to draw.

2. Position the mouse pointer at the place on the page where you want a corner or edge of the shape to start.

3. Click and drag diagonally until the object is the size and shape you want.
    - The direction and distance you drag determines the shape and size of the object.
    - When drawing a circle or oval shape, the point of the click is the top left edge of its bounding box.

Draw a Predefined Shape by Dragging from Its Center

You can draw a rectangle, circle, arc, line segment, rectangular grid, and polar grid starting from the center of the shape rather than its corner. Simply hold down the ⬚ key as you start to drag.

- If you start a regular drag (from the top left) and then press the ⬚ key, the object automatically readjusts to become a center drag.
- If you start a center drag by holding down the ⬚ key, then release the ⬚ key, the shape reverts to what it would have been if you had started a regular drag.

Move a Predefined Shape as You Draw It

To "freeze" the drawing of a shape at a specific size and move it to a new location, press the spacebar and move the object before releasing the mouse. If you want to resize it again, after releasing the spacebar, move the mouse until the object is the desired size. You can continue pressing and releasing the spacebar until the shape is the size and in the position you want.

Create Predefined Shapes Numerically

You can create a predefined shape with specific dimensions by entering those dimensions in that tool's Options dialog box. You can't, however, make changes to an existing shape using the tool's Options dialog box. To specify exact dimensions for a shape you are going to draw using one of the shape tools in the Toolbox:

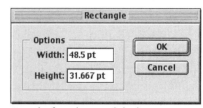

Example of a tool options dialog box

1. Select the tool in the Toolbox that corresponds to the shape you want to draw.

2. Click without dragging at the spot on the page where you want to start your shape. If you want to draw the shape from its center point, press the ⌥ key as you click on the page.

   ■ The Options dialog box corresponding to the selected tool display.

     ▪ Options dialog boxes are context-sensitive, which means only fields that apply to the selected tool are displayed.

     ▪ Some fields have arrows you can click to enter values.

   ■ The units of measurement used in the fields can be changed in the Document Setup dialog box (⌥⌘p) (see the discussion about Rulers in Step 6, *Rulers, Grids, & Guides*.

   ■ The numbers already present in the fields are the specifications of the last shape you drew with that tool.

3. Enter the appropriate values in the fields.

4. Click OK or press *return/enter*.

Create Multiple Shapes as You Drag

You can multiply the number of shapes you draw by holding down the ` (grave accent) key as you drag.

   ■ The speed at which you drag determines how many additional paths are created. Fewer shapes are created the faster you drag.

   ■ Release the mouse before releasing the ` key or all the paths except the original one will disappear.

   ■ Create additional shapes around the outside of the original shape by holding down the ` key and the *Shift* key.

read this!

A Radius field in an Options dialog box means the value entered in the field is measured from the point of the click to the outside of the shape, making the size of the entire shape double the value in the field.

Multiple shapes created by holding down the ` key when dragging to create the shape. (A) rotated when dragging; (B) Shift key held down when dragging

fyi The copied objects are separate paths so they can be deleted, colored, moved, and so on, individually.

Rectangle Tool and Ellipse Tool

There are two tools for drawing rectangles and squares — the Rectangle tool (keyboard command: letter *m*) for drawing rectangles or squares with square corners () and the Rounded Rectangle tool for drawing rectangles or squares with rounded corners (). The Ellipse tool () (keyboard command: letter *l*) is used to draw ovals and circles. All of these shapes are closed-path objects.

The Rounded Rectangle tool and the Ellipse tool are hidden under the Rectangle tool in the Toolbox. These tools are hidden under the Rectangle tool so you must press the arrow on the Rectangle tool to display the hidden tools before you can select it. Or you can use Illustrator's tear-off feature and make the shape tools appear in a separate palette.

Draw a Perfect Square or Circle

You can draw perfect squares with the Rectangle tool or Rounded Rectangle tool and perfect circles with the Ellipse tool in two ways:

1. Press the *Shift* key as you drag.
   - If you start to drag and then press the *Shift* key, the shape instantly becomes an exact square or a perfect circle.
   - Hold down the *Shift* key and the ⌥ key to draw a perfect square or circle starting from its center point.
     - Release the mouse before releasing the *Shift* and ⌥ keys.
2. Enter the same value in the Height field that you entered in the Width field of the Rectangle or Ellipse Options dialog box.

The Center Point

When you draw a shape with the Rectangle tool or the Ellipse tool, Illustrator calculates the exact center of the shape and places a center point. When the Selection tool is active, the center point is always solid (active) and is visible in the center of the bounding box, not necessarily in the center of the shape.

When the Direct Selection tool is used to select a shape, the center point is hollow (inactive) until you select it. When you click on the center point, the center point and all the anchor points in the path become solid. If the object has a fill color (even white), you can click inside the shape to select it.

The center point of an active shape can be visible or invisible by changing that option in the Attributes dialog box.

1. Display the Attributes palette:
   - Choose **Window ➪ Attributes**.
   - Click the Attributes folder tab in the Color palette.
2. Click the Show Center button () or the Don't Show Center button () on the left side of the palette.

Rectangle tool
icon in the
Toolbox palette

Ellipse tool
icon in the
Toolbox palette

timesaver

When entering values in the Rectangle Options or Ellipse Options dialog boxes, you can create perfect squares or circles by entering a value in the Width field, then clicking on the word Height. This will copy the Width value into the Height field. It also works to enter a value in the Height field, then click on the Width field to copy it to that field.

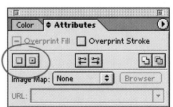

Display or hide the center point in an object by pressing the appropriate button in the Attributes palette

Step 3 — BASIC SHAPES

activity 3.2

1. Create a new document: Letter size, CMYK color mode.

2. If it seems like your screen is filled with palette groups, you can close them by clicking in their Close boxes. Leave the Navigator and Color palettes open. The others can be closed because you won't be using them in this chapter.

3. Enlarge the View to 400%.

4. Select the Rectangle tool (▣).
   - Click the Rectangle tool in the Toolbox or press _m_ on the keyboard.

5. Click in the document page and drag down and to the left to create a rectangle. Release the mouse when the rectangle is about 2" wide and 1" high.
   - A black border appears on the rectangle you drew because the program default applies a 1 point black stroke around any shape you draw. If your rectangle doesn't have a black border, click the Default Fill and Stroke button on the Toolbox palette. Refer to page 30, if necessary, for its location on the palette.
   - Notice the corner points in the corners of your shape and the center point in the middle.

6. Click on the Ellipse tool (◉) in the Toolbox or choose it by pressing _l_ (el) on the keyboard.

7. Draw a perfect circle about 1" in diameter on another spot on your page by holding the _Shift_ key down as you drag to create the shape.
   - Notice the anchor points on the path and the center point in the middle.

8. Choose the Rectangle tool, and in a new position on the page, draw a rectangle from its center point by holding the ⬚ key down when you drag, but don't release the mouse yet.

9. Release the ⬚ key, but not the mouse.
   - Toggle back and forth by pressing and releasing the ⬚ key. The shape changes from one that is created from the center at the point of the click to one that is created from the corner.

10. Without releasing the mouse, move it back and forth and up and down to change the shape of the rectangle.

11. Without releasing the mouse, press and hold the spacebar.

12. Move the mouse, which moves the shape. Move it to a new position on the page.

13. Release the spacebar and the mouse to drop the shape in its new position.

14. Select the Ellipse tool in the Toolbox, and click on the upper left corner of the rectangle, without dragging the mouse.
   - The Ellipse Options dialog box displays with the Width field highlighted.

15. Type 65 in the Width field.

16. Click the word Height in the dialog box. The same value (65) is entered in the Height field.

17. Click OK or press _return/enter_.

18. Select the circle with the Selection tool so its bounding box displays.
   - Notice that upper left corner of the bounding box is at the point of your click (the upper left corner of the rectangle).

19. Select the Rectangle tool, press the ⬚ key down, and click in a clear spot on your page.

20. When the Rectangle Options dialog box displays, type 72 in the Width field and press the tab key to highlight the Height field. Type 28 in this field.

21. Click OK or press _return/enter_.
   - The shape displays on the screen with its center located at the spot of your click.

22. Practice drawing circles, ovals, squares, and rectangles until you are comfortable drawing them by dragging and by entering numbers in their dialog boxes.

23. Return the View to 100% by pressing ⌘1, then close the document without saving it to a file.

Rounded Rectangle Tool

With the Rounded Rectangle tool, you can create shapes with rounded corners the same way square-cornered rectangles are created. The roundness (radius) of the corners of a rounded rectangle can be adjusted in several ways:

1. You can adjust the roundness of the corners as you draw the shape:

   ■ Select the Rounded Rectangle tool.

   ■ Click on the page where you want the object to be positioned and start dragging.

   ■ As you drag:

     ▪ Press the Left arrow (←) to change to the minimum radius (square) instantly.

     ▪ Press the Right arrow (→) to instantly change to the maximum radius (most roundness) instantly.

     ▪ Press the Up arrow (↑) to adjust the radius to more roundness gradually as you drag.

     ▪ Press the Down arrow (↓) to adjust the radius to less roundness gradually as you drag.

   ■ Release the arrow keys when the corners are the roundness you want.

2. You can change the roundness of the corners numerically:

   ■ Display the Rounded Rectangle Options dialog box by selecting that tool in the Toolbox and clicking in the document where you want the shape to be drawn.

   ■ Enter the Width and Height values.

   ■ Enter a number in the Corner Radius field.

     ▪ The value in the field reflects the radius of the last rectangle that was created. The default Corner Radius is 12 pt.

     ▪ A Corner Radius of 0 creates a shape with square corners.

     ▪ To determine the roundness of the corner you want, visualize a circle of that diameter drawn in the corner of a rectangle or square.

3. You can also change the Corner Radius value by displaying the General Preferences dialog box (**Edit ⇨ Preferences ⇨ General**) and entering a different number in the Corner Radius field. The new value is displayed in the Corner Radius field of the Rounded Rectangle Options dialog box.

Rounded rectangle tool icon in the Toolbox palette

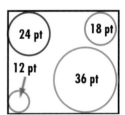

Visualize circles in the corner of a square to determine the corner radius value

Rounded rectangle Options dialog box

Adjust the corner radius of rounded-corner rectangles by changing the Corner Radius value in the General Preferences dialog box

fyi *The value entered in the General Preferences dialog box changes the value in the Rounded Rectangle Options dialog box, and vice versa. If you enter a value in the Rounded Rectangle Options dialog box, the same value is entered in the General Preferences dialog box, too.*

Step 3 — BASIC SHAPES

 *activity* 3.3

1. Create a new document: Letter size, CMYK color mode.

2. Select the Rounded Rectangle tool () in the Toolbox.

3. Click and drag to draw a rounded rectangle about 2" wide and 3" high in the upper left corner of the page.

4. Draw another rounded rectangle inside the first one, starting the drag from the center of the new shape, except press the spacebar and move the shape outside the border to the right of the first shape and drop it by releasing the spacebar. Before releasing the mouse, enlarge it to approximately the same size as the first shape.

   - Press the ⌥ key down before starting the drag to draw from the center.
   - Release the mouse before releasing the ⌥ key.

5. To the right of the second shape, draw another rounded rectangle about 2" square. Change the corner radius as you draw by pressing the up arrow (↑).

6. Using the Rounded Rectangle Options dialog box, draw a new shape below the existing shapes: 2½" square, with a corner radius of 24.

   - Remember: If you type in "2.5 inches" or "2.5 in," Illustrator will convert it to points for you.

   - Because you want to draw a square, type the numbers in the Width field then click the word Height to repeat the value in that field.

7. With the Rounded Rectangle tool selected, start to drag in the artwork window to create a shape. Before releasing the mouse, hold down the ` key and continue to drag. Vary the speed you move the mouse and notice the difference in the spacing of the new shapes.

8. Close the document without saving it to a file.

Polygon Tool

A polygon is a shape having a specified number of sides of equal length and all sides are an equal distance from the center of the shape. The Polygon tool is hidden under the Rectangle tool in the Toolbox. Press the ⌥ key and click on the Rectangle tool until the Polygon tool displays.

All polygons are drawn from the center rather than the top edge. You don't have to hold down the ⌥ key to get that feature. Click on your page where you want the center of the polygon to be, and drag to create the shape, or display the Polygon Options dialog box and enter values in the fields.

Adjust the Number of Sides in a Polygon

You can add or subtract the number of sides a polygon has as you draw it by pressing the up and down arrows before releasing the mouse. Hold the arrow keys down or press-and-release the arrow keys until the desired number of sides is reached. A polygon can have as few as 3 sides and as many as 1000 sides.

   - ↑ arrow = adds sides
   - ↓ arrow = subtracts sides

Polygon tool icon in the Toolbox palette

fyi *The Polygon Options dialog box has a Radius field, indicating that values entered will create a polygon that is twice the size of that value. For example, entering 1 inch in the field results in a polygon that's 2 inches wide.*

Rotate a Polygon as You Draw It

1. Rotate the polygon visually as you draw it by moving the pointer around.

2. To rotate the polygon as you draw it so that one side is always horizontal on the bottom, press the *Shift* key before you release the mouse. You can press the *Shift* key at any time before releasing the mouse to snap a side of the polygon to the horizontal position. That happens because the Constrain Angle field in the General Preferences dialog box is 0°, which restricts the angle to only preset values (0°, 45°, 90°).

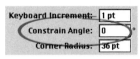

Constrain Angle field in the General Preferences dialog box

   ■ To specify a different angle of rotation, enter a new angle number in the Constrain Angle field of the General Preferences dialog box (**Edit ⇨ Preferences ⇨ General**).

3. Keep the polygon from rotating at all by holding down the *Shift* key as you drag to create it.

fyi *When you create a polygon or star by specifying its dimensions in Options dialog boxes, you cannot rotate the object as you create it. You can rotate it by selecting it with the Selection tool so that the bounding box displays. Then rotate the bounding box.*

activity 3.4

1. Create a new document: Letter size, CMYK color mode.

2. Zoom to 200%.

3. Select the Polygon tool (◙) in the Toolbox.

4. Click in the document page and drag down to create a polygon. Release the mouse when the polygon is about 2" in diameter.

5. Click and drag to draw another polygon and, without releasing the mouse, move it back and forth and up and down to change its size.

6. Without releasing the mouse, press and hold the spacebar.

7. Move the mouse to move the object to a new position on the page.

8. Release the spacebar and the mouse to drop the shape in its new position.

9. Move to a clear spot on your page and click without dragging.

   ■ The Polygon Options dialog box displays.

10. Type 1 inch in the Radius field (Illustrator converts the value to points automatically).

11. Type 11 in the Sides field.

12. Click OK or press return/enter.

   ■ A 2" polygon with 11 sides displays on the screen.

13. Click in a blank area of the page and drag to draw a polygon. Don't release the mouse.

14. Press the ↑ arrow to increase the number of sides on the polygon.

   ■ Value in Options dialog box is also changed.

15. Press the ↓ arrow until you have only three sides, creating a triangle.

16. Release the mouse.

17. Practice drawing polygons until you are comfortable drawing them by dragging and by entering numbers in the Options dialog box and increasing and decreasing the number of sides.

18. Return the View to 100% by pressing the arrow in the View Percent field and choosing 100% in the pop-up menu.

19. Close the document without saving it to a file.

Star Tool

Another predefined shape you can create with a tool in the Toolbox is a star. The Star tool is hidden under the Rectangle tool. All stars are drawn from the center rather than the top edge so you don't have to hold down the ⌥ key to get that feature. To position the star, click on your page where you want the center of the star to be. You can rotate a star as you draw it the same way you rotate a polygon — by moving the mouse around.

Star tool icon in the Toolbox palette

Adjust the Star as You Drag

Add/Subtract the Number of Points You can add or subtract points from a star as you draw it by pressing the up and down arrows before releasing the mouse. Hold the arrow keys down or press-and-release the arrow keys until the desired number of points is reached. You can specify as few as 3 points or as many as 1000 points.

- ↑ arrow = adds points
- ↓ arrow = subtracts points

Keep the Sides Straight Keep the sides of a star straight by holding down the ⌥ key as you drag.

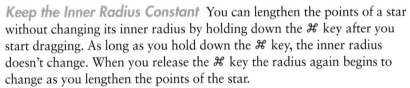

Normal star   Straight-sided star

Keep the Inner Radius Constant You can lengthen the points of a star without changing its inner radius by holding down the ⌘ key after you start dragging. As long as you hold down the ⌘ key, the inner radius doesn't change. When you release the ⌘ key the radius again begins to change as you lengthen the points of the star.

- Unfortunately, a glitch in the program causes the radius to "get stuck" at that inner radius. To release it, start dragging a new star, then hold down the ⌥ key, then the ⌘ key and drag a little more. The new star reverts back to the default inner radius.

Star with small inner radius

Create a Star Numerically

1. Select the Star tool (⭐) in the Toolbox and display the Star Options dialog box by clicking on the page where you want the center of the star to be.

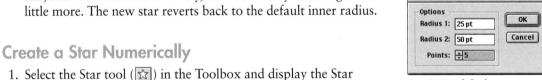

Star Options dialog box

2. The numbers you enter in the Radius 1 and Radius 2 fields control the dimensions of the star. The largest number you enter in one of the fields is the length of the points of the star. The smallest number you enter becomes the size of the center radius and the distance between the bottom of each arm of its points. It's best, though, to be consistent with entering the numbers so you are sure to get the shape you want. For instance, always enter the value for the length of

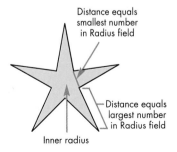

Distance equals smallest number in Radius field

Distance equals largest number in Radius field

Inner radius

the points in the Radius 1 field and enter the value for the center radius in the Radius 2 field. *Remember that a value in a radius field creates a shape that's twice the size of that value.*

3. Specify how many points you want in the star by typing a number in the Points field or by clicking the arrows on the left side of the field to select a number.

4. Click OK or press *return/enter.*

activity 3.5

1. Create a new document: Letter size, CMYK color mode.

2. Zoom to 400%.

3. Select the Star tool (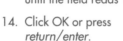) in the Toolbox.

4. Click in the document page and drag to create a star. Without releasing the mouse, move it back and forth and up and down to change its size and rotation. Release the mouse when the star is about 1" in diameter.

5. Click and drag to draw another star and, without releasing the mouse, press and hold the spacebar. Move the mouse to move the star to a new position on the page. Release the spacebar and the mouse to drop the star in its new position.

6. Click in a blank area of the page and drag to draw a star. Don't release the mouse.

7. Press the ↑ arrow to increase the number of points on the star to 7 or 8.

8. Press the ↓ arrow until you have only three points, creating a triangle.

9. Release the mouse.

10. Move to a clear spot on your page (press *h* and drag). Reselect the Star tool and click on the page without dragging.
    - The Star Options dialog box displays.

11. Enter .5 inch in the Radius 1 field. Illustrator converts to points unless you changed the units of measurement in Units & Undo Preferences to something other than points.

12. Enter 9 in the Radius 2 field.
    - Because the unit of measurement is already points, you just have to enter the number 9.

13. Type 11 in the Points field or click the "up" arrow until the field reads 11.

14. Click OK or press *return/enter.*
    - A pointy star is created.

15. With the Star tool, click in a blank area on your page, and drag the mouse only a short distance.

16. Press the ⌘ key to keep the center radius from getting any larger, and continue dragging until the points of the star are about 1" long. Release the mouse.

17. Press the ⇧ ⌘ a to deselect everything.

18. Draw another star the same way, except press the ⌥ key before releasing the mouse to keep the sides straight.

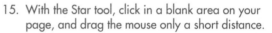

19. Practice drawing stars with different specifications until you are comfortable drawing them by dragging and using combinations of the ⌘ key and ⌥ key to create different kinds of stars. Also practice creating stars by entering numbers in the Options dialog box.

20. Return the View to 100% by pressing ⌘ 1, then close the document without saving it to a file.

Line Segment Tool

The Line Segment tool is used to draw individual straight segments by clicking and dragging the mouse or clicking in the artwork window with the tool selected and entering values in the Line Segment Options dialog box.

Line Segment
tool icon in the
Toolbox palette

Draw a Straight Line Segment by Dragging

To draw a single line segment, select the Line Segment tool in the Toolbox and click in the artwork window to establish the point of origin. Drag the mouse in the direction you want the segment to be placed. Release the mouse when the segment is the length you want it to be.

- Hold down the *Shift* key to draw line segments only at 0°, 45°, and 90° angles from the point of origin.
  - Changing the Constrain Angle field in the General Preferences dialog box doesn't have any effect on the Line Segment tool.

Create a Line Segment Numerically

You can create an individual line segment by specifying its length and angle in the Line Segment Options dialog box:

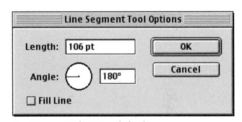

Line Segment Tool Options dialog box

1. Select the Line Segment tool in the Toolbox.

2. Display the Line Segment Options dialog box by clicking in the artwork window.

3. Enter a value in the Length field to specify how long you want the segment, measured from the point of the click in the artwork window.

4. Enter a value in the Angle field to specify the slant of the segment from the point of the click.

5. Click in the Fill checkbox to apply a fill color to the line segment.
   - This isn't particularly useful for a single straight segment. But in Step 4, *The Pen & Pencil Tools*, you'll learn how to add anchor points and this feature will have a purpose.

timesaver

Hold down the ⌥ key when the Line Segment or Arc Segment Tool Options dialog boxes are displayed to change the Cancel button to a Reset button. Click it to reset the values in the fields to their default values.

Arc Tool

The Arc tool enables you to create single curved segments. You can draw a curved segment by dragging with the mouse, or by displaying the Arc Tool Options dialog box and specifying its length and shape.

Arc tool icon
in the Toolbox
palette

Draw a Curved Segment by Dragging

1. Select the Arc tool in the Toolbox and click in the artwork window to establish the point of origin.

2. Drag the mouse until the curved segment is the length and shape you want it to be. Smooth anchor points, with direction lines and direction points, are placed on each end of the arc, which means you can select it with the Direct Selection tool and manipulate the shape of the curved segment.

   ■ Hold down the *Shift* key to draw curved segments at only 0°, 45°, and 90° angles from the point of origin.

     ▪ Changing the Constrain Angle field in the General Preferences dialog box doesn't have any effect on the Arc tool.

   ■ To increase the angle of the arc: Before releasing the mouse, press the up arrow (↑). To decrease the angle of the arc, before releasing the mouse, press the down arrow (↓).

     ▪ The curve increases until it reaches its maximum, a 90° angle.

   ■ To flip the arc: Before releasing the mouse, press the letter *f* on the keyboard. The point of origin and the ending point remain fixed.

   ■ To make the curved segment a closed path: Before releasing the mouse, press the letter *c* on the keyboard. A square-cornered path is added to connect the point of origin and the ending point of the curved segment.

     ▪ It isn't necessary to hold down the letter *c*, just tap it once to close the path. Tap it again to revert to an open path.

     ▪ If you hold down the letter *c* and release the mouse before releasing the letter *c*, the Scissors tool becomes selected in the Toolbox.

     ▪ Once you close an arc path, all arcs you draw after that will also be closed until you change it by pressing the letter c again as you draw an arc.

   ■ Create multiple curved arcs by holding down the ` key (grave accent) as you drag. Release the mouse before releasing the ` key or all arcs except the original one disappear.

   ■ Create multiple curved segments at 45° angles by holding down the *Shift* and the ` key as you drag. Release the mouse before releasing the *Shift* and ` keys or all the arcs except the original one disappear.

Closed path created
with the Arc tool

Step 3 — BASIC SHAPES

Create a Curved Segment Numerically

To draw a curved path with exact specifications:

1. Display the Arc tool Options dialog box by selecting the Arc tool in the Toolbox and clicking in the artwork window.

2. Fill in the fields to achieve the arc shape you want:

   ■ **Length X-Axis:** This value determines how far horizontally from the point of origin the endpoint will be placed.

   ■ **Length Y-Axis:** This value determines how far vertically from the point of origin the endpoint will be placed.

   ■ **Type:** Choose Open (open path) or Closed (closed path with a square corner) from the pop-up submenu.

   ■ **Base Along:** Choose X-Axis or Y-Axis from the pop-up submenu.

   ▪ **X-Axis:** Arc path extends vertically then curves horizontally (convex).

   ▪ **Y-Axis:** Arc path extends horizontally then curves vertically (concave).

   ■ **Slope:** The value in this field determines how pronounced the slope of the curve will be. Enter a positive number for a convex curve or a negative number for a concave curve.

   ▪ You can move the slider rather than entering a value in the field.

   ■ **Fill:** Click this checkbox to apply a fill color between the two endpoints of an open curved segment or to the inside of a closed path.

3. **Point of Origin box:** Click in the tiny square in a different corner of the box to change the direction of the arc. The sample shown here was created with the point-of-origin click in exactly the same spot for each arc.

4. Click OK or press *return/enter.*

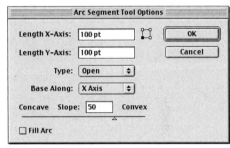

Arc tool Options dialog box

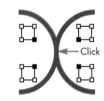

Arc paths drawn with X-Axis selected (A), and with Y-Axis selected (B) in the Arc tool dialog box

Resulting arc paths when point of origin is changed

Step 3 — BASIC SHAPES

85

activity 3.6

1. Create a new document: Letter size, CMYK color mode.

2. Enlarge the View to 400%.

3. Choose the Line Segment tool (▨) in the Toolbox.

4. Click on the document page and draw a segment about an inch long.

5. Click again near the first segment and draw another segment about the same size, but before releasing the mouse, press the ⌥ key.

   ■ The length of the segment doubles because it's being drawn from the center rather than the top left corner.

6. Click again on a blank spot and draw another segment about the same size, but before releasing the mouse, hold down the *Shift* key and drag the mouse around in a circle, before releasing it.

   ■ Notice that the segment pauses at certain angles because you're constraining the angle to 0°, 45°, and 90°.

7. Click again on a blank spot and draw another segment about the same size, but before releasing the mouse, hold down the ` (grave accent) key and drag the mouse around in a circle, before releasing it.

8. Click in a blank spot on the document page and draw a curved segment with the Arc tool (▨).

9. Draw another curved segment with the Arc tool, but before releasing the mouse move it around and notice how the shape of the curved segment changes, depending upon how far away and at what angle you drag from the point of the click.

10. Draw another curved segment, but before releasing the mouse, press the letter *c* on the keyboard to close the path.

11. Select the Arc tool again, and draw another path with the Arc tool.

    ■ It's still a closed path.

12. Draw another path with the Arc tool, but before releasing the mouse, press the letter *c* on the keyboard.

13. Select the Arc tool and draw another path, but before releasing the mouse, press the letter *f* on the keyboard.

    ■ The arc flips across so the curve is on the opposite side.

14. Draw another curved segment and press the up arrow key (↑) several times before releasing the mouse.

    ■ The curve is increased each time the arrow key is pressed.

15. Draw another curved segment with the Arc tool and hold down the ` (grave accent) key and drag around in a circle, but every so often press the *f* key to flip the curve as you drag.

16. With the Arc tool selected, click on a blank spot on the page to display the Arc tool Options dialog box.

    ■ The values in the fields are the values left over from the last curved segment you drew with the Arc tool.

17. Enter the following values in the fields:

    ■ Length X-Axis: 50
    ■ Length Y-Axis: 100
    ■ Type: Open
    ■ Base Along: X Axis
    ■ Slope: Convex: 50

18. Click OK or press *return/enter* to exit the dialog box and create a curved segment extending from the point of the click.

Continued

19. Click on the page again to display the Options dialog box, hold down the ⌥ key to change the Cancel button to Reset and click it to reset the values in the field to the defaults, then click OK or press *return/enter*.

■ Notice the shape of the curve.

20. Display the Options dialog box again and change the Base Along field to Y Axis, then click OK or press *return/enter*.

■ Notice the difference in the shape of the curve when only that one change was made. It's basically the same as pressing *f* on the keyboard to flip the curve.

21. Practice drawing straight and curved segments using the Line Segment tool and the Arc tool. Display their Options dialog boxes and create segments by entering different values in the fields.

22. When you're familiar with how the tool works, close the artwork window without saving changes.

Spiral Tool

Another predefined shape you can create with a tool in the Toolbox is a spiral. The Spiral tool is hidden under the Line Segment tool in the Toolbox. You can move and rotate a spiral as you draw it the same way you move and rotate a polygon or star.

Spiral tool icon in the Toolbox palette

All spirals are drawn from the center rather than the top edge. You don't have to hold down the ⌥ key to select that option. Position your spiral by clicking on your page where you want the center of the spiral to be.

All the values in a spiral work together. If you specify a Decay value (tightness of the coil) that is too low for the number of segments specified, a default spiral is drawn. If the number of segments specified in a spiral with a Decay value that is too high for its Radius, a default spiral having the most segments that can be drawn with the given specifications is created.

Decay Value

The Decay value determines the amount each coil of the spiral decreases relative to the previous coil. The higher the number, the tighter the coil. The decay value must be between 5 and 150.

Segments

A complete spiral with one wind is 4 segments (the same number of anchor points in a circle drawn with the circle tool). You can have as few as 2 segments in a spiral and as many as 1000 segments, but I've never managed to create a spiral having that many segments.

Spiral shape drawn with Spiral tool showing 10 segments

Adjust a Spiral as You Draw It

You can use keyboard commands to adjust the shape and appearance of a spiral you create as you drag. There are limitations, though. You can't put more segments in a spiral than is allowed by the decay value, and vice versa. It takes practice to understand how the values all work together.

Add/Subtract Segments Add or subtract the number of segments (coils) in the spiral as you draw it by pressing the up or down arrow before releasing the mouse. Hold the arrow keys down or press-and-release the arrow keys until the desired number of segments is reached.

- ↑ arrow = adds segments
- ↓ arrow = subtracts segments

Control How Tight a Spiral Winds Adjust the Decay value as you create a spiral by pressing the ⌘ key as you drag.

Create a Spiral Numerically

You can create a spiral by specifying its characteristics numerically.

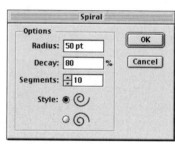

Spiral tool Options dialog box

1. Select the Spiral tool (⊚) in the Toolbox and display the Spiral Options dialog box by clicking on the page where you want the center of the spiral to be.

2. In the Radius field, enter the distance you want from the center of the object to the outermost anchor point of the spiral.

3. The number (percentage) you enter in the Decay field controls how tightly the spiral winds. You can enter a number from 5–150.

4. Enter a number in the Segments field or click the arrows to determine how many times the spiral winds around (revolutions).

   - For example, if you want two complete turns around the spiral, enter the number 8 because each complete revolution of a spiral contains 4 segments.

5. In the Style area, click the clockwise or counter-clockwise radio buttons to specify the direction the spiral winds from the center point.

6. Click OK or press *return/enter.*

activity 3.7

1. Create a new document: Letter size, CMYK color mode.

2. Zoom to 400%.

3. Select the Spiral tool (⊚) in the Toolbox.

4. Click in the document page and drag to create a spiral. Without releasing the mouse, move it back and forth and up and down to change its size and rotation. Release the mouse when the spiral is about 2" long.

5. Click and drag to draw another spiral and, without releasing the mouse, press and hold the spacebar.

6. Move the mouse to move the spiral to a new position on the page. Release the spacebar, but not the mouse.

7. Resize the spiral, making it larger, by dragging more before releasing the mouse.

8. Move to a clear spot on your page (press h and drag). Reselect the Spiral tool and click on the page without dragging.

   ■ The Spiral Options dialog box displays.

9. Enter 72 in the Radius field, 80 in the Decay field, and 15 in the Segments field. Press *return/enter.*

10. Count the number of segments in the spiral.

11. Click in a blank area of the page to display the Spiral Options dialog box.

   ■ Notice that the specifications you entered before are still there.

12. Change the Segments field to 150 and press *return/enter.*

13. Count the number of segments in this spiral.

   ■ Even though you entered 150 in the Segments field, a spiral with that many segments couldn't be created with a radius of 72 points and a Decay value of 80.

14. Click to display the Spiral Options dialog box again, and leave 72 entered in the Radius field, change the Decay value to 99, and leave the Segments value at 150. Press *return/enter.*

   ■ The shape of the spiral changes considerably by altering only one number. Now the spiral can accommodate 150 segments.

15. Click to display the Spiral Options dialog box again, and enter 60 in the Radius field, change the Decay value to 85, and change the Segments value to 18. Press *return/enter.*

16. Click and drag to create a new spiral. Don't release the mouse.

   ■ It will have the same specifications as the last spiral you drew except the radius, because that depends on how far you drag.

17. Holding the mouse steady, press the ↓ arrow to decrease the number of segments until it stops removing segments. Don't release the mouse.

18. Press the ↑ arrow to increase the number of segments until it stops adding segments. Then release the mouse.

19. Count the number of segments in the spiral.

20. Click to open the Spiral Options dialog box, and you will see that the number in the Segments field kept increasing, but the number of actual segments added stopped.

21. Enter a Decay value of 100 and a Segments value of 2. Press *return/enter.*

   ■ A perfect half-circle is drawn.

   ■ To skew the curve, enter a larger or smaller number in the Decay field.

22. Practice drawing spirals until you are comfortable drawing them by dragging and by entering numbers in the Options dialog box and changing specifications.

23. Return the View to 100% by pressing ⌘1, then close the document without saving it to a file.

The Grid Tools

A *grid* is a framework of lines and Adobe Illustrator 10 has two tools that create grids. The Rectangular Grid tool, used for drawing rectangular or square grids, contains a specified number of equally-spaced horizontal and vertical dividers. The Polar Grid tool, used for drawing circular grids, creates a specified number of concentric circles and equally-spaced radial dividers.

You can create grids by dragging with a grid tool or by entering values into its options dialog box. Dragging with a grid tool creates a grid having the same values as the last one that was created.

As with the other shape creation tools, you can:

- Keep the rectangular grid to a square and the polar grid to a perfect circle by holding down the *Shift* key before releasing the mouse.

- Create a grid from its center point rather than from the lower left edge by holding down the ⌥ key before you release the mouse.

- Create a perfect square or round circle grid from its center point by holding down the *Shift* key and the ⌥ key as you drag.

- Move a grid as you draw it by holding down the spacebar and moving the shape before releasing the mouse.

- Create multiple grids by holding down the ` key and dragging. Release the mouse before releasing the ` key or the added grids will disappear.

- Reset the fields in the grid Options dialog boxes to their default values by changing the Cancel button to a Reset button by holding down the ⌥ key and clicking it.

- Line segments in grids can be moved individually by selecting them with a Direct Selection tool and dragging to a new position.

- *Skew* means to deviate from symmetry or to distort. When working with the grid tools, to adjust the skew is to change the spacing between lines or circles in the grid automatically so they're spaced unevenly. A skew value of 0% means that all lines or circles are spaced evenly.

Rectangular Grid Tool

To create a rectangular grid by dragging:

1. Select the Rectangular Grid tool in the Toolbox and click in the artwork window.

2. Drag diagonally until the desired shape is reached.

3. You can adjust the grid's dividers as you drag (before releasing the mouse).
   - Add horizontal lines by pressing the up arrow (↑).
   - Remove horizontal lines by pressing the down arrow (↓).

Rectangular Grid tool icon in the Toolbox palette

- Add vertical lines by pressing the right arrow (→).
- Remove vertical lines by pressing the left arrow (←).
- Decrease the skew value of the horizontal dividers by pressing the letter *f* on the keyboard.
- Increase the skew value of the horizontal dividers by pressing the letter *v* on the keyboard.
- Decrease the skew value of the vertical dividers by pressing the letter *x* on the keyboard.
- Increase the skew value of the vertical dividers by pressing the letter *c* on the keyboard.

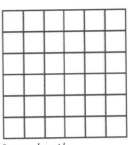

Rectangular grid

Create a Rectangular Grid Numerically Display the Rectangular Grid Options dialog box by selecting the Rectangular Grid tool (▦) in the Toolbox and clicking in the artwork window. Enter the appropriate values and make selections to create the grid you want then click OK or press *return/enter* to exit the dialog box.

- Enter values in the Width and Height fields for the overall size and shape of the rectangular grid you are creating.
- Click one of the tiny boxes in the corners of the Point of Origin box (⊡) to determine the point from which the grid is created. The default is the lower left corner instead of the upper left corner.
- Enter the number of horizontal dividers in the Number field of the Horizontal Dividers section.
- Enter a positive or negative value in the Skew field to cause the horizontal dividers to be unevenly spaced. A negative value places the largest space at the top of the grid; a positive value places the largest space at the bottom of the grid.
  - Move the sliders to change the Skew value.
- Enter the number of vertical dividers in the Number field of the Vertical Dividers section.

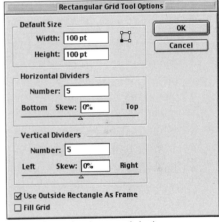

Rectangular Grid Tool Options dialog box

- Enter a positive or negative value in the Skew field to cause the vertical dividers to be unevenly spaced. A negative value places the largest space on the left side of the grid; a positive value places the largest space on the right side of the grid.
  - Move the sliders to change the Skew value.
- When the Use Outside Rectangle As Frame checkbox is checked, the outside edges of the grid is a single box. When it is unchecked, the outside edges of the grid are divider lines and they're not connected.

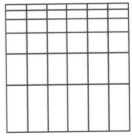

Rectangular grid with a horizontal skew of 51% (top)

- The Fill checkbox doesn't perform any useful service that I could find. When Use Outside Rectangle As Frame is unchecked, the grid won't be filled with color even if the Fill box is checked. And when the Use Outside Rectangle As Frame is checked, the grid is filled with the fill color whether or not the Fill checkbox is checked or not. Go figure.

Polar Grid Tool

To create a polar grid by dragging:

1. Select the Polar Grid tool in the Toolbox and click in the artwork window.

2. Drag diagonally until the desired shape is achieved.

3. You can adjust the grid's dividers as you drag (before releasing the mouse).

   - Add concentric circles by pressing the up arrow (↑).
   - Remove concentric circles by pressing the down arrow (↓).
   - Add radial lines lines by pressing the right arrow (→).
   - Remove radial lines by pressing the left arrow (←).
   - Change the skew value of the concentric dividers outward by pressing the letter x on the keyboard.
   - Change the skew value of the concentric dividers inward by pressing the letter c on the keyboard.
   - Change the skew value of the radial dividers counterclockwise by pressing the letter f on the keyboard.
   - Change the skew value of the radial dividers clockwise by pressing the letter v on the keyboard.

Create a Polar Grid Numerically Display the Polar Grid Options dialog box by selecting the Polar Grid tool () in the Toolbox and clicking in the artwork window. Enter the appropriate values and make selections to create the grid you want then click OK or press *return/enter* to exit the dialog box.

- Enter values in the Width and Height fields for the overall size of the circular grid you are creating.

- Click one of the tiny boxes in the corners of the Point of Origin box (⌐⌐) to determine the point from which the grid is created. The default is the lower left corner.

- Enter the number of circular dividers in the Number field of the Concentric Dividers section.

- Enter a positive or negative value in the Skew field to cause the circular dividers to be unevenly spaced. A negative value places

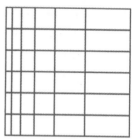

Rectangular grid with a vertical skew of –51%

Polar Grid tool icon in the Toolbox palette

Polar grid

Polar grid with a concentric divider skew value of 50% (right)

Polar grid with a radial divider skew value of –50% (bottom)

the largest space at the top of the grid; a positive value places the largest space at the bottom of the grid.

- Move the sliders to change the Skew value.

■ Enter the number of radial dividers in the Number field of the Radial Dividers section.

■ Enter a positive or negative value in the Skew field to cause the radial dividers to be unevenly spaced. A negative value places the largest space on the outside side of the grid; a positive value places the largest space at the center of the grid.

- Move the sliders to change the Skew value.

■ When the Create Compound Paths From Ellipses checkbox is checked, elements of the grid can be moved independently, but if you select them with the Selection tool, they're still connected to the whole; the entire shape is a single unit.

- A *compound path* is a combination of two or more paths that function as though they are a single path.

■ If a fill color has been specified, and Create Compound Path From Ellipses is unchecked, the entire grid is filled with the current fill color, whether or not the Fill Grid box is checked. You can select each ring separately with the Direct Selection tool and fill each ring with different colors.

■ When the Create Compound Path From Ellipses checkbox is checked, alternating circles are filled with the current fill color. Selecting a single ring with the Direct Selection tool and changing its color changes the colors of all colored rings in the grid.

- When the Fill Grid checkbox is unchecked when a polar grid is created and you select one of the concentric circles with the Direct Selection tool, the fill color in the Color palette and the Toolbox switches to None. If Fill Grid is checked, the fill color doesn't change in the Color palette and the Toolbox.

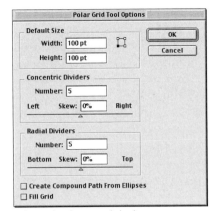

Polar Grid Tool Options dialog box

 *activity 3.8*

1. Create a new document: Letter size, CMYK color mode.

2. Enlarge the View to 200%.

3. Choose the Rectangular Grid tool (▦) in the Toolbox, click on the page to display the tool Options dialog box. Hold down the ⌥ key and press the Reset button to restore the fields to their default values. Click OK or press *return/enter* to create a rectangular grid.

4. Click in a blank spot on the page, hold down the *Shift* key on the right side of the keyboard, then drag down and to the right to create a square grid, but don't release the mouse or the *Shift* key.

5. Press all the arrow keys several times. Still don't release the mouse, but release the Shift key.

   ■ Notice that the up and down arrows add and remove horizontal dividers and the right and left arrows add and remove vertical dividers.

Continued

6. With the mouse still pressed, press the letters *f* and *v* several times to increase and decrease the skew value of the horizontal dividers.

7. With the mouse still pressed, press the letters *x* and *c* several times to increase and decrease the skew value of the vertical dividers.

8. Release the mouse and deselect all.

9. With the Selection tool, click on one of the lines of the grid.

   ■ Notice that all the paths in the grid are selected.

10. Deselect all.

11. With the Direct Selection tool, click on the right-most vertical line (outside line) of the grid.

   ■ Notice that the outside path is selected but the interior vertical and horizontal lines are not.

12. With the Rectangular Grid tool selected, click on the page about ½" to the right of the bottom of the first grid to display the Rectangle Grid tool Options dialog box. Uncheck Use Outside Rectangle As Frame, and click OK.

13. Deselect all, then select the Direct Selection tool, and click on the rightmost vertical path.

   ■ Only that vertical path is selected because Use Outside Rectangle As Frame was unchecked when this grid was created.

14. Press *z* on the keyboard to select the Zoom tool, then draw a very small marquee at the lower left corner of the third grid. Using the scroll sliders, move the contents of the artwork window so that both the bottom right corner of the second grid and the bottom left corner of the third grid are visible.

   ■ Notice that the corner of the third grid is not as smooth as the corner of the second grid that had Use Outside Rectangle As Frame checked.

15. Press ⌘1 to return the View to Actual Size (100%).

16. Select all and press delete to remove all the rectangular grids.

17. Choose the Polar Grid tool (⬚) in the Toolbox, click on the page to display the Polar Grid tool Options dialog box. Hold down the ⌥ key and press the Reset button to restore the fields to their default values. Click OK or press *return/enter* to create a polar grid.

18. With the Polar Grid tool selected, click on a blank spot on the page and drag to create a polar grid about 2" in diameter, but before releasing the mouse, press each arrow key several times.

   ■ Notice that the up and down arrows add and remove circles and the right and left arrows add and remove radial lines.

19. Release the mouse and deselect all.

20. Drag to create another polar grid, but before releasing the mouse, press the letters *x* and *c* to change the skew of the concentric (circular) dividers.

21. Keeping the mouse pressed, press the letters *f* and *v* to change the skew of the radial dividers.

22. Release the mouse and deselect all.

23. Zoom to 200%, then choose the Rectangle tool in the toolbox.

24. Hold the *Shift* key down, then click and drag on a blank spot on the page to create a very small square.

25. Choose the Polar Grid tool and click in the middle of the small square you just drew. The Polar Grid tool Options dialog box displays.

26. Hold down the ⌥ key and click the Reset button to restore the tool to its default values. Notice that the Point of Origin is in the lower left corner. Press *return/enter*.

27. Create three more polar grids by clicking in the small square to display the Options dialog box and changing the position of the Point of Origin each time to a different corner.

   ■ Notice that the grids are displayed around the small square according to which corner in the Point of Origin box was chosen.

28. Move the artwork window so that one of the polar grids is visible in the middle of your screen.

29. Press the letter *d* on the keyboard to change to the default colors (white fill and 1 pt black stroke).

   ■ I know you haven't learned that yet, but take my word for it for now.

Continued

94

30. With the Direct Selection tool, click in each of the concentric circles.

   - Notice that when you click in a circle, only that circle is selected.

31. With the Polar Grid tool selected, click on a blank spot on the page to display the Polar Grid Options dialog box. Click the Create Compound Path From Ellipses checkbox, then click OK or press *return/enter*.

32. Click in the CMYK Spectrum bar to choose a fill color.

   - Alternating rings are colored.

33. Click on a blank spot on the page to display the Polar Grid tool Options dialog box and check the Fill Grid checkbox. Click OK or press *return/enter*.

   - The entire object is colored.

34. Continue creating rectangular and polar grids by dragging and by entering different values in the Polar Grid tool Options dialog boxes until you are familiar with the objects created with the tools.

35. Close the artwork window without saving it to a file.

Move or Modify the Shape of a Path

You can change the shape of any path you've created by moving its curved or straight segments, by moving any of its anchor points, or by adjusting direction lines associated with anchor points. The path or its anchor points must be selected before any modifications can be made to its segments or anchor points.

Moving Paths When the Bounding Box is Visible

When the Selection tool is highlighted in the Toolbox, you can move selected paths. Unselected paths in an object with more than one path are not moved.

- Position the cursor inside the bounding box of an active path until the arrowhead cursor displays (▶), then click and drag to a new position.

- You can also move a selected path by pressing the arrow keys (↑ , ↓ , ←, →) corresponding to the direction you want to move the path. Each time you press the arrow key, the path (and bounding box) moves 1 point. If you press and hold the arrow key down, the path moves continuously in 1-point increments. If you hold the *Shift* key down while pressing an arrow key, the path moves in larger increments.

  - If you find that you need more precision when moving a path, you can change the value in the Keyboard Increment field in the General Preferences dialog box (**Edit** ⇨ **Preferences** ⇨ **General**). The default is 1 point, but you can change it to as little as .001 point (which is barely visible even at 6400%) to as many as 1296 points. The larger the number, the farther the path moves each time you press the arrow key.

Changing the Keyboard Increment value changes how far an object moves when pressing the arrow keys

Other ways to move paths are discussed in Step 9, *Reshape, Combine, & Distort Objects*.

Moving Paths With the Direct Selection Tool

When the Direct Selection tool is highlighted in the Toolbox, you can move selected paths or individual anchor points by clicking and dragging them to a new position. Remember, though, that when the Direct Selection tool is active, anchor points are hollow unless they are selected. Then they become solid. To make an entire path move without reshaping, make sure all anchor points in the path are solid (selected), then click and drag. If anchor points are hollow, the attached curved segments are reshaped rather than moved.

You can also move anchor points or paths when the Direct Selection tool is selected by pressing the arrow keys, the same as when the Selection tool is active.

Only selected anchor points move when the Direct Selection tool is active

Moving Anchor Points

To move an anchor point:

1. Choose the Direct Selection tool in the Toolbox.

2. Click on a segment of a path to make the path active.

3. Click on an anchor point to select it, or ⇧-click on multiple anchor points to make more than one anchor point active.

   ■ Selected anchor points are solid.

4. Drag the anchor point in any direction. Release the mouse to drop it where you want it.

   or

   Press the arrow keys (↑ , ↓ , ←, →) to move selected anchor points in the direction corresponding to the direction the arrow points.

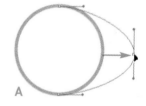

Move anchor points by selecting and dragging them with the Direct Selection tool. A, curved segments; B, straight segments

   ■ All selected (solid) anchor points move. Unselected (hollow) anchor points remain in their original positions.

   ■ Moving an anchor point affects the segments on both sides of the anchor point.

   ■ To keep an anchor point moving horizontally, hold down the *Shift* key while dragging. This allows the anchor point to move at only 45° angles (0°, 45°, 90°, and so on). If you move up or down drastically, the anchor point snaps to the nearest 45° angle increments.

   ■ The program default is to move the selected anchor point 1 point at a time when the arrow keys are pressed. You can change this default by entering a different value in the Keyboard Increment field of the General Preferences dialog box.

Moving a Straight Segment

To move a straight segment:

1. Choose the Direct Selection tool in the Toolbox.

2. Click and drag a straight segment of a path.

   or

   Press the arrow keys (↑ , ↓ , ←, →) to move the selected segment in the direction corresponding to the direction the arrow points.

   - The points anchoring each end of the segment moves with the segment.

   - To keep the segment moving in only 45° increments, hold down the *Shift* key while dragging.

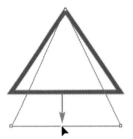

Hold down the Shift key to move a straight segment in a straight line

Reshaping Paths When the Bounding Box is Visible

When the Selection tool is active and the bounding box is visible on a selected path or paths, you can reshape the path by dragging the handles of the bounding box.

- Position the Selection tool cursor over a bounding box handle until the arrows (↔, ↕, or ↘) display. Then click and drag in the direction the arrows point.

  - An outline of the path displays and changes as you move the bounding box handle.

  - If more than one path is selected, all are reshaped at once.

  - Hold the *Shift* key down when moving the arrows to reshape the path proportionally.

  - Flip the object by dragging to the opposite side (horizontally or vertically). Hold the *Shift* key down to flip the object proportionally.

  - Hold the ⌥ key down to reshape from the center point rather than at the point of the drag. Drag clear across to flip the object and the bounding box.

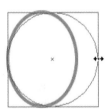

Reshape a path by moving its bounding box

Adjusting the Shape of a Curve

You can change the shape of a curve by moving a segment or by adjusting the Direction lines associated with an anchor point on a curved path.

Move a Curved Segment Move a curved segment in the same manner you do a straight segment:

1. Choose the Direct Selection tool in the Toolbox.

2. Click on a segment of a curved path and drag it to a new position.

Click and drag a segment with the Direct Selection tool to reshape a curve

97

or

Press an arrow key to move the segment in the corresponding direction (↑ , ↓ , ←, →).

- Direction lines associated with the anchor points on both ends of the curved segment are adjusted automatically.

Adjust Direction Lines To change a curved segment by adjusting its direction lines:

1. Choose the Direct Selection tool in the Toolbox.

2. Click on the segment of a curved path to make it active.

    - Direction lines and direction points associated with that segment display on the anchor points at both ends of the segment.

3. Click and drag a direction point at the end of a direction line to reshape the curve. If the anchor point is a Smooth point, a direction line displays on both sides of the point.

    - Lengthen the direction line to enlarge the curve.

        - Even though a direction line displays on both sides of the anchor point, only the segment on the same side of the anchor point as the direction line is adjusted.

    - Shorten the direction line to reduce the curve.

    - Change the angle of the direction line to change the shape of the curve.

        - Unlike when you lengthen or shorten a direction line and only the side you're adjusting changes, the handles on both sides of a smooth anchor point move together, changing the curve on both sides of the anchor point.

Rotating Objects Using the Bounding Box

When the Selection tool is active and the bounding box is visible on a selected path or paths, you can rotate the path by dragging the handles of the bounding box.

- Position the Selection tool cursor a little to the outside of a bounding box handle until the rotate arrows (↵⌐) display. Then click and drag in the direction the arrows are pointing.

    - The larger the View magnification, the more control you have over the amount of rotation.

    - Press the *Shift* key to rotate the bounding box in 45° increments.

Lengthen a direction line to enlarge the curve

Shorten a direction line to reduce the curve

Rotating a direction line changes the curves on both sides of the anchor point

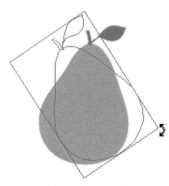

An object can be rotated using its bounding box

Copying Paths

You can create a copy of an object by pressing the ⌥ key before you drag a path or multiple paths. When you start dragging with the ⌥ key pressed, the pointer changes to a double arrowhead (▶), indicating that a duplicate will be created. The copied object remains selected and the original object becomes deselected. Release the mouse before you release the ⌥ key, or the object is moved rather than duplicated.

You can drag-copy an object by clicking its fill or by clicking its edge with either the Selection tool or the Direct Selection tool. Don't drag a bounding box handle, though.

You also can make multiple copies of a path using the arrow keys:

1. Choose the Selection tool.

2. Select the path you want to copy.

3. Hold down the ⌥ key.

4. Press the appropriate arrow key to copy the path, moving it by the Keyboard Increment value that's currently specified in General Preferences (**Edit ⇨ Preferences ⇨ General**). The default is 1 point. Each time you press the arrow key with the ⌥ key held down, another copy is made.

Copy a path by holding down the ⌥ key and dragging

Multiple stars created by holding down both the ` (grave accent) and the Shift key when dragging

Deleting Paths or Anchor Points

To delete an entire path:

1. Select an object with the Selection tool

2. Press the *delete* key on the keyboard.

To delete part of a path by deleting an anchor point:

1. Select an anchor point with the Direct Selection tool.
   - ■ The anchor point will be solid.

2. Press the *delete* key on the keyboard.
   - ■ Segments attached to the anchor point are also deleted.
   - ■ When a fill color is applied to an open path, Illustrator simulates a closed path by filling in color between the endpoints.

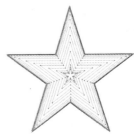

fyi The copied objects are separate paths so they can be deleted, colored, moved, and so on, individually.

Fill color applied to an open path simulates a closed path

99

activity 3.9

1. Create a new document: Letter size, CMYK color mode.

2. Click the Default Colors button ( ) on the Toolbox palette.

3. Select the Rectangle tool ( ) in the Toolbox and draw a 1" square.

4. Deselect the object.

5. Press the letter *v* on the keyboard to make the Selection tool in the Toolbox active.

6. Click on the rectangle and drag it to a new location on the page.

7. Hold down the key, click in the rectangle, and drag to create a copy of the shape.

   ■ Release the mouse before releasing the key.

8. Deselect both objects.

9. Press the letter *a* on the keyboard to select the Direct Selection tool in the Toolbox.

10. Click in the middle of the right segment of one rectangle and drag it up and to the right. Release the mouse to drop the segment.

11. Undo that action to restore the object to a square.

12. Deselect the shape.

13. Hold the *Shift* key down, click on the right vertical segment again, and drag it to the right horizontally. Release the mouse to drop the segment.

   ■ The movement is kept at a 0° angle, or perfectly horizontal.

14. Undo that action to restore the object to a square.

15. Click on the anchor point that forms the bottom right corner of the object.

16. Drag it down and to the left.

17. Undo.

18. Deselect the shape.

19. -click on the bottom left anchor point and the top right anchor point. Drag up and to the right.

20. Deselect all.

21. In a blank area on the document page, draw an oval about 2" long and 1" high, then deselect the object.

22. Press the letter *a* on the keyboard to select the Direct Selection tool in the Toolbox.

23. Click on the bottom right segment of the oval.

24. Drag it up and down and around so you can see what happens to the shape of the segment and how the Direction lines change, depending on where you move the segment.

25. Undo that action. If you deselected at any time while you were moving the segment around, keep performing the Undo command until you get back to the original oval shape.

26. With the Direct Selection tool active (press *a*), select the oval, click on a Direction point, and move it up and down and around to see what effect that has on the shape of the oval.

   ■ Notice that as you lengthen the Direction line, the Direction line on the other side of the anchor point doesn't lengthen simultaneously. But if you change the angle of the Direction line, the Direction line on the other side of the anchor point changes correspondingly.

27. Deselect all objects.

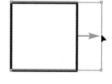

Continued

28. Choose the Polygon tool in the Toolbox and draw a polygon.

29. Press v to select the Selection tool, then move the cursor to a corner of the bounding box until the rotate arrows ( ) display.

30. Click and drag around in a circle to rotate the polygon, then release the mouse.

31. With the Selection tool still active and the polygon selected, move the cursor over a corner handle on the bounding box until the resizing arrows ( ) display.

32. Drag up diagonally up and to the right to reshape the polygon, but don't release the mouse.

33. Hold down the *Shift* key, then release the mouse. The polygon is enlarged, keeping its original shape.

34. Deselect the object.

35. With the Direct Select Lasso tool, select the anchor point at the top of the polygon.

36. Press the delete key to delete the anchor point.

37. Deselect the object.

38. Continue creating shapes and moving anchor points, segments, and direction lines until you feel comfortable with how the different shapes can be altered.

39. Close the document without saving it to a file.

40. Open the file named Sheep.eps that's stored in the Student Files folder on the CD-ROM that came with this book.

41. With the Arc tool, add curved segments to the interior of the sheep to give it some dimension. Use the sheep shown here as a guide.

- Put grass in the sheep's mouth.

- Add the curved segment to the sheep's right hoof.

- Use the bounding box to rotate segments.

- Move direction points to change the shape of the segments after they've been created.

42. When you're satisfied with your results, name your file and save the file into your Practice folder.

Add Color to Your Artwork

There are many options you can use to add color to objects you draw with Illustrator 10. Step 7, *Add Color to Artwork* is devoted to that subject. When you get to that chapter, you'll learn about CMYK, RGB, spot color, and so on. Until then, I want you to concentrate on drawing shapes. In this section, I'll give you a brief overview of a few of the basics so you can add basic color to the shapes you draw.

The color you specify for the interior of an object is called Fill. The border along the path of an object is called the Stroke. For example, the shapes you've created thus far have had a 1 point stroke and a fill of white because that's the program default.

When a fill color is applied to an object, the color extends to the edge of the path. A stroke on a path defines its outline. You can specify thickness (weight) and color on the outline of a selected object. When a stroke is applied to a path, it is centered on the path, which means that half of the stroke is on the inside of the path and half is on the outside. This means that the stroke overlaps the fill color by half the weight of the stroke.

Fill and stroke selections made in either the Color palette or the Toolbox are applied immediately to the selected path. You don't have to press *return/enter* or click an OK button.

If the Use Area Select checkbox is checked in General Preferences (**Edit** ➪ **Preferences** ➪ **General**) and an object is filled with white or a color, you can click within the object, rather than its path, to select it. If the Use Area Select checkbox in General Preferences is unchecked, or if an object has a fill of None, you must select the object by clicking on its path.

Check Use Area Select in General Preferences to be able to select objects by clicking on them

A Value of None

The None button (▱) in the Color palette and in the Fill and Stroke section of the Toolbox removes the fill or stroke from the selected object. When an object has a fill selection of None, it becomes transparent, which allows you to see objects stacked beneath it. See the discussion about *Stacking Order* in Step 4, *The Pen & Pencil Tools*.

- To apply None using the keyboard, select the path and press the Slash key (/).

Fill of None

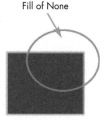

Objects that have no fill (None) are transparent

Color Palette

The Color palette that displayed on your screen when you launched Illustrator the first time is the default palette. Changes you make in the palette are remembered the next time you open Illustrator unless you delete the Preferences file to restore program defaults. Refer to Step 2, *Introducing Adobe Illustrator 10* for instructions on this procedure.

The Fill box is active because it's in front of the stroke box

- The Fill box and Stroke box in the Color palette (Figure 3.4A) display the current fill and stroke colors applied to the selected object or objects and update immediately as you make changes in the Color palette. The box that displays in front of the other box is the active attribute that is affected.
  - Toggle between the fill box and the stroke box by pressing *x* on the keyboard.
- Click the None button (⬜) on the left side of the CMYK Spectrum bar to specify a transparent fill or to remove a stroke.
- The CMYK field allows you to create custom colors. The default is CMYK, but other color models, such as RGB and HSB, are available. Refer to Step 7, *Add Color to Artwork*, for more information.
  - C = cyan, M = magenta, Y = yellow, K = black, the four colors that are used for process-color printing.
- Click or click and drag in the CMYK Spectrum color bar to select a color. Release the mouse when the desired color is displayed in the fill or stroke box.
  - When you select a color by clicking in the CMYK Spectrum bar, its makeup is displayed as percentages of color in the CMYK fields.
  - You can create your own colors by entering values in the fields.
  - Create your own process colors by moving the sliders under C, M, Y, or K.
  - The cursor becomes an empty eyedropper (𝄽) when you position it over the CMYK Spectrum bar. When you click to select a color, the eyedropper appears to be filled (𝄽).

timesaver Change the fill color when the stroke box is active, and vice versa, by holding down the ⌥ key and clicking on the CMYK Spectrum bar.

fyi The colors displayed in the slider bars change as you drag them. That's to help you judge which slider to move and how far to move it in order to get the color you want.

Step 3 — BASIC SHAPES

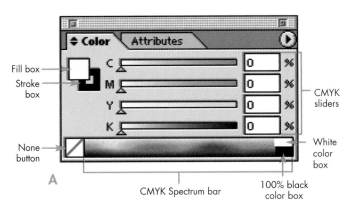

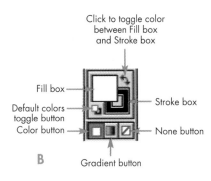

FIGURE 3.4 (A) The default Color palette and (B) Toolbox color and stroke controls.

- The values in the CMYK fields represent the color mix required to create the color you selected.
- Move the sliders in the CMYK fields to adjust colors.

■ Click the White or Black button (▭) on the right side of the CMYK Spectrum bar to specify a fill or stroke of white or 100% black.

  - The cursor becomes an empty eyedropper until you click to select the color, then it becomes a half-full eyedropper.
  - When you click in the white area, the values entered in the CMYK fields are 0.
  - When you click in the black area, the values entered in the CMY fields are 0 and K (black) is 100%.
  - To create shades of gray, move the K (black) slider to the left.

■ When you select a color of None for a fill or stroke, a Last Color box (↖▪) displays on the Color palette above the None box. Click this box to restore the last color applied before None was applied.

Toolbox Controls

The Toolbox also has controls for editing color in your illustration (Figure 3.4B). Changes made to the controls in the Color palette also change the corresponding controls in the Toolbox, and vice versa.

■ Click the unselected Fill or Stroke box to bring it to the front and make it the active box.

■ Click the arrow (↰) to switch the colors in the Fill and Stroke boxes.

■ Click the Default Fill and Stroke button (▭) to reset fill and stroke attributes to the default of white fill and 1 pt black stroke.

  - The keyboard command to change to Default Fill and Stroke is the letter *d*.

■ When an active path has a color of None applied to it, you can click the Color button (■) to apply the last solid color selected.

  - The keyboard command to select the Color button is a comma (,).

■ Click the Gradient button (▣) to apply the last gradient applied to an active object.

  - The keyboard command to select the Gradient button is a period (.).

■ Click the None box (▨) to remove the stroke or fill of a selected object, depending upon which attribute is active.

  - The keyboard command to select the None button is a slash (/).

timesaver

Change the intensity (tint) of a color by holding the Shift key down while dragging a slider in the Color palette. The other sliders automatically readjust as necessary to lighten the color.

read this!

If two objects with different fill values or different stroke values are selected, a question mark displays in the Fill or Stroke box in the Color palette in the Toolbox.

Applying Color by Dragging and Dropping

Changing color on a path that's selected is easy. Just pick a color in the CMYK Spectrum bar and the color is applied automatically to the selected path. But how about applying color to an object that isn't selected? You can do that by dragging and dropping the color onto it. This procedure applies only to changing the color, it doesn't have any effect on the weight of a stroke.

1. Choose your color in the CMYK Spectrum bar or by mixing it using the sliders. The color must appear in the Fill box on the Color palette and in the Fill box in the Toolbox.

2. Click in the Fill box on the Color palette or on the Fill box in the Toolbox and drag the pointer over the object to which you want to apply the color, and release the mouse to drop it.

   ■ To drag and drop a fill or stroke color on a path having a fill of None, you must release the mouse over its path, not inside the shape.

   ■ Drag and drop a stroke color if the Fill box is active (in front) and vice versa by holding down the *Shift* key while dragging.

   ■ When the Stroke box is active (in front), color a stroke with the current Fill color by clicking and dragging the color from the Fill box. The stroke changes to the Fill color. This works when the Fill box is active, you can change the fill to the stroke color by dragging from the Stroke box.

Stroke Weight

The weight of a stroke (how thick it is) is specified in the Stroke palette attached to the Color palette (in its default state). You can tear it off and make it its own palette, which you can then close if you wish. To add a stroke to a path:

1. Select the path to which you want to add or change the stroke.

2. Click the Stroke box in the Color palette or in the Toolbox.

3. Type a value in the Weight field of the Stroke palette.

---

read this!

There's a glitch in the program that will probably be fixed by Adobe in an update. When you drag and drop a color from the Swatches palette on the path line of a SELECTED object having a stroke of None and the Stroke box active in the Color palette, the entire artboard is changed to that color, rather than just the stroke.

timesaver

   ■ To toggle between Fill and Stroke, press x on the keyboard.

■ To swap Fill and Stroke colors, press Shift-x.

■ Using the Stroke/Fill boxes on the Color palette or on the Toolbox, make the stroke and fill colors the same by dragging one box over the other.

read this!

Another glitch: When you drop a stroke color from the Swatches palette on the path line of an unselected object, the stroke weight doesn't register in the Stroke palette until you deselect then reselect the object, even though a default stroke weight of 1 pt was applied.

fyi A stroke weight of less than .3 can be difficult to "hold" when it's output for printing. Check with your output provider for minimum stroke weight specifications.

- If you type in a value other than points, Illustrator converts it to its equivalent value in points.
- If you enter a value of 0, it is changed to None.

or

Click the arrows to select a preset weight.

or

Click the menu arrow to display the pop-up menu and drag to select a preset weight.

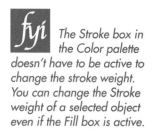

fyi The Stroke box in the Color palette doesn't have to be active to change the stroke weight. You can change the Stroke weight of a selected object even if the Fill box is active.

activity 3.10

1. Create a new document: Letter size, CMYK color mode. Enlarge the View to 200%.

2. Select the Rectangle tool and draw a rectangle about 2" wide and 1" high.

3. Fill the rectangle with a color by clicking in the CMYK Spectrum bar.
   - The color is applied to the object immediately.
   - Notice that the color extends to the edge of the path.
   - Notice the numbers in the CMYK fields.

4. Adjust the color by moving the CMYK sliders back and forth.

5. Change the Stroke weight to 6 point.
   - You can change the Stroke weight when the Fill box is selected in the Color palette.
   - Notice that the path line goes down the middle of the stroke. The color extends under the stroke to the path line.

6. Click the Stroke box to make it the active selection and click in the CMYK Spectrum bar to choose a different color for the stroke.

7. Click the Fill/Stroke toggle arrow (↱) in the Toolbox to switch the colors.
   - The Stroke color is now the Fill color and the Fill color is the Stroke color.

8. Click the Default Colors button in the Toolbox.
   - Fill is white and Stroke is black — the default colors.

9. With the Ellipse tool draw a circle so that at least part of it is over the rectangle you drew.

- The Fill is white and Stroke is black because those are the last colors used.

10. Press the letter *v* on the keyboard (to choose the Selection tool in the Toolbox) and click on the rectangle. Choose a Fill and Stroke color from the CMYK Spectrum bar.
    - The path is visible under the circle but the color is covered by the fill and stroke of the circle.

11. Make the circle the active object, click the Fill box to make it active, then click the None button either on the Toolbox or the Color palette to place a transparent fill in the circle.
    - The colors of the rectangle are now visible through the circle.

12. Click the Last Color box in the Color palette to restore the white fill in the circle.

13. Draw a polygon with the Polygon tool. Deselect it.

14. Click on yellow in the CMYK Spectrum bar to make it be the current Fill color.

15. Click in the Fill box on the Color palette and drag it over the polygon.
    - The polygon changes to yellow even though it wasn't selected.

16. Experiment with adding colors in different combinations, using the controls and colors in the Color palette and the Toolbox.

17. Close the document without saving it to a file.

PRACTICE ACTIVITY 3-1 — Bulls-Eye Logo

1. Create a new document. Save it into your practice folder as an Illustrator EPS file and name it Ferdinand.eps.

2. Change the fill color to 100% black and the stroke color to None.

3. Draw a 5" polar grid with the following specifications:
   - Width: 5"
   - Height: 5"
   - Concentric Dividers:
     - Number: 4
     - Skew: 0%
   - Radial Dividers:
     - Number: 0
     - Skew: 0%
   - Create Compound Path from Ellipses: Checked
   - Fill Grid: Checked

4. With the Direct Selection tool, click on the path line of the smallest circle, then *Shift*-click on its anchor points to select them (make them solid).
   - Because we checked Create Compound Path from Ellipses, you have to select the path line to select the path.

5. Press the *delete* key to delete that path.

6. Move to a blank spot on the page and choose the Star tool in the Toolbox.

7. Click on the document page to display the Star options dialog box. Enter the following specifications:
   Radius 1: 1"
   Radius 2: 3"
   Points: 3

8. Apply a 3 pt black stroke and a white fill.

9. Move the shape so it's centered on the circles.
   - Zoom in and out as necessary to position paths.

10. Draw two .5" circles to form the eyes, apply a 1pt black stroke, white fill, and move them to the approximate position as indicated in the sample.

11. Draw 2 more circles, .125" in diameter, fill with 100% black, no stroke, and using the center points, position them in the center of the two .5" circles you just drew.

12. Using the Line Segment tool, draw the eyebrows with a 3 pt black stroke.
    - You can move the lines around and rotate them with the selection tools until they're positioned like you want them. They don't have to be exactly like ours.

13. To create the bull's horns, draw an oval with the Ellipse tool that's 1.5" long and .75" high. Fill the shape with 100% white and apply a 3 pt black stroke.

14. Deselect the shape.

15. With the Direct Selection tool, select the top anchor point and drag it down until it snaps to the center point.

Continued

16. With the Direct Selection tool, select the right-most anchor point. Click on the direction point and drag the top direction line down until it creates a point.

   ■ You can move the anchor points and adjust the curves after you've drawn the basic shape.

   ■ Remember you can use the Undo command until you get it to look like you want it.

17. With the Selection tool, rotate the shape and place it on the bull's face

18. Repeat for the other horn, except modify the opposite end.

19. To create the nostrils, select the Spiral tool, click on the document page, and enter the following specifications in the fields:

   Radius: .2"

   Decay: 70

   Segments: 6

   Style:

20. Verify that a 3 point black stroke has been applied (that's the last stroke size you used) and make sure it's filled with white.

21. Move the spiral into position on the nose of the bull.

22. Choose the Spiral tool again and click on the document page to display the Spiral Options dialog box. The specifications you entered for the first spiral are still there. The only change you have to make is to select the other Style ( ).

23. Rotate the bounding box of the spiral you just created to about 180°.

24. Verify that a 3 point black stroke has been applied and the fill is 100% white.

25. Move the spiral into position on the nose of the bull.

26. Create another spiral with the following specifications:

   Radius: .6"

   Decay: 70

   Segments: 10

   Style:

27. Apply a 1 pt black stroke and a fill of None.

28. Create a duplicate of this spiral using drag-copy.

29. Rotate and drag spirals into position under the bull's left nostril.

30. Repeat steps 26–29 for the right side except use the other spiral style ( ).

31. Save your file.

32. Print your document.

33. Close the document window.

PRACTICE ACTIVITY 3-2 — Sailboat

1. Create a new document. Save it into your practice folder as an Illustrator EPS file and name it Sailboat.eps.

2. Click the Default Colors button on the Toolbox palette.

3. Create a circle 3" in diameter and, using the CMYK sliders in the color palette, fill it with 76 C (cyan), 90 M (magenta), 0 Y (yellow), 0 K (black).

4. Apply a 2 pt stroke and color it 100 C, 9 M, 0 Y, 0 K.

5. To create the sun, choose the Star tool and click on a blank spot on the page to display the Star Options dialog box. Enter the following specifications:
   Radius 1: .5"   Radius 2: .2"
   Points: 25

6. Fill the sun with 0 C, 15 M, 75 Y, 0 K, no stroke (click the None button with the Stroke box active).

7. Drag the sun into position in the circle.

8. To draw the large sail, display the Polygon Options dialog box and enter the following specifications:
   Radius: .5"   Sides: 3

9. With the Direct Selection tool selected, drag the top anchor point up and to the left, until the left side of the sail straight up and down and approximately 1.5" tall and .875" wide at the bottom. Zoom in so you can verify that the line is straight.

10. Fill the sail with 100 C, 9 M, 0 Y, 0 K, no stroke.

11. Move the shape into position in the circle.
    ■ You can adjust the size, shape, and position later if necessary.

12. Create the small sail in the same manner as the large sail, except the Radius in the Polygon Options dialog box should be .3" wide. Drag the top anchor point up and to the right approximately 1".

13. Verify that the sail is filled with 100 C, 9 M, 0 Y, 0 K, no stroke.

14. Move the shape into position in the circle.

15. To create the boat, draw a rectangle 1.5" wide and .25" high.

16. With the Direct Selection tool active, modify the shape to match the sample illustration by dragging its anchor points.

17. Move into position under the sails in the circle.

18. Create the waves with the Spiral tool. Display the Spiral Options dialog box and enter the following specifications:
    Radius: .25"
    Decay: 60
    Segments: 5
    Style: ◎

19. Apply a 2 point stroke and color it 100 C, 9 M, 0 Y, 0 K, no fill.

20. Rotate as necessary and move it into position in the circle under the bottom of the boat.

21. Drag-copy as many spirals as you need to fill the space. Move them into position in the circle.

22. To create the stripes in the small sail, draw four rectangles about .4" wide and .05" high. Fill them with 76 C, 90 M, 0 Y, 0 K and a stroke of None.

23. Move them into position on the sail.

24. Create the nautilus shell on the large sail by drawing a spiral with the following specifications:
    Radius: .2"
    Decay: 75
    Segments: 20
    Style: ◎

25. Press *d* on the keyboard to choose default colors. Then apply 100 C, 9 M, 0 Y, 0 K to the stroke, and a fill of 76 C, 90 M, 0 Y, 0 K.

26. Move it into position on the large sail.

27. Save your file, print it, and close the window.

EXERCISE 3-1 — Pencil

Pencil Point

Step 1
Create the pencil point by drawing a rectangle. Delete one of the top anchor points and drag the remaining point at the top of the shape horizontally over to the center to make a triangle. Fill it with the appropriate color. Use the same procedure to create the black tip and position it at the very top of the triangle. Zoom in so you can position it precisely.

Step 2
Draw a rectangle, with a 1 pt black stroke. Apply the appropriate color.

Step 3
Draw another rectangle, 1 pt black stroke, and center it horizontally on top of the first rectangle. Hold the *Shift* key down and drag one of the CMYK sliders to the left to lighten the color slightly.

Step 6
Draw a small rounded rectangle with a 3 pt corner radius, 1 pt black stroke. Drag-copy 3 more and position as shown.

Step 5
Draw a rectangle, 1 pt black stroke.

Step 4
Draw a rounded rectangle with a 6 pt corner radius, 1 pt black stroke.

The Pen & Pencil Tools

Chapter Outline

- The Bézier Path
- Pen Tool
- Draw Straight Segments
- Draw Curved Paths
- Convert Anchor Points
- Add and Delete Anchor Points
- Add Segments to an Open Path
- Join Endpoints of a Path or Paths
- Pencil Tool
- Smooth Tool

- Erase Tool
- Stroke Palette
- Delete a Path
- Copy a Path
- The Paste Command
- Stacking Order
- Select All Paths Having Similar Characteristics
- Group/Ungroup Paths
- Lock/Unlock Objects
- Hide/Show Artwork

The Bézier Path

A path created with the Pen tool has the same components as a path created with the other creation tools (Rectangle, Ellipse, Polygon, and so on). That is, it has straight segments, curved segments, and anchor points. The difference is that when you draw a path with the Pen or Pencil tools, *you* determine the shape of the path.

Pen Tool

The keyboard command to select the Pen tool in the Toolbox is the letter *p*. As with other tools, there are related tools hidden under the Pen tool. To select them, press the arrow on the lower right edge of the Pen tool. You can also tear them off to create a new palette by clicking on the tearoff bar at the right edge of the palette.

With the Pen tool you can create straight segments, curved segments, corner anchor points, smooth anchor points, and anchor points that are a combination of corner points and smooth points. When you learn how and when to use each of them, you can create virtually any shape you want easily.

Anchor Points

As you already know, all segments of a path — straight segments and curved segments — are connected by anchor points, with each segment having a minimum of two anchor points, one at the beginning and one at the end. When you click to create a corner point, it doesn't have any direction lines or direction points for you to manipulate. When you click-and-drag to create a smooth point, direction lines and direction points display on two sides of the anchor point, which you can manipulate to change the shape of a curved segment.

You can move an anchor point after you've clicked to establish it: before releasing the mouse, press and hold the spacebar down, then move the mouse to move the anchor point to a new location. Release the mouse.

■ The cursor changes to a solid arrowhead unless you position it over the first anchor point. Then it becomes hollow. The path is not closed at this point because the two endpoints are still there.

Corner Point When you click on your document page to draw a path with the Pen tool, a corner point is placed where you clicked. When you click again (without dragging) in a different spot, another corner point is created with a straight segment between the two points.

Corner points connect three kinds of segments:

■ Two straight segments (A).

■ A straight segment and a curved segment (B).

■ Curved segments where an abrupt change of direction is needed (C).

Smooth Point A smooth point connects two curved paths to form a smooth, continuous curve. When a smooth point is drawn, direction lines with direction points on the ends extend from two sides of the point, creating "handles." You manipulate these handles to control the size and shape of the curve.

■ The direction in which you drag when creating a smooth point determines the direction of the curve of the path that is drawn from the anchor point. As you can see in the illustration, the direction you drag is the side the hump of the curve is on. In this example, the curve was created by dragging straight up and down.

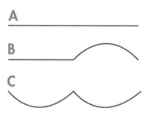

Three kinds of segments connected by a corner point: A, two straight segments; B, a straight segment and a curved segment; C, two curved segments

Curved segments connected by a smooth point

When drawing a curved segment, drag in the direction you want the hump of the curve to appear

- The angle at which you drag when creating a smooth point determines the shape of the curved segment. The curves in the example at the right were created by dragging the handle at an angle.

- How far you drag the handle determines how high the curve will be from the anchor point. It can also affect the shape of the curve. Notice that a short handle creates a small hump and dragging the handle farther from the anchor point creates a larger hump.

The angle at which you drag the direction handles determines the shape of the curve

Closing a Path

To close a path:

1. Move the point of the Pen tool pointer directly over the first anchor point you created until a small circle displays next to the pen tip (⬥₀).

2. Click. The path closes, ending creation of that path.
   - The Pen tool and the path you just closed remain selected, but when you click to start another path, the previous path deselects, allowing you to start a new path.

How far you drag the direction handles determines the height of the curve

Ending an Open Path

To end an open path:

- ⌘-click on the page away from the path.

or

- Choose **Select** ➪ **Deselect**.

When you end a path without closing it, the Pen tool remains selected, so you can create new paths.

Draw Straight Segments

Straight segments are the easiest to draw with the Pen tool. A straight segment has only corner points with no direction lines to manipulate. You can draw straight open paths, such as a simple straight line, or straight closed paths, such as a triangle.

To draw straight segments:

1. Select the Pen tool in the Toolbox (press *p*).
   - The pointer changes to the Pen tool pointer (⬥ₓ). The small ✕ beside the pen tip indicates you're drawing a new path.

2. Move the point of the Pen tool pointer to the spot on the page where you want the path to start, then click.
   - A corner anchor point is placed at the point of the click.

Pen tool icon in the Toolbox palette

- Don't move the mouse at all when you click or direction handles will display, indicating that a curved segment will be created.

3. Position the point of the Pen tool pointer where you want the first segment of the shape to end, and click again.

   - To keep segments perfectly aligned at 0°, 45°, or 90°, press the *Shift* key before you click. The anchor point will be placed at the nearest 45° angle, which is 0° if you want a horizontal line, or 90° for a vertical line.

   - To create a perfectly straight horizontal line, move to the approximate position you want and eyeball it to be as straight as possible before you *Shift*-click. It snaps to 0°. If you're closer to 45° from the starting point, it snaps to 45° rather than 0°.

4. Continue moving the Pen tool pointer and clicking to create as many straight segments as you need to complete your shape.

activity 4.1

1. Create a new document: Letter size, CMYK color mode.

2. Select the Pen tool in the Toolbox (press *p*).

3. Without moving the mouse as you click, click somewhere on the page.

   - A corner point is placed on the page.

4. Hold the *Shift* key down and click about 2" to the right of the click, as close to horizontal as you can.

   - A perfectly horizontal straight segment is drawn between the two corner points created when you clicked.

   - Remember that you can Undo any point you place in error.

5. ⌘-click somewhere on the page away from the path you just created to deselect the path, allowing you to create a new path.

6. Draw a straight segment at a 45° angle:

   - Click on a blank spot on the page.

- Hold the *Shift* key down and make the second click away from the horizontal baseline. In the example shown here, the click was made where the Pen tool icon is shown, but the segment was positioned at a 45° angle from the original anchor point.

7. ⌘-click on the page away from the path you just created to deselect the path.

8. Draw a straight segment at a 90° angle:

   - Click on a blank spot on the page.

   - Hold the *Shift* key down and make the second click perpendicular to the horizontal baseline. In the example shown here, the click was made where the Pen tool icon is shown, but the segment was positioned at a 90° angle (straight up) from the original anchor point.

Continued

9. Deselect the path by ⌘-clicking in a blank spot on the page.

   - If you don't have a stroke or fill applied to the path, it will disappear when you deselect it. You can make it reappear by selecting it again. The easiest way to do that is to marquee it with a selection tool.

10. Click on a blank spot on your page to start a new path.

11. Move the mouse to the right and click to create a horizontal segment.

12. Move the mouse up about ½" and click but, before releasing the mouse, hold the spacebar down. Move the point up and down and around, then release the mouse and the spacebar to drop the point.

13. Delete the path by pressing the *Delete* key on the keyboard.

   - Only the last segment you created will be deleted because that's the only segment that has a solid anchor point (indicating that it's selected). The other two anchor points in the path are hollow, indicating they are not selected.

   - Notice that when you delete the segment, the anchor points on the remaining segment become solid, indicating they are now selected.

14. Press *Delete* again to delete the remaining segment.

15. On a clear spot, draw a triangle:

   - With the Pen tool selected, click on a blank spot on the page to establish a new corner point.

   - Apply a 1 point yellow stroke to this path.

   - Hold the *Shift* key down and click again about 2" to the right to draw a perfectly horizontal segment.

   - With the *Shift* key still pressed, move the mouse pointer up about 1" and click.

   - Release the *Shift* key.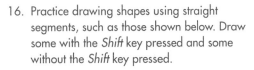

   - Position the pointer directly over the first anchor point you created. When the pointer displays a small circle beside it (⟨△₀⟩), you know you're directly over the anchor point.

   - Click to close the path.

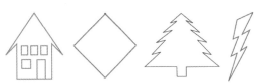

16. Practice drawing shapes using straight segments, such as those shown below. Draw some with the *Shift* key pressed and some without the *Shift* key pressed.

17. Close this document without saving it to a file.

Draw Curved Paths

Drawing smooth curved paths is a little more difficult than drawing straight paths. When you drag the Pen tool, even a little, as you click to establish a point, a smooth point is created. The angle at which you drag and how far you drag when creating the point, determines the shape of the curve.

To draw a curved segment:

1. Select the Pen tool (⬚) in the Toolbox (press *p*).
   - ■ The pointer changes to the Pen tool pointer (⬚). The small × beside the pen tip indicates you're drawing a new path.

2. Move the point of the Pen tool pointer to the spot on the page where you want the path to start.

3. Click and drag to establish a smooth point.
   - ■ When you drag, the anchor point remains fixed. You're actually dragging a direction point.

   - ■ When you begin to drag the mouse, the pointer changes to an arrowhead (▶), indicating that it's an active path.
   - ■ When you create the first anchor point of a curved path, always drag in the direction you want the curve to go. If you want the hump of the curve to go *up* from the point, drag up; if you want the hump of the curve to go *down* from the point, drag down.
   - ■ The angle of the direction lines extending from the point determines the shape of the curve.

   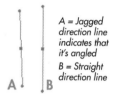

   A = Jagged direction line indicates that it's angled

   B = Straight direction line

   - ■ If you want the direction lines to be perpendicular or at a 45° angle so you can create a uniform series of curves, press and hold the *Shift* key before releasing the mouse when creating an anchor point.
     - ▪ You can tell if the direction line is at 0°, 45°, or 90° because the line is smooth. If the direction line is jagged, it isn't at 0°, 45°, or 90°.

   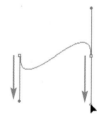

   - ■ To draw an s-shaped curve, drag the second anchor point the same direction you dragged when you created the first anchor point.

4. Create only as many anchor points as you need to make the shape you want. Unneeded anchor points can cause a curve to be bumpy.

   Drag direction lines in the same direction to create an s-shaped curve

   - ■ To draw an oval, you need only two anchor points, one on each side of the shape, creating only two segments.
     - ▪ Notice that there is no center point in the oval shown here. The program default is to put a center point in a circle or oval drawn with the Ellipse tool (⬚), but not in one created with the pen tool. If you want a center point, you can add one by clicking the Show Center Point button (⬚) in the Attributes palette. You may have to click the Attributes palette Options arrow to display the menu and choose Show All to display the portion of the palette that contains the center point buttons.

   This oval has only two smooth anchor points

   - ■ A perfect circle requires four anchor points. If you draw a circle with more than four anchor points, it's likely to be bumpy and uneven.

   A perfect circle with its four smooth anchor points and direction lines

 activity 4.2

1. Create a new document: Letter size, CMYK color mode.

2. With the Pen tool selected (press *p*), draw a uniform wavy line using the "c" curve:

   - Press the *Shift* key, click somewhere near the left side of the document page, then drag straight down to create the anchor point.

   - With the *Shift* key still pressed, move to the right about 1", click and drag straight up about the same distance you moved when you dragged down to create the first anchor point.

     - The distance you drag the handle determines how big the humps of the curve are.

     - Visually line up the direction point you're drawing with the direction point that's visible on the last anchor point you created.

   - Repeat the last step until you have a wavy line across the page. Deselect (⌘ click).

3. Draw a uniform wavy line using the "s" curve:

   - Press the *Shift* key, click somewhere near the left side of the document page, then drag straight down to create the anchor point.

   - With the *Shift* key still pressed, move to the right about 1", click and drag straight down again about the same distance you moved when you dragged down to create the first anchor point.

   - Repeat the last step until you have a wavy line across the page. Deselect.

4. Draw another uniform wavy line using the "s" curve:

   - Press the *Shift* key, click somewhere near the left side of the document page, then drag down and to the left at a 45° angle to start the curve.

   - With the *Shift* key still pressed, move to the right about 1", click and drag at a 45° angle again about the same distance you moved when you dragged down to create the first anchor point.

   - Repeat the last step until you have a wavy line across the page. Deselect all.

5. Practice drawing curved shapes, using "c" curves and "s" curves, both with the *Shift* key pressed and without the *Shift* key pressed.

6. Using only smooth anchor points, practice drawing non-uniform shapes by drawing a shape similar to "Blobby boy" shown here.

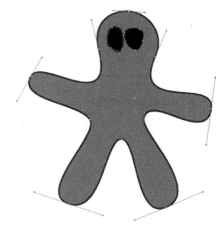

   - Notice where the anchor points are positioned and the angle of the direction lines.

   - Close the path by positioning the Pen tool over the first anchor point you drew until the circle displays beside the tool icon (🖊), then click.

7. Change "Blobby boy's" shape by moving anchor points and by changing the angle of the direction lines.

8. Close your document without saving it to a file unless you want to save your "Blobby boy." In that event, name the file and save it into your Practice Folder.

Convert Anchor Points

You can change a corner anchor point to a smooth anchor point, and vice versa, on an existing selected path or as you're drawing a new path.

Converting Anchor Points on an Existing Path

You can convert anchor points on an existing path only if the path is active (selected). You can use the Pen tool ([✎]) or the Convert Anchor Point tool, which is a hidden tool under the Pen tool, to convert an anchor point in a closed path or in the middle of an open path. To convert an endpoint, you must use the Convert Anchor Point tool.

Convert a Smooth Point to a Corner Point

1. With the Pen tool selected, position the pointer over a smooth point in an active curved path. Press and hold the ⌥ key.

   ■ The pointer changes to the Convert Anchor Point pointer (⌐).

2. Click. The smooth point changes to a corner point. Direction lines that were attached to the smooth point disappear and the shape of the path changes to reflect the change of anchor point.

Convert a Corner Point to a Smooth Point

1. With the Pen tool selected, position the pointer over a corner point in an active path that has a corner point. Press and hold the ⌥ key.

   ■ The pointer changes to the Convert Anchor Point pointer (⌐).

2. Click and drag away from the anchor point to display direction lines, thus changing it to a smooth point.

   ■ If the path twists around the anchor point, just click on a direction line and rotate it to untwist it.

Convert a Smooth Point to an Anchor Point with Independent Direction Lines

1. With the Pen tool selected, position the pointer over an active smooth point (solid) in a curved path to display its direction lines.

2. Hold down the ⌥ key and click on one of the direction *points*. Release the ⌥ key.

   ■ The smooth point converts to an anchor point with direction lines that you can manipulate independently of each other.

Convert Anchor Point tool icon in the Toolbox palette

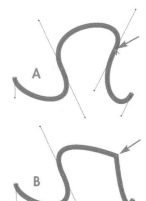

Smooth point (A) converted to corner point (B)

Corner point (A) converted to a smooth point (B)

Corner point (A) converted to anchor point with independent direction lines (B)

activity 4.3

1. Create a new document: Letter size, CMYK color mode.

2. Select the Pen tool (press *p*) and click on the page to create a corner anchor point. Apply a green stroke color.

3. Move to the right about 1½", click and drag down to create a smooth anchor point.

4. Move to the right another 1½", then click and drag down to create another smooth point, which creates an s-shape curved segment.

5. Position the pointer over the middle anchor point, hold down the ⌥ key, and click on the anchor point. Release the ⌥ key.

   ■ The first segment of the path is changed to a straight segment because the points on each end of the segment are now corner points.

6. Select the Direct Selection tool (press *a*).

7. Click on the middle anchor point (the one you just converted), and drag it down about 1". Release the mouse.

   ■ Notice how the shape of the path changed.

8. Select the Pen tool (press *p*) and hold down the ⌥ key. Click on the middle anchor point, drag down, then release the ⌥ key and the mouse.

   ■ Direction handles display on the anchor point.

   ■ Notice how the shape of the path changed.

9. With the Direct Selection tool selected (press *a*), hold down the ⌥ key, click on the top direction point of the middle anchor point, and drag it around to the left and down. Release the mouse when the direction point is near the bottom direction point.

   ■ Notice how the shape of the path changed.

10. With the Convert Anchor Point tool (⌐) selected, position the pointer over the smooth anchor point at the right endpoint of the path, and click on the anchor point to change it to a corner point.

    ■ Notice that the curved segment attached to the last anchor point has disappeared.

11. Deselect the path (⌘-click). Then, with the Direct Selection tool selected (press *a*), click on a segment of the path.

12. Click on the right endpoint (it should be hollow), and move it up and down and in and out.

    ■ Notice that the shape of the curve changes where it extends from the middle anchor point, depending on how far you drag the last anchor point away from it, and at what angle you drag the anchor point.

    ■ Notice that only one direction line extends from the middle anchor point.

13. Click on the lefthand segment of the path.

    ■ The other direction line displays.

14. *Shift*-click the middle anchor point to display both direction lines. Move their handles around and notice the changes that are made to the path.

15. Close the document without saving it to a file.

Converting Anchor Points as You Draw a Path

You can convert anchor points as you draw a path with the Pen tool, enabling you to create (a) a curved segment followed by a straight segment, (b) a straight segment followed by a curved segment, or two curved segments connected by a corner point.

Curved Segment Followed by a Straight Segment

1. With the Pen tool selected, click and drag to create the first anchor point of the curved segment.

2. Move the pointer to the place you want the curved segment to end, then click and drag to draw the curve you want. Release the mouse.

3. Move the pointer so it's over the active endpoint (solid). The pointer icon changes and a small Convert Anchor Point icon displays beside the pen tip (⟁ₙ).

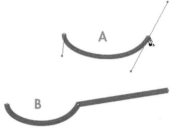

4. Click the anchor point.

   ■ The smooth point changes to a corner point.

5. Move the pointer to the place on the page where you want the straight segment to end, and click without dragging.

   ■ To keep the segment horizontal (0°) or at a 45° or 90° angle, hold down the *Shift* key when you click to create the endpoint.

Creating a curved segment (A) followed by a straight segment (B)

Hold down the Shift key when creating the endpoint of the straight segment to make the straight segment perfectly horizontal

Straight Segment Followed by a Curved Segment

1. With the Pen tool selected, click in two places to create a straight segment.

   ■ To keep the segment horizontal (0°) or at a 45° or 90° angle, hold down the *Shift* key before clicking to place the second corner point.

2. Move the pointer over the active endpoint (solid) until the Convert Anchor Point pointer (⟁ₙ) displays.

3. Click and drag. A direction line is pulled from the anchor point as you drag. The length and angle of this direction line determines the shape of the curved segment that is created.

   ■ You can adjust the length and angle of this direction line after the path is complete, if necessary.

4. Click and drag where you want the new curved segment to end, creating a smooth point.

   ■ Adjust the direction lines to change the shape of the curve.

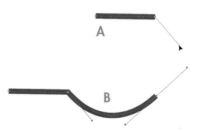

Creating a straight segment (A) followed by a curved segment (B)

Draw Two Curved Segments Connected by a Corner Point

If you want to draw two curved segments that abruptly change direction at the anchor point, such as a scallop shape, you have to connect the two curved segments with a corner point. You can do it as you draw the path or you can convert a smooth point to a corner point after you've finished drawing your path.

To connect two curved segments with a corner point:

1. With the Pen tool selected, click and drag to create a smooth point.

2. Click and drag in another spot on the page to create a curved segment but, before releasing the mouse, hold down the ⌥ key. This allows you to move the direction handle on only one side of the point.

3. Drag the direction point to a new position. The length and angle of this direction line determines the slope of the next curved segment in the path.

   ■ If you have released the mouse before realizing you want to make the point an anchor point, leave the Pen tool selected, press the ⌥ key. The cursor changes to the Convert Anchor Point icon (⌐). Click on the direction point and move it into a new position.

4. Click and drag a new smooth point to complete the path.

Curved segments connected by corner points

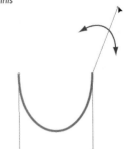

Hold down the ⌥ key, click on a direction point, and drag to move the direction handle on one side of an anchor point

The angle of the direction handle when you release it determines the shape of the curve

activity 4.4

1. Create a new document: Letter size, CMYK color mode.

2. Select the Pen tool in the Toolbox (press *p*).

3. On the page, click and drag down about half an inch to create a smooth point.

4. Hold the *Shift* key down and move the cursor to the right about an inch.

5. Click and drag straight up about the same distance you dragged when you created the first point (line up the direction points at the bottom of the path).

6. Release the *Shift* key, but not the mouse.

7. Hold down the ⌥ key, and move the direction point down until it is positioned over the direction point on the bottom of the anchor point.

8. Release the ⌥ key and the mouse.

9. Hold down the *Shift* key, then click about an inch to the right of the last anchor point, release the *Shift* key, and drag straight up to form another curved segment.

10. Hold down the ⌥ key, and drag the direction point down and position it over the direction

Continued

point on
the bottom
of the anchor
point.

11. Add several more curved segments to the scallop shape.

12. Deselect (⌘-click).

13. Draw a cloud by creating smooth points, converting them to corner points with independent direction lines and adjusting the lines to form a cloud shape.

14. Close the document without saving it to a file.

Add and Delete Anchor Points

You can add or delete anchor points from any active path. If you've created too many smooth points and your path is bumpy, remove the ones you don't need. In addition, fewer anchor points in a path makes the path less complex, file size is smaller, and it prints faster. Add anchor points when you need more control over the shape of the path.

Adding Anchor Points

You can add anchor points to segments of a selected path in three ways. First, choose the Direct Selection tool and click on the path to which you want to add anchor points. Then:

1. Select the Pen tool and position the pointer over the segment of the path where you want to add an anchor point until the Pen tool displays a plus sign beside the pen tip (♧₊). Click on the segment. A new, selected anchor point is added on the path.

   ■ If you want to start a new path on top of an existing path, without connecting it to the existing path, you can temporarily disable the automatic Add Anchor Point feature by holding down the *Shift* key as you move the pointer over the segment of a path. Release the *Shift* key before releasing the mouse or the new path snaps to 0°, 45°, or 90°.

   ■ To turn off the ability of the Pen tool to add anchor points in an existing path permanently, check the Disable Auto Add/Delete checkbox in the General Preferences dialog box (**Edit** ⇨ **Preferences** ⇨ **General**).

or

2. Select the Add Anchor Point tool (▨) in the Toolbox. It's hidden under the Pen tool. The cursor changes to the Add Anchor Point pointer (♧₊). Position the pointer over the spot on the segment where you want to add the anchor point, and click. A new, selected anchor point is added on the path.

Add an anchor point to an existing path with the Pen tool

☐ **Disable Auto Add/Delete**
☐ Japanese Crop Marks
☐ **Transform Pattern Tiles**
☐ **Scale Strokes & Effects**
☐ **Use Preview Bounds**

Check this box in the General Preferences dialog box to turn off the ability of the Pen tool to add anchor points to an existing path

■ To change the Add Anchor Point tool to the Delete Anchor point tool temporarily, hold down the ⌥ key when you position the pointer over an anchor point in a path.

or

3. To add an anchor point to each segment of a selected path, evenly spaced between existing anchor points, choose **Object** ➪ **Path** ➪ **Add Anchor Points**. All anchor points added to the path are selected.

An anchor point that's added to a straight segment will be a corner point. An anchor point added to a curved segment will be a smooth point with direction lines.

Deleting Anchor Points

You can delete anchor points manually in a selected path in two ways:

1. With the Pen tool selected, position the pointer over the anchor point that you want to delete. The Pen tool displays a minus sign beside it (✒₋). Click on the anchor point.

   ■ To temporarily disable the automatic Delete Anchor Point feature, hold down the *Shift* key as you move the pointer over an anchor point on the path.

   ■ To turn off the ability of the Pen tool to change to the Delete Anchor Point pointer, check the Disable Auto Add/Delete checkbox in the General Preferences dialog box (**Edit** ➪ **Preferences** ➪ **General**).

2. Select the Delete Anchor Point tool ( ) in the Toolbox (hidden under the Pen tool). The cursor changes to the Delete Anchor Point pointer (✒₋). Position the pointer over the anchor point you want to delete, and click.

   ■ The shape of the path is changed to reflect the absence of the anchor point.

   ■ To change the Delete Anchor Point tool to the Add Anchor Point tool temporarily, hold down the ⌥ key.

If you attempt to delete an anchor point by clicking on a segment of a path rather than an anchor point, an alert displays telling you to click on an anchor point of a path.

Deleting an anchor point when the Pen tool is selected

☐ Disable Auto Add/Delete
☐ Japanese Crop Marks
☐ Transform Pattern Tiles
☐ Scale Strokes & Effects
☐ Use Preview Bounds

Check this box in the General Preferences dialog box to turn off the ability to delete anchor points with the Pen tool selected

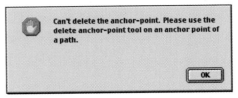

Can't delete the anchor-point. Please use the delete anchor-point tool on an anchor point of a path.

[OK]

Alert message that displays when you click on something other than an anchor point with the Delete Anchor Point tool selected.

Simplifying Paths

Many times, imported paths that have been created in other programs — and sometimes by users who don't know any better — have too many anchor points, making the path ragged and difficult to manipulate. Illustrator can smooth the shape of a selected path by removing unnecessary anchor points automatically using the Simplify command.

To delete anchor points from a selected path, choose **Object** ⇨ **Path** ⇨ **Simplify** to display the Simplify dialog box (Figure 4.1).

Preview Click the Preview box to see the results of your changes before clicking OK or pressing *return/enter*. When checked, the Original/Current values under the Angle Threshold slider change to indicate how many points were in the original path and how many points will remain after the command has been applied.

Curve Precision This value determines how drastically curved paths are altered. You can enter a value between 0% and 100%, or move the slider to the desired value. The default is 50% but if you want to leave the path exactly as it was drawn, change the Curve Precision value to 100%. Then only unnecessary anchor points are removed.

Angle Threshold Move the slider to control the smoothness of corner points. The lower the Angle Threshold value, the smoother sharp angles become.

Straight Lines Straight lines will be created between anchor points.

Show Original Displays the original path so you can see how much was changed.

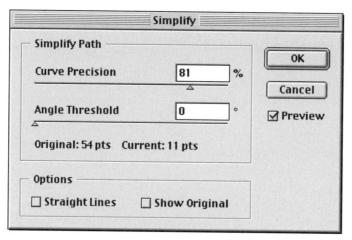

FIGURE 4.1 Change values in the Simplify dialog box to delete anchor points from a path automatically, making it less complex.

 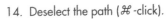 *activity 4.5*

1. Create a new document: Letter size, CMYK color mode.

2. Draw a curved segment, followed by a straight segment (somewhat like a crude spoon).

   ■ Don't forget to convert the second smooth anchor point of the curved segment so you can create a straight segment.

   ■ If you want the straight segment to be perfectly horizontal, hold the *Shift* key down when creating the last anchor point.

3. With the Pen tool, add an anchor point anywhere in the straight segment.

   ■ Notice that no direction lines or direction points are displayed on the anchor point, indicating that it's a corner point.

4. Add an anchor point somewhere in the curved segment.

   ■ Notice that there are direction lines and direction points extending from the anchor point, indicating that it's a smooth point.

5. Deselect the path (⌘-click on a blank spot on the page).

6. Move to a blank spot on the page.

7. Choose the Ellipse tool (⬛) in the Toolbox.

8. Draw a perfect circle on the page. Color the stroke yellow, no fill.

9. Deselect the path.

10. With the Direct Selection tool (press *a*), select the path.

11. Make the Pen tool active (press *p*).

12. Position the pointer over the anchor point at the top of the circle (it should be hollow) until the pointer changes to the Delete Anchor Point pointer.

13. Click to delete the anchor point.

14. Deselect the path (⌘-click).

15. Repeating #10–14 above, delete the bottom anchor point.

16. Deselect all, then move to a blank space on the page.

   ■ Press the letter *h*, then click and drag to move the document window around on the screen.

17. Click the Default Fill & Stroke button on the Toolbox palette.

18. With the Pen tool, draw an exaggerated wave like the one shown here.

19. Display the Object menu, scroll down to Path, and select Add Anchor Points.

   ■ Notice that anchor points were added, equally spaced, between each of the anchor points you created when drawing the path.

20. Repeat #18 above two more times, taking note of how many anchor points are added and where they're placed in the path.

21. Press *p*, then position the Pen tool pointer over one of the anchor points in the right side of the path until the Delete Anchor Point pointer displays.

22. Click to remove that anchor point.

23. Remove several more of the anchor points and notice what happens to the shape of the path.

24. Close this document without saving it to a file.

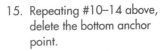
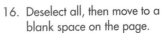
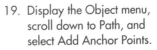
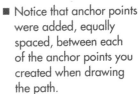
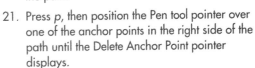

Add Segments to an Open Path

You can add segments to an existing path with the Pen tool, whether the path is selected or deselected.

1. Choose the Pen tool in the Toolbox (press *p*).

2. Position the Pen tool pointer over the last anchor point at the end of a selected or unselected path to which you want to add a segment until the pen tip displays a small diagonal slash next to it (⟁).

3. Click the anchor point. If the path was deselected, it becomes active, with the endpoint solid (active). Continue adding segments to the path the same as if you hadn't stopped drawing the original path.

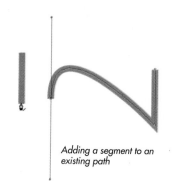

Adding a segment to an existing path

Join Endpoints of a Path or Paths

To join the endpoints of an open path or the endpoints of two separate open paths:

1. Choose the Pen tool in the Toolbox (press *p*).

2. Position the Pen tool pointer over the endpoint of a deselected path until the pointer displays a small diagonal slash next to it (⟁). This is the Add Segments pointer.

3. Click the anchor point.

4. Position the pointer over the endpoint that you want to connect to. When you're precisely over the other endpoint in the same path, the pointer displays a small circle next to it (⟁₀). If you're joining two separate open paths, the pointer displays a small square with lines extending from the sides (⟁).

5. Click the anchor point. An open path becomes a closed path or two separate paths become one continuous path.

or

1. Select the two endpoints of a path (anchor points are solid when selected).

2. Choose **Object ⇨ Path ⇨ Join**.

If the endpoints of the paths are corner points, the new segment will be a straight segment. If the endpoints are smooth points, the new segment will be a curved segment.

Joining endpoints of an open path

This command works on two selected endpoints of the same open path or two selected endpoints of separate open paths. A warning (shown here) may display (a) if two endpoints are not selected, (b) if they are on text paths, or (c) if they are in graphs. If the paths are grouped, the endpoints must be in the same group. Groups are discussed later in this chapter.

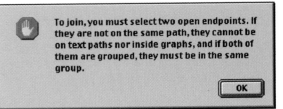

To join, you must select two open endpoints. If they are not on the same path, they cannot be on text paths nor inside graphs, and if both of them are grouped, they must be in the same group.

OK

Warning message that displays when you attempt to join two endpoints improperly

activity 4.6

1. Create a new document: Letter size, CMYK color mode.

2. Press *p* on the keyboard (to select the Pen tool), and draw a curved horizontal path on the page. Apply a 2 pt green stroke.

3. Deselect the path (⌘-click).

4. Move the pointer over the right endpoint of the path until the Add Segments pointer (✑) displays, and click and drag to create a smooth point.

5. Add more segments to the path, but don't close the shape.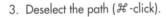

6. Deselect the path (⌘-click).

7. Join the endpoints of this path by moving the Pen tool pointer over one of the endpoints of the path until the Add Segments pointer displays, then click.

8. Position the Pen tool pointer over the other endpoint of the path until the Close Path pointer displays (✑), then click to close the path.

9. Deselect the path (⌘-click).

10. Draw two more open paths on the page, similar to the ones shown here. Apply 2 pt pink strokes.

11. Select the two endpoints of each path where it looks like a gap in the circle.

12. Choose Object ⇨ Path ⇨ Join.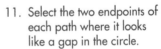

13. Close the document without saving it to a file.

Pencil Tool

With the Pencil tool, you can perform two functions.

1. You can draw freeform paths like when you draw with a pencil on paper, giving a hand-drawn look to your artwork, but it doesn't work too well for drawing straight lines.

2. You can change the shape of an existing path or add to it.

Pencil tool icon in the Toolbox palette

Draw an Open Path

To draw an open freeform path with the Pencil tool.

1. Select the Pencil tool in the Toolbox.

   ■ The mouse pointer changes into the Pencil cursor (✐ₓ).

2. Click on the page where you want the path to start, and drag to create the shape.

   ■ As you move the mouse, a dotted line follows the pointer.

   ■ When you want to draw a new path near an existing selected path and the Pencil cursor loses its ×, becoming a plain pencil, the existing path is changed rather than a new one drawn. To draw a new path, make sure the × is visible on the Pencil cursor. The larger you make the View percentage, the easier it is to draw a new path close to an existing path.

3. Release the mouse when you have finished drawing the shape.

   ■ Anchor points are placed automatically on the path. You can't specify where they are positioned along the path. It's determined according to the length and complexity of the path and by the settings that are entered in the Pencil Tool Preferences dialog box. Refer to Setting Pencil Tool Preferences later in this chapter for information about Pencil tool preferences.

Add to an Existing Open Path To add segments to any existing path (not just paths drawn with the Pencil tool):

1. Select the path with one of the selection tools (the anchor points are visible).

2. Choose the Pencil tool (*n*), click on the endpoint that you want to add to, and drag.

   ■ Anchor points are adjusted according to the shape of the new path. In fact, the anchor point that you clicked on to add to the path may be moved.

3. Release the mouse when the shape is complete.

Connect a New Path to an Existing Path To connect a new path to an existing path:

1. With one of the selection tools, select an existing path.

2. Choose the Pencil tool (*n*) and drag to create a new path. Before releasing the mouse, hold down the ⌘ key and drag to connect the new path to an anchor point on the selected path.

   ■ When the ⌘ key is pressed, the pointer changes to a Pencil with a hollow anchor point beside it (⌀).

3. Release the mouse when the shape is complete.

You can connect a new path to a closed path, such as a rectangle, a star, a circle, a closed freeform shape, and so on, or an open path.

Draw a Closed Path

To draw a closed freeform path with the Pencil tool:

1. Select the Pencil tool (🖉) in the Toolbox.

   ■ The mouse pointer changes into the Pencil pointer (🖉ₓ).

2. Click on the page where you want the path to start, hold down the ⌥ key, and drag to create the shape.

   ■ The mouse pointer changes into the Pencil pointer with a solid eraser and with a small circle (o) instead of an × (🖉ₒ), indicating that the path is continuous.

3. Release the mouse when you have finished drawing the shape. Don't release the ⌥ key until after you have released the mouse.

   ■ You don't have to be near the other end of the path to close the shape. It'll find it.

   ■ To close a path and form a smoother intersection, press the ⌥ key but don't release the mouse until you are almost on top of the starting point.

   ■ If you release the ⌥ key first, the path won't close.

Edit an Existing Path

You can adjust the shape of an existing selected path with the Pencil tool by placing the Pencil cursor within 2 pixels of the existing path, then redrawing where you want the path to go. You don't have to position the Pencil cursor on an anchor point to edit a path.

   ■ The × disappears from the Pencil cursor when you are close enough to an existing path to edit it.

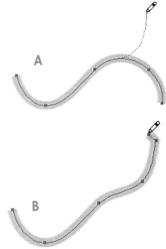

Position the Pencil tool pointer within two pixels of a selected path (A) and drag to edit the path (B)

- If, when you edit a path, you come within 2 pixels of another spot on the same path, the curve is changed to reflect the new path you drew, but the rest of the original path is left intact.

- You don't have to make drastic changes such as I have displayed. You can use this technique to make subtle changes to smooth out a path.

- You can split a closed path and make it an open path by placing the Pencil cursor on an anchor point in a selected path and drawing in a different direction.

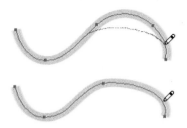

Reshape a selected path by drawing a new path between two points on the path

Setting Pencil Tool Preferences

You can adjust how many anchor points are placed in paths drawn with the Pencil tool and how smooth the path is by changing the value in the Fidelity field (pixels) and Smoothness field (percentage) of the Pencil Tool Preferences dialog box. Only paths drawn after changes are made to the settings are affected. Paths already drawn are not changed.

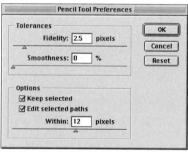

Pencil tool Preferences dialog box

To display the Pencil Tool Preferences dialog box:

- Double-click the Pencil tool ( ) in the Toolbox.

or

- Press the letter *n* on the keyboard to select the Pencil tool in the Toolbox, then press *return/enter*. If the Pencil tool is already selected, just press *return/enter*.

Fidelity The number in the Fidelity field determines how closely the movement of the mouse is followed when the path is rendered on the screen. A lower number in the Fidelity field causes a greater number of anchor points to be placed in the path, resulting in a more ragged curve. A higher number in the Fidelity field causes fewer anchor points to be placed in the path, thus creating a smoother path. See Figure 4.2 and Figure 4.3.

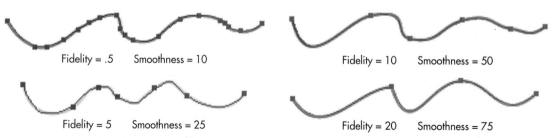

FIGURE 4.2 Samples of similar lines drawn with different fidelity and smoothness values.

Fidelity = .5   Smoothness = 100
(minimum fidelity)

Fidelity = 10   Smoothness = 100
(mid-range fidelity)

Fidelity = 20   Smoothness = 100
(maximum fidelity)

Fidelity = .5   Smoothness = 0
(minimum fidelity default)

Fidelity = 10   Smoothness = 50
(mid-range fidelity)

Fidelity = 20   Smoothness = 100
(maximum fidelity)

FIGURE 4.3   Samples of similar shapes drawn with varying fidelity and smoothness values.

You can enter a number from .5–20 in the Fidelity field or you can move the Fidelity slider by clicking and dragging its triangle up and down the line until the desired number is displayed.

Smoothness   Smoothness controls the amount of smoothness applied when drawing with the Pencil tool. The lower the value, the more uneven the path appears. The higher the value, the smoother the path. If a path is drawn with a higher smoothness value, it may have fewer anchor points than the same path drawn with a lower smoothness value. See Figure 4.2 and Figure 4.3.

You can enter a number from 0–100 in the Smoothness field or you can move the Smoothness slider by clicking and dragging its triangle up and down the line until the desired number is displayed.

Values entered in this dialog box remain until new values are entered or the Reset button is clicked to restore the options to program defaults.

Keep Selected Checkbox   The Keep Selected checkbox at the bottom of the Pencil Tool Preferences dialog box, when checked, keeps a path selected after you've drawn it so you can make adjustments to the path. If you uncheck this box, the path deselects and you have to select it again before you can make changes to it.

Edit Selected Paths   The Edit Selected Paths checkbox allows you to turn off the ability to edit paths with the Pencil tool by unchecking the box. When the box is checked, you can enter a value in the field to specify the distance, in pixels, from a selected path that you must be within to be able to edit the path. The default is 12, which means you must be within 12 pixels of a path in order to edit it with the Pencil tool. The minimum is 2 and the maximum is 20.

1. Create a new document: Letter size, CMYK color mode. Zoom to 200%.

2. Select the Pencil tool (⬚) in the Toolbox.

3. Click and drag the mouse to draw three curvy open paths on the page.

4. Add more curved segments to the first path you drew:

   ■ Hold the ⌘ key down, position the cursor over the first path you drew, and click to select it.

     • Remember that pressing the ⌘ key allows you to use a selection tool to select a path without actually switching to the tool in the Toolbox. The selection tool used is the last one you selected in the Toolbox. You can continue selecting paths as long as you have the ⌘ key depressed.

   ■ Click on an endpoint and continue drawing more curvy segments on the path.

5. Smooth out the curve of the second path you drew:

   ■ Select the path.

   ■ Position the Pencil cursor over one side of a curve on the path until the × beside the cursor disappears.

   ■ Click and drag to the other side of the curve on the path to flatten it out a little.

   ■ Release the mouse when the cursor is positioned over the path on the other side of the curve.

6. Change the direction and shape of the path:

   ■ Select the third path you drew.

   ■ Position the Pencil cursor over an anchor point in the middle of the path until the × beside the cursor disappears.

   ■ Click on the anchor point and drag in a different direction than the original path, then release the mouse.

7. Draw a closed path with the Pencil tool:

   ■ Draw a half-circle, press the ⌥ key, then release the mouse.

   • The path is closed in a straight line from the endpoint where you stopped drawing to the endpoint where you started drawing.

8. Split a closed path:

   ■ With the last path you drew still selected, click on an anchor point with the Pencil tool, drag the mouse in a different direction from the original path, then release the mouse.

9. To verify that the path was split, deselect the path, then select the path with the Direct Selection tool (press *a*), click on the anchor point at the end of the original path you drew, and move it.

10. Adjust the number of anchor points that are placed in a path you draw with the Pencil tool:

    ■ With the Pencil tool (press *n* to select the tool), draw a curvy path about 2" long. Count the anchor points in the path.

    ■ Press *return/enter* to display the Pencil Tool Preferences dialog box.

    ■ Change the Fidelity value to 15 and press *return/enter*.

    ■ Draw the same curvy line again (match it as close as you can).

    ■ Count the anchor points in this path. There should be fewer anchor points in this path.

    ■ Display the Pencil Tool Preferences dialog box again, change the Fidelity value to 1 and press *return/enter*.

    ■ Draw the same curvy line again (match it as close as you can).

    ■ Count the anchor points in this path. There are more anchor points than in the other two paths.

11. Repeat the steps in #10 above, except change the Smoothness value in the Pencil Tool Preferences dialog box and compare the number of anchor points in the similar paths.

12. Practice drawing shapes with the Pencil tool, both open paths and closed paths, editing them, and splitting the closed paths.

13. Return the View to 100% by pressing ⌘1, then close the document without saving it to a file.

Smooth Tool

The Smooth tool is hidden under the Pencil tool in the Toolbox. You can use this tool to smooth out existing open or closed paths or portions of existing paths, while retaining most of the shape of the original path. Settings for this tool can be adjusted in the Smooth Tool Preferences dialog box (see below for information). Only paths drawn after changes are made to the settings are affected. Paths already drawn are not changed.

Smooth tool icon in the Toolbox palette

To smooth an existing path:

1. Select a path.
2. Choose the Smooth tool in the Toolbox.
3. Drag the Smooth tool along the portion of the path that you want to smooth out.
4. Repeat the action until the path is as smooth as you want it to be.

Smooth Tool Preferences

Controls to set tolerances for the Smooth tool are located in the Smooth Tool Preferences dialog box. To display the Smooth Tool Preferences dialog box, double-click the Smooth tool in the Toolbox or, if the Smooth tool is already selected, press *return/enter*.

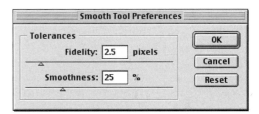

Smooth tool Preferences dialog box

Fidelity The number in the Fidelity field determines how closely the smoothing action retains its original shape. A lower number in the Fidelity field causes fewer anchor points to be removed from the path, resulting in a more ragged path. A higher number in the Fidelity field results in more anchor points being removed from the path, thus creating a smoother path.

You can enter a number from .5–20 in the Fidelity field or you can move the Fidelity slider by clicking and dragging its triangle up and down the line until the desired number is displayed.

Smoothness Smoothness controls the amount of smoothness applied when smoothing a path with the Smooth tool. The higher the value, the more smoothing is applied to the path. A lower value results in less smoothing applied to the path.

You can enter a number from 0–100 in the Smoothness field or you can move the Smoothness slider by clicking and dragging its triangle up and down the line until the desired number is displayed.

Click the Reset button to reset the options to program defaults.

1. Create a new document: Letter size, CMYK color mode. Zoom to 200%.

2. Select the Pencil tool in the Toolbox.

3. Draw several wavy paths similar to the one shown here.

4. Select one of the wavy paths you just drew.

5. Choose the Smooth tool in the Toolbox and drag the cursor over the curves to flatten them out. Continue dragging over the path until the curves are almost flat.

6. Display the Smooth Tool Preferences dialog box by pressing *return/enter* with the Smooth tool selected in the Toolbox.

7. Change the Fidelity value to 10 and the Smoothness value to 50. Click OK or press *return/enter*.

8. Select another of the paths you drew and apply the Smooth tool.

9. Display the Smooth Tool Preferences dialog box again and click the Reset button to return the options to the program defaults. Click OK or press *return/enter*.

10. Select the Star tool in the Toolbox and draw a star about 1" in diameter.

11. Select the Smooth tool in the Toolbox and apply smoothing to the points of the star. Keep smoothing until it looks something like the one displayed here.

   - Dragging the smooth tool close to the base of the points of the star works best.

   - You can smooth across the pointy ends of the star and make them rounded, too.

12. Experiment with smoothing different shapes, using the creation tools you've learned.

13. Return the View to 100% by pressing ⌘1, then close the document without saving it to a file.

Erase Tool

The Erase tool, hidden under the Pencil tool in the Toolbox, performs the function its name implies — it erases. If you erase part of a closed path, it becomes an open path. If you erase the middle portion of an open path, it becomes two separate paths, with anchor points added to the ends of each new path. Erase an entire selected closed path at one time by clicking on it with the Erase tool selected. Or you can erase sections of a selected open or closed path:

Erase tool icon in the Toolbox palette

1. Drag the Erase tool along a selected path or a portion of a selected path. The portion you "erased" disappears.

2. To erase sections of a selected path, drag across the area you want to remove. When you release the mouse, that section of the path is erased.

   - You must be within the pixel range specified in the Pencil Tool Preferences dialog box when you begin your drag across the path.

■ How you drag with the Erase tool from one side of a shape to the other side determines which part of the shape is erased. If you curve into one side of the shape when you drag, that portion of the shape is erased.

3. Split an active open path into two paths or an active closed path into an open path by dragging the cursor across it, like you were cutting through it with a knife.

 *activity 4.9*

1. Create a new document: Letter size, CMYK color mode. Zoom to 400%.

2. Select the Ellipse tool (⬤) in the Toolbox and draw a circle on the page of any size and shape.

3. Select the Erase tool (✎) and drag the eraser across one side so the closed path becomes an open path.

   ■ You could also drag along the path to make a larger opening, but if you just want to split the path, drag across it.

   ■ Notice that anchor points were placed at both ends of the path where you bisected it.

4. Select the Pencil tool and draw a wavy shape on the page.

5. Select the Erase tool and drag along the curved portions of the path to erase them.

6. Press the letter *h* and drag to move to a blank area on your page. Select the Polygon tool (⬤), and draw a six-sided polygon about 1" wide. Rotate the shape before you release the mouse so that two sides of the shape are vertical.

7. Position the Erase tool over the anchor point at the top of the lefthand vertical side. Click and drag to the anchor point at the top of the righthand vertical side, then release the mouse.

   ■ The top part of the polygon is deleted.

8. Undo (⌘z) to restore the polygon to its original shape.

9. Position the Erase tool over the middle of the path on the lefthand vertical side. Be sure you're very close but not touching the path. Click and drag down in an arc and end up in the middle of the path on the right-hand vertical side, then release the mouse.

   ■ The bottom part of the polygon is deleted.

10. Undo (⌘z) to restore the polygon to its original shape.

11. Position the Erase tool over the middle of the path on the lefthand vertical side. Click and drag up in an arc and end up in the middle of the path on the righthand vertical side, then release the mouse.

   ■ The top part of the polygon is deleted.

12. Practice drawing paths in varying shapes and erasing portions of them.

13. Return the View to 100% by pressing ⌘1, then close the document without saving it to a file.

135

Stroke Palette

In addition to specifying the weight of strokes you apply to paths, the Stroke palette provides options for creating (a) pointed, round, or bevel junctions, (b) pointed, round, or blunt ends (caps) on open paths, and (c) paths with dashed rather than solid strokes. To change stroke appearance from the program default of mitered corner, blunt end, and solid stroke, display the entire Stroke palette (Figure 4.4) by (a) clicking the palette Options arrow at the top left side of the palette and choosing Show Options, or (b) double-clicking the Stroke palette tab. To hide the options and revert the palette to showing only Stroke weight, (a) click the palette Options arrow and choose Hide Options, or (b) double-click the Stroke palette tab again.

Determining the Appearance of Segment Joins

When you draw two segments that are joined together, you must specify the kind of corner you want the junction (join) to have. The program default is a Miter join (▣), a pointed corner. To change the corner to one of the other two available, Round join (▣) or Bevel join (▣), simply click its icon in the Stroke palette and click OK. Refer to Figure 4.5 to see examples of the three types of joins.

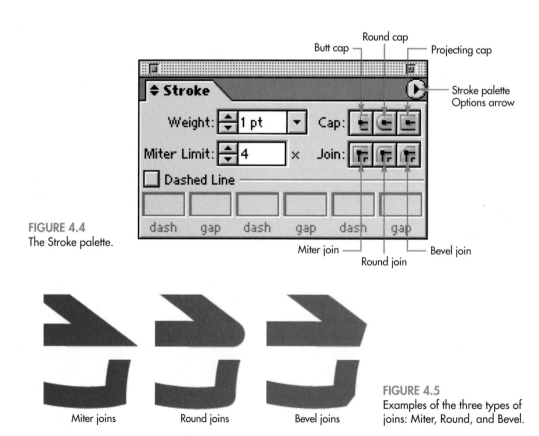

FIGURE 4.4
The Stroke palette.

Miter joins　　Round joins　　Bevel joins

FIGURE 4.5
Examples of the three types of joins: Miter, Round, and Bevel.

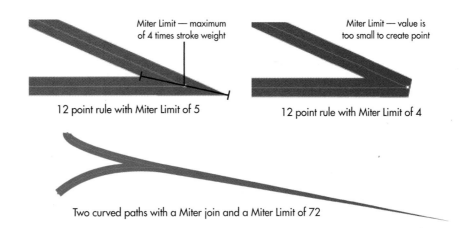

FIGURE 4.6
Examples of corners with different Miter Limit values.

Miter Limit — maximum of 4 times stroke weight

12 point rule with Miter Limit of 5

Miter Limit — value is too small to create point

12 point rule with Miter Limit of 4

Two curved paths with a Miter join and a Miter Limit of 72

Miter Limit The value entered in this field determines how far a mitered join can extend before it switches automatically from a pointed corner to a beveled corner. See Figure 4.6. You can enter a value from 1 to 500 in this field. This value applies only to a Miter join. The field turns gray (unavailable) when a Round or Bevel join is specified.

A path with a heavy stroke or a stroke on a path with a tight angle needs more room to complete a pointed corner than a path with a lightweight stroke or a path with a wider angle. If the Miter Limit is too small, there isn't enough room to extend the stroke to a point. In that event, a pointed corner switches to a Bevel join. To force a Miter join to have a bevel corner, enter a low value in the Miter Limit field.

Line Caps

The Stroke palette offers three options for the appearance the end of a stroke on an open path:

- **Butt cap** (▣) — square ends — the stroke ends precisely at the endpoint of the path.

- **Round cap** (▣) — round ends — the stroke extends beyond the end of the path half the width of the stroke weight. For example, if the weight of the stroke is 12 point, the path extends 6 points beyond the anchor point at the end of the path.

- **Projecting cap** (▣) — square end — the stroke extends beyond the end of the path half the width of the stroke weight.

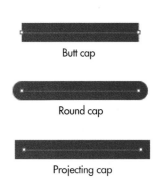

Butt cap

Round cap

Projecting cap

Creating Dashed Lines

Dash patterns that can be applied to strokes are created using options available in the Stroke palette (see Figure 4.7). Click on the Dashed Line checkbox to activate the Dash/Gap fields at the bottom of the palette. Press the *tab* key to move to the next field. Press *return/enter* to apply the values to a path.

The value in a Dash field is the length of the dash and the value in the Gap field is the length of the space between the dashes. If you specify a gap value smaller than the stroke weight, the dashes will overlap. You can specify three different sets of dashes and gaps to create varying dash lengths and gap spaces in one path.

The default value for a dash is 12 point, so if you don't enter a value in a Dash field, you'll have a dashed line with 12 point dashes and 12 point gaps. If you don't enter a Gap value, the dash value is used as the gap value. Once values have been entered in the Dash and Gap fields, they remain in effect until you change them or quit Illustrator and relaunch the program.

■ If you apply a Round cap or Projecting cap to the Stroke, the Gap is visually reduced by the amount of the projection of the cap. See Figure 4.7D.

■ To create a dotted line, choose a Round Cap for the shape of the dash and enter a value of 0 in the Dash field. Enter a Gap value that is larger than the Stroke weight. See Figure 4.7F.

■ Avoiding crashing dashes in closed paths is sometimes frustrating. The only way is by trial and error. Adjust the values by as little as +.01 or +.01 increments until the dashes and gaps in the path become evenly spaced along the path.

A. Dash 6 (no other values entered)

B. Dash 6, Gap 12, Dash 4, Gap 8, Dash 12, Gap 6

C. Same values as B. above, except Round Cap applied. Values are too small to allow for extension of end cap.

D. Dash 15, Round Cap applied

E. Dash 18, Gap 6

F. Dash 0, Gap 12, Round Cap

FIGURE 4.7 Examples of dash patterns.

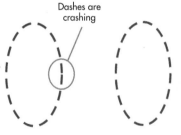

Dashes are crashing

Dash 9, Gap 6

Dash 9, Gap adjusted to 5.7 for consistent spacing

 *activity 4.10*

1. Create a new document: Letter size, CMYK color mode.

2. With the Star tool, draw a star about 3" in diameter. Apply an 18 point Stroke.

3. Display Stroke palette options and change to a Round join.

4. Change to a Bevel join.

5. Switch to a Miter join.

6. Change the Miter Limit value to 2. Press *return/enter*.

   ■ The ends of the star change to a bevel because the Miter Limit isn't large enough to create a pointed end.

7. Delete three points of the star so you have two open paths.

   ■ Use the Erase tool to delete the points of the star.

8. Apply a Round cap to one path and a Projecting cap to the other path.

   ■ Notice that the stroke extends beyond the anchor points at the ends of the paths.

9. Select both paths and change to a Butt cap, and a Miter join with a Miter Limit of 4. Press *return/enter*.

   ■ The junctions of the two segments on each path are now pointed because the Miter Limit is set large enough to allow room for the points to extend.

10. Click the Dashed Line checkbox.

    ■ Notice how awkward the dash pattern is at the junction of the two segments of each path.

11. On one of the paths, enter a Dash value of 6 and a Gap value of 9. Press *return/enter*.

    ■ Notice the interesting pattern at the join.

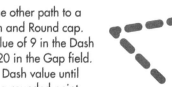

12. Change the other path to a Round join and Round cap. Enter a value of 9 in the Dash field and 20 in the Gap field. Adjust the Dash value until the join is a rounded point.

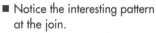

13. Draw paths and apply different combinations of end caps and join types. Vary the Miter Limit value. Practice drawing open and closed paths and creating dash patterns.

14. Close this document without saving it to a file.

Delete a Path

Cut

The Cut command (press ⌘ x or choose **Edit** ⇨ **Cut**) performs the obvious function its name implies. You can remove a selected path, selected multiple paths, or part of a selected path, by "cutting" it out. Objects you cut are placed in a temporary storage file called the Clipboard (see the following section).

To delete an entire object with the Cut command:

1. Select it with the Selection tool (bounding box displays).

2. Press ⌘ x

    or

    Choose **Edit** ⇨ **Cut**.

    or

    Press the *delete* key.

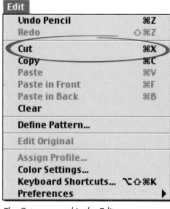

The Cut command in the Edit menu

When you select a path with the Direct Selection tool, the segment of the path you clicked on displays the direction lines and direction paths that pertain to that portion of the path. When you press ⌘ x, only that segment is cut. If the segment you cut was part of a closed path, the path becomes an open path.

The Clipboard

The Clipboard is a temporary storage area in the computer's memory. When an object is cut (⌘ x) or copied (⌘ c), its PostScript language description is placed in the Clipboard. When the Paste command (⌘ v) is executed, the object is retrieved from the Clipboard and placed in the document.

The Clipboard can hold only one item at a time. The next time you cut or copy an object, the current contents of the Clipboard are replaced by the new items. Until you replace an item with new objects or quit the program, though, it remains in the Clipboard.

When copying from one Illustrator document to another, it's not necessary to change any Preferences settings. If you're copying artwork from an Illustrator document and pasting it into a document in another application, you may want to change some of the default settings in Files & Clipboard Preferences.

Setting Clipboard Preferences To change default settings that control how information is copied to the Clipboard, display the Files & Clipboard Preferences dialog box (**Edit** ⇨ **Preferences** ⇨ **Files & Clipboard**) (see Figure 4.8). Choose options in the Clipboard section of the dialog box.

- **Clipboard** — The default setting for copying files is PDF, which retains transparency information in the file. Files using older programs may not

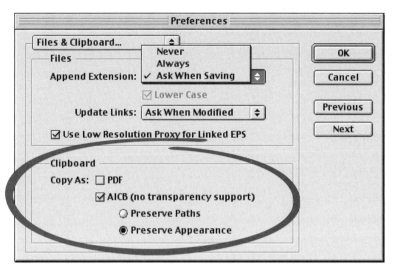

FIGURE 4.8 This is an example of the Files & Clipboard Macintosh Preferences dialog box. *Note:* The Windows version doesn't have the Append Extension section because extensions are automatically appended to Windows documents.

be able to use this format. AICB is a format similar to EPS that keeps the *appearance* of transparency, but doesn't keep the actual transparency information in the artwork. If you check both boxes (PDF *and* AICB), the application you're pasting the artwork into will choose the format it prefers. This may slow down the copying and pasting process, however.

In addition, AICB allows you to either preserve the paths in the artwork or the appearance of the artwork.

- Click the Preserve Paths radio button to copy the selection as a set of paths — useful when pasted into a Photoshop document.

- Click the Preserve Appearance radio button to keep the overall appearance of the selection when it's pasted into a document created in another program.

- Click OK or press *return/enter* to exit the dialog box.

Delete

Pressing the *delete* key on the keyboard deletes selected anchor points or segments of a path, but does not put them in the Clipboard. *Windows* users can also press the *backspace* key. The only way to retrieve an object you've deleted with the *delete* key (or *backspace* key) is to use the Undo command ($\mathcal{H}$ z).

- You can split a path by selecting an anchor point or a segment with the Direct Selection tool and pressing the *delete* key. An open path results when an anchor point or segment is deleted from a closed path. Two open paths result if the original path was an open path.

Clear

The Clear command, **Edit ⇨ Clear**, removes a selected path or paths from the artwork window, but does not put them in the Clipboard. There is no keyboard command for this function. The only way to retrieve an object you've deleted with the Clear command is to use the Undo command (⌘ z).

Copy a Path

There are several ways you can copy a path or set of paths. You can (1) press the keyboard command (⌘ c), (2) drag down the Edit menu and select the Copy option, (3) use drag and drop, or (4) perform the drag-copy function you learned in Step 3, *Basic Shapes*.

When you want to copy a path, leaving the original path intact, and want to paste the path back into the document, use the Copy command (press ⌘ c or choose **Edit ⇨ Copy**). The item you copied is then stored in the Clipboard temporarily until you paste it into a document, replace it with another copied object, or until you quit the program.

Macintosh: You can drag an object onto the desktop to make a copy, but the resulting copy of the object is converted to a picture clipping file in PICT format. This file format is used primarily by Macintosh users as an intermediary file for transferring files between applications. If your document is going to be printed on a PostScript printer, you should avoid using this file format.

Drag and Drop

When you use the drag-and-drop feature to copy objects from one file to another, the objects are not placed into the Clipboard. If any objects currently reside in the Clipboard when dragging and dropping, those objects are unaffected.

From Illustrator File to Illustrator File To copy objects from one Illustrator document to another using the drag-and-drop feature:

1. Open both documents and position them so both pages are visible on the screen.

2. With the Selection tool, select all the paths you want to copy onto another document page.

3. Click and drag the selected paths to the new document and release the mouse.

From Illustrator to Other Applications You can also copy artwork created in Illustrator into other programs using the drag-and-drop feature. In Mac OS, the application you're dropping the art into must support Macintosh Drag Manager. In Windows, the application must be OLE compliant.

From Illustrator to Photoshop To drag and drop selected objects from Illustrator into a Photoshop image or image window:

1. Open the Photoshop image or window into which you want to copy the Illustrator artwork.

2. In Illustrator, select the objects you want to copy.

3. Drag the objects into the Photoshop window.

4. Release the mouse when a black outline displays around outside of the Photoshop window.

   ■ To position the artwork in the center of the Photoshop window, hold down the *Shift* key when you release the mouse and drop the artwork in the Photoshop window.

   ■ Artwork copied into a Photoshop window, whether empty or containing a bitmap image, is converted into a bitmap image with the specifications of the existing Photoshop image or specifications of the file; that is, resolution, color mode, and so on.

From Illustrator to Photoshop as Paths To convert selected objects into a Photoshop path as you drag from Illustrator into a Photoshop image or image window:

1. Open the Photoshop image or window into which you want to copy the Illustrator artwork.

2. In Illustrator, select the objects you want to copy.

3. Hold down the ⌘ key as you release the mouse to drop the artwork into the Photoshop image or window.

   ■ The copied artwork is placed in the center of the active layer.

The Paste Command

To insert cut or copied objects that are stored in the Clipboard into a document, use the Paste command (⌘ v). When cut or copied objects are pasted into a document, they are placed in the center of the visible portion of the active document *window* (not the center of the document *page*). The pasted object remains selected.

If you paste more than one object onto a page without moving the document window, the objects are pasted one on top of the other. You can separate them by selecting the top one and moving it.

 You can cut or copy an object in one Illustrator window and paste it into another active window. The shape remains selected in both windows.

 *activity 4.11*

1. Create a new document: Letter size, CMYK color mode.

2. With the Ellipse tool selected, draw a perfect circle by holding down the *Shift* key and dragging the mouse.

3. Deselect the shape (⌘-click).

4. Using the Direct Selection tool (press *a*), select two segments of the circle.
   - Hold down the *Shift* key when clicking on the segments to select them.
   - Selected segments display direction lines.

5. Press ⌘ x to cut the selected segments.
   - Notice that the points connecting the segments you deleted are still there.

6. Deselect everything (click on a blank area).

7. Select the segments that remain.

8. Press ⌘ c to copy them.
   - They are stored temporarily in the Clipboard.
   - Notice that the segments you copied remain in place in your document.

9. Create a new document. Size and position both documents so you can see both windows at the same time.

10. Using the Selection tool (press *v*), drag the two selected segments to the new document and release the mouse.
    - The original shape stays in position on the original document and a copy is placed in the new document.

11. In the original document, draw a circle and fill it with 100% yellow.
    - Use the CMYK slider to achieve the percentage of color.

12. With the Direct Selection tool selected (press *a*), hold down the ⌥ key, click in the circle, and drag to create a duplicate circle.

13. Draw a 2" polygon.

14. Cut the polygon (⌘ x) and paste it back into the document using the Paste command (⌘ v).
    - Notice that it was pasted in the center of the document window, not the center of the page.

15. Move the document page to a new position in your document window and paste the object again.
    - The object was pasted in the center of the document window, regardless where your document page is located in the window.

16. Draw a Spiral on a clear spot on your page.
    - Press the *h* key to select the Hand tool, then click and drag the mouse to move to a blank spot on the page.

17. Copy the spiral using the Copy command (⌘ c).

18. Paste the object into the document using the Paste command (⌘ v).
    - The original spiral remained on the page and a new one was pasted in the center of the document window.

19. Draw paths on the page and practice drag-copying them.

20. Close both documents without saving them.

Stacking Order

When you draw multiple objects on a page, they are stacked in order as they are drawn, one in front of the other. The first object drawn is at the back of the stack. Each time another path (object) is created, it is stacked in front of the last object drawn. It's important to understand how this works because the order in which multiple objects are drawn determines how they overlap, thus how they display.

You can change the stacking order of objects in your document, however, in several ways. You can cut objects then paste them in front of or in back of selected objects. Or you can use one of the Arrange commands: Bring to Front, Bring Forward, Send Backward, and Send to Back. Changing the position of an object in the stacking order doesn't change that object's position from the margins of the page. It just changes its stacking relationship to other objects on the page.

Paste in Front

When you cut an object ($\mathcal{H}$x), you have an option to place that object in front of another object in the stack rather than in the center of the document window. If an object is selected when you execute the Paste in Front command, the object that was cut is placed in front of the selected object. If no object is selected when the Paste in Front command is used, the object that was cut is placed on top of the stack.

1. Select the object in a stack of multiple objects that you want to reorder.

2. Press $\mathcal{H}$x to delete the object and place it temporarily in the Clipboard.

3. Click the object that you want to place the contents of the Clipboard in front of.

4. Choose the Paste in Front command (press $\mathcal{H}$f or choose **Edit ⇨ Paste in Front**).

   ■ The object that was cut is pasted back into exactly the same position on the page from which it was cut, except it is placed *in front of* the active object.

Paste in Back

When you cut an object ($\mathcal{H}$x), you have an option to place that object behind another object in the stack rather than in the center of the document window.

fyi Sometimes stacking order is defined as "above" or "below" and sometimes it's indicated by "in front of" or "in back of." "Above" is the same as "in front of" and "below" is the same as "in back of."

fyi If you select and cut only a portion of a path and use the Paste in Front or Paste in Back command, the segments pasted back into the document become separate paths.

145

1. Select the object in a stack of multiple objects that you want to change its stacking order.

2. Press ⌘ x to delete the object and place it temporarily in the Clipboard.

3. Click the object that you want to place the contents of the Clipboard in back of.

4. Choose the Paste in Back command (press ⌘ b or choose **Edit** ⇨ **Paste in Back**).

   ■ The object that was cut is pasted back into exactly the same position on the page from which it was cut, except it is placed *behind* the active object.

 *activity 4.12*

1. Create a new document: Letter size, CMYK color mode.

2. Draw a rectangle about 2" long and 1" high. Fill it with a blue color from the CMYK Spectrum bar in the Color palette.

3. Draw about a 1½" round circle so it overlaps the right half of the rectangle you just drew. Fill it with yellow from the CMYK Spectrum bar in the Color palette.

4. Draw about a 1" star and position it so it overlaps the circle. Fill it with green from the CMYK Spectrum bar in the Color palette.

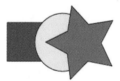

5. Select the rectangle and cut it (⌘ x).

6. Click on the circle to select it, then paste the rectangle in front of the circle (Edit ⇨ Paste in Front or press ⌘ f).

   ■ The rectangle retains its position on the page but it moves up one level in the stacking order and is placed in front of the circle.

7. Cut the star and paste it to the bottom of the stack (Edit ⇨ Paste in Back or press ⌘ b).

   ■ Don't select any of the other objects. The object that was cut is placed on the bottom of the stack when the Paste in Back command is used. If you have another path selected, the item you paste is placed in back of the selected path.

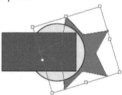

8. Undo (⌘ z) your last action (the Paste in Back command).

   ■ The star is still on the Clipboard.

9. Click on the rectangle to select it.

10. Choose Edit ⇨ Paste in Back to paste the star back onto the page.

   ■ Because the rectangle was selected, the star is pasted behind the rectangle instead of at the bottom of the stack.

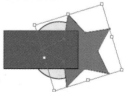

11. Close this document without saving it.

Arrange Stacking Order

In addition to the Paste in Front and Paste in Back commands, you have even more flexibility for arranging the stacking order of objects — using the four Arrange commands in the Object menu. To display the Arrange commands:

1. Choose **Object** ➪ **Arrange** to display the pop-up submenu.

2. Display the context-sensitive menu that contains the Arrange option pertaining to the object drawn.

   - *Macintosh:* ⌃-click on the page.
   - *Windows:* Right-click on the page.

Bring to Front The Bring to Front command (⇧⌘]) moves the selected object to the front of the stack, regardless of its position in the stack. Other objects in the stack are moved back one step in the stacking order.

Bring Forward The Bring Forward command (⌘]) moves the selected object one position toward the front of the stack. For instance, if the selected object is the first of three objects drawn and you execute the Bring Forward command, the object is moved one position toward the front of the stack to the #2 position. Using the Bring Forward command again brings the object to the #3 position. You can continue using the Bring Forward command until the selected object is at the front of the stack.

Send Backward The Send Backward command (⌘[) functions the same as the Bring Forward command except it moves the selected object one level toward the back of the stack.

Send to Back The Send to Back command (⇧⌘[) functions the same as the Bring To Front command except it moves the selected object to the back of the stack as if it were the first object drawn on the page.

Send to Current Layer The Send to Current Layer command moves selected items to the layer currently selected in the Layers palette. Layers are discussed in Step 8, *Layers & Links*.

The Arrange command in the Object menu

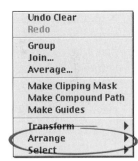

The Arrange command in the context-sensitive menu

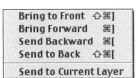

Options available in the Arrange command submenu

Restack Multiple Objects

If you select more than one object and execute one of the restacking commands, the objects are reordered according to their relative positions. For example, if you have four items on a page, give them imaginary numbers of 1-2-3-4, #1 being the first object drawn and #4 the last object drawn. If you select Object #2 and Object #4 and execute the Send Backward command, the objects end up 2-1-4-3.

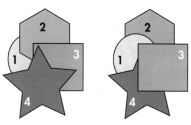

Examples of restacking multiple objects. (A) Original stacking order; (B) Objects #2 and #4 sent backward in stacking order.

Selecting Objects in a Stack

You can select objects in a stack using the options available in the Select menu and by displaying the context-sensitive menu and choosing one of its Select options.

Use Options in the Select Menu The options for selecting objects in a stack are:

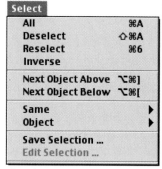

The Select menu

1. **Next Object Above** (⌥ ⌘]) — This option deselects the currently selected object and selects the object or path that is above it in the stacking order (that is, it was drawn after the selected object).

2. **Next Object Below** (⌥ ⌘ [) — This option deselects the currently selected object and selects the object or path that is below it in the stacking order (that is, it was drawn before the selected object).

3. **Object submenu** — Display the submenu to have even more ways to select specific objects.

   ■ **All on Same Layer** — Selects all the objects that are placed on the same layer as the currently selected object. A layer is not the same as stacking order. Layers are discussed in Step 8, *Layers & Links*.

   ■ **Direction Handles** — Displays all the direction handles, if the path has any, on a selected object. All anchor points and the center point become visible, but are deselected (hollow).

   ■ **Brush Strokes** — Selects all brushstroked paths. Brushstrokes are discussed in Step 10, *Brushes, Patterns, & Symbols*.

   ■ **Stray Points** — Selects all anchor points that don't have a segment attached to them. Stray anchor points occur when only segments of a path are deleted. Stray points should be deleted frequently. This command should be used immediately before sending a file to be printed to avoid having anchor points with attributes applied (font, color, and so on) that may cause printing problems.

Options available in the Object submenu in the Select menu

For example, an anchor point with a spot color applied to it that isn't used anywhere else in the file may cause an additional color plate to be generated when the file is output.

- **Text Objects** — Selects all type objects in the document. Type is discussed in Step 5, *Add Type to Artwork*.

Use the Context-Sensitive Menu To select a path that's hidden or partially hidden under another path in a stack:

1. Display the context-sensitive menu.
   - *Macintosh*: ∧-click.
   - *Windows*: Right-click.
2. Click the Select option to display the pop-up submenu.
3. Drag to select the option you want.

This procedure works only if:

- You ∧-click (or right-click) on a portion of the path that overlaps the path you actually want to select,

  and

- the path you want to select has a fill color,

  and

- the mouse pointer is directly over the path or fill of the lower object.

| First Object Above |
| Next Object Above |
| Next Object Below |
| Last Object Below |

Options available in the Select pop-up menu in the context-sensitive menu

Some of these options are not available in the Select menu. The only way you can access them is by displaying the context-sensitive menu. (I think it's easier to select objects using the options available in the Select menu.)

 *activity 4.13*

1. Create a new document: Letter size, CMYK color mode. Name it Stacking Practice.eps and save it into your Practice folder.

2. Draw, in order, the following shapes: a circle, a polygon, a rectangle, and a star. Position them as you draw them so they are similar to the example shown here.

3. Fill each shape with a different color and apply a 1 point black stroke to each shape.

4. Click on the polygon (the second object you drew) and Bring to Front (Object ⇨ Arrange ⇨ Bring to Front).

Continued

- The polygon was moved from the #2 position to the top of the stack.

5. Click on the rectangle (the third object you drew) and Bring Forward (Object ⇨ Arrange ⇨ Bring Forward).

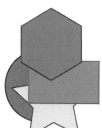

- The rectangle was moved up only one level in the stack.

6. Click on the star and send it back one level in the stack (Object ⇨ Arrange ⇨ Send Backward).

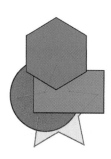

- The star was moved back one level which is the bottom of the stack.

7. Click on the polygon and send it to the bottom of the stack (Object ⇨ Arrange ⇨ Send to Back).

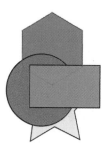

- The polygon was moved to the bottom of the stack.

- You could also cut the polygon (⌘x) then use the Paste in Back (Edit ⇨ Paste in Back) command to move it to the bottom of the stack as long as no other paths are selected.

8. Bring the star to the front of the stack (Object ⇨ Arrange ⇨ Bring to Front), and move the polygon up one level in the stack (Object ⇨ Arrange ⇨ Bring Forward). This restores the objects in the stack to their original positions.

9. Save the file.

10. *Shift*-click the star and the circle so they are both selected. Send them both backward one level (Object ⇨ Arrange ⇨ Send Backward).

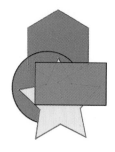

- They both moved back in the stack one level.

11. Select the rectangle, display the Object submenu in the Select menu, and choose Direction Handles.

- All the anchor points become hollow.

12. Select the circle, then choose Direction Handles in the Object submenu of the Select menu.

- All direction lines and direction points are displayed and all anchor points are hollow.

13. Click on the star shape, then choose Next Object Above in the Select menu.

- The star is deselected and the rectangle becomes selected.

14. Select the circle and bring it to the front of the stack.

15. With the Direct Selection tool, *Shift*-click to select two anchor points on opposite sides of the circle.

16. Press the delete key to delete the segments.

- Stray anchor points remain.

17. Deselect all objects.

18. Select the stray anchor points by choosing Stray Points from the Object submenu in the Select menu.

19. Close the artwork window without saving the changes.

Select All Paths
Having Similar Characteristics

You can search for paths that have characteristics similar to the path you have selected using the Select option in the Edit menu. The title of each command tells you what it searches for.

1. Click on a path in your document with any selection tool.

   ■ If a path is not selected when you choose the Select command, the last path that had been selected is used for the search.

2. Choose **Select** ⇨ **Same** to display the submenu.

3. Drag to select the option that searches for other paths having the same characteristics as the selected path or the last-selected path.

   ■ **Blending Mode** — searches for and selects only paths having the same blending mode as the selected path or last-selected path. Blends will be discussed in Step 12, *Meshes, Masks, Blends, & Transparency*.

   ■ **Fill and Stroke** — searches for and selects paths having the same fill color, stroke weight, and stroke color as the selected path or last-selected path.

   ■ **Fill Color** — searches for and selects only paths having the same fill color as the selected path or last-selected path.

   ■ **Opacity** — searches for and selects only objects having the same opacity (transparency) as the selected path or last-selected path. Transparency will be discussed in Step 12, *Meshes, Masks, Blends, & Transparency*.

   ■ **Stroke Color** — searches for and selects only paths having the same stroke color as the selected path or last-selected path.

   ■ **Stroke Weight** — searches for and selects only paths having the same stroke weight as the selected path or last-selected path.

   ■ **Style** — searches for and selects all paths with the same attributes (fill color, stroke, etc.) as the selected path or last-selected path. Styles will be discussed in Step 11, *Filters & Filter Effects*.

   ■ **Symbol Instance** — searches for and selects masking paths. Masks are discussed in Step 10, *Brushes, Patterns, & Symbols*.

If you have the Selection tool selected in the Toolbox when you use the Select command, a bounding box displays around the outermost edge of the shapes that are selected. If you have the Direct Selection tool selected, no bounding box displays.

| Blending Mode |
| Fill & Stroke |
| Fill Color |
| Opacity |
| Stroke Color |
| Stroke Weight |
| Style |
| Symbol Instance |

Use the "Same" submenu in the Select menu to select paths having similar characteristics

1. Open the Select samples.eps file located in the Student Files folder on the CD-ROM attached to the back of this book.

2. Choose the Direct Selection tool (press *a*).

3. Click in the red star in the upper left corner of the page to select it.

4. Choose Select ⇨ Same ⇨ Fill & Stroke. Four objects on the page are selected, including the original object.

   ■ The red polygon in the fourth row was not selected because it has a different stroke weight.

5. Select the purple circle in the top row.

6. Choose Select ⇨ Same ⇨ Fill Color.

   ■ All the purple objects on the page are selected.

7. Click on the spiral in the top row.

8. Choose Select ⇨ Same ⇨ Stroke Weight.

   ■ Thirteen of the objects have the same stroke weight as the selected object.

9. Select the rectangle in the top row.

   ■ You can't click within the rectangle to select it. You have to click on its path because it doesn't have a fill color applied to it. The fill is None (▱).

10. Choose Select ⇨ Same ⇨ Fill Color.

    ■ The round-corner rectangle in the third row is now selected, too.

    ■ Notice that there are several stray anchor points that became visible. They have a fill value of None so they displayed when the Select Same Fill Color command was executed.

11. Deselect all.

12. Choose ⇨ Select ⇨ Object ⇨ Stray Points.

    ■ Only the stray anchor points are now selected.

13. Press the *delete* key on the keyboard to eliminate the stray points.

14. Select all the yellow objects on the page.

15. Choose Select ⇨ Inverse.

    ■ The yellow objects become deselected and all the other objects on the page become selected.

16. Close this document without saving changes.

Group / Ungroup Paths

Combining more than one object so that it acts as a single unit is called grouping. A bounding box surrounds the outside of all the objects in the group when the group is selected with the Selection tool or the Group Selection tool. Attributes you apply when a group is selected apply to all objects in the group. Grouped objects can be moved as a unit without changing the position of objects within the group.

All objects in a group are automatically placed on the same stacking layer as the frontmost layer in the group. If you group two or more objects leaving an ungrouped object between them, the ungrouped object is moved behind the group. This means some objects may not display correctly when groups are created.

Grouping Objects

To create a group:

1. Select at least two paths with the Selection tool.

   ■ If you choose the Direct Selection tool and select only part of an object, the entire object is grouped.

2. Choose **Object** ⇨ **Group**.

   or

   Press ⌘g.

   or

   Display the context-sensitive menu and click on Group.

   ■ *Macintosh:* ⌃-click the page.
   ■ *Windows:* Right-click the page.

You can also create groups of groups by selecting two or more groups and grouping them.

Ungrouping Objects

To separate the objects in a group (ungroup):

1. Select a group.

2. Choose **Object** ⇨ **Ungroup**.

   or

   Press ⇧⌘g.

   or

   Display the context-sensitive menu and click on Ungroup.

If you add objects to a group and then apply the Ungroup command, the objects are ungrouped in the order they were grouped. Repeat the Ungroup command until all objects are ungrouped.

Selecting Grouped Objects

   ■ To select an entire group, click on any object in the group with the Selection tool.

   ■ To select individual objects or individual anchor points of an object in a group, click on them with the Direct Selection tool.

   ■ To select entire groups nested within other groups, use the Group Selection tool in the Toolbox and click on an object. Continue clicking in the same spot to select successive groups. The first click selects the object you clicked on, the second click selects the other objects grouped with the object you clicked on, and successive clicks select any groups that are grouped with that object.

Group Selection tool icon in the Toolbox palette

activity 4.15

1. Open the file named Stacking Practice.eps that you saved into your Practice folder.

2. Marquee to select all the objects.

3. Group all the objects of this set together (press ⌘ g, choose Object ➪ Group, or display the context-sensitive menu and click on the Group option).

4. Deselect all objects.

5. With the Selection tool selected (press v), move the group by clicking and dragging it.

6. Drag-copy a new set of objects and move to a blank spot on the page.

   ■ The original objects are deselected and the new set of objects is selected.

7. With the group selected, click on the red color at the right end of the CMYK Spectrum bar in the Color palette.

   ■ All objects in the group changed to red.

8. Change the stroke weight to 3 point for all the objects in the group.

9. Ungroup the objects (press ⇧ ⌘ g, choose Object ➪ Ungroup, or display the context-sensitive menu and click on Ungroup).

10. Deselect all paths.

11. *Shift*-click to select the polygon and the star in the red set of objects. Group them then deselect all.

12. *Shift*-click to select the rectangle and the circle in the same set of objects and group them. Deselect.

13. Click on the polygon.

   ■ Both the polygon and the star are selected and the bounding box surrounds both.

14. Choose Object ➪ Arrange ➪ Send Backward.

   ■ Both items in the selected group move behind the other two objects, because they are both on the topmost level of the group.

15. Deselect the group (click off). Choose the Direct Selection tool and click on a segment of the circle.

   ■ When the Direct Selection tool is active, the objects are treated as individual objects.

16. Select both groups by choosing the Selection tool, holding the *Shift* key down, and clicking somewhere in an object in both groups. Group these two groups, then click off to deselect them.

17. Choose the Group Selection tool (▨) in the Toolbox and click on the circle. Click on the same spot to select the rectangle. Click again on the same spot to select the polygon/star group that is grouped with the circle/rectangle group.

18. Ungroup everything.

   ■ Apply the command 3 times or until everything is ungrouped.

19. Don't save or close this document.

Lock / UnLock Objects

If you want to be certain that you don't mistakenly alter an object, you can isolate it and use the Lock command. When the Lock command is applied to an object or path, it cannot be selected or modified. If you close and reopen a document containing locked objects, those objects remain locked. Locked objects remain visible and they print the same as if they were not locked.

You cannot lock anchor points or segments of a path. If you have only a portion of a path selected when you apply the Lock command, the entire path gets locked.

Lock Objects

To lock *selected* objects:

■ Choose **Object** ➪ **Lock** ➪ **Selection**

or

■ Press ⌘2.

To lock all objects *above* or *in front of* the selected object in the stacking order:

■ Choose **Object** ➪ **Lock** ➪ **All Artwork Above**

To lock all objects on other layers:

■ Choose **Object** ➪ **Lock** ➪ **Other Layers**. Layers are not the same as stacking order and they are discussed in Step 8, *Layers & Links*.

If you have difficulty selecting an object, it's probably locked. To check it, display the Object menu. If the Unlock All option is black (available), the object is locked. Unfortunately, you can't tell whether objects are locked by looking at them.

Unlock All

Unlike grouping, you cannot unlock individual objects. Your only option is to unlock everything at once and objects become selected after they are unlocked. If you have other objects selected when you apply the Unlock All command, they become deselected.

■ To unlock *all* locked objects, choose **Object** ➪ **Unlock All** or press ⌥⌘2.

 *activity 4.16*

1. Open the file named Stacked Fish.eps that's in the Student Files folder on the CD-ROM that accompanies this book.

2. With the Selection tool, *Shift*-click on the orange fish and the green fish to select them.

3. Choose Object ➪ Lock ➪ Selection or press ⌘2 to lock these objects.

  ■ Notice that the anchor points and direction lines disappeared.

4. With the Selection tool active, try to select the orange or green fish.

5. Marquee all the fish.

  ■ The two fish that were locked won't select.

6. Choose Object ➪ Unlock All or press ⌥⌘2 to unlock all the objects on the page.

  ■ Notice that the set that was locked is now selected and the other objects that had been selected are deselected.

7. Select the red-purple fish, then choose Object ➪ Lock ➪ All Artwork Above.

8. Marquee all the fish.

  ■ The green fish and the yellow/orange fish aren't selected because they're above (in front of) the green fish in the stacking order. The orange fish is behind the green fish, so it can be selected.

9. Save the file and close the document.

Hide / Show Artwork

To make an object invisible so you can more easily work on overlapping objects, apply the Hide Selection command (⌘ 3). Hidden paths won't print and cannot be seen in Outline or Preview views. When you close and reopen a document in which objects have been hidden using this command, the hidden objects remain invisible.

To hide *selected* objects:

■ Choose **Object** ⇨ **Hide** ⇨ **Selection**

or

■ Press ⌘ 3.

To hide all objects in *above* or *in front of* the selected object in the stacking order:

■ Choose **Object** ⇨ **Hide** ⇨ **All Artwork Above**

To hide all objects on other layers:

■ Choose **Object** ⇨ **Hide** ⇨ **Other Layers**. Layers are not the same as stacking order and they are discussed in Step 8, *Layers & Links*.

Show All

To make all hidden objects visible:

■ Choose **Object** ⇨ **Show All**.

or

■ Press ⌥ ⌘ 3.

You cannot show individual hidden objects. Your only option is to show them all at once. The hidden objects become selected after they are visible and any selected object become deselected.

 *activity 4.17*

1. Open the file named Stacked Fish.eps that's in the Student Files folder on the CD-ROM that accompanies this book.

2. Select, ungroup, and unlock all the fish, then deselect all.

3. *Shift*-click to select three of the fish.

4. Choose Object ⇨ Hide ⇨ Selection or press ⌘ 3 to hide the selected fish.
   ■ Only the unselected fish is visible.

5. Choose Object ⇨ Show All or press ⌥ ⌘ 3 to show the hidden fish.

6. Select the orange fish and choose Object ⇨ Hide ⇨ All Artwork Above.
   ■ Only the orange fish is visible because all the other fish are stacked in front of it (above it) in the stacking order.

7. Save the file and close the document.

8. Reopen the file (Stacked Fish.eps).
   ■ The hidden objects are still not visible.

9. Close the document.

PRACTICE ACTIVITY 4-1 — Toothpaste Tube

1. Create a new document: Letter size, CMYK color mode. Name it Toothpaste Tube.eps and save it into your Practice folder as an .eps file.

2. Draw a rounded rectangle 36 pt wide by 30 pt high, with a 2 pt corner radius. Press *d* on the keyboard to apply a white fill and 1 pt black stroke.

3. Draw a standard rectangle 9 pt wide and 36 pt high using the same default colors. Align the center points of the shapes so the new rectangle is centered horizontally and vertically on the rounded rectangle. Deselect all paths.

4. With the Direct Selection tool, click on the path line of the standard rectangle so all anchor points are hollow. Then click on the top left anchor point, hold down the *Shift* key to keep the movement vertical (90°), and drag the anchor point downward until it lines up with the top of the rounded rectangle.

5. Using the same method, move the bottom left anchor point up to line up with the rounded rectangle.

6. Drag-copy the smaller rectangle to place one to the left of the original shape and one to the right of the original shape. Align the vertical lines of each rectangle, as shown.

7. Draw an oval that's 21 pt wide by 72 pt high. Place it against the large rectangle, centered vertically, and so the strokes of both paths barely touch each other, as shown. Deselect all paths.

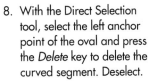

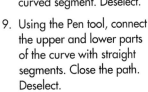

8. With the Direct Selection tool, select the left anchor point of the oval and press the *Delete* key to delete the curved segment. Deselect.

9. Using the Pen tool, connect the upper and lower parts of the curve with straight segments. Close the path. Deselect.

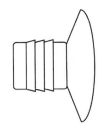

10. With the Pencil tool, start at one corner of the oval and draw the rest of the tube. Draw straight segments at the end of the tube with the Pen tool.

11. Send To Back (press ⇧ ⌘ [).

12. Adjust anchor points and curved segments as necessary.

13. Add a vertical straight line at the end of the tube, as shown, for the crimp line. Also add a line or two with the Pencil tool for detail.

14. With the pencil tool, draw toothpaste coming out of the tube. Set the Stroke weight to 20 pt with a round cap and assign a color. Start at the mouth of the tube and draw a line with only a few anchor points. Send to Back to put the toothpaste behind the mouth of the tube.

15. Save, then print the file, and close the artwork window.

EXERCISE 4-1 — Miscellaneous Shapes

Draw the items shown on this page. They don't have to match exactly, but should be recognizable as the item you're attempting to create. Create new documents for each item and save them into your Practice folder. You'll use them later.

158

Add Type to Artwork

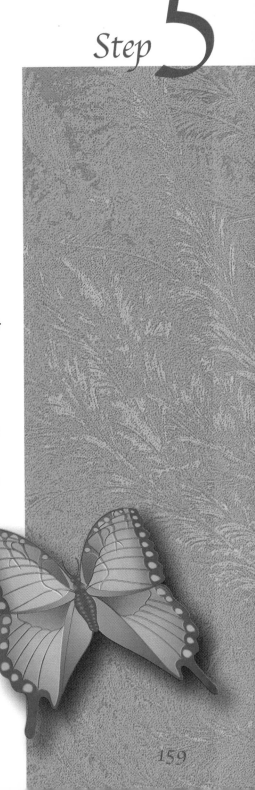

Chapter Outline

- The Type Tools
- Creating Type in a Document
- Adding Color to Type
- Selecting and Deselecting Type
- Add, Delete, and Replace Type
- Move Type Objects
- Resize and Reshape Type Manually
- Type Formatting in Illustrator
- Character-Based Type Formatting
- Paragraph-Based Type Attributes
- Word Hyphenation
- Smart Punctuation
- Importing Type
- Link Multiple Text Blocks
- Exporting Type
- Tabs
- Find and Replace Text
- Find and Replace a Font
- Check Spelling
- Create Outlines
- Wrap Type Around an Object
- Multiple Master Fonts

Although Illustrator isn't intended as a page layout program, the tools and commands available in Illustrator 10 enable you create, format, and edit text that adds to the visual impact of your artwork. Programs such as QuarkXPress and InDesign are better suited for use when large amounts of text are required.

Type can be created as stand-alone characters and lines where you determine its line endings, or it can be entered as text blocks that wrap automatically from one line to the next. Type can be placed inside objects and along freeform paths that you draw, and it can be displayed horizontally or vertically.

You can apply different attributes for individual characters or for entire blocks at one time. Type characters are colored by applying a fill color. You can apply a stroke color and weight to characters, too.

The Type Tools

Illustrator 10 has six type creation tools in the Toolbox, three for creating type horizontally and three for creating type vertically.

Vertical type tools create type that reads from right to left in a vertical format for use with languages that are read that way. Type tools are hidden under the regular Type tool and each type tool has its own unique cursor icon so you know immediately which type tool is active in the Toolbox. Samples of the kind of type that is created with the various type tools are depicted in Figure 5.1.

- **Type Tool** — The is the tool that you'll use most often to create type in your artwork. Using this tool, you can create type that can be floating, it can be contained in a block you define, or it can be placed inside a closed path. To choose this tool using the keyboard shortcut, press the letter *t*. The cursor changes to the I-beam cursor displaying a dotted box ([I]).

- **Area Type Tool** — Creates type inside open or closed paths. The cursor changes to the I-Beam with a dotted circle ([I]).

- **Path Type Tool** — Type flows along the outside edge of open or closed paths. The cursor changes to the I-Beam with a dotted curved line ([I]).

- **Vertical Type Tool** — This tool functions the same as the Type tool except that type is created from top to bottom rather from left to right. When the *return/enter* key is pressed to create a new line, the type flows from right to left. The cursor changes to a horizontal I-Beam with a dotted box ([H]).

- **Vertical Area Type Tool** — Type flows vertically from right to left inside open or closed paths. It's generally used only for certain languages that require it, such as Japanese. The cursor for this tool displays as a horizontal I-Beam with a dotted circle ([H]).

- **Vertical Path Type Tool** — Type flows vertically along the outside edge of open or closed paths. The cursor displays as a horizontal I-Beam with a dotted curved line ([H]).

Type tool icon in the Toolbox palette

Area type tool icon in the Toolbox palette

Path type tool icon in the Toolbox palette

Vertical type tool icon in the Toolbox palette

Vertical Area type tool icon in the Toolbox palette

Vertical Path type tool icon in the Toolbox palette

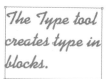

The Type tool

Floating type attached to a point

The Type tool creates type in blocks.

Type set inside a user-defined block

Type set along a user-defined path — Path type tool

The Area Type tool creates type inside an object you've drawn.

Type set inside a graphic object — Area Type tool

Type set using the Vertical Area Type tool

The Vertical Type

Type set using the Vertical Type tool

The Vertical Path

Type set using the Vertical Path Type tool

FIGURE 5.1 Samples of type using the various type tools in the Toolbox.

FIGURE 5.2
Parts of a character.

Figure 5.2 displays the difference between *serif* type (serif is a Latin word meaning *feet*), *sans serif* characters (Latin, meaning *without feet*), and names the different parts of a character.

Creating Type in a Document

Type in an Illustrator document can be attached to an anchor point, called an *alignment* point, it can flow along a freeform path, or it can be surrounded by a container that determines the shape of the text block. The element that type is attached to or contained within is called a type object. For example, when type flows along a path, the path itself is the type object.

Creating Type Attached to a Point

Type that's attached to an alignment point is called *Point* type. It can be entered in any blank spot in in the work area and dragged to its final position. This kind of type is generally used for text that has only one or two words or lines, such as a heading.

Type attached to an alignment point is treated as a single type object when the alignment point is selected. It flows in a straight horizontal or vertical line from its alignment point, but you can enter a paragraph return to create multiple lines. To create Point type:

1. Choose the Type tool (T) or Vertical Type tool (⊞) in the Toolbox.

   ■ The cursor changes to an I-beam cursor (⌶). A crossbar marks the baseline of the characters. Character baseline is depicted in Figure 5.2.

2. Click in a blank area of the document page where you want the type to start.

   ■ An *alignment point* is placed where you clicked to start entering the type and all characters connected to that alignment point display a non-printing underline at the baseline of the characters.

   ▪ In Preview mode, the alignment point displays only when the type is selected.

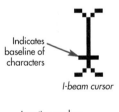

Indicates baseline of characters

I-beam cursor

Insertion marker

William

Alignment point (Outline mode)

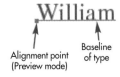

Alignment point (Preview mode)

Baseline of type

- A blinking insertion marker displays to the right of each character that indicates where the next character will be inserted.

3. Type the characters and words you want.

    - Text is entered on a single line.

    - To begin a new line, press *return/enter*. The new line aligns with the first line.

    - To insert a character between two existing characters, click between the two characters so the Insertion marker displays, then enter the new character. You can press the *return/enter* key to send the remainder of the line to a new line, too.

    - The object layer in the Layers palette displays the text of the type block as the name of the layer.

read this!

When you've finished entering type and a type tool is still selected, you can't press the keyboard commands to switch to the Selection tool or the Direct Selection tool.

activity 5.1

1. Create a new document: Letter size, CMYK color mode. Name the file Type Practice.eps and save it into your Practice folder as an .eps file.

2. Choose the Type tool in the Toolbox ([T]) (press *t*), then click on the document page, without dragging, and type your full name. If you don't have a middle name, enter your mother's maiden name or make one up. I want you to end up with three names.

    Mallory Kristene Granger

    - Notice that the cursor changed to the Type tool icon (I).

3. Zoom in so you can see your name easily.

4. Choose the Direct Selection tool in the Toolbox.

    - Notice the alignment point that displays at the baseline to the left of the first character. All characters display a blue underline at the baseline.

5. Choose the Type tool (press *t*) and click after the first space to display the Insertion marker. Press *return/enter* to send the rest of the characters on the line to a new line. Insert a return before your last name so you end up with three lines.

    Mallory
    Kristene
    Granger

6. Click the Direct Selection tool in the Toolbox.

    - Notice that even though there are three lines, there is only one alignment point.

7. Choose the Vertical Type tool ([IT]) in the Toolbox. Click on a blank spot on the page and type your name again.

    - The characters are aligned one beneath the other with the alignment point above the first character.

    - The line that connects the text characters to the alignment point runs vertically through the characters rather than at the baseline.

8. Click above the first character of your second name and press *return/enter*.

    - Your second and third names were placed to the left of your first name.

9. Click above the first character of your third name and press *return/enter*.

    - Your third name was placed to the left of your second name.

10. Save the file, but don't close the document.

```
G  K  M
r  r  a
a  i  l
n  s  l
g  t  o
e  e  r
r  n  y
   e
```

Entering Type in a Text Rectangle

When a paragraph or more of text is required, you can define the shape of the type container before entering the type. A text rectangle is a non-printing container created specifically for holding type. The text rectangle is the text object for this kind of type. Line endings are determined by the width of the container and any text that doesn't fit on a line automatically wraps down to the next line. The only shape you can create is a rectangle, but the shape of the rectangle can be changed, if necessary, after it has been created.

1. Choose the Type tool (T) or Vertical Type tool (T) in the Toolbox.
   - The cursor changes to the appropriate cursor for the tool selected (I or ⊞).
   - Type entered into a rectangle with the Vertical Type tool is entered with the characters one beneath the other, and columns reading from right to left.

2. Drag to create a rectangle, just as if you were creating a rectangle with the Rectangle tool.
   - The rectangle defines the height and width of the text block.
   - The rectangle has anchor points in each corner the same as other rectangles drawn with the Rectangle tool.
   - The Insertion marker blinks in the upper left corner (Type tool) or upper right corner (Vertical Type tool) as soon as you release the mouse.

3. Start typing the text. Press *return/enter* only when you want to begin a new paragraph.
   - The object layer in the Layers palette displays some of the type as the layer name.

The size and shape of the text rectangle can be modified. Refer to the section called Resizing and Reshaping Type Blocks later in this chapter.

Overflow Text

If the text doesn't all fit in a type rectangle or a type container, a small overflow symbol (⊞) displays at the bottom right corner of the container, indicating that type is missing. To solve this problem, you can:
   - Resize the type container until all the text fits inside it (see the section on *Resizing and Reshaping Type* blocks later in this chapter).

We the People of the United States, in Order to form a more perfect Union, establish Justice, insure domestic Tranquility, provide for the common defence, promote the general Welfare, and secure the Blessings of Liberty to ourselves and our Posterity, do ordain and establish this Constitution for the United States of America.

Text rectangle

read this!

Don't hold the Shift key down to try to create a perfectly square type container. Holding the Shift key down when drawing a type container temporarily changes the Type tool to the Vertical Type tool, and vice versa.

fyi *If a single word in a text container is too long to fit on one line, a ⊟ icon displays along the edge of the container at the end of the line.*

or

- Link the text to another text block (see the section called Link Multiple Text Blocks later in this chapter)

or

- Make the type smaller (see the section on *Enlarging or Reducing Type Size* later in this chapter).

Show Hidden Characters

If you like to see the spaces and paragraph returns as you enter type, choose **Type ➪ Show Hidden Characters**. When this feature is turned on, a checkmark displays to the left of the command name. To turn it off, click the command again to remove the checkmark. Some of the characters you'll be able to see are

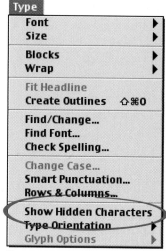

Type menu

- ¶ — Standard paragraph return (hard return)
- ↵ — Soft paragraph return
- · — Space
- → — Tab
- ∞ — End of text block

Entering Special Characters

All fonts are not created with exactly the same set of characters and most standard character sets don't contain some of the characters you need. Special fonts, such as Windings, Universal Pi, Zapf Dingbats, Carta, and so on, contain sets of special characters.

Macintosh The Macintosh Operating system has a feature called Key Caps that allows you to locate all characters available for a particular font installed on your computer. An alias for this utility is in the Apple menu ().

Windows Windows has a utility, called the Character Map, that you can use to enter special characters into the text in a document. It involves a number of steps and I don't like having to use it.

There's another way to enter special characters on the Windows platform, though. Each ASCII character is assigned a numeric code. You can enter a special character by holding down the ⌥ key and pressing its numeric code on the keypad on the right side of your keyboard. You can't use the standard numbers across the top of the keyboard, only the numbers on the keypad.

Sample character sets, instructions for using the font utilities that give you access to the special characters, and the ANSI Code Set can be found in Appendix B: *Character Sets & Utilities*.

 activity 5.2

1. In the file named Type Practice that you still have open (or reopen it if you've already closed it), verify that the Type tool in the Toolbox is still selected, then click on a blank area of the page and drag down and to the right to create about a 1" × 1" text rectangle. Use the Info palette to verify the size of your text rectangle.

   - Notice that the cursor changed to the Arrow cursor until you release the mouse. Then it changes to the I-beam cursor (I).

   - The Insertion marker blinks in the upper lefthand corner of the text rectangle.

2. Type your name full again in the text rectangle. Let Illustrator wrap to the next line automatically if your name doesn't fit on one line.

   Mallory.
   Kristene.
   Granger

3. Choose Type ⇨ Show Hidden Characters.

   - Notice the spacebar symbols and the end-of-text-block character.

   - The Insertion marker blinks after the last character entered.

4. Save the file, but don't close the document.

Entering Type Into an Irregularly Shaped Container

Using the Type tool, the Vertical Type tool, the Area Type tool, or the Vertical Area Type tool, you can convert a shape drawn with any of the creation tools (Ellipse, Rectangle, Pencil, Paintbrush, and so on) to a type container. The shape of the container determines the shape of the text block. If the path is an open path, Illustrator draws an imaginary line from its endpoints and uses that imaginary line to wrap the text in the shape of the path. Any fill and stroke attributes applied to the original path are removed.

To enter type into a previously-drawn shape:

1. Choose the Type tool (), the Vertical Type tool ([T]), the Area Type tool ([T]), or the Vertical Area Type tool ([T]) in the Toolbox.

   - The pointer changes to the Area Type tool icon (I) or the Vertical Area Type tool (⊕) icon.

   - If the type is a closed path, you can enter type into the container using the Type tool or the Vertical Type tool. If the path is an open path, enter type with the Area Type tool or Vertical Area Type tool.

2. Click anywhere on the pathline of the container.

   - The Insertion marker blinks at the top of the container, regardless where you clicked on the pathline of the container.

   - If the object contains multiple paths, only the path you click on with one of the Type tools is converted to a type container. The other paths of the object are unaffected.

3. Start typing new text or paste copied text. Press *return/enter* only when you want to begin a new paragraph.

   - The type stays inside the container and conforms to its shape.

Pear:
The juicy, edible, fleshy fruit of a tree of the rose family, cultivated in many varieties.

— Funk & Wagnalls New Comprehensive International Dictionary of the English Language

Type can be entered into an irregularly shaped container

fyi You can't enter both horizontal and vertical type in the same type container. New type entered conforms to the kind of type already existing regardless of the tool that's selected.

165

activity 5.3

1. In the file named Type Practice that you still have open, draw a vertical oval about .75" wide and 1.5" high.
   - It doesn't matter what the fill and stroke color is because it'll be removed as soon as you click on it with the Type tool.

2. Choose the Type tool (press *t*), then position the pointer anywhere on the edge of the oval.
   - Notice that the pointer was the Type tool pointer (⬚) until it was positioned over the edge of the oval. Then it changed to the Area Type tool pointer (⬚), indicating that type will be entered into a container.

3. Click the edge of the oval and type your full name again in the oval. Let Illustrator wrap to the next line automatically if your name doesn't fit on one line.
   - Fill and stroke attributes are removed.
   - The Insertion marker blinks at the top of the container.
   - The type follows the shape of the container. If a line is too long to fit into the widest part of the container, a word is divided and wrapped to the next line at the widest part of the container.

4. Save the file, but don't close the document.

Entering Type Along a User-Defined Path

Type can be entered along an open freeform path that is drawn with the Pen, Pencil, or Paintbrush tools. You can't convert a compound path, a mask object, a gradient mesh object, or a blend into a type path. And only one line of type at a time can be placed on a path. All fill and stroke attributes that were previously applied to a path are removed when type is placed on it.

Once a regular path is converted to a type path, it can't be changed back. The only way to return it to a regular path is to apply the Undo command.

1. Choose the Type (T), Path Type (⬚), Vertical Type (IT), or the Vertical Path Type tool (⬚).
   - The dotted box on the I-beam cursor changes to a curved line (⬚), indicating type will flow along a path rather than inside a rectangle or other container.

2. Click anywhere along the pathline of an open horizontal or vertical path. After you click, and the insertion marker displays, start entering type.
   - The type follows the contours of the path from the point where you clicked and in the direction the path is drawn.
   - A path having smooth shallow curves works best. Paths with sharp angles or radical curves causes characters to bunch up or overlap.

Type flows along
a path drawn
with the Pen tool

166

- If the type is too long for the path, it disappears. You can lengthen the path to get it back, though. See the section about Reshape Only the Type Path later in this chapter.

- The object layer in the Layers palette displays the text entered on the type path as the name of the layer.

- Pressing *return/enter* adds space between characters or words. It doesn't create a new line.

The path of this curve is too sharp for the type to flow smoothly

Adding Color to Type

Type is colored by applying the fill color in the Color box in the Color palette to selected type the same as other objects created in Illustrator.

- To apply color to all the type in a type block, select it with the Selection tool.

- To apply color to only selected text, highlight it with a Type tool.

- To apply color to the type container but not the type, click on the pathline of the container with the Direct Selection tool.

activity 5.4

1. In the file named Type Practice that you still have open, choose the Pencil tool and draw a shallow wavy path on a blank area of the document page.

   - It doesn't matter if the path has a fill or stroke color applied to it. In fact, it's easier to see if it does have a stroke applied.

2. Choose the Type tool (press *t*), and position the cursor over the left end of the path.

   - Notice that the cursor changes to the Path Type tool cursor ( ) when the cursor is over the edge of the path.

3. Click on the path and type your full name again.

   - As soon as you click on the path, fill and stroke attributes are removed and the Insertion marker starts blinking.

   - The type follows the contours of the path.

4. Highlight the text and apply a color of 100% cyan, 0% magenta, 40% yellow, 0% black.

   Mallory Kristene Granger

5. Save the file and close the document.

Selecting and Deselecting Type

You can use the Selection tool, the Direct Selection tool, or any of the Type tools to select type. Each tool, however, is used to select different elements.

Selecting Type and Its Type Object

Click anywhere in the type object with the Selection tool to select the type and its alignment point, container, or path. Use this method of selecting type when you want to select everything in the type container. A bounding box displays just like it does when you select other objects. You can drag the handles of the bounding box to reshape the type and its object.

Type and type container are selected.

- Point type that's selected with the Selection tool displays a bounding box, a solid alignment point, and a solid line displays along the baseline of all type attached to the alignment point.

- When type objects linked to other type objects are selected with the Selection tool, all linked type objects are selected.

Alignment point

Multiple lines of type attached to a single alignment point

Selecting a Type Object But Not Its Type

If you want to select a type container or path (not Point type), choose the Direct Selection tool and click on the edge of the type container or path. If the Direct Selection pointer displays a solid square beside the hollow pointer (▸▪), it's over a segment. If the square is hollow (▸▫), it's over an anchor point. To select the type container with all its anchor points solid, hold down the ⌥ key when clicking on its pathline with the Direct Selection tool.

When only the container is selected, any changes you make affect only the container or path, not the type. You can apply a background color or apply a stroke to the container path.

If you have trouble selecting only the type container, change to Outline view and select the container. If you *still* can't seem to select the container without selecting the type, display the Type & Auto Tracing Preferences dialog box (**Edit** ⇨ **Preferences** ⇨ **Type & Auto Tracing**) and uncheck the Type Area Select checkbox. See Figure 5.5 later in the chapter. You can't select type by clicking on it when this option is unchecked.

Only the type container is selected

- If you select Point type with the Direct Selection tool, the alignment point and all the type attached to it are selected, too. The only difference between selecting Point type with the Direct Selection tool and the Selection tool is that with the Direct Selection tool, the bounding box doesn't display.

Selecting Only the Type

Choose one of the Type tools to select only the type but not its container, alignment point, or path. You can select all the type at once, or individual characters. Characters are highlighted when they're selected. Changes you make when only the type is selected are applied only to those selected characters.

Individual characters can be selected in a line of type

- Click in the text where you want to start highlighting and drag along the characters to select one or more characters in a line.

- Double-click in a word to select an entire word and the space following it.

- To select multiple lines in a text block, click in the text where you want to start highlighting and drag down (for horizontal type) or left and right (for vertical type).

- In a block of text containing paragraph returns, triple-click anywhere in a paragraph to select the entire paragraph.
  - A paragraph is defined as all text between hard paragraph returns.
  - A *soft return* (*Shift-return*) is a forced return of type in a line, without affecting character attributes that have been applied to the paragraph. You can also press the *enter* key on the numeric keypad to enter a soft return.
  - A paragraph may consist of a single character.

- In Point type containing only one line, triple-clicking selects all the type in the line.

- To select all the type in a type container, even if it isn't all visible, press ⌘a or choose **Select** ⇨ **All**.

- Click in the line or paragraph where you want to start selecting text, then *Shift*-click where you want the type selection to end. All type between the clicks is selected.

Deselecting Type

To deselect type when you're finished entering it or when your modifications are complete:

- Hold down the ⌘ key and click anywhere on the page. Then release the ⌘ key.
  - The type and the Type tool remain selected, but you can click in a new spot or draw a new type container.

or

read this!

When a Type tool is active, you can't access the Hand tool by pressing its keyboard shortcut (the spacebar). Pressing the spacebar adds spaces in your text. Instead, press the ⌘ key and the spacebar, then release the ⌘ key and drag with the mouse.

- Click the Type tool in the Toolbox.
  - The Type tool remains selected.

or

- To deselect the type and deselect the Type tool, choose the Selection tool or the Direct Selection tool in the Toolbox, then click on a blank spot on the page.

or

- Press ⇧ ⌘ a or choose **Select** ➪ **Deselect**.

Add, Delete, and Replace Type

Use the Clipboard feature in Illustrator to copy type, store it on the Clipboard, then paste it to a different place in the current document, place it into a different Illustrator document, or paste it into another application document, such as Photoshop. You can cut, copy, paste, and delete individual type characters, or the container or path, or both at the same time, depending upon what is selected.

When type is cut or copied, character-based attributes, such as fill and stroke color, are retained when it's pasted into a new type block. When type and its container or path is cut or copied, character-based and paragraph-based type attributes are retained. Character-based and paragraph-based type attributes are discussed later in this chapter.

To cut or copy, then paste type, containers, or paths:

1. Select the type, type container, or type path you want to copy.

2. To copy selected elements, press ⌘ c or choose **Edit** ➪ **Copy**. To cut selected elements, press ⌘ x or choose **Edit** ➪ **Cut**.
   - Cut or copied elements are placed on the Clipboard.

3. To paste cut or copied elements into the same Illustrator document or into a different Illustrator document:
   - To add copied type to a new position in the same type block or to a different type block, click in the type block or type path where you want the type to be inserted. The Insertion marker displays where the type will be inserted. Press ⌘ v or choose **Edit** ➪ **Paste**.
   - To convert cut or copied type in a type container or along a path to stand-alone Point type, click on a blank area of the page, then paste the type. The type is attached to an alignment point.
   - If you highlight type with the Type tool and copy or cut it, deselect the highlighted type (⌘ -click) before pasting back into the document as Point type.

read this!

If nothing happens when you type, copy, or delete text, it may mean that a field in the Character palette or Paragraph palette is active. To deactivate the palette field and return to the document, press return/enter.

- To paste the cut or copied type back into the document at a specific spot, click again to establish a point to attach the point. If you don't click to establish a point, the type is pasted into the center of the screen.

■ To replace existing type with cut or copied type, highlight the characters you want replaced, then press ⌘v or choose **Edit** ⇨ **Paste** to paste the cut or copied type.

4. To paste type and its container or path (stored on the Clipboard) into an open Photoshop document:

■ Click in the document where you want the type placed.

■ Press ⌘v or choose **Edit** ⇨ **Paste**.

■ When the Paste dialog box displays, choose Paste as Pixels and check the Anti-Alias checkbox. Then click OK or press *return/enter*.

5. To add type to an existing type block, click so the Insertion marker blinks where you want to add the type. Then type, paste, or import the new type.

■ To add type to the end of a type block, click before the end-of-text-block symbol (∞).

6. To delete selected type and its container or path, press the *Delete* (or *del*) key (*Windows* users can also press the *Backspace* key). Elements removed this way are not placed on the Clipboard and cannot be pasted back into a document.

 *activity* **5.5**

1. Open the file named Type Practice.eps that you saved into your Practice file.

2. With the Selection tool (press *v*), click on the 3-line Point text that's your name and drag the text block to a new position on the page.

■ All three lines moved as a block because they're all attached to the same alignment point.

■ A bounding box surrounds the text block.

3. With the Direct Selection tool (press *a*), select the vertical text block that's on the page. Press the *delete* key to delete it.

■ All lines connected to the alignment point are deleted.

4. Choose the Type tool (press *t*), then in the type that's in the type rectangle, click in the middle of your first name and drag across three or four characters to select them.

> Mallory.
> Kristene.
> Granger∞

5. Press ⌘c to copy the characters, then ⌘-click in a blank area of the page, click again to establish a point, and paste (⌘v).

■ The copied characters are now attached to an anchor point where you clicked.

6. In the type that's on the curved path, select three or four characters (with the Type tool selected)

Continued

and cut them (⌘x). Click between two characters in a different place on the path and paste them back into the line (⌘v).

- The type adjusts to the contours of the path as you remove or insert characters in the text.

7. With the Direct Selection tool, click on the type rectangle with your name in it so that only the rectangle object is selected, not any of the type.

- The pointer displays a solid box next to it when its over a segment of the path.

- If a line displays at the baseline of the type it's selected.

8. Apply a fill of 30% yellow and a stroke weight of 3 pt and stroke color of 100% cyan.

- The type is still black because it wasn't selected.

9. Select the type without selecting the type rectangle by choosing the Type tool in the Toolbox and clicking before the first character, then *Shift*-clicking after the last character (before the end-of-text-block symbol).

10. Apply a fill color of 90% cyan, 75% magenta.

11. Save the file and close the document.

```
Mallory.
Kristene.
Granger∞
```

Move Type Objects

Type attached to an alignment point, a type container, or a type path can be moved by selecting it and dragging it to a new position or by pressing the arrow keys on the keyboard. Each time an arrow key is pressed, the block of type moves in the direction of the arrow key by the Keyboard Increment value that's specified in the General Preferences dialog box (**Edit** ⇨ **Preferences** ⇨ **General**).

- Select Point type with the Selection tool or the Direct Selection tool to move it by dragging or by pressing the arrow keys.

- To move an entire container or path and its type, select it with the Selection tool or the Direct Selection tool.

- Hold the *Shift* key down while dragging to keep the movement horizontal, vertical or at a 45° angle.

Resize and Reshape Type Manually

By selecting only the type container, you can change the shape of the type block inside it by dragging its anchor points. The size and shape of the individual characters are unchanged. You can change the size and shape of type attached to a point or type along a path by selecting it with the Selection tool and dragging a handle.

The transform tools and the transform commands in the Object menu (shear, rotate, reflect, scale, and move) can be applied to type the same way they're applied to other objects drawn in Illustrator. Transform tools and commands are covered in more detail in Step 9, *Reshape, Combine, & Distort Objects*.

Resizing and Reshaping Type Attached to a Point

The size and shape of Point type can be changed by selecting it with the Selection tool and dragging the handles of its bounding box. In the example shown here, the purple type is the original size, and the blue is the new size and shape after it was dragged by the lower corner handle.

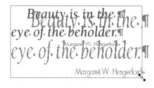

Type resized by dragging its bounding box handles

Resizing and Reshaping Type Blocks

Change the shape of a type container the same way you change the shape of any other object created in Illustrator. Changing the shape of the type container changes the shape of the text block that's inside it. The type reflows to conform to the new shape.

When you select a type container with the Selection tool, the bounding box displays and you can change the shape of the type container by dragging its handles. Drag a corner handle to enlarge or reduce the size of the type container proportionally or drag a side handle to enlarge or reduce in only one direction.

Click on the pathline of a type container with the Direct Selection tool and drag a segment or an anchor point. Click on an anchor point to make it solid to move only that anchor point.

- Press the arrow keys to nudge a segment or anchor point by the value in the Keyboard Increment field of the General Preferences dialog box (**Edit** ⇨ **Preferences** ⇨ **General**).

- Turn on Smart Guides to make it easier to see the pathline of the type container. Refer to Step 6, *Rulers, Grids, & Guides*, for information about Smart Guides.

  - Make sure the Object Highlighting checkbox in the Smart Guides Preferences dialog box is checked (**Edit** ⇨ **Preferences** ⇨ **Smart Guides & Slices**).

- Add or delete anchor points on the path, then move them, to change the shape of a container.

The term funny bone was coined as a pun on the name for the bone running from the shoulder to the elbow, the humerus. Humerus — humorous. Get it?

From *Dictionary of Word and Phrase Origins*, William & Mary Morris, 1962, New York, Harper & Row.

Drag the bounding box of a type container to change the size of the type block

1. Create a new document: Letter size, CMYK color mode (press ⌥⌘n) and save it into your Practice folder as an .eps file named Type Practice2.eps.

2. With the Type tool (press *t*), draw about a 1" × 2" type rectangle.

   ■ It doesn't have to be exactly that size, just approximately that shape.

   ■ You can use the Rulers or the Info palette to gauge the size of the container.

3. Enter the following text into the type rectangle.

   ■ Changing the shape of the type container changes the shape of the text block that's inside it. The type reflows to conform to the new shape.

   ■ Don't be concerned if all the type doesn't fit inside the container. Type it all anyway.

   ■ It doesn't matter what size the type is or which font is used.

4. Select the type rectangle with the Selection tool and press the right arrow key (→) several times to nudge the type block to the right. Press the other arrow keys to move it around on the page.

5. Deselect all.

6. Click on the right vertical segment of the type rectangle with the Direct Selection tool to select the container without selecting the type inside the container.

   ■ All the anchor points should be hollow.

7. Press the right arrow key to widen the text box, causing the type to reflow inside the container.

8. Click on the top righthand anchor point to select it, then press the up arrow key (↑) 12 times to move just that anchor point up.

   > Changing the shape of the type container changes the shape of the text block that's inside it. The type reflows to conform to the new shape

9. Click and drag that anchor point up and to the right about ½".

   ■ The type block conforms to the new shape.

10. With the Add-Anchor-Point tool, add an anchor point at approximately the midpoint in the lefthand vertical segment of the type rectangle.

    ■ It should be the only solid anchor point of the path.

11. With the Direct Selection tool (press *a*), drag that anchor point to the left about 1" and drop it.

    > Changing the shape of the type container changes the shape of the text block that's inside it. The type reflows to conform to the new shape

    ■ The type conforms to the new shape of the type container.

12. With the Type tool, drag across a line of the text inside the rectangle to select the whole line. Copy it (press ⌘c).

13. Click the Type tool, then click on a blank area of the page, and paste the words.

    ■ The words are now attached to an alignment point.

14. Select the words you just pasted with the Selection tool and drag the bottom right corner anchor point down and to the right about ½".

    ■ The size and shape of the characters change as you dragged.

15. With the Type tool, drag across the characters to select them, then press ⌘x to cut them. Click in the middle of the text in the type rectangle, then press ⌘v to paste them back inside the type rectangle.

    ■ The pasted characters retained their size and shape.

16. Save the file and close the document.

Modifying Type on a Path

Type that's placed along a path can be reshaped and resized by dragging its bounding box handles the same as other type objects. The shape of the path is changed at the same time. But you can also change the shape of the type path without changing the shape or size of the type that's placed along it. And you can reposition the type on the path.

Reshape Only the Type Path To change the shape of a path after type has been placed on it, deselect the path, then select it with the Direct Selection tool and move the anchor points or adjust the position of the direction points. Lengthen a path by selecting its endpoint and dragging it to a new position. Or, you can add to the path with the Pen tool or the Pencil tool.

Reposition Type Along the Path You can change the position of the type as it flows along the path. You can even make it flow upside down along the underside of the path. In the section about the Baseline Shift function, discussed later in this chapter, you will learn how you can move the characters down just a little to make them flow along the center of the path or move them up a little to sit above a stroke that you apply to the path.

To reposition the type as it flows along the path:

1. Deselect the path.

2. With the Direct Selection tool, click on the text to display the I-beam handle.

3. Click on the I-beam handle and drag it back and forth so the starting point of the text is in a new position along the path.

   ■ The type appears to fall off the end of the path if you move the I-beam handle to the right far enough that the path becomes too short.

4. To position the type upside down along the path, drag the I-beam handle around the end of the path.

   or

   Double-click the I-beam handle.

   ■ If the type doesn't display, drag the I-beam handle to the right or left.

Original path (top) was lengthened so all the type would fit on it (bottom)

Type was repositioned along the path by moving the I-beam handle

I-beam handle was dragged around the end of the path to position the type upside down along the path

Shorten a Path That's Too Long Normally, you don't have to do anything if a path is longer than the type that flows along it. But if you want to apply a stroke to the path, the path shouldn't be longer than the type that sits on it. To shorten a path that's too long:

1. With the Selection tool or the Direct Selection tool, select the type path.

2. Choose the Add Anchor Point tool in the Toolbox, and click in the path where you want the path to end to add a new anchor point. Deselect the path.

3. With the Direct Selection tool, select the path (anchor points are hollow). Then, with the Direct Select Lasso tool, circle all the anchor points that extend beyond the new anchor point you added to the path.

4. Press the *Delete* key to delete those selected anchor points, making the anchor point you added the new endpoint of the path.

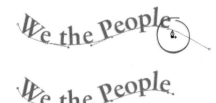

Type path was shortened by adding an anchor point where I wanted the path to end, then deleting the unnecessary anchor point

Convert a Horizontal Path to a Vertical Path and Vice Versa

Horizontal point type or type that's been placed along a horizontal type path can be converted to a vertical orientation. First, select the alignment point, baseline, or path of the stand-alone type, then choose **Type** ➭ **Type Orientation** ➭ **Vertical** (or **Horizontal**).

activity 5.7

1. Locate and open the file you saved into your Practice folder as Type Practice2.eps.

2. Verify that hidden characters are still displayed.

3. With the Pencil tool or Pen tool, draw a wavy horizontal path on a blank area of the page.

4. Choose the Type tool (press *t*) and click at the left end of the path. When the Insertion marker displays, start typing: Fourscore and seven years ago
    ■ Type all five words. Even if they don't all fit on your path.

5. Choose the Direct Selection tool (press *a*).
    ■ Notice the I-beam marker that displays before the first character.

Fourscore and seven years

6. Click on the bottom crossbar of the I-beam marker and, keeping the pointer below the path, drag it slowly to the right so the type falls off the end of the path.

7. Drag it back to its approximate starting position. Then, without releasing the mouse, move the

Continued

176

pointer above the path and drag to the right again.

Fourscore and seven years (appears upside down/reversed)

- The type displays upside down and backwards on the path.

8. Drag the type so it reads right-side up and from left to right in a normal orientation.

9. Deselect the path, then choose the Direct Selection tool (press *a*).

10. Click at the baseline of the text to select only the path, not the type.
    - All the anchor points are hollow because you selected a segment of the path.

11. Click the right endpoint to select it, then drag it to the right to extend the path so that all the type fits on the path. Adjust it's direction handle to restore a smooth shallow curve to the path.

Fourscore and seven years ago

12. Choose the Type tool and click in the type just to the left of the "s" of the word "seven". Drag to the right until the entire word is highlighted.

13. Deselect all.

14. Double-click anywhere in the word "seven" to select the word and the spacebar following the word.

15. Enter a 7 and a space to replace the characters in the word with the number.

Fourscore and 7 years ago

16. With the Direct Selection tool, click the text of the path. Click the Fill box in the Color palette to bring it to the front, then click a swatch in the Swatches palette to apply a color.
    - The text is filled with that color.

17. Undo the last action (press ⌘z) and deselect the path.

18. With the Direct Selection tool, click the baseline of the type to select only the path, not the type.

19. In the Color palette, click the Stroke box to bring it to the front. Apply a stroke color by clicking on a swatch in the Swatches palette. Change the Stroke weight to 6 pt.

Fourscore and 7 years ago

20. Because the path is too long for the type that's on it, choose the Add Anchor Point tool in the Toolbox and add an anchor point to the path just to the right of the last character.

21. Deselect the path, then reselect it by clicking the baseline of the type with the Direct Selection tool.

22. Click on the right endpoint to select it (it becomes solid).

23. Press the *delete* key to delete the endpoint and the segment that's attached to it.

Fourscore and 7 years ago

24. Draw a 1" square on the page.
    - Don't worry about any fill or stroke attributes that might be applied to the path.

25. With the Type tool, triple click the type on the path you created, and copy it (press ⌘c).

26. With the Path Type tool, click in the middle of the top segment of the square you just drew, and paste the type (press ⌘v).
    - The type is wrapped around the outside of the square.

27. Choose the Direct Selection tool in the Toolbox, click on the I-beam marker and drag inside the square so the type flips to the inside of the square.

28. Select the square with the Selection tool and rotate it so the type is readable.

29. Practice drawing paths and entering type on them. Draw vertical paths. Draw horizontal paths with the Vertical Type tool and see the results.

30. Save the file and close the document.

Type Formatting in Illustrator

Character-based formatting refers to attributes that are applied to selected characters, such as typeface and point size. *Paragraph-based formatting* is formatting changes, such as alignment and leading, that are applied to entire paragraphs.

Character-based attributes are contained in the Character palette and paragraph-based attributes are in the Paragraph palette. Palettes are displayed by choosing **Window** ⇨ **Type** ⇨ **Character** or **Window** ⇨ **Type** ⇨ **Paragraph**. Unlike other palettes, these palettes have their own keyboard shortcut:

- **Character** — Press ⌘t
- **Paragraph** — Press ⌘m

To make changes quickly in the palettes, use the following techniques:

- To apply a value in a field and move to the next field in the palette, press the *Tab* key.

- Press *Shift-Tab* to apply a value, and move to the previous field.

- Press *return/enter* to apply a value and exit the palette.

- Press *Shift-return/enter* to apply a value, but keep the current field highlighted.

In addition to the fields in the Character palette, separate Font and Size pop-up menus can be displayed using options in the Type menu. Choose **Type** ⇨ **Font** or **Type** ⇨ **Size**. As soon as you make a selection from the pop-up menu, the attribute is applied to selected type and the menu closes. In the Size pop-up menu, choosing Other highlights the Size field in the Character palette. If the Character palette is not displayed when Other is selected, the Character palette displays on the screen automatically.

Character-Based Type Formatting

Attributes in the Character palette (Figure 5.3) are applied to selected (highlighted) text by entering values in the fields, by choosing a value from the pop-up submenu to the right of each field, or by clicking the up or down arrows to the left of each field. When you click an up/down arrow and when you choose a value from a pop-up menu, the values are applied to selected characters immediately. If you enter a value in a field, press *return/enter* or click in another field to apply the attribute to selected type.

When a Type tool in the Toolbox is active, point size, font, and tracking information for type is

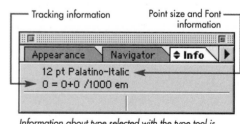

Information about type selected with the type tool is displayed in the Info palette

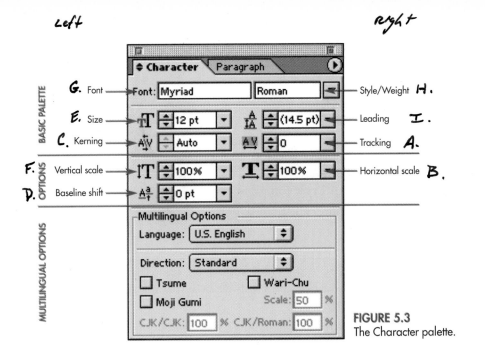

Left *Right*

FIGURE 5.3
The Character palette.

displayed in the Info palette. If the palette is expanded, color information is also displayed. If all type is deselected, information for the last-selected type block is displayed when a Type tool is selected.

General Information About Fonts

Serif and sans serif fonts (see Figure 5.2) are generally available in *families*. A font family is a complete set of characters, including any special characters created for that typeface design. Each family contains variations of the typeface such as *italic*, **bold**, ***bold italic***, and so on. Some families have extensive family members consisting of many different weights of the typeface, such as light, book, book italic, medium, medium italic, ultra, compressed, condensed in each weight, extended in each weight, and on, and on, and on.

For each font you use in an Illustrator document, you must have a printer font stored in the same location as its screen font so Illustrator can find it. If a style or weight of a typeface is not displayed in the Style/Weight pop-up menu on the Character palette, it's not available on your computer.

Illustrator doesn't like True Type fonts very much. This type of font is more commonly found on the Windows platform, but some Macintosh users also use True Type fonts.

Because most True Type fonts cannot be output on high-resolution imagesetters, they should be avoided in projects to be output on these devices. If a project is to be displayed only on a monitor or projection equipment, True Type fonts are acceptable.

True Type font icon

PostScript Type 1 font icon

fyi *Instructions for using special characters can be found in the Font Utilities folder on the CD-ROM that accompanies this book.*

179

The Illustrator CD-ROM that was used to install the Illustrator program has a folder containing several PostScript Type 1 fonts. To install these fonts on your computer:

- **Macintosh:** Drag them to the fonts folder in the System folder on your hard drive.

- **Windows:** Add the fonts to the *psfonts* folder on your hard drive. If you don't have a font utility to add the fonts, the folder on the CD-ROM contains a *Light* version of the ATM (Adobe Type Manager) utility. Install the utility and use it to add the fonts to the *psfonts* folder.

  - Type 1 fonts cannot be added to the regular Fonts folder in the Windows folder.

Font Printing Problems Improper font usage is the most common problem encountered by output providers when generating film from digital files. The following general guidelines will help you avoid problems when outputting your artwork to a high-resolution imagesetter.

- Use only PostScript Type 1 fonts when sending artwork to be output on a high-resolution imagesetter. Most True Type fonts won't print on these devices. Don't mix True Type and Type 1 fonts in the same document.

- Don't rename printer fonts. You can change the names of screen fonts if you want to (*why?*), but if you change the name of a printer font, it won't print correctly. Screen fonts are linked to their respective printer fonts and if you rename the printer font, the link is destroyed.

- It is illegal to give fonts to output providers to use when processing your files, unless the output provider holds a license for that font. Check with your output provider before handing over any fonts.

- In some cases, you can avoid the font usage problem entirely by converting type used in a document to outlines. See the section about Create Outlines later in this chapter.

Illustrator's Default Font When you enter type in a newly-created Illustrator document, the program's default font, Myriad, is used. This is one of the fonts that's automatically stored in a folder in your computer's system files. Adobe uses these fonts for internal operations within the program and only Adobe products have access to the fonts in this folder.

- **Macintosh:** **System** [folder] ⇨ **Application Support** ⇨ **Adobe** ⇨ **Fonts** ⇨ **Reqrd** ⇨ **Base**

- **Windows:** **Program Files** ⇨ **Common Files** ⇨ **Adobe** ⇨ **Fonts** ⇨ **Reqrd** ⇨ **Base**

Choosing a Font

You can change the font of existing type or choose a typeface before you start entering type. First, highlight the type with the Type tool or click on the type block with the Selection tool or the Direct Selection tool so the type is underlined. Because this is a character-based attribute, only selected characters are affected by font changes.

timesaver

Highlight the Font field in the Character palette by pressing ⇧ ⌥ ⌘ m. If the character palette isn't displayed, it opens automatically with the Font field highlighted.

1. Choose a font using the Character palette:
   - **Macintosh:** Display the Style/Weight pop-up menu and choose a font family, then, if one is available for that font, choose a font style or weight from the font submenu.

      or

      Windows: Display the Font pop-up menu and choose a font family. Then, if one is available for the chosen font family, choose a font style or weight from the Style/Weight submenu.

   - Highlight the Font field and start typing a few characters of the font name. Illustrator finds the font, or at least it finds a font name closest to the characters you entered. When the name displays in the field, press the *Tab* key to move to the Style/Weight field. Enter a few characters of the style or weight or choose a style/weight from the Style/Weight pop-up submenu.

   or

2. Choose a font by displaying the context-sensitive menu and choosing a font from the Font pop-up submenu.
   - **Macintosh:** ⌃-click in a type block.
   - **Windows:** Right-click in a type block.

   or

3. Choose **Type ➪ Font** and select a font from the pop-up submenu.

Choose a font style or weight from the font's pop-up menu

Changing Case

Select an option in the Change Case dialog box (**Type ➪ Change Case**) to switch characters highlighted with the Type tool to UPPER CASE, lower case, or Mixed Case (initial caps). Then click OK or press *return/enter*.

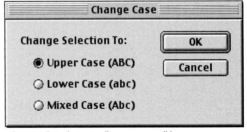

Change selected type to all upper case, all lower case, or initial caps on each word using the Change Case dialog box

1. Locate and open the file you saved into your Practice folder as Type Practice.eps.

2. With the Type tool, double-click on your first name in the Point type block to highlight the characters.

3. Display the Character palette with the Font field highlighted by pressing ⇧ ⌥ ⌘ m and change the font to Times Italic (*Windows:* Times New Roman Italic).

4. Select the characters in your second name and change them to Times Bold (*Windows:* Times New Roman Bold).

5. Select the characters in your last name and change them to Times Bold Italic (*Windows:* Times New Roman Bold Italic).

   Mallory. ¶
   Kristene. ¶
   ***Granger*∞**

6. With the Type tool, highlight all the characters of your last name.

7. Choose Type ⇨ Change Case to display the Change Case dialog box. Click the Upper Case radio button (it's the default selection, so it may already be selected), then click OK or press *return/enter*.

   Mallory. ¶
   Kristene. ¶
   ***GRANGER*∞**

8. Select the block with the Direct Selection tool and change all the type in the block to a typeface you have on your computer that you like.

9. Save the file and close the document window.

Enlarging or Reducing Type Size

In the United States, type is measured in points, which is why it's called *point size*. Other options in the Units & Undo Preferences dialog box for measuring type (**Edit** ⇨ **Preferences** ⇨ **Units & Undo**) are inches, millimeters, Q, or Pixels. Refer to information in Step 6, *Rulers, Grids, & Guides*, for more information about units of measurement. Until you change the point size of type, Illustrator's default size is 12 point.

Different typefaces specified as the same point size can actually be different heights. Times Roman in 9 point measures differently than Lubalin Graph in 9 point. If you measure the ascenders, x-height, and descenders of most typefaces, the total will be the point size of the type, but it can vary from typeface to typeface. See Figure 5.4 for the measurement of the typeface Sabon.

FIGURE 5.4
Measurement of type (60 point Sabon).

To resize type, select the type with the Type tool or with the Selection tool, and

1. Use the keyboard shortcut. Hold down the *Shift* and ⌘ keys and press > to enlarge selected text, and press < to reduce selected type.

   ■ The amount the selected text enlarges or reduces is determined by the value entered in the Size/Leading field in Type & Auto Tracing Preferences (**Edit** ⇨ **Preferences** ⇨ **Type & Auto Tracing**). See Figure 5.5. The default is to increase or decrease the point size by 2 points each time the > or < key is pressed.

     ▪ Hold down the ⌥ in addition to the *Shift* and ⌘ keys when pressing the > or < keys to increase or decrease the point size of selected text by five times the current increment value in the Size/Leading field.

2. Specify a point size Size field (T) in the Character palette.

   ■ Highlight the field, enter a new value, and press *return/enter*.

     ▪ You can enter a value from .1 to 1296.

     ▪ If selected type contains more than one point size, the field is blank and the value you enter changes all selected type.

   ■ Click the up (⬆) or down (⬇) arrows to the left of the Size field.

   ■ Click the arrow on the right side of the Size field to display the pop-up submenu and choose a preset size.

3. Display the context-sensitive menu and choose a preset size from the Size pop-up submenu.

   ■ *Macintosh:* ⌃-click with type selected.

   ■ *Windows:* Right-click with type selected.

fyi To speed up the display of type on the screen, Illustrator displays small type as a gray bar. This is called Greeking and affects type only as it's viewed on the screen. It has no effect on the type when it's printed.

You can control the point size at which type is greeked by changing the value in the Greeking field of the Type & Auto Tracing Preferences dialog box.

Font Size icon in the Character palette

Step 5 — ADD TYPE TO ARTWORK

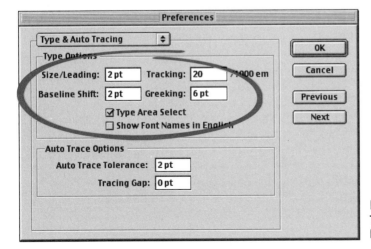

FIGURE 5.5
Type options in the Type & Auto Tracing Preferences dialog box.

183

- If you choose Other in the pop-up submenu, the Size field in the Character palette is highlighted. If the Character palette isn't displayed, it opens automatically with the cursor in the Size field.

4. Choose the Size option in the Type menu (**Type ⇨ Size**) and choose a size from the pop-up submenu.

- If you choose Other in the pop-up submenu, the Size field in the Character palette is highlighted. If the Character palette isn't displayed, it opens automatically with the cursor in the Size field.

activity 5.9

1. Create a new document: Letter size, CMYK color mode. Save it into your Practice Folder as an .eps file named Type Size Practice.eps.

2. Choose the Type tool (press *t*) and type your name again, in three lines.

3. Select the first line, display the Character palette, and change the Font to Times and the Size to 24 point, Auto leading.

4. With the Type tool still selected, double-click on the second line to select it and, by clicking the down-pointing arrow to the left of the field, change its point size to 8 point.

5. Select the third line and change it to 36 point by pressing ⇧ ⌘ > until the value in the field reaches 36 point.

   - Notice that the value in the Size field changes as you press the keys.

6. Select all three lines.

   - Notice that the Size field in the Character palette is blank because type having more than one size is selected.

7. Press ⇧ ⌘ > three times.

   - Click on each line and notice that the point size of all three lines increased by 6 points

from their original size (2 pts each time the command was pressed).

8. Select the last letter of your first name and enlarge it using the keyboard command until it's x-height is approximately the same size as the uppercase first letter.

Mallor**Y**
Kristene

Granger

9. In a blank area of the page, draw a type rectangle with the Type tool that's about 1" wide and 1½" high.

10. Change the fields in the Character palette to 14 pt Times Italic, then type

    Home is where the heart is. Pliny the Elder

11. Insert a hard return before Pliny, then select Pliny the Elder and change it to 8 pt Helvetica (Windows: Arial).

12. Save this file. This file will be used in the next activity so you can leave the artwork window open on your screen or you can close it.

Home is where the heart is.
Pliny the Elder

Specifying the Amount of Space Between Lines of Type

Spacing between lines of type is called leading (pronounced *ledding*). The term originated when type was set using metal, either handset a letter at a time or on a hot-lead typesetting machine such as a Linotype. A thin strip of lead was placed between the lines of type to space it out. Leading is usually measured in points, and it's calculated from the baseline of one line to the baseline of the line *above* it.

Readability can be affected by the amount of leading used. Too little space between lines can be difficult to read, but too much space can unintentionally break up continuous text. It's usually better, though, to have too much space between lines rather than too little. A long line of text requires more leading than a short line to enable the eye to easily follow across.

In layout programs such as QuarkXPress, leading is a paragraph attribute because a leading value applies to each line in the paragraph. But in Illustrator, each line of type in a block can have a different leading value, usually expressed in points. When Auto is the leading value, you can select as little as a single character to change the leading for an entire line. When characters in a line of type have different leading values, the leading value of the largest character is applied to the line and the field in the Character palette is empty.

To specify leading between one or more lines of type:

1. With any Type tool, select at least one character in a line. You can triple-click in a paragraph to select the entire paragraph.

   or

   With the Selection tool or the Direct Selection tool, click in a type block to select all the type attached to an alignment point, along a path, or in a container.

2. Use the keyboard shortcut. Hold down the ⌥ key and press the up arrow (↑) to *decrease* the leading and the down arrow (↓) to *increase* the leading.

   - The amount the leading increases or decreases is determined by the value entered in the **Size/Leading** field in Type & Auto Tracing Preferences (**Edit** ➪ **Preferences** ➪ **Type & Auto Tracing**). See Figure 5.6. The default is to increase or decrease the leading by 2 points each time the arrow keys are pressed.

     - Hold down the ⌘ in addition to the ⌥ key when pressing the arrow keys to increase or decrease the leading of selected text by five times the current increment value in the **Size/Leading** field.

fyi When Auto leading is applied to a block of type, all characters in a line must be highlighted to decrease the leading using the Up arrow key. If a single character remains unhighlighted, pressing the Up arrow key changes the value in the leading field of the Character palette, but the leading doesn't actually change.

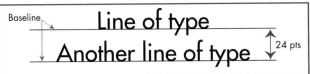

FIGURE 5.6
Leading measurement is from baseline to baseline.

185

3. Change the leading value in the Character palette:

■ Enter a number in the Leading field () and press *return/enter* to exit the palette. Press the *Tab* key to move to the next field.

or

■ Click the pop-up submenu arrow on the right side of the Leading field and choose a preset value.

▪ Choosing Auto sets the leading value at 120% of the largest character on each line. This setting works fairly well for font sizes smaller than 14 pt, but for point sizes larger than 14 pt, it's usually too much space.

or

■ Click the up (▲) or down (▼) arrows to the left of the Leading field.

or

■ Double-click the Leading icon () to assign a leading value that's the same as the point size of the type in the line. This only works if all the selected type is the same size. Specifying a leading that's the same as the point size of the type is called *solid* leading.

 fyi You can add leading above a paragraph by selecting a character in the first line and increasing the leading of that character.

Leading icon in the Character palette

 *activity 5.10*

1. If the document you created in Activity 5.9 is not still open on your screen, open it now. Unless you changed the value in the Leading field from the program default, the leading for the lines on this page were set with Auto leading.

■ Notice that the space above your middle name reduced proportionally to the point size of the type, and the space above your last name increased because the point size was made larger.

Mallory
Kristene
Granger

2. Select all three lines and change the leading in the Leading field to 36 pt.

■ Now the space from the baseline of one line to the baseline below it is the same regardless of the point size of the type on the line.

3. Change the point size of one letter in your middle name to 48 pt.

■ The leading wasn't affected by the change in type size.

4. Select the larger character in your middle name and display the menu of preset options by clicking

the arrow at the right side of the Leading field in the Character palette. Choose Auto.

■ The space between the lines was adjusted to accommodate the larger size character.

5. In the last activity you changed the last character of your first name to a larger size. Restore it to the same size as the rest of your first name (30 pt).

■ The leading between your first and middle name wasn't affect by changing the leading of a character in the top line. Leading is calculated upward.

6. Select a character in the second line of the type in the type rectangle and change it to 48 pt.

■ Even though the character is in the middle of a paragraph, the size of individual characters in a line affect the leading for that line when Auto leading is selected.

Home is

wh*e* re the

heart is.
Pliny the Elder

7. Save the file and close the document window.

Adjusting Space Between Characters

Kerning Adjusting the space between two characters (called a *pair*) is called kerning. When fonts are designed, some pairs, such as WA, have kerning values built in. These built-in kerning values work well at smaller sizes, but additional kerning may be necessary at larger sizes. If built-in kerning values are established between characters of a kerning pair, the value is displayed in parentheses in the Kerning field of the Character palette. Choosing Auto in the Kerning field applies the built-in kerning values to selected type.

Kerning is accomplished by clicking between two characters to position the Insertion marker between them, then entering values in the Kerning field (A̅V̅) in the Character palette.

Tracking When the space between three or more characters is adjusted, it's called *tracking*. Highlight the characters you want to squeeze or spread by dragging with a Type tool, or select all type in a container or text block with the Selection tool or Direct Selection tool so that all characters are underlined. Then enter a value in the Tracking field (A̅V̅) of the Character palette.

Specify Kerning or Tracking Values Enter a negative value to squeeze characters together; enter a positive value to spread characters apart. You can enter or choose values between –1,000 and 10,000 in .01 increments.

To specify a kerning or tracking value:

- Hold down the ⌥ key and press the left arrow key (←) to squeeze two characters together or press the right arrow key (→) to spread two characters apart.
  - Each time you press an arrow key, the amount of space that's added or removed is determined by the increment value in the Tracking field of Type & Auto Tracing Preferences (**Edit ⇨ Preferences ⇨ Type & Auto Tracing**). The default is 20/1000 of an em space and you can change this value but there's really very little reason to do so.

  or
- Press ⇧ ⌘ [to squeeze characters and press ⇧ ⌘] to spread characters by the increment value in the Tracking field in the Type & Auto Tracing dialog box each time the key is pressed.

  or
- Click the up (▲) or down (▼) arrows to the left of the respective field.
  - Each time you click, the selected type changes to the new value immediately.

Kerning icon in the Character palette

Tracking icon in the Character palette

Kern pair with no kerning applied

Kern pair with Auto kerning applied

Kern pair with additional manual kerning applied

read this!

The default Tracking unit of measurement is not points as it is with size and leading. It's 20/1000 of an em space. An em space is as wide as the point size of the type. In other words, an em space in 12-point type is 12 points wide.

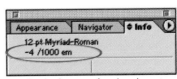

Kern/track information for selected type is displayed in the Info palette

or

- Click the arrow on the right side of the field to display the pop-up submenu and choose a preset value.
  - If a manual kerning value has been entered in the Kerning field and you want to return to the factory specifications, choose *Auto*.
- Highlight the Kerning or Tracking field in the Character palette and enter a value. Press *return/enter* or the *Tab* key to apply the value.

The Fit Headline Command Using the Fit Headline command in the Type menu, you can add or delete space between characters (track) so a type block consisting of a single line automatically fits in its container. You can't select a line in the middle of a paragraph. It works on only a single line of type in a container. The amount of tracking necessary to fit the headline to its container is displayed in the Tracking field of the Paragraph palette. When this command is applied to a Multiple Master font (see that section later in this chapter), the weight of the characters is adjusted as well as the inter-character space.

fyi Type specs for type size and leading are usually written as 12/14. Type size is always first followed by the leading value separated by a slash. Verbally, specs are given as: "Twelve on fourteen . . . (usually the font is given next).*

Fit Headline

Space is added automatically between characters to make the text fill the type block when the Fit Headline command is applied

activity 5.11

1. Create a new document: Letter size, CMYK color mode. Save it into your practice folder as an .eps file and name it Kerning Practice.eps.

2. Choose the Type tool (press *t*), click on the document page, and type

   The price of greatness
   is responsibility.
   Winston Churchill

3. Change the quotation to 24/24 Times Italic. Change Winston Churchill's name to 12/20 pt Myriad Roman.

4. With the Type tool, highlight the capital T in The and change the size to 48 pt.

   *T*he price of greatness
   is responsibility.
   Winston Churchill

5. Highlight both lines of the quotation and reduce the space between the characters to −20 by clicking the down arrow to the left of the Tracking field in the Character palette.

6. Because there's still too much space between the capital T and the "h", click between the two characters so the Insertion marker is blinking there. Then hold down the ⌥ key and press the left arrow key until the value in the Kerning field is −120.

7. Reduce the spacing between characters in Winston Churchill's name to −40.

8. Highlight the quotation and change the fill color to 95% cyan, 65% magenta, 0% yellow, and 0% black.

   *T*he price of greatness
   is responsibility.
   Winston Churchill

9. Save the file and close the document window.

Scaling Type Using the Character Palette

Scaling type changes the width or height of characters by distorting them so they're wider or narrower (horizontal scaling) or taller or shorter (vertical scaling). Scaled characters don't have the same appearance as a designer-created condensed or expanded font in a typeface family. For this reason, whenever possible, use the condensed or expanded font in a typeface family rather than applying scaling.

Type can be scaled in three ways:

■ Select it with the Selection tool and drag the side handles (horizontal scaling) and the top or bottom handles (vertical scaling) of its bounding box.

or

■ Apply the Scale command or by use the Scale tool in the Toolbox.

or

■ Enter values or choose preset values in the Character palette.

You can scale type by dragging the handles of its bounding box like other objects you draw, but you can specify Horizontal Scale and Vertical Scale using the Character palette, too. The Horizontal Scale and Vertical Scale options are located in the Options panel of the Character palette. To display it if it's not visible, click the arrows (‡) on the Character palette folder tab, double-click the folder tab, or click the Options arrow at the top right corner of the palette and choose Show Options.

Using one of the selection methods described previously, select the characters to be scaled, then

■ Highlight the Horizontal Scale field in the Character palette and enter a value. Press *return/enter* or the *Tab* key to apply the value. You can enter values from 1 to 10,000 percent of its original size.

▪ A higher value in the Horizontal Scale field widens the type. A lower value condenses it.

▪ A higher value in the Vertical Scale field makes the type taller. A lower value makes it shorter.

or

■ Click the up (▲) or down (▼) arrows to the left of the respective field.

▪ Each time you click, the selected type changes to the new value immediately.

or

■ Click the arrow on the right side of the field to display the pop-up submenu and choose a preset value.

60

Helvetica Heavy scaled horizontally to 83% of its original width

60

Helvetica Heavy Condensed with no scaling applied

T

Horizontal Scale icon in the Character palette

T

Vertical Scale icon in the Character palette

189

Restore Normal Scaling Normal scaling is 100%. To restore the type to its normal state, select the type you want to restore, and

- Press ⇧ ⌘ x

or

- Enter 100% in the Vertical Scale and Horizontal Scale fields in the Character palette.

1. Create a new document: Letter size, CMYK color mode. Save it into your Practice folder as an .eps file named Scale Type Practice.eps.

2. Draw a 1" circle on the page.
   - It doesn't matter what fill and stroke attributes are applied to the circle.

3. Choose the Path Type tool in the Toolbox, click on the edge of the circle, and type

   Type Around a Circle

4. With the Type tool, highlight the text and change it to 18 pt Times.

5. With the Direct Selection tool, select the type (not the path) so the I-beam marker displays. Drag the type around the circle until the first character is lined up with the leftmost anchor point of the circle.

6. With the Type tool, highlight all the characters and click the down arrow on the left side of the Horizontal Scale field until the last character of the text is lined up with the rightmost anchor point of the circle.

7. Highlight the text again, then enter 500% in the Vertical Scale field in the Character palette.

8. With the Direct Selection tool, select the text, but not the circle. Move the I-beam marker until the text is centered at the top of the circle.

9. Save the file and close the document window.

Adjusting the Baseline of Type

When it's necessary to move characters above or below the baseline, use the Baseline Shift command. Illustrator doesn't provide a typestyle option for creating subscript ($_3$) or superscript (^{3}) characters, so you can use this command to create them. You can also use this command to reposition characters along a type path and to create fractions.

The Baseline Shift command ($\frac{A}{\div}$) is located in the Options panel of the Character palette. To display it if it's not visible, click the arrows ($\updownarrow$) on the Character palette folder tab, double-click the folder tab, or click the Options arrow at the top right corner of the palette and choose Show Options.

To reposition characters above or below the baseline, select the characters, and

$$H_2O$$
$$CA^{2+}$$

Use Baseline Shift to create subscripts and superscripts

■ Hold down the *Shift* and ⌥ keys and press the up arrow key (↑) to move selected characters upward off the baseline. Press the down arrow key (↓) to shift characters downward off the baseline.

Baseline Shift

The Baseline Shift command can be used to center characters on a path

- Each time you press an arrow key, the distance the characters are shifted is determined by the increment value in the Baseline Shift field of Type & Auto Tracing Preferences (**Edit** ➭ **Preferences** ➭ **Type & Auto Tracing**). The default is 2 pt.

- Add the ⌘ key to the *Shift* and ⌥ keys when you hold them down and press an arrow key to shift the characters by 10 times the value in the Baseline Shift field of Type & Auto Tracing Preferences.

or

■ Highlight the Baseline Shift field in the Character palette and enter a value. Press *return/enter* or the *Tab* key to apply the value. You can enter values from −1296 to 1296. Press *return/enter* or the *Tab* key to apply the values.

- A positive value shifts characters upward.
- A negative value shifts characters downward.

Baseline Shift icon in the Character palette

or

■ Click the up (⬆) or down (⬇) arrows to the left of the respective field.

- Each time you click, the selected type changes to the new value immediately.

or

■ Click the arrow on the right side of the field to display the pop-up submenu and choose a preset value.

Create a Fraction The Baseline Shift function can be used to create fractions.

1. Enter all the numbers in the fraction, including a slash character.
2. Select the numbers and change the type size to about half the current type size.

$5/16$

Fractions are created using the Baseline Shift command

3. Select only the numerator (all the numbers to the left of the slash).

4. In the **Baseline Shift** field of the Character palette, enter a value that's ⅓ the current type size.

5. The slash character isn't the correct character to use in a fraction, but I find it's easier to keep track of what I'm doing if I use it until this point when I'm creating a fraction. The proper character is called a *virgule*. It's more slanted than the slash character and looks better in a fraction. To insert a virgule in the fraction, select the slash character and replace it as follows:

   ■ *Macintosh:* Press ⇧ ⌥ 1

   ■ *Windows:* Change the font to Symbol, hold down the ⌥ key, and press 0164 on the numeric keypad. Then release the ⌥ key. The character displays when the ⌥ key is released.

fyi *Windows users only: Adobe typefaces include three fraction characters that you can display using the ANSI equivalent:*

¼ = ⌥ 0188
½ = ⌥ 0189
¾ = ⌥ 0190

activity 5.13

1. Create a new document: Letter size, CMYK color mode. Save it into your Practice Folder as an .eps file and name it Baseline Shift Practice.

2. Display the Character palette, including its options. Verify that the Baseline Shift field is set to 0.

3. With the Pencil tool draw a slightly curvy path on the page.

4. Choose the Type tool (press *t*), click on the path, and type the words

   Baseline Shift

5. Change the type to 12 pt Times Bold.

6. If necessary, click on the type with the Direct Selection tool so the I-beam Marker displays and move it to center the type on the path.

7. With the Type tool, highlight the words, then click the down arrow to the left of the Baseline Shift field in the Character palette. Keep clicking the down arrow until the path runs through the center of the characters.

   ■ If you can't seem to get it exactly centered, select the value in the field and enter a half-point value, such as 3.5.

8. With the Direct Selection tool, select the path without selecting the type. Apply a 12 pt blue stroke to the path.

9. Change the color of the type to white.

10. Change the Baseline Shift value back to 0.

11. In a blank area of the screen, click with the type tool and enter the following type

    11415/32

12. Select all the type and change it to 18 pt Times Roman.

13. Highlight the last four numbers (not the slash) and change them to 9 pt.

14. Select the two numbers to the left of the slash and, in the Character palette, click the up arrow until the value in the Baseline Shift field is 6 (⅓ the point size of the whole number, not the fraction numbers).

15. Change the slash character to a virgule by selecting the slash, then:

    ■ *Macintosh:* Press ⇧ ⌥ 1

    ■ *Windows:* Change the font to Symbol, hold down the ⌥ key, and press 0164 on the numeric keypad. Then release the ⌥ key. The character displays when the ⌥ key is released. $114^{15}/_{32}$

16. Save the file and close the artwork window.

Multilingual Options

To display the Multilingual Options panel of the Character palette, click the folder tab arrows (⬍), double-click the folder tab, or click the arrow at the top right corner of the palette to display the Character palette Options menu, and choose Show Multilingual.

Multilingual section of the Character palette

- Change the selection in the Language pop-up menu to apply hyphenation rules for a different language to selected type.

  - To change hyphenation rules for the whole document, display Hyphenation Preferences (**Edit ➪ Preferences ➪ Hyphenation**) and change the selection in the Default Language pop-up menu.

- The Tsume checkbox is used to change text using Japanese fonts in which all the characters are the same width and height to proportionally spaced, or varying, spaced text.

- The Moji Gumi option is also used for Japanese fonts to specify the amount of spacing placed between characters and punctuation.

- Click the Wari-Chu option to reduce the point size of selected characters and stack them on two lines, centered vertically in the line. In the sample shown here, the words FOR THE were scaled to 37% so they aligned at the baseline and at the top of the cap letter.

  - Enter a value in the Scale field below the Wari-Chu checkbox to specify the size of the selected characters, as a percentage of the current type size.

A Photographic Atlas FOR THE **Anatomy & Physiology Laboratory**

Wari-Chu applied to text

activity 5.14

1. Create a new document: Letter size, CMYK color mode.

2. Choose the Type tool (press *t*) and create about a 3" × 2" type rectangle. Type the following text in the type rectangle:

   . . . law is most commonly represented by the following equation: Rate of effusion of ARate of effusion of B, which applies equally well to rates . . .

3. Change all the type to 18 point with Auto leading.

4. Highlight the words Rate of effusion of ARate of effusion of B (not the comma), display the Multilingual panel of the Character palette, and click the Wari-Chu checkbox.

- Selected characters decreased in size and are stacked in the line.

5. Adjust the percentage value in the Scale field in the Character palette until the characters are aligned with the baseline and with the top of the ascenders of the regular type.

  - You can use the Baseline Shift feature, too, to align the characters differently than the default if you don't want to change the size.

6. With the Line Segment tool, draw a horizontal line between the stacked characters to finish the equation.

   ...law is most commonly represented by the following equation $\frac{\text{Rate of effusion of A}}{\text{Rate of effusion of B}}$, which applies equally well to rates ...

7. Close the document without saving changes.

Paragraph-Based Type Attributes

Options available in the Paragraph palette (Figure 5.7) are applied to entire paragraphs of type, whether or not individual characters are selected. To make paragraph-based changes, click in a paragraph so the Insertion marker is blinking. To apply paragraph attributes to more than one paragraph, select the type block with the Selection tool or highlight a portion of all paragraphs with a Type tool.

To display the Paragraph palette,

- Choose **Window** ➪ **Type** ➪ **Paragraph**

or

- Press ⌘ m

To display the options panel of the palette,

- Click the arrows (⬍) on the Character palette folder tab

or

- Double-click the folder tab

or

- Click the palette options arrow at the top right corner of the palette to display the Paragraph palette Options menu, and choose Show Options.

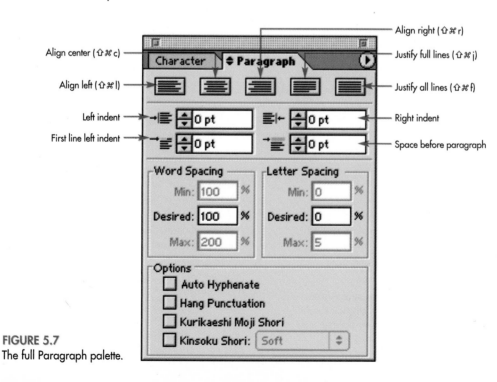

FIGURE 5.7
The full Paragraph palette.

A *paragraph* encompasses all type between the beginning of a type block or type rectangle until a paragraph return is reached, all type between paragraph returns, or until an end-of-text-block symbol is encountered. A soft return (press *Shift-enter* or press the *enter* key on the numeric keypad) acts like a paragraph return except that it doesn't end the paragraph. It's ignored when paragraph attributes are applied to the paragraph.

Paragraph Alignment

The alignment commands found at the top of the Paragraph palette align lines of text in a paragraph, along a text path, or text that's attached to an alignment point. A sample of each is shown here.

- When applied to text attached to an alignment point, the alignment point is used as the point of origin for aligning its text.

- When applied to text along a path, the endpoints of the path are used as the reference points. For example, if you apply the Align Center command, the text is centered between the two endpoints of the path.

- **Align left** — Often referred to as *flush left, ragged right*, or just *ragged right* and is often written as *fl rr*, or *fl*, or *rr*. All lines of the paragraph line up on the left edge of the alignment point, of the type container, or the left endpoint of a path. Keyboard command: ⇧⌘l (el)

- **Align center** — All lines of the paragraph are centered.
  - Keyboard command: ⇧⌘c

- **Align right** — It's often referred to as *flush right, ragged left*, or just *ragged left*. All lines of the paragraph line up on the right edge of the alignment point, of the type container, or the right endpoint of a path. Keyboard command: ⇧⌘r
  - When lines are aligned right, any spaces at the end of automatically wrapped lines are ignored.

- **Justify full lines** — This command aligns all lines of text with the right *and* left edges of its container, *except* the last line. This command doesn't apply to type attached to an alignment point or to type along a path. Keyboard command: ⇧⌘j

- **Justify all lines** — Often referred to as *force justify*, this command aligns all lines of text, *including* the last line, with the right *and* left edges of its container. This command doesn't apply to type attached to an alignment point or to type along a path. Keyboard command: ⇧⌘f

Align Left icon in the Paragraph palette

"When you start arguing with a fool, the other guy's doing the same thing."

Align left — Flush left, ragged right

Align Center icon in the Paragaph palette

"When you start arguing with a fool, the other guy's doing the same thing."

Centered

Align Right icon in the Paragraph palette

"When you start arguing with a fool, the other guy's doing the same thing."

Align right — Flush right, ragged left

Justify Full Lines icon in the Paragraph palette

"When you start arguing with a fool, the other guy's doing the same thing."

Justified

Justify All Lines icon in the Paragraph palette

"When you start arguing with a fool, the other guy's doing the same thing."

Justify all lines — Force justify

1. Create a new document: Letter size, CMYK color mode. Save it into your Practice Folder as an .eps file named Paragraphs Practice.eps.

2. In the Character palette, make the following changes: 12 point Times, 15 pt leading, uncheck the Wari-Chu option in the Multilingual section.

3. Choose the Type tool (press *t*) and create about a 1"×1" type rectangle. Enter the following text:

   > To be or not to be, that is the question . . . Shakespeare

   To be or not to be, that is the question . . . Shakespeare

4. With the Type tool, click in the second line, display the Paragraph palette, then click the Align Center button.

   - Each line in the paragraph is center-stacked. The name Shakespeare, though, didn't change because it's a different paragraph.

5. Show the hidden characters (Type ⇨ Show Hidden Characters).

   To be or not to be, that is the question . . . Shakespeare

6. Click anywhere in Shakespeare's name and click the Align Right button in the Paragraph palette.

   - Notice that the space symbols hang outside the edge of the container so that the characters are flush with the container.

7. Change the point size of Shakespeare's name to 9 point.

8. Click anywhere in the quotation (not Shakespeare's name), and press ⇧ ⌘ l [el].

9. Press ⇧ ⌘ j [jay] to justify the paragraph.

10. With the Selection tool, select all the type in the container, then press ⇧ ⌘ f to justify everything in the container, even Shakespeare's name.

    To be or not to be, that is the question . . . Shakespeare

11. With the Type tool, click in the container and press ⌘ a to select all the type.

12. Press ⌘ c to copy the type, click the Type tool in the Toolbox, then click somewhere else on the document page and paste the copied text.

13. With the Type tool, click before the word "that" (after the space). Press *return/enter* to create a second line.

14. Click the Direct Selection tool to select the type block, then drag a vertical ruler guide onto the page and position it on the alignment point.

15. With the Type tool, click anywhere in the first line, and press ⇧ ⌘ c to center that line.

    - Notice that only the first line was affected by the change in alignment — because there was a hard return (regular paragraph return) at the end of the first line.

    - The line is centered on the alignment point.

16. With the Type tool, click anywhere in the second line and press ⇧ ⌘ r.

    - The last character in the second line is aligned with the alignment point.

17. Save the file and close the document.

Indenting Text

The Paragraph palette contains fields for specifying left, right, and first line indents. All of these indents can be used with type in a container, but they don't work at all on type that's along a path. Only the Left Indent can be applied to type attached to an alignment point.

Left Indent icon in the Paragraph palette

To apply indent values, at least a portion of each paragraph must be selected. To apply a value to a single paragraph, click anywhere before the paragraph return so the Insertion marker is blinking somewhere in the paragraph. To apply the same indent value to all paragraphs in a container, select them with the Selection tool.

You can enter values between –1296 and 1296 in the indent fields. To indent paragraphs:

Right Indent icon in the Paragraph palette

■ Enter new values in the Left Indent, Right Indent, or First Line Left Indent fields.

 ▪ **Left Indent** — Shifts all lines in selected paragraphs to the right of the left margin by the value specified in the field.

 ▪ **Right Indent** — Shifts all lines in selected paragraphs to the left of the right margin by the value specified in the field.

First Line Left Indent icon in the Paragraph palette

 ▪ **First Line Left Indent** — Indents only the first line of a paragraph. Use this field for specifying standard paragraph indents. A positive number shifts type to the right. A negative number shifts type to the left. See the following section about Hanging Indent.

or

■ Click the up (▲) or down (▼) arrows to the left of the respective field.

 ▪ Each time you click, the selected type changes to the new value immediately.

Hanging Indent A hanging indent means that all lines of a paragraph are indented *except* the first line. You can even hang text outside its container and it will still print.

1. Click in the paragraphs that you want to hang.

2. Enter a positive value in the Left Indent field.

3. Enter the same value in the First Line Left Indent field, except make it a negative value by entering a minus in front of it.

To format multiple paragraphs with hanging indents so that characters, such as numbers or bullets, hang outside the margin to the left of the paragraph:

1. Click in the paragraphs that you want to hang.

2. Enter 0 in the Left Indent field.

3. Enter a negative value in the First Line Left Indent field.

> We the People of the United States, in Order to form a more perfect Union, establish Justice, insure domestic Tranquility, provide for

fyi Specifying a negative value in the First Line Left Indent field to create a hanging indent works only if the text to which it's applied is flush left rather than justified.

4. After the number or bullet characters, press the Tab key. The text of the paragraph automatically aligns with the left edge of the container.

Hanging Punctuation   Illustrator provides a Hang Punctuation checkbox in the Paragraph palette that automatically hangs punctuation outside its container. Punctuation can hang out of the left side and the right side of the container. Characters that are affected when this option is checked are: quotation marks, apostrophe, em dash, period, comma, hyphen, colon, and semicolon.

1. Click in the paragraph for which you want the punctuation to hang.

2. Click the Hang Punctuation checkbox in the Paragraph palette.

| 1. Guest Seating¶ |
| 2. Dedication¶ |
| 3. Welcoming Remarks¶ |
| 4. Keynote Speaker¶ |
| - Intermission∞ |

> "To be or not to be, that is the question . . . ¶
> Shakespeare∞

activity 5.16

1. Create a new document: Letter size, CMYK color mode.

2. Choose the Type tool (press *t*) and draw a type container that's 2½" × 2½".

   ■ Refer to the Width and Height information in the Info palette to draw the type container the correct size.

3. Enter the following type into the container:

   Use *who, whom,* and *whose* when referring to people; use *which* when referring to animals or things; use *that* when referring to animals or things (though it can refer to people). For example: He is a governor who is looking for a fiscal miracle. Once the levee burst, dozens of snakes that floated to the surface clung to treetops.

4. Format the type to 10 pt, 12 leading, Times, align left, and press *return/enter* to apply the characteristics.

   ■ *Windows:* Use Times New Roman. The text may flow slightly differently.

5. Select the words that are italics in the paragraph in #3 above, and format them as Times Italic.

   ■ *Windows:* Times New Roman Italic.

6. Indent the paragraph by entering 1p in the First Line Left Indent field in the Paragraph palette and pressing *return/enter.*

7. Position the cursor after the colon and the space following "For example:" and press *return/enter* twice so the sentence beginning "He is a . . ." starts a new paragraph with space above it.

8. Position the cursor after the period and space following "miracle." and press *return/enter* twice to begin the sentence "Once the levee . . ." as a new paragraph with space above it.

9. With the Type tool selected, highlight at least a portion of both of the bottom two paragraphs.

10. Enter 1p in the Left Indent field of the Paragraph palette and 0p in the First Line Left Indent field, then press *return/enter.*

    ■ All lines of the bottom two paragraphs are indented 1p.

11. Highlight the bottom two paragraphs again, enter 2p in the Left Indent field and −1p in the First Line Left Indent field, and press *return/enter.*

    ■ The first lines of the bottom two paragraphs are indented from the main paragraph above them, and the rest of the lines of the paragraphs are indented even more.

12. Display the Save As dialog box, name the file Indenting Practice.eps, and save the file into your Practice folder as an .eps file. Print it, then close the artwork window.

Adding Space Before Paragraphs

You can highlight a character on the top line of each paragraph in a block of type and change the leading value to add space between the paragraphs. But the Paragraph palette has a field — Space Before Paragraph field — that accomplishes the same thing and it can be applied to the entire text block at once. You can add or subtract space before selected paragraphs. Values in this field don't apply to type attached to an alignment point or type along a path. You don't have to highlight type, just click somewhere in a paragraph, to apply this command.

Space Before Paragraph icon in the Paragraph palette

- Enter a positive number to add space between paragraphs.

- Enter a negative number to subtract space between paragraphs.

Adjusting Word Spacing and Letter Spacing

The middle section of the Paragraph palette contains options for manipulating the space between words in a line (Word Spacing) and between characters (Letter Spacing). The space you add or subtract between characters when you apply Tracking is a fixed amount, but letter spacing is flexible and can vary from line to line. The values entered into the fields in this section of the palette determine how much the spacing can vary.

The value in the Desired field in both sections is the value applied to type that's attached to an alignment point, type along a path, and nonjustified lines (flush left, flush right, or centered) in paragraphs. If no justified lines are selected, the Min (minimum) and Max (maximum) fields are unavailable. If a nonjustified line is selected along with justified lines, the fields also become unavailable.

The values in these fields tell Illustrator how to adjust spacing in lines of a paragraph when the lines are to be justified. Values are calculated as a percentage of the width of the standard space as designed for that particular font. The width of the space can vary from typeface to typeface.

Whenever possible, the value in the Desired field is used. But if a line can't be justified using the value in the Desired field, Illustrator will squeeze the characters together or squeeze the space between words up to the amounts specified in the Min. fields. Or Illustrator can add space between characters or between words up to the amount specified in the Max. fields.

When in the
Normal spacing between letters

When in the
Word spacing increased to +175

When in the
Word spacing reduced to −95

- **Minimum Word Spacing** — Value can't be less than 0 percent.

- **Maximum Word Spacing** — Value can't be more than 1000 percent.

- **Minimum Letter Spacing** — Value must be 0 percent or a negative value.

- **Maximum Letter Spacing** — Value must be 0 percent or a negative value.

activity 5.17

1. Locate and open the file you saved into your Practice folder as Indenting Practice.eps.

2. Select all the type in the type container, display the Paragraph palette, and change the values in the Indent fields to 0.

3. Choose the Justify Full Lines option (▤) at the top of the palette.

   ■ Notice that the words are too widely spaced and don't look very good.

4. Display the Word Spacing and Letter Spacing options in the Paragraph palette, and enter −3 in the Min Letter Spacing field. Press *return/enter*.

   ■ Notice that the characters in the first line were squeezed enough to allow the first word in the next line to move up to the top line. The rest of the lines rewrapped to justify in the type container.

5. With all the text in the type container selected, enter 70 in the Min Word Spacing field and press *return/enter*.

   ■ Space between the words in the top line didn't change because the change wasn't enough to allow another word to move up and fit on that line. But the space between the words in the second line squeezed together enough to allow another word to fit on the line.

6. There's too much space above the last two paragraphs. So, place the cursor before the first character in the second paragraph and press delete to remove the paragraph return above it.

7. Remove the paragraph return above the last paragraph the same way.

8. Highlight at least a portion of all paragraphs and enter 6 pt in the Space Before Paragraph field of the Paragraph palette. Press *return/enter*.

9. Save the file, print it, and close the document window.

Word Hyphenation

When setting type in a document, it's sometimes necessary to break a word to achieve balance in a block of text or for pleasing visual appearance. Too many hyphens, though, becomes difficult to read, so they should be used sparingly. See Figure 5.8 for general guidelines for hyphenating words.

In Adobe Illustrator 10, there are three ways to break words at the ends of lines of text in text blocks: (1) Discretionary hyphen; (2) Automatic hyphenation; and (3) Manual hyphenation. I'll describe all three methods, but only discretionary hyphenation is recommended.

Discretionary Hyphenation

A *discretionary hyphen* is an invisible character that's inserted into a word for use when the word falls at the end of a line and it's necessary for Illustrator to break the word in order to justify the line. If it's not needed, you never see it. When it is needed, a regular hyphen displays where the discretionary hyphen command (⇧ ⌘ -) was inserted. This is the most efficient hyphenation method available.

You can insert a discretionary hyphen in more than one place in a word and Illustrator uses the one that works best. When the word is broken at the discretionary hyphen, a "shadow" hyphen displays behind the hyphen character, indicating that it's a discretionary hyphen (₋).

Automatic Hyphenation

Automatic hyphenation sounds good, but it doesn't work very well. The hyphenation rules that Illustrator uses sometimes create weird hyphenations. You have to scan the type manually and correct them by entering discretionary hyphens anyway, so why not just enter discretionary hyphens in the first place?

The Auto Hyphenation feature affects highlighted text or text created after the option is turned on.

1. With a Type tool, highlight the text you want to hyphenate.

2. Check the Auto Hyphenate checkbox at the bottom of the Paragraph palette.

   ▪ If the option isn't visible, click the arrows to the left of the name on the folder tab or display the Paragraph palette Options menu and choose Show Options.

3. Display the Paragraph palette Options menu and choose Hyphenation to set hyphenation options in the Hyphenation Options dialog box that displays (Figure 5.9).

   ▪ **Hyphenate [   ] letters from beginning** — This value specifies the minimum number of characters in a word that must occur before a hyphen is inserted.

   ▪ **Hyphenate [   ] letters from end** — This value specifies the minimum number of characters in a word that remain after the hyphen is inserted.

   ▪ **Limit consecutive hyphens to [   ]** — More than two hyphens in a row at the ends of lines of a paragraph is called a *ladder* and is considered poor typography.

4. Click OK or press *return/enter*.

Hyphenation Preferences In the Hyphenation Preferences dialog box (**Edit** ⇨ **Preferences** ⇨ **Hyphenation**) (Figure 5.10) you can control hyphenation of words you use frequently.

1. Display the Hyphenation Preferences dialog box (**Edit** ⇨ **Preferences** ⇨ **Hyphenation**).

2. In the New Entry field, enter the word for which you want to specify the hyphenation.

▪ Never hyphenate a word after only one character.

▪ The second half of a hyphenated word must have at least three characters — and punctuation doesn't count.

▪ Don't hyphenate a compound word (two words joined by a hyphen), such as *moderate-impact*, except at the hyphen. In other words, don't hyphenate a hyphenated word.

▪ If possible, avoid hyphenating the last word in a paragraph.

▪ Don't hyphenate words when the result affects readability. For example, even though the word *people* has two syllables and can "legally" be hyphenated, peo-ple can make for awkward reading. So can mus-cle.

FIGURE 5.8
General guidelines for word hyphenation.

- Enter the word with the hyphens inserted between the characters you will allow hyphenation to occur.

- To keep a word from hyphenating at all, enter the word without any hyphens.

3. Click the Add button to add the word to the scroll list.

4. To remove a word from the scroll list, highlight it in the scroll window, then click the Delete button.

5. Click OK or press *return/enter* when you're finished.

Unfortunately, hyphenation specifications are saved in the preferences for the application that created the document. This means that if the file is opened using an application with different preferences, such as at the output provider, type may reflow because hyphenation specifications are different. This is the reason I never use this option.

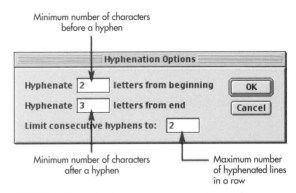

Minimum number of characters before a hyphen

Minimum number of characters after a hyphen

Maximum number of hyphenated lines in a row

FIGURE 5.9 Set hyphenation options in the Hyphenation Options dialog box.

fyi Default rules for hyphenation are for English as it's spoken in the United States. To apply hyphenation rules for a different language, display the Multilingual Options panel in the Character palette and choose a different option from the Language pop-up submenu. You can also switch language hyphenation rules in the Hyphenation Preferences dialog box (Edit ⇨ Preferences ⇨ Hyphenation).

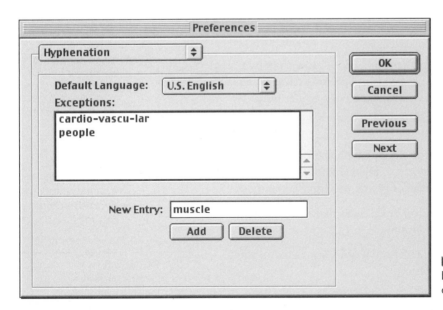

FIGURE 5.10 Hyphenation Preferences dialog box.

Manual Hyphenation

Manual hyphenation is simply inserting a regular hyphen character (-) where you want a line to break. Use this method for type attached to an alignment point. Don't use this method for text in a container. If you make changes to the text, you may end up with hyphens in the middle of words because those words no longer occur at the end of a line.

 *activity* **5.18**

1. Create a new document: Letter size, CMYK color mode. Name it Hyphenation Practice.eps and save it into your Practice Folder as an .eps file.

2. Choose the Type tool (press *t*) and draw a container that's 1.75" wide and 5.5" high.

3. Enter the text of Figure 5.8 on page 201 into the container. Use any style bullet you like, but don't put any space between the bullet and the first character.

   ▪ In the finished sample at the end of this activity, I used a round bullet (*Macintosh:* ⌥8; *Windows:* ⌥-0149), increased its size to 18 point, then baseline shifted it down 2 points so it's centered vertically on the cap height of the first line.

4. Format the type to 11 pt, 14 leading, Times, justified, with 50 Max. Letter Spacing. Add an additional 8 points between each paragraph.

   ▪ Notice the extreme letter spacing in the last paragraph.

5. Hang indent the bullet outside the container.

   ▪ The bullet in the sample shown has a negative value of −9 pt.

6. Click the Auto Hyphenate box in the Paragraph palette to let Illustrator hyphenate the text using the specifications in the Hyphenation Options dialog box.

7. Display the Hyphenation Options dialog box and change the fields to match the fields as shown in Figure 5.9. Click OK or press *return/enter.*

8. Place the cursor in the paragraph that begins "If possible . . ." and check the Hang Punctuation checkbox in the Paragraph palette.

   ▪ Notice that the hyphens at the ends of the lines extend outside the righthand side of the container.

9. Uncheck the Hang Punctuation checkbox.

10. Select all the text in the container and uncheck the Auto Hyphenate box.

    ▪ Notice what happens to the text.

11. Position the cursor between the *y* and the *p* in *hyphenated* on the second line of the second paragraph, and press ⇧⌘- to hyphenate the word to make the spacing better.

    ▪ Turn on the Show Hidden Characters option in the Type menu if you want to see the discretionary hyphen character and the spacebars.

12. Hyphenate the word *compound* (compound) in the third paragraph, the word *hyphenating* (hyphenating) in the fourth paragraph by entering discretionary hyphens.

    ▪ The spacing still looks pretty awful.

13. Select all the type in the container and change the alignment to flush left.

    ▪ Notice that the Min. and Max. fields in the Word Spacing and Letter Spacing sections of the Paragraph palette are gray, because those values are only applied to justified type.

14. Save the file, print it, and close the artwork window.

> • Never hyphenate a word after only one character.
>
> • The second half of a hyphenated word must have at least three characters—and punctuation doesn't count.
>
> • Don't hyphenate a compound word (two words joined by a hyphen), such as moderate-impact, except at the hyphen. In other words, don't hyphenate a hyphenated word.
>
> • If possible, avoid hyphenating the last word in a paragraph.
>
> • Don't hyphenate words when the result affects readability. For example, even though the word people has two syllables and can "legally" be hyphenated, peo-ple can make for awkward reading. So can mus-cle.

Smart Punctuation

When typing on a typewriter, "dumb" punctuation is all that is available because of the limitations of the keys on the typewriter. For example, an em dash (—) key isn't available so two hyphens are used instead. Quotation marks are straight and look more like inch marks than the more professional "curly" quotes. Adobe Illustrator 10 has a command in the Type menu called Smart Punctuation that allows you to convert typewriter punctuation into professional typesetting characters.

Unfortunately, the Smart Punctuation feature is not automatic. When you type characters in your document, typewriter punctuation is used. You have to apply the Smart Punctuation command (**Type ➪ Smart Punctuation**) to convert the characters to professional typesetting characters. Changes you make in the Smart Punctuation dialog box (Figure 5.11) that displays are remembered for future documents until you restore default Preferences.

You can choose to convert only highlighted characters to Smart Punctuation by choosing Selected Text Only in the Replace In section of the dialog box. To convert all characters in the document without having to highlight them, choose the Entire Document option. Attempting to apply the Smart Punctuation command to text selected with the Direct Selection tool causes an alert box to display warning that the text hasn't been selected, indicating that the text must be *highlighted* with the Type tool. Because of the problem with the En, Em Dashes (--) option (see the next section), I prefer to keep the default Selected Text Only option chosen.

Typewriter quotes

"Curly" quotes

 Once characters are converted to Smart Punctuation, they can't be converted back to "dumb" punctuation by unchecking the option in the Smart Punctuation dialog box. You have to select the characters and re-enter them manually.

FIGURE 5.11
Smart Punctuation dialog box.

Replace Punctuation

When checked, the option is on. If the checkbox is blank, characters aren't automatically converted.

- **ff, fi, ffi Ligatures** (fl, fi, ffi) and **ff, fl, ffl Ligatures** (fl, fi, ffi) — Converts the particular combinations of letters into single distinctive characters.

  - *Macintosh only:* Most serif fonts contain fi and fl ligatures. The ff, ffi, and ffl ligatures are present only on the Adobe Expert font set for a particular typeface.

  - *Windows:* The Adobe Expert font set for the font you're using must be available on your computer to have access to ligatures.

- **Smart Quotes** (" ") — Converts straight quotes (") and straight apostrophes (') to curly quotes (" ") and curly apostrophes (' ').

  - *Macintosh only:* You can type curly quotes and apostrophes from the keyboard: ⌥[= "; ⇧ ⌥[= "; ⌥] = '; ⇧ ⌥[= '.

- **Smart Spaces** (.) — Converts two spaces after a period to one space.

- **En, Em Dashes** (--) — This option is the reason I apply Smart Punctuation only to highlighted text and not the entire document. The traditional typewriter method of displaying an em dash (also called a long dash) is by typing two hyphens. Unfortunately, Illustrator converts two hyphens to an *en* dash rather than an *em* dash when the Smart Punctuation command is applied to text. An em dash and an en dash are not interchangeable grammatically, so an en dash should never be used in place of an em dash.

  Illustrator converts three hyphens in a row (---) to an em dash. If you don't want to enter three hyphens in a row, you can type the em dash character by pressing ⇧ ⌥- (hyphen) (*Macintosh*) or hold down the ⌥ key and press 0151 on the numeric keypad (*Windows*).

  - An em dash is used to separate a parenthetical phrase — a phrase that is unnecessary but adds clarity to the sentence. It's also used to denote a sudden break in thought or before an expression such as *that is*, *namely*, and so on.

  - An en dash is longer than a hyphen but is shorter than an em dash and is most commonly used between numbers denoting continuing times, dates, and so on. Examples of where an en dash should be used are: June–July 2002, pp. 65–45, 10:00–11:00 A.M.

- **Ellipses** (...) — Replaces three periods in a row — the way most people type an ellipsis — with the special ellipsis symbol (...), which has thin spaces on each side of the three "dots" in the string. Generally accepted typography allows the use of a period with regular spaces before and after each period (. . . . . .) in type that is set flush left.

Ligature characters

- **Expert Fractions** — If you have the Adobe Expert font set for the font you're using loaded on your computer, click this checkbox to access the fractions on that font. If you don't have the Adobe Expert font set, build your own fractions as described previously in the Baseline Shift section of this chapter.

Report Results

When this checkbox at the bottom of the dialog box is checked, a box displays after characters are converted telling you how many and what kind of characters were replaced. If you don't want to see this box, uncheck the Report Results checkbox. I usually uncheck this option because I don't usually care how many characters were changed.

 *activity 5.19*

1. Create a new document: Letter size, CMYK color mode.

2. In the Character palette, specify the type to be 24 pt Times Roman with Auto leading.
   - *Windows:* 24 pt Times New Roman

3. Choose the Type tool (press *t*) and create a type container that's approximately 5" × 3". Enter the following text in the type container:

   "Plan a week's stay in two of Colorado's premier winter vacation cities--Vail and Aspen. During your flight over our majestic mountains, you'll see crystalline lakes, fields of flowers..."

   - Put two spaces after the period at the end of the first sentence.
   - Notice that the quotes are straight typewriter quotes.

4. Zoom in as much as possible and still be able to see all the type and turn on the Show Hidden Characters option in the View menu.

5. With the Type tool, select (highlight) the two hyphens in the first sentence.

6. Display the Smart Punctuation dialog box and click the Selected Text Only button. Click the En, Em Dashes (--) checkbox and uncheck all other checkboxes. Uncheck Report Results. Click OK or press *return/enter*.
   - The hyphens are replaced with an en dash.

7. Because we want an em dash rather than an en dash, highlight the en dash character and replace it by entering the em dash character.
   - *Macintosh:* Press ⇧ ⌥- (hyphen)
   - *Windows:* Hold down the ⌥ key and press 0151 on the numeric keypad.

8. Highlight the two spaces after the end of the first sentence.

9. Display the Smart Punctuation dialog box and check the Smart Spaces checkbox. Click OK or press *return/enter*.
   - One space is removed, leaving only one.

10. Deselect all the type.

11. Display the Smart Punctuation dialog box and check all the checkboxes except Expert Fractions in the Replace Punctuation section. Click the Entire Document button then click OK or press *return/enter*.
   - It may take several seconds to complete the conversions so don't get impatient.

12. Notice that the quotes are now "curly" quotes. Look at the words *flight, fields,* and *flowers* in the last sentence. The "fl" and "fi" characters have been converted into ligatures.
   - To see the original and then the converted characters, toggle the Undo and Redo commands: Undo is ⌘z, and Redo is ⇧⌘z.

Continued

- **Windows:** The ligature function isn't available.

13. Try to place the Insertion marker between the fl or fi characters in these words. You can't because they're now a single combined character.

14. Notice the difference in the ellipses (...). You can't put the insertion marker between the periods because they're combined into a single character, too.

15. Close the document without saving it to a file.

Importing Type

Type created in other programs and saved in ASCII text format, including SimpleText (Macintosh) and WordPad (Windows), and Microsoft Word files can be imported into Illustrator documents using the Place command. ASCII text files retain minimal text formatting, but Microsoft Word documents, including those saved in the Rich Text format, keep most of their text formatting.

fyi ASCII is pronounced ask-ee and is an acronym for American Standard Code for Information Interchange.

1. Choose **File ➪ Place**.
   - The Place dialog box displays (similar to the Open dialog box).

2. Navigate through your files to locate the name of the file you want to import, and highlight it.

3. Click the Place button.
   - If the file you're importing is ASCII text, the Text Import Options dialog box displays (Figure 5.12). Choose the options you want and click OK or press *return/enter*.
     - **Encoding** — Choose the platform (Windows or Macintosh) that was used to create the file. Choose a Character Set from the pop-up submenu. ANSI is the selection for most files.

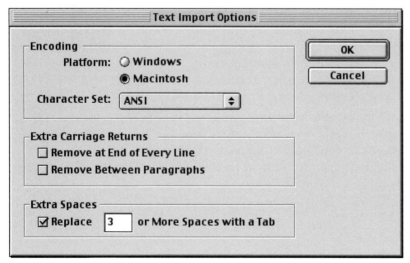

✓ ANSI
UNICODE
Shift JIS
GB2312
Chinese Big 5
Cyrillic

Options available in the Character Set pop-up submenu

FIGURE 5.12 The Text Import Options dialog box displays when you place text saved in the ASCII format.

207

- **Extra Carriage Returns** — Two options are provided for determining how carriage returns in the imported file will be handled by Illustrator.

- **Extra Spaces** — Click to check the Replace checkbox if you want multiple spaces in a row replaced with a tab. Enter a number in the field to specify the minimum number of spaces in a row that will be replaced with a tab.

- Click OK or press *return/enter* to exit the dialog box.

■ The file is displayed on the Illustrator page in a type rectangle. You can change its size and shape the same way you would if you had drawn the type rectangle with the Type tool.

■ If a font is used in the imported file that isn't available when the file is imported, a warnings box displays telling you that a default font will be substituted.

■ To put the placed type inside an irregularly shaped text container, select the text with the Type tool, then copy and paste it into the type container. Formatting, if there is any, is kept intact.

Importing Text Created in Microsoft® Word

Illustrator supports files created in Microsoft Word 6, 95, 97, 98, and 2000, and it's coded file format, Rich Text Format. Most formatting commands are successfully retained when imported into an Illustrator document. Some exceptions are:

■ **Typeface** — The typeface of the original document is retained unless it isn't installed on your computer. In that event, the default font, Myriad, is substituted.

■ **Type styling** — Some type styles, such as italic, bold, superscript, and subscript, are imported successfully. Others, such as small caps, underline, and so on, are not.

■ **Tabs** — The *Tab* character is imported successfully, but the tab stops and tab leaders are not. Tab stops must be reset in Illustrator. Refer to the Tabs section later in this chapter.

■ **Automatic leading** — If automatic leading is applied to text in the Microsoft Word document, Illustrator assigns its default automatic leading of 120% of the point size of the type.

■ **Special characters and functions specific to Microsoft Word** — Special characters that aren't part of the standard character set, such as em spaces, and special functions, such as automatic page numbering and page breaks, aren't imported with the text. Discretionary hyphens, though, are imported.

If fonts used in the imported document are not installed on your computer, a warning displays indicating that fonts will be substituted.

Importing Text Created in a Page Layout Program

You can import type that was created in a page layout program, such as QuarkXPress, and saved in EPS format. Open the file as an Illustrator EPS file using the Open command to open the file. Unfortunately, though, the type displays as Point type blocks. In most cases, each line has its own alignment point. Changes in typeface generate a new alignment point for text, too.

Link Multiple Text Blocks

When type overflows a type container, you can enlarge the container or you can flow it into another linked container. This allows you to create several columns of text or to flow type to additional pages. You can't link type attached to an alignment point or type that flows along a path. You can flow type into two or more containers by linking selected objects or by drag-copying the original container.

- Select one of the linked type containers with the Selection tool to select all type containers that are linked to it.

- To select an individual container in a linked chain of text blocks, select it with the Direct Selection tool.

- Triple-clicking with the Type tool selects an entire paragraph, even if part of it is in another linked type container.

- If you click in one of the linked type containers and apply the Select All command ($\mathcal{H}$a), all type in all linked type containers is selected.

Using the Link Command

1. With the Direct Selection tool, select the type container (not the type).

2. *Shift*-click to select another path or marquee so both paths are selected.

3. Choose **Type ➪ Blocks ➪ Link**.

   - Overflow text from the first path automatically flows into the second object.

   - The second path doesn't have to be a type container, because it's automatically converted to one when the Link command is applied. Any fill or stroke attributes are removed automatically.

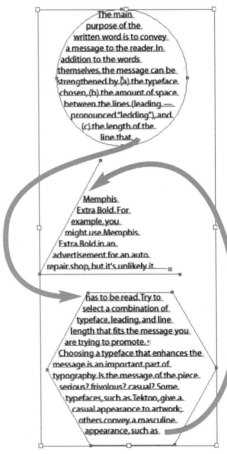

Type is linked from the top shape to the bottom shape, then to the middle shape, causing the text to flow into the shapes in that order

209

- Paths are filled according to their stacking order, starting with paths at the back of the stack and working forward. If the second path was created before the original text container, which places it behind the original text container, the beginning of the text block shifts to start in the second path.

- Using the Arrange commands in the Object menu (**Bring to Front, Send to Back, Bring Forward, Send Backward**), rearrange the stacking order of the type containers until they flow through the containers in the proper order.

- You can move object layers in the Layers palette to rearrange stacking order of objects on a page, too.

Drag-Copying to Link Text Blocks

1. Deselect all type containers.

2. With the Direct Selection tool, hold down the ⌥ key and click on the pathline of the type container to select it, with all the anchor points solid (selected).

   - Verify that the type isn't underlined, because you don't want it to be selected.
     - If the type inside a container is selected when you drag, a duplicate copy of the object and the type is created, but text won't be linked.

3. Drag the container to a new position. Release the mouse before releasing the ⌥ key.

   - Type flows automatically into the cloned type container and it's automatically linked to the original container.

   - Because the cloned type container is always created after the original type container, there's never a problem with the stacking order of the type containers like there is when the Link command is used.

4. Continue drag-copying type containers until all the type is visible.

   - To create additional linked clones, press ⌘d or choose **Object** ⇨ **Transform** ⇨ **Transform Again**. Transform commands are discussed in Step 9, *Reshape, Combine, & Distort Objects*.

Unlinking Text Blocks

Unlink text blocks by selecting the text blocks and choosing **Type** ⇨ **Blocks** ⇨ **Unlink**. When type containers are unlinked, type no longer flows from one to the other. They're independent text blocks and behave as if they were created separately from the others in the chain. There's no way to relink them automatically.

To relink text that's in text containers that have been unlinked, cut the text from the unlinked containers (one container at a time), and paste it back into the original container (in the proper order, of course). Then choose new containers and link them to reflow the type.

read this!

If unlinked type containers are deleted, the type in those containers is lost. It can't reflow to another container because it's no longer linked.

Deleting a Linked Text Container

If you delete a container containing linked type, the text flows automatically to the next container in the chain. If there isn't another container linked after the deleted container, the overflow symbol displays in the last remaining container.

 *activity 5.20*

1. Create a new document: Letter size, CMYK color mode.

2. Choose File ⇨ Place, locate the file named Typography ASCII.txt that's in the Student Files folder on the CD-ROM that accompanies this book, and click Place or press *return/enter*.

3. When the Text Import Options dialog box displays, verify that the platform is correct and that ANSI is the Character Set. Click OK or press *return/enter*.

   ■ The file is imported into the open Illustrator document in a type rectangle.

4. Select the rectangle with the Selection tool and drag it out of the way.

5. Draw about a 2½" circle on the page. Apply the Blue color swatch from the Swatches palette. Deselect the path.

6. Skip about 3" below the circle and draw a 2½" polygon. Apply the 75% Yellow swatch, then deselect the shape.

7. Between the circle and the polygon draw two legs of a triangle with the Pen tool. Click first at the top then move down about 2" and to the left about 1" and click, then horizontally to the right 2" and click. Apply the Red color swatch. Deselect the path.

   ■ Leave the shape as an open path.

8. With the Type tool, click in the text that was Placed on the page and press ⌘a to select all the type.

9. Copy the type by pressing ⌘c.

10. Choose the Area Type tool in the Toolbox, and click on the pathline of the circle.

    ■ The fill color is removed and the Insertion marker blinks at the top left of the shape.

11. Press ⌘v to paste the copied text into the shape.

    ■ Notice the Overflow symbol at the bottom right side of the container.

12. With the Selection tool, marquee to select all the shapes.

13. Choose Type ⇨ Blocks ⇨ Link.

    ■ The triangle and the polygon are converted to type containers and, if you read through the text, you'll find that the type flows from the first shape that was drawn (the circle) into the second shape that was drawn (the polygon), and then into the triangle.

    ■ Notice that Illustrator pretended that the two endpoints of the triangle were connected and the type was wrapped according to this imaginary line.

14. With the Direct Selection tool, click on the polygon, then choose Object ⇨ Arrange ⇨ Bring to Front. Deselect all.

    ■ The stacking order of the objects is rearranged and the type flows through the objects in the proper order.

15. With the Direct Selection tool, ⌥-click on the path of the triangle to select it with its anchor points solid.

    ■ To find the pathline of the type container, move the pointer around the edge of the triangle until the solid box displays on the pointer (▸▪). Then press the ⌥ key and click.

    ■ Make sure the type is not selected (underlined) or it will be erased in the next step, too.

Continued

16. Press the *delete* key to delete the container.
    - The type automatically flowed to the next container in the chain.

17. Using the Place command, import the file named Typography Word.doc that's in the Student Files folder on the CD-ROM that accompanies this book.
    - Notice that formatting attributes such as typeface, point size, leading, and alignment was retained when the Microsoft Word file was imported into the Illustrator document.

18. Select the rectangle with the Selection tool and drag it out of the way.

19. With the Type tool, click in the imported type rectangle, press ⌘ a to select all the text, then copy it (⌘ c).

20. In a blank area of the page, draw a 2" wide × 2" high type rectangle with the Type tool.
    - Use the Info palette to verify the size of the rectangle as you draw it.

21. Paste (⌘ v) the copied type into the type rectangle.
    - Notice the Overflow symbol at the lower right edge of the rectangle, indicating that the type didn't all fit into the container.

22. Deselect the rectangle.

23. Choose the Direct Selection tool (press *a*) and position the pointer over the path of the container until the black box displays. Hold down the ⬦ key and click and drag the container down to a blank spot on the page so that it doesn't overlap the original shape. Release the mouse before you release the ⬦ key.
    - A copy of the first container is created and overflow type from the original container flows into it.

24. Continue drag-copying containers until all the type is visible in a container.

25. With the Selection tool (press *v*), marquee to select all of these containers.

26. Choose Type ⇨ Blocks ⇨ Unlink to unlink the type containers.

27. With the Selection tool, select one of the middle containers and press the *delete* key to delete it.
    - The container and the type are deleted and the type doesn't flow into another container because it's no longer linked. It's a stand-alone object.

28. Close this document without saving it to a file.

Creating Rows and Columns

The Rows and Columns command in the Type menu converts one or more objects into a specified number of equally sized and spaced linked objects that are aligned in columns and rows. If the original object contains type, any overflow text flows to the next container in the manner you specify in the Rows & Columns dialog box.

- All selected objects, regardless of their original shape, are converted to rectangles or squares.
- If you select more than one type container, the containers must be linked to be able to convert them to Rows & Columns.

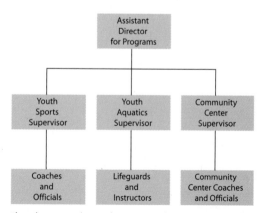

Flow chart created using the Rows & Columns command

- Units of measurement are displayed in the current units specified for the document. Units of measurement are discussed in Step 6, *Rulers, Grids, & Guides*.

- The alignment of type in the original container(s) is retained when the Rows & Columns command is applied. That is, if the type was centered in the type container before the Rows & Columns was applied, it will be centered in the rectangles after the Rows & Columns command is applied.

- Fill and stroke attributes applied to a selected object are retained when the Rows & Columns command is applied. For example, if the selected object has a 1 pt black stroke, the resulting rectangles after the Rows & Columns command is applied have a 1 pt black stroke, too.

To create objects in a specified number of rows and columns:

1. Select one or more objects.

2. Display the Rows & Columns dialog box (Figure 5.13) by choosing **Type ⇨ Rows & Columns**.

3. Check the Preview checkbox so you can see your changes immediately.

4. Enter values in the Rows and Columns fields or click the arrows to the left of the fields to change field values.

   - **Number** — The number of rows and the number of columns you want to create.

   - **Height/Width** — The height of each row and the width of each column.
     - The value in the Height field must be less than the value in the Total field in the Rows section divided by the number of rows.
     - The value in the Width field must be less than the value in the Total field in the Columns section divided by the number of columns.

fyi To create a checkerboard pattern, the values in both Number fields and both Total fields must be the same; the values in the Height and Width fields must be equal and they must match both Gutter values.

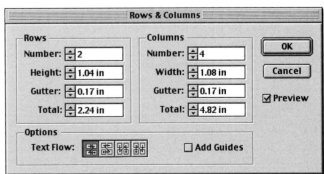

FIGURE 5.13
Rows & Columns
dialog box.

- Values entered into the fields that are too large, based on the size specified in the Total field, will be rejected. But you can change the overall size of the objects by increasing the value in the Total field.

■ **Gutter** — Specify the amount of space you want between each row and between each column.

- To keep the space between each object, the value in the Rows Gutter field should be the same as the Columns Gutter field.

■ **Total** — These fields determine the overall size of all the objects. When the dialog box is first displayed, the values in these fields is the overall size of the bounding box that surrounds the selected objects.

- In the Rows section, enter the overall height of all the rows of objects.

- In the Columns section, enter the total width of all the columns.

■ **Text Flow** — Click one of the buttons to choose how you want the text to flow from one object to another In the sample at the right:

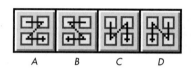

- **A** — Text flows from left to right, then to the next row.

- **B** — Text flows from right to left, then to the next row.

- **C** — Text flows from top to bottom of the first column, then from top to bottom of the next column on the right.

- **D** — Text flows from top to bottom of the last column, then from top to bottom of the next column on the left.

■ **Add Guides** — When this checkbox is checked, ruler guides are placed around each object. Ruler Guides are discussed in Step 6, *Rulers, Grids, & Guides*.

■ **Preview** — When this checkbox is checked, you can enter a value in a field, then click in a different field to see your changes applied to the object. Or you can click the checkbox to turn Preview off, then click again to turn it back on to see the changes to the object.

- Values entered into the fields in the Rows & Columns dialog box are adjusted automatically to fill the size specified in the Total field in the Rows section (height) and the Columns section (width). The Number fields and the Total fields in both sections remain constant, with the Height/Weight and Gutter fields adjusting. That is, if the Gutter value is increased, the Column width or Row width decreases, and vice versa.

5. Click OK or press *return/enter*.

Exporting Type

Type created in Illustrator can be exported as plain text (ASCII text). Text characters in a container, along a path, or attached to an alignment point can be exported, but the characters must be highlighted. You can't select text with the Selection tool or the Direct Selection tool to export it. With the Type tool active, select them:

- By dragging across them.
- By clicking, then *Shift*-clicking to select chunks at a time.
- By clicking in a type container and pressing ⌘ a or choosing **Select** ⇨ **All**.

When the type you want to export is selected:

1. Choose **File** ⇨ **Export** to display the Export dialog box, which looks like the Save dialog box.
2. Navigate to the folder or disk where you want the file saved.
3. Choose Text Format (TXT) from the Format pop-up menu (***Windows:*** Save as type)
4. *Macintosh:* Check the Append File Extension checkbox if you want the .txt file extension added to the file name.
   - If Append File Extension is checked, the Lower Case checkbox is available. Check this box if you want the file extension to appear in lower case characters.
   - ***Windows:*** The .txt file extension is automatically added to the file name.
5. Enter a name for the text file in the Name field (***Windows:*** File name).
6. Click Export (***Windows:*** Save) or press *return/enter.*

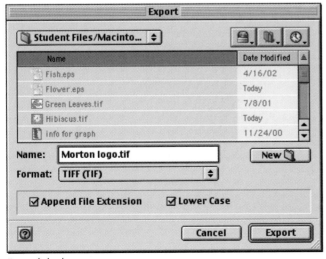

Export dialog box

AutoCAD Drawing (DWG)
AutoCAD Interchange File (DXF)
BMP (BMP)
Computer Graphics Metafile (CGM)
Enhanced Metafile (EMF)
JPEG (JPG)
Macintosh PICT (PCT)
Macromedia Flash (SWF)
PCX (PCX)
Photoshop (PSD)
Pixar (PXR)
Targa (TGA)
Text Format (TXT)
✓ TIFF (TIF)
Windows Metafile (WMF)

File formats available for exporting Illustrator 10 files for use in other programs

activity 5.21

1. Create a new document: Letter size, CMYK color mode. Name it Rows & Columns Practice.eps and save it into your practice folder as an .eps file.

2. Draw a rectangle on the page that's about 5" × 3" and fill it with 100% cyan, 15% magenta, 45% yellow, and 0% black. Specify a 2 pt 50% black stroke.

3. If possible, position the Rows & Columns dialog box and the selected object on the screen so you can see both of them, or at least most of the object.

4. With the rectangle still selected (select it with the Selection tool if it isn't selected), choose Type ⇨ Rows & Columns to display the Rows & Columns dialog box.

5. Enter 4 in both Number fields and enter 12 pt in both Gutter fields. Click OK or press *return/enter*.

   ■ Notice that the fill and stroke color and the stroke weight are the same as what you applied to the rectangle before applying the Rows & Columns command.

6. With the objects selected, display the Rows & Columns dialog box again and change the Rows Gutter field to 6 pt, then click in a different field so you can see the changes it makes to the object.

   ■ Notice that the value in the Height field changed to accommodate the new Gutter size and the space between the rows became narrower.

7. Change the Columns Gutter field to 18 pts and click in a different field.

   ■ Notice that the value in the Width field changed to accommodate the new Gutter size and the space between the columns became wider.

8. Change the number of Columns to 5.

   ■ Notice that the value in the Width field changed to accommodate the increased number of objects, but the gutter value remained the same.

9. Click OK or press *return/enter*.

10. Delete all the objects.

11. Choose File ⇨ Place and locate the file named Addresses.doc that's in the Student Files folder on the CD-ROM that came with this book. Click Place or press *return/enter*.

   ■ The type is imported into the document inside a type container. It's centered, with the phone numbers boldface.

12. With the Selection tool, select the type container and display the Rows & Columns dialog box.

   ■ If possible, position the Rows & Columns dialog box and the imported type on the screen so you can see both of them, or at least most of the type.

13. Change the values as follows:

Rows	Columns
Number: 2	Number: 3
Height: 45 pt	Width: 132 pt
Gutter: 18 pt	Gutter: 18 pt
Total: 108 pts	Total: 432 pts

Flow Options: Select the first button (By Rows, Left to Right)

Add Guides: Unchecked

14. Uncheck and recheck the Preview checkbox to see the changes that were applied.

   ■ Notice the order the names were placed into the separate type containers. They flowed across the first row then down and across the second row.

15. Click the second Flow Options button (By Rows, Right to Left). If necessary, uncheck and recheck the Preview checkbox to see how the type flowed through the type containers.

16. Repeat #15 with the other Flow Options buttons, and pay attention to how the type was placed in the type containers.

17. Click OK or press *return/enter*.

18. Save the file and close the document window.

Tabs

Because characters have varying widths, using spaces to align columns isn't efficient and actually takes more time than storing tab stops. Using the Tab Ruler palette (Figure 5.14), you can set custom tabs that align left, center, right, and at a decimal point in type set horizontally. When applied to vertical type, the tabs are top, center, bottom, and decimal point.

	Game 1	Game 2	Game 3
Mary	136	153	142
Patricia	160	154	172
Donna	168	174	220

If you have a type container selected when the Tab Ruler palette is displayed, the palette displays the same width as the selected type container. If you display the Tab Ruler palette before selecting a type container, you can widen or shorten it by dragging the Reshape box at the bottom right corner of the palette.

Tab stops are specified in the Tab Ruler (**Window ⇨ Type ⇨ Tab Ruler** or press ⇧ ⌘ t). Default tab stops are set every half inch, but they disappear from the tab marker in the area of the Tab Ruler where tab stops are set. They still display on the right side of the last tab marker. To move text from one tab stop to the next press the *Tab* key on the keyboard.

 When you zoom in or out, the Tab Ruler palette doesn't adjust size to match. You have to resize the palette manually and move it into position.

Setting Custom Tab Stops

You can set up the tab stops before you enter text or enter the text, select it, then specify the tab stops. You can select all the text in a container, even if it isn't to be tabbed, because tabs don't affect text until a tab character is inserted.

To specify custom tab stops:

1. Select the type container holding the tabbed type.

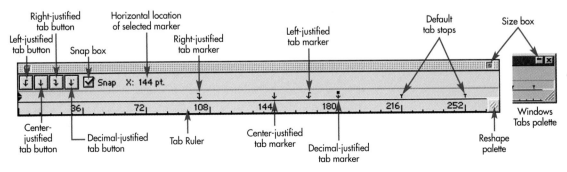

FIGURE 5.14 The Tab Ruler palette — Macintosh.

2. Choose **Window** ⇨ **Type** ⇨ **Tab Ruler** or press to display ⇧ ⌘ t to display the Tab Ruler.

   ■ Measurements in the Tab Ruler use the Artboard Units selection in the pop-up submenu of the Document Setup dialog box. This selection may be different from the unit of measurement in the Units & Undo Preferences dialog box. Units of measurement are discussed in Step 6, *Rulers, Grids, & Guides*.

3. Click in the Tab Ruler at the bottom of the palette (or in the blank area just above it) to place a Left-justified tab marker at the point of your click.

4. Click a tab alignment button (Center, Right, Decimal) to assign a different alignment to the tab marker.

   or

   ⍓-click a tab marker to cycle through the alignment types.

   ■ Click the Snap box to cause a tab marker to snap to the nearest ruler tick mark as you drag the marker to the left or right.

      ▪ If the Snap box is checked, turn it off temporarily by holding down the ⌘ key as you drag a tab marker. If the Snap box is unchecked, turn the Snap feature on temporarily by holding down the ⌘ key as you drag a tab marker.

   ■ The position of a selected tab marker from the edge of a container or from an alignment point is displayed in the Horizontal Location area (X) of the palette.

Move a Tab Marker To move an existing tab marker, drag the marker to the left or right along the Tab ruler and release the mouse. To move all the markers that are to the right of the selected marker at the same time you drag the selected marker, hold the *Shift* key down as you move a marker.

   ■ When a tab marker is moved, a vertical line displays in the text to indicate the new position of the tab marker.

   ■ A question mark displaying in the tab marker area of the Tabs palette indicates that not all selected lines have the same tab stops applied to them. Click the question mark to apply the same tab stops to every line.

Delete a Tab Marker To delete an existing tab marker, drag the marker up and off the Tabs ruler. When you hold the *Shift* key down as you drag a tab marker off the palette, all tab markers to the right of the selected tab are deleted, too. So to delete all the tab markers at the same time, *Shift*-drag the leftmost tab marker.

   ■ The Horizontal Location area displays *delete* when a tab marker is dragged off the palette.

activity 5.22

1. Create a new document: Letter size, CMYK color mode. Name it Tabs Practice.eps and save it into your Practice Folder as an .eps file.

2. Choose the Type tool in the Toolbox and create a type rectangle about 396 pt (5.8") wide, 90 pt (1.25") high. Type the following text in the type rectangle (insert a tab character in place of [tab]):

   Dress shoes[tab]Oxfords[tab]Brown[tab]$69.95
   Shoes[tab]High-Top Athletic[tab]Black[tab]44.95
   Shoelaces[tab]Long[tab]White[tab]2.95

3. Format the type to 12 pt Myriad, 24 pt leading.

4. Display the Tab Ruler (choose Window ➪ Type ➪ Tab Ruler or press ⇧⌘t). Move the Tab Ruler palette so it's just above the type block. Lengthen it so it's the same width as the type container.

5. Select the text.

6. Click on the left-justified tab button, then click in the marker area of the Tab Ruler palette to place a left-justified tab marker. Drag to position it at 108 pt (1.5"), then release the mouse.
   - Watch the horizontal location display at the top of the palette to position the tab marker.
   - Numbers may include decimals when you position a tab on the Tab Ruler. Position the tab marker as close as you can to the whole number.

7. Click in the tab marker area and place a tab marker at 223 pt (3.09"). Then click the right-justified tab button to change the tab marker to right-justified.

8. Place a decimal tab at 336 pt (4.667").
   - Notice that the figure aligns at the decimal point, regardless how many characters are in the number.

9. Click on the right-justified tab marker you placed in #7 above, and drag it off the Tab Ruler palette.
   - Notice that "delete" displays in the location area at the top of the palette.

10. Click in the tab marker area and place a tab marker at 262 pt (3.6"). Then click the center-justified tab button to change the tab marker to center-justified.

11. Close the Tab Ruler palette.

12. Choose the Rectangular Grid tool (▦) in the Toolbox. Click on the page to display the Rectangular Grid Tool Options dialog box. Enter the following values, then click OK or press return/enter.
    - Width: 375 pt (5.2")
    - Height: 77 pt (1.07")
    - Horizontal Dividers: 2, no skew
    - Vertical Dividers: 3, no skew
    - Check Use Outside Rectangle As Frame
    - Uncheck Fill Grid

13. Change the fill of the rectangular grid object to None and apply a 1 pt black stroke. Drag it into position over the tabbed text.

14. Deselect the rectangular grid object. Choose the Direct Selection tool (press a), hold the Shift key down, then click and drag the vertical dividers (one at a time) into position to separate the columns.

Dress shoes	Oxfords	Brown	$69.95
Tennis shoes	High-top athletic	Black	44.95
Shoelaces	Long	White	2.95

15. Save the file and close the artwork window.

Find and Replace Text

Use the Find/Change command in the Type menu to search for and replace words and characters in a document. Or, you can use the dialog box to locate text in the document without replacing it with new text. You can search the entire document or only part of it.

To search all text in an entire document, select a type block or type container with the Selection tool. To search only part of a document, click in a type block at the point you want to begin the search. Illustrator searches from that point forward and doesn't search any text entered before the Insertion marker.

To search for text and replace it with new text:

1. Select a type block with the Selection tool or click in a type block.

2. Choose **Type** ⇨ **Find/Change** to display the Find/Change dialog box (Figure 5.15).

3. In the Find what field, enter the text you want to search for.

4. In the Change to field, enter the text you want to change the "found" text to.

    ■ You can copy text in the document and paste it into either the Find what or Change to field.

    ■ If you are trying to find text and don't want to make changes to it, leave this field blank.

5. Make desired changes in the checkboxes:

    ■ **Whole Word** — Check this box to find text only if it's a whole word, not part of a larger word. For example, if *part* is the word in the Find what field, *party* won't be found if this box is checked.

    ■ **Search Backward** — To search before the Insertion marker rather than after it, check this box.

    ■ **Case Sensitive** — When this box is checked, only the exact match with regard to uppercase and lowercase letters will be found. For example, when checked, if *Party* is the word in the Find what field, *party* won't be found.

read this!

Illustrator can't find words or characters that have been converted to outlines. See Create Outlines later in this chapter.

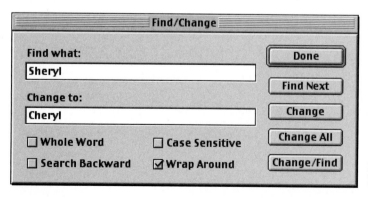

FIGURE 5.15
Find/Change dialog box.

- **Wrap Around** — When this box is checked, Illustrator searches from the Insertion marker to the end of the type block or linked type objects, then wraps around to the top and searches until it reaches the Insertion marker.

6. Click the Find Next button to highlight the first occurrence of the word.

7. Click Find Next to skip that occurrence and search for the next occurrence.

   or

   Click Change to replace the text with the text in the Change to field.

   or

   Click Change All to replace all occurrences of the text in the Find what field with the text in the Change to field at one time.

   or

   Click Change/Find to replace the text and search for the next occurrence. If one is found, you have the option again of clicking any of the four buttons.

   - Changed text retains the type attributes of the text it's replacing.

8. Click Done or press *return/enter* when you're finished searching.

 *activity 5.23*

1. Create a new document: Letter size, CMYK color mode. Name it Find/Change Practice.eps and save it into your Practice folder as an .eps file.

2. Choose File ➪ Place and locate the file named Find/Change text.txt that's in the Student Files folder on the CD-ROM that's in the back of this book.

3. Choose Macintosh platform, ANSI character set, and uncheck all the other checkboxes. Click OK or press *return/enter*.

   - The type container displays with the text selected.

4. With the type still selected, choose Type ➪ Find/Change to display the Find/Change dialog box. Check the Case Sensitive and Wrap Around checkboxes.

5. Position the dialog box so you can see both the text and the dialog box at the same time.

6. Type *illustrator* — lower case i — in the Find What field and click the Find Next button.

   - Nothing can be found because there's no word illustrator with a lower case i in the document.

7. Type *document* in the Find What field and *documents* in the Change To field.

8. Click the Change/Find button.

   - The first occurrence of the word *document* is changed to *documents* and the next occurrence is highlighted.

9. Continue clicking the Change/Find button 10 or 12 times.

   - Because Wrap Around is checked, Illustrator starts back at the top and continues searching and replacing.

10. Uncheck the Case Sensitive and Wrap Around checkboxes. Click Done or press *return/enter*.

11. Choose the Type tool in the Toolbox and click after the period at the end of the first paragraph.

12. Display the Find/Change dialog box again and type *text* in the Find What field. Then click the Find Next button to find the first occurrence of the word *text* after the Insertion marker. Continue clicking the Find Next button until all occurrences have been located.

   - The search stopped at the end of the document because the Wrap Around checkbox was unchecked.

13. Click Done or press *return/enter*.

14. Save the file and close the artwork window.

Find and Replace a Font

The Find Font command in the Type menu can be used to generate a list of the fonts used in a document or to replace one font with another font. You can also save a list of the fonts as a separate text file, which is helpful if you take the file to a service bureau for printing.

1. Choose **Type** ⇨ **Find Font** to display the Find Font dialog box (Figure 5.16).

2. To display only certain types of fonts in the Fonts in Document window, check that specific box at the bottom of the dialog box. To display Multiple Master fonts, check both the Type 1 and the Multiple Master checkboxes because Multiple Master fonts are Type 1 fonts.

3. Choose Document in the Replace Font From pop-up submenu to display all fonts used in the current document.

    or

    Choose System in the Replace Font From pop-up submenu to display all fonts currently installed on the computer — of the type selected in the checkboxes at the bottom of the dialog box.

4. To replace a font used in a document with another font, highlight the font you want to replace in the Fonts in Document window and choose the font you want to replace it with in the Replace Fonts From window. The first instance of

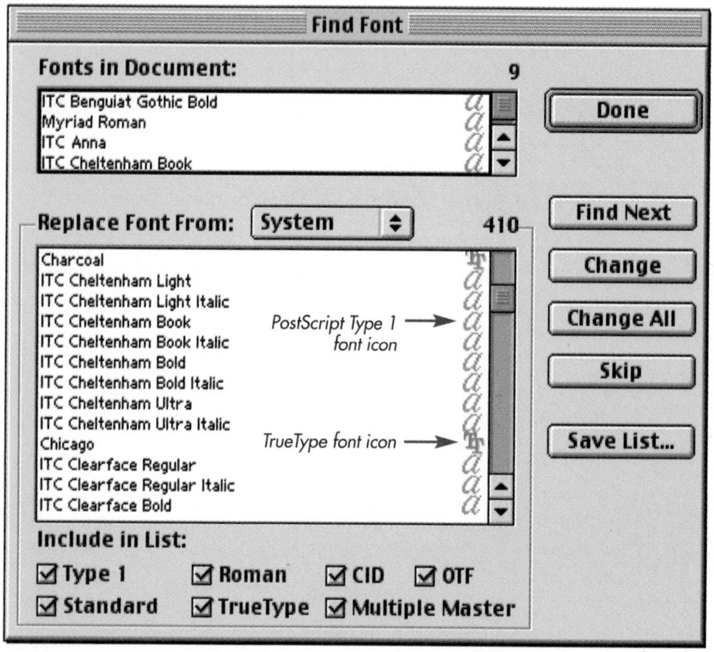

FIGURE 5.16
Find Font dialog box.

type in the document using that font is highlighted. Then do one of the following:

- Click the Find Next button to select the next type using that font.
- Click the Change button to replace only the type selected in the document with the new font.
- Click the Change All button to replace all type in the document using the highlighted font with the new font.
  - When all instances of a highlighted font have been replaced, the font name is removed from the list of fonts in the Fonts in Document window.
- Click the Skip button to leave the current instance of the font unchanged and find the next instance of the font.
- Click the Save List button to save a list of the fonts used in the document (shown in the Fonts in Document window). When the Save Font List dialog box displays, enter a file name, specify a location, and click Save or press *return/enter*.

 *activity 5.24*

1. Open the document named Find a Font.eps that's stored in the Student Files folder on the CD-ROM that's in the back of this book.

2. Display the Find Font dialog box and highlight ITC Benguiat Bold in the Fonts in Document window.

3. Choose System from the Replace Font From pop-up submenu and wait until the font list displays. If you have a lot of fonts installed, this could take a few minutes.

4. If you have all the fonts installed that came on the Illustrator 10 CD, highlight ITC Eras Bold in the Replace Font From window. If you don't have ITC Eras Bold installed, choose a bold font that you do have installed.

5. Click the Change All button.
   - All type in the document that has Benguiat Bold applied to it is changed to ITC Eras Bold.

6. Change type that's Friz Quadrata Bold to ITC Eras Bold.
   - Notice that the listing for Friz Quadrata Bold was removed from the Fonts in Document window.

7. Save a list of the fonts into your Practice folder. Name the file Save Fonts List.

8. Save the file into your Practice folder and close the artwork window.

Check Spelling

The Check Spelling command in the Type menu checks the spelling of words in an entire document. The default dictionary that comes with Illustrator 10 cannot be modified, but you can add, edit, or delete words you use frequently in a user-defined dictionary. You can even check the spelling of several foreign languages. The Check Spelling command can't be used with Japanese, Chinese, or Korean fonts, though.

1. Choose **Type** ⇨ **Check Spelling** to check the spelling of all words in the document.

   ■ Words used in the document that aren't in the dictionary are treated as misspelled words.

   ■ If Illustrator didn't detect any misspelled words, an alert displays telling you that no spelling errors were found. Then the Check Spelling dialog box displays (Figure 5.17).

Alert that displays if no misspelled words were found when the Check Spelling command was used

2. If a misspelled word was found in the document, the Check Spelling dialog box displays (Figure 5.17) with that misspelled word highlighted. A list of suggested replacement words is shown in the bottom window.

   ■ The misspelled word is highlighted in the document.

   ■ Only the first occurrence of the misspelled word is displayed in the list.

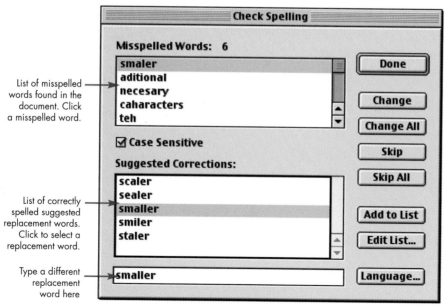

List of misspelled words found in the document. Click a misspelled word.

List of correctly spelled suggested replacement words. Click to select a replacement word.

Type a different replacement word here

FIGURE 5.17
Check Spelling dialog box.

3. Double-click the correctly spelled word in the Suggested Corrections window.

or

If the correct word isn't displayed in the Suggested Corrections window, highlight the field at the bottom of the dialog box and type in the correctly spelled word. If the misspelled "word" displays because a space is missing between two words and the correct spacing isn't listed in the Suggested Corrections list, add a space between the words in the field at the bottom of the dialog box.

or

Click the Skip button to leave that instance of the misspelled word unchanged. Click the Skip All button to leave all instances of the word unchanged. The next misspelled word is highlighted.

4. Click the Change button to correct that instance of the misspelled word and move to the next instance of that word (if any).

or

Click the Change All button to correct all instances of the selected misspelled word.

■ When all instances of the misspelled word are corrected, the word is removed from the Misspelled Words window.

5. If the Case Sensitive checkbox is checked, and the capitalization of words doesn't match the capitalization of words in the dictionary, those words appear in the Misspelled Words list.

6. Click the Add to List button to add the current misspelled word to the user-defined dictionary file.

■ To add more than one word at a time, ⌘-click them to select them.

■ The word is skipped automatically and removed from the Misspelled Words list. The next time the word is encountered, it won't appear as a misspelled word.

7. If you've cleared all the words from the Misspelled Words list, an alert displays telling you that you're finished and how many words were corrected or skipped. Click OK or press *return/enter*.

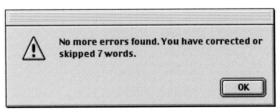

Alert that displays when all spelling errors have been corrected

8. Click the Done button or press *return/enter* to exit the Check Spelling dialog box.

Editing the User-Defined Dictionary

The only way to add new words or to modify existing words in the user-defined dictionary is by clicking the Edit List button in the Check Spelling dialog box. The dictionary cannot be edited using a word processing program. You can add words to the user-defined dictionary even when the current document page is blank.

The default dictionary file for each language supported is stored in the Plug-Ins folder in the Adobe Illustrator 10 folder on your hard drive. The user-defined dictionary is named AI User Dictionary and is stored in the same folder as soon as the first word is added to it.

- *Macintosh:* **Adobe Illustrator 10** ⇨ **Plug-Ins** ⇨ **Text Filters** ⇨ **AI User Dictionary**

- *Windows:* **Program Files** ⇨ **Adobe** ⇨ **Adobe Illustrator 10** ⇨ **Plug-ins** ⇨ **Text Filters** ⇨ **AIUser.dct**

fyi Words added to the user-defined dictionary remain in the dictionary file even after the file has been deleted.

To edit the user-defined dictionary:

1. Choose **Type** ⇨ **Check Spelling** to display the Check Spelling dialog box, if isn't already displayed.

2. Click the Edit List button to display the Learned Words dialog box.

3. **Add a new word** — Type a new word in the field at the bottom of the dialog box, then click the Add button.

   or

   Change an existing word — Click a word listed in the window and change its spelling, capitalization, or hyphenation (in compound words) in the field at the bottom of the dialog box, then click the Change button.

   or

   Delete an existing word — Click a word listed in the window, then click the Remove button.

4. Click Done or press *return/enter* when you're finished.

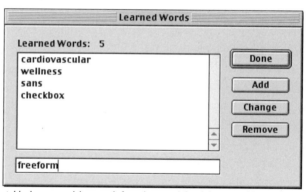

Add, change, or delete words from the user-defined dictionary file in the Learned Words dialog box

activity 5.25

1. Open the file named Spell Check text.txt that's in the Student Files folder on the CD-ROM that's in the back of this book.

   - The font used for the text in the file is Friz Quadrata Medium. If you don't have that font installed on your computer, any font will work.

2. Choose Type ⇨ Check Spelling to display the Check Spelling dialog box.

   - Uncheck the Case Sensitive checkbox.

   - Adjust the position the Check Spelling dialog box and the size of the block of type so you can see as much as possible of the block of type.

3. The first misspelled word in the list of Misspelled Words is *kernng*. Verify that the correct spelling of the word (kerning) is highlighted in the Suggested Corrections list of words.

   - Notice that the first word in the second paragraph is *Kernng* (with a capital *K*).

4. Click the Change All button to change all occurrences of *kernng* to *kerning*.

   - Notice that the word Kerning (capital K) was changed to kerning (small k).

5. Click the Case Sensitive checkbox.

   - Notice that the word *Caharacter* in the last line of the second paragraph has the same misspelling as other instances of the word *caharacters*, except it has a capital *C* and it isn't plural.

6. Highlight the word *caharacters* in the Misspelled Words list, verify that the proper spelling of the word is highlighted in the Suggested Corrections list, and click the Change All button.

   - Notice that this time the word *Caharacter* wasn't changed because its capitalization didn't match the word in the list.

7. Correct the spelling of the rest of the words in the Misspelled Words list.

8. Sans isn't misspelled, so add it to the user-defined dictionary so it won't come up again as a misspelled word.

   - Highlight the word in the Misspelled Words list, then click the Add to List button.

9. Click the Edit List button to display the Learned Words dialog box.

10. Add the following words to the user-defined dictionary:

freeform	nonjustified
artboard	spacebar
unsatisfied	neurons
gherkins	analyses

11. Remove the word neurons from the list.

12. Click Done when you're finished adding words to the list, then click Done again to exit the Check Spelling dialog box.

13. Close the artwork window without saving the file.

Create Outlines

The Create Outlines command in the Type menu lets you convert type characters into a compound path (two or more separate paths that function as a single unit). You can modify type that's been converted to outlines the same way you modify any path drawn with an object creation tool. You can reshape individual paths, apply fill and stroke attributes, and you can even fill the characters with type. Existing attributes, such as fill and stroke, are retained after type has been converted to outlines, but the type container, if any, is deleted.

Type converted to outlines

The font you are using—both Type 1 and TrueType fonts—must be installed on your computer. If they aren't, Illustrator substitutes a font. In addition, for Type 1 fonts, both the screen font *and* printer font must be installed.

Once type has been converted to outlines, you can't convert the paths back into type characters, which means type editing procedures no longer work. You can apply the Undo command, though. All type in a type container, along a freeform path, or attached to a point is converted when the Create Outlines command is applied. You can't pick out just one letter or word and convert it to outlines.

When the Create Outlines command is applied to type, the *hinting* information that's built in to most Type 1 fonts is lost. Hinting ensures that type prints correctly when set at small sizes. So when small type is converted to outlines, character shapes may not be preserved. In addition, character outlines are usually slightly heavier than the type character and small type outlines may not be legible.

Type characters converted to outlines become a compound path, that is, multiple paths functioning as a single unit. Separate paths are created if a type character requires more than one path to create its shape, such as *A* or *e*.

When a single path is selected with the Selection tool, all paths in the set are selected. To separate the characters into its individual paths, choose **Object ⇨ Compound Path ⇨ Release**. When you do that, though, characters requiring two paths to form the inner portions of the letter, such as *O*, *A*, *e*, and so on, become the same color as the outside of the character. You have to select them individually and apply white or another color.

You can reassemble the parts so they function as a single unit by choosing **Object ⇨ Compound Path ⇨ Make**.

By converting type to outlines, you can avoid font conflicts and, in addition, you can use a font for which you only have the screen font. Just convert it to outlines before sending it to your output provider. Because the type becomes a path, the printer font isn't necessary.

fyi When converting type to outlines, work on a copy of the file so you still have the original in the event you need to edit the text.

fyi Type converted to outlines causes the file size to be larger.

To convert type to outlines:

1. Select the type with the Selection tool.

2. Choose **Type** ➪ **Create Outlines**

   or

   Press ⇧⌘o

activity 5.26

1. Create a new document: Letter size, CMYK color mode.

2. Choose the Type tool (press *t*), click to establish a point, and type WOW.

3. Format the type to be 72 pt Friz Quadrata Bold, and apply a fill color of 90% cyan, 10% magenta.

4. Select the type (if it isn't already selected) and choose Type ➪ Create Outlines.

   ■ The type characters are converted to paths.

5. Deselect the paths.

6. With the Selection tool (press *v*), click on one of the characters.

   ■ The paths for all the characters are selected.

7. Deselect the paths.

8. Choose the Direct Selection tool (press *a*) and ⬉-click on the pathline of the inner circle of the o.

   ■ The path is selected with all the anchor points solid.

9. Drag it to a new location inside the o character.

10. Deselect all.

11. Press *v* to select the Selection tool and click on one of the characters.

12. Choose Object ➪ Compound Path ➪ Release to separate each character into it's own object.

13. In the Character palette, change to: 6 pt Friz Quadrata Medium, Auto leading, Horizontal Scale 80%, flush left.

14. Press *t* to choose the Type tool, then position the pointer over the pathline of the first *W* until the Area Type icon (⬚) displays, then click the pathline to convert the character into a type container.

    ■ Fill color is removed.

15. Type *This is really cool.*

16. Name the file, Outlines.eps and save it into your Practice folder as an .eps file. Close the artwork window.

Wrap Type Around an Object

When type is placed beside an object or a placed image, the bounding box of the image determines the line endings or beginnings of the type. You can make area type or type in a type container follow the contours of one or more vector objects or a placed image rather than their bounding boxes using the Wrap command in the Type menu. The Wrap command doesn't work, though, with type attached to a point or type on a path. And you can't wrap type around an open path.

- The object or image must be in front of the type in stacking order.

- The object(s) or image(s) and the type container(s) function as a single graphic object.

- Type wraps around both sides of an object that's in the middle of a type block.
  - If a word is too small to fit on one side or the other of the object or image, it leaves a blank space. To fix the problem, (a) widen the type container, (b) make the object or image smaller, or (c) make the type smaller.

- The Wrap command wraps type around paths. If you want to wrap type around a raster image, draw a vector object with one of the drawing tools that's the shape you want to wrap. Apply a fill and stroke of None. Use that object to wrap the type around.
  - Use the Direct Selection tool to move or reshape the object the type is wrapping around.

- Change the amount of space between the object and the type by changing the Left or Right Indent value of the type in the Paragraph palette. Of course, doing that also creates an indent from the edge of the container, but you can simply adjust the size of the container to compensate.
  - Type wrapped around an object having a heavy stroke may cause the type to run into the object.

To wrap type around an object or image:

1. Make sure the object or image is in front of the type container.
   - Select the object or image and choose **Object** ⇨ **Arrange** ⇨ **Bring to Front** or press ⇧⌘]

2. Select the type container and the wrapping object or image.
   - Marquee the type container and the object or image with the Selection tool or Direct Selection tool to be sure all paths are selected.

3. Choose **Type** ⇨ **Wrap** ⇨ **Make**.
   - A graphic object is created that functions as a single object.

Remove Type Wrap Around an Object

If you decide you don't want the type to wrap around an object or image:

1. With the Selection tool, select the type container and the object or image.

2. Choose **Type** ➪ **Wrap** ➪ **Release**.

   ■ The graphic object reverts back to its separate components.

activity 5.27

1. Create a new document: Letter size, CMYK color mode. Name it Type Wrap Practice.eps and save it into your Practice folder as an .eps file.

2. Place the text file named Grid information.txt that's in the Student Files folder on the CD that's in the back of this book.

3. Reshape the type container to 340 pt wide and 155 pt high.

   ■ Use the Info palette to move the boundaries of the type container to the proper size.

4. Format the type to 10 pt Cushing, 14 pt leading, flush left, 12 pt paragraph indent.

5. Choose the Polar Grid tool (⊕) in the Toolbox and draw a polar grid that's 100×100 pt, 5 concentric dividers, and 5 radial dividers with no skew. Check the Create Compound Paths from Ellipses checkbox.

6. Place the grid object with the top of the grid even with the top of the type container and centered horizontally.

7. With the Selection tool or the Direct Selection tool, marquee to select all paths in the type container and the grid object.

8. Choose Type ➪ Wrap ➪ Make.

   ■ The type wraps around the polar grid, but some text is too close to the grid.

9. Display the Paragraph palette and change the Left Indent and Right Indent values to 6 pt.

   ■ The type rewraps around the object.

A grid is a framework of lines and Adobe Illustrator 10 has two tools that create grids. The Rectangular Grid tool, used for drawing rectangular or square grids, contains a specified number of equally-spaced horizontal and vertical dividers. The Polar Grid tool, used for drawing circular grids, creates a specified number of concentric circles and equally-spaced radial dividers. You can create grids by dragging with a grid tool or by entering values into its options dialog box. Dragging with a grid tool creates a grid having the same values as the last one that was created.

10. Save the file and close the artwork window.

Multiple Master Fonts

The MM (Multiple Master) Design palette allows you to alter the weight and width of characters in multiple master fonts, which are special PostScript fonts designed by Adobe. The names of Multiple Master fonts can be distinguished from regular PostScript fonts by the "MM" in its name.

To modify multiple master fonts:

1. Choose **Window** ➪ **Type** ➪ **MM Design** to display the MM Design palette.

2. Adjust the sliders to modify the weight or width of selected characters.

   ■ Sliders that are available vary from font to font, but the options most commonly available are width and weight.

   ■ Changes are applied as soon as you release the mouse after moving the slider.

3. Close the palette when you're satisfied with your font changes.

read this!

Check with your output provider to make sure they accept projects using Multiple Master fonts. Many do not.

PRACTICE ACTIVITY 5-1 — Mink Information Sheet

1. Open the file named Mink Information Sheet.eps that's stored in the Student Files folder on the CD-ROM that's in the back of this book.

2. Create a rectangle that's 6½"wide × 9" high, fill of None, 1 pt black stroke.

3. Position it so the bottom right corner of the rectangle aligns with the bottom right corner of the dotted box on the page.

4. The type in the sample shown is wrapped around the image of the mink. But this is a bitmap image so it doesn't have paths to select to create a wrapping object, so we need to draw one.

5. Draw a shape with the Pen tool or the Pencil tool that's about ⅛" away from the top and back of the mink. Apply a fill of None and a stroke of None.

The complex actions and interactions of organ systems in vertebrates must be precisely controlled to meet the specific needs of the animal. We have examined one of the major systems responsible for coordinating these processes—the nervous system. The endocrine system is another major player in the body's attempt to co-ordinate the activities of its many organs and organ systems. In that respect, the endocrine and nervous systems are very much alike.

The similarities between the two systems do not go very far beyond that, however. Unlike the nervous system which has its own contained system for information transfer (the nerves), the endocrine system is ductless and therefore must rely on another neighboring system to send its messages throughout the body.

The glands of the endocrine system produce and secrete their hormones directly into the bloodstream to be carried to their target organs. These hormones are chemical compounds that interact with target cells in the body to produce a myriad of behavioral, neurological and physiological responses. In this way, they influence many of the same behaviors and processes that the nervous system regulates. However, due to the nature of hormones, the effects produced by the endocrine system are generally not short-lived.

Nervous responses are instantaneous and degrade immediately, but hormones circulating through the bloodstream may take some time to produce a response and anywhere from minutes to hours to break down. Thus hormonal effects tend to be much longer in duration and the processes that are under hormonal control are typically processes that occur over hours, days, weeks or even years (e.g., sexual maturation, metabolic rate, growth rate, ovulation). In addition, the degree of response shown by the target organ is directly proportional to the amount of hormone released by the endocrine gland—the more hormone a gland releases, the more pronounced the effect.

This is a fundamental distinction from the all-or-nothing response of nerve cells and illustrates why both systems, the nervous system and the endocrine system, are essential for complex organisms to coordinate different aspects of their lives.

6. Choose File ⇨ Place, locate the file named Mink Information.txt that's stored in the Student Files folder on the CD-ROM that's in the back of this book.

7. Verify that the Platform selection is Macintosh (because that's the platform on which the file was created), the Character Set is ANSI, and everything else is unchecked. Click OK or press *return/enter.*

8. Position the type container so it's horizontally centered in the rectangle and so there's approximately the same amount of space between the top of the type container and the top of the rectangle as there is on each side.

9. Format the type: 11.5 pt ITC Galliard Roman, 15 pt leading, flush left, 18 pt paragraph indent, track −1.

10. Because the type container was placed on the page after the path was drawn around the mink, it's in the front of the stack. A wrapping object must be in front of the type container, so select the path and bring it to the front of the stack (Object ⇨ Arrange ⇨ Bring to Front).

11. With the Selection tool, select the path you drew around the mink and the type container. Make sure you don't select the bounding box of the mink.

■ *Shift*-click the objects or marquee to select.

12. Choose Type ⇨ Wrap ⇨ Make.

13. You may have to adjust the width of the text container or adjust the shape of the path of the text wrap to make all the type fit on the page.

14. Check the spelling and fix any misspelled words in the document.

15. Save the file into your Practice folder as an .eps file named Mink Information Sheet.eps.

16. Turn on Smart Punctuation (Type ⇨ Smart Punctuation). In the Replace Punctuation section uncheck everything except Smart Quotes, Smart Spaces, and En, Em Dashes. Select Replace in Entire Document, and uncheck Report Results. Click OK or press *return/enter.*

17. The text document had two hyphens (--) instead of three hyphens, so the Smart Punctuation

command changed them to en dashes. Highlight the en dashes. There's one in the third line of the first paragraph, and one near the end of the fourth paragraph.

18. *Macintosh:* Copy the character (⌘c), display the Find/Change dialog box (Type ⇨ Find/Change), click in the Find What field, and paste the character (⌘v). Enter the keystrokes for an em dash (⇧⌘-) in the Change to field.

   Windows: Enter the ANSI code for an en dash in the Find What field and the ANSI code for an em dash in the Change to field.

19. Click the Find Next button, then click the Change All button. Click Done to exit the dialog box.

20. Save the file.

21. Highlight the first character in the document. Change it to 34 pt and baseline shift is −15 pts.

22. In the paragraph palette, change the First Line Left Indent value to 0.

23. Turn on Show Hidden Characters.

24. After the space at the end of the last character in the first line, enter a soft return (⇧-return).

25. Zoom in close on the first character in the document, Enter several spaces before the first character of the second line to move the first word over to align it with the second character in the first line (h). Get it as close as you can.

26. Place the Insertion marker between two of the spaces and adjust the kerning (+ or −) until the stem of the *p* lines up with the stem of the *h*. In the next chapter, you'll learning about using guides, but for now, just eyeball it.

27. Reduce the view.

28. Check each line ending to make sure that no compound (hyphenated) words were broken except at the hyphen. Enter a discretionary hyphen or a soft return wherever necessary to adjust where a line wraps around.

29. Save the file, print it, and close the artwork window

EXERCISE 5-1 — Aquarium Ad

Create an ad for the Gala Opening of the Lighthouse Point Aquarium. The sample shown here is merely an example of what you can do. Design your own ad piece.

    We have supplied the artwork for the fish shown here, or you can draw your own. They are saved in the Student Files folder on the CD-ROM in the back of this book as an .eps file named Aquarium ad.eps. The text is saved in the same folder and is named Aquarium ad.txt.

- To rotate the fish, select them with the Selection tool and rotate the bounding box.

- The seaweed was drawn with the Pencil tool. Draw any kind of plant life you'd like, or none at all.

Note: The large red fish was drawn with the mesh tool, which is discussed in Step 12, Meshes, Masks, Blends, & Transparency.

Rulers, Grids, & Guides

Chapter Outline

- Rulers
- The Info Palette
- The Measure Tool
- Grids
- Guides

- Smart Guides
- Change Artboard Specifications
- Create Crop Marks
- Create a Custom Startup File

Rulers

When creating artwork, it is sometimes important that you position artwork or pieces of an illustration precisely. Illustrator 10 has rulers that display across the top and along the left side of the document window to help you do just that. The default, though, when you open a new document is for rulers to be hidden. To make the rulers visible:

1. Choose **View** ➪ **Show Rulers**.

or

2. Press ⌘r

or

3. If nothing in the document is selected, you can display the context-sensitive menu (*Macintosh:* ⌃-click; *Windows:* right-click) and choose Show Rulers.

You can make the rulers visible on new documents by creating a Custom Startup file. See Create a Custom Startup File later in this chapter.

The Rulers command is a toggle, so to hide the rulers, press ⌘r again or choose Hide Rulers in the View menu or context-sensitive menu. Even if you've created a new Startup file and rulers display when a new file is opened, you can hide them with the Hide Rulers command or by pressing ⌘r.

As you move around in the document window or zoom to enlarge or reduce the View, the rulers adjust at the same time. When you enlarge or reduce the View, the tick marks indicating the increments in the rulers enlarge or reduce proportionally, too. The pointer is tracked on both rulers by a dashed line that moves when you move the pointer.

Dashed line in the ruler bars that moves when you move the pointer

Ruler Origin

All measurements are calculated from the zero point on the rulers — called the *ruler origin*. The position of the ruler origin is dependent upon the Artboard Setup settings in the Document Setup dialog box (the box that displays when you create a new document, Figure 6.1). If Single Full Page or Tile Full Pages is selected in the View area of the Document Setup dialog box, 0 is at the bottom left corner of the first page. You can move the ruler origin to any position on the page.

Measurements are calculated from the bottom of the document page to the top and from the left side to the right side.

fyi Moving the ruler origin may affect the printing of pattern fills in objects. See the Crop Marks section later in this chapter. You should restore the ruler origin back to its default position before sending a document to the printer.

Set Ruler Origin Sometimes it's more efficient to measure placement of artwork from a 0-point at the edge of the object than from the default ruler origin — when creating a business card, for instance. Once the rulers are displayed on the document window, the ruler origin can be set to any position on the page. Just click and drag the Ruler Origin box (top left corner of the document window) to a new position (bottom left or top left corner of the business card, for example), and release the mouse.

Ruler origin box

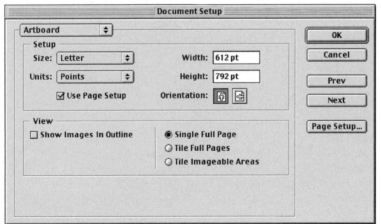

FIGURE 6.1
Document Setup dialog box.

As you drag, a dotted crosshair displays, indicating the point of ruler origin. The 0 markers in the ruler bar at the top and left side of the document window move to reflect the point where you release the mouse. The new position of the ruler becomes the default for that document only. Other documents aren't affected.

Restore Ruler Origin To restore the ruler origin to its default position, double-click the Ruler Origin box in the upper left corner of the document window.

Ruler Units of Measurement

The default unit of measurement for the rulers, measure tool, size or distance values fields in dialog boxes is points. But you can change it to picas, inches, millimeters, centimeters, or pixels for the current document only or for all new documents you create after you make the change.

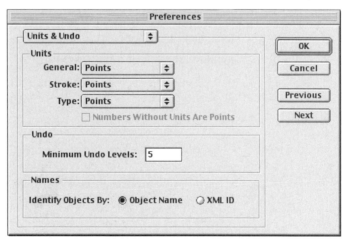

✓ Points
Picas
Inches
Millimeters
Centimeters
Pixels

Units of measurement available in Illustrator 10

Change Unit of Measure for Current Document Only To change the measurement scale for the current document only, change the selection in the Units pop-up menu in the Document Setup dialog box (see Figure 6.1:

1. Choose **File** ⇨ **Document Setup**.
   or
   Press ⌥⌘p

2. Choose Units ⇨ General to display the pop-up submenu and choose the unit of measurement you want to use.

3. Click OK or press *return/enter*.

Change Unit of Measurement for All Future Documents To change the default measurement scale for the current document *and* all new documents created thereafter:

1. Display the Units & Undo dialog box (**Edit** ⇨ **Preferences** ⇨ **Units & Undo**; *Mac OS X users:* **Illustrator** ⇨ **Preferences** ⇨ **Units & Undo**) (Figure 6.2).

2. Choose Points in the General pop-up submenu.

3. Click OK or *press return/enter*.

FIGURE 6.2 Units & Undo Preferences dialog box.

- Stroke weight and type size should always be measured in points, so don't make any changes in the Stroke and Type pop-up menus.

Units of Measurement Available There are six units of measurement available in Illustrator 10:

- **Points:** 72 points = 1 inch, 12 points = 1 pica
- **Picas:** 1 pica = 12 points, 6 picas = 1 inch
    - When specifying picas and fractions of a pica, enter numbers on one or both sides of the letter p. Numbers entered to the left of the p are full picas, and numbers entered to the right of the p are fractions of a pica expressed in points. For example, 3½ picas is typed 3p6. Half a pica is 6 because a full pica is 12 points. Zero is implied if either side of the p is blank; for example, ½" is 3p.
    - When Picas is the measurement unit, increase the magnification of the document window until the tick marks are displayed in pica increments, because at a View of 100% or lower, ruler increments are displayed in increments of 8, which is not a usable increment when measuring in picas.
- **Inches:** 1 inch = 6 picas, 1 inch = 72 points
- **Millimeters:** 1 mm = .03937 inch
- **Centimeters:** 1 cm = .3937 inch
- **Pixels:** size of pixel depends upon resolution of image

Measurement Symbols You can mix any of the measurement units, regardless of the selection in the Units & Undo dialog box or the Document Setup dialog box. To enter a value in a field that's a different unit of measurement from the document preferences, add the appropriate abbreviation after the number. Illustrator translates the new value into the equivalent of the default unit of measurement when you press *return/enter*.

- Points   pt or points
- Picas   p or picas
- Inches   inch, inches, in, or "
- Millimeters mm, millimeters, or millimetres
- Centimeters cm, centimeters, or centimetres
- Q   q
- Pixels   px or pixels

fyi A Q is equal to 0.25 mm.

For example, if Inches is specified as the unit of measurement, either in Document Setup or Units & Undo Preferences, and you enter a value of 3p in a dialog box field, Illustrator converts the value of 3p to its equivalent value in inches: .5 inch.

Illustrator Does the Math In any field in a dialog box in which you enter numeric (number) values, you can instruct Illustrator to perform mathematical operations. Enter the symbols for add (+), subtract (-), multiply (*), or divide (/) in the field. You can even ask Illustrator to calculate a percentage (%). For example, if you enter 38-6 in a field, Illustrator subtracts 6 from 38 and enters the result (32) in the field in whatever measurement system you have selected.

You can even mix up the measurement values. Let's say, for instance, you have specified Inches as your default unit of measurement. If you type 48pt+18mm in a field and press *return/enter*, Illustrator performs the calculation, translates the result into inches, and enters that value in the field (1.375 in). If you enter 16p*50%, Illustrator multiplies 16 picas by 50% and enters the result of 1.333 inches in the field (16p × 50% = 8p = 1.333 inches). If you enter 12.5 in + 60%, Illustrator calculates the total of 12.5 inches plus 60% of 12.5 and enters a total of 20 inches in the field.

 *activity 6.1*

1. Create a new document: Letter size, CMYK color mode.

2. Display the Units & Undo dialog box in the Preferences file (Edit ➪ Preferences ➪ Units & Undo — *Mac OS X users:* Illustrator ➪ Preferences ➪ Units & Undo.

3. Change the General Units of Measurement to Inches.
   - In general, the measurement system you'll use when completing the activities and exercises in this book is inches.
   - Leave the measurement system as Points for Stroke (weight) and Type measurements.
   - Click OK or press *return/enter* to exit the dialog box.

4. Press ⌘ r to show the rulers.

5. With one of the Selection tools selected, move the pointer around the document page and find the dashed lines in the rulers that move when you move the pointer.

6. Click in the Ruler Origin box at the top left corner of the document window and drag the ruler origin down to the "8" on the left ruler and the "2" on the top ruler and release the mouse.
   - Notice that the 8 and the 2 became 0, indicating that measurements are calculated from that point.

7. Double-click in the Ruler Origin box to restore the rulers to the default.

8. Click the Rectangle tool in the Toolbox to make it active, then click in the document to display the Rectangle Options dialog box.
   - Notice that measurements are now given in inches rather than points.

9. Type 40 mm in the Width field and 16p in the Height field. Click OK or press *return/enter*.

10. Click in the document to display the Rectangle Options dialog box again. The measurements have been changed to their equivalents in inches (Width = 1.575 inches, Height = 2.667 inches).

11. Type 3+1.5p in the Width field and 16p-3mm in the Height field. Click OK or press *return/enter*.

12. Click in the document to display the Rectangle Options dialog box again. The measurements have been calculated and their equivalents in inches have been entered in the fields (Width = 3"+1.5p = 0.292 in; Height = 16p–3mm = 2.549 in).

13. Hide the rulers using the context-sensitive menu.

14. Close this document without saving it to a file.

The Info Palette

The Info palette, included, by default, as a tab in the Appearance/Navigator palette, displays information about selected objects. Depending upon which tool is selected, the exact position of an object on the page using X/Y coordinates, its width, height, angle of rotation, and so on, may be displayed. You can even measure the distance between two points using the Measure tool in the Toolbox. Measurements are expressed in the unit of measurement currently specified for the document. Fill and stroke information for selected objects is also displayed.

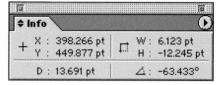

Info palette

Display the Info palette in one of 3 ways:

■ Choose **Window** ⇨ **Info**.

or

■ Click the Info tab in the Appearance/Navigator/Info palette if it's visible.

   • Click and drag the Info tab in the Appearance/Navigator/Info palette to display the Info palette as a separate palette.

X/Y Coordinates

The pointer's position on a document page can be described in the document's unit of measurement by using its X/Y coordinates. These coordinates are calculated based upon the X/Y axes. By default, the X/Y axes are parallel to the horizontal and vertical sides of the artwork window.

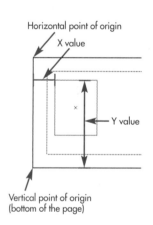

Horizontal point of origin

X value

Y value

Vertical point of origin
(bottom of the page)

■ X describes the horizontal position of the pointer, beginning at the 0 point of the ruler origin; that is, how far from the left edge of the page a point is if the ruler origin is 0 at the left edge of the page. If you move the ruler origin away from the left edge of the page, calculations are made from wherever the 0 point is located.

■ Y describes the vertical position of the pointer, beginning at the 0 point of the ruler origin, or how far up from the bottom of the page (when 0 ruler origin is at the bottom of the page boundary as determined by the page size setting of the output device). The 0 point is not necessarily the bottom of the page if the value entered into the Height field of the New dialog box is not the same as the page size of the printer.

   • If you change the default position of the ruler origin at the bottom of the page, calculations are made upward from wherever the 0 point is located.

What's Displayed in the Info Palette?

Different information is displayed in the Info palette depending upon which tool is selected. The following list tells what is displayed when specific tools are active:

- **Selection tool** (▶ or ▷) — X/Y coordinates of the pointer are displayed and change as you move the pointer.
  - If an object is selected, the width (W) and height (H) of the object are displayed.
  - If a selected object is moved, the absolute horizontal distance and the absolute vertical distance (how far up or down and how far left or right) the object was moved is displayed in the W and H areas, the total distance it is being moved is displayed in the D area, and the angle at which it is being moved is displayed in the △ area.
  - A negative value (minus) displayed in the W area as an object is moved indicates the object was moved to the left of its point of origin.
  - A negative value (minus) displayed in the H area when an object is moved indicates the object was moved down from its point of origin.
  - When an object is moved, the D area never displays a negative (minus) value because it measures the *total* distance an object moved, regardless of direction.
- **Pen tool** () — X/Y coordinates of the pointer are displayed and change as you move the pointer.
- **Pencil tool** (✎) — X/Y coordinates of the pointer are displayed and change as you move the pointer.
- **Zoom tool** (🔍) — X/Y coordinates of the pointer are displayed, as well as the magnification percentage of the artwork window. When you enlarge or decrease magnification, X/Y coordinates don't change because you're not actually changing the size of the object, just the size at which it's viewed on the screen.

Info Palette Options

Display the Info palette Options menu by clicking the Options arrow at the top righthand side of the palette. Color values for the Fill (□) and the Stroke (■) of a selected object are displayed. If no object in the document is selected, values of the last object that had been selected are shown.

- If more than one object on a page is selected, these sections are blank, unless the information for all selected objects is the same.

fyi To display Width and Height information for a selected object in the Info palette, including its stroke, check the Use Preview Bounds checkbox in General Preferences (Edit ⇨ Preferences ⇨ General). Then the measurements will include the width of the stroke that hangs outside the path line.

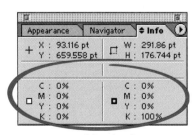

Options section of the Info palette

241

The Measure Tool

You can determine how far it is between two points in the document window or the angle between two points using the Measure tool, which is hidden under the Eyedropper tool () in the Toolbox. When you click on the document page with the Measure tool selected, the Info palette opens automatically and displays the specifications for the point of the click.

Measure tool icon in the Toolbox palette

Use one of the following methods to select the Measure tool.

■ Click the arrow on the Eyedropper tool icon to display the pop-up menu, then drag to select the Measure tool.

or

■ Tear off the tools, creating a new palette, then click on the Measure tool in the new palette.

To measure the distance between two points:

■ Click starting and ending points to measure the distance or the angle between them. The distance and angle between the first click and the second click is displayed in the Info palette.

  ▪ To keep the angle between the two points straight or in increments of 45°, hold the *Shift* key down while clicking.

or

■ Click the first point, drag to the second point, and release the mouse.

  ▪ To keep the angle between the two points straight or in increments of 45°, hold the *Shift* key down while dragging.

The distance between the two points is displayed in the D area of the Info palette. The angle between the two points is displayed in the ∠ area.

 activity 6.2

1. Create a new document: Letter size, CMYK color mode.

2. Choose the Selection tool, then display the Info palette, if it isn't already visible.

3. Move the cursor around the page.

   - Notice that the values in the X area and Y area change, depending upon where the cursor is on the page, even if you move outside the printable page.

4. Draw a rectangle.

   - Notice that the values in the X area and Y area didn't change once you clicked to start drawing the shape, but the values in the W and H areas did. That's because the point where the shape started (X/Y coordinate) didn't change. Just the size of the rectangle changed as you drew it.

5. Deselect the shape.

6. Choose the Direct Selection tool and click inside the shape so that the Center point displays. Without releasing the mouse move the shape to the right and down a little bit.

   - The values in the X area and Y area changed to reflect where the pointer is positioned on the page as it moved.

   - The values in the W area and H area show how far the shape moved up or down (H) and sideways (W).

   - The value displayed in the ∠ area indicates the angle at which you moved the shape.

7. When the object is released, W/H fields revert to displaying the size of the object and Angle and Distance values disappear.

8. Select the Zoom tool and notice that the percentage of magnification is indicated in the Info palette. The value changes as you increase or decrease the magnification.

9. Draw two rectangles side by side on the page, a couple of inches apart.

9. Select the Measure tool.

10. Click on the top right corner of the leftmost rectangle, then click on the top left corner of the rightmost rectangle.

    - How far apart are your rectangles?

    - At what angle are they positioned?

11. Hold down the *Shift* key, click on the right side of the leftmost box, drag to the left side of the rightmost box, then release the mouse and *Shift* keys.

    Click here
    Drag to here and release

    - How far apart are your rectangles?

    - At what angle did you measure the two boxes?

12. Don't save or close this document.

Grids

A grid in Illustrator is a non-printing set of lines or dots that display on your document like a piece of graph paper and all Illustrator documents have a grid, but the default is for them to be invisible. To show or hide the grid:

- Choose **View** ⇨ **Show Grid** (or **Hide Grid** if the grid is visible on the screen)

or

- Press ⌘ " (quote)

or

- Display the context-sensitive menu and choose Show Grid.

You can use the grids to measure and align objects in your artwork. You can snap objects to the grid for quick placement and measurement, specify the color of the grid lines, and determine how far apart the grid lines are. You can even turn the grid at an angle to draw objects in perspective.

Snap To Grid

The Snap to Grid feature causes an object that is moved close to a grid line to move quickly (snap) to the grid line and stick there. If you move the object close to another grid line, it snaps to the one it's closest to. Objects snap to the grid defined by the settings in Guides & Grid Preferences.

You can turn on the Snap to Grid function even though the grid is not displayed on the screen. :

- Choose **View** ⇨ **Snap to Grid**

or

- Press ⇧ ⌘ " (quote)

Turn off the Snap to Grid feature by choosing that option again from the View menu or pressing ⇧ ⌘ " (quote) again.

Setting Grid Preferences

You can choose how your grid displays on your screen by changing the preferences in the Guides & Grid Preferences dialog box. To display the Preferences dialog box (Figure 6.3):

- Choose **Edit** ⇨ **Preferences** ⇨ **Guides & Grid**.

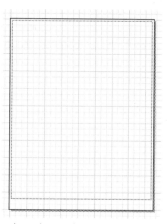

The grid covers the entire artboard

  A quick way to see if an object or part of an object in your artwork has a None fill or a White fill is to show the Grid. If the object has a None fill, it is transparent and the grid lines show through the object.

View	
Outline	⌘Y
Overprint Preview	⌥⇧⌘Y
Pixel Preview	⌥⌘Y
Proof Setup	▶
Proof Colors	
Zoom In	⌘+
Zoom Out	⌘-
Fit in Window	⌘0
Actual Size	⌘1
Hide Edges	⌘H
Hide Artboard	
Hide Page Tiling	
Show Slices	
Lock Slices	
Hide Template	⇧⌘W
Show Rulers	⌘R
Hide Bounding Box	⇧⌘B
Show Transparency Grid	⇧⌘D
Guides	▶
Smart Guides	⌘U
Hide Grid	⌘"
Snap to Grid	⇧⌘"
✓ Snap to Point	⌥⌘"
New View...	
Edit Views...	

View menu

244

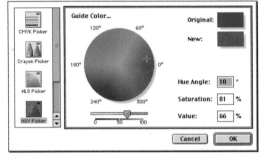

FIGURE 6.3 Guides & Grid
Preferences dialog box.

Color You can change the color of the grid lines by pressing the submenu arrow to display the submenu in the Color area of the Grid section of the dialog box. If you have objects in your artwork that are the same colors as the preset selections, making the grid lines difficult to see, you can select your own color. Choose Other to display the Color Picker dialog box, then click in the color wheel to select a new color.

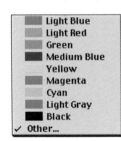

Color Picker dialog box

Style There are only two choices in this submenu — Lines and Dots — and they display as their name implies. The only major difference is that subdivision grid lines don't display when Dots is the selection.

Increments You can define how widely spaced the grid lines are by entering values in the Gridline every and Subdivisions fields of the Guides & Grid dialog box. The Gridline every number sets the distance between the major grid lines. The default is 72 pt (1 inch), so if the unit of measurement is points, the field displays 72 pt (1 inch = 72 points), picas = 6p0, millimeters = 25.4 mm, and so on.

The value in the Subdivisions field determines how many lines are displayed between the major grid lines (when the Style selected is Lines). The default in the Subdivision field is 8. That means, then, that when Inches is the unit of measurement and Gridline every specifies 1 inch for the major grid line, a grid line is displayed every 1/8 inch.

If you are using Picas as your unit of measurement, you may want to change the Subdivisions value to 6 so you have a grid line every pica.

| Light Blue |
| Light Red |
| Green |
| Medium Blue |
| Yellow |
| Magenta |
| Cyan |
| Light Gray |
| Black |
| ✓ Other... |

Grid colors available in Illustrator 10

| ✓ Lines |
| Dots |

Styles of guides available in Illustrator 10

245

There are 6 picas to an inch, so it makes more sense to have a division at the pica mark, rather than an eighth of an inch.

Grids in Back The Grids in Back checkbox can be unchecked if you want to display the grid in front of your artwork rather than behind it.

Changing Constrain Angle

You can change the angle of the grid lines rather than using the 0°, 45°, 90° default, making it easier to draw objects in perspective.

1. Display the General Preferences dialog box (**Edit ⇨ Preferences ⇨ General**).

2. Change the value in the Constrain Angle field.

3. Click OK or press *return/enter*.

Changes in the Constrain Angle value apply to the current document, to all new documents created, and to any existing document opened after the changed was made. In addition, when you change the Constrain Angle value, tool behaviors and other operations are also affected, such as:

- Shapes drawn with the rectangle and ellipse tools and paths drawn with the Pen tool snap to the new angle value (axes) when the *Shift* key is held down.

- Moving objects with *Shift* key held down snaps them to the new angle value.

Using Angled Grids to Draw Objects in Perspective Draw objects in perspective quickly by changing the angle of the grid lines from the default angle of 0°. Use the angled grid lines to align the paths of the object.

timesaver

To change the Constrain Angle value to the same as an object in your artwork, select the object, then change the Constrain Angle field to the same angle displayed in the Info palette.

activity 6.3

1. If the document you had open in Activity 6.2 has been closed, create a new document.

2. Display the grid (View ⇨ Show Grid or press ⌘ " or display the context-sensitive menu and choose Show Grid).

   - Notice that the major grid lines are placed every inch and that there are 7 lines between each major grid line, creating eight "cells" between the major grid lines.

3. Display the Guides & Grid Preferences dialog box. Change the grid color to Light Gray and the Style to Dots. Click OK or press *return/enter*.

   - Notice that there are no indications of any subdivisions.

4. Move to a section of the document page where there is no artwork.

Continued

5. Draw a rectangle. Apply a 1 point black stroke and fill it with White by clicking the Default Fill and Stroke button in the Toolbox.

   - Notice that the grid lines are blocked out by the rectangle.

6. Change the fill color of the rectangle to None.

   - Notice that the grid lines show behind the rectangle because the object is transparent.

7. Turn on the Snap to Grid option (View ⇨ Snap to Grid).

8. With the Selection tool, select the rectangle and move it slowly to the right until it sticks (snaps) to the grid line.

   - You have to click on the edge of the object to select it because the fill is None. To be able to click and move from within an object, the fill must be White or a color.

9. Delete the rectangle you just drew.

10. Display the General Preferences dialog box (Edit ⇨ Preferences ⇨ General) and change the value in the Constrain Angle field to 25.

11. Display the Guides & Grid Preferences dialog box (Edit ⇨ Preferences ⇨ Guides & Grid) and change the color of the grid to a light pink.

    - Display the Color Picker and click on a light pink color in the color wheel.

12. Change the Style to Lines.

13. With the Rectangle tool, draw a rectangle along the major grid lines that is two sections long and 1 section wide (see illustration #1). Apply a fill of White.

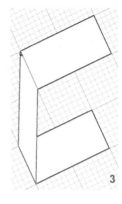

14. With the Direct Selection tool, click in the rectangle and drag-copy it straight down two sections. Align it along major grid lines (see illustration #2).

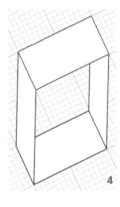

15. With the Pen tool, draw another rectangle from the top left corner of the first rectangle you drew, down to the top left corner of the second rectangle, then to the bottom left corner of the second rectangle, up to the bottom left corner of the first rectangle, then over to the top left corner and close the path (see illustration #3).

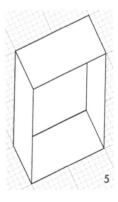

16. With the Direct Selection tool, click in rectangle #3 and drag-copy it straight across to align it along the right edge of the first two rectangles to create the fourth side of the box.

17. Click on the first rectangle you drew and bring it to the front of the stack (see illustration #4).

18. Deselect all.

19. With the Pen tool, click on the top left corner of the first rectangle, then click on the top left corner of the second rectangle, then click on the top right corner of the second rectangle, then move up and click on the top right corner of the first rectangle, and move over to the top left corner and close the path.

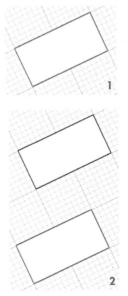

20. Send this rectangle to the bottom of the stack (illustration #5).

21. Turn off Snap to Grid and hide the grid.

22. Close this document without saving it to a file.

247

Guides

In addition to using grids to align objects, you can create and display guides, which are non-printing lines like the grid, but instead of being placed at predefined intervals on the page, you can place them where you want them. There are two kinds of guides: ruler guides and object guides, and they are locked into place when you create them. But you can unlock them so you can move, delete, or modify them.

Ruler Guides

Ruler guides are straight lines, either horizontal or vertical, and are solid or dotted lines along which you can align paths. The guides extend to the edge of the Pasteboard. The rulers must be displayed in order to create ruler guides, but the Rulers command doesn't have to be turned on for guides already created to be visible. If the Snap to Grid option is on, the ruler guide snaps to the nearest grid line.

To create a ruler guide:

1. If rulers are not visible in the document window, choose **View** ⇨ **Show Rulers** or press ⌘r to display them.

2. *Vertical guides:* Position the pointer somewhere in the ruler on the left side of the document window. Click and drag the pointer to where you want it to be placed, then release the mouse to drop it there.

   Horizontal guides: Position the pointer somewhere in the ruler at the top of the document window. Click and drag the pointer to where you want it to be placed, then release the mouse to drop it there.

You can switch a guide from horizontal to vertical, or vice versa, by pressing the ⌥ key before releasing the mouse. That means that you can place a vertical guide by dragging from the horizontal ruler and pressing the ⌥ key before you release the mouse. A vertical ruler is placed rather than a horizontal one.

Object Guides

You aren't limited to horizontal and vertical lines as guides. Any path you create, except type, can be converted to a guide and you can convert object guides back to graphic objects easily. Paths snap to object guides the same as they do ruler guides or grids.

To create a guide object:

1. Select an object, multiple objects, a group of objects, or a combination of objects and groups of objects.

2. Choose **View** ⇨ **Guides** ⇨ **Make Guides**
   or
   Press ⌘5

 A path created without a stroke or fill applied to it disappears when it's deselected and reappears when it's reselected. Making an object into a guide causes the path to remain visible when its deselected, allowing you to create a preliminary layout plan of your artwork.

Any paint attributes (stroke and fill) applied to the object are invisible. They're still there; you just can't see them. To edit the shape of a guide object, Lock Guides must be unchecked (**View** ➪ **Guides** ➪ **Lock Guides**). When you're finished editing the guide object, lock the guides again (**View** ➪ **Guides** ➪ **Lock Guides**). The checkmark reappears beside the menu item.

Show/Hide Guides

Guides are visible only when Show Guides is turned on in the View menu. It's a toggle with Hide Guides. You can place guides when Hide Guides is turned on, but you can't see them until you choose Show Guides.

Snap to Point

When Snap to Point is turned on, a checkmark appears next to the Snap to Point option in the View menu. The Snap to Point command is a toggle. When Snap to Point is turned on, a checkmark displays beside the option in the View menu. When it is turned off, the checkmark is absent.

The point at which you click on an object to move it (the point directly under the pointer) snaps to guides placed on the document page whenever it is moved to within 2 pixels of the guide. The pointer turns white when it snaps to the guide. If you have the Direct Selection tool selected, you can drag an anchor point and snap it to a point on another object.

How close you need to be to a guide before a path or anchor point snaps to it can be changed in the Smart Guides Preferences dialog box (**Edit** ➪ **Preferences** ➪ **Smart Guides & Slices**). Change the value in the Snapping Tolerance field. Enter a larger number (0 to 10 pt) to snap from farther away from the point or a smaller number, which requires that you're closer to the guide before a path snaps to it.

If both Snap to Point and Snap to Grid are turned on, it may be difficult to determine whether the object is snapping to the grid or snapping to the point. You should turn off one or the other so you're sure what your object is snapping to, the guide or the grid. In most cases, I prefer to snap the object to the guides I place in the document, rather than the grid. So I turn off Snap to Grid and leave Snap to Point on.

Unlocking Guides

When guides are created, they are locked into the position they were originally placed so you don't move or delete them accidentally. You can, however, unlock them so they can be moved, copied, or deleted. The Lock Guides command is a toggle, so when guides are locked, a checkmark displays in the View menu next to the Lock Guides command. When guides are unlocked, there is no checkmark. If one guide is locked, they all are. You can't selectively choose which guides are locked and which are not.

Hide Guides	⌘;
✓ Lock Guides	⌥⌘;
Make Guides	⌘5
Release Guides	⌥⌘5
Clear Guides	

Guides submenu options

249

Moving and Copying Guides

Once guides have been unlocked, they can be selected so you can move, copy, or delete them. Select, move, copy, and paste guides the same way you would an object:

- Click on a single guide or *Shift*-click to select multiple guides.
- Marquee one or more guides to select them.
- Click and drag selected guides to move them.
- Press ⌘c to copy selected guides.
- Press ⌘v to paste guides that have been cut or copied into the current document or another document.

Deleting Guides

Guides can be deleted in the following ways:

- To delete all guides at once, choose **View** ⇨ **Guides** ⇨ **Clear Guides**. This command does not store the guides in the Clipboard and they cannot be pasted into the document.

- Unlock the guides, select the ones you want to delete, and do one of the following:

  - Press delete (*Windows: Backspace* or *del*). Guides that have been deleted are not stored in the Clipboard and cannot be pasted back into the document.

  - Choose **Edit** ⇨ **Cut**. Guides that have been cut are stored in the Clipboard and can be pasted back into the current document or a different document.

  - Choose **Edit** ⇨ **Clear**. This command does not store the guides in the Clipboard and they cannot be pasted into the document.

- Delete the Guide layer in the Layers palette. Layers are discussed in Step 8, *Layers & Links*.

Converting a Guide Object Back to a Graphic Object

To convert a guide object back to a graphic object:

1. Unlock guides.

2. Select the guide (or guides) you want to convert back to a graphic object.

3. Choose **View** ⇨ **Guides** ⇨ **Release Guides**.
   or
   Press ⌥⌘5
   or
   Display the context-menu and choose Release Guides from the menu.

read this!

When you select a Ruler Guide with the Direct Selection tool, anchor points display on both ends of the Guide the same as an open path. When you press delete, the anchor points remain. These stray anchor points can cause all sorts of problems. Believe me, you want to get rid of them. Either press delete twice, or select the stray points (Select ⇨ Object ⇨ Stray Points) and press the delete key.

Any paint attributes (stroke and fill) applied to the object before it was converted to a guide object are restored.

Setting Guide Preferences

Guide Preferences are located in the Guides & Grid Preferences dialog box.

Guide colors available in Illustrator 10

Color You can change the color of guides by pressing the submenu arrow to display the submenu in the Color area of the Guides section of the dialog box. If you have objects in your artwork that are the same colors as the preset selections, making the grid lines difficult to see, you can create your own color. Choose Other from the submenu to display the color picker dialog box. Click in the color wheel (**Windows:** in the Color field) to select a new color.

Options for guides styles available in Illustrator 10

Style As with Grid Styles, there are only two choices in this submenu — Lines and Dots.

fyi When you're displaying a grid and using ruler guides, make them different colors and change the Guide Style to Dots so you can tell which is a guide and which is the grid.

activity 6.4

1. Create a new document: Letter size, CMYK color mode.

2. Choose Edit ⇨ Preferences ⇨ General to display the General Preferences dialog box. Change the value in the Constrain Angle field back to 0 (it was changed in the last activity).

3. Verify that the Snap to Point option is turned on (checked) in the View menu.

4. Draw a rectangle in the center of the page. Paint it blue and apply a 1 point black stroke.

5. If rulers are not visible, display them (press ⌘ r).

6. Click in the ruler on the left side of the page and drag to create a vertical ruler guide. Drop it somewhere between the 1" mark and the 2" mark.

7. With the Selection tool, click on the left side of the rectangle you drew and move it so it snaps to the ruler guide you created.

   ■ The pointer becomes hollow when it snaps to the guide.

8. With the rectangle still selected, make it an object guide (View ⇨ Guides ⇨ Make Guides).

   ■ The guide is locked if a checkmark displays next to the Lock Guides option in the View menu.

9. Unlock the guides.

10. Copy the rectangle object guide and paste it into the document twice.

    ■ The two guides you pasted back into the document were placed one on top of the other.

11. Select and move these rectangle object guides into new positions.

12. Draw an oval beside one of the rectangle object guides.

13. With the Direct-Selection tool, drag an anchor point of the oval to the rectangle until it snaps to it.

14. Delete two of the rectangle object guides you created.

15. Close this document without saving it to a file.

Smart Guides

Smart Guides help you align objects with one another as you draw, move, or duplicate them. They are temporary guides that, when turned on, display when you pass the pointer over an object to which you want to align another object. The point at which you click the second object is the point that snaps to the first object, either on its path, its anchor point, or at a specified angle.

Smart Guides are temporary and disappear so quickly they seem to flash off and on. You can't lock them to make them visible permanently either. When turned on, they are applied to objects already drawn as well as any new objects you draw. They are the same color as the ruler guides and you can change the color the same as you do ruler guides — in the Guides & Grid Preferences dialog box (**Edit** ➪ **Preferences** ➪ **Guides & Grid**).

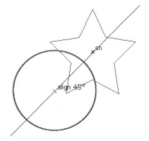

read this!

Snap to Grid must be turned off for Smart Guides to be visible.

To turn Smart Guides on or off:

- Choose **View** ➪ **Smart Guides**

or

- Press ⌘u

Smart Guide Preferences

You can define how far from a Smart Guide the second object must be to snap to it (Snapping Tolerance) and the angles at which the guides display by changing those settings in the Smart Guides Preferences dialog box. To display the Smart Guides Preferences dialog box:

- Choose **Edit** ➪ **Preferences** ➪ **Smart Guides & Slices**.

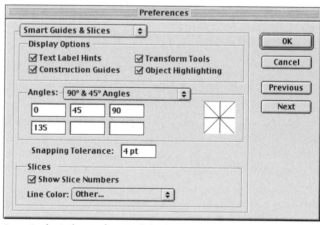

Smart Guides & Slices Preferences dialog box

Display Options

Text Label Hints Text Label Hints are labels that display on the Smart Guides to help you align objects. They display when you pass the pointer over the first object and again when the second object is aligned at that point. For example, the word Path displays when the pointer is passed over the path of the object to which you want to align another object. When the point where you clicked the second object to drag it is exactly over the path of the first object, the word Path displays again.

Center points of star and circle are aligned on 45° angle

- Turn Text Label Hints off by clicking its checkbox to uncheck it. The labels won't display on the Smart Guides.

To align an object along a specified angle relative to another object, drag the pointer over the object to which you want to align a second object (before clicking the mouse). Click at the point on the second object where you want to align it to the first object, then drag it until the Smart Guide for the angle you want displays on the first object. Snap to the Smart Guide angle line and drag along it to the position you want.

Construction Guides When Construction Guides are on (the program default), angle lines display when you are drawing a shape with the Pen tool, allowing you to align anchor points as you draw an object.

- Turn Construction Guides off by clicking its checkbox to uncheck it.

Transform Tools When checked, it allows you to use Smart Guides with the Transform tools, scale, rotate, shear, and so on. Transform functions are discussed in Step 9, *Reshape, Combine, & Distort Objects.*

- Turn Transform Tools off by clicking its checkbox to uncheck it.

Object Highlighting On

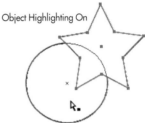

Object Highlighting When Object Highlighting is on (the program default), the first object is highlighted when you pass the pointer over it. When you turn Object Highlighting off in the Smart Guides Preferences dialog box, the first object is not highlighted when you pass the pointer over it but Text Label Hints still display.

- Turn Object Highlighting off by clicking its checkbox to uncheck it.

Notice that the path of the circle, created first so it's on the bottom of the stacking layer, is displayed even though the star has a white fill applied to it

Angles

Choose a selection from the pop-up submenu to determine the angle at which the guides display when Smart Guides are turned on. The angles associated with the choice you make in the submenu are displayed in the fields below the pop-up menu.

If you want to set your own angle, change one of the preset angles in the fields. You also can choose Custom Angles from the submenu and enter these pre-defined angle values in the fields. If you specify your own set of angles, switch to a pre-defined set of angles, then switch to Custom Angles again, the custom angle values you entered the last time are used.

| 90° Angles |
| 45° Angles |
| ✓ 90° & 45° Angles |
| 60° Angles |
| 60° & Horizontal Angles |
| 30° Angles |
| 90° & 15° Angles |
| Custom Angles |

Preset angle options for displaying Smart Guides

Snapping Tolerance

The value entered in this field determines how close the point of the second object has to be to snap to the first object. The default is 4 points, but you can enter a lower number (as low as 0) to require the pointer to be closer for the snap to take effect, or enter a higher number (as high as 10) to snap to the object from a greater distance. A higher value means you don't have to be as close to a path to see the Smart Guides.

253

activity 6.5

1. Create a new document: Letter size, CMYK color mode.

2. Verify that Snap to Grid is not checked in the View menu.

3. Turn Smart Guides on.
   - Choose View ⇨ Smart Guides or press ⌘ u.

4. Draw a rectangle on the page. Apply a 1 point stroke and fill it with white.
   - Click the Default Fill and Stroke button in the Toolbox.

5. With any of the Selection tools selected, click in the rectangle and drag it around in a small circular motion to see the angle guides.
   - Notice that the axis point of the angles is the point where you clicked to select the rectangle.
   - The word "origin" and a degree of angle display at the point of the click.

6. Move the rectangle up along the 45° angle guide about an inch. Release the mouse to drop the rectangle in its new position.

7. Because you can accomplish this same thing by holding down the *Shift* key (when the default of Constrain Angle in the General Preferences dialog box is 0°), display Smart Guide Preferences (Edit ⇨ Preferences ⇨ Smart Guides & Slices) and choose 30° Angles from the Angles pop-up menu.

8. Draw a second rectangle and move it around its original position in a circular motion.
   - The new set of angles display as you pass over them, but the 45° angle also displays because that's the default in the Constrain Angle field of the General Preferences dialog box.

9. Delete one of the rectangles so there's only one left.

10. Draw an oval to the right directly beside the remaining rectangle. Make it slightly smaller than the rectangle. Apply a 1 point stroke and fill it with None.

11. Without clicking the mouse, move the pointer over the rectangle. Move it over the center point until the Text Label Hint displays. Then move it over each side of the outside path of the rectangle so you can see the word Path on each side.

12. With the Direct Selection tool, click on the path of the oval between the left anchor point and the top anchor point.
    - The path should be selected (all anchor points solid). If it isn't, marquee it so all anchor points are solid.
    - You can't select the oval by clicking in the center of the oval because it isn't filled with a color.

13. Move the oval just a little bit and then move it back to where you originally clicked to select it, but don't release the mouse.
    - You can tell when you are in the exact same position because the word "origin" displays.

14. Drag the oval to the path of the rectangle along the guide that displays at "origin 0°" until you see the word "intersect" appear.
    - When "intersect" appears, the point of your click on the oval is intersecting with the path of the rectangle.

15. Move the oval up and down along the path of the rectangle and release the mouse.

16. Delete all the shapes on the page (press ⌘ a, then the delete key).

17. Draw a perfect circle 1½" in diameter. Apply a 2 point purple stroke and fill it with 100% yellow.

18. Click on the center-point of the circle and drag-copy a new circle, align it on 150° angle and drop it so outside paths are about ¼" apart.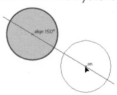

19. Drag copy five more circles, place them so outside paths are about the same distance apart and so they're aligned on the 30°, 90°, 150° angles around the original circle.
    - If you get them close to the same distance from the original circle, they will then be that same distance from each other, too.

20. Close this document without saving it to a file.

Change Artboard Specifications

Changing Size of Artboard

To change the size of the artboard in an existing document, its orientation, the units of measurement used in the document, and other specifications, display the Document Setup dialog box (**File ⇨ Document Setup** or press ⌥⌘ p).

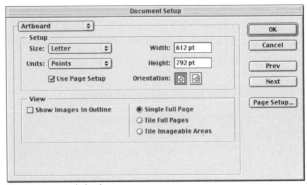

Make sure Artboard is the selection in the pop-up menu at the top left corner of the dialog box. The other two options will be discussed later. Choose one of the following methods to change the size of the artboard:

Document setup dialog box

1. Choose a preset size from the Size pop-up menu.

2. Enter values in the Width and Height fields to create a Custom artboard.

3. Check the Use Page Setup checkbox (***Windows:*** Use Print Setup). This option matches the artboard size and orientation specifications to the page size and orientation set in the Page Setup (***Windows:*** Print Setup) dialog box.

   ■ You can change the size of the page in the Page Setup (***Windows:*** Print Setup) only if the printer you are currently using accepts custom sizes.

     • Click the Page Setup button in the Document Setup dialog box to display the Page Setup dialog box for the printer.

     • Change the options in the Paper pop-up menu.

     • Click OK or press *return/enter* to exit the Page Setup dialog box.

   ■ If you change the size in the Artboard Size field to a size larger than the size in the Page Setup dialog box of the printer, the artboard in your document window (solid line) reflects that size. The page size in the document window, however, reflects the size of the page as selected in the Page Setup dialog box, with the imageable area represented by a dotted line inside the dotted line of the page border.

read this!

The size of the page and the imageable area is important only if you're going to print directly from Illustrator 10. If the file is imported into a page layout program (such as QuarkXPress), any object in the file is available for import, regardless of the size or position of the artboard, page border, or imageable area. The object doesn't even have to be on the artboard; it can be in the scratch area.

Artboard is smaller than the page size of the printer as determined by the printer's Page Setup dialog box

255

- If the size you make the artboard is smaller than the page size as indicated in the Page Setup dialog box of the printer, the artboard (solid line) is the size you select. But the dotted line representing the imageable area is visible only on the top and left side, indicating that the paper is larger than the size of the artboard.

Changing Units of Measurement

To change the system of measurement used in the document, make a different selection from the Units pop-up menu in the Document Setup dialog box: Points, Picas, Inches, Millimeters, Centimeters, or Pixels.

- When you change from one system of measurement to another, Illustrator converts the present measurement into the new one. For example, if you want to know how wide 692 points equal in inches, change the selection in the Units pop-up menu from Points to Inches.

  - Changing the unit of measurement here saves the changes only in the current document. To change the unit of measurement in all new documents, see *Ruler Units of Measurement* previously discussed in this chapter.

Changing Orientation

There are two orientations for a document page: Portrait (⊞) (taller than it is wide) and Landscape (⊞) (wider than it is tall). The default is Portrait because a standard sheet of printer paper is taller than it is wide.

To change the orientation of your *artboard*:

1. Display the Document Setup dialog box.

2. Click the Landscape button (⊞).

3. Click OK or press *return/enter* to exit the dialog box.

To change the orientation of your *page*:

1. Display the Document Setup dialog box.

2. Click the Page Setup button (**Windows:** Print Setup) and display the printer's Page Setup dialog box.

   - Printers have different print drivers and the Page Setup information can be located in different places. You should be familiar with your printer's Page Setup dialog box.

3. Click the Landscape Orientation icon in the Page Setup dialog box.

Measurement options available in the Units submenu of the Document Setup dialog box

Artboard orientation is Portrait but orientation in Print Setup dialog box is Landscape. With this setup, only objects within the dotted lines will print

4. Click OK or press *return/enter*.

5. Click OK or press *return/enter* again to exit the Document Setup dialog box.

activity 6.6

1. With a document window open, display the Document Setup dialog box (File ➪ Document Setup or press ⌥ ⌘ p).

2. Verify that the Units pop-up menu selection is Inches.

3. In the Size pop-up submenu, change the Artboard Size to Legal.

  ■ Notice that the Use Page Setup checkbox becomes unchecked.

4. Click OK or press *return/enter*.

5. Using the scroll arrows, move the contents of the document window until you can see the bottom of the artboard.

  ■ Notice that the solid line showing the edge of the artboard is 3″ below the bottom of the page because the page size of the printer is 8½″ × 11″.

6. Display the Document Setup dialog box again.

7. Change the Artboard Size to Tabloid.

8. Click OK or press *return/enter*.

  ■ The dotted lines indicating the page border are considerably smaller than the artboard.

9. Display the Document Setup dialog box.

10. Click the Page Setup (**Windows:** Print Setup) button to display the Page Setup dialog box for the printer you're currently using.

11. Does your printer support Tabloid paper size? If so, perform the steps listed below. If not, proceed to #12.

  ■ Change the paper size to Tabloid. Click OK or press *return/enter* to exit the Page Setup/Print Setup dialog box.

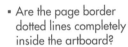

  ■ Click OK or press *return/enter* to exit the Document Setup dialog box.

    • Are the page border dotted lines completely inside the artboard?

  ■ Display the Document Setup dialog box again.

  ■ Click the Page Setup button to display the printer's Page Setup dialog box.

  ■ Change the Paper Size back to Letter or 8½″ × 11″.

  ■ Click OK or press *return/enter* to return to the Document Setup dialog box.

12. Click the Landscape icon in the Orientation field.

13. Click OK or press *return/enter*.

  ■ The artboard turned sideways. It's now 17″ × 11″ but because the printer's Page Setup is 8½″ × 11″, Portrait, so are the dotted lines for the page size in the Illustrator document. Objects placed outside the dotted lines — indicating the paper size for the printer — will not print.

14. Don't save or close this document.

Creating a Multi-Page Document

The program default for a new document in Illustrator 10 is a single page. You can, however, create a multi-page document that prints as individual pages. This process is called *page tiling*.

1. Display the Document Setup dialog box.

   ■ Choose **File** ⇨ **Document Setup** or press ⌥ ⌘ p.

2. Change the artboard size to a width and height that is at least as large as the combined size of the individual pages you want to create.

   ■ If you want to create a 4-page 8½" × 11" document with all the pages side by side, the artboard should be at least **34"** wide and **11"** deep (8½" + 8½" + 8½" + 8½" = 34").

   ■ A document that is two pages across and two pages down should have an artboard that is at least **17"** wide and **22"** high (width: 8½" + 8½" = 17"; height: 11" + 11" = 22").

     ▪ The small numbers at the bottom of each page on the artboard indicate its page number. These numbers don't print.

     ▪ Any part of an object that extends into the nonimageable area (the gutter) between two pages won't print (because of the limitations of the printer).

   ■ If you want to add crop marks to the document, make sure the artboard is larger than the sum of the pages so the crop marks fit inside the artboard borders.

3. Click the Tile Full Pages button in the View section of the Document Setup dialog box.

   ■ As many *full* pages as can fit on the artboard are displayed (dotted lines) (Figure 6.4A).

4. Click the Tile Imageable Areas button to display as many full pages and as many *partial* pages as are visible based on the size of the artboard (Figure 6.4B). Gutter areas don't display because you're requesting *imageable* areas.

timesaver

To display the entire artboard on the screen, double-click the Hand tool icon in the Toolbox.

Choose Tile Full Pages to display as many full pages as can fit on the artboard

Step 6 — RULERS, GRIDS, & GUIDES

Show/Hide Page Tiling

You can choose to show the nonprinting tiling guidelines on the screen or hide them. Choose **View** ➪ **Show Page Tiling** or **View** ➪ **Hide Page Tiling**. This option in the View menu is a toggle. If page tiling is visible on the screen, the option reads Hide Page Tiling. If page tiling is invisible, the option reads Show Page Tiling.

And don't forget, if you want to work with no boundaries at all, you can hide the entire artboard by choosing **View** ➪ **Hide Artboard**.

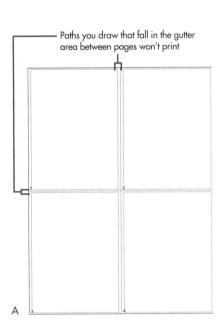

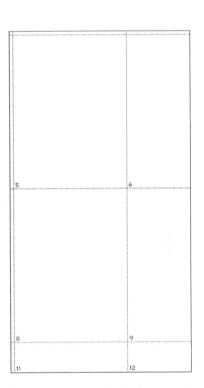

FIGURE 6.4 Examples of page tiling. (A) Tile Full Pages is selected in the Document Setup dialog box. (B) Tile Imageable Areas is selected in the Document Setup dialog box.

activity 6.7

1. If the document you used in Activity 6.6 is not still open on your screen, create a new document.

2. Display the Document Setup dialog box (choose File ⇨ Document Setup or press ⌥ ⌘ p).

3. Change the Artboard Size to accommodate 3 standard 8½" × 11" pages across and 3 pages down.

   ■ Add the widths of the three pages together to get the total width of the artboard.

   ■ Add the height of the three pages together to get the value to enter in the Height field.

4. Click the Tile Full Pages checkbox.

5. Click OK or press *return/enter*.

   ■ Your artboard should look like the one displayed below.

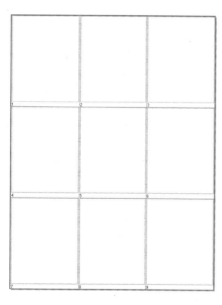

6. Change the artboard size to 30" wide by 36" high.

   ■ Your artboard should look like the one displayed below.

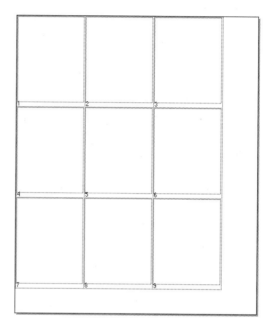

   ■ Illustrator 10 calculated the page positions based on the page size as set in the printer's Page Setup dialog box, with the excess left blank.

7. Display the Document Setup dialog box.

8. Change the artboard size to 20" wide by 27" high and click the Tile Imageable Areas button.

   ■ Illustrator 10 calculated how many pages fit on the artboard, based on the page size as set in the printer's Page Setup dialog box, with the excess left blank.

9. Close this document without saving it to a file.

Repositioning Pages on the Artboard

You can't move the artboard (pretend it's pinned to the pasteboard); it's always in the center of the pasteboard. But you can move pages around on the artboard (providing the artboard is big enough) using the Page tool. It's hidden under the Hand tool () in the Toolbox.

This feature is useful when you create artwork in the middle of the page but before you're finished, it extends beyond the boundaries of the page. You can move the page boundaries to encompass the artwork so the entire illustration prints.

1. Select the Page tool in the Toolbox.

2. Click, or click and drag, inside the artboard where you want the lower left corner of the imageable area of the page to be placed.

   - Enlarge the size of the artboard if necessary to accommodate the new position of the page.

   - The point of the click is the lower left corner of the imageable area of the page.

   - To line up the lower-left page boundary with the lower left corner of the artboard automatically, double-click the Page tool in the Toolbox.

   - If Tile Imageable Areas is selected in the Document Setup dialog box when you click with the Page tool, as many partial pages as can fit are displayed to the left, right, top, and bottom of the point of the click.

Page tool icon in the Toolbox palette

Artwork extends beyond page boundaries and off artboard

Page boundaries are moved so artwork fits within printable page

activity 6.8

1. Open the file named Fish.eps that's located in the Student Folder on the CD-ROM that accompanies this book.

   - Notice one of the fish didn't fit on the page, which means the tail won't print.

2. Display the Document Setup dialog box (File ⇨ Document Setup or press ⌥⌘p).

3. Change the Artboard Size to 15" wide and click OK or press *return/enter*.

   - The fish are now all within the artboard boundaries, but not the page boundary.

4. Select the Page tool in the Toolbox (▢).

5. Click on the artboard and drag the page boundaries to the left until all the fish fit within the page boundaries, then release the mouse.

   - Now all the fish will print.

6. Save this file into your Practice folder and print this page.

7. Close the document.

Create Crop Marks

Crop marks, also called trim marks or cutmarks, are short vertical and horizontal lines printed ⅛" outside an object's or page's edges that indicate where the object or page should be trimmed after it's printed. Illustrator 10 has two ways to create crop marks: (a) the Crop Marks command in the Object menu and (b) the Trim Marks filter.

Creating Crop Marks Using the Crop Marks Command

The Crop Marks command in the Object menu creates crop marks at the corners of a rectangle that you draw (Figure 6.5), and they become part of your artwork (A). You can specify only one set of crop marks per artwork file using this command. Applying the Crop Marks command a second time replaces the existing crop marks, even if there are multiple pages in a file. To create more than one set of crop marks on a page, use the Trim Marks filter (see *Creating Crops Marks Using the Trim Marks Filter* later in this chapter).

Crop marks created with the Crop Marks command in the Object menu aren't visible when the artwork is imported into page layout programs.

To create crop marks:

1. With the Rectangle tool (▣), draw a rectangle around the artwork that will be the final shape and size after it's printed.

   ■ For example, if you're designing a business card, draw the rectangle 3½" × 2" (standard size business card) and position it around your business card art and text to indicate its edges.

   ■ If you don't create a rectangle, the crop marks are placed at the corners of the artboard.

   ■ The rectangle can be filled with color or have a stroke applied, but it disappears when crop marks are specified.

> **read this!**
>
> *Crop marks created with the Crop Marks command in the Object menu cannot be selected or edited. If they have to be changed, release them and create new ones.*

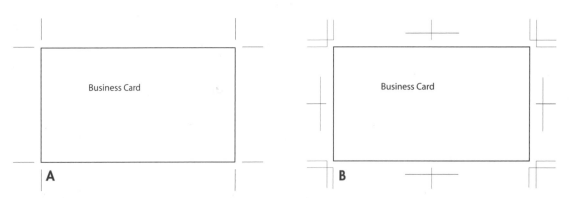

FIGURE 6.5 Artwork displaying crop marks: (A) standard crop marks; (B) Japanese crop marks

2. With the rectangle still selected, choose **Object** ⇨ **Crop Marks** ⇨ **Make**.

- The rectangle disappears and crop marks display ⅛" from the corners of the rectangle.

Japanese Crop Marks Japanese crop marks (see Figure 6.5) perform the same function as standard crop marks; they just look different. Check with your output provider before using this style of crop marks. If they are unfamiliar with them, errors could occur.

To create Japanese crop marks, check the Japanese Crop Marks checkbox in the General Preferences dialog box (**Edit** ⇨ **Preferences** ⇨ **General**).

Creating a Bleed A *bleed* is an image or screen that extends beyond the boundaries of the artwork or page. Most output providers require that images remain at least ¼" from the edge. Portions of the artwork, including screens, that bleed (extend beyond the trim marks), should extend at least ⅛". Some output providers require even more bleed. Check with your output provider for the exact specifications.

Image and screen that bleeds
(extends beyond its crop marks)

Removing Crop Marks Created with the Crop Marks Command

To delete existing crop marks that were created with the Crop Marks command in the Object menu, choose **Object** ⇨ **Crop Marks** ⇨ **Release**. The rectangle reappears with a fill and stroke of None, even if it had a fill or stroke applied to it before the Crop Marks command was applied.

- If the rectangle becomes deselected and you can't find it, display artwork in Outline mode, then select the rectangle and return to Preview mode.

- You can add a fill color or stroke to the rectangle, resize it, or delete it.

Creating Crop Marks Using the Trim Marks Filter

Trim marks are placed around selected objects in a document and, using the Trim Marks filter, you can create multiple sets of crop marks in an artwork file. You don't have to draw a rectangle around objects for which you want trim marks. Illustrator uses the the smallest rectangle that can enclose all objects (including the half of the stroke weight that extends outside the pathline) as a guide for placing the trim marks.

Crop marks created with the Trim Marks filter can be selected, moved, edited, colored, and so on, the same as other objects. The crop marks are grouped together so selecting one of the marks with the Selection tool, selects all of them. To select individual crop marks, select them with the Direct Selection tool. They are visible when the artwork is imported into a page layout program.

To create crop marks using the Trim Marks filter:

1. Select the object or objects for which you want crop marks.

2. Choose **Filter** ⇨ **Create** ⇨ **Trim Marks**.

   ▪ Crop marks are placed ¼" away from the edges of its "surrounding rectangle."

   ▪ Group the crop marks and the artwork so they move with the artwork if it's moved.

   ▪ If Japanese Crop Marks is checked in the General Preferences dialog box, Japanese crop marks are created (see Figure 6.5B)

Trim marks surrounding artwork. Blue box is imaginary rectangle Illustrator used for placing trim marks.

activity 6.9

1. Open the file containing the hammer you created as part of the exercise in Step 4, *The Pen & Pencil Tools*.

2. Draw a rectangle that's ¼" larger all the way around than the actual artwork. Fill it with 100% cyan and apply a 2 pt black stroke.

   ▪ Display the grid to help you determine the correct size for the rectangle. Change the value in the Subdivisions field of the Guides & Grid Preferences dialog box to 4 (resulting in ¼" grid lines). Then position the left edge and the top edge of the hammer precisely on grid lines. Draw the rectangle one grid line (or partial grid block) beyond the edges of the hammer.

3. Choose Object ⇨ Crop Marks ⇨ Make.

   ▪ The rectangle disappears and crop marks display at the corners of the artwork.

4. Choose Object ⇨ Crop Marks ⇨ Release.

   ▪ The crop marks disappear and the rectangle returns, but the original fill and stroke attributes are gone and replaced by None.

5. Press the Delete key to remove the rectangle.

6. With the Selection tool, select all the objects of the hammer.

7. Choose Filter ⇨ Create ⇨ Trim Marks.

   ▪ Crop marks are placed ¼" away from the corners of the imaginary rectangle that surrounds the object.

8. With the Selection tool, select the upper left vertical crop mark. Change the stroke color to 100% magenta.

   ▪ Selecting a single trim mark with the Selection tool causes all trim marks to become selected.

9. Deselect all.

Continued

10. With the Direct Selection tool, select the bottom right crop mark and change its color to 100% black.

11. Close the file without saving it.

Create a Custom Startup File

If you find you're always working with the rulers on, grids on, and other document settings that are different from the default settings, you can create a Custom Startup file so that these elements are automatically part of every new document you create. You can change Document Setup and Page Setup options, such as Show Rulers, Show Grid, and so on. You can also add color swatches from Swatch libraries, patterns, gradients, brushes. The procedures for adding these elements to the Custom Startup File are covered in Step 7, *Add Color to Artwork*. Custom graph designs also can be saved in the Custom Startup file. Graphs are discussed in Step 13, *Graphs*.

To create a Custom Startup file for a document using CMYK color mode, make changes to the Adobe Illustrator Startup_CMYK file (printed pages). To create a Custom Startup File for a document with RGB color mode, make changes to the Adobe Illustrator Startup_RGB file (Web pages). The instructions listed below for the CMYK color mode can be used for the RGB mode, too.

1. Locate the Adobe Illustrator Startup_CMYK file in the Plug-ins folder that's stored in the Adobe Illustrator 10 folder on your hard drive.

   ■ *Windows:* Choose **My Computer** ⇨ **Program Files** ⇨ **Adobe** ⇨ **Illustrator 10** ⇨ **Plug-Ins**

2. For insurance, make a copy of this file and store it "loose" in the Adobe Illustrator 10 folder or in another folder. Use this file copy if something happens to the new Custom Startup file you're creating.

   ■ *Macintosh:* Choose **File** ⇨ **Duplicate** or press ⌘d

   ■ *Windows:* Right-click the file, choose Copy from the menu that displays. Right-click to display the menu again and choose Paste.

3. Open the Adobe Illustrator Startup_CMYK file that's still in the Plug-ins folder (see Figure 6.6).

4. Change specifications according to your needs. Some examples are listed below, but you don't have to change all of them. I suggest showing rulers and changing the size of the artwork window to fit on your monitor screen.

   ■ Show Rulers

   ■ Show Grid

- Turn on Smart Guides

- If you consistently work on a page size different than standard Letter size, change the Page Setup, artboard size, and imageable area sizes.

- Change the size of the artwork window, position it to best advantage on your screen, and display only those palettes you use frequently.

5. Save the file as an Adobe Illustrator document with exactly the same name back into the Plug-ins folder to overwrite the original file. It's okay; you made a copy of the original for future use, if necessary.

6. Quit the Illustrator 10 program and relaunch it. Create a new file and see if your changes appear in the new document.

   - Changes won't take effect until you quit and relaunch Illustrator 10.

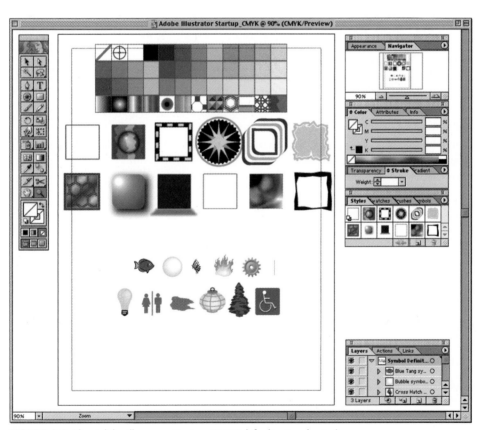

FIGURE 6.6 The Adobe Illustrator Startup_CMYK default artwork window.

activity 6.10

1. Locate the Adobe Illustrator Startup_CMYK file in the Plug-ins folder that's stored in the Adobe Illustrator 10 folder on your hard drive.

2. Make a copy of this file and save it "loose" in the Adobe Illustrator 10 folder.
   - **Macintosh:** Choose File ⇨ Duplicate or press ⌘d
   - **Windows:** Right-click the file, choose Copy from the menu that displays. Right-click to display the menu again and choose Paste.

3. Open the Adobe Illustrator Startup_CMYK file that's still in the Plug-ins folder.

4. Show Rulers (View ⇨ Show Rulers).

5. Display the Document Setup dialog box and change the Units pop-up menu to Inches.

6. Size the artwork window to fit onto your screen.

7. Save the file and close the window.

8. Quit Illustrator and reopen it.

9. Create a new CMYK document.
   - Are rulers displayed showing increments in inches?
   - Does the artwork window fit the way you changed it in the Startup file?

10. Close the file without saving it.

PRACTICE ACTIVITY 6-1 — Videotape

1. Create a new document. Name it Videotape.eps and save it into your Practice folder.

2. Show smart guides, grid, and rulers. Display the Info palette. Unit of measurement should be inches.

3. Change the View mode to Outline.

4. Create a duplicate window and change the View mode to Preview so you can see the changes take place in Preview mode in the duplicate window as you make them in Outline on the original window.

5. Draw a rounded rectangle 7" wide × 4" high, with a corner radius of ¼". Fill with 100% black, no stroke.

6. Drag a vertical ruler guide to the 8" mark.

7. Drag a horizontal ruler guide to the 4" mark.

8. Align the right side of the rounded rectangle with the 8" guide. Align the center point vertically on the 4" guide.

9. Create a second rounded rectangle, 6½" × 2", corner radius 2". Align the center points of the two rectangles.

10. With the Direct Selection tool, select only the top right and bottom right anchor points of the smaller shape. Drag them to the right and align at the 7" vertical guide.

11. With the Direct Selection tool, select only the top left and bottom left anchor points of the smaller shape. Drag them to the left and align at the 2" vertical guide.

12. Fill this shape with 30% black.

13. Draw a circle 2¼ in diameter. Fill with 100% black, no stroke.

14. Draw another circle 1" in diameter. Fill with white and drag over the black circle. Align center points.

15. Draw a third circle ½" in diameter. Apply a 2 point black stroke with a white fill. Drag over the other two circles and align center points.

16. Highlight all three circles (marquee) and drag over rectangles. Align center points of the circles with 3" horizontal mark and 4" vertical mark.

17. With all three circles still highlighted (and nothing else), drag-copy another set of circles. Align their center points on the 6" horizontal mark and the 4" vertical mark.

18. Draw a rectangle 3" wide and 2½" high. Fill with 100% black, no stroke. Drag to align the center point with the center point of the first rounded rectangle.

19. With the Line Segment tool, draw a straight line from the left edge of the shape to the right edge, aligned at the 5½" vertical mark on the ruler. Apply a 4 point, 60% black stroke, no fill.

20. Draw a 1.111" long, 24 point wide, 60% black, dashed stroke. Enter 6 in the first dash field. Align on the 4" vertical mark and horizontally on the left side similar to the illustration below.

21. Copy the dashed rule, paste and align it on the 4" vertical mark on the right side, similar to the one below.

22. Save the file, print it, and close the document window.

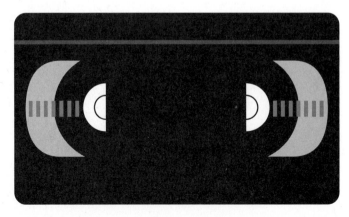

PRACTICE ACTIVITY 6-2 — Umbrella

1. Create a new document, name it Umbrella.eps and save it into your practice folder.
2. Show rulers, grid, and smart guides, and ruler guides. Display the Info palette. Unit of measurement should be inches.
3. Drag vertical ruler guide to the middle of the page.
4. Create a 3" circle and align its center point on the vertical ruler guide. Apply a 1 point black stroke and a fill of None.
5. Select Erase tool in the Toolbox and erase the bottom half of the circle.

   or

   Choose the Direct Selection tool in the Toolbox, select only the bottom anchor point of the circle, and press *delete*.
6. Highlight the bottom-left anchor point. Using the Convert Anchor Point tool, drag the direction line up and to the right, toward the middle of the shape.
7. With the Pen tool, click on the bottom-left anchor point. Move 6 "cells" to the right, aligned at 0°. Click and drag down to the right until the top of the curved path is 2 cells up and centered on the third cell. Using the Convert Anchor Point tool, drag the bottom direction point up to the right.
8. Move 6 cells to the right, and click and drag down. Using the Convert Anchor Point tool, drag the lower right-hand direction point up and to the right.
9. Move 6 cells to the right, and click and drag down, but don't move the Direction point with the Convert Direction Point tool.
10. With the Pen tool, click on the righthand anchor point of the half-circle to close the path. Then, with the Convert Anchor Point tool, click on the lower righthand direction point of the point you created in #9, and drag up to reshape the curve into the scallop shape.
11. Adjust direction points so the scallops are consistently shaped.
12. At the top of the umbrella, click, without dragging, with the Pen tool to create a corner point. Click and drag at the point of the first scallop to create a gradual curve for the umbrella panels.
13. Repeat for the right side.
14. With the Line Segment tool, draw a straight segment from the top of the umbrella to the bottom of the center scallop for the center panel.

15. Apply a color to the top of the umbrella.
16. Draw a rectangle .153" (or something close) wide (check the Info palette) and 2.5" high, starting just above the center scallop and center the point of the scallop in the center of the rectangle. Apply 1 pt black stroke and fill with 20% black. Send to back.
17. At the bottom of the rectangle, aligned with the grid, draw a horizontal straight line with the Pen tool, from left to right 2 cells wide. No fill.
18. Drop straight down 4 cells and click to place a corner point.
19. Drop down 4 more cells and move to the left 3½ cells and place a smooth point. Adjust the curve so it's smooth and is approximately like the one shown here.
20. Move to the left 3½ more cells and up 5 cells. Click to establish a corner point. Adjust curve.
21. Move to the right 2 cells and click to establish a corner point.
22. Move down 3 cells and to the right 1½ cells. Click to establish a smooth point. Adjust curve so it's parallel with the bottom curve.
23. Move to the right 1½ cells and up 3 cells. Click to establish a corner point. It should be directly across from the anchor point on the other side. Adjust the curve so it's parallel with the other side of the handle.
24. To close the path, move up and click on the first anchor point you drew.
25. Fill with 100% black.
26. Save the file, then print it, and close the document window.

EXERCISE 6-1 — Herb Pot

- Use Smart Guides or Grid with Snap to Grid command to create the rim of the pot. The rim of the pot has round corners.

- For the bottom of the pot you can create a rectangle then move the bottom anchor points toward the center the same amount for both sides. Or you can use the Pen tool and a Grid.

- Draw the stems with the Pencil tool or the Pen tool.

- Draw three or four of the leaves with the Pencil tool or the Pen tool, then drag-copy to make duplicates and move them to different stems. Rotate them, when necessary, using the bounding box.

- Save the file into your practice folder.

EXERCISE 6-2 — Circus Tent

- Use the Pen tool, Guides and a Grid to draw the bigtop.

- Draw the flags with the Pencil tool.

- Use the Convert Direction Point to control angle of the top of the tent and the flaps.

- Save the file into your practice folder.

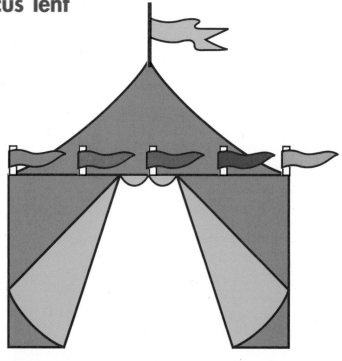

Add Color to Artwork

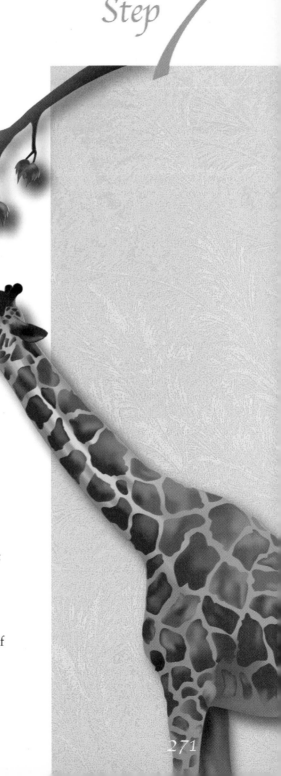

Chapter Outline

- Additive Color
- Subtractive Color
- Color Modes
- Spot Color
- Grayscale
- Display the Best Color
- Choose Your Color
- Swatch Libraries
- Swatches Palette
- Automatic Color Changes
- Gradient Fills
- Artwork with a Flare
- Magic Wand
- Save and Edit Selections
- Color Blends

The three primary colors in nature are red, green, and blue. Most colors in the spectrum visible by the human eye can be created using these three colors. Combinations of these three colors, with varying intensities of each of them, create the different colors.

The color you see is your brain's interpretation of the light waves it receives, as registered by structures in your eye, called cones. Some of these cones react to red light, some to blue, and some to green. People see colors differently, depending on the sensitivity level of the cones in their eyes. Some people are colorblind and can't tell the difference between some colors. The cones in their eyes aren't sensitive to those colors.

Additive Color

A light source (in nature, the sun) projecting a combination of *all* colors is seen as white. The more you add intensity to the three primary colors, the lighter the resulting color becomes. This is called *additive color*. If there is no light, the eye sees black.

The eye registers colors other than the three primary colors when lightwaves of two or more colors are received together. For example, when a red-sensitive cone and a green-sensitive cone receive lightwaves, the brain registers the color as yellow, which is a lighter color than either red or blue.

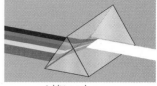
Additive colors

Subtractive Color

Subtractive colors — cyan, magenta, and yellow — filter out colors of lightwaves to create additional colors. They're opaque colors — you can't see through them — so the filtered colors are reflected back to the eye. The three subtractive colors filter out different kinds of light (red, green, blue), and your eye sees what's left over.

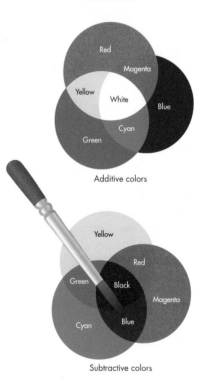
Additive colors

Subtractive colors

- Cyan ink filters red lightwaves and reflects all lightwaves that are not red, that is, green and blue.

- Magenta ink filters green lightwaves, leaving red and blue.

- Yellow ink filters blue lightwaves, leaving red and green.

For example, to create true red ink, you have to filter the blue and green lightwaves. Magenta ink filters the green lightwaves, but leaves red and blue. To filter the blue light-waves, you have to add yellow. Increase the percentage of yellow to make the color more orange; increase the red to make it a deeper red.

Color Modes

Illustrator offers you the choice of working in one of two color modes, RGB or CMYK. When you create a new document, you must choose which mode you will work in for that document. Choose RGB for artwork that will be displayed using a light source (monitor, as in a Web page; screen, as with a PowerPoint project; slide projector, for images converted to slides; and so on). Choose CMYK for artwork that will be printed.

You can create colors for your artwork in only one mode at a time. You can, however, switch color modes (**File ⇨ Document Color Mode**). When you switch modes in a document, all colors in that document are converted automatically to the new color mode and changes in colors used in the document are likely to occur. Colors you mix in the Color palette in a mode other than the current document color mode automatically conform to the document color mode.

RGB Color Mode

RGB color in Illustrator is additive color. Values of RGB colors range from 0 to 255, with 0 representing black and 255 representing white. Other colors range in between, depending upon their intensity.

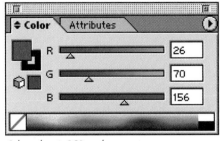

Color palette in RGB mode

Because 100% of all three colors, when combined, is perceived as black, equal values of all three in lesser intensities create shades of gray. For example, 30% red, 30% green, and 30% blue create gray, but it's a lighter shade of gray than 60% red, 60%, green, and 60% blue.

Adobe Illustrator 10 supports two variations of the RGB color model: HSB and Web-Safe RGB.

HSB (Hue, Saturation, Brightness) This color model is based on the way the human eye perceives color.

- Hue is the name of the color, expressed as a degree, between 0° and 360°, measured from its location on the standard color wheel.

- Saturation is the intensity or purity of a color (how rich it is). It's measured as a percentage from gray (0%) to saturated (100%). The greater the saturation, the more intense the color.

- Brightness is the lightness or darkness of a color (luminosity), measured in percentages with 0% representing black and 100% representing white.

Web-Safe RGB Not all RGB colors are the same on Mac OS and Windows platforms. When an image is going to be displayed on the Web, you don't know if the viewer is using a Macintosh or a Windows computer. And some older monitors display only 256 colors. To be certain the colors used in your image will display the same on all platforms and all monitors, choose colors in the Web-Safe color model.

If you choose a color that isn't web-safe (not one of the 216 colors common to all color monitors), two of the closest colors available will be mixed together to simulate your color. This is called *dithering*, and it sometimes results in a blotchy, uneven color. A dithered color applied to text is especially difficult to read.

Colors in the Web-Safe RGB palette are defined using the Hexidecimal color-naming system, which names colors with a combination of numbers (0–9) and letters (A–F). So the name of a color could be #CC66CC (pink). Each slider in the palette has tick marks to which the slider snaps when you drag it and the value for that tick mark is displayed in the field.

timesaver
When you click in the Spectrum color bar at the bottom of the Web-Safe RGB color palette, you automatically get the closest Web-safe color.

CMYK Color Mode

CMYK color in Illustrator is subtractive color and the CMYK color mode should be used when images are going to print on paper or other reflective material. Black has been added to the three subtractive colors because combining cyan, magenta, and yellow doesn't create a solid black. Adding black to the CMYK color model ensures nice, deep blacks and true grays, but it can also make colors look dull.

Process Colors

Cyan, Magenta, Yellow, and Black are the four standard inks used in the printing process and they're often called *process* colors. Printing using combinations of these four colors is called 4-color process printing. Process colors are measured in percentages, with 100% being the maximum intensity of a color and 0% the minimum intensity.

Projects that contain continuous-tone color bitmap images (photographs) should always be printed using process colors, that is, the CMYK color mode. There are color-matching systems available, such as Trumatch®, that define colors using percentages of the four process colors, which means you don't have to rely on the colors that display on your monitor to determine the color that will actually be printed.

Global Process Colors A global process color () (displays a white triangle on the lower right corner of the swatch) is linked to a swatch in the Swatches palette. If you change the swatch of a global process color, all elements, selected or unselected in the document, to which that color was applied are updated automatically. You don't have to select each individual object to change it. A global process color displays only one slider in the Color palette that you can adjust to create tints (shades) of the process color. See the section about Swatch Options later in this chapter.

Non-Global Process Colors A non-global process color () (no triangle in the lower right corner of the swatch) is a color that doesn't update other objects in the document that have that color applied to them when the color is modified — only the color of selected objects changes. A process color, when created in Illustrator, is a non-global process color, but you can convert it to a global process color using the Swatch Options dialog box.

fyi A general printer's rule of thumb: The total percentage of all your colors, including black, shouldn't add up to more than 300%. It helps keep your colors from looking "muddy."

read this! Because color displayed on your monitor is additive color and printed color is subtractive color, don't depend on your monitor to choose colors for projects that will be printed. Sometimes the conversion from RGB to CMYK changes colors drastically.

fyi Global process colors and spot colors cannot have the same name. Either of them can, however, have the same name as a non-global process color, resulting in two swatches in the Swatches palette with the same name.

Spot Color

Spot colors are separate, pre-mixed inks used when color accuracy is critical or when only one, two, or three colors are required for printing. Colors outside the gamut (range) of process colors can sometimes be achieved by using spot colors. Use a color-matching system to choose spot colors, not the colors displayed on your monitor, which only simulate the actual printed color.

Color-matching systems are libraries of pre-mixed inks that include a preselected range of colors. Inks in PANTONE® colors are the most popular spot color inks used in the United States. Most commercial printers use the PANTONE MATCHING SYSTEM® for printing spot colors, but other Swatch libraries are supported in Illustrator 10. See the section on Swatch Libraries later in this chapter.

Even if your project doesn't include color photographs, if you use a lot of colors of type, backgrounds in boxes, colored rules, and so on, using the 4-color process colors might be less expensive than using four spot colors. Check with your printer.

Spot colors should always be created as a named swatch in the Swatches palette to make them easy to identify and edit. Each spot color prints on its own plate (separation) when the document is output for printing.

All tints (shades) of a spot color output to the same plate. This means that if you're producing a 2-color job, you can use as many shades of the two colors as you want. It still counts as only two colors.

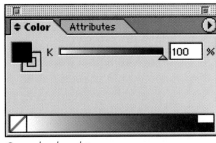

read this!

You do not have to use those spot colors only available in spot color Swatch Libraries. An imagesetter outputs film (or paper) in black and white, no matter what color you specify in the document. As long as a spot color separates to its own plate, you can tell the printer what color you want to use to print that plate. For instance, if you prepare a project using the colors Black and Blue and, at the last minute, the client changes his or her mind and wants Black and Red. The job doesn't have to be redone. Just tell the printer to print the blue plate with red ink.

Grayscale

Grayscale is shades of black, expressed in percentages, ranging from 0% to 100%, with 0% representing white and 100% representing black. Tints of gray are achieved in the Grayscale palette by moving the slider to the desired shade of gray. You can achieve the same result in the CMYK palette by setting the CMY values to 0 and moving the K slider to the desired shade or entering a percentage in the field. In the RGB and Web-Safe RGB palettes, set equal amounts for all three sliders.

Grayscale color palette

Display the Best Color

Illustrator has provided several commands that enable you to choose settings so your monitor displays its best color. You can then make more accurate color choices when colorizing your artwork. For best results, keep lighting in the work environment as consistent as possible from session to session, and change the background pattern on your monitor to a plain neutral gray.

If accurate color for your artwork is really critical, you can go to more extreme steps to assure consistent color. For example, work in a room without windows to avoid variations in the amount and color of sunlight; paint the walls of your work environment a neutral color because a room's color can affect your perception of color as displayed on your monitor; wear clothes in neutral colors because some colors may reflect back onto the screen and affect your perception of colors.

Calibrating Your Monitor

The first step in displaying accurate color is to calibrate your monitor. There are many ways to accomplish calibration, and some are quite expensive. For most people, though, the calibration utility that comes with Illustrator is adequate. Most specifications have been preset by the monitor manufacturer and I don't recommend you change them unless you know specifically that they're incorrect.

Anytime you change your monitor's Contrast (◖) or Brightness (☼) settings (usually buttons or knobs on the exterior of the monitor), you should recalibrate your monitor.

1. *Macintosh:* Display the Apple menu and choose Control Panels, then Adobe Gamma (🍎 ➪ **Control Panels** ➪ **Adobe Gamma**).

   Windows: Display all the files and folders on your hard drive. Then open the following folders to display the Adobe Gamma.cpl file, located in the Adobe Calibration folder. Choose **Program Files** ➪ **Common Files** ➪ **Adobe** ➪ **Calibration** ➪ **Adobe Gamma.cpl**.

2. Click on the Step by Step button to display instructions for each section of the procedure.

3. Click the Next button to proceed to the next section.

   ■ In the section that begins, "The gamma setting of your monitor . . .", uncheck the View Single Gamma Only checkbox to display a color box and slider for each color (Red, Green, Blue).

   ■ Once you've been through the Step by Step procedure, the next time you calibrate, you may want to click on the Control Panel button. All sections will display in one dialog box with no instructions, which makes it quicker to make changes.

4. Click Finish to exit the Adobe Gamma Utility. You're asked to save the new display profile.

- *Macintosh:* Save your new profile in the ColorSync Profiles folder, which is in the ColorSync Profiles folder within the System folder (**System Folder ⇨ ColorSync Profiles**).

- *Windows:* Save your new profile in the Color folder, which is in the System folder within the Windows folder (**Windows ⇨ System ⇨ Color**).

- The correct path should display when the Save As dialog box displays.

- I strongly recommend you save it with a slightly different name so the original display profile is retained for use as a starting point if you want to recalibrate. *Windows:* Be sure to include the .icm extension on your new name.

Choose Your Color

Illustrator 10 has provided separate color palettes for Grayscale, RGB, HSB, CMYK, and Web-Safe RGB so you can mix your own colors using the sliders in each palette. Display the Color palette Options menu and choose the color palette you want to use. Sometimes it's easier to mix the desired color in RGB or HSB palettes. Even though you mix the color in a palette different from the color mode you specified when you created the document, the resulting color conforms automatically to the color mode of the document.

Color palettes available in the Color palette Options submenu

- *Shift*-click the Spectrum color bar to cycle through the Color modes in the Color palette.

Out of Web Color

If you mix a color that is not safe for the Web, that is, doesn't display the same on all platforms, the Out of Web Color warning (⬡) displays on the Color palette (Figure 7.1). The color box to the right of the warning icon displays the Web-safe color that's closest to the color you mixed. Click in that Color box to change to that web-safe color.

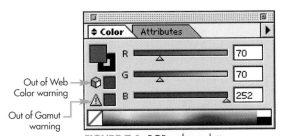

Out of Web Color warning

Out of Gamut warning

FIGURE 7.1 RGB color palette.

Out of Gamut

The Out of Gamut warning icon (⚠) displays on the RGB and Web-safe RGB color palettes when a color is mixed that is out of the CMYK color range (it can't be printed on a press). Click the warning icon and Illustrator substitutes the closest printable (CMYK) color. If your artwork is strictly for the Web and you're never going to print it, you can ignore this warning. When you convert the RGB or Web-safe RGB palette to the CMYK palette, the color is automatically converted to a color within the CMYK color gamut (range).

Using the Color Picker

The standard Color Picker (Figure 7.2) is another way to specify colors in Illustrator. To display the Color Picker, double-click the Fill or Stroke box in the Toolbox or in the Color palette.

Clicking a radio button next to the HSB or RGB components determines the color that displays in the Color field. The vertical Color slider displays the range of color available for the selected component. The color in the Color field is the range available for the remaining two components of the color model. For example, if the R radio button is clicked, the colors in the Color slider are the red component of the colors displayed in the Color field, which is a combination of G and B.

To define color in the Color Picker:

■ Move the color slider to the desired color.

or

■ Click in the Color field to select the color at the point of the click.

or

■ Enter the Hexadecimal color name in the # field.

The Out of Web Color warning (⬡) and the Out of Gamut warning (⚠) icons display when a defined color is not web-safe or is not a printable CMYK color. Check the Only Web Colors checkbox on the bottom lefthand corner of the Color Picker to display only Web-safe colors.

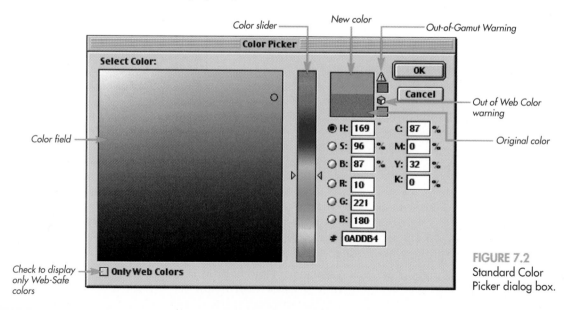

FIGURE 7.2
Standard Color Picker dialog box.

As you adjust the slider or click in the Color field to choose a color, its numerical value is displayed in the fields. You can see the original color and the new color in the rectangle at the top of the color rectangle to the right of the slider. In the sample shown here, the new color is green, and the original color is red.

Using the Eyedropper Tool

The function of the Eyedropper tool is to "read" (sample) the attributes of an object to make them the current attributes, which means they're applied automatically to any selected objects. The Eyedropper tool (keyboard command = *i*) samples an object's appearance attributes (fill and stroke color, gradient, and so on), as well as text attributes, if any. Whatever is under the eye-dropper when you click is what gets sampled.

Eyedropper tool icon in the Toolbox palette

When you click with the Eyedropper tool selected, the eye-dropper icon changes to half full (), indicating that attributes have been picked up. If you click on an object having a None fill or on a blank spot on the document page, the eyedropper icon displays a small dot ( ). The color of an object under the None object, if any, is what gets sampled.

Bitmap images imported (embedded or linked) in your Illustrator document can't be sampled. Vector artwork containing a gradient mesh and even some gradients don't sample, or don't sample accurately. You can, however, sample colors in bitmap images by following the instructions in the section below.

Sampling Colors From Images in Opened Documents You can sample colors from images created and opened in other applications, including photographs, as well as Illustrator artwork containing a gradient mesh. You can even sample the color of your monitor's desktop. As long as you can see a color on your screen, you can probably sample it.

1. Create an Illustrator document or open the Illustrator document into which you want to sample a color.

2. Open an existing document in Illustrator or another application, such as Photoshop, and position it so the portion containing the color you want to sample is visible.

3. Select the Eyedropper tool in the Toolbox (press *i*).

4. Click in the object in the Illustrator document into which you want to sample the color. Drag the eyedropper icon outside the artwork window and over the image containing the desired color. Release the mouse when the color you want is displayed in the Fill box in the Color palette and in the Toolbox.

5. To keep the color for future use, create a new swatch in the Swatches palette. See the section on Create a New Swatch later in this chapter.

read this!

When you sample colors of images in other applications or on the desktop, the eyedropper picks up the RGB color from the screen, even if the object in the other application was colored in CMYK mode. Illustrator converts it to the current color mode of your document.

Sample Only Color Attributes To sample only color attributes, ignoring other attributes, such as a Style, *Shift*-click with the Eyedropper tool. (Styles are predefined sets of attributes; they are discussed in Step 11, *Filters & Filter Effects*.)

Using the Paint Bucket Tool

The Paint Bucket tool allows you to apply fill and stroke attributes without displaying the Color or Stroke palettes. An object doesn't even have to be selected in the document page. The tool is hidden under the Eyedropper tool in the Toolbox and its keyboard command is *k*. Current fill and stroke settings are used when you use the Paint Bucket tool to apply color.

Paint Bucket tool icon in the Toolbox palette

1. Deselect all objects on the document page.

2. Choose the Paint Bucket tool in the Toolbox.

3. Specify fill and stroke colors.

4. Specify stroke weight and any other desired stroke options, such as dashed lines, endcaps, or joins.

5. Click on an object (it doesn't have to be selected).

   ■ Current color and stroke attributes are applied to the object.

timesaver
To toggle from the Eyedropper tool to the Paint Bucket (and vice versa), hold down the ⌥ key when you click.

To apply fill and stroke colors to an object with a fill color of None, position the spill of paint on the Paint Bucket pointer over the path line of the object when you click.

Eyedropper/Paint Bucket Options

You can determine which attributes the Eyedropper samples and the Paint Bucket applies to objects.

1. Double-click the Eyedropper tool or Paint Bucket tool in the Toolbox to display the Eyedropper/Paint Bucket Options dialog box (Figure 7.3).

2. Click the Expand arrow (▷) to display the list of attributes that can be sampled and applied.

3. Uncheck the ones you don't want to use.

4. Click OK or press *return/enter*.

   ■ Only checked attributes are sampled with the Eyedropper tool and applied with the Paint Bucket tool.

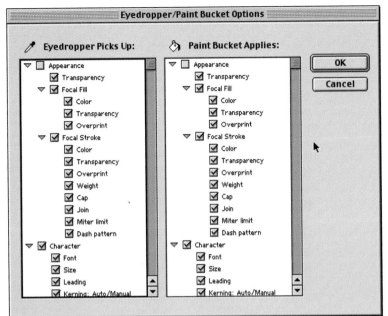

Eyedropper/Paint Bucket Options

Eyedropper Picks Up:	Paint Bucket Applies:

Eyedropper Picks Up:
- Appearance
  - Transparency
  - Focal Fill
    - Color
    - Transparency
    - Overprint
  - Focal Stroke
    - Color
    - Transparency
    - Overprint
    - Weight
    - Cap
    - Join
    - Miter limit
    - Dash pattern
  - Character
    - Font
    - Size
    - Leading
    - Kerning: Auto/Manual

Paint Bucket Applies:
- Appearance
  - Transparency
  - Focal Fill
    - Color
    - Transparency
    - Overprint
  - Focal Stroke
    - Color
    - Transparency
    - Overprint
    - Weight
    - Cap
    - Join
    - Miter limit
    - Dash pattern
  - Character
    - Font
    - Size
    - Leading
    - Kerning: Auto/Manual

OK
Cancel

FIGURE 7.3
Eyedropper/Paint Bucket
Options dialog box.

activity 7.1

1. Create a new document: Letter size, CMYK color mode. Name it My Posie.eps and save it into your Practice folder as an .eps file.

2. Open the file named Rose.tif that's in the Student Files folder on the CD-ROM that accompanied this book.

   ■ If you get an alert warning you that the color profile will be discarded, click OK.

3. Reduce the size of the windows of the two documents and position them until you can see most of the rose and still have an area of the My Posie.eps document on which to work. If necessary, reduce the View size of the document containing the rose.

4. On the My Posie.eps document page, turn on Smart Guides.

5. Draw a 1" circle having default colors (white fill, 1 pt. black stroke).

   ■ Click the Default Fill and Stroke button on the Toolbox to apply the fill and stroke.

6. With the Selection tool (press v), drag-copy a new circle and position it so it's aligned on the 45° angle with the center point on the stroke of the first circle.

7. Drag-copy two more circles, always aligning on the 45° angle and positioning the center point on the stroke of the previous circle.

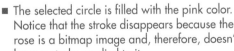

8. With the last circle still selected, select the Eyedropper tool (press i), click on the document page, and drag to a pink edge of the rose in the other document until the pink color displays in the Fill box of the Toolbox and the Color palette. Then release the mouse.

   ■ The selected circle is filled with the pink color. Notice that the stroke disappears because the rose is a bitmap image and, therefore, doesn't have a stroke applied to it.

Continued

9. Hold down the ⌥ key to change to the Paint Bucket tool (even though the Eyedropper is still selected in the Toolbox), and click the remaining three circles to fill them with the new color.

10. Draw a ½" circle and position it in the center of the four circles. It should snap in place.

11. With the Eyedropper tool, drag from the current document to the Rose and sample a light yellow color.

- Because the small circle was still selected, it should automatically change to yellow when you release the mouse.

12. Save the My Posie.eps file and close the document. Close the Rose.tif document.

Swatch Libraries

A swatch library is an Illustrator document containing a set of predefined colors. When you install Illustrator 10, 25 swatch libraries are installed, too. Some sets, such as Earthtones, Harmonies, and Pastels, were put together for you by Adobe. Others, such as PANTONE, correspond to printing inks and they have printed swatch color books that you can use to choose colors.

Display the Swatch Library menu by choosing Swatch Libraries from the Window menu (**Window ⇨ Swatch Libraries**). Each swatch library displays in its own palette that you can enlarge, reduce, close, dock, and so on. You can't edit the swatches in a swatch library, though.

You can add a complete swatch library to the Swatches palette by dragging its folder tab into the Swatches palette and dropping it when the black line displays around the palette window.

- PANTONE® — PANTONE® Color Systems are used by most commercial printers in the United States. PANTONE® Digital Color Libraries in Illustrator correspond to PANTONE Color guides, which is what you should use to choose color. Colors displayed on screen are not always accurate.

  Eight PANTONE Digital Color Libraries are available. Names given to these libraries refer to the paper upon which the color will be printed. Colors in "PANTONE Process" correspond to process colors in the Process color guide coated/uncoated. Colors in "PANTONE Solid" correspond to spot colors in the PANTONE formula guide solid coated/uncoated and matte. Colors in "PANTONE Metallic Coated"

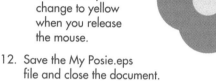

```
Default_CMYK
Default_RGB
Diccolor
Earthtones_1
FOCOLTONE
Harmonies_1
HKS E
HKS K
HKS N
HKS Z
PANTONE Metallic Coated
PANTONE Pastel Coated
PANTONE Pastel Uncoated
PANTONE Process Coated
PANTONE Process Uncoated
PANTONE Solid Coated
PANTONE Solid Matte
PANTONE Solid Uncoated
Pastels
System (Macintosh)
System (Windows)
Toyo
Trumatch
VisiBone2
Web
Other Library...
```

Swatch libraries available in Illustrator 10 (Window ⇨ Swatch Libraries) correspond to spot colors in the PANTONE metallic guide + chips coated. Colors in "PANTONE Pastel" correspond to spot colors in the PANTONE pastel guide + chips coated/uncoated.

- Trumatch® — Use this matching system when choosing Process colors. Many spot colors are out of gamut when converted to Process colors. Colors in the Trumatch Swatching System were created using standard CMYK process colors, so no conversion from a spot color is required. The Trumatch Colorfinder swatch book contains more than 2000 colors arranged according to hue, saturation, and brightness. Swatches in the Trumatch library are non-global process colors.

- Diccolor (Japan), FOCOLTONE (England), HKS (Germany), and Toyo (Japan) are color systems used in countries other than the U.S.

- Visibone2 and Web — Use for creating Web graphics. Both of these libraries contain the 216 Web-safe colors. The Adobe Web library is arranged according to the hexidecimal names of the colors. The Visibone2 library is arranged according to hue.

Display Swatch Library When Launching Illustrator

If you consistently use the same Swatch Library and want to have it displayed on your screen each time Illustrator is launched (in addition to the Swatches palette), choose Persistent from the Swatch library Options menu.

read this!

You can't edit swatches in a swatch Library (note the non-edit icon (🏃) in the lower left corner of the Swatch Library palette). Once a swatch is placed in the Swatches palette of a document, however, it can be edited. Editing it in the Swatches palette does not affect the swatch in the swatch library.

fyi Swatch books can be purchased at most art supply stores, or they can be ordered directly from the manufacturer via the Internet or by mail.

Pantone, Inc.
(201) 935-5500
http://www.pantone.com

Trumatch, Inc.
(800) 878-9100
(631) 204-9100
(631) 204-0002 (Fax)
http://www.trumatch.com
e-mail: info@trumatch.com

Swatches Palette

A swatch is a small square containing a predefined color or pattern used for selecting a color to apply to a path. Swatches in Illustrator are displayed on the Swatches palette (see Figure 7.4) or in swatch libraries that can be displayed on-screen. You can add swatches from swatch libraries to the Swatches palette or you can create a new swatch from colors you mix using the sliders in the Color palette.

The Swatches palette contains swatches for colors, gradients, and patterns, and they are saved only with the current document file. Default color swatches for the current document color mode (CMYK or RGB) are displayed in the default Swatches palette.

Most of the buttons on the Swatches palette are self-explanatory, with the possible exception of the Registration color button (⊕). Registration color is used

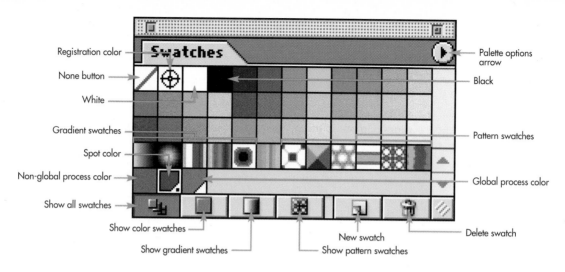

Labels (left side, top to bottom): Registration color, None button, White, Gradient swatches, Spot color, Non-global process color, Show all swatches

Labels (right side, top to bottom): Palette options arrow, Black, Pattern swatches, Global process color, Delete swatch

Labels (bottom): Show color swatches, Show gradient swatches, New swatch, Show pattern swatches

FIGURE 7.4 The Swatches palette.

to color crop marks. For example, on a dark illustration use this swatch to change the color of the crop marks to white.

Applying Colors Using the Swatches Palette

To choose a predefined color (rather than mixing a new one), click on its swatch in the Swatches palette or on a swatch in a swatch library if one is displayed on your screen. That color then becomes the current fill or stroke color, whichever is active (in the Color palette and Toolbox).

You can also drag-and-drop a swatch over an object to change its fill or stroke (whichever is active), even if the path is unselected. When you drop a swatch on a selected object, the color in the active Fill or Stroke box in the Color palette changes to the swatch color. When you drag a swatch over an *unselected* object, the color in the Fill or Stroke box of the Color palette doesn't change to that color.

- To change the color (fill or stroke) of an unselected object having a stroke of None and a fill of None, you must drop the swatch on the path of the object.

- When you drag-and-drop a swatch from a Swatch Library to colorize an object, that swatch, in most cases, is added to the Swatches palette. The exception is a swatch that's dragged from a swatch library containing only non-global process colors (Default_CMYK, Default_RGB, Earthtones, Harmonies, Pastels, Trumatch, Visibone2, or Web libraries). Swatches from these palettes are not added to the Swatches palette. This means you can't add colors from these palettes to the Swatches palette of an Illustrator document by dragging an object from one Illustrator document to another. See the Adding Swatches to the Swatches Palette section later in this chapter.

Displaying Swatches in the Palette

Swatches can be displayed in the Swatches palette a number of ways. Click the buttons at the bottom of the palette to show only color swatches (▯), to show only gradient swatches (▯), to show only pattern swatches (▦), or to show them all (▦). You can display swatches using small (default) or large color blocks or you can display them by their names. And you can sort them so they display alphabetically or by type — gradient, color, pattern, and so on.

To change how swatches are displayed in the Swatches palette, display the Swatches palette Options menu:

- ■ Small Thumbnail View — Displays swatches using small color blocks. Swatches in Figure 7.4 are displayed using small thumbnails.

- ■ Large Thumbnail View — Displays swatches using large blocks of color (Figure 7.5).

- ■ List View — Displays color alphabetically by name (Figure 7.6).

Sorting Swatches To sort swatches so all swatches of the same type are together, display the Swatches palette Options menu and choose Sort by Kind. To sort swatches alphabetically, display the Swatches palette Options menu and choose Sort by Name.

- ■ Sort By Name — Displays swatches alphabetically by name.

- ■ Sort By Kind — Displays swatches in groups according to their type (gradients, process colors, and so on).

- ■ Show Find Field — Displays Font field into which you can type font name or number to search for and display the desired swatch.

Selecting Swatches in the Swatches Palette

- ■ Click a swatch then *Shift*-click the last swatch in a series to select all swatches between the two clicks.

- ■ ⌘-click swatches to select random swatches or to deselect selected swatches

- ■ Deselect all swatches by clicking in an empty area of the Swatches palette.

Options available in the Color palette Options menu

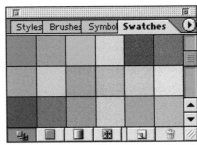

FIGURE 7.5 Swatches palette displayed in Large Thumbnail View.

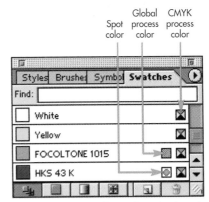

FIGURE 7.6 Swatches palette displayed in List View, sorted by Kind, with Find field displayed.

Moving Swatches Around in the Swatches Palette Click and drag swatches to reposition them in the Swatches palette. Drop the swatch when a dark line displays where you want it repositioned.

Locating Swatches in the Palette

Some Swatch libraries, such as PANTONE and Trumatch, contain a large number of color swatches. In addition, you may have added a large number of swatches to the Swatches palette and have difficulty finding them. To find a swatch without having to scroll through them all:

1. Display the Swatches palette Options menu and choose Show Find Field to display the Find field at the top of the palette.

2. Enter the number of a swatch if it's categorized that way. For example, enter 345 to find PANTONE 345 C in the PANTONE Solid Coated palette. Enter the first few characters of a swatch name for swatches categorized by name rather than a number. For example, enter *az* for the Azure swatch.

   ■ The located swatch is displayed in the top row of the palette and displays a white border.

Entering numbers or letters in the Find field doesn't seem to work as well as it used to. Maybe Adobe can improve it in an update.

Adding Swatches to the Swatches Palette

Swatches added to the Swatches palette are saved with the document. When you reopen it, the swatches are still there.

Drag and Drop The easiest way to add swatches to the Swatches palette is to use the drag-and-drop method. Click on a swatch in a Swatch library, on the Fill box in the Colors palette, or on the Fill box in the Toolbox. Drag it to a blank area of the Swatches palette, and release the mouse to drop it. A dark line displays around the window area of the Swatches palette and the new swatch becomes the last swatch in the palette. Or, you can insert the swatch between two existing swatches when the dark line displays between them.

   ■ You can drag-and-drop swatches from another open Illustrator document to the current document.

   ■ Colors added from a Swatch Library are automatically converted to the color mode of the document.

   ■ To replace an existing swatch with another one, ⌥-drag the new swatch over the existing one and drop it. A colored border displays around the swatch you're replacing.

Create a New Swatch When new swatches are created, they are automatically in the color mode of the document — CMYK or RGB — regardless of the mode displayed in the Color palette. If colors are created in a mode different from the document mode, they're automatically converted to the document's color mode.

There are a few ways to create a new swatch in the Swatches palette:

1. Drag the currently active color in the Color palette — the Fill box or Stroke box — and drop it over the New Swatch button ([⬜]) at the bottom of the Swatches palette. The new swatch becomes the last swatch in the palette. If the active color in the Fill or Stroke box is a spot color, the new swatch is a spot color swatch (▨) and displays a white triangle with a dot on the lower right corner of the swatch. If the active color is a process color, it is a non-global process color (▨) — no triangle displays on the swatch. It can then be converted to a global process color. See the Swatch Options section later in this chapter.

   ■ Drop the new swatch between two existing swatches (a dark line displays between the two swatches).

   ■ Hold the ⌘ key down as you drag to convert a process color into a spot color swatch when you drop it in the Swatches palette.

   or

2. Display the Swatches palette Options menu and choose New Swatch. The New Swatch dialog box displays showing the currently active color in the Color palette — the Fill box or Stroke box — as the color of the new swatch. It's positioned as the last swatch in the palette.

   or

3. To display the Swatch Options dialog box when creating a new swatch, ⟋-click the New Swatch button ([⬜]) at the bottom of the Swatches palette. When the Swatch Options dialog box displays, enter a name, choose a color type, and move the sliders to create a new color. Click OK or press *return/enter* when finished.

Add Swatches from Another Illustrator Document Drag an object with the color you want from another Illustrator file and place it on the document page. If a spot color swatch or a global process color swatch for the color was created on the original document, it displays in the destination document's Swatches palette. (Non-global process colors won't transfer when the object is copied). Then delete the copied object.

   ■ Even if the color in the copied object is not associated with a swatch (because it's the active object), its color is displayed in the Fill box in the Color palette. Drag and drop the Fill box onto the Swatches palette. Then delete the copied object.

Add Swatches from the Swatches Palette of Another Illustrator File

1. Open the Illustrator file into which you want to add swatches from another *unopened* Illustrator file.

2. Display the Swatch Libraries menu, and choose Other Library.

3. Navigate until you find the file from which you want to copy swatches. Click Open.

   ■ The file doesn't display on your screen, but the Swatches palette associated with that document does display.

4. Select the swatches you want to copy.

   ■ Click to select a single swatch; click the first swatch in a series, then *Shift*-click to select the last swatch in a series, which selects all swatches between the two clicks; ⌘-click to select random multiple swatches.

5. Drag the selected swatches to the original file's Swatches palette.
   or

   Choose Add to Swatches from the Swatches palette Options menu of the palette in which you selected the swatches.

Resolving Swatch Conflicts

When copying an object from an Illustrator file into your current document, any spot color or global process color swatches used in the copied object transfer to the Swatches palette of your current document. If a swatch associated with the copied object has the same name but is a color different from that of a swatch in the current document's Swatches palette, the Swatch Conflict dialog box displays. To resolve the conflict:

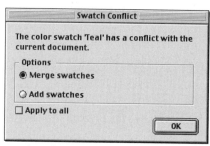

Swatch Conflict dialog box

■ **Merge swatches** — Click this option to apply the color of the swatch in the existing document to the copied object.

■ **Add swatches** — When this option is clicked, the swatch is added to the Swatches palette and a number is added to the name of the swatch. The actual color in the copied object doesn't change.

■ **Apply to all** — Check this box to apply the selection you made in the Options section of the dialog box if any other conflicts occur when copying the object into the current document. When this box is checked, the Swatch Conflict dialog box won't display again until you copy another object.

Merging Spot Color Swatches

Unfortunately, when you resolve spot color swatch conflicts by adding swatches having the same name to the Swatches palette, each color outputs to a separate plate. Because this is usually not a desirable outcome, Illustrator has provided a command to merge the colors into one swatch, which then output to only one plate.

1. In the Swatches palette, select the swatches you want to merge.

   - *Shift*-click to select swatches in a series; ⌘-click to select random swatches.

2. Display the Swatch palette Options menu, and choose Merge Swatches.

   - The *first* swatch you select replaces the other swatches. Any colors (or patterns or styles) applied to objects in the document are replaced by the remaining swatch.

Swatch Options

The Swatch Options dialog box enables you to change the name of a swatch, change its color type from a spot color to a process color, specify a color as a global process color, and view the CMYK breakdown of a spot color. To display the Swatch Options dialog box, double-click a swatch in the Swatches palette or a Swatch library palette, or ⌥-click the New Swatch button (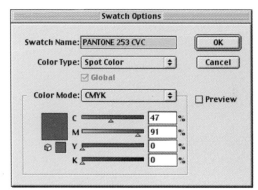) at the bottom of the Swatches palette when creating a new color.

Swatch Options dialog box

- **Swatch Name** — Enter a new name for the swatch. If the Show Tool Tips option is still checked in the General Preferences dialog box (**Edit ⇨ Preferences ⇨ General**), the new name displays when the pointer is passed over that swatch in the Swatches palette.

- **Color Type** — Choose either Spot Color or Process Color. Use this option to change a Spot color to a Process color or a Process color to a Spot color.

- **Global checkbox** — Check to convert a process color to a global process color.

- **Color Mode** — Choose a color mode to display the appropriate sliders for mixing a new color in that color mode. Keep in mind, though, that this section is only for mixing a new color in that color mode. The color is converted to the color mode of the document automatically.

  - The Out of Gamut warning icon and the Out of Web warning icon display, if appropriate, when mixing colors.

- **Preview** — When checked, the Fill (or Stroke) box in the Color palette and the Toolbox is automatically updated to the new color when you release the slider. If an object is selected in the document, its color is also updated automatically to the new color.

  - If you create a new swatch by ⌥-clicking the New Swatch button on the Swatches palette, the Preview button isn't present on the Swatch Options dialog box.

Converting Colors

In addition to changing the selection in the Swatch Options dialog box to change a spot color to a process color, and vice versa, you can use an option in the Color palette to do the same thing. Click the Spot color button (⊙) or the Process color button (⊠) (see Figure 7.7) to convert the spot color to its process color equivalent. Clicking either of these buttons doesn't change the swatch, just the color that's applied to selected objects. Drag the Fill box onto a blank area of the Swatches palette to create a swatch of the process color equivalent of the spot color.

The Global Process color button (▦) displays in the Color palette in place of the Spot color button (⊙) when the current color is a Global Process color (Figure 7.7).

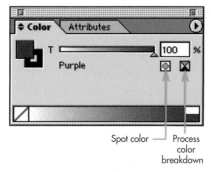

Spot color — Process color breakdown

FIGURE 7.7 Color palette displaying a spot color.

Replacing Swatches

You can replace swatches in the Swatches palette with swatches of a different color. When you replace a spot color swatch or a global process color swatch with a swatch of a different color (same type of swatch), all objects in the document update to the new color. The objects don't have to be selected. If the original color was a tint of the color, the same tint percentage is used for the new color.

When you replace a non-global process color swatch with a different color swatch, only objects *selected* in the document are changed. If no objects in the document are selected, no colors are affected by replacing a swatch with a different color.

To replace a swatch in the Swatches palette with a swatch of a different color:

- ⌥-drag one swatch and drop it over another swatch.

or

- Create a new color in the Color palette, then ⌥-drag the Fill box over the swatch you want to replace in the Swatches palette.

  - A border displays around the swatch you're replacing with the new color.

  - To convert the new color to a spot color and replace a swatch in the Swatches palette at the same time, hold down both the ⌥ key and ⌘ key when dragging.

Deleting Swatches from the Palette

Swatches can be deleted in several ways. First, select the swatch you want to delete by clicking on it (a white border displays). Click a swatch, then *Shift*-click the last swatch in a series of swatches to select all swatches between the two clicks. To select random multiple swatches, hold down the ⌘ key and click on the swatches.

- Click the Delete button (🗑) at the bottom of the Swatches palette. Click Yes when the warning box displays asking if you want to delete the swatch.

or

- Display the Swatches palette Options menu and choose Delete Swatch. Click Yes when the warning box displays asking if you want to delete the swatch.

or

- ⬝-click the Delete button (🗑) at the bottom of the palette. The warning box doesn't display.

or

- Drag the swatches you want to delete and drop them on the Delete button (🗑) at the bottom of the palette. The warning box doesn't display.

Delete All Unused Swatches To delete all swatches not used in the document, display the Swatches palette Options menu and choose Select All Unused. Then delete them in one of the ways listed above.

- To make sure you don't delete swatches of different types, such as pattern swatches or gradient swatches, click the Show button at the bottom of the palette that corresponds to the type of swatches you want deleted. For example, if you want to delete only color swatches, click the Show Colors button (▣) before choosing Select All Unused.

Restore Default Swatches If you've deleted the default swatches and want to add them back into the Swatches palette:

1. Display the Swatch Libraries menu (**Window ⇨ Swatch Libraries**)

2. Choose Default_CMYK or Default_RGB, depending upon which color mode you're working in.

3. Select the swatches you want to restore to your open document.
   - Click on the first swatch in a series, then *Shift*-click on the last swatch in a series to select all swatches between the two clicks.
   - To select random multiple swatches, ⌘-click on the swatches.

4. Drag the selected swatches to the open document's Swatches palette.

   or

   Display the Library's Swatches palette Options menu and choose Add to Swatches.

fyi The None and Registration swatches cannot be deleted from the Swatches palette.

Duplicating Swatches

To copy an existing swatch in the Swatches palette:

- Select the swatch you want to duplicate. Display the Swatches palette Options menu and choose Duplicate Swatch.

or

- Select the swatch you want to duplicate, and click the New Swatch button ([⊒]) at the bottom of the Swatches palette.

or

- Select the swatch you want to duplicate and drag it over the New Swatch button ([⊒]) at the bottom of the Swatches palette.

The copied swatch (or swatches) displays as the last swatch in the palette.

Creating Your Own Swatch Library

You can create swatch libraries containing the colors you use consistently. For example, if a client specifies the same colors for every project you do for that client, create a library of those colors and give it a name unique to that client.

1. Create a new document.

2. Add or delete colors from the Swatches palette until you have only the swatches (colors, gradients, patterns) you want.

3. Name the file and save it as an .ai file into the Presets folder in the Adobe Illustrator 10 program folder on your hard drive.

   - The file isn't visible until Illustrator is closed and relaunched.

That swatch library is listed in the Swatch Library submenu just like the other libraries. Display it on your screen by choosing it from the submenu like you would any of the other libraries.

Adding Swatches to Your Custom Startup File

If you find you're adding the same colors, gradients, or patterns to the Swatches palette each time you create an illustration, you can add those swatches to your Custom Startup File so they display in the Swatches palette each time you launch Illustrator.

1. Open the Custom Startup file you created in Step 6, *Rulers, Grids, & Guides.* Or, if you didn't create one in that chapter, follow the instructions given there to create one.

   - It's located in the Plug-ins folder in the Adobe Illustrator 10 program folder on your hard drive.

2. Add swatches (colors, gradients, or patterns) to the Swatches palette using any of the methods described in this chapter.

3. Save the file (without changing its name) back into the Plug-ins folder.

activity 7.2

1. Create a new document: Letter size, CMYK color mode. Display the Swatches palette.

2. Draw a circle then a rectangle on your page and apply the default colors.
   - Click the Default Fill and Stroke button in the Toolbox (⌷).

3. Deselect the objects.

4. Display the PANTONE Solid Coated swatch library palette.

5. Apply a PANTONE 312 C fill to the circle by dragging the swatch from the library palette and dropping it on the circle.
   - Locate the color by displaying the Find field in the PANTONE palette (if it's not visible) and typing 312.
   - Notice that the swatch was added to the document's Swatches palette and that it displays as a spot color.

6. Select the rectangle.

7. Display the palette Options menu on the PANTONE Solid Coated swatch library, and choose List View.
   - Notice the icons on the right side of the palette. ◉ denotes that the color is a spot color and ⊠, when placed in the Swatches palette, can be clicked to display the color's CMYK breakdown.
   - Notice the non-editable icon (✗) in the bottom left corner of the palette.
   - As you click on swatches in the Swatches palette or on swatches (or names) in the PANTONE Solid Coated library palette, the color in the rectangle changes (because it's selected), as well as the color in the Fill box (or stroke) in the Color palette and the Toolbox.
   - Notice that each swatch is added to the document's Swatches palette as you click on it in the Library palette.

8. Display the CMYK Color palette and mix a red color: 0% C, 85% M, 85% Y, and 0% K.

9. Create a spot color swatch for the color you just mixed.
   - Hold down the ⌘ key as you drag the color from the Fill box to the Swatches palette.

10. Display the Swatch Options dialog box for the red swatch you just created. Change its name to Warm Red and convert it to a global process color swatch. Click OK or press *return/enter*.
    - Notice that the swatch displays a blank white triangle in the lower right corner.
    - If you left Tool Tips turned on, the name of the swatch displays when you pause as you pass the pointer over each swatch in the Swatches palette. Swatch names display on all swatches in the palette.

11. On the document page, draw a star and apply a None fill and a None stroke.

12. In the color palette, make sure the Fill box is in front, then drag the red color you just created and drop it on the path line of the star.
    - The star is filled with the color.

13. Display the Find field in the document's Swatches palette and find the swatch named Azure.

14. Select the rectangle in the document. Then display the Swatch Options dialog box of the Azure swatch by double-clicking it. Position the dialog box so you can see at least a portion of the rectangle as well as the Swatch Options dialog box.

15. Click the Preview checkbox, change it to a global process color, and move the Y slider to 30% and release.
    - Notice that the fill color in the rectangle changes to the new color when you released the slider.

16. Rename the swatch Teal. Click OK or press *return/enter*.
    - The Azure swatch was replaced by the new Teal global process swatch.

Continued

- The Color palette displays only one slider (named Teal), even though it's a process color, enabling you to create a tint of the color.

17. Verify that the rectangle is still selected in the document, and move the slider in the Color palette to 75%.

   - When you release the slider, the color in the rectangle is 75% of its original color.

18. Display the Swatches palette Options menu and choose Sort by Kind.

   - The three swatches you added to the palette are displayed after the default swatches and before the Gradient and Pattern swatches.

19. Display the Swatches palette Options menu again and choose Sort by Name.

   - Swatches are now displayed alphabetically by their names, and the gradient and pattern swatches are all mixed in.

20. Click the Show Color Swatches button on the bottom of the Swatches palette.

   - The Gradient and Pattern swatches disappear and only color swatches are left, sorted alphabetically by name.

21. Display the Swatches palette Options menu and choose Large Thumbnail View.

   - You may have to lengthen the palette to see all the swatches.

22. Drag the Teal swatch and drop it on the New Swatch button at the bottom of the palette to duplicate the swatch.

   - A duplicate swatch is created and named Teal 1.

23. Drag and drop the duplicate Teal 1 swatch on the circle to change it's color. Don't select the circle first. Both objects should be the Teal color, but the rectangle is still set to 75%.

24. Deselect both objects.

25. Click on one of the non-global process colors in the Swatches palette.

   - Notice that the colors of the two objects on the page didn't change at all.

26. Display the Swatch Options dialog box for the Teal 1 swatch and move the sliders to change its color. Click OK or press *return/enter*.

   - Even though the objects in the document weren't selected, the fill color of the circle changed, as well as the swatch in the Swatches palette, because the swatch is a global process color swatch.

27. Delete the currently selected swatch by dragging it to the Delete button at the bottom of the palette.

28. Click on the 75% Green non-global process color in the Swatches palette. ⌥-drag it over the 75% Orange non-global process color to replace it.

   - Now you have two swatches with the same color breakdown of the 75% Green color, but the name of the replaced swatch is still 75% Orange.

29. Display the Swatches palette Options menu and choose Select All Unused to select all the swatches not used in the document. Then select Delete Swatch from the Options menu or drag and release them on the Delete button.

30. Click the Show All Swatches button at the bottom of the Swatches palette.

   - Because the Gradient and Pattern swatches were hidden, none of them were deleted when the Select All Unused command was used.

31. Display the Default CMYK swatch library. Click on the first color swatch in the library palette, then hold the *Shift* key down and click on the last color swatch in the palette to select all the color swatches. Don't select any Gradient or Pattern swatches.

32. Display the library palette's Options menu and choose Add to Swatches. Then close the library palette.

   - All the selected swatches are added to the document's Swatches palette.

33. Display the Swatches palette Options menu and choose Sort by Kind to organize the swatches.

34. Close the Pantone Swatches library palette.

35. Close the document without saving it to a file.

Automatic Color Changes

Once you've applied a color to an object in your Illustrator document, there are various commands you can use to alter those colors, such as Invert, Complement, Convert to CMYK, and others.

Inverting Colors

Invert means to *change to the opposite*. Black becomes white; white becomes black. You can't toggle between the original color and the inverted color. When you apply an Invert command, then apply it again to the same object, the original color doesn't return. You have to apply the Undo command to return to the original color.

The Invert Command in the Color Palette The results that are achieved when the Invert command is applied, depends upon the color mode currently in effect.

Color palette Options menu

- **Grayscale mode** — Values are subtracted from 100%. For example, if you invert a grayscale value of 56%, it becomes 43.92%; 24% black becomes 76.08% black.

- **RGB color mode** — The value of each color channel is subtracted from the maximum of 255, the highest RGB value, or white. For example, an R value of 44 is inverted to a value of 211 ($255 - 44 = 211$); a G value of 38 is inverted to a value of 217 ($255 - 38 = 217$); and a B value of 214 is inverted to a value of 41 ($255 - 214 = 41$).

- **HSB color mode** — The Invert command exchanges the S and B values and the Hue value changes to 180° from its original value, based on their equivalent values in RGB color mode.

- **CMYK color mode** — CMYK colors are inverted using their equivalent RGB values. Even if you're working in the CMYK color mode, RGB values are used, then the colors are automatically converted to the color mode of the document.

This command can be applied to a stroke color *or* to a fill color, whichever element is active in the Color palette; but not both stroke and fill at the same time. Multiple objects with different colors are treated differently, depending upon the color mode being used. And it depends upon whether you *Shift*-click to select multiple objects or whether you marquee to select the objects.

The Invert command in the Color palette menu can be applied to global process colors, spot colors, and non-global process colors. When it is applied to objects filled with a gradient or a pattern, Illustrator inverts the last solid color that was used in the document (see the last-color-used box (⬆-■) on the palette).

All in all, this command is very confusing and you can obtain some undesirable results if you're not careful. The main thing to remember, though, is that RGB values are used for calculating the inverted colors.

The Invert Colors Command in the Filter Menu

This command (**Filter ⇨ Colors ⇨ Invert Colors**) converts only non-global process colors. It doesn't work on spot colors, global process colors, gradients, or patterns. A warning box displays if you apply the command to any color that isn't a non-global process color.

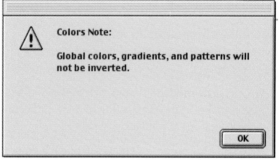

Options available in the Colors submenu in the Filter menu

Calculations are made the same way as the Invert Command in the Color palette. The difference between the two commands is that if an object has a stroke *and* a fill color, the Invert Colors in the Filter Menu inverts both colors with this one command, rather than applying only to the one that's active in the Color palette. If more than one object is selected, or a group is selected when the Invert Colors command is applied, all colors in all the objects are inverted individually.

> ⚠ **Colors Note:**
>
> **Global colors, gradients, and patterns will not be inverted.**
>
> OK

Warning alert that displays when you attempt to Invert global colors, gradients, or patterns using the Invert command in the Filter menu

Using the Complement Command

The Complement command in the Color palette Options menu is one of those commands you'll probably never use. But in the interest of information, it works like this: Colors are calculated using values in the RGB color mode, but the color mode of the document isn't changed and colors are converted automatically to the current color mode of the document.

Original color, R114, G38, B222

The highest and lowest values are added together, and that sum is subtracted from each separate value, which results in the complementary color. For example, in the samples shown here, the values of the original color are R = 114, G = 38, B = 222. When the Complement command is applied, the G (lowest) and B (highest) values are added together (equalling 260) and the other values are subtracted, creating its complementary color: 260 − 114 = 146 (R), 260 − 38 = 222 (G), and 260 − 222 = 38 (B).

Complementary color, R146, G222, B38

Convert to Grayscale

The Convert to Grayscale command in the Filter menu (**Filter ⇨ Colors ⇨ Convert to Grayscale**) changes the fill color *and* stroke color of an object into shades of gray. The Color palette displays the Grayscale slider and field.

Convert to CMYK / Convert to RGB

These two commands in the Filter menu (**Filter** ➪ **Colors** ➪ **Convert to CMYK** and **Filter** ➪ **Colors** ➪ **Convert to RGB**) allow you to change the color mode of selected paths to the color mode of the document. Use this command to convert a Spot color into its CMYK (or RGB) breakdown.

Adjust Colors

The Adjust Colors command in the Filter menu (**Filter** ➪ **Colors** ➪ **Adjust Colors**) can be applied to selected paths and text objects, or to opened or placed TIFF, EPS, and .psd images that have been flattened in Photoshop. Change the color of a photograph, for example, to a different color or make it lighter or darker. Darken or lighten spot colors. You can also use this command to convert colors from one mode to another and to convert spot colors to process color or to grayscale.

To adjust colors:

1. Select the object or objects whose colors you want to adjust.

2. Display the Adjust Colors dialog box (**Filter** ➪ **Colors** ➪ **Adjust Colors**).

3. Click the Preview checkbox to see your changes as you make them.

4. Click the Convert checkbox to convert all objects selected in the document to the same color mode. In other words, you can convert spot colors (global) to process CMYK colors, or to RGB, or to Grayscale.

5. In the Adjust Options section, check the attributes you want to change: fill color, stroke color, or both.

6. The Color Mode pop-up menu shows the color mode of selected objects and its corresponding sliders. If selected objects have more than one color mode, the bottommost one on the pop-up menu displays first. For example, if a spot color is present in selected objects, Global displays in the pop-up menu. Move sliders or enter values in the fields to adjust the intensity of colors. Only colors in the active mode (global, spot, and so on) are adjusted. When you're finished adjusting colors in one mode, choose a different mode in the pop-up menu and adjust those colors.

   ■ A positive number increases the percentage of color (darkens); a negative number decreases the percentage of color (lightens).

 You can change the color of a black and white line art (1-bit) TIFF image that's opened by Illustrator or that has been embedded into an Illustrator document by selecting it's bounding box and applying a fill color from the Color palette.

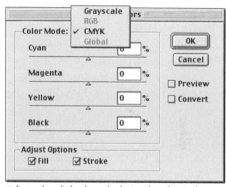

Adjust colors dialog box, displaying the color modes available

 To change colors of objects on layers in a placed Photoshop image (not a photograph), choose Convert Photoshop layers to objects when asked in the import procedure.

- The numbers displayed in the fields reflect the percentage of change applied to the color, not the actual percentage value of the color. For example, if a color is 80% cyan, a +10% color change increases the color value to 88% (10% of 80 is 8). A –10% color change decreases the color value by 8% to 72%.

- A color tint can never be more than 100% or less than 0%. If, by adjusting a color, the resulting value is more than 100% or less than 0%, the maximum (100%) or minimum (0%) values are applied.

7. Click OK or press *return/enter*.

Saturate

Choose this command in the Filter menu (**Filter** ⇨ **Colors** ⇨ **Saturate**) when you want to intensify (darken) or lighten the color (by percentage) of a selected object. Even process colors can be saturated or desaturated using this command.

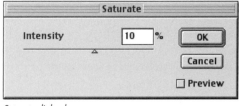

Saturate dialog box

1. Display the Saturate dialog box (**Filter** ⇨ **Colors** ⇨ **Saturate**).

2. If you want to see the results of your changes as you make them, click the Preview checkbox. (I don't know why Illustrator doesn't have Preview boxes checked as the default. You always want to see what you're doing.)

3. Move the slider or enter a value in the field.

- A larger number darkens a color (up to a maximum of 100%), and a smaller number lightens a color (to a minimum of –100%, or white).

4. Click OK or press *return/enter*.

Overprint Fill / Stroke

When one object is placed on top of another object on a page, Illustrator, by default, deletes the portion of the object that's underneath so the colors won't mix and create a different color. Sometimes that's a desirable effect but, in most cases, it isn't what you want. You'll usually want a black stroke to overprint, however, to avoid possible misregistration on press. Refer to Appendix A, *Output: Printing & Exporting Files*, for more information about trapping, color separations, and printing.

Controls for setting overprint are located in the Attributes palette. The overprint option, by default, is turned off. To turn it on for fill or stroke, or both:

1. Select the object for which you want to specify whether or not its fill or stroke overprints.

2. Display the Attributes palette.

   ■ Click the Attributes folder tab in the Color palette.

   or

   ■ Choose **Window ➪ Attributes**.

3. Check Overprint Fill to cause any portion of the selected object that overlaps another colored object to mix its colors with the object underneath.

4. Check Overprint Stroke to cause a stroke applied to an object to overprint (mix) its fill or the fill and/or stroke of a colored object underneath it.

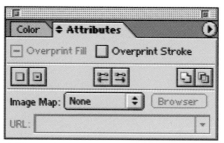

Attributes palette

Overprint Preview To show on your screen how your overprint choices affect the colors of your objects, choose Overprint Preview in the View menu (**View ➪ Overprint Preview**). The objects on your screen display how the colors mix when printed.

Pixel Preview Choose the Pixel Preview option in the View menu (**View ➪ Pixel Preview**) to see how your artwork displays after it has been rasterized for display in a Web browser. If you work in Pixel Preview mode rather than Preview or Outline, the "Snap to" option in the View menu is Snap to Pixel rather than Snap to Grid.

   ■ When the Pixel Preview option is checked (turned on), images may appear blurry because anti-aliasing is automatically applied.

      ▪ Anti-aliasing is the addition of blurred pixels along the edges of paths to soften the edge and make it look less jagged.

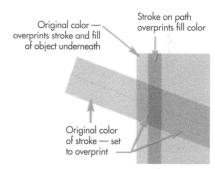

Original color — overprints stroke and fill of object underneath

Stroke on path overprints fill color

Original color of stroke — set to overprint

When Overprint Preview is turned on, you can determine how the colors will mix when printed

Pixel Preview unchecked (off)

Pixel Preview checked (on)

activity 7.3

1. Create a new document: Letter size, CMYK color mode.

2. Draw a cloud shape and fill it with the 50% Yellow swatch. Apply a 12 point stroke and color it with the 25% Blue swatch.

3. Zoom in until you can see the edge of the path easily. Display the Attributes palette and click the Overprint Stroke button.

4. Choose Overprint Preview in the View menu.

   - Notice the different color created where the stroke overlaps the fill color.

5. Make a copy of your cloud shape and position it so it overlaps the first shape.

6. Change the stroke to None and the fill to 25% Green (swatch). Send this object to the back of the stack.

7. Select the first cloud shape, display the Attributes palette, and check the Overprint Fill checkbox.

   - The overlapping colors create a different color.

8. Reduce the view, then display the Color palette Options menu and choose Invert.

   - Only the fill color was changed because that was the active element.

9. Undo the last command (press ⌘ z).

10. Click the Stroke box in the Color palette and apply the Invert command.

    - Only the stroke color was changed because that was the active element.

11. Apply the Invert Colors command in the Filter menu (Filter ➪ Colors ➪ Invert Colors).

    - The stroke color and the fill color were changed.

12. Apply the Complement command to your object.

    - Only the Stroke color changed because it was the active element.

13. Undo the last command (press ⌘ z).

14. Display the Saturate dialog box (Filter ➪ Colors ➪ Saturate), check the Preview box, and move the slider to the left to lighten the colors, then to the right to darken the colors.

    - Notice that both the stroke and the fill colors were altered.

15. Click Cancel to exit the dialog box without applying changes.

16. Choose Filter ➪ Colors ➪ Convert to Grayscale.

    - Colors of the selected objects were changed to shades of gray.

17. Close the document without saving it to a file.

18. Locate and open the file named My Rose.eps that is in the Student Files folder on the CD-ROM that came with this book. Select the image.

19. Display the Saturate dialog box (Filter ➪ Colors ➪ Saturate), click the Preview checkbox, then move the slider back and forth.

    - Notice that all colors in the image are lightened or darkened.

20. Click Cancel to exit the dialog box without applying any changes.

21. Display the Adjust Colors dialog box (Filter ➪ Colors ➪ Adjust Colors). Click the Preview checkbox, then move the sliders back and forth one at a time.

    - Notice what happens to the colors in the image.

22. Click Cancel to exit the dialog box without applying any changes.

23. Close the document without saving changes.

Gradient Fills

A gradient fill is a gradual fading or blending of one color into another color or a shade of the same color. In Illustrator, you can specify multiple colors in one gradient fill, restricted only by the amount of RAM on your computer. Applying gradient fills to objects gives them depth and a more realistic look. Gradient fills can be created using two or more CMYK process colors, RGB process colors, or tints of a single spot color. If color modes are mixed in a single gradient fill, all colors are converted to CMYK process color.

Gradients can be applied to a single object or to several objects, using the same procedures for applying a color swatch; that is, select an object in the document and click a gradient swatch in the Swatches palette or drag a gradient swatch and drop it on a selected or unselected object. You can adjust where one color blends into another color and you can change the direction of the gradient.

Several gradients have been created for you. They can be found on the Swatches palette and in libraries that can be displayed on your screen the same way you display swatch libraries. Choose **Window ➪ Swatch Libraries ➪ Other Library**, then locate the Presets folder in the Adobe program folder on your hard drive and open the Gradients folder. Choose one of the libraries and click Open or press *return/enter*. Add swatches to the Swatches palette of your document by clicking on them in the library palette or by displaying the library palette's Options dialog box and choosing Add to Swatches.

Using the Gradient palette (**Window ➪ Gradient**), you can modify the default gradients or create your own. Display Gradient options (click the Options menu arrow) to see the controls for modifying existing gradients or creating new ones. The Gradient palette (Figure 7.8) offers two types of gradients: Radial and Linear. A Radial gradient is circular and extends out from the center. A Linear gradient extends in a straight line, at any angle, from left to right.

The Gradient tool (▣) in the Toolbox enables you to change the angle of a linear gradient or reposition the starting point of a radial gradient.

Linear gradient

Radial gradient

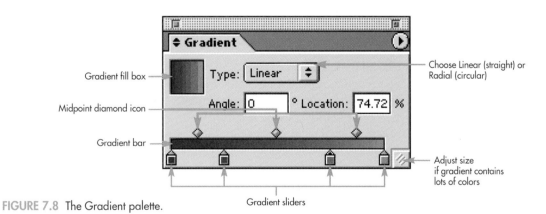

FIGURE 7.8 The Gradient palette.

301

Banding

When an object containing a gradient fill or a color blend is printed, a phenomenon called *banding* can occur. That is, colors don't transition smoothly from one to the next and stripes of color are created. Line screen frequency versus resolution, the difference in color from one end of the gradient or blend to the other, and the length of the gradient fill or color blend can all affect banding.

- Higher screen frequencies generate fewer levels of gray (an imagesetter outputs only in black or shades of gray), which means a higher resolution is necessary to generate 256 shades of gray. For example, an imagesetter outputting a page with a resolution of 1270 dpi and a specified screen frequency of 79 lpi can achieve the maximum of 256 shades of gray. However, an imagesetter outputting a page with a resolution of 1270 dpi and a specified screen frequency of 133 lpi can achieve a maximum of only 82 shades of gray. The maximum of grays a PostScript printer can output is 256, so there's no benefit in having more steps than 256.

Blend of two colors in which there aren't enough steps to create a smooth transition, so banding occurs

  So when you're creating blends, keep in mind the resolution of the printer and the screen frequency at which it will be output. Try to output objects containing gradient fills and color blends on a printer that's capable of printing 256 levels of gray at the desired screen frequency. Check with your output provider for the correct specifications.

- At least one component in the color breakdown should change by at least 50% from the start of the gradient or blend to its end. That is, if the blend is a CMYK color, either the cyan, magenta, yellow, or black should be 50% more (or less) at the end of the gradient or blend than it is at its beginning. This means you can have at least 50 steps in the gradient or blend (one step for each percentage shade of gray).

- The number of steps allocated by Illustrator to a gradient or blend is calculated based on the percentage of change between the colors used. The number of steps, therefore, determines the maximum length a gradient or blend can be before banding occurs. The greater the difference in percentage of change in a color, the more potential steps can be allocated, and the longer the blend can be. The general rule of thumb is to keep gradient fills and blends to a maximum of 7½" because that's the length a blend can be with 256 transition steps (shades of gray).

 If gradients look banded on your screen but print okay, your monitor is probably set to display too few colors. To adjust the color display settings:

Mac OS 9: Monitors control panel

Mac OS X: Displays panel of System Preferences

Windows: Settings ➪ Control panel ➪ Display Settings tab

The number of steps that are allocated to a gradient fill or color blend can be calculated by this formula:

Number of levels of gray generated by the printer at a specified resolution and screen frequency × Change in color (percentage) = Number of steps

For example, if the process color at the start of a blend is 80% cyan, 60% magenta, 21% yellow, 0% black and the ending process color is 25% cyan, 40% magenta, 50% yellow, 0% black, the greatest percent of change is in cyan, from 80% to 25% (55%) or .55. If the levels of gray generated by the printer is 256, the number of steps required to create a smooth blend is 140.8. According to the chart supplied in the Adobe Illustrator User Guide (page 372), the gradient fill or color blend can be a maximum of 4.2 inches.

Creating a Gradient Fill

To create a new Gradient fill:

1. Display the full Gradient palette by clicking its Options menu arrow and choosing Show Options.

2. Display the gradient sliders:

   ■ Click the Gradient Fill box on the Gradient palette.

   or

   ■ Click the Gradient bar on the Gradient palette.

   or

   ■ Click the Gradient button on the Toolbox (■) or press >.

3. Choose the type of Gradient fill you want by choosing Radial or Linear in the Type pop-up menu.

4. Specify a color for the gradient sliders:

   ■ Drag a swatch from the Swatches palette and drop it on the Gradient slider (⌂).

   or

   ■ Click on the Gradient slider (⌂), then mix a color in the Color palette or click in the Spectrum color bar.

   or

   ■ Click on the Gradient slider (⌂), then *Shift*-click a color on a document page with the Eyedropper tool.

   or

   ■ Click on the Gradient slider (⌂), then ✎-click a swatch in the Swatches palette.

Two examples of gradient fills

5. Move the Midpoint Diamond icon (◈) along the Gradient bar to adjust the how much of each color is used. A Midpoint Diamond icon is always placed in the middle between one Gradient slider and the next Gradient slider. When you move a Gradient slider, the Midpoint Diamond icon is adjusted accordingly to keep it in the middle between the two colors.

6. Enter a percentage value in the Location field to specify a percentage of color to the active Gradient slider. The slider moves automatically to that position on the Slider bar.

7. If the new gradient is a Linear Gradient, enter a value in the Angle field to change the angle from 0°, if desired.

Save the New Gradient When you create a Gradient fill, it's applied to selected objects in the document, but if you click on another swatch or on another object in the document, the new Gradient fill isn't saved. To save the newly created Gradient fill:

■ Drag the Gradient Fill box from the Gradient palette onto a blank area in the Swatches palette to create a swatch.

or

■ Click the Gradient Fill box in the Gradient palette, then click the New Swatch button at the bottom of the Swatches palette.

Name the New Gradient Name a newly created gradient (or rename an existing one) by double-clicking its swatch in the Swatches palette to display the Swatch Options dialog box, then enter a name in the field. All other options in the dialog box are unavailable (dimmed). To display the Swatch Options dialog box as you save a swatch, ⬚-click the New Swatch button.

Editing an Existing Gradient Fill

Editing an existing Gradient fill is simple.

1. Display the Gradient fill you want to edit in the Gradient Fill box in the Gradient palette.

■ Click the Gradient swatch you want to change in the Swatches palette.

or

■ Click an object in the document containing the Gradient fill you want to change.

or

■ Click on a similar gradient swatch in the Swatches palette, display the Swatches palette Options menu, and choose Duplicate Swatch. Edit the copied swatch.

fyi Gradient swatches can be added to your Custom Startup file.

fyi To remove a Midpoint diamond, remove a color slider under the gradient bar by dragging it down and off the palette.

2. Change the colors of the Gradient sliders or adjust the Midpoint Diamond icon using the procedures described in Creating a Gradient Fill.

3. To add a Gradient slider so you can add a new color to the gradient fill:

   ■ Click along the bottom of the Gradient bar. A new Gradient slider is added containing the color currently in the Fill box in the Color palette. New Midpoint Diamond icons display.

   ■ Drag a swatch from the Swatches palette and drop it on the Gradient bar in the Gradient palette. Additional Midpoint Diamond icons display.

4. To rearrange colors in a Gradient fill containing multiple colors, ⬎-drag one slider over another to reverse their positions along the Gradient bar. The gradient is updated automatically.

5. Adjust the Midpoint Diamond icons and the Gradient sliders to produce the desired colors and blends.

6. To delete a Gradient slider, drag it down until it's off the Gradient palette.

Using the Gradient Tool

The Gradient tool is used to change the direction or angle of a linear Gradient fill or reposition the center point of a Radial gradient fill. You can also use the Gradient tool to apply a single Gradient fill to more than one object.

Gradient tool icon in the Toolbox palette

Change the Angle of a Linear Gradient Fill To change the angle in an object to which a Gradient fill has been applied:

1. Choose the Gradient tool in the Toolbox.

2. Click in a selected object containing a Gradient fill and drag across it. Release the mouse where you want the Gradient fill to end.

   ■ The point you start dragging is where the Gradient fill starts blending. Any portion of the object to the left of the first click is 100% of the color of the lefthand Gradient slider. Any portion of the object to the right of the point where you release the mouse is 100% of the color of the righthand Gradient slider.

   ■ The angle at which you drag is the new angle of the Gradient fill.

   ■ Hold down the *Shift* key as you drag to keep the angle of the Gradient fill to 0°, 45°, or 90° (or the angle specified in the Constrain Angle field in General Preferences).

   ■ You can start or finish the drag outside the boundaries of the selected object. But the colors start blending at the point of the click, so you won't have 100% of the beginning and ending colors.

   ■ You can drag across an object with the Gradient tool as many times as necessary to achieve the Gradient fill you want. You don't have to use the Undo command between drags unless you want to start fresh each time.

Reposition the Center of a Radial Gradient Fill

1. Choose the Gradient tool in the Toolbox.

2. Click in a selected object containing a Gradient fill and drag to the outside edge of the object. Release the mouse where you want the Gradient fill to end.

   ■ The point of the click is the color of the lefthand Gradient slider and the point at which you release the mouse is the color of the righthand Gradient slider.

   ■ If you don't drag clear to the outside of the object, the righthand color extends, without a gradation of color, to the edge of the object.

   ■ If you drag outside the object, some colors on the righthand side of the Gradient bar won't display in the object.

Applying a Gradient Fill Over Multiple Objects
You can apply a single Gradient fill to multiple objects so that the Gradient fill starts in the first object and ends in the last object. This works with both types of gradients, Linear and Radial.

1. *Shift*-click or marquee to select all objects to which you want to apply the Gradient fill.

2. Click the desired Gradient swatch in the Swatches palette to fill all objects with the same Gradient fill.

3. Choose the Gradient tool in the Toolbox and drag across all the objects.

   ■ The angle at which you drag determines the angle of the gradient and you can *Shift*-drag to keep the angle to 0°, 45°, or 90° (or the angle specified in the Constrain Angle field in General Preferences).

   ■ You can start the drag or end the drag outside the first and last objects.

 *activity* 7.4

1. Create a new document: Letter size, CMYK color mode.

2. Draw three rectangles side by side on the document page, fill them with 50% black and a 1 pt black stroke. Leave one of them selected.

3. Display the Gradient palette (Window ⇨ Gradient) or click its folder tab in the Transparency/Stroke/Gradient palette. Show Options to display the full palette by clicking the Options arrow.

4. In the Swatches palette, click the Copper gradient swatch.

   ■ Notice where the Gradient sliders and the Midpoint Diamond icon are positioned along the Gradient bar in the Gradient palette.

5. In the Swatches palette, click the Violet Eye gradient swatch.

   ■ Notice where the Gradient sliders and the Midpoint Diamond icon for this gradient are positioned along the Gradient bar in the Gradient palette.

6. Display the Trumatch swatch library.

Continued

7. Add Trumatch swatches 9b, 27b, and 38e to the Swatches palette.

8. In the Gradient palette, drag all the sliders off except three. Position them so there's one on each end and one in the middle of the slider bar.

9. Choose Linear in the Type pop-up menu.

10. Drag the Trumatch 27b swatch and drop it on the lefthand Gradient slider.

11. Drag the Trumatch 9b swatch and drop it on the middle Gradient slider.

12. Drag the Trumatch 38e swatch and drop it on the righthand Gradient slider.

   ■ The new Gradient fill you created is applied to the selected rectangle.

13. Click on the middle Gradient slider and move it back and forth. Then click on the Gradient sliders on each end of the Gradient bar and move them toward the center.

   ■ The Midpoint Diamond icons adjust relative to the middle point between the lefthand and middle Gradient sliders and the middle and righthand Gradient sliders.

   ■ The closer you move the Gradient slider toward the middle, the darker the color on the end becomes. That's because the color on the end remains at 100%, but you're telling Illustrator to start the blend at a lower percentage of color.

   ■ Notice that when you click on a Gradient slider, the Fill box in the Color palette changes to the color of the slider.

14. Click on the Gradient Fill box in the Gradient palette.

   ■ Now the Gradient fill you've just created is displayed in the Fill box of the Color palette.

15. Click on one of the other rectangles, then click in the Gradient Fill box in the Gradient palette to fill the rectangle with the new Gradient fill.

16. Click in the Gradient Fill box in the Gradient palette and drag it onto a blank spot on the Swatches palette and drop it.

   ■ Now you have a new Gradient fill swatch that you can select to fill other objects. You can also transfer it to other documents using the drag-and-drop method, or create a swatch library containing this Gradient fill.

17. Double-click the new gradient swatch and name it Teal, Yellow, Violet.

18. Select one of the rectangles containing the Gradient fill.

19. Choose the Gradient tool in the Toolbox.

20. Click at the bottom left side of the selected rectangle and drag up and to the right. Repeat two or three times, beginning and ending the click-and-drag in different places on the rectangle. Even click outside the rectangle and drag outside the rectangle before you drop.

   ■ Notice how the angle of the gradient changed and how dragging outside the rectangle changed the spread of the colors of the Gradient fill.

21. Click and drag one more time from left to right, holding down the *Shift* key as you drag, to return the Gradient fill to a 0° angle.

22. Click on the right side this time and drag to the left.

   ■ Now the colors have reversed positions. The Violet is on the left side of the rectangle and the Teal is on the right side.

23. Select the third rectangle that's filled with 50% black, then click on the Teal, Yellow, Violet swatch in the Swatches palette.

24. Remove the middle (Yellow) Gradient slider in the Gradient palette by dragging it down and off the palette.

25. Adjust the remaining Midpoint Diamond icon so that more of the Violet color is visible than the Teal color.

26. Change the Gradient Type to Radial.

27. With the Gradient tool still selected, click in a corner of the rectangle.

Continued

- The Teal center moves to the position of the click.

28. Draw a circle. The current Gradient fill applies to the new object automatically because it's the current fill color in the Fill box in the Color palette.

29. With the Gradient tool selected, click somewhere toward the outside of the circle to move the Teal center.

30. Select all three rectangles and apply the new Gradient fill swatch you created.

31. With the Gradient tool selected in the Toolbox, click on the left edge of the first rectangle, drag across all three rectangles, and release at the right edge of the last rectangle.

   - The gradient is applied as if the objects were all one object with no spaces between them.

32. Practice creating gradient fills, at least one having six or seven colors.

33. Close this document without saving it to a file.

Convert a Gradient Fill into Separate Objects

To simplify a gradient fill that is too complex to print, use the Expand command in the Object menu to convert the gradient into separate objects. Each step in the gradient is converted to a separate object with a different color or shade from the step object next to it and is grouped with a clipping mask. Clipping masks are discussed in Step 12, *Meshes, Masks, Blends, & Transparency.*

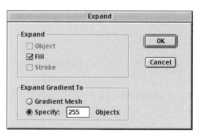

   These separate objects can be selected, modified, deleted, and so on, independent of the other step objects that were created. You can create a design by expanding the gradient fill and deleting some of the step objects or applying a different color.

Convert a gradient to separate objects by expanding it's fill into a specified number of objects

1. Choose **Object ➪ Expand** to display the Expand dialog box.

2. In the Expand Gradient To section, enter the number of objects you want to be created from the gradient in the field.

   - The number must be high enough to create enough shapes to produce smooth color transition.

   - To use the same value that was entered the last time the dialog box was displayed, hold down the ⌥ key while displaying the Object menu and choosing the Expand command.

3. Click OK or press *return/enter.*

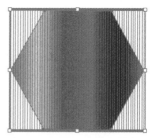

Shape containing a gradient fill that was converted into separate objects and selected to display the clipping mask

activity 7.5

1. Create a new document: Letter size, CMYK color mode.

2. Draw about a 2" star on the document page and apply the Rainbow gradient swatch, no stroke.

3. Choose Object ➪ Expand to display the Expand dialog box. Enter 50 in the Specify [ ] Objects field to convert the gradient into 50 separate objects.

4. Deselect the shape and zoom in to about 2400% (or larger if your monitor is big enough). You need to be able to see the individual paths.

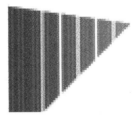

5. With the Direct Selection tool, select the fifth path to the left of the right side of the star and delete it.

6. Move across the star from right to left and delete every fifth path.

7. Zoom out to see the results.

8. Close the document without saving it to a file.

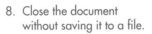

Artwork with a Flare

The new Flare tool, hidden under the Rectangle tool in the toolbox, creates an effect similar to a lens flare in a photograph. A flare object created in Illustrator consists of rings, rays, and halos around a bright center (see Figure 7.9). You can create a flare without rays or rings but not without the center and its halo. The components of the flare are filled with a fill color at varying opacity settings.

    Flare objects are intended to be placed over existing objects. Their appearance varies, depending on the fill color of the object that's behind it.

    You can move individual elements of an existing flare object, you can add more rays or rings, and you can completely change it by changing its options in the Flare dialog box. But keep in mind that the more complex the flare object is, the more difficult it is to print. Don't make it any more complex than necessary to achieve the desired results.

    You can create a flare (a) by dragging with the Flare tool selected, (b) numerically by entering values in the Flare dialog box, or (c) using current settings in the Flare Options dialog box. There are settings in the Flare Tool Options dialog box to control the appearance of each component of the flare object.

Flare tool icon in the Toolbox palette

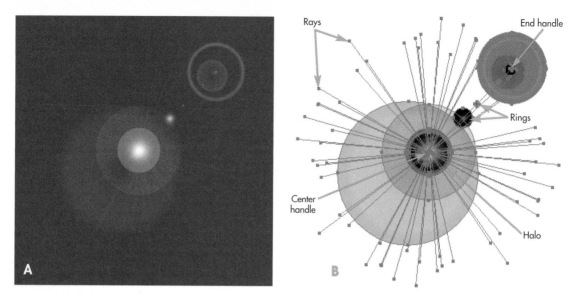

Rays

End handle

Rings

Center handle

Halo

B

FIGURE 7.9 (A) A flare created with Flare tool default values; (B) Components of the flare shown in A.

Dragging to Create a Flare

1. Choose the Flare tool (⊡) in the Toolbox.

2. Click on the page where you want the center handle of the flare to be located, and drag until the center of the flare is the size you want it. The farther you drag, the larger the center and its halo become.

   ■ Rings are created in a random pattern.

3. Before releasing the mouse, you can:

   ■ Drag in a circular motion to change the angle of the rays.

   ■ Press the Up arrow (↑) to add rays.

   ■ Press the Down arrow (↓) to remove rays.

   ■ Hold down the spacebar and drag to move the position of the center handle.

   ■ Hold down the *Shift* key as you drag to keep the angle of the rays constant.

   ■ Hold down the ⌘ key as you drag to freeze the center handle and center halo while enlarging the other elements as you continue to drag.

4. Click again on the page to establish the end handle and rings of the flare object.

   ■ Before releasing the mouse, move the handle around to change the length or angle of the end handle part of the flare.

- Press the Up arrow (↑) to add rings.
- Press the Down arrow (↓) to remove rings.

Creating a Flare Numerically

You can create a flare object with specific dimensions and angles by setting options in the Flare Tool Options dialog box (Figure 7.10). Click the arrows to the left of the fields to change the value one increment at a time. Click the arrow to the right of the field to display a slider. Click and drag the triangle to change the value in the field.

fyi *The Preview checkbox is not available when creating a new flare object.*

1. Select the Flare tool (🔍) in the Toolbox (under the Rectangle tool).

2. Display the Flare Tool Options dialog box:

   - By double-clicking the Flare tool in the Toolbox

   or

   - By clicking (without dragging) on the page where you want the center handle of the flare to appear.

3. Enter values in the fields of the four sections:

   - **Center** — These values apply to the inner portion of the flare object. Diameter determines the size of the center of the object, Opacity determines how transparent the center portion of the object will be, and Brightness is how light or dark the center is.

   - **Halo** — The Growth field determines the radius of the halo as a percentage of the overall size of the flare object. Fuzziness determines the sharpness the halo. You can enter a percentage value from 0 to 100; 0% is crisp (no fuzziness applied) and 100 is fuzzy.

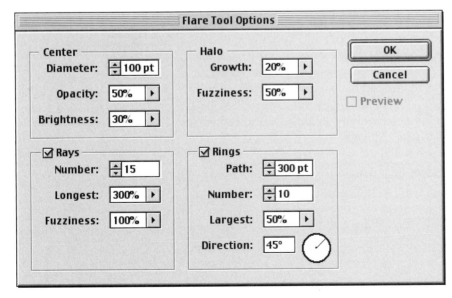

FIGURE 7.10 Flare Tool Options dialog box displaying default values. You can change the values to alter the size and appearance of a flare.

- **Rays** — If you don't want the flare object to have rays, uncheck the Rays checkbox. You can specify:
  - **Number** — how many rays the object will have.
  - **Longest** — how long the longest ray will be (as a percentage of the average ray).
  - **Fuzziness** — how fuzzy they'll be (0 (crisp) to 100 (fuzzy).
- **Rings** — If you don't want the flare object to have rings, uncheck the Rings checkbox. You can specify:
  - **Path** — Enter a value or click the arrows to control how far the end handle appears from the center handle of the flare object.
  - **Number** — Controls how many rings the flare object will have.
  - **Largest** — Sets the size of the largest ring (as a percentage of the size of the average ring).
  - **Direction** — Enter a value in the field or move the pointer in the Direction icon to control the angle at which the end handle projects from the center of the flare.

4. Click OK or press *return/enter.*

Create a Flare Using Current Values Create a flare using the values currently set in the Flare Tool Options dialog box by holding down the ⌥ key and clicking on the page where you want the center handle of the object to appear.

Create a Flare Using Default Values Display the Flare Tool Options dialog box, and hold down the ⌥ key. The Cancel button changes to Reset. When you click the Reset button, all values change to the program default values.

Edit an Existing Flare With the Selection tool, select an existing flare object and double-click the Flare tool in the Toolbox to display the Flare Tool Options dialog box. Change values in the fields, then click OK or press *return/enter.* You can move a single component of the flare object by clicking on its pathline with the Direct Selection tool, clicking each anchor point, making them solid, then dragging them to a new location. If you select a ray with the Direct Selection tool, you can change its length and angle.

- To see the results of your edits more easily, choose Hide Edges in the View menu to hide the path lines of the objects.

The Preview checkbox is available when modifying an existing flare object. Check and uncheck it to see the results of your changes. A flare object is complex, so it may take a few seconds.

Expanding a Flare

You can also edit individual components of a flare object by converting it into its individual components.

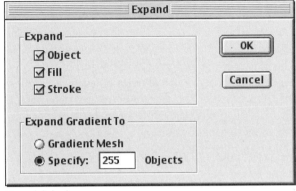
Expand dialog box

1. With the Selection tool, select the flare object.

2. Choose **Object** ⇨ **Expand** to display the Expand dialog box.

3. Check all three checkboxes in the Expand section.

4. Click OK or press *return/enter*.

5. Choose **Object** ⇨ **Ungroup** or press ⇧ ⌘ g to ungroup them.

Once a flare object has been expanded, it can't be edited by changing values in the Flare Tool Options dialog box.

1. Create a new document: Letter size, CMYK color mode.

2. Choose the Flare tool (⬚) in the Toolbox, then click on the page and drag about ½" to create the center part of a flare. Before releasing the mouse:

   ▪ Move it up and down to increase the size of the flare

   ▪ Move it in a circular motion to rotate the rays

   ▪ Press the Up arrow key (↑) five or six times to add rays

   ▪ Press the Down arrow key (↓) twice to reduce the number of rays

   ▪ Move the mouse until the flare is about 1½" in diameter, then release the mouse.

3. Position the pointer about an inch away from the rays and click. Before releasing the mouse:

   ▪ Move it up and down like a yo-yo to change the length of the handle.

   ▪ Move it in a circular motion to rotate the handle around the center of the flare.

   ▪ Press the Up arrow key (↑) five or six times to add rings.

   ▪ Press the Down arrow key (↓) twice to reduce the number of rings.

   ▪ Position the mouse until the handle is about 1" away from the rays, then release the it.

4. With the Rectangle tool, draw a rectangle that covers the flare, apply a fill of 90% cyan, 90% magenta. Send it to the back of the stack (Object ⇨ Arrange ⇨ Send to Back).

   ▪ Notice the colors in the flare.

5. Change the color of the rectangle to 100% cyan, 60% yellow.

   ▪ Notice the change in the colors of the flare.

6. Change the color of the rectangle several times and notice the changes in the color of the flare.

7. Open the file named Mountain Flare.eps that's in the Student Files folder on the CD-ROM that's in the back of this book.

8. Add a flare to the sun peeking over the mountain.

9. Save the file into your Practice folder, same name, same format. Print it, then close the artwork window.

Magic Wand

The Magic Wand tool allows you to select all objects in a document having the same or similar fill color, stroke color, stroke weight, blending mode, or opacity as the object you click on. The keyboard command for this tool is *y*. The advantage to using the Magic Wand instead of the Same options in the Select menu is that you can select objects with *similar* attributes, not just objects that match the selection. You can determine how similar the objects are by setting tolerance levels for these attributes in the Magic Wand palette (**Window ⇨ Magic Wand**).

Magic Wand tool icon in the Toolbox palette

Setting Magic Wand Tolerances

Before using the Magic Wand, options must be chosen in the Magic Wand palette (Figure 7.11) to determine which characteristics will be used to select objects.

1. Check the checkbox for the attribute to use when making the selection.

    ■ To select objects having only the same fill color, a checkmark should appear only in the Fill Color checkbox.

    ■ To select all objects having the same fill color and stroke color as the original object, check Fill Color and Stroke Color checkboxes. And so on.

2. Enter a value in the Tolerance field to specify how similar the attribute must be to the original object to be selected.

    or

    Click the arrow to the right of the field (▶) to display the slider bar. Click on the slider and drag it back and forth to change the Tolerance value in the field.

    ■ A value of 0 selects objects that match the original object exactly.

    ■ A low value selects objects similar to the original object.

    ■ A high value selects objects having a broader range of colors, weights, or opacities.

    ■ Fill and Stroke color values range from 0–100 for CMYK colors or 0–255 for RGB colors.

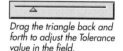

Drag the triangle back and forth to adjust the Tolerance value in the field.

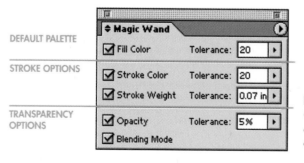

DEFAULT PALETTE

STROKE OPTIONS

TRANSPARENCY OPTIONS

| Hide Stroke Options |
| Hide Transparency Options |
| Reset |
| ✓ Use All Layers |

Options available in the Magic Wand palette Options menu

FIGURE 7.11 The complete Magic Wand palette. Change values in the Tolerance fields to select only objects with matching attributes (lower values) or objects with similar attributes (higher value).

- Stroke weight tolerances range from 0–1000 points.
- Percentages for Opacity tolerance range from 0–100%.

3. If you want the Magic Wand tool to select objects on all layers in the document, the Use All Layers option in the Magic Wand palette Options menu should be checked. It's a toggle command: if it's checked, click it to uncheck it, and vice versa. If it's unchecked, the Magic Wand selects only objects on the same layer as the original object that's selected.

4. To reset all values in the Tolerance fields to their default values, display the Magic Wand palette Options menu and choose Reset.

Using the Magic Wand

To select objects using the Magic Wand tool:

1. Select the Magic Wand tool (🔲) in the Toolbox and select an object.
   - Depending upon the options and settings in the Magic Wand palette, other objects having the same or similar characteristics are selected.

2. To select additional objects having different characteristics, *Shift*-click an object having attributes different from the original object.

3. To eliminate a set of selected objects from the selection, ⌥-click one of the objects.

 *activity* 7.7

1. Open the file named Magic Wand samples.eps that's in the Student Files folder on the CD-ROM that came with this book.

2. Choose the Magic Wand tool (🔲) in the Toolbox and click on one of the yellow objects on the page.
   - All the yellow objects are selected.

3. Display the Stroke Options section of the Magic Wand tool palette, uncheck Fill Color and check Stroke Color. Then click on the circle in the second row.
   - It has a black stroke color, so all objects having a black stroke are selected, regardless of the weight of the stroke.

4. Uncheck Stroke Color and check Stroke Weight, then click on the polygon in the first row.
   - All objects with the same stroke weight are selected.

5. Uncheck Stroke Weight and check Fill Color. Enter 5 in the Tolerance field and click on the oval in the first row.
   - No other objects are selected because none are within 5% of the selected color.

6. Click on the circle in the third row.
   - The polygon in the first row and the oval in the fourth row are also selected because the selected object is 95% cyan and the polygon and oval are 100% cyan, which is within the 5% tolerance value.

7. Change the Fill Color Tolerance value to 20% and click one of the cyan-colored objects.
   - Now the oval in the first row is selected because it's within the tolerance value.

8. Continue selecting objects by changing selection option checkboxes and tolerance values.

9. Close the artwork window without saving changes.

Save and Edit Selections

The Save Selection and Edit Selection commands in the Select menu allow you to name and save the set of selections so you can select those same objects again with one command. This comes in handy if you have many objects in a document that have the same attributes where if you change one, you have to change them all. Selection sets are saved with the document.

Create and Save a Selection Set

To create and save a selections set:

1. Select one or more objects in the document using one of the selection methods: *Shift*-click multiple objects, marquee the objects, use the Magic Wand tool to select similar objects, and so on.

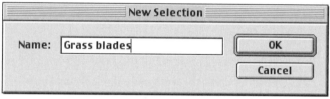

Enter a name for the selection set in the Name field of the New Selection dialog box

2. Choose **Select** ➪ **Save Selection** to display the New Selection dialog box.

3. Enter a name for the selection in the Name field.

4. Click OK or press *return/enter*.

    ■ The selection set is saved and appears at the bottom of the Select menu.

    ■ When you click on the selection name in the Select menu, the objects in the document that were saved in that selection set become selected.

    ■ Selected objects can be modified without affecting the selection set. If an object in the selection set is deleted, the selection set is not affected.

New selection sets appear at the bottom of the Select menu

Edit a Selection Set

To change the name of a selection set or to delete a selection set:

1. Choose **Select** ➪ **Edit Selection** to display the Edit Selection dialog box.

2. Highlight a selection set and edit its name in the Name field, then click OK or press *return/enter*.

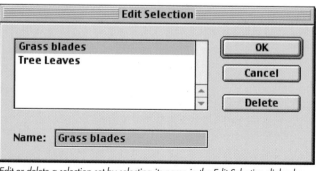

Edit or delete a selection set by selecting its name in the Edit Selection dialog box

or

Highlight the name of a selection set you want to delete, then click the **Delete** button.

activity 7.8

1. Open the file named US Flag.eps that's in the Student Files folder on the CD-ROM that came with this book.

2. With the Selection tool or the Direct-Selection tool, marquee to select all the stars and the background.

3. Display the Select menu and choose Save Selection. When the New Selection dialog box displays, enter Stars & Background in the field.

4. Deselect everything, then marquee to select all the stripes and save this selection as Stripes.

5. Deselect everything.

6. Display the Select menu and choose the Stars & Background option at the bottom of the menu.

   ■ In the document, all the stars and the background are selected.

7. Without deselecting the stars and the background, choose Stripes from the Select menu options.

   ■ The stars and the background are deselected and the stripes are selected.

8. In the Select menu, choose Stars & Background, *Shift*-click the background behind the stars to deselect it.

9. In the Select menu, choose Save Selection and name it Stars.

10. In the Selection menu, choose Edit Selection. When the dialog box displays, highlight the Stars & Background selection and delete it.

11. Save the file into your Practice folder with the same name, then close the artwork window.

Color Blends

In addition to Gradient fill, Illustrator provides commands to blend colors from one object to another. In addition to blending colors, the Blend command and the Blend tool also allow you to actually morph from one object shape to another object shape. In this chapter, though, you'll learn about blending colors. More complete information about blending shapes is discussed in Step 12, *Meshes, Masks, Blends, & Transparency*.

Blending Colors

The three Blend commands in the Filter menu enable you to create continuous color blends between three or more separate objects. Each object is filled with a flat color (no gradient), but it is a transition color from the first object to the last object. The more intermediate objects you have selected, the more gradual the color change from one object to the next.

You must have at least three objects selected to use these commands, and all objects must have a fill color. Objects with a fill of None are ignored. Intermediate objects are filled with blends of the first (topmost, leftmost, frontmost) and last (bottommost, rightmost, backmost) objects. Stroke colors applied to selected objects are not affected by these commands.

The beginning and ending objects (top and bottom, left and right, and so on) cannot be filled with global process colors, patterns, gradients, or two different spot colors. They must be process colors or tints of the same spot color. Objects between the first and last object can be filled with any color, pattern, or gradient because when the command is applied to selected objects, fill colors in intermediate objects are converted to the blend of the first and last object anyway.

Blend Front to Back (**Filter ➩ Colors ➩ Blend Front to Back**)
Selected objects are colorized based on their stacking order, from the frontmost object to the backmost object in the stack.

Blend Horizontally (**Filter ➩ Colors ➩ Blend Horizontally**)
Objects are colorized from the leftmost selected object to the rightmost selected object.

Blend Vertically (**Filter ➩ Colors ➩ Blend Vertically**)
Objects are colorized from the topmost selected object to the bottommost selected object.

fyi *Once one of these Blend commands has been applied to objects, rearranging them on the document page doesn't affect the color of the objects.*

activity 7.9

1. Create a new document: Letter size, CMYK color mode. Name it Leaf.eps, and save it into your Practice Folder as an .eps file.

2. In the Color palette, change the fill color to None and specify the stroke as 1.5 pt black.

3. Draw a leaf similar to the one shown here.

   ■ Draw the veins with the Pencil tool, and apply round endcaps to those paths. Remove unnecessary anchor points to make smoother paths.

   ■ Adjust the Miter Limit of the outside path so all the joins have pointy corners. If you can't get pointy corners that look right, then adjust the angle of the intersecting paths.

4. When you're finished with the entire leaf, click on the outside path and change the fill to white. Save your file (⌘ s).

   ■ If you change the fill to white before drawing the veins of the leaf, they will have a fill of white and you don't want the veins to have a fill.

5. Marquee with the Selection tool to select all the paths in the leaf, then drag-copy five more leaves while holding down the *Shift* key. Position them to the right of the first leaf so they overlap the first one about halfway.

6. Apply the Orange swatch (M=50, Y=100) to the leftmost leaf.

7. Apply the 75% Yellow swatch to the rightmost leaf.

Continued

8. Marquee across the top of all the leaves to select the outside paths. Don't select any veins in the leaves.

9. Choose Filter ⇨ Colors ⇨ Blend Horizontally.

  - Colors in the intermediate leaves change gradually from the orange on the left to the yellow on the right.

10. Create a linear gradient using these two colors and apply it individually to each of the 6 leaves.

  - Put the orange color in the left Gradient slider and the yellow in the right Gradient slider.

11. Select the outside paths of all 6 leaves (no veins).

12. Select the Gradient tool and drag horizontally from left to right.

  - See the difference between applying a gradient and applying the Blend Horizontally command? When a gradient is applied, each leaf contains a gradient, depending upon where it falls in the Gradient bar. When a Blend is applied, each leaf is a flat color that's a gradual change from one leaf to the next until the first color is morphed to the last color.

13. Select all the leaves (not the veins) and change the fill to white.

14. Apply the Orange swatch to the leftmost leaf and 75% Yellow swatch to the rightmost leaf and Blend Horizontally again.

15. Marquee to select the outside paths of all the leaves.

16. Apply Blend Front to Back command (Filter ⇨ Colors ⇨ Blend Front to Back).

  - Oops! You got a Colors Error: Patterns, global colors, and gradients cannot be processed by this filter.

17. Click on the leaf next to the leftmost leaf in the row. Apply the Orange swatch to that leaf and send it to the back of the stack (Object ⇨ Arrange ⇨ Send to Back).

18. Click on the leaf in position #3 (next to one you just sent to the back of the stack) and apply the 75% Yellow swatch to that leaf. Bring it to the front of the stack (Object ⇨ Arrange ⇨ Bring to Front).

19. Select the outside paths of all of the leaves and apply the Blend Front to Back command again.

  - The leaves are recolored according to their stacking order.

20. Rearrange the leaves on the document page vertically, overlapping them slightly.

21. Click on the leaf closest to the top of the page (topmost) and apply the Orange swatch to that leaf.

22. Click on the leaf closest to the bottom of the page (bottommost) and apply the 75% Yellow swatch to that leaf.

23. Click on the outside path of each leaf (make sure no veins are selected).

24. Apply the Blend Vertically command (Filter ⇨ Colors ⇨ Blend Vertically).

  - The leaves are recolored from the top to the bottom, regardless of their stacking order.

25. Save the file and close the document.

319

PRACTICE ACTIVITY 7-1 — Ghosting

1. Create a new document: Letter size, CMYK color mode. Name it Ghosting.eps and save it into your practice folder as an .eps file.

2. With the Rectangle tool, draw a rectangle that's approximately 4½" × 3", no stroke.

3. Create the following linear gradient:
   - Left slider: 100% cyan, 50% magenta, 0% yellow, and 0% black.
   - Right slider: White
   - Midpoint Diamond location: 35%
   - Angle: −90°

4. Choose the Type tool, click on the page and type ICE, all caps. Format it to be 180 pt. Myriad Bold. Convert it to outlines (⇧ ⌘ O).

5. Select both the type outlines and the rectangle and apply the gradient.

6. Deselect the rectangle and move the type into position inside the rectangle.

   - Different positions inside the rectangle gives different effects.
   - You can also change the location of the Midpoint Diamond of the gradient to alter the effect of the type within the rectangle.

7. Save the file, print it, and close the artwork window.

PRACTICE ACTIVITY 7-2 — Simple Creamer

1. Create a new document: Letter size, CMYK color mode. Name it Creamer.eps and save it into your practice folder as an .eps file.

2. With the Pen tool, draw the body of the creamer, similar to the one shown here. It should be about 5" high from the top of the spout to the bottom of the "foot". Don't apply a stroke to the shape.

3. Create the following radial gradient swatch and name it Creamer Gradient:
   - Left slider: 18% cyan, 11% magenta, 0% yellow, and 0% black.

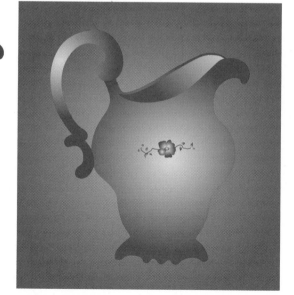

320

- Right slider: 91% cyan, 80% magenta, 0% yellow, and 0% black.
- Midpoint Diamond location: 57%

4. Apply it to the body of the creamer with its center in the middle of the body of the creamer, as shown.

5. With the Pen tool, draw the handle as a separate piece. Apply the same gradient, with the center of the radial in the middle of the handle, as shown. Don't apply a stroke.

6. Drag the handle into position on the body of the creamer.

7. Create a new Linear gradient, using the same color specifications as the radial gradient you created earlier, except change the angle to 135°. Save it as a swatch and name it Spout Gradient.

8. Draw the spout showing the inside of the creamer as a separate piece and apply the Spout Gradient. Again, no stroke.

9. Press ⌘s to save your file.

10. With the Pencil tool, draw the flower, stems, and leaves. You can draw them in place on the body of the creamer by locking the creamer first, or you can draw them separately and drag them into position when you're finished. Apply the Creamer gradient to the flower petals and apply the purple color to the stems (91% cyan, 80% magenta, 0% yellow, and 0% black).

- I moved each section apart so you could see the shape of each piece.

11. Draw a square around your creamer at least 1" beyond each side of the object. Apply the following radial Gradient:
    - Left slider: 17% cyan, 30% magenta, 0% yellow, and 0% black.
    - Right slider: 52% cyan, 80% magenta, 0% yellow, and 12% black.
    - Midpoint Diamond location: 48%

12. Send to back.

13. Press ⌘s to save your file. Print it, then close the artwork window.

EXERCISE 7-1 — Banana

Draw a banana. Obtain a fresh banana or use
the one shown here as an example.

EXERCISE 7-2 — Fruit or Vegetable

Obtain a piece of fruit or a vegetable, and draw it.

EXERCISE 7-3 — China

Draw a piece of china from a decorative set of dishes. Find a
piece that has a unique shape, not just a simple piece.

Layers & Links

Chapter Outline

- The Layers Palette
- New Layers
- Layer Options
- Layer Management

- Import Images Into Illustrator
- The Links Palette
- The Document Info Palette
- Trace Imported Images

In previous chapters, you drew artwork on a flat artwork page containing only one layer. In Chapter 4, you learned about stacking objects and the order in which they're placed on an artwork page — the first path drawn is on the bottom of the stack. As you create more complex artwork, having only one layer to work on can be restricting.

Adobe Illustrator 10 has a feature, called Layers, that allows you to draw artwork on independent, self-contained levels of the same artwork page. It's like each layer is a clear piece of glass upon which you draw objects. Unless objects overlap, you can see from the top layer clear through to the bottom layer. This allows you to draw pieces of an illustration without affecting any other part of the artwork.

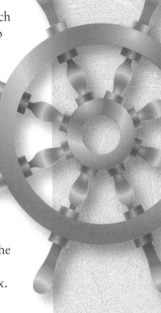

You can have as many layers as your computer's memory will allow, and each top-level layer or sublayer can contain any number of objects, each on their own object layer. Each individual layer can be named, edited, reordered, hidden, locked, printed, and so on, independently of objects on other layers. You can even have different display modes for different layers.

Layers can have sublayers, which are nested under the top-level layer, and even sublayers within sublayers. Up to 29 sublayers are allowed under a top-level layer, numbered in the order in which they were created. But don't get carried away with creating layers; your artwork could become unnecessarily complex.

The Layers Palette

Layers are created, organized, selected, and so on, using the Layers palette (**Window** ⇨ **Layers**). See Figure 8.1. The appearance of the elements in the Layers palette can be changed by making choices in the Palette Options dialog box.

Layers Palette Options

To access the Layers Palette Options dialog box (Figure 8.2), click the Palette Options arrow at the top right corner of the palette. Scroll to the bottom of the pop-up menu that displays and choose Palette Options.

- **Show Layers Only** — Check to list only top-level layers and sublayers, without displaying individual objects and paths contained on individual layers.

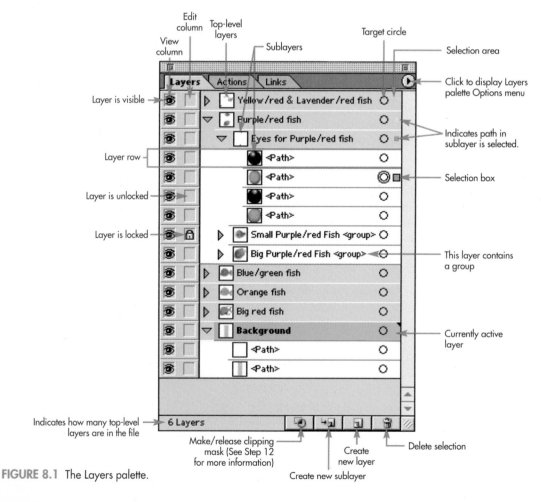

FIGURE 8.1 The Layers palette.

New Layer...
New Sublayer...
Duplicate "Background"
Delete "Background"

Options for "Background"...

Make Clipping Mask

Locate Object

Merge Selected
Flatten Artwork
Collect in New Layer

Release to Layers (Sequence)
Release to Layers (Build)
Reverse Order

Template
Hide Others
Outline Others
Lock Others

Paste Remembers Layers

Palette Options...

Layers palette Options menu

Layers Palette Options

☐ Show Layers Only   [OK]
┌─ Row Size ──────────   [Cancel]
  ○ Small
  ● Medium
  ○ Large
  ○ Other: [   ] pixels

┌─ Thumbnails ──────────
  ☑ Layers
     ☐ Top Level Only
  ☑ Groups
  ☑ Objects

FIGURE 8.2 The Layers palette can be customized for each file by changing options in the Layers Palette Options dialog box.

- **Row Size** — Choose the size of the thumbnail preview of layer icons and objects on individual layers.
  - When you choose Small the Thumbnails section of the dialog box turns gray (dims), indicating that thumbnail previews are not available.
  - Choose Other, then enter a custom size, between 12–100 pixels, in the adjacent field to display the icons at a specific size.
- **Thumbnails** — Specify which layers will have thumbnail previews.
  - **Layers** — Show thumbnails on all layers and sublayers.
  - **Top Level Only** — Show thumbnails only on top-level layers.
  - **Groups** — Show thumbnails of groups on a layer.
  - **Objects** — Show thumbnails of objects (paths) on layers.

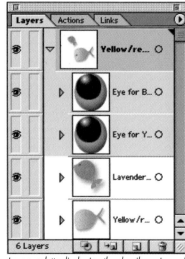

Layers palette displaying thumbnail previews of 50 pixels

New Layers

When a document is created, it automatically has a top-level layer in the Layers palette. Layers can be nested one inside another, like the folders where you store files. A layer is a top-level layer when it isn't inside another layer. Sublayers are part of a top-level layer, but they can be manipulated (edited, printed, and so on) independently of the top-level layer.

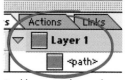
Layers cannot be added to your Custom Startup file. See Step 6, Rulers, Grids, & Guides, for information about creating a Custom Startup File.

Nesting

A thumbnail preview of objects placed on a layer is displayed on the Layers palette, indented (nested) under the Layer on which it's placed. Each individual path has a thumbnail view, so each layer has as many thumbnails as it has individual paths. You can view these thumbnails by clicking the triangle arrow to the left of the Layer name to open the layer. If the Layers palette gets too long, click the Expand Layer arrow (▷) to hide some of the nested paths.

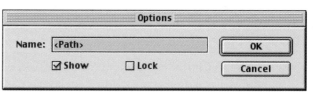

A name is assigned to the path thumbnail, by default, that describes what's on the object layer (path, text, image, and so on). You can change the name of its thumbnail and hide or lock the object layer by double-clicking on it to display its Options dialog box. Enter a name in the Name field. It's a good idea to leave the descriptive name assigned by Illustrator as part of the name for easy identification of the element.

A sublayer nested in another layer

Options dialog box that displays when you double-click an object layer

Uncheck the Show checkbox to hide the path on the document page. Checking the Lock checkbox locks the path so it can't be selected or edited. The Show and Lock checkboxes perform the same functions as the Show/Hide and Lock/Unlock commands in the Object menu. Changing the options for a particular path doesn't have any effect on other paths on the same layer.

A layer in the Layers palette must be active to be able to draw paths on it. The active layer is designated on the Macintosh platform by a black triangle in the upper right corner of the layer row. On the Windows platform, this triangle is white.

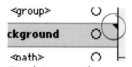

Triangle in upper right corner of layer row designates the active layer

Creating New Layers

New top-level layers are added above the active layer in the Layers palette. When you add new layers you need to choose options that apply to the layer, such as name, color, order, and so on. Or you can add new layers and let Illustrator make the choices for the these options. When Illustrator makes the choices, the next number in order of creation is assigned to the new layer and the next available color from the list of colors in the Color pop-up menu in the Layer Options dialog box is applied to the new layer.

To create a new layer:

1. Click on the name of the top-level layer above which you want to add the new layer.

2. Click the Create New Layer button ([□]) at the bottom of the Layers palette. The Layer Options dialog box doesn't display and Illustrator assigns default option choices (see the section on Layer Options).

   or

   Choose New Layer from the Layers palette Options menu (click arrow at the top right corner of the palette to display the menu). The Layer Options dialog box displays (see the section on Layer Options).

   or

   Hold down the ⌥ key and click the Create New Layer button ([□]) at the bottom of the palette. The Layer Options dialog box displays (see the section on Layer Options).

3. Make choices from the options in the Layer Options dialog box (see the section on Layer Options).

Creating Sublayers

If your artwork needs only a few layers (you should keep it as simple as possible), you'll rarely need to use sublayers. Sublayers are components of, and are nested within, the top-level layer. You can have as many as 29 levels of sublayers (hopefully, you'll never need that many), and every level is indented under the layer or sublayer of which it's a part. Sublayers are named, by default, the same way as top-level layers — numerically in the order they were created.

Elements placed on sublayers also have thumbnail previews to show what's on the sublayer. They're nested under the sublayer just as elements placed on top-level layers and the same options are available for them (name, show, hide). Display or hide the thumbnails on the palette by clicking the Expand Layer arrow (▷) to the left of the name of the layer. You can tell it's a sublayer rather than an object layer because an object layer doesn't have the Expand Layer arrow.

To create a new sublayer:

1. Click on the name of the top-level layer or sublayer into which you want to nest the new sublayer.

2. Click the Create New Sublayer button ([+□]) at the bottom of the Layers palette. The Layer Options dialog box doesn't display and Illustrator assigns default options.

   or

Choose New Sublayer from the Layers palette Options menu (click arrow at the top right corner of the palette to display the menu). The Layer Options dialog box displays (see the section on Layer Options).

or

Hold down the ⌥ key and click the Create New Sublayer button (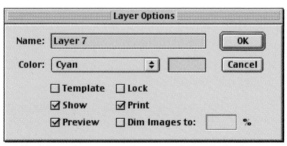) at the bottom of the palette. The Layer Options dialog box displays.

3. Make choices from the options in the Layer Options dialog box (see the section on Layer Options).

Drawing Objects on Layers

With respect to stacking order, drawing objects using layers is the same as drawing objects on a page containing a single layer, except you have to be aware of which layer it's placed onto. Objects are nested in layers or sublayers in the same stacking order they're created, with the first object that's created placed on the bottom of the stack.

- If a top-level layer, but no sublayer, is active when a new object is created, the new object is nested directly below the top-level layer.

- If a sublayer, but no objects nested in the sublayer, is active when a new object is created, the new object is nested directly below the sublayer.

- If an object or group is active when a new object is created, the new object is placed directly above the active object or group.

All groups are nested as sublayers and individual paths are displayed as nested objects. The sublayer is named by Illustrator as <Group> rather than numbered numerically in the order it was created. You can change the name of the group sublayer as well as its individual paths.

Layer Options

The Layer Options dialog box displays when:

- You choose New Layer in the Layers palette Options menu.

- You double-click a layer or sublayer in the Layers palette.

- You choose Options for "<Layer name>" in the Layers palette Options menu.

In the Layer Options dialog box, you can assign a descriptive name to a layer to make it easier to identify the objects on each layer and choose a color for anchor points and path lines for objects that appear on a layer, as well as other options.

Double-click on a layer name in the Layers palette to display the Layer Options dialog box

Name

Enter a name for the new layer in the field. A descriptive name for what appears on the layer works best, for example Leaves, Stem, Petals, and so on. If you don't enter a name, Illustrator assigns a name numerically according to the order in which the layer was created, for instance, Layer 1, Layer 2, Layer 3, and so on.

Color

This option chooses the color of unstroked paths, anchor points, and Direction lines of paths you draw. The default color for a page having a single layer is light blue. For ease in telling which layer or sublayer is selected, each layer is assigned a different color. Colors are assigned to layers according to the order in which they appear in the pop-up menu. Layer 1 is the first color (Light Blue), Layer 2 is the second color (Red), and so on. In the example shown to the right, Cyan is checked, indicating that Layer 7 is the active layer.

You may want to define your own color if artwork on a layer is similar to the the layer color. Choose a color from the pop-up menu, click on Other at the bottom of the pop-up menu, or double-click in the color box next to the pop-up menu. When the Illustrator Color Picker displays, click in the color wheel to choose a color (**Windows:** click in the color spectrum box), then click OK or press *return/enter*.

- The color assigned to each layer is designated by the Selection box on the righthand side of the Layers palette when an object on that layer is selected.

- Selection boxes on Object layers within a layer or sublayer display the same color as the layer or sublayer.

Selection box in the Layers palette

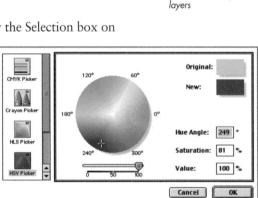

The Color Picker displays when Other is chosen in the Color pop-up submenu in the Layer Options dialog box

Template

A *template* is a pattern or guide; a *template layer* is a non-printing, locked layer on which you can place objects you want to trace. Template layers are identified on the Layers palette by the 🖼 icon and their names are displayed in italics. You can also designate a layer as a Template layer by displaying the Layers palette Options menu (click the arrow at the top right corner of the palette) and choosing Template.

Objects on this layer are dimmed for ease in tracing over them. You can specify how gray images appear by changing the value in the Dim images to field. You'll learn about tracing images later in this chapter.

Light Blue
Red
Green
Blue
Yellow
Magenta
✓ Cyan
Gray
Black
Orange
Dark Green
Teal
Tan
Brown
Violet
Gold
Dark Blue
Pink
Lavender
Brick Red
Olive Green
Peach
Burgundy
Grass Green
Ochre
Purple
Light Gray
Other...

Default colors available for anchor points and path lines on object layers

 fyi Changes made in the Layer Options dialog box when more than one layer is selected apply to all selected layers.

Show

Uncheck this box to hide all objects on the layer. Show/Hide can also be controlled on the Layers palette without opening the Layer Options dialog box. To Show or Hide a layer using the Layers palette, click the eye icon (👁) in the first box to the left of the Layer name. If the eye icon is present, the layer is visible. If the box is empty, the layer is hidden.

Objects on hidden layers are not visible and hiding a layer hides all objects drawn on it.

- If artwork on a layer has the Hide Selection command in the Object menu (**Object ⇨ Hide Selection**) applied individually to objects, that command is preserved when the eye icon is clicked to hide the layer. For example, a layer has a square and a circle drawn on it, but the **Object ⇨ Hide Selection** command has been applied to the square so it isn't visible. If you Hide the layer, the circle disappears. When you Show the layer again, the circle reappears but the square retains the Hide Selection command that had been previously applied to it so it's still invisible. To make the square visible again, you must apply the Show All command in the Object menu (**Object ⇨ Show All**).

activity 8.1

1. Create a new document: Letter size, CMYK color mode. Save it as a native Illustrator file, put it into your Practice folder, and name it Layers Practice.

2. If the Layers palette is not displayed on your screen, display it (Window ⇨ Layers).

3. Draw about a 2" circle somewhere on the page. Fill it with yellow from the CMYK Spectrum bar in the Color palette. No stroke.

   - Notice that the object that you drew on the layer is shown in thumbnail view in the Layer 1 row of the Layers palette.

   - Notice that the Selection box on the righthand side of the Layers palette is Light Blue because that's the default color of the first layer and the object on the layer is selected.

4. Create a new top-level layer by clicking the Create New Layer button on the bottom of the Layers palette.

   - The new layer becomes the active layer.

5. Draw about a 2" wide × 1" high rectangle on this new layer. Color it red from the CMYK Spectrum bar in the Color palette. No stroke.

6. Click the Expand Layer arrow to the left of the Layer 2 thumbnail to display the path drawn on that layer.

   - Notice that the Selection box on the righthand side of the Layers palette for both the Layer row and its object row is Red. The object on the document page is selected so the Selection box displays on the Layers palette.

   - You can tell which object is on a particular layer by matching the color in the Selection box to the color of the anchor points and path lines of an object on a layer.

7. With the Selection tool, select both objects.

   - Notice that the Selection boxes on both layer rows display because items on both layers are selected.

   Continued

- Notice that the bounding box enclosing both objects is the color of the topmost selected object (red).

8. Display the Layer Options dialog box by double-clicking the Layer 1 name, then change the name to Circles. Click OK or press *return/enter.*

9. Change the name of Layer 2 to Red Rectangles. And, because the rectangle is red and the anchor points and path lines are also red, making them difficult to see, change the color in the pop-up menu to Purple. Click OK or press *return/enter.*

   - Notice that because the rectangle is still selected, the Selection box on the righthand side of the Layers palette changed to Purple and the anchor points and path lines of the red rectangle are Purple.

   - The Selection box on the object layer remains red until you click the Expand Layer arrow to close the layer, then click it again to reopen it.

10. Make sure the Red Rectangles layer is still active (the black (or white on the Windows platform) triangle is in the upper right corner). Create a Sublayer by displaying the Layers palette Options menu and choosing New Sublayer.

    - Notice that the new sublayer is indented (nested) under the top-level Red Rectangles layer and is named Layer 3 (because it's the third layer you created).

11. The Layer Options dialog box displays.

    - Notice that the color in the Color pop-up menu is the third color listed (Green).

12. Don't make any changes in the default options. Click OK or press *return/enter.*

13. Draw a star on the sublayer. Color it Purple from the CMYK Spectrum bar on the Color palette. No stroke.

    - Notice that the red rectangle and the purple star are both displayed in the thumbnail of the Red Rectangles top-level layer.

14. Hide the layer named Circles by clicking its eye icon.

    - The yellow circle disappears from the page.

    - The View column (thumbnail) for the top-level layer still shows the circle.

15. Show the Circles layer. Hide the layer named Red Rectangles.

    - Notice that the nested sublayer and the red rectangle disappear, too, and their eye icons are gray (dimmed).

16. Display the Object menu so you see that you can't make the objects reappear by applying the Show All command, because it's not available.

17. Show the Red Rectangles layer. Click on the eye icon for the Layer 3 sublayer to hide the star.

    - You can hide a sublayer without hiding the top-level layer or other sublayers nested under the top-level layer. Sublayers and objects nested under the hidden sublayer, however, are also hidden.

18. Click the eye icon again to show the star on Layer 3.

19. With the Selection tool, click on the red rectangle on the page to make it active.

20. Hide the red rectangle by choosing Object ⇨ Hide ⇨ Selection.

    - The View column on the object layer is blank because the object is hidden.

    - Notice that the eye icon is still in the View column of the Red Rectangles top-level layer because the layer isn't hidden, just the object that was on the layer.

21. Click on the Red Rectangles eye icon to hide all the objects on the layer.

    - The star on the sublayer disappears.

22. Choose Object ⇨ Show All.

    - The red rectangle and the star still don't display because the layer is hidden.

23. Click the eye icon for the Red Rectangles layer.

    - The star reappears, but the red rectangle still doesn't display because it's still hidden.

24. Choose Object ⇨ Show All.

    - The red rectangle now displays.

    - This may seem confusing, but if you have trouble getting an object to display, remember to check both places, the View column in the Layers palette and the Object menu command.

25. Save the file and close the document.

Preview

In the Layer Options dialog box, uncheck the Preview checkbox to display objects drawn on the layer in Outline mode, regardless of the View mode that's selected in the View menu. The View mode chosen for a top-level layer applies to all of its sublayers, so objects on these layers are displayed in Outline mode, too.

- You can change the View mode of a top-level layer to Outline using the Layers palette by ⌘-clicking the Show/Hide eye icon (👁). The eye icon becomes hollow (👁). Restore to Preview mode by ⌘-clicking the icon again.

- You can choose to display all top-level layers in Outline view except one by ⌥⌘-clicking a top-level layer. All layers display in Outline view except the one you clicked on. To restore all layers to Preview, ⌥⌘-click on the eye icon again.

  or

  You can display all layers in Outline except the active top-level layer by choosing Outline Others from the Layer palette Options menu.

- You can change all layers from Outline to Preview mode at once by choosing the Preview All Layers option in the Layers palette Option menu (click the arrow at the top right edge of the Layers palette).

  - This selection toggles with Outline Others. If any layers are in Outline mode, Preview All Layers is an option. If no layers are in Outline mode, Outline Others is the option in that position in the menu.

- If all objects in a document have been converted to Outline view using the Outline command in the View menu (**View ➪ Outline**), objects on individual layers can be restored to Preview mode by ⌘-clicking the eye icon in the Layers palette. As long as some objects in the document are in Outline view, the toggle command in the View menu reads Preview. When all objects in the document are changed to Preview mode by changing the eye icons in the Layers palette, the command reverts to read Outline.

- Template layers display in Preview mode even when Outline is the chosen View mode in the View menu or when Preview All Layers is the selection in the Layers palette menu. To display objects on a Template layer in Outline mode, ⌘-click its icon (🗺) in the Layers palette.

Lock

When checked in the Layer Options dialog box, objects on this layer or sublayer cannot be selected or edited and remain locked even if you close and reopen the file. A padlock icon (🔒) displays in the Edit column of that layer in the Layers palette when the layer is locked.

- When a top-level layer is locked, objects on sublayers are locked also. You can't unlock objects on a sublayer if the top-level layer is locked. You have to unlock the top-level layer first.

*Lock icon in
Layers palette*

- To select and edit objects on a locked layer or sublayer, uncheck the Lock checkbox in the Layers Options dialog box.

- You can also lock or unlock layers or sublayers on the Layers palette by clicking in the Edit column box. When the padlock icon (🔒) displays, the layer is locked. When the box is blank, the layer is editable.

- Lock objects on all layers except the selected layer (selection box is visible in the layer) by choosing **Object ⇨ Lock ⇨ Other Layers**.

- ⌥-click in the Edit column of a top-level layer to lock or unlock all other top-level layers except the one you clicked on.

- If artwork on a layer has the Lock command in the Object menu (**Object ⇨ Lock**) applied individually to objects, that command is preserved when the Lock command is applied to a layer.

  - For example, a layer has three locked rectangles and two unlocked stars drawn on it. If you lock the layer, all objects on the layer are locked. When you Unlock the layer, the stars become unlocked but the rectangles retain the Lock command that had been previously applied to them using the Lock command in the Object menu. To unlock the rectangles, you must apply the Unlock All command in the Object menu (**Object ⇨ Unlock All**).

- When a layer is locked, the Selection box on the righthand side of the Layers palette doesn't display because objects can't be selected when they're locked.

  - If an object on the page is selected when it's locked, the object becomes deselected.

- If you attempt to add an object to a locked layer with any of the drawing tools (Pen tool, Pencil tool, Ellipse tool, Star tool, and so on), the pointer changes to a Blocked Pencil icon (✎), indicating that paths cannot be drawn on that layer.

- Gray (dimmed) Padlock icons in the Edit column of the Layers palette indicate that locking control for those layers has been set by a higher-level layer.

Print

When checked in the Layer Options dialog box, everything on the layer prints. Uncheck the box to prevent any objects on the layer

fyi *The Unlock All commands in the Object menu lock and unlock selected objects in a document. The Lock and Unlock commands in the Layers palette lock and unlock entire layers. You can lock and unlock objects on a layer using the Object menu commands without locking or unlocking other objects on the same layer.*

timesaver *You can quickly lock or unlock layers by clicking in the Edit column of the Layers palette and dragging up or down to pass over all the layers you want locked or unlocked.*

fyi *The Object ⇨ Lock ⇨ All Artwork Above command doesn't work on layers. Apply this command to lock objects above the selected object in the stacking order of objects on a single layer.*

from printing, even when they're visible. Layer names display in italics when the layer is non-printing. Objects on non-printing layers still export in other formats when the Export command in the File menu (**File ⇨ Export**) is used. See Appendix A, *Output: Printing & Exporting Files* for information regarding exporting artwork.

- You can also prevent a layer from printing by hiding it.

Dim Images To...

When checked, placed images or rasterized objects on the layer display as gray. The default percentage is 50%, but you can change the value if you want the placed image to be lighter (higher number) or darker (lower number). Use this feature for tracing placed images so you can differentiate what you're creating from the "pattern" underneath. Unlike images placed on Template layers, you can still select, edit, and print images that have been dimmed. Placed images are discussed later in this chapter.

1. Open the Layers Practice file that you saved in Activity 8.1.

2. Click on the yellow circle with the Selection tool to make that layer active.

3. Double-click the layer named "Circles" in the Layers palette to display the Layer Options dialog box. Uncheck the Preview box. Click OK or press *return/enter*.
   - The yellow circle is displayed in Outline mode, with only the bounding box and its path line visible. Fill and stroke attributes are hidden.
   - Notice that the eye icon in the View column for the Circles layer is hollow.

4. ⌘-click the eye icon in the View column for the Circles layer to restore the Preview mode.

5. Deselect all objects.
   - Notice that the Circles layer is still active, but there are no Selection boxes visible because no objects on the document page are selected.

6. Choose View ⇨ Outline to convert all objects to Outline view.
   - All objects on the document page display only path lines.

7. ⌘-click the eye icon for the Circles layer.
   - The circle is restored to Preview mode and its eye icon in the Layers palette is solid.

8. Display the Layers palette Options menu by clicking the arrow in the top right corner of the palette. Choose Preview All Layers from the pop-up menu.
   - All objects in the document are restored to Preview mode.
   - Display the View menu and notice that the command now reads Outline.

9. Click in the circle to make it active, and apply a 1 point black stroke.

10. Draw three smaller circles on the Circles layer and position them so they all touch the first circle you drew.
    - The new circles automatically have the same color attributes as the first circle you drew.

11. Draw three smaller rectangles on the Red Rectangles layer with the same color and stroke attributes as the first red rectangle. Position the new rectangles so they overlap the first rectangle.

Continued

Step 8 — LAYERS & LINKS

12. Draw two smaller stars on Layer 3 with the same color and stroke attributes as the first star you drew. Position the stars so they don't overlap the first star.

- Notice that the thumbnails for each layer display all objects drawn on the layer and any sublayers nested within it.

13. The objects are difficult to distinguish because the thumbnails are so small, so let's make them bigger. Display the Layers palette Options menu and choose Palette Options.

14. Change Row Size to Large. Click OK or press *return/enter*.

- Elements in the Layers palette are larger.

15. They're still not large enough to see easily, so let's make them even bigger. Display Palette Options again and click on Other in the Row Size section. Enter 80 in the field. Click OK or press *return/enter*.

- Elements in the Layers palette are really big now.

16. Change the Size back to the default of Medium by displaying Palette Options again and clicking the Medium button.

17. Lock Layer 3 by clicking in the Edit column of Layer 3 in the Layers palette so the Padlock icon displays.

18. Layer 3 with the stars on it should still be the active layer, so try to draw a third star with the Star tool.

- The Blocked Pencil icon displays (✘), indicating that you can't draw a path on that layer.

19. Unlock Layer 3 by clicking in its Edit column in the Layers palette then lock the Red Rectangles layer.

20. Click on the Red Rectangles layer in the Layers palette to make it active.

21. Choose the Pen tool in the Toolbox and pass the pointer over the circles, rectangles and stars.

- The Blocked Pencil icon displays (✘) even when you pass over the yellow circles because you're working on the Red Rectangles layer.

22. Click on the Circles layer in the Layers palette to make it the active layer.

- The Blocked Pencil icon (✘) changes back to the Pen tool pointer (✎×), even when you pass it over the stars and rectangles, because the Circles layer is the active layer and it isn't locked so paths can be drawn on that layer.

23. Unlock all locked layers by displaying the Layers palette Options menu and choosing Unlock All Layers from the pop-up menu.

- The Padlock icon disappears and the Edit column for all layers is blank.

24. Lock the Red Rectangles layer in the Layers palette.

25. Marquee to select all the yellow circles and lock them using the Lock command in the Object menu (Object ⇨ Lock ⇨ Selection).

- The Padlock icon doesn't display in the Circles layer Edit column of the Layers palette, because the objects are locked, not the layer. You can still draw new paths on the layer.

26. Choose the Unlock All command from the Object menu (Object ⇨ Unlock All).

- Objects on the Circles layer are unlocked and are editable, but the rectangles on the Red Rectangles layer are still locked.

27. Unlock the Red Rectangles layer.

28. Display the nested paths under Layer 3.

- Click the triangle (▷) to the left of the Layer name.

29. Double-click the middle path to display the Options dialog box.

30. Name the path "Star <Path>" and uncheck the Show checkbox.

- The thumbnail preview for the object layer didn't change, but the star disappears from the Layer 3 thumbnail, indicating there is a path on the layer but it's hidden.

- This must have been a "fix" in the 9.0.2 update. In version 9.0, when you hide the object layer, the thumbnail image disappears from the object layer as well as the Layer.

31. Choose Object ⇨ Show All.

32. Save the file and close the document.

Layer Management

Explaining how to manipulate items listed in the Layers palette can be confusing. You can activate layers, select layers, select objects and groups on the Layers palette, or select objects and groups on the page using the Layers palette, copy layers, objects, and groups, delete . . ., etc., etc., etc. By the time you complete the activities in this section, though, you'll understand how they all work together to make drawing artwork easier.

Activating a Layer, Sublayer, Object Layer, or Group Layer

Click the name of a top-level layer, the name of a sublayer, or the name of an object to activate the layer. Only one layer, sublayer, object layer, or group layer can be active at a time. Other layers can be selected (highlighted), but unless they display the current layer icon in the upper right corner of the layer row, they're not the active layer.

The current layer icon in the Layers palette. Triangle is white on the Windows platform

Selecting Multiple Layers, Sublayers, Object Layers, and Group Layers

You can select (highlight) multiple top-level layers, multiple sublayers nested under one top-level layer, multiple objects, or multiple groups nested under one top-level layer or sublayer, but you can't mix-and-match between layers and sublayers. Highlighting layers, sublayers, object layers, or group layers in the Layers palette doesn't actually select any objects on the document page.

If no Selection box displays when you click the Selection area of a top-level layer or sublayer, there is no path on that layer or sublayer; it's object layer thumbnail is blank.

- You *can* select two or more top-level layers.
- You *can* select two or more sublayers nested under the same top-level layer.
- You *can't* select two or more sublayers that are nested under different top-level layers.
- You *can* select two or more object layers nested under the same top-level layer or sublayer.
- You *can't* select multiple object layers in two different layers or sublayers.
- You *can* select sublayers and object layers under the same top-level layer as long as they're on the same hierarchy level in the Layers palette.

To select more than one layer (of the same type) at a time, *Shift*-click two top-level layers or two sublayers nested under the same top-level layer. The layers you clicked on and all layers in between are highlighted. To select layers or sublayers that aren't next to each other, ⌘-click their names, keeping in mind that they have to be on the same nesting level.

You can select sublayers, object layers, or group layers by ⌥⌘-clicking anywhere in the Layers palette (a dark line displays around the inside of the palette window) and typing the first few characters of its name. The layers don't have to be visible if the palette is too short, but the Expand Layer arrow (▷) on the top-level layer or sublayer has to be clicked so the names of nested sublayers and object layers are listed.

■ If you haven't renamed the layers and the name is still the default Layer [#], you don't have to type the word "Layer". You can simply type the number.

Selecting Objects on the Page Using the Layers Palette

You can select objects or groups on your document page by clicking (with any tool active) in the Selection area of a layer, sublayer, object, group, or an individual path in a group in the Layers palette. Paths selected on the document page display a Selection box in the Selection area of the Layers palette.

When a path in a layer is selected in the document, a small box displays in the Selection area of the layer (and sublayer, if any) letting you know that an object in the document is on that layer. That's handy if the Layer is closed so you can't see a list of the objects on the layer. Click the Expand Layer arrow (▷) to see the contents of the layer.

Even though you can't select objects on the document page when they're hidden, you can select them in the Layer's palette. Click in the Selection area of the hidden object's layer and a bounding box displays around its path on the document page. The object isn't visible, but the bounding box tells you where it is on the page.

Select All Objects or Groups in a Layer If you click in the Selection area of a top-level layer, all sublayers, objects, and groups nested within that top-level layer display a Selection box in the Selection area and all objects and groups on those layers are selected on the document page. If you click in the Selection area of a sublayer, all sublayers, objects, and groups nested within that sublayer display the Selection box, and all objects in those sublayers are selected on the document page.

■ If an object on the document page is selected, choose **Select** ⇨ **Object** ⇨ **All on Same Layer** to select all other objects on that object's top-level layer.

Select One Object, Group, or an Individual Path in a Group To select a single object or an individual path in a group using the Layers palette, the object name must be visible on the palette. Click the Expand Layer arrow (▷) to the left of a layer or sublayer name to open the layer or sublayer, making the object names visible. Click in the Selection area of the object name. The Selection box displays and the object is selected on the document page.

Select Multiple Objects *Shift*-click in the Selection area of objects visible in the Layers palette. If an object name isn't visible in the palette, click the triangle arrow (▷) to open its layer or sublayer. You can *Shift*-click to select multiple objects at a time. They don't have to be in the same layer or sublayer and they don't have to be next to each other. *Shift*-clicking allows you to select random individual objects (not random multiple layers, just random multiple objects).

Another way to select more than one object at a time is to hold down the ⌥ key and drag through layer or sublayer names (to select all objects on those layers or sublayers) or object names. You can select a series of objects this way, then *Shift*-click individual Selection boxes to deselect objects you don't want included.

Create a Group *Shift*-click in the Selection area of objects visible in the Layers palette to select objects on the document page that you want to group together. If an object name isn't visible in the palette, click the triangle arrow (▷) to open its layer or sublayer. Then choose **Object** ⇨ **Group** (or press ⌘g). A new sublayer is created in the Layers palette in place of the bottommost object that was grouped.

Deselecting Objects Using the Layers Palette

To deselect an object or group that's selected in a document, *Shift*-click the Selection box for that object in the Layers palette. To deselect all the objects in a layer, including objects in sublayers,*Shift*-click the Selection box for the layer in the Layers palette. All objects on the document page that are in that layer are deselected. If you have several objects selected and want to remove one or more from those selected, *Shift*-click again. This procedure works the same as if you're *Shift*-clicking to select an object directly on the document page.

Deleting Layers

To delete a layer, sublayer, or object:

1. Select the layer, sublayer, or object you want to delete by clicking on its name in the Layers palette.

2. Display the Layers palette Options menu and choose Delete [   ].
   or
   - Click the Delete Selection button (🗑) at the bottom of the Layers palette.
     - If a layer or sublayer has objects placed on it, a warning box displays asking if you want to delete these objects.
   or
   - Drag the selection over the Delete Selection button (🗑) at the bottom of the Layers palette until the button is highlighted, then release the mouse.
     - The warning box doesn't display.

Just deselecting a layer in the Layers palette doesn't deselect a selected object on the document page. To deselect an object on the document page using the Layers palette, you must Shift-click in the Selection area and remove the Selection box.

read this!

When you delete a top-level layer, all sublayers and objects nested in the top-level layer and sublayers are also deleted.

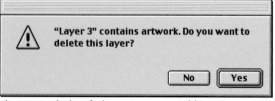

This warning displays if a layer you're trying to delete contains artwork

To delete more than one element at a time, ⌘-click each item (layer, sublayer, or object). You can select multiple top-level layers, multiple sublayers nested under one top-level layer, or multiple objects nested under one top-level layer or sublayer, but you can't mix-and-match between layers and sublayers.

Duplicating Layers

Using the Layers palette, you can copy the contents of (a) an entire layer, including all sublayers and objects nested under it, (b) a sublayer, including all sublayers and objects nested under it, or (c) an object on a layer or sublayer, and place them on a new layer. Or you can copy these elements and place them on an existing layer that you choose.

Place Copied Elements on a New Layer

- Activate the top-level layer, sublayer, or object on a layer and choose Duplicate "<Selection>" in the Layers palette Options menu (click arrow at the top right corner of the Layers palette). A new layer, sublayer, or object is created and is stacked above the original element.
  - All sublayers and objects nested in them are copied to the new layer or sublayer.
  - The new layer or sublayer has the same name as its original, but the word "copy" is added to the end of its name. The word "copy" is not added to the name of an object when it's duplicated, only to the names of layers and sublayers.

or

- Drag a top-level layer name, sublayer name, or object name over the Create New Layer button at the bottom of the Layers palette. A new layer, sublayer, or object is created and is stacked above the original layer.
  - The pointer changes to a closed hand (🖑) when you drag the Layer name and a plus box is added (🖑) when you're over the Create New Layer button.
  - All sublayers and objects on them are copied to the new layer or sublayer.
  - The new layer or sublayer has the same name as its original, but the word "copy" is added to the end of the name. The word "copy" is not added to the name of an object when it's duplicated, only to the names of layers and sublayers.

Place Copied Elements on an Existing Layer

- Click in the Selection area of a top-level layer, sublayer, or object to display the Selection box. The entire contents of the layer or sublayer are selected, including sublayers and all objects on them. ⌥-click-and-drag the Selection box up or down until you reach

read this!

When you drag-copy a layer or sublayer to an existing layer, the contents of the layer become individual object layers. To keep the sublayer intact, duplicate it onto a new layer (see above), then move it to its new layer.

the layer upon which you want to drop the copied elements. Release the mouse when the Selection box of the layer upon which you want to drop the copies becomes hollow.

- The pointer changes to a pointing hand with a plus box when you start dragging the Selection box.

- Objects copied to an existing layer or sublayer are placed in the same x/y location as the objects on the original layer or sublayer.

■ The artwork on the document page redraws with the objects in their new position in the stacking order.

 *activity 8.3*

1. Locate and open the file named Fish.eps in the Student Files folder on the CD-ROM that came with this book.

2. Adjust the View and position the artwork so you can see all the fish.

3. Hide all layers except Blue/green fish and Orange fish.

4. On the document page, *Shift*-click to select the orange fish at the bottom of the illustration and the blue/green fish near the top. Don't marquee to select the fish because you don't want the eyes selected for this step.

   ■ Notice that a Selection box displays in the Selection areas of both group layers that are nested under their top-level layers. Expand the top-level layers, if necessary, to see the sublayers.

   ■ A small Selection box displays in the top-level layer Selection areas, letting you know that something on that layer is selected on the document page.

5. Expand the group layers by clicking the Expand Layer arrow on each group layer.

   ■ All objects in the group display Selection boxes in their Selection areas because they're selected on the document page.

6. *Shift*-click the Selection area of the top-level layer named Orange fish to deselect the group layers.

   ■ Oops! Not everything in that layer was selected, so when you *Shift*-clicked, you caused the unselected items in that layer to become selected.

7. *Shift*-click the Selection area of the Orange fish layer again to deselect everything in that layer.

8. Click in a blank spot on the document page to deselect everything.

9. Show the Background layer at the bottom of the Layers palette by clicking its eye icon, then expand the layer.

10. One of the thumbnails in that layer appears to be blank, so delete that object layer.

    ■ Oops! That layer is locked, so the object layer can't be deleted.

11. Unlock the layer, then delete the object layer.

    ■ Uh oh. That deleted the path that created the splash of water at the top of the illustration.

12. Restore it by pressing ⌘ z.

13. Click in the Selection area of the Orange fish layer to display the Selection box.

14. Duplicate the objects in that layer and place them as a sublayer in the Big red fish layer by ⬃-clicking the Orange fish layer Selection box and dragging it over the Selection box of the Big red fish layer. Release the mouse when the Selection box in the Big red fish layer becomes hollow.

    ■ Oops! The Big red fish layer is hidden so you can't add anything to it. Notice the icon (⊘) that displays when you drag the Orange fish selection box over it.

Continued

15. Show the Big red fish layer by clicking its eye icon, then try duplicating the Orange fish objects again.

    ■ Now you have two orange fish on the document page — one on top of the other.

16. Click in the Selection area of the Orange fish top-level layer to select the fish at the front of the stack.

    ■ Because the copied Orange fish was placed in a layer below it in the Layers palette, it's behind the original Orange fish. The original Orange fish is on top of it.

17. With the Selection tool, drag the selected Orange fish down a little and to the right so you can see both Orange fish.

18. Look at the blue/green fish at the top of the illustration. Where is his eye? It's not on the Blue/green fish layer or it would be visible.

19. Delete the layer named Eye for Blue/green fish in the Blue/green fish top-level layer because it's empty.

20. Close the document without saving changes.

Moving Layers, Sublayers, Objects, and Groups

In Step 4, *The Pen & Pencil Tools*, you learned about the stacking order of objects on a document page, and about the Paste In Front and Paste in Back commands. The Layers palette also allows you to move layers, sublayers, objects, and groups around, thereby rearranging the stacking order of objects on the document page.

Layers are added in the palette according to the stacking order (the order in which they're drawn) and objects drawn on these layers are placed in front of objects drawn on previous layers. You can change the front-to-back order of objects or groups in a document simply by moving things around in the Layers palette.

Move an Object Layer or Group Layer To move an object or group to a new position in the Layers palette:

1. Select an object or a group by clicking on its name in the Layers palette and drag it up or down (the pointer turns into a closed hand).

2. Release the mouse to drop the object or group over another object.

    ■ An indicator bar displays, telling you where in the palette list the object will be placed, above or below a layer row. In the example to the right, the moved object was placed below the Yellow circle path and above the Pink polygon path in Layer 4. How far the insertion bar is indented tells you what nesting layer you're placing the moved object on. If it extends to the left margin, for example, it will be placed on a top-level layer.

    ■ When you drag an object layer or group layer over the name of a layer or sublayer, a large black triangle

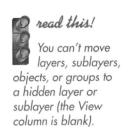

A

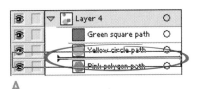

B

The indicator bar (A) tells you that the moved layer will be placed below the Yellow circle path layer as a sublayer (B)

341

displays on both sides of the layer name. The moved object is placed at the top of the stacking order for that layer.

A large black triangle displays next to the layer name when another layer, sublayer, object layer, or group layer is moved into it

- An object or multiple objects dragged into a sublayer consisting of a group becomes part of the group.
- The artwork on the document page redraws with the objects in their new position in the stacking order.

Move a Layer or Sublayer You can move a top-level layer to a different position in the stacking order but keep its top-level status, or you can nest it under a different top-level layer or a sublayer, which converts the moved top-level layer into a sublayer. Change a sublayer to a top-level layer by dropping it between two top-level layers.

- When you're nesting a layer or sublayer inside a different layer or sublayer, a large black triangle displays on both sides of the layer name.
- Moving a layer or sublayer moves all sublayers, groups, and objects nested within them.

Reverse Order of Layers With one command, you can reverse the order of top-level layers or sublayers, objects, and groups in single layer or sublayer.

1. *Shift*-click to select the layer names of all objects, layers, sublayers, or groups, for which you want to reverse the order. Don't click in the Selection area to select them.

   - ⌘-click the names of objects, layers, sublayers, or groups to select layers that aren't next to each other.
   - Objects and groups must be in the same top-level layer or sublayer. You can't select objects or groups from different layers or sublayers.

2. Display the Layers palette Options menu and choose Reverse Order.

   - The order of the selected listings in the Layers palette are reversed.
   - The order of sublayers, objects, or groups within a top-level layer are not reversed, just the top-level layers themselves.
   - Artwork on the document page redraws with the objects in their new position in the stacking order.

Move Layers, Sublayers, Objects, or Groups to New Layer With a single command — Collect in New Layer — you can move selected top-level layers (with all nested sublayers, objects, and groups), sublayers, objects, or groups into a new layer. The new layer is named automatically by Illustrator and given the next number in order of creation. You can rename the new layer by displaying its Option dialog box.

To move selected layers, sublayers, objects, or groups and create a new layer for them:

1. Click on two or more top-level layers, two or more sublayers in one top-level layer, two or more objects or groups in a layer or sublayer to select them.

2. Display the Layers palette Options menu and choose Collect in New Layer.

   - Top-level layers become sublayers in the new top-level layer.

   - Sublayers are combined into a new sublayer nested in the same top-level layer.

   - Objects and groups are collected into a new sublayer nested in the same top-level layer.

   - Artwork on the document page redraws with objects in their new position in the stacking order.

fyi You can move selected objects to the active layer by choosing Object ⇨ Arrange ⇨ Send to Current Layer.

Move Objects or Groups onto Separate Layers within the Active Layer There are two commands in the Layers palette Options menu for putting all objects in a layer onto their own separate layers within the active layer. These functions are necessary when exporting artwork for use in creating Web animation. If the selected objects are in an active sublayer, they are moved onto individual sublayers nested within that active sublayer. You can't select sublayers on different top-level layers or sublayers. They must be on the same layer (indent) level.

1. In the Layers palette, click a top-level layer, sublayer, or group to make it the active layer.

2. Display the Layers palette Options menu and

   - Choose Release to Layers (Sequence) to nest each object on its own layer within the original active layer.

     - The object's original stacking order is kept intact.

     - If the released objects were a group, <Group> is removed from the name.

     or

   - Choose Release to Layers (Build) to nest objects in an increasing sequence, starting with the bottommost object in the stacking order on the first layer. The next layer contains the bottommost object and the next object above it in the stacking order; the third layer contains the first two objects plus the next object in the stacking order. And so on.

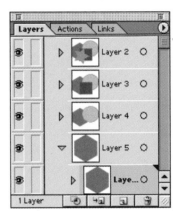

The Release to Layers (Sequence) command applied to four objects on a single layer

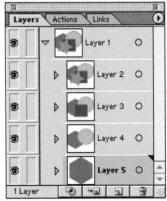

The Release to Layers (Build) command applied to four objects on a single layer

343

Use the Clipboard to Move Objects You can cut (⌘x) and paste (⌘v) objects in the artwork window and move them to different layers by turning on (checked) or turning off (unchecked) the Paste Remembers Layers command in the Layers palette Options menu. The objects can be nested in different layers and sublayers. In the artwork window, select an object or objects and cut them (⌘x). Then do one of the following steps:

To paste objects at the top of the active layer:

1. Display the Layers palette Options menu and verify that Paste Remembers Layers is turned off (unchecked).

2. Click the name of the top-level layer or sublayer into which you want to move the object(s) that were cut.

3. Paste the object(s) back into the artwork window.

   ■ If you use the Paste command (⌘v), the object(s) is pasted back into the center of the document window, regardless of the original x/y coordinates of the object(s).

   ■ If you use the Paste in Front command (**Edit ⇨ Paste in Front**) or Paste in Back command (**Edit ⇨ Paste in Back**), the object(s) is pasted back into the document window in front of or in back of the selected layer or sublayer without changing its respective x/y coordinates. In other words, you've changed the stacking order.

To paste objects at the top of its own layer or sublayer:

1. Display the Layers palette Options menu and verify that Paste Remembers Layers is turned on (checked).

2. Paste the object or objects back into the artwork window.

   ■ If you use the Paste command (⌘v), the object(s) is pasted back into the center of the document window, regardless of the original x/y coordinates of the object(s).

   ■ If you use the Paste in Front command (**Edit ⇨ Paste in Front**) or Paste in Back command (**Edit ⇨ Paste in Back**), the object(s) is pasted back into the document window in front of or in back of the selected layer or sublayer without changing its respective x/y coordinates. In other words, you've changed the stacking order.

fyi If the original layer from which an object(s) was cut is deleted before the object(s) is pasted back into the artwork window, a new layer is created on which to paste the object(s).

Add a New Object to a Group To automatically place a new object into a group, expand the group layer, activate the object layer in the group layer above which you want to add the new path, and draw the object. The new object layer is displayed directly above the object layer you activated and the new object is automatically grouped with the other objects in that group.

To add multiple objects to a group, after adding the first path, click the group layer again to add another object at the top of the group. You can't just draw paths one after the other because after the first path is drawn, additional paths are placed in the top-level layer. Click the group layer or click a different path in the group between each path drawn.

When you drag an object layer into a group layer, it automatically becomes part of the group. Drop the object layer between two layers in the group to position it in the stacking order.

Ungroup Objects Using the Layers Palette To ungroup objects that have been grouped together:

1. Select the layer in the Layers palette containing the grouped objects.

2. Display the Layers palette Options menu and choose Release to Layers (Sequence or Build), depending on how you want the objects nested.

The objects are ungrouped and placed as individual objects in a sublayer of the layer in which the original group was located. If you changed the name of the group from the one supplied by Illustrator, the sublayer retains that name. If you didn't rename the group (it's still *<Group>*), Illustrator renames the Sublayer numerically according to the order in which it was created.

Ruler Guides as Objects on the Layers Palette When you drag Ruler Guides onto a document page, they are displayed as separate objects on the Layers Palette. Illustrator assigns the name *<Guide>*, which you can change by displaying the Layer Options dialog box. They can be hidden and shown, deleted, locked and unlocked, and moved in the Layers palette hierarchy, the same as other objects.

The same rules apply, with regard to the Guide commands in the View menu, as those for objects in the Object menu; that is, if a command is applied in the View menu, it can't be overridden by commands in the Layers palette. For example, if Guides are locked using the View command (**View ⇨ Guides ⇨ Lock Guides**), you can't unlock them using the Layers palette.

Finding Objects on the Layers Palette

If you have lots of layers in your document, the listing in the Layers palette can become quite long, making it difficult to find an object's layer. The Locate Object command in the Layers palette Options menu solves the problem. To locate an object in the Layers palette:

1. Choose the Selection tool in the Toolbox.

2. Select the object on your document page that you want find in the Layers palette.

   ■ *Shift*-click or marquee to select several objects.

 If Locate Layer appears on the Layers palette Options menu instead of Locate Object, it's because Show Layers Only is checked in the Layer Options dialog box. Display that dialog box (double-click the layer), uncheck it and click OK or press return/enter. The Locate Object command then becomes available in the Layers palette Options menu.

Display the Layers palette Options menu (click the arrow at the top right corner of the Layers palette) and choose **Locate Object**.

The Layers palette scrolls to display the object's top-level layer. It expands to show all sublayers and object listings, and a Selection box appears in the selected object's Selection area.

- If more than one object is selected, the top object in the stacking order may be the only one displayed in the Layers palette window, but all selected objects have a Selection box in their Selection areas to indicate that they're selected.

Merging Layers

If you find you've been overzealous when creating layers and now you have a Layers palette with far too many layers, you can combine some of them into one layer. You can even combine locked or hidden layers.

1. Select two or more top-level layers or two or more sublayers in one top-level layer (you can't select two sublayers under different top-level layers).

2. Display the Layers palette Options menu and choose **Merge Selected**.
   - Objects on merged layers keep their original stacking order.

All objects appear on a single layer. Objects on the other selected layers are combined onto the active layer and the now-empty layers are deleted automatically. When merging top-level layers, you can determine which layer remains by clicking it last, making it the active layer (the one with the black triangle in the upper right corner of its row).

Flattening Layers

This command is similar to merging the layers, except that all layers visible in the Layers palette are combined into one top-level layer (the one that's active). If a layer is hidden, it's discarded, along with any objects on that layer or its nested sublayers. A warning box displays, though, giving you the opportunity to keep the hidden objects in the document.

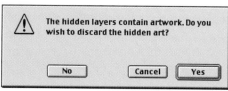

The hidden layers contain artwork. Do you wish to discard the hidden art?

No   Cancel   Yes

You get a second chance to keep your artwork

To flatten artwork:

1. Make sure all layers you want included in the final layer are visible in the Layers palette.

2. Activate the layer into which you want the other layers merged.

3. Display the Layers palette Options menu and choose **Flatten Artwork**.
   - Sublayers are nested under the single new top-level layer.

read this!

When you flatten artwork, transparency and clipping mask attributes are lost. These features are discussed in Step 12, Meshes, Masks, Blends, & Transparency.

- If a sublayer is the active layer when the Flatten Artwork command is used, its top-level layer becomes the new single flattened layer.
- Stacking order of the objects is kept intact.

Targeting an Object on a Layer

This section of the Layers palette is reserved for applying Appearance attributes (other than stroke and fill) to grouped objects or envelopes. The target circle (◎) in the Layers palette identifies which groups, envelopes, or objects are going to have the Appearance attributes applied to them.

 *activity 8.4*

1. Locate and open the file named Fish.eps in the Student Files folder on the CD-ROM that came with this book. Name it My Fish.eps and save it into your practice folder.

2. Adjust the View and position the artwork so you can see all the fish.

3. Because we know that the Eye for the Blue/green fish object layer in the Blue/green fish top-level layer is blank, delete it again.

4. In the document, click on the eye of the Blue/green fish. Then look in the Layers palette to locate its actual layer.

5. Move its sublayer into the Blue/green fish top-level layer where it belongs.
   - Be sure to put it above the group layer in the Layers palette. Otherwise, it will be under the fish on your page and you won't be able to see it.

6. Take a good look at the stacking order of the fish on the background. Make note of which fish are in front of other fish.

7. In the Layers palette, click in the name area of the uppermost layer in the palette (the Yellow/red & Lavender/red fish layer).

8. *Shift*-click in the name area of the Big red fish top-level layer.
   - All top-level layers between the first one you clicked and the last one you clicked are highlighted.

9. Display the Layers palette Options menu and choose Reverse Order.
   - The top-level layers are rearranged in the Layers palette so the bottommost layer is now the topmost layer.
   - Notice that the layers within the top-level layers were not affected by the Reverse Order command.

10. Look at the stacking order of the fish in the document.
    - The Big red fish is now in front of the two Purple/red fish because its layer is higher in the Layers palette.

11. Expand the Orange fish top-level layer and click on the Fish <Group> sublayer. Draw three small white circles in a row vertically (should look like bubbles) above the mouth of the orange fish.
    - Activate an object layer for the first circle, then activate the group layer and draw the second circle, then activate the first object layer you drew before drawing the third circle.

12. Draw a fourth white circle without clicking the group layer or an object layer in the group.
    - The object layer is at the top of the top-level layer.

Continued

13. Click on the object layer and drag it into the group layer, dropping it between two of the other "bubble" object layers.

   ■ It's now part of the group with the rest of the "bubbles".

14. On the document page, with the Selection tool, click on one of the white circles you just drew.

   ■ The circles are grouped with the orange fish.

15. Click on the Big Purple/red Fish <Group> sublayer in the Purple/red fish top-level layer. Display the Layers palette Options menu and choose Release to Layers (Build).

   ■ Objects steadily build from the original object that was on the bottom of the stack on the bottom layer, then adding an object to it in each succeeding layer, until all objects are on a single layer.

   ■ The objects are no longer grouped and <Group> has been removed from the name in the Layers palette.

16. In the Layers palette, highlight the two sublayers in the Big red fish layer. Display the Layers palette Options menu and choose Merge Selected.

   ■ All paths in both sublayers are now in one layer.

17. Display the Layers palette Options menu and choose Flatten Artwork.

   ■ All top-level layers, sublayers, and object layers are placed into one top-level layer in the Layers palette, keeping the same stacking order.

18. Save and close the document.

Import Images Into Illustrator

One of the best uses for layers is when tracing images that were created in other programs and imported into Illustrator as a template. You can import images created in programs such as Adobe Photoshop, Macromedia FreeHand, CorelDRAW. You can also import and edit PDF files.

Import images into Illustrator in one of the following ways:

■ Performing the Open command (choose **File ⇨ Open** or press ⌘o) opens a file created in other applications as a new Illustrator 10 file.

■ Using the Place command (choose **File ⇨ Place**) imports an image created in another program and places it inside a bounding box in the Illustrator file.

■ Copying a bitmap image (a raster image comprised of pixels) in a program such as Photoshop and placing it on the Clipboard, then pasting it into an Illustrator file.

   ▪ The image is imported inside a bounding box the same as a Placed image.

   ▪ The resolution of a TIFF image is reduced (downsampled) to 72 ppi when it's pasted into an Illustrator document. The resolution of the original image is not altered. This resolution (72 ppi) is suitable for display on a screen (for example, the web), but not for a project that is to be printed.

   ▪ A bitmap image that has been imported into Illustrator doesn't have paths that can be edited in Illustrator.

- Drag-copying an image from a Photoshop file to an Illustrator file.
  - The image is displayed inside a bounding box the same as a Placed file.
  - The resolution of a TIFF image is reduced (downsampled) to 72 ppi when it's copied to Illustrator, but the resolution of the original image isn't affected. This resolution (72 ppi) is suitable for display on a screen (for example, the web), but not for artwork that is to be printed.

The two most common ways to import files are by using the Place command and the Open command, and those are the only methods discussed here.

Opening Files Created in Other Programs

When you open a file in Illustrator that was created in another program (**File ⇨ Open**), it becomes a new Adobe Illustrator file. If the opened file has been created in another vector program, any paths that existed in that file become Illustrator paths and can be modified as if they were created in Illustrator.

The default selection in the Show menu (*Windows:* Files of type) of the Open dialog box is All Readable files, which means that all files visible in that folder or on that level on the disk can be opened by Illustrator. If the file you're searching for is not listed, click on All Documents (*Windows:* All Formats) to display all documents filed in that location to make sure your document is listed.

If you've verified that the document you want to open is in the folder you're viewing but the name disappears from the list when you click All Readable Documents, it's not stored in a file format that Illustrator can read. If you want to list only files saved in a particular format, choose that file format from the Show menu. If it isn't listed, it can't be opened by Illustrator.

Open a PDF File Unless specified otherwise in the Save As dialog box, artwork saved as a PDF (Portable Document Format) file can be opened and edited as an Illustrator document. Open these files as though they were created in Illustrator (choose **File ⇨ Open** or press ⌘o).

All Documents
✓ All Readable Documents

Adobe PDF (PDF)
AutoCAD Drawing (DWG)
AutoCAD Interchange File (DXF)
BMP (BMP,RLE)
Computer Graphics Metafile (CGM)
CorelDRAW 5,6,7,8,9,10 (CDR)
Encapsulated PostScript (EPS,EPSF,PS)
Enhanced Metafile (EMF)
Filmstrip (FLM)
FreeHand 4,5,7,8,9 (FH4,FH5,FH7,FH8,FH9)
GIF89a (GIF)
JPEG (JPG)
Kodak PhotoCD (PCD)
Macintosh PICT (PIC,PCT)
Microsoft RTF (RTF)
Microsoft Word (DOC)
PCX (PCX)
Photoshop (PSD, PDD)
Pixar (PXR)
PNG (PNG)
SVG (SVG)
SVG Compressed (SVGZ)
Targa (TGA,VDA,ICB,VST)
Text (TXT)
TIFF (TIF)
Windows Metafile (WMF)

File formats that can be opened as an Illustrator file or placed into an Illustrator document

Enter the page number of the page you want to open or place

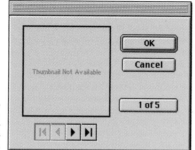

When a PDF file contains more than a single page, specify the page you want to open or place

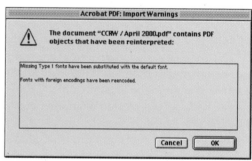

Warning box that displays when opening a PDF document having objects using both color modes. Choose one.

An alert displays if fonts used in a document are not available

If the PDF file you want to open has more than one page, a box displays. Use the arrows at the bottom of the box to locate the desired page (the ▶| arrow takes you directly to the last page of the document; the |◀ arrow takes you directly to the first page of the document), then click OK or press *return/enter*. You can also click the 1 of [#] button (# = the number of pages in the document), which displays the Go to page number dialog box. Enter the document page number you want to Place in the Illustrator document, and click OK or press *return/enter*.

If the file you're opening contains elements using both CMYK and RGB color modes, an alert box displays that gives you a choice of which color mode you want the Illustrator file to be. Click the radio button of the color mode you want to use, then click OK or press *return/enter*.

If the PDF file you're opening in Illustrator contains fonts that are missing or not opened on your computer, an alert displays warning you what will happen to the fonts when the file is opened. To make sure the file opens with the correct fonts, click Cancel to stop the operation, then open the necessary fonts and open the file again.

Open an EPS (Encapsulated PostScript) File A vector file that was created by another application and saved as an EPS file can be opened by Illustrator as though it were created in Illustrator (choose File ⇨ Open or press ⌘o). Vector paths are converted to Illustrator vector paths and can be modified using any of the tools available in Illustrator. When the file is saved, it becomes a new Adobe Illustrator file.

Open a Photoshop File Bitmap images (photographs, scanned line art, etc.) when opened in Illustrator display in a bounding box and do not have paths that you can edit. Some transformation tools, such as scale and rotate, can be applied to bitmap images, as well as some of the filters in the Filters menu.

- Some filters available in Illustrator (discussed in Step 11, *Filters & Filter Effects*) can be applied *only* to imported bitmap images.

- You can use the object transformation tools available in Illustrator (see Step 9, *Reshape, Combine, & Distort Objects*) to alter the bounding box that surrounds the image, thus changing the appearance of the contents of the bounding box.

- Photoshop images that contain layers can be opened in Illustrator with its layers intact.

Placing Files in an Illustrator Document

You can put files created in other programs into an open Illustrator file using the Place command (**File ⇨ Place**). The dialog box that displays (Figure 8.3) gives you options for *linking* the original file to the Illustrator document or *embedding* the file into the Illustrator document. The Links palette (discussed later in this chapter) helps keep your embedded and linked files organized.

To Place a file into an open Illustrator document:

1. Locate the file you want to place the same way you would if you were opening a file.

   - If the file you want is not visible in the window when All Readable Documents (*Windows:* All Formats) is chosen in the Show (*Windows:* Files of type) menu, it's been saved in a file that Illustrator can't read. You can't place an unreadable file into an Illustrator file.

   - If an image you're Placing in the Illustrator file was saved in its original application with a Preview format

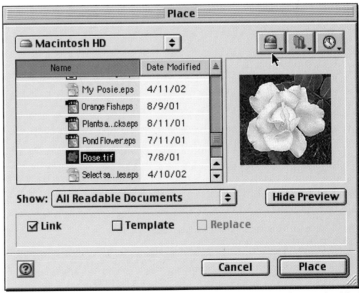

FIGURE 8.3 Place dialog box; this file will be linked rather than embedded.

351

Illustrator recognizes, it displays in the Preview box on the right side of the Place dialog box. If the image was saved with a preview that Illustrator doesn't recognize (or without any preview at all), a line in the Preview area says No preview available.

If you don't want to see what's on the file, click Hide Preview. The Preview of the file disappears and the file name and date modified information spreads to fill the entire area.

2. Check or uncheck the Link checkbox.

   ■ When you Place a file into an Illustrator document, you have the choice of embedding (uncheck) the Placed file into the document or linking (check) the file to the document.

   • *Linked file* — A preview of the image is placed in the Illustrator document and is "linked" to the original image that's saved elsewhere. A linked file remains independent of the Illustrator file, so the size of the linked image is not included in the size of the Illustrator file and the file is smaller. An image that's linked in an Illustrator file must accompany the file when it's exported to another format or imported into a page layout file (such as QuarkXPress). If you modify and resave a linked image in its native program, it updates automatically in the Illustrator document.

Linking files containing objects that have transparency effects applied to them is not as efficient as embedding them. This alert displays warning you that printing is more accurate if the file is embedded.

   • *Embedded file* — The imported image is placed directly into the Illustrator document and becomes a part of the file. When you embed an image, the size of the Illustrator document increases to include the size of the Placed file.

3. Check or uncheck the Template checkbox.

   ■ When the Template box is checked, the Placed image is automatically placed on a template layer for ease in tracing. Both linked and embedded images can be templates.

   ■ An unchecked Template checkbox places the image on a separate new layer.

4. Check or uncheck the Replace checkbox.

   ■ When checked, this option allows you to replace an image that was placed previously. In the document, simply select the image you want to replace, then choose the Place command (**File ⇨ Place**), locate and select a new image, and click Place or press *return/enter*.

 If a file can be linked, it can also be embedded. But not all embedded files can be linked, such as

CGM	*RTF*
DOC	*SVG*
DXF/DWG	*WMF*
Freehand	

352

5. Highlight the name of the file you want to import and click Place or press *return/enter*.

   or

   Double-click the name of the bitmap or vector file.

   ■ The selected image displays in the center of the artwork window. Linked bitmap EPS images display with an "X" across the bounding box when the bounding box is selected; embedded bitmap images do not.

   ■ If the color mode (RGB or CMYK) of a Placed file is different from the Illustrator document, it's converted to the color mode of the Illustrator document.

   ■ Placed artwork (vector) files that are embedded (Link option unchecked) display with paths selected. These files can be edited as if they had been created in Illustrator.

   ■ Placed artwork (vector) files that are linked (Link option checked) display in a bounding box. Paths are not available for selection so the image cannot be edited, even though it's vector artwork. To change Placed artwork that is linked, edit the original artwork file and update the Illustrator file using the Links palette (discussed later in this chapter).

   ■ Placed bitmap files (photographs, scanned line art, Photoshop artwork) display in a bounding box and do not have paths that can be edited in Illustrator.

      ▪ Placed TIFF and Photoshop EPS files keep their original resolution, color, and detail, so this is the best method to use for importing images saved in these formats. A PICT file downsamples to the multiple of 72 ppi that is closest to its original resolution. For example, a placed file with a resolution of 240 ppi is downsampled to 210 ppi.

      ▪ Placed bitmap images can be modified by tools that modify a bounding box, such as rotate, shear, and scale. You can change the size of a Placed bitmap image by moving the bounding box handles like you would if the contents of the bounding box was an object you created in Illustrator.

      ▪ If you enlarge or reduce a TIFF or EPS image that has been Placed in an Illustrator document, its resolution changes, too. Enlarging an image reduces its resolution and reducing an image increases its resolution.

      ▪ Some filters available in the Filter menu can be applied to Placed bitmap images. In fact, some filters available in Illustrator can be applied only to Placed bitmap images. Filters are discussed in Step 11, *Filters & Filter Effects*.

      ▪ When you Place a file created in Photoshop (not scanned art or scanned photographs, but art actually created using Photoshop tools), with the Link option deselected, a dialog box displays that gives you two choices. You can convert photoshop layers to objects or you can flatten photoshop images to one layer.

If layers were used to create the art in Photoshop, choose Convert Photoshop layers to objects to retain those layers in Illustrator. They are placed on separate nested layers, but they aren't paths that can be edited. These images can be edited by applying appearance attributes via the Appearance palette (see Step 11, *Filters & Filter Effects*).

When importing art created in Photoshop, you must choose to convert the layers to objects or to flatten the layers to a single image

Choosing Flatten Photoshop layers to single image places the entire image on a nested layer within the currently active layer in the Illustrator document.

Check the Import Image Maps or Import Slices checkboxes to retain those elements when importing the file into Illustrator.

Display a Placed Image in Outline View

If a Placed image is imported into an Illustrator document whose View mode is Outline rather than Preview, the image displays as a blank bounding box. To display the imported image in a black-and-white format when the document is in Outline view:

1. Display the Document Setup dialog box (⌥⌘ p).

2. Check the Show Images in Outline checkbox.

3. Click OK or press *return/enter.*

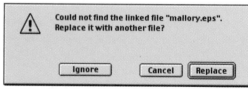

A Placed image displayed in Outline view (Show Images in Outline is checked in the Document Setup dialog box), displays in black and white

Open a File Containing a Linked Image

Opening an Illustrator document containing a linked image whose original image file has been moved since the Illustrator file was saved causes a warning box to display. To relink the image or substitute a different image, click Replace and locate the desired image.

If you click Ignore, the Illustrator document still opens, but the bounding box in which the image was contained is blank. In Outline view, the bounding box is visible; in Preview, the bounding box is visible only when it's selected.

If a linked file is moved since the Illustrator file was saved, this alert displays when reopening the file

Saving a Document Containing a Placed Image as an EPS File If you're going to import images created in Illustrator into another program, such as QuarkXPress, save your file in EPS format. Unless file size is a consideration, images should be embedded rather than linked to avoid missing files. The original file for linked images must be transported along with an Illustrator file. If it isn't located in the same folder with the Illustrator EPS file, the image doesn't print.

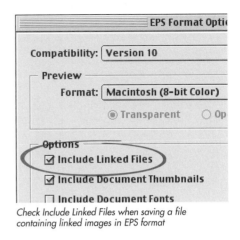

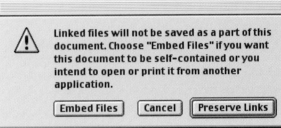

Check Include Linked Files when saving a file containing linked images in EPS format

- There's an option in the EPS Format Options dialog box that allows you to include linked files when you save a document containing a linked image, thus embedding the placed file. A checked box changes linked images to embedded images. If the box is unchecked, placed images remain linked rather than embedded. A box displays asking, yet again, if you're sure you don't want to embed the images.

- If you've placed a file (linked or embedded) with a color mode different from the Illustrator document into which you placed it, a warning displays when you save the document as an EPS file. The color mode of the imported image must be the same as the color mode of the Illustrator document or it may not print or display correctly. Click Cancel and change one or the other so they match, or click Continue to save with differing color modes anyway.

Warning that displays if Include Linked Images is unchecked in the EPS Format dialog box

The Links Palette

The Links palette (Figure 8.4) keeps placed images organized for you. Using the palette, you can find, sort, and change the embedded status of all Placed images in your document. All linked or embedded images are listed by name and include a thumbnail display. Show or hide the Links palette using the option in the Window menu. By default, it's in the same palette as the Layers and Actions palettes, but you can drag it to appear in a different palette or as a stand-alone palette.

fyi *Only embedded images saved in TIFF format and linked images display file names.*

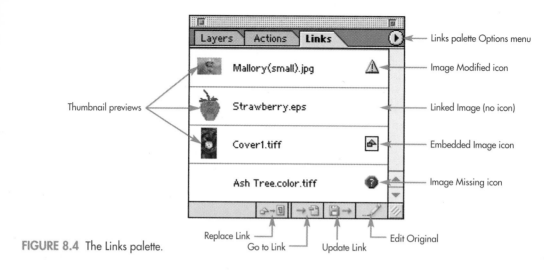

Links palette Options menu

Image Modified icon

Linked Image (no icon)

Thumbnail previews

Embedded Image icon

Image Missing icon

Replace Link

Go to Link

Update Link

Edit Original

FIGURE 8.4 The Links palette.

Identifying Palette Icons

Each image placed in an Illustrator document is listed on the Links palette and you can see information about the status of each image by the icons displayed on the righthand side of the palette.

- **No icon** — A linked image is properly linked, and the original hasn't been modified.

- **Embedded Image icon** (⬛) — The image has been embedded into the Illustrator document and is a part of it.

- **Image Modified icon** (⚠) — The original file of a linked image has been modified since it was placed in the Illustrator file.

- **Image Missing icon** (❓) — The original file of a linked image has been moved from its location on the disk since it was placed in the Illustrator file.

Change Preview Icons You can change the size of the thumbnail preview icons in the Links palette and you can choose to see (in the Links palette) how transparent objects interact with solid objects:

1. Display the Palette Options dialog box by choosing Palette Options from the bottom of the Links palette Options menu.

2. Choose a different size by clicking its radio button or on its icon.

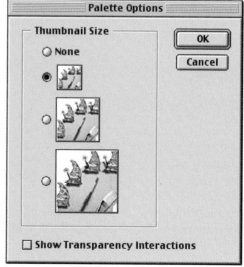

Change the size of thumbnail preview icons in the Links palette in the Palette Options dialog box

- Choose None if you don't want to display a thumbnail preview at all. Only the name of the linked image will display.

3. Click the Show Transparency Interactions to see the transparency interactions in the thumbnail preview.

4. Click OK or press *return/enter*.

Organizing the Links Palette

Using the options contained in the Links palette Options menu, you can decide which Placed images are displayed and you can group them together in different ways.

Show Images To display only certain types of images in the Links palette, choose from the four options available in the Links palette Options menu:

- **Show All** — Displays all placed images. Unless one of the Sort options (see below) is chosen, images are displayed in the Links palette according to their stacking order; that is, the first item placed is at the bottom of the list, with additional images displayed above it.

- **Show Missing** — Displays only linked images whose link to the original file has been broken.

- **Show Modified** — Displays only linked images whose original file has been modified since it was placed in the Illustrator file.

- **Show Embedded** — Displays only images that have been embedded rather than linked.

Sort Images To gather images placed in the Illustrator file into groups in the Links palette, select the images in the Links palette and choose from one of the three options:

- **Sort by Name** — Displays images in alphabetical order.

- **Sort by Kind** — Displays images according to file format.

- **Sort by Status** — Displays images in the following order: Missing, modified, embedded, properly linked.

You can select links by *Shift*-clicking to select more than one image in a row, or ⌘-click to select multiple random images.

| Go To Link |
| Update Link |
| Edit Original |
| Replace... |
| Placement Options... |
| Verify Workgroup Link |
| Save Workgroup Link... |
| Embed Image |
| Information... |
| ✓ Show All |
| Show Missing |
| Show Modified |
| Show Embedded |
| Sort by Name |
| Sort by Kind |
| Sort by Status |
| Palette Options... |

Links palette Options menu

Step 8 — LAYERS & LINKS

fyi The Workgroup options in the Links palette Options menu refer to linked files saved on a WebDAV server. Refer to the Adobe Illustrator 10 User's Manual for information.

Using the Links Palette

Using options available in the Links palette, you can update a linked image that has been modified, edit the original file of a linked image, locate a placed image in the document, replace a linked image with a different image, change the status of an image from a linked image to an embedded image, and display file information about a linked image.

Locate a Linked Image To find a linked image in an Illustrator document:

1. Click on the name of the linked image in the Links palette to highlight it.
2. Click on the Go to link button ([→🗐]) on the bottom of the Links palette.

    or

    Display the Links palette Options menu and choose Go To Link.

The document page moves so the linked image displays in the center of the artwork window and it becomes selected.

Update Modified Linked Images How linked files are updated is controlled by options in the Update Links section of the Files & Clipboard dialog box (**Edit ➪ Preferences ➪ Files & Clipboard**). You can choose to have modified linked files updated automatically, manually, or have a warning box display asking if you want to update them. The default is Ask When Modified.

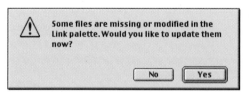

An alert displays if linked files are missing or if they have been modified since they were placed in the document

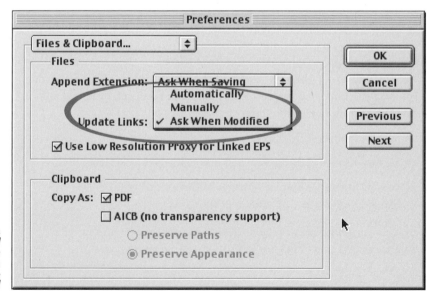

Change the Update Links option in the Files & Clipboard Preferences dialog box if you want to update linked files automatically when they've been modified

- **Automatically** — A linked image that's been modified is updated automatically without notifying you that it's being updated. Be careful when choosing this option. If you want to use one image in more than one piece of artwork with slight changes to fit into a new illustration, all documents that use that image are updated without informing you. You can save a changed image with a different name, but what if you forget you've already used it in a different document?

- **Manually** — With this preference option, the "modified image" warning icon (⚠) displays in the Links palette. That's the only way you'll know the link connecting the original of a linked image to the image placed in the Illustrator document is broken. No warning box displays. Update the link by clicking on the name of the modified image in the Links palette, then:

  - Click on the Update Link button (🔳→) at the bottom of the Links palette.

  or

  - Display the Links palette Options menu and choose Update Link.

  The image is updated immediately.

Edit the Original File of a Linked Image If you determine a linked image needs to be modified, using controls in the Links palette, you can launch the application in which it was created (if it's on your computer, that is), and open the file.

1. Click on the name of the linked image in the Links palette to select it.
2. Click on the Edit Original button (▱) on the bottom of the Links palette.

   or

   Display the Links palette Options menu and choose Edit Original.

   or

   Display the Edit menu and choose Edit Original.

When the original image displays on your screen, make the changes, save the file, then return to your Illustrator document. A warning box displays letting you know that an image in the Links palette is missing or has been modified, and asks if you would like to update it now. Click Yes.

Replace a Linked Image With a Different Image To replace one linked image in an Illustrator document with a different image:

1. Click on the name of the linked image in the Links palette to select it.
2. Click on the Replace Link button (📄→🗑) on the bottom of the Links palette.

   or

   Display the Links palette Options menu and choose Replace.

   or

Click on the image in your Illustrator document, and choose Place from the File menu. When the dialog box displays, check the Replace box. Then locate the new file and click Place or press *return/enter.*

Any Effects or modifications, such as scaling, that were made to the original placed image are applied to the new image, too.

Update a Linked Image Whose Original File Has Been Moved
If you move the original file of a linked image, the "missing" icon () displays in the Links palette because Illustrator can't find the original image, indicating the link has been broken. To relink the file:

- Move the original file back to where it was when it was placed in the Illustrator file

or

- Replace the image. Follow the instructions for Replace a Linked Image With a Different Image (above) except locate the same image in its new location and replace it.

Replace a Linked Image with an Image Having Different Dimensions
If you choose an image with different dimensions to replace the current linked image, you can determine how the new image is positioned on the page, relative to the current image using Placement Options in the Links palette Options menu.

1. Display the Placement Options dialog box by choosing Placement Options from the Links palette Options menu.

   - You can choose placement options *after* the image has been replaced, too.

fyi *Placement Options are available only when replacing a linked image with another linked image.*

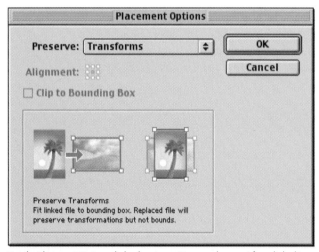

Use the Placement Options dialog box to position a replacement for a linked image

✓ **Transforms**
  Proportions (Fit)
  Proportions (Fill)
  File Dimensions
  Bounds

Options available for positioning a replacement image

2. Choose an option from the Preserve pop-up submenu. A description of the option is displayed at the bottom of the dialog box.

- **Transforms** — The bounding box of the original image is ignored and the bounding box of the replacement image is used, preserving any transformations (stretching or squeezing) that had been applied to the original image.

Replacement image positioned using the Proportions (Fit) placement option

- **Proportions (Fit)** — Reduces or enlarges the image so that its largest side fits in the bounding box of the original image, while preserving the shape of the image. This means that the image will fill the bounding box in one direction, but may not fill it in the other direction. That is, its width may fit, but its height may be too short, and vice versa.

- **Proportions (Fill)** — The bounding box of the original image is filled with the smallest side of the replacement image, while preserving its shape. This means that part of the image may overlap the bounding box.

Replacement image positioned using the File Dimensions placement option. The image overlaps the original bounding box.

- **File Dimensions** — The bounding box of the replacement image is used; the shape is not changed.

  - To determine how the new image is placed, relative to the original image, click a point on the Alignment icon (see below).

  - The bounding box of the original image displays so you can see how the replacement image is positioned relative to the original image.

- **Bounds** — Changes the shape of the replacement image to fit in the bounding box of the original image. The replacement image may be stretched in one direction and squeezed to fit in another direction.

Replacement image positioned using the Proportions (Fill) placement option

3. Click a point on the Alignment icon (⌗) to determine where to align the replacement image, relative to the bounding box of the original image.

- For example, to place the center point of the replacement image over the center point of the original image, click the center of the Alignment icon (the default). To place the top left corner of the bounding box of the replacement image in the same spot as the top left corner of the bounding box of the original image, click the top left corner of the Alignment icon.

- This option is not available for every selection in the Preserve pop-up submenu.

Replacement image positioned using the Bounds placement option. The image is altered to fit in the original bounding box.

361

4. To prevent the replacement image from overlapping the bounding box of the original image, without changing the shape of the image, click the Clip to Bounding Box checkbox.

   ■ This option is not available for every selection in the Preserve pop-up submenu.

5. Click OK or press *return/enter* to apply your changes and exit the dialog box.

Change a Linked Image to an Embedded Image To convert a linked image in an Illustrator document to an embedded image using the Links palette:

1. Click on the name of the linked image in the Links palette to select it.

2. Click on the Replace Link button (⟨⟩⟨⟩) on the bottom of the Links palette.

   or

   Display the Links palette Options menu and choose Replace.

   or

   Click on the image in your Illustrator document, choose Place from the File menu and when the dialog box displays, check the Replace box. Then locate the new file and click Place or press *return/enter*.

Any Effects or modifications, such as scaling, that were made to the original placed image are applied to the new image, too.

Display File Information About a Placed Image To display information about an embedded or linked Placed image, display the Link Information palette:

   ■ Click on its row in the Links palette, display the Links palette Options menu, and choose Information.

   or

   ■ Double-click its row in the Links palette.

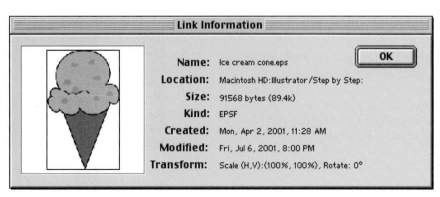

The Information option in the Links palette Options menu displays information about the linked image

The Document Info Palette

In addition to the information provided when you choose the Information option in the Links palette Options menu, you can obtain information about an element selected in a document or general information about the document itself. This palette is used only for displaying information.

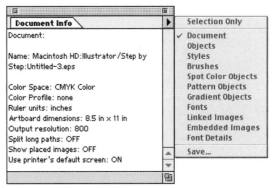

Information displayed in the Document Info box when Document is selected in the Document Info palette Options dialog box

1. To obtain information about an object or imported image, select it in the document.

2. Choose **Window ➪ Document Info** to display the Document Info palette.

3. Display the palette Options menu by clicking the arrow in the upper righthand corner of the palette.

   ■ To display information about all elements in the document, deselect Selection Only.

   ■ To display general information about the document, uncheck Selection Only and check Document (displays a checkmark).

   ■ To display information about an element selected in the document, choose Selection Only (displays a checkmark). This option can be selected along with options listed below the dividing line.

4. Choose one of the other options to display information pertaining to it.

5. If you want to save the information about the document, or its objects, fonts, and so on, choose Save at the bottom of the palette Options menu. The Save As Document Info dialog box opens. Navigate to the folder in which you want to save the information or create a new folder, and click Save or press *return/enter*.

   ■ The information (more than is displayed on the Document Info palette) is saved as a text document that you can import into a word processing program, a page layout program, or open it using your computer's default text editor (usually SimpleText on a Macintosh).

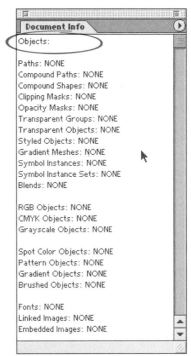

Document Info palette displaying general information about all objects on the page. Selection Only is deselected.

activity 8.5

1. Create a new document: Letter size, CMYK color mode.

2. Display the Place dialog box (File ⇨ Place), locate the file named Flower.eps that's stored in the Student Files folder on the CD-ROM that came with this book, and place it in the document by linking it.

   ■ Click OK when the alert regarding transparency displays.

3. Display the Links palette.

4. Copy the file named Flower.eps from the Student Files folder on the CD into your Practice folder on the hard drive.

5. Eject the CD from the machine.

6. Click Yes when the alert displays asking if you want to update the link.

7. Click Replace when the alert displays telling you the link is missing, then locate the Flower.eps file you copied onto your hard drive, highlight it, and click Replace.

8. Click the Edit Original button (⬚) at the bottom of the Links palette.

   ■ The file opens automatically.

9. With the Selection tool, click on the righthand leaf and drag-copy another leaf. Drop it down the stem from the original leaf. Send it to the back, then save the file.

10. The "missing or modified" alert displays before you can even close the artwork window. Click No, then close the artwork window.

    ■ Notice that the name in the Links palette displays the Image Modified icon (⚠).

11. Highlight the listing in the Links palette, then click the Update Link button (⬚) at the bottom of the palette.

12. Move the flower to the top center area of the page.

13. Reinsert the CD-ROM that came with this book. Locate the file named Hibiscus.tif that's in the Student Files folder on the CD, and copy it into your Practice folder.

14. Display the Place dialog box again, and link the file named Hibiscus.tif into your open document.

    ■ Both are images are displayed in the Links palette.

15. Move the hibiscus to the bottom of the page.

16. Display the Links palette Options menu and choose Palette Options.

17. Click on the large icon, then click OK or press *return/enter* to close the dialog box.

    ■ Notice how large the thumbnail previews in the Links palette are.

18. Delete the hibiscus.

19. Display the Links palette Options menu and choose Placement Options. When the dialog box displays, make sure that Transforms is the selection in the Preserve pop-up submenu. Click OK or press *return/enter*.

20. With the Selection tool, select the flower, then drag the lower left anchor point to the left to skew the image.

21. Press the Replace Link button (⬚) at the bottom of the Links palette and locate the Hibiscus.tif file that's in your Practice folder, make sure the Link checkbox is checked, and click the Replace button.

    ■ The flower is replaced by the hibiscus and is skewed the same as the flower.

22. Display the Placement Options dialog box again and choose the Proportions (Fill) option. Click OK or press *return/enter*.

    ■ The hibiscus redisplays, but the image is not skewed and it is positioned where the original flower was placed before it was skewed.

Continued

Step 8 — LAYERS & LINKS

23. Display the Placement Options dialog box again and check the Clip to Bounding Box checkbox. Click OK or press *return/enter*.

   ■ The hibiscus doesn't change position, but its edges are clipped to fit inside the bounding box of the skewed image.

24. Continue placing linked images using different placement options until you're familiar with how they work.

25. Display the Document Info palette (Window ⇨ Document Info) and display the information available for linked images.

26. Close the document without saving it to a file.

Trace Imported Images

Images opened in Illustrator or images imported into an Illustrator document with the Place command can be traced manually with drawing tools (the Pen tool and the Pencil tool) or by using the Auto Trace tool, hidden under the Blend tool (⬚) in the Toolbox. Put an image you want to trace on a template layer or a locked regular layer so you don't inadvertently move it while you're tracing the image. Then delete the layer when you're finished. Hide the layer whenever you want to see how you're new artwork is progressing.

Whether you use drawing tools or the Auto Trace tool, you should start tracing with a Fill of None and a black stroke. If the fill is a color, you won't be able to see the image underneath to be able to trace it. A black stroke defines the traced path more readily. You can change these attributes after the tracing is finished.

Using the Auto Trace Tool

When you use the Auto Trace tool, paths created usually have more anchor points than is necessary and sometimes they're in strange places on the path. There's generally a lot of cleanup that has to be done. This tool works well for simple objects, but more complex shapes and images, such as a photograph, are easier to draw manually with the Pen tool and the Pencil tool.

You can control the sensitivity of the Auto Trace tool by changing values in the Auto Trace Options section of the Type & Auto Tracing Preferences dialog box (**Edit** ⇨ **Preferences** ⇨ **Type & Auto Tracing**).

   ■ **Auto Trace Tolerance** — Enter a value from 0–10 pt. A value of 0 tells Illustrator to trace every pixel of a bitmapped image, creating a lot of anchor points. A value of 10 traces less precisely and creates fewer anchor points, but it also ignores some of the details. It's usually better to have more anchor points than you need, rather than fewer than you need, because you can always delete them later. The default value of 2 pt is a good place to start.

Auto Trace tool icon in the Toolbox palette

fyi *Embedding an EPS for tracing is better than linking it because a linked image usually isn't as clear.*

365

Control how the Auto Trace tool performs by changing values in the Type & Auto Tracing Preferences dialog box

- **Tracing Gap** — Enter a value from 0–2 pt. This is the minimum width a break in the image must be for Illustrator to ignore it and jump over it. A value of 0 tells Illustrator to never trace over a gap. A value of 2 pt allows Illustrator to jump a 2 point gap.

Trace an Image with the Auto Trace Tool

1. Open an image in Illustrator or import it into an Illustrator document using the Place command (**File ⇨ Place**). Choose to embed the image rather than linking it.

   - Put the placed image on a Template layer by clicking the Template checkbox in the Place dialog box or change the layer on which it's imported to a Template layer by choosing Template from the Layers palette Options menu.

2. Verify that the Fill is None and stroke is black (and change if necessary).

3. Select the Auto Trace tool (▨) in the Toolbox.

   - The pointer changes to the Target pointer (-¦-).

4. Click in an area of the image to be traced.

   - Illustrator automatically encircles the area with a closed path.

   or

   Click and drag from one point on the edge of an image (within 6 pixels of the edge of the color you're tracing) to within 6 pixels of a different edge on the image.

- Illustrator automatically traces an open path between the two points — clockwise around an outside edge and counterclockwise around interior edges.

5. Adjust anchor points and curves, add or delete anchor points, and change options in the Stroke palette (miter limit, join type, and end caps) until you're satisfied with the results of the shape.

1. Create a new document: Letter size, CMYK color mode. Save it into your Practice Folder and name it Green Leaves.eps.

2. Locate the file named Green Leaves.tif in the Student Files folder on the CD-ROM that accompanied this book.

3. Embed it into your new document as a template. Zoom in as large as you can and still see all of the top leaf on your screen.

4. Change the Fill to None and the stroke to 1 pt black.

5. Choose the Auto Trace tool () in the Toolbox and click close to the outside edge of the black outline of the top leaf.

   - A path is drawn around the outside of the leaf.

6. With the Auto Trace tool still selected, click in the interior of the leaf (the green part) to draw a path around that section of the leaf.

   - A path is drawn around the outside of the green area.

7. Adjust the position of the anchor points and direction lines to follow the path of the original image a little more accurately. A few anchor points in the point of the leaf and on the stem can be deleted.

8. Using the Layers palette, hide the template. Deselect all paths and check to make sure your curves are all smooth.

9. With the Selection tool, select the path that defines the interior of the leaf. Change the fill to 85% cyan, 0% magenta, 85% yellow, and 0% black. Change the Stroke to None.

10. With the Selection tool, click on the path that defines the outline of the leaf. Change the fill to 100% black and the stroke to None.

11. Show the template.

12. In the Layers palette, create a new layer.

13. With the Auto Trace tool, click in the middle of the green area of the middle leaf to outline the interior. Oops! Change the fill back to None and the Stroke to 1 pt black.

14. Zoom in to about 1200% so you can see the point of the leaf easily.

   - Notice the Miter join on the stroked path. It's very pointed. If you were going to leave the stroke on this path, you would want to change that point.

15. Display the entire Stroke palette and change the Miter join to the Round join ().

   - Notice how the point is now rounded.

16. Adjust anchor points and direction lines to follow the image more accurately. Delete anchor points that aren't necessary. Change the corner point at the bottom of the leaf to a smooth point to form a more rounded corner.

Continued

17. With the Auto Trace tool selected, click somewhere in the black area to outline the outside of the leaf. Then adjust the anchor points and direction lines.

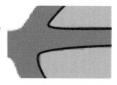

18. Change the fill to 100% black and the stroke to None.

19. Send to the bottom of the stack (Object ⇨ Arrange ⇨ Send to Back).

20. Create a new layer.

21. Choose the Auto Trace tool, then click on the outer edge of the black area of the smallest leaf and drag to the outer edge of the black area on the bottom of the leaf.

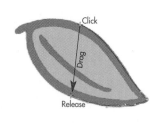

- A path is drawn clockwise around the right half of the leaf because this is an exterior path. Dragging with the Auto Trace tool draws a path only between the points of the click.

22. Click and drag from the inside edge of the black area at the top of the leaf to the black area on the bottom of the leaf.

- A path is drawn counterclockwise around the left half of the leaf because this is an interior path.

23. Click and drag from the inside edge of the green area at the top of the leaf to just inside the green area on the bottom of the leaf. It has to be within 6 pixels of the edge of the color you want to outline. If you release more than 6 pixels into the black area, a path is drawn around the entire green area.

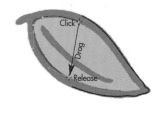

24. Delete the paths you drew on the bottom leaf and, following the same procedures as for the first two leaves, trace and color the bottom leaf to complete the illustration.

25. Save this file and close the document.

PRACTICE ACTIVITY 8-1 — Swan on a Pond

All the components to recreate the scene pictured here, except the swan and the pond, have been created and placed on the CD-ROM that accompanies this book.

1. Create a new document and save it into your Practice folder. Name it Swan on a Pond.eps.

2. Locate the file named Swan.tif in the Student Files folder on the CD-ROM that accompanies this book. Embed it on a new template layer by clicking the Template checkbox on the Place dialog box.

3. Rename Layer 1 Swan <Path>.

4. Change fill to None and stroke to 1 pt black.

5. Choose the Auto Trace tool in the Toolbox.

6. Click in the middle of the swan's neck to trace the outline of the swan.

7. Zoom in so you can see the endpoints of the swan's wing easily. Then, with the Auto Trace tool, click in the white area a few pixels (within 6 pixels) below the top endpoint and drag to within 6 pixels above the bottom endpoint.

   ■ If you've done it right, a clockwise path is drawn, outlining the swan's wing.

8. Change the stroke weight of the swan's outline to 2 point. Change the swan's wing to a 1.5 pt stroke.

9. Adjust anchor points and curves, removing anchor points that aren't necessary, until you're satisfied with the shape of the paths.

10. Draw or trace the swan's face area with the Pen tool. Apply a 1 point black stroke and a fill of 0% cyan, 30% magenta, 95% yellow, and 2% black to its beak.

11. Change the color of the swan to white.

12. When you're satisfied with your swan, hide the template layer.

13. Create a new layer and name it Pond. Draw the pond around your swan with the Pen tool. Color it 100% cyan, 65% magenta, 0% yellow, and 0% black. Using the Layers palette, put this layer to the back of the stack.

14. Create a new sublayer in the Pond layer and name it Lilypads. Draw three lilypads that closely resemble those shown here. Color them green.

15. Locate the file named Pond Flower and embed it on the middle lilypad in the same layer as the lilypads.

16. Create a new layer and name it Plants and rocks. Locate the file named Plants and rocks.eps that's in the Student Files folder on the CD-ROM. Embed it in the new layer and drag to place it in approximately the same position on the pond as pictured here.

   ■ Clicking on the large rock on the righthand side of the image is an easy place to grab the image.

17. Save your file.

369

EXERCISE 8-1 — City Scene

1. Re-create the city scene as shown here.

2. Place each building on a separate layer.

3. Displaying a grid may be helpful.

Additional Exercise:

Using your city or neighborhood, draw a simple city scene.

Reshape, Combine, & Distort Objects

Chapter Outline

- Transform Objects
- Move Objects
- Step-and-Repeat
- Point of Origin
- Scale Objects
- Rotate Objects
- Square Up the Bounding Box
- Reflect Objects
- Slant Objects
- The Free Transform Tool
- The Transform Palette
- Illustrator Does the Math
- The Twist Tool

- The Reshape Tool
- Split a Path
- Divide Objects Below
- Offset a Copy of a Path
- Convert a Stroke Into an Object
- Average and Join Anchor Points
- Compound Paths
- The Knife Tool
- The Pathfinder Palette
- Align and Distribute Objects
- The Liquify Tools
- Envelopes

So far, you've learned all the basic information about creating artwork in Illustrator. In this chapter, you'll learn how to change, combine, and transform the objects you create. In other words, here's where it starts getting fun.

Transform Objects

In previous chapters you learned to move objects by dragging with the Selection tool and to rotate, scale, and reflect objects by adjusting an object's bounding box. In this section, you'll learn how to use tools, menu commands, and the Transform palette to do those things — and more.

Transform Again

Once one of the following transformations on an object is performed, you can continue making additional transformations using the same values by performing the Transform Again command. It's the same as the duplicate command in other programs.

■ Press ⌘ d

or

■ Choose **Object** ➪ **Transform** ➪ **Transform Again**

or

■ Display the context-sensitive menu and choose **Transform** ➪ **Transform Again** in the menu that displays.

  ▪ *Macintosh:* ⌃-click on the document page.

  ▪ *Windows:* Right-click on the document page.

Move Objects

Even though moving an object is not transforming it, Illustrator has placed this command in the Transform menu, so we'll discuss it here with the rest of the real Transform tools.

In addition to moving objects by dragging them to a new position, you can display a dialog box and specify numerically exactly how far and in which direction the objects move. You can also use the Transform palette to move objects, but that procedure is discussed in the Transform palette section later in this chapter. Values in the Move dialog box remain until you (a) enter new values, (b) move an object by dragging with the mouse, or (c) use the Measure tool.

To move objects using the Move dialog box:

1. Select the item you want to move.

2. Display the Move dialog box (Figure 9.1):

   ■ Press ⇧ ⌘ m (any tool in the Toolbox can be active)

   or

   ■ Press *return/enter* with the Selection tool or the Direct Selection tool selected in the Toolbox

   or

   ■ Double-click the Selection tool or the Direct Selection tool in the Toolbox

   or

   ■ Choose **Object** ➪ **Transform** ➪ **Move**

   or

 Distance and angle values calculated using the Measure tool (see Step 6, Rulers, Grids, and Guides), are displayed in the Move dialog box. Then use the Transform Again command (press ⌘ d) to automatically move a selected object by the amount of the measurement.

- Display the context-sensitive menu and choose **Transform** ⇨ **Move** in the menu that displays.
  - *Macintosh:* ∧-click on the document page.
  - *Windows:* Right-click on the document page.

3. Click the Preview checkbox to see the results of your changes as you make them.

   - As soon as you click the Preview checkbox after entering new info in fields, the object moves, leaving behind an outline path of its original position.

   - If the Preview checkbox is still checked from the last move that was made, the object moves by the values left over from the last move. If the object was selected with the Selection tool, its bounding box displays in the object's original position.

   - Toggle the Preview checkbox (check/uncheck) to get a quick visual of exactly how much the object moved.

4. Enter values in the Horizontal and Vertical fields to specify how far side to side (horizontal) or up and down (vertical) you want to the object to move.

   or

   Enter values in the distance and angle fields.

   - Enter positive values to move the object up or to the right. Enter negative values to move the object down or to the left.

   - Enter a 0 in a field if you don't want the object to move in that direction.

   - You can enter values up to three digits after the decimal. More than three numbers after the decimal get rounded off.

   - If the Preview checkbox is checked, click in another field or press the *Tab* key (which moves you to another field) to see the results of your changes before exiting the dialog box.

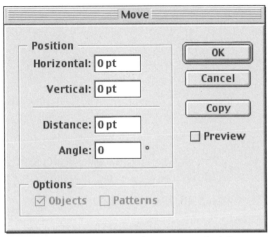

FIGURE 9.1 Move selected objects a specified distance by entering values in the Move dialog box.

fyi *You can enter values in the fields using any of the standard units of measurement. Illustrator converts values to the document's current unit of measurement automatically.*

■ If the Preview checkbox is checked and the object moved when you displayed the Move dialog box because values remained from the last move that was made, new values entered in the fields are calculated from the original position of the object, not from the move that was made when the Move dialog box was opened.

5. Click the Copy button to exit the dialog box and make a copy of the selected object that's positioned the distance away from the original object according to the values in the fields. The original object stays where it was.

6. The two choices shown in the Options section of the dialog box relate to Pattern fills and are discussed in Step 10, *Brushes, Patterns, & Symbols.*

7. Click OK or press *return/enter.*

activity 9.1

1. Create a new document: Letter size, CMYK color mode.

2. Draw a star and apply a fill of 100% cyan, 80% yellow, and a 1 pt black stroke.

3. Choose the Selection tool to display the star's bounding box, then press ⇧ ⌘ m to display the Move dialog box.

4. If the Preview box isn't checked, click it now.

   ■ The star moves according to the values remaining in the fields from the last move but the bounding box remains in its original position.

5. Enter .5" in both the Horizontal and Vertical fields. Press the *Tab* key.

   ■ Notice that the values in the Distance and Angle fields adjusted according to the values entered in the Horizontal and Vertical fields. If you entered .707 in the Distance field and 45 in the Angle field, .5 in would automatically display in the Horizontal and Vertical fields.

6. Click OK or press *return/enter.*

   ■ The star moved to the right ½" and up ½", and as soon as you exited the dialog box, the bounding box moved to surround the star in its new position.

7. Display the Move dialog box again and enter a minus (hyphen) before the values in the Distance and Angle fields. Press the Tab key.

   ■ The star moved to the left ½" and up ½". Why didn't it move down instead of up? Because it's still on a −45° angle. To move the star down, enter 135° in the Angle field.

8. Click the Copy button.

   ■ A new star was created and placed in position according to the values in the fields.

9. Close this document without saving it to a file.

Step-and-Repeat

Step-and-repeat is a phrase you may hear from your output provider. It means to move and copy. For example, a business card is usually printed at least four on a sheet of paper, sometimes more, so you need to place four exact copies of the artwork on the document page.

1. With the Selection tool, select all the paths that make up the artwork.

2. Display the Move dialog box, using one of the methods described previously.

3. In the Horizontal field of the Move dialog box, enter a value equal to the width of the trim size of the artwork.

   ■ A standard business card is 3½" × 2", so the horizontal value should be 3.5" or 21 pt if you're stepping and repeating business card artwork.

4. Enter 0 in the Vertical field.

5. Click the Copy button.

   ■ An exact copy of the selected artwork is positioned to the right of the original path the precise distance specified in the Horizontal field.

     ▪ To position the copied artwork to the left of the original object, enter a minus sign (-) preceding the value in the field.

6. Repeat #2–6 for as many copies of the artwork you want across the page.

   or

   Press ⌘d repeatedly until you have the desired number of copies.

   ■ This is the Transform Again command. See information about the Transform Again command later in this chapter.

7. Select all the copies of the artwork and display the Move dialog box again.

8. Enter 0 in the Horizontal field and enter the height of the trim size of the artwork in the Vertical field.

9. Click the Copy button.

   ■ An exact copy of the selected artwork is positioned above the original artwork the precise distance specified in the Vertical field.

     ▪ To position the copied artwork below the original artwork, enter a minus sign (-) preceding the value in the field.

10. Repeat #7–9 until you have as many vertical copies of the artwork as you need.

    or

    Press ⌘d repeatedly until you have the desired number of copies.

activity 9.2

1. Create a new document: Letter size, CMYK color mode. Save it into your Practice folder as an .eps file named Step and Repeat Practice.eps.

2. To ensure that you have a white fill and black stroke, press d or click the Default Fill & Stroke button (⬜) at the bottom of the Toolbox palette.

3. Draw a rectangle that's $3\frac{1}{2}" \times 2"$.

4. With the rectangle still selected, press ⇧ ⌘ m to display the Move dialog box and enter 3.5" in the Horizontal field, and enter 0 in all the other fields.

5. Click the Copy button.

   ■ A copy of the rectangle is placed to the right of the original rectangles so that the touching vertical strokes overlap by the width of the stroke.

6. Select both rectangles and display the Move dialog box. Enter −2" in the Vertical field and 0 in all the other fields.

7. Click the Copy button.

   ■ A copy of both rectangles is placed below the original rectangle so that the touching horizontal strokes overlap by the width of the stroke.

8. With the rectangle tool, draw a single rectangle that's the exact size and shape of the four rectangles. Send to the back of the stack.

   ■ Crop marks can only be attached to a single object, so you have to make a single object the correct size that surrounds the four individual objects.

9. Choose Object ⇨ Crop Marks ⇨ Make.

   ■ Crop marks are placed at the four outside corners of the rectangles.

10. With the Line Segment tool, draw a straight .5 pt wide horizontal line that's $\frac{1}{2}"$ long. Position it $\frac{1}{8}"$ to the left of the rectangles at exactly the center of the four rectangles where they overlap.

■ Hold the *Shift* key down to get a perfectly straight line.

■ Display the Info palette and watch the Width value to draw a line exactly $\frac{1}{2}"$ long (36 pt).

■ To position the line exactly $\frac{1}{8}"$ from the left edge of the rectangles, move it so the right end of the line touches the left side of the rectangles. Then deselect the line. Reselect the line and move it to the left, watching the Info palette D (distance) value. Stop when the D value is 9 pt or .125".

11. Change the stroke to a dashed line by entering 4 in the dash field, leaving the other fields blank.

   ■ Dashed lines are used to indicate a "cut" mark between two or more items on a single sheet of paper that are butted together. In printing terms, this is called a "chop".

12. With the stroke still selected, display the Move dialog box and enter 7.75" in the Horizontal field and 0 in the vertical field. Click Copy.

   ■ The value was calculated by adding the width of the rectangles ($3\frac{1}{2}" + 3\frac{1}{2}" = 7$), plus the length of the rule ($\frac{1}{2}"$), plus the amount of space between the original line and the rectangles ($\frac{1}{8}"$), plus the space between the rectangles and the copied dashed line ($\frac{1}{8}"$). That's how far I want the left edge of the original dashed line to be from the right edge of the copied dashed line.

13. Using the same procedures you performed in #10–12 for creating the horizontal "cut" marks, place vertical cut marks.

   ■ When you're finished, the artwork is ready to send to the output provider.

14. Save the file, print it, and close the artwork window.

Point of Origin

When changes are made to objects using the Transform tools (scale, rotate, shear, reflect), calculations for those changes are made from a point of origin. By default, the point of origin (✛) of a single object is its center point; in grouped objects, the center is defined by the group's overall bounding box. When you click an object or grouped objects with a Transform tool selected, the point of origin icon displays.

When using one of the four Transform tools — not the Free Transform tool (📧) — you can establish a new point of origin:

1. Select an object or group.

2. Choose a transform tool in the Toolbox — scale (📧), rotate (📧), reflect (📧), and shear (📧).

3. Click in or near the object where you want to establish the point at which calculations are made to transform the object.

   or

   Drag the existing point of origin to a new position.

   ■ After establishing a new point of origin, the pointer changes to an arrowhead (▶).

Scale (Enlarge/Reduce) Objects

In addition to enlarging or reducing the size of an object by adjusting its bounding box, you can use the Scale tool (📧) in the Toolbox, which gives you more flexibility. You can scale objects by entering values in the Scale dialog box or by dragging with the Scale tool.

■ To use Smart Guides when scaling objects with the Scale tool, make sure the Transform Tools checkbox is checked in the Smart Guides Preferences dialog box (**Edit** ⇨ **Preferences** ⇨ **Smart Guides & Slices**). The program default is for the box to be checked.

Small leaf on the left is enlarged uniformly to the size of the large leaf on the right

Scale by Dragging

To scale an object by dragging:

1. With the Selection tool or the Lasso tool, select an object.

2. Choose the Scale tool in the Toolbox.

3. Establish the point of origin. Leave it in the center of the object's bounding box or click to reposition it.

   ■ If multiple individual objects are selected, the point of origin is the center point of the bounding box that surrounds all selected objects.

Scale tool icon in the Toolbox palette

4. Click and drag the selection. You don't have to click on the object to drag it. In fact, the farther away from the object you click to start the drag, the finer the control you have over its shape and size.

- Scale a copy of the object by pressing the ⌥ key any time after you start dragging to resize the shape and before you release the mouse. Release the mouse before releasing the ⌥ key.

  - The original shape is unchanged.

- Flip the object as you scale it by dragging completely across it.

- Press the *Shift* key down as you drag to resize the object proportionally. Drag up and down to resize vertically, sideways to resize horizontally, or diagonally to resize horizontally and vertically at the same time.

  - If you've changed the Constrain Angle value from the default of 0 in the General Preferences dialog box (**Edit ⇨ Preferences ⇨ General**), *Shift*-drag in the direction of the new angle specification to resize the object proportionally.

- To have even more control over the size of an object, drag just a tiny bit with the Scale tool, and release. Then press ⌘d repeatedly until it's the size you want.

Scale Selected Anchor Points in an Object You don't have to scale entire objects when dragging with the Scale tool. You can select anchor points with the Direct Selection tool or the Direct Select Lasso tool and drag with the Scale tool to scale only those anchor points. The point of origin displays in the center of the selected anchor points, but you can reposition it to achieve the shape you want. This technique allows you to reshape portions of an object in equal amounts. Even if the Scale Strokes & Effects checkbox is checked in General Preferences, strokes don't scale when only part of an object is scaled.

Scale Numerically

Another method of scaling objects, or portions of an object, is to display the Scale dialog box and enter values in the fields, which means you can scale objects by exact amounts. You can also use the Transform palette to accomplish the same thing.

To scale an object using the Scale dialog box (Figure 9.2):

1. With any of the Selection tools, select an object or select anchor points in an object.

read this!

If you scale an object, then select another object and use the Transform Again command (⌘ d) to scale it by the same percentage as the first object, the original point of origin of the first object is used for the calculations.

fyi When scaling objects, by dragging the bounding box or by using the Scale dialog box, the default is to not scale strokes or effects that have been applied to those objects. You can choose to scale strokes and effects by clicking the checkbox in the General Preferences dialog box or in the Scale dialog box. Checking or unchecking the box in one location automatically turns it on or off in the other location.

2. Display the Scale dialog box:

- Double-click the Scale tool (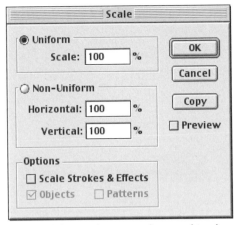) in the Toolbox

or

- Choose **Object** ➪ **Transform** ➪ **Scale**

or

- ⍓-click near the object to reposition the point of origin and automatically display the Scale dialog box.

  - If multiple objects are selected, all selected objects are scaled from that common point of origin.

3. Check the Preview checkbox to see the results of your changes as you make them.

- Click the checkbox off and on to toggle the selection.

4. Enter values in the fields.

- **Uniform** — Enter a value in the Scale field to resize the height and width of the selected object or part of an object by the same amount.

- **Non-Uniform** — Enter a value in the Horizontal (width) and Vertical (height) fields to resize the selected object or part of an object by those percentages.

- Enter negative values to flip the selection. This feature doesn't work too well when only a portion of the object is selected.

- Enter 100 in a field to leave that dimension of the object unchanged.

- You can enter up to three digits after the decimal.

5. Decide whether you want to scale any Strokes or Effects that have been applied to the object. A checkmark in the Scale Strokes & Effects checkbox indicates that strokes and effects are scaled. Blank indicates they will remain at their original values. Effects are discussed in Step 11, *Filters & Filter Effects*.

- When a Uniform scale value is entered, and Scale Strokes & Effects is checked, strokes are scaled differently than when Non-Uniform values are specified.

6. The Objects and Patterns checkboxes relate to pattern fills and are discussed in Step 10, *Brushes, Patterns, & Symbols*.

FIGURE 9.2 To enlarge or reduce an object by a specified amount, enter values in the Scale dialog box.

fyi *To display Width and Height information for a selected object in the Transform palette, INCLUDING ITS STROKE, check the Use Preview Bounds checkbox in General Preferences (Edit ➪ Preferences ➪ General). Then the measurements will include the width of the stroke that hangs outside the path line.*

Step 9 — RESHAPE, COMBINE, & DISTORT OBJECTS

7. When you're satisfied with the results of your changes, click OK or press *return/enter* to exit the dialog box.

8. Click the Copy button to resize a copy of the selected object, leaving the original object untouched. This action also closes the dialog box.

 *activity* 9.3

1. Open the document named Orange Fish.eps in the Student Files folder on the CD-ROM that accompanies this book.

2. Zoom in so you can see the fish easily, then select it with the Selection tool.

   ■ All the paths that created the fish are grouped, so all paths are selected when clicked with the Selection tool.

3. Select the Scale tool in the Toolbox.

   ■ Notice that the point of origin icon (✛) is positioned in the middle of the fish (according to the group's bounding box).

4. Position the mouse pointer about an inch to the right of the tail of the fish, click, then move the pointer up and down, from side to side, and diagonally. Don't release the mouse yet, though.

   ■ All paths in the object are scaled uniformly because the point of origin is in the exact center of the object.

5. Move the pointer up and down far enough that the fish is flipped vertically. Move the pointer back to its original position, then move it to the left until the fish is flipped horizontally. Move the pointer back to approximately it's original position. Then move it down and to the right.

6. Release the mouse when you've resized the fish to be proportionally larger.

7. Undo the last action.

8. Select the Fish again with the Selection tool.

9. Select the Scale tool and click in the open mouth of the fish to reposition the point of origin. Position the mouse pointer to the right of the fish's tail in approximately the same position you did before, and click and drag around. Release the mouse.

   ■ Notice the distinctly different shape you achieved when you moved the point of origin.

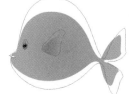

10. Double-click the Scale tool to display the Scale dialog box.

    ■ If the Preview box is checked in the dialog box, the fish was resized again by the values that remained in the fields when you released the mouse after the last resizing option.

11. Enter 100 in the Scale field of the Uniform section of the dialog box and click OK or press *return/enter*.

    ■ The fish reverted back to the size it was before the Scale dialog box was opened, but not to its original size and shape.

12. Press ⌘ z repeatedly until the fish is back to its original size and shape.

13. ⌥-click at the top of the fish's tail to reposition the point of origin and display the Scale dialog box.

14. Enter 85 in the Horizontal field and 125 in the Vertical field. Click the Copy button.

    ■ A copy was made that was 15% narrower (100-85) and 25% taller (100+25) than the

Continued

original fish. The top of the tail is in the same position on both fish because that's the point of origin.

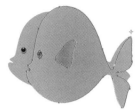

15. With the Selection tool, move the copy of the fish to a clear spot on the page and deselect all paths.

16. With the Direct Select Lasso tool, select the anchor points that make up the tail of the fish.

17. Double-click the Scale tool.

   ■ The tail of the fish changed by 15% horizontally and 25% vertically because those were the values that were in the Scale dialog box.

   ■ Notice that the position of the point of origin icon is in the center of the selected anchor points.

18. Click the Preview checkbox off and on to see the difference it made in the shape of the tail.

19. Click the Cancel button to exit the Scale dialog box without making any changes.

20. Position the pointer to the right of the fish's tail and drag it around.

21. It doesn't really create a very good shape for the tail, so release the mouse and press ⌘ z to undo the scale action.

22. Reposition the point of origin in the narrow part of the tail (where it joins the body). Then position the pointer in about the same spot again and drag to scale the tail.

   ■ That's much better.

23. Close this document without saving it to a file.

Rotate Objects

You already know how to rotate an object using its bounding box. Using the Rotate tool in the Toolbox, you can rotate a selected object or selected anchor points in an object. Drag to rotate an object visually or display the Rotate dialog box and enter values to rotate an object in precise increments.

Rotating an Object by Dragging

To rotate an object or portion of an object by dragging:

1. Select the entire object or select certain anchor points in the path.

2. Select the Rotate tool in the Toolbox.

3. Establish the point of origin around which the object is rotated. Leave it in the center of the object's bounding box or click to reposition it.

   ■ If multiple objects are selected, the point of origin is the center point of the bounding box surrounding all selected objects.

Rotate tool icon in the Toolbox palette

4. Click and drag the selection. Don't click on the object to drag it. The farther away from the object you click to start the drag the finer the control you have over its movement.

■ To rotate an object in 45° increments, hold down the *Shift* key while you drag. Or you can press the *Shift* key at any time before you release the mouse to snap to the nearest 45° angle. Release the mouse before you release the *Shift* key.

▪ If you've changed the program default of 0 in the Constrain Angle field in the General Preferences dialog box, the object snaps to multiples of the new angle value.

5. To copy the selected object, applying the rotation value to the copied object, and leaving the original object untouched, press the ⌥ key before releasing the mouse. Then release the mouse before you release the ⌥ key.

Point of origin icon

Rotating an Object Numerically

To rotate a selected object or a portion of an object by specifying precise increments:

1. Select the entire object or select individual anchor points in the path.

2. Display the Rotate dialog box (Figure 9.3).

■ Double-click the Rotate tool () in the Toolbox.

▪ By default, the point of origin is the object's center point.

or

■ Establish a new point of origin and display the Rotate dialog box by selecting the Rotate tool in the Toolbox and ⌥-clicking near the object.

▪ If multiple objects are selected, all selected objects are rotated from that common point of origin.

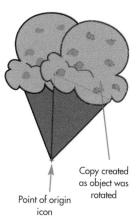

Copy created as object was rotated

Point of origin icon

3. Click the Preview checkbox to see the results of your changes as you make them.

4. Enter a value in the Angle field.

■ Enter a positive value to rotate the selected object counterclockwise.

■ Enter a negative value to rotate the selected object clockwise.

```
┌─────────────── Rotate ───────────────┐
│                                        │
│                              ┌───────┐ │
│                              │  OK   │ │
│    Angle: ┌──────┐ °         └───────┘ │
│           │  0   │           ┌───────┐ │
│           └──────┘           │Cancel │ │
│                              └───────┘ │
│  ┌─ Options ──────────┐      ┌───────┐ │
│  │ ☑ Objects ☐ Patterns│     │ Copy  │ │
│  └────────────────────┘      └───────┘ │
│                              ☐ Preview │
└────────────────────────────────────────┘
```

FIGURE 9.3 Enter a new value in the Angle field to change the angle of an object.

5. Click OK or press *return/enter* to exit the dialog box.

   ■ The two items in the Options section of the dialog box relate to pattern fills and are discussed in Step 10, *Brushes, Patterns, & Symbols.*

6. To apply the rotation value to a copy of the selected object, leaving the original object untouched, and exit the dialog box, click the Copy button.

Square Up the Bounding Box

Normally the bounding box of an object or group of objects is aligned with the page, that is, straight vertical/horizontal. When you rotate objects with the Rotate tool or the Transform tool, the bounding box may rotate also. To realign the bounding box so it's square with the document page, select the object, then:

■ Choose **Object ⇨ Transform ⇨ Reset Bounding Box**

or

■ Display the context-sensitive menu and choose **Transform ⇨ Reset Bounding Box.**

   • *Macintosh:* ⌃-click
   • *Windows:* Right-click.

Resetting the bounding box has no effect on the artwork contained within the bounding box. It just resets it square with the page so you have a zero-point to work with.

activity 9.4

1. Create a new document: Letter size, CMYK color mode. Save it into your Practice folder as an .eps file named Rotate Practice.eps.

2. With the Pen tool, draw a shape like the one shown here.
   ■ You should use only two anchor points.

3. If the center point of the shape isn't visible, display the Attributes palette and click the Show Center button (□).

4. Drag-copy to create a second shape. Put one of the shapes aside to use again later.

5. Select one of the shapes, then choose the Rotate tool (○) in the Toolbox.
   ■ Notice that the point of origin icon displays over the center point of the selected object.

6. Fill the object with 80% cyan, 95% magenta, no stroke. Convert the color to a global process color and name it Plum Purple.

7. Position the pointer about 2" to the right of the shape, then click and drag up and to the left to rotate the shape. Before releasing the mouse, press the ⬿ key to copy the original shape for the rotation.
   ■ Release the mouse before releasing the ⬿ key.

8. Press ⌘d as many times as necessary to copy the object enough times to complete a circle.

9. Unless you're real lucky, the "petals" won't end up evenly spaced between the first one and the last one.

10. Press ⌘z repeatedly until you get back to the original colored shape.

11. Double-click the Rotate tool to display the Rotate dialog box. Enter 20 in the Angle field and click the Preview checkbox.

Continued

12. Click the copy button to apply the rotation to a copy of the original object.

13. Press ⌘d as many times as necessary to copy the object enough times to complete a circle.

    ■ If the angle value divides 100 by an equal amount, the "petals" will end up symmetrical. For example, $100 \div 25 = 4$, so an angle of 25° can be used to achieve a symmetrical shape. $100 \div 30 = 3.333$, so an angle of 30° won't achieve a symmetrical shape.

14. Change the View to Outline.

    ■ If you applied a black stroke and a fill of None to the original shape, what you see on the screen is what it would look like.

15. Change the View back to Preview.

16. Click the original petal (the one in the back), and change the color to 10% Plum Purple.

17. Marquee to select all the objects. Choose Filter ➪ Colors ➪ Blend Front to Back.

18. To have a different "look" to the object, select all the objects and choose Object ➪ Blend ➪ Make.

19. Click on the shape that you put aside. Apply a fill of 100% cyan, 65% yellow. Create a global process color swatch and name it Teal Green.

20. Apply a stroke of 100% Teal Green.

21. Select the Rotate tool in the Toolbox and ⬐-click the bottom anchor point to establish a new point of origin and display the Rotate dialog box.

22. Verify that 20 is the value in the Angle field and click the Copy button. Press ⌘d until the circle is complete.

23. To demonstrate how to reset the bounding box, click on one of the petals in the object with the Selection tool to display it's bounding box.

    ■ Notice that the bounding box is rotated and is no longer square with the page.

24. Display the context-sensitive menu and choose Transform ➪ Reset Bounding Box.

    ■ Notice that the position of the object didn't change.

25. Change the fill color of the last petal to 10% Teal Green.

26. Blend the colors front to back.

27. Save the file, print it, and close the artwork window.

Reflect Objects

To reflect an object is to flip it. In Illustrator, you can reflect an object so it's a mirror image of the original object, either horizontally or vertically, or reflect it at a different angle from the original object. As with the other transformation tools, you can create a copy of the object as you reflect it.

Leave the point of origin in the center of the object's bounding box if you want the object to pivot from its center. Reposition the point of origin to pivot the object from a different point, even a point outside the object. You can flip an object visually by dragging it with the Reflect tool or by making selections or entering values in the Reflect dialog box.

Reflect an Object by Dragging

To reflect an object or portion of an object by dragging:

1. Select the entire object or select certain anchor points in the path.

2. Select the Reflect tool in the Toolbox, hidden under the Rotate tool (⊙).

3. Establish the point of origin. Leave it in the center of the object's bounding box or click to reposition it.

4. Click and drag the pointer up, down, or sideways.

   ■ To create a mirror image of the selected object without changing its angle or x/y position on the page, leave the point of origin at the center point, align the mouse with the point of origin above or below it, then drag sideways just a tiny bit.

   ■ To turn the object upside down without changing its angle or x/y position on the page, leave the point of origin at the center point, align the mouse to the side of the point of origin, then drag up or down just a tiny bit.

   ■ To keep the object's rotation to perfectly horizontal or perfectly vertical as you reflect it, hold down the *Shift* key.

5. To reflect the object and create a copy of it simultaneously, leaving the original object untouched, press the ⬿ key before you release the mouse. Then release the mouse before you release the ⬿ key.

Reflect an Object Using the Reflect Dialog Box

1. Select the entire object or select certain anchor points in the path.

2. Display the Reflect dialog box (Figure 9.4) by double-clicking the Reflect tool (⬚) in the Toolbox

   ■ By default, the point of origin is the object's center point.

   or

Reflect tool icon in the Toolbox palette

Establish a new point of origin and display the Reflect dialog box simultaneously by selecting the Reflect tool in the Toolbox and ⬦-clicking near the object.

- If multiple objects are selected, all selected objects are reflected from that common point of origin.

3. Verify that the Preview checkbox is checked so you can see the results of your changes as you make them.

4. Click the button of one of the options in the Axis section of the dialog box.

- Click the Horizontal button to flip the along the imaginary line that's the horizontal axis — which means the object flips upside down.

  - When the Horizontal button is clicked, the default angle in the Angle box is 0°, which is perfectly horizontal.

- Click the Vertical button to flip the along the imaginary line that's the vertical axis — which means the object flips sideways.

  - When the Vertical button is clicked, the default angle in the Angle box is 90°, which is perfectly vertical.

- Enter a positive value, up to 360, in the Angle field (the button is checked automatically if the Preview box is checked) to reflect the selected object counterclockwise, measured from the horizontal axis.

- Enter a negative value, up to −360, in the Angle field to reflect the selected object clockwise, measured from the horizontal axis.

5. Click OK or press *return/enter* to exit the dialog box.

- The two items in the Options section of the dialog box relate to pattern fills and are discussed in Step 10, *Brushes, Patterns, & Symbols*.

6. To reflect a copy of the object, leaving the original object untouched, and exit the dialog box, click the Copy button.

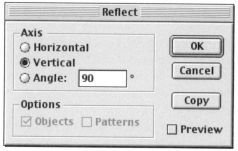

FIGURE 9.4 Choose the axis across which to reflect an object and its angle in the Reflect dialog box.

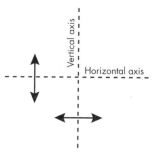

Arrows show how an object is reflected, depending upon which axis is used

 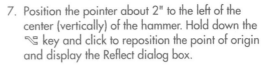

activity 9.5

1. Open the document you created when you drew the hammer in Step 4, *The Pen & Pencil Tools*.

2. With the Selection tool, select the hammer.

3. Click on the Reflect tool ( ) in the Toolbox.

   ■ The point of origin icon is at the center point.

4. Position the pointer just outside the bottom of the object. Click and drag just a tiny bit, then release the mouse.

   ■ The hammer flipped across the vertical axis, creating a mirror image of the original.

5. Click to establish the point of origin at the bottom right edge of the handle of the hammer.

6. Position the pointer about 2" down and to the right of the bottom of the hammer. Click and drag the hammer in a circle around the shape. Move the pointer close to the point of origin and drag around the circle, then move it 2" or so away from the point origin and drag around. Release the mouse wherever you want.

   ■ Notice that the closer you were to the point of origin when you dragged, the more exaggerated the moves the hammer made. The further away you were, the finer its movements were.

Location of click

7. Position the pointer about 2" to the left of the center (vertically) of the hammer. Hold down the ⌐ key and click to reposition the point of origin and display the Reflect dialog box.

   ■ If the Preview box was checked when the dialog box opened, your hammer flipped according to the value in the Angle field, which is the leftover angle from the last reflect command performed.

8. If the Preview box wasn't checked when the Reflect dialog box displayed, check it now.

   ■ Your hammer flipped according to the value in the Angle field.

9. Click the Horizontal button, then click the Preview checkbox off and on.

   ■ Notice the movements your hammer makes as it flips on the Horizontal axis.

10. Click the Vertical button, then click the Preview checkbox off and on.

    ■ Notice the movements your hammer makes as it flips on the Vertical axis.

11. Enter different values in the Angle field and click the Preview checkbox off and on between each entry to see the movements of your hammer.

12. Click the copy button to make a copy of your hammer, reflected according to the specifications you entered, and exit the dialog box.

13. Close this document without saving it to a file.

Slant Objects

To shear an object is to slant it, not just rotate it, but actually alter its shape. This action is performed with the Shear tool (), which is hidden under the Scale tool (🔲) in the toolbox. As with the other transformation tools, you can specify a point of origin from which the object is slanted, and you can determine the angle at which it is slanted. You can slant an object at any angle by dragging it with the Shear tool to slant it visually or by entering values in the Shear dialog box to slant the object numerically.

Shear angle: 20° along horizontal axis

Slant an Object by Dragging

Slanting an object by dragging it is easily accomplished, but it isn't easy to control the results. If you leave the point of origin in the center, you may not get the results you want. I find it easier to move the point of origin to one of the object's corners before slanting it.

Shear angle: −20° along horizontal axis

Two examples of how the shear angle affects artwork

The procedure for slanting an object with the Shear tool is basically the same as for the other transformation tools:

1. Select the entire object or select certain anchor points in the path.

2. Select the Shear tool in the Toolbox.

3. Establish the point of origin around which the object is rotated. Leave it in the center of the object's bounding box or click to reposition it.

Shear tool icon in the Toolbox palette

4. Click and drag the selection. The farther away from the object you click to start the drag, the finer the control you have over its movement.

   - How far you drag determines how much the object is slanted.

   - The angle at which you drag determines the direction of the slant.

     - The shape gets a little funky at certain angles. For example, if you compare it to the face of a clock, about 2 o'clock is where it gets haywire.

   - Holding down the *Shift* key as you drag slants the object in 45° increments, and it's much easier to control the angle of the slant. Or you can press the *Shift* key at any time before you release the mouse to snap to the nearest 45° angle. Release the mouse before you release the *Shift* key.

5. To copy the selected object and apply the slant value to the copied object, leaving the original object untouched, press and hold the ⌥ key before you release the mouse. Then release the mouse before you release the ⌥ key.

Slant an Object Numerically

To slant a selected object or a portion of an object by specifying precise increments:

1. Select the entire object or select certain anchor points in the path.

2. Display the Shear dialog box (Figure 9.5) by double-clicking the Shear tool (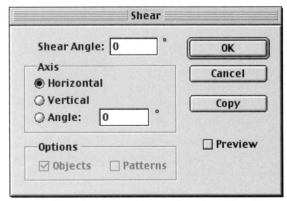) in the Toolbox.

   ▪ By default, the point of origin is the object's center point.

   or

   Establish a new point of origin and display the Shear dialog box by selecting the Shear tool in the Toolbox and ⌥-clicking in or near the object.

   ▪ If multiple objects are selected, all selected objects are slanted from that common point of origin.

3. Verify that the Preview checkbox is checked so you can see the results of your changes immediately.

4. Enter a value between 360 and −360 in the Shear Angle field.

   ▪ Enter a positive value to slant the selected object clockwise.

   ▪ Enter a negative value to slant the selected object counterclockwise.

5. Click OK or press *return/enter* to exit the dialog box.

   ▪ The two items in the Options section of the dialog box relate to pattern fills and are discussed in Step 10, *Brushes, Patterns, & Symbols*.

6. To apply the slant value to a copy of the selected object, leaving the original object untouched, and exit the dialog box, click the Copy button.

FIGURE 9.5 Change the values and options in the Shear dialog box to slant an object by a specified amount.

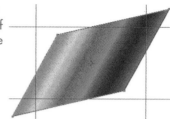

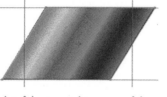

1. Create a new document: Letter size, CMYK color mode.

2. With the Rectangle tool, draw a rectangle twice as wide as it is high. Fill it with the Rainbow swatch (█), no stroke.

3. If rulers are not visible in your artwork window, show the rulers (press ⌘r or choose View ▷ Show Rulers).

4. Drag ruler guides along all four sides of the rectangle.

5. Select the Shear tool (🖅) in the Toolbox, then display the Layers palette and expand its layer. In the Layers palette, click in the Selection area of each guide layer, one at a time.

   ■ Notice that the point of origin icon shifts to display on each guide as you select it.

6. Delete a guide layer in the Layers palette to remove a guide from the page.

   ■ I just wanted to remind you that you could remove guides from the page using the Layers palette.

7. Replace the ruler guide that you deleted.

8. Select the object, then select the Shear tool in the Toolbox. Position the pointer about an inch to the right of the top right corner of the rectangle and drag to the right as straight as possible.

   ■ The point of origin is at the center point.

   ■ If you move the pointer up or down when you drag, the baseline angle of the rectangle changes.

   ■ Notice that because the point of origin was in the center, both vertical edges extended beyond the starting point.

9. Drag the pointer up and down, then release.

   ■ Notice that the angle of the baseline changes when you move up and down.

10. Click and drag in different directions and around in a circle and notice how the shape of the object changes with the different directions and angles you drag.

11. Perform the Undo command until you're back to the original shape.

12. ⬉-click the bottom left corner of the rectangle to reposition the point of origin and display the Shear dialog box.

13. Make sure the Preview box is checked.

14. Enter 35 in the Shear Angle field and click the Horizontal button. Click the Preview checkbox on and off.

    ■ Notice how the rectangle slants.

15. Click the Vertical button and click the Preview checkbox on and off.

16. Enter a minus sign (hyphen) before the 35 in the Shear Angle field, making it a negative number. Then click the Vertical button. Click the Preview checkbox on and off between each change.

    ■ Notice how the rectangle slants with each change of the Shear angle.

17. Enter a value in the Angle field. Click the Preview checkbox on and off.

    ■ Notice how the rectangle slants with the change in angle value.

18. Change the specifications several times by entering different values in the Shear Angle field and the Angle field, and by clicking the Horizontal and Vertical buttons with different values in the fields.

Continued

- Notice how the rectangle slants with each change.

19. Click the Copy button to apply the last specifications you entered in the Shear dialog box to a copy of the rectangle and exit the dialog box.

20. Close the document without saving it to a file.

21. Open the Pear you drew in Exercise 4-1.

22. Apply a couple of different Shear specifications to slant this shape. Reposition the point of origin in several places and drag in different directions. Then ⬚-click to reposition the point of origin and display the Shear dialog box. Then enter several different combinations of specifications.

- Notice how the object changes shape with each change.

23. Close the document without saving the changes.

The Free Transform Tool

With the Free Transform tool, you can do most of the same things you can do when you drag the other transformation tools (scale, rotate, shear, and reflect), plus more. What you can't do is specify an exact point of origin or apply changes to a copy of the original object. If you don't want the original object changed, make a copy of it before reshaping it with the Free Transform tool. There is no dialog box associated with the Free Transform tool; it's all done by dragging the selection.

Free Transform tool icon in the Toolbox palette

An object in the document that's selected when you click on the Free Transform tool in the Toolbox, displays a bounding box like the standard bounding box that displays when an object is selected with the Selection tool. You can square up the bounding box when the Free Transform tool is selected the same way you can when the bounding box is displayed when the Selection tool is selected. Choose **Object** ➪ **Transform** ➪ **Reset Bounding Box**.

The same handles and icons display on the Free Transform bounding box, too, plus a few new ones. The standard reshape icons on the bounding box (↔, ↕, ↖, and ↘), perform the same functions as the standard bounding box, with a few new functions added when you use the Free Transform tool.

Using the Free Transform Tool

To reshape objects using the Free Transform tool, select the object, then select the Free Transform tool (⬚)in the Toolbox.

Scale Scale with the Free Transform tool the same way you do when the object is selected with the Selection tool.

- Drag a corner handle to enlarge or reduce the size of an object in both directions. Hold down the *Shift* key to scale both directions proportionally. The opposite corner acts as the point of origin.

- To enlarge or reduce only horizontally, drag a side handle (not a corner handle) of the object.

- To enlarge or reduce only vertically, drag a top or bottom handle (not a corner handle) of the object.

Rotate When an object is selected with the Selection tool, you can rotate it only by dragging a corner handle (when the ↵⟋ icon displays). When the Free Transform tool is selected, the rotate icon displays anywhere along the outside of the object's bounding box, which means you can click and drag anywhere to rotate the object. All rotations pivot around the center point of the object.

- Hold the *Shift* key down to rotate in 45° increments (providing the value in the Constrain Angle field in General Preferences is still 0).

  - Calculations of rotation angles (entered in Constrain Angle field) are based on the orientation of the bounding box, not the orientation of the page. If your bounding box is not aligned with the page, *Shift*-dragging won't align it with the bottom of the page.

Shear To Shear an object with the Free Transform tool, start to drag a side handle (not a corner handle), then hold down the ⌘ key and continue dragging until the shape is like you want it. When you press the ⌘ key, the pointer changes to ▶₊₊ when you drag a handle on the horizontal side, and to ▶↕ when you drag a handle on the vertical side, indicating the direction of the slant. Release the mouse before releasing the ⌘ key. You can press the ⌘ key any time before releasing the mouse. The opposite corner handles act as the point of origin.

- To keep the object or objects you're dragging from enlarging or reducing in the direction you're dragging, start the drag, then hold down the ⌘ and *Shift* keys as you continue to drag.

- To shear an object from its center point, start the drag, then hold down the ⌘ and ⌥ keys as you drag. Keep the sides horizontal (or vertical) when shearing from the object's center by holding down the ⌘, ⌥, and *Shift* key as you continue to drag.

fyi Hold down the ⌥ key to enlarge or reduce an object from its center point.

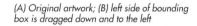

(A) Original artwork; (B) left side of bounding box is dragged down and to the left

Reflect Flipping objects with the Free Transform tool is performed the same way you flip an object with the Selection tool. You don't have to start the drag before holding down the modifier keys (⌥, *Shift*)

- Drag a handle of the bounding box to the opposite side of the object.
  - If you drag from a corner handle, the object is anchored at the opposite corner.
  - If you drag from a middle handle, the object is anchored along the opposite side.
- Hold down the *Shift* key as you drag to flip the object proportionally.
- Hold down the ⌥ key as you drag to flip the object from its center point.

Distort To move one corner handle (not a side handle) independently of the other three corners, hold down the ⌘ key after you start dragging. You can distort the shape of the object in any direction. Release the mouse before you release any modifier keys.

- Hold down the *Shift* and ⌘ keys to keep the movement to 0°, 45°, or 90° (or to the angle specified in the General Preferences dialog box).
- Hold down the ⌘ and ⌥ keys to distort the object proportionally from opposite corners.

Put Objects in Perspective To apply perspective to selected objects with the Free Transform tool, start to drag a corner handle (not a side handle), then hold down the ⌘, ⌥, and *Shift* keys as you continue to drag until the object is reshaped. The corner handles on the opposite side of the bounding box are anchored in place. Release the mouse before you release the ⌘, ⌥, and *Shift* keys.

read this!

You can't apply the Distort or Perspective features to type unless the characters have been converted to outlines. See Step 5, Add Type to Artwork for more information.

Type can be put in perspective by first converting to outlines

1. Open the file you stored in your Practice Folder named Leaf.eps.

2. Select all the leaves with the Selection tool.

3. Select the Free Transform tool () in the Toolbox.

4. Drag the left side handle of the bounding box just a little bit, then hold down the ⌘ key and drag down about an inch to slant the leaves. Before you release the mouse, hold down the *Shift* key. Then release the mouse.

5. Drag a corner handle a little bit, then hold down the ⌘ key and drag the handle around. Add in the other modifier keys before you release the mouse.

6. Revert to the last saved version of the file (press *F12*).

7. Select all the leaves with the Selection tool.

8. Select the Free Transform tool in the Toolbox.

9. Drag a corner handle a little bit, then press all three modifier keys: *Shift*, ⌥, and ⌘. Drag horizontally and vertically to see how the perspective changes depending upon the direction you drag.

10. Practice using the Free Transform tool. Open other objects you've drawn and play around with them, too.

11. Close the file without saving changes.

Apply Multiple Transformations

You can make multiple changes to multiple objects simultaneously in the Transform Each dialog box. You can't apply separate options in the Transform Each dialog box to individual objects in a group. The group is treated as a single object and all transformations are applied to the whole group.

1. Select one or more objects or groups, or a combination.

2. Display the Transform Each dialog box (Figure 9.6):

   ■ Choose **Object** ⇨ **Transform** ⇨ **Transform Each**

   or

   ■ Press ⇧ ⌥ ⌘ d

   or

   ■ Display the context-sensitive menu and choose **Transform** ⇨ **Transform Each**.

      ▪ *Macintosh:* ⌃-click

      ▪ *Windows:* Right-click.

3. Check the Preview checkbox.

4. Enter the appropriate specifications. Press the *Tab* key to move to the next field.

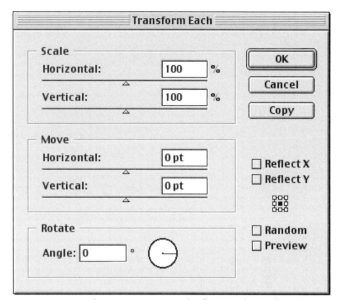

FIGURE 9.6 Scale, move, rotate, and reflect an object all at the same time by changing options in the Transform Each dialog box.

- **Point of Origin** (⊞) — Click one of the boxes of the icon to establish the point of origin for each individual object, not for the bounding box surrounding the selected objects.

- **Scale** — Move the Horizontal and Vertical sliders or enter values in the fields to resize the selected objects.

- **Move** — Move the sliders or enter values in the fields to move the selected objects.

  - Enter a larger number in the Horizontal field to move selected objects to the right. Enter a smaller number to move selected objects to the left.

  - Enter a larger number in the Vertical field to move selected objects up. Enter a smaller number to move selected objects down.

- **Rotate** — Enter a value in the Angle field or drag the dial marker to rotate the selected objects around their individual points of origin.

- **Reflect** — Check the Reflect X checkbox to flip selected objects on the vertical axis. Check the Reflect Y checkbox to flip selected objects on the horizontal axis.

  - Change the value in the Rotate Angle field to change the angle of the baseline of selected objects as they're flipped.

  - You can't access these checkboxes by pressing the *Tab* key.

- **Random** — This is the best thing about this command. Click this checkbox to have Illustrator apply the transformation you specified in the Transform Each dialog box randomly to selected objects. For example, if you specified a Horizontal Scale of 60% for 5 selected objects, a different scale value will be applied to each object.

  - Each time you click the Preview checkbox, new random values are applied to selected objects. So if you don't like how they looked the first time, keep turning the Preview checkbox on and off until you like what you see.

- You can leave the Preview button checked and click the Random button off and on to force Illustrator to change how settings are applied, too.

■ **Copy** — Click this button to apply specified transformations to a copy of the selected objects, leaving the original objects untouched.

■ Click OK or press *return/enter* to apply specified transformations to the original object or objects and exit the dialog box.

activity 9.8

1. Create a new document: Letter size, CMYK color mode.

2. Open the file named Plants and rocks.eps that's in the Student Folder on the CD-ROM that accompanies this book.

3. Copy (⌘ c) one of the larger rocks and paste it (⌘ v) into the new document you created.

4. Close the file named Plants and rocks.eps without saving changes.

5. Press ⌘ v several more times to paste more rocks into the document. Position them however you want, even overlapping some if you like.

6. Marquee to select all the rocks.

7. Display the Transform Each dialog box (press ⇧ ⌥ ⌘ d or choose Object ⇨ Transform ⇨ Transform Each).

■ Settings remaining in the dialog box from the last time it was used are applied to selected objects.

8. Enter the following specifications in the dialog box:

■ Scale: Horizontal — 50%, Vertical — 50%

■ Move: Horizontal — .25 in, Vertical, 0%

■ Rotate: Angle — 10°

9. Check the Random checkbox.

10. Check the Preview checkbox several times, forcing Illustrator to reapply the specifications in a different way each time.

11. Change the specifications a couple of times and click the Preview and Random checkboxes off and on several times which each specification change.

12. When you're finished experimenting, close the document without saving it to a file.

The Transform Palette

By entering values in the fields of the Transform palette (Figure 9.7), you can control the transform tools numerically. Display the palette by displaying the Window menu and choosing Transform. A check-mark displays to the left of the menu option. To hide the palette, click its close box or display the Window menu and choose Transform again. The checkmark beside the menu option disappears.

There is no Preview available when you move, scale, rotate, shear, or reflect objects using the Transform palette. You have to Undo the last action and enter a new value. To apply new values entered into the fields, click in another field in the palette. Press the *Tab* key to apply the new values and move to the next field. To apply the new values and leave the same field highlighted, press *Shift-return/enter.*

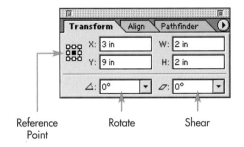

Reference Point   Rotate   Shear

FIGURE 9.7 You can also move, scale, rotate, shear, and reflect an object all at one time by changing options in the Transform palette.

- To copy a selected object and apply the new values, press ⌥-*return/enter*, exiting the palette.

- To copy a selected object and apply the new values, and highlight the next field, press ⌥-*Tab.*

The Reference Point

The reference point (point of origin) is displayed in the Transform palette and you can reposition the reference point for the selected object by clicking one of its hollow squares. The point of origin icon doesn't display on the artwork when its position is changed in the Transform palette.

Move Selected Objects

Enter values in the X and Y fields in the Transform palette to move selected objects.

- To move a selected object to the right, enter a value in the X field that's higher than the current value. Enter a lower value or a negative value to move a selected object to the left.

- To move a selected object upward, enter a value in the Y field that's higher than the current value. Enter a lower value or a negative value to move a selected object down.

Flip Horizontal
Flip Vertical

Scale Strokes & Effects

Transform Object Only
Transform Pattern Only
✓ **Transform Both**

Options available in the Transform palette Options menu

Scale Selected Objects

Enter values in the W and H fields in the Transform palette to resize selected objects.

- Enter values larger than the current values in the W (width) *and* H (height) fields to scale a selected object uniformly. To scale an object non-uniformly, enter different values in the fields.

- To scale the width of strokes and any effects applied to scaled objects, display the Transform palette Options menu by clicking the arrow in the upper right corner and click Scale Strokes & Effects on (with checkmark). Choose again to turn it off.

Rotate Selected Objects

Enter a value in the Rotate field or click the submenu arrow to display a menu of preset increments that you can scroll to select.

- Establish the point of origin around which to rotate the object by clicking one of the boxes in the Reference Point section of the palette.

- To rotate the selected object counterclockwise, enter (or choose from the submenu) a positive value.

- To rotate the selected object clockwise, enter (or choose from the submenu) a negative value.

Slant Selected Objects

Enter a value in the Shear field or click the submenu arrow to display a menu of preset increments that you can scroll to select.

- Establish the point of origin for the slant to originate from by clicking one of the boxes in the Reference Point section of the palette.

- To slant the selected object to the right, enter (or choose from the submenu) a positive value.

- To slant the selected object to the left, enter (or choose from the submenu) a negative value.

- To change the angle of the baseline of the object, enter a positive (upward) or negative (downward) value in the Rotate field.

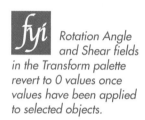

fyi   *Rotation Angle and Shear fields in the Transform palette revert to 0 values once values have been applied to selected objects.*

Flip Selected Objects

To reflect selected objects, display the Transform palette Options menu and choose Flip Horizontal or Flip Vertical. Enter values in the X and Y fields to move the object as it's reflected. Enter a value in the Rotate field to change the object's angle in relation to the bottom of the page.

Transform Objects and Patterns

The three options at the bottom of the Transform palette Options menu affect objects filled with patterns, which are discussed in the next chapter (Step 10, *Brushes, Patterns, & Symbols*).

- **Transform Object Only** — changes apply to the object only, leaving the pattern fill unrotated, unscaled, and so on.
- **Transform Pattern Only** — changes apply to the pattern fill without altering the shape, orientation, etc, of the object itself.
  - An icon (🔲) displays in the lower left corner of the palette.
- **Transform Both** — changes made in the Transform palette are applied to both the object and its pattern fill.

Illustrator Does the Math

You can let Illustrator calculate values for you in the fields of the dialog boxes for the transform tools and in the Transform palette.

- To increase a value in a field, enter a positive number to the right of the current number. For example, if the number currently in the field is 2.5 in, enter +3 after it so it reads 2.5 in+3. When you exit the field, Illustrator calculates the value and changes it to read 5.5 in.

- To decrease a value in a field, enter a negative number to the right of the current number.

- To change the current number by a percentage value, type an asterisk, then the percentage of change, to the right of the current value. For example, type *50% in a field to reduce the current value by 50% or half the current value. This works only in the scale or move fields in the palettes and dialog boxes. It doesn't work in fields in which you specify angles.

- Multiply the current value by another value by entering a * between the numbers, for example, 2 in*2.

- Divide the current value by another value by entering a / between the numbers, for example, 4 in/2.

2.5 in+3	5.5 in
Math entry – Add	Calculated result

3 in–1	2 in
Math entry – Subtract	Calculated result

7 in*50%	3.5 in
Math entry – Multiply	Calculated result

2 in*2	4 in
Math entry – Multiply	Calculated result

8 in/2	4 in
Math entry – Divide	Calculated result

activity 9.9

1. Create a new document: Letter size, CMYK color mode.

2. With the Rectangle tool, draw a rectangle twice as wide as it is high. Fill it with the rainbow Gradient swatch (), no stroke.

3. Display the Transform palette (Window ⇨ Transform).

4. If the Reference Point isn't in the center of the point of origin icon in the Transform palette, click the center box now.

5. Enter 4" in the X field and 6" in the Y field. Press *return/enter* to register the changes.

   ■ The center point of your rectangle should be aligned 4" from the left edge and 6" up from the bottom of your page.

   ■ The object remained selected.

6. Click the top left Reference Point box.

   ■ Notice that the numbers in the X and Y fields changed because measurements now are from the top left corner of the object rather than its center point.

7. Enter 30 in the Rotate field, then click on the document page to register the change.

   ■ Notice that the rectangle pivoted at the upper left corner and became deselected.

8. Reselect the object with the Selection tool.

9. Display the Transform palette Options menu and choose Flip Vertical.

10. Display the Shear pop-up menu and select 30°.

    ■ Notice that value in the Shear field momentarily displayed the 30°, then quickly reverted back to 0°.

11. Apply a 4 pt black stroke to the rectangle.

12. Enter *2 after the last number in the W field and after the last number in the H field. Illustrator will scale the object to twice it's original size.

    ■ Notice that the stroke weight remained the same as the original shape.

13. Return the rectangle to the size and shape it was before you scaled it by performing the Undo command twice.

14. Display the Transform palette Options menu and choose Scale Strokes & Effects.

15. Scale the shape to twice its size again.

    ■ Notice that the stroke weight scaled to twice its original size, too.

16. Practice making changes to the rectangle by entering different values in the Transform palette. Change the Reference Point around and make changes.

    ■ Notice what happens to the rectangle when you make different changes.

17. Close this document without saving it to a file.

The Twist Tool

Hidden under the Rotate tool in the Toolbox is the Twist tool. With this tool, you can reshape the points of an object by twisting it around its center point. It's similar to a whirlpool where the center of an object twists more sharply than its outside edges. You can drag an object clockwise or counterclockwise with the Twist tool.

Twist tool icon in the Toolbox palette

- You can't make a copy of the original object with this tool like you can with the transformation tools.

- You can't apply the Twist tool to selected anchor points in a path — it applies to the entire object.

- Gradient or pattern fills don't twist automatically when you drag with the Twist tool, just the object's outer shape.

- You will also find Twist commands in the Filter menu and the Effect menu, discussed in Step 11, *Filters & Filter Effects*. These commands produce an effect similar to the results of using the Twist tool, but a dialog box displays so you can enter absolute angle values.

Sailboat activity created in Practice Activity 3-2 with sun twisted using the Twist tool

Twist the Fill in an Object

You can make the fill pattern or gradient twist along with an object's outside edges by performing the Expand command (**Object ➪ Expand**) before dragging with the Twist tool. The results consume a lot of RAM and will slow down output of your project substantially, so use this feature sparingly.

You can twist the fill in a selected object

Step 9 — RESHAPE, COMBINE, & DISTORT OBJECTS

401

activity 9.10

1. Create a new document: Letter size, CMYK color mode.

2. Turn on Smart Guides.

3. Draw a star with the following specifications:
   - Radius 1: 1.037 in
   - Radius 2: 0.88 in
   - Points: 58

4. Apply a white fill, no stroke.

5. With the object still selected, choose the Twist tool in the Toolbox. Click on the page about an inch to the right of the object and drag down and to the left. Stop dragging and release the mouse when you are straight below the object.

6. Draw a .2" circle and apply a white fill, no stroke.

7. Align the center point of the small circle with the center point of the star.

8. Apply a radial gradient to the star with the following specifications. A visual is supplied.
   - Lefthand slider: 28% black, Location: 13.5

- Second slider from left: 10% black, Location: 40.5
- Third slider from left: 25% black, Location: 63
- Righthand slider: 15% black, Location: 82.5
- Lefthand Midpoint Diamond icon: 50
- Middle Midpoint Diamond icon: 37
- Righthand Midpoint Diamond icon: 62

9. Choose the Gradient tool (▨) in the Toolbox and drag from the top left corner to the bottom right corner to reposition the center of the radial gradient.
   - Repeat dragging with the Gradient tool until you're satisfied with how the gradient is positioned on the shape.

10. Save the document into your practice folder as Sawblade.eps. Close the file.

The Reshape Tool

The Reshape tool, hidden under the Scale tool in the Toolbox, allows you to change the shape of a path by selecting and dragging individual anchor points without distorting the original shape of the path any more than necessary. You can also change the shape of a path without having to add, then drag, anchor points.

When you click on an existing anchor point in a selected path with the Reshape tool selected, a small square displays around the anchor point. If you click on a segment of a selected path, a new anchor point is created that displays the small square, indicating it was created or selected with the Reshape tool.

Reshape tool icon in the Toolbox palette

Anchor points that aren't selected with the Reshape tool (no square around it) are not moved when the shape is changed.

- When you select all the points in an open path, the two endpoints become stationary anchor points and don't move when the path is reshaped.

- You can make a copy of the original object as you reshape it, leaving the original unchanged, by holding down the ⌥ key as you drag.

To change the shape of a path with the Reshape tool:

1. Select the path using any Selection tool.

2. Deselect any anchor points that you don't want to move when the path is reshaped.

3. Choose the Reshape tool () and position the cursor over the element in the path (anchor point or segment) that you want to use to reshape the path, and click.

- Anchor points or segments selected with the Reshape tool display a box around them and keep their original positions with respect to one another.

- Anchor points selected with a Selection tool (are solid), adjust according to the anchor points that were selected with the Reshape tool and the unselected anchor points.

- Anchor points that aren't selected, don't move at all.

- If all anchor points in a path are selected, the entire path moves — just as if you were moving it with the Selection tool.

4. *Shift*-click to select additional anchor points or path segments, or select them with the Direct Select Lasso tool and the *Shift* key held down.

- You can select an unlimited number of anchor points or path segments.

5. Drag the selected anchor points to reshape the path.

activity 9.11

1. Create a new document: Letter size, CMYK color mode.

2. Draw a small rectangle and apply a fill of a pink color and 1 pt black stroke. Deselect the path.

3. Click on the path line of the rectangle with the Direct Selection tool (press *a*) to select it with all anchor points hollow.

4. Choose the Reshape tool (⬚) in the Toolbox.

- It's hidden under the Scale tool (⬚) in the Toolbox.

5. Click on the righthand vertical segment (not an anchor point) and drag to the right.

Continued

- A selected anchor point with a square around it is added to the segment.
  - You could accomplish the same thing by adding a smooth anchor point to the path, then selecting it with the Direct Selection tool and dragging it.

6. Delete the rectangle.

7. With the Pen tool, draw a wavy line with anchor points at the top of five peaks and the bottom of four valleys. Apply a 4 pt green stroke, no fill. Apply a Round Cap (just because it's prettier).

8. Drag copy two clones of the wavy line and position them so they're about an inch apart.

9. With the Selection tool, select the top wavy line so all anchor points are solid.

10. Choose the Reshape tool and select the anchor point at the top of the third peak and move it down before releasing the mouse.

  - The anchor point displays a box around it.

  - The two endpoints remain anchored in place and the other anchor points adjust according to the position of the anchor point moved with the Reshape tool, trying to keep the original shape as closely as possible.

11. With the Selection tool, select the middle wavy line.

12. With the Reshape tool, *Shift*-click the anchor points in the second and third valleys and on the third peak. Drag down the same distance.

- The shape between the selected points were not changed at all, but the rest of the path was reshaped as it was moved.

13. With the Selection tool, select the top wavy line and move it to position the top of the third peak over the top of the third peak of the bottom wavy line.

  - Notice how the path was distorted from the original path.

14. Undo the last function (press ⌘ z).

15. With the Selection tool, select the middle wavy line and move it to position the top of the third peak over the top of the third peak of the bottom wavy line.

  - Notice that the path from the anchor point of the second valley to the anchor point of the third valley, which includes the third peak, are exactly the same as the original path.

16. Undo the last function (press ⌘ z).

17. With the Direct Selection tool, select the path line of the bottom wavy line so all anchor points are hollow. Then *Shift*-click to select the anchor points at the bottom of the second and third valleys and the top of the third peak.

18. Drag down. See the difference between reshaping with the Reshape tool and dragging selected anchor points with the Direct Selection tool?

19. Close this document without saving it to a file.

Split a Path

In Step 4, *The Pen & Pencil Tools*, you learned how to split a path by selecting an anchor point with the Direct Selection tool and pressing the *Delete* key. But that deleted the segments attached to the anchor point, too. Using the Scissors tool in the Toolbox, you can split a path, leaving all segments intact. You can split the path in the middle of a segment, not just at an anchor point.

Scissors tool icon in the Toolbox palette

- A path doesn't have to be selected (active) to split it with the Scissors tool.
  - If the path is not active when you split it with the Scissors tool, one of the split segments becomes selected.

- The pointer changes to a target pointer (-¦-).

- Clicking on an open path with the Scissors tool in one place changes it to two open paths. Clicking on a closed path with the Scissors tool in one place converts it to an open path. Clicking on a closed path with the Scissors tool in two places creates two open paths. And so on.

- If you attempt to split a path by clicking on an endpoint, a warning box displays telling you that you must click on a segment or an anchor point, not an endpoint.

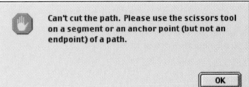

Can't cut the path. Please use the scissors tool on a segment or an anchor point (but not an endpoint) of a path.

OK

 *activity 9.12*

1. Create a new document: Letter size, CMYK color mode.

2. Draw a square. Apply a 3 pt red stroke, yellow fill.

3. Choose the Scissors tool (✂) in the Toolbox.

4. Click in the middle of the top segment of the square.

5. With the Direct Selection tool, move the anchor points up and away from each other.
   - The closed path becomes an open path.
   - Notice that the fill extends across the gap.

6. With the Scissors tool selected, click on the bottom right anchor point of the shape.
   - The open path becomes two separate open paths with the same attributes as the original path.

7. With the Selection too, drag the new path away from the original shape.

8. Close this document without saving it to a file.

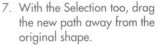

Divide Objects Below

The Divide Objects Below command in the Object menu (**Object ➪ Path ➪ Divide Objects Below**), when applied to an object, makes that object act like a cookie cutter on any objects underneath it. Then the dividing object is deleted and the resulting paths are selected. If you want to keep the path you used as the cutting pattern, make sure a copy of it is saved elsewhere.

- Stroke and fill attributes applied to the objects being divided are applied to the new "pieces" that were cut.

- Any fill or stroke attributes applied to the top object are ignored.

- The Divide Objects Below command doesn't work when the dividing object is placed on an open path having a fill of None. It does work, though, on a closed path with a fill of None.

Objects placed on top of other objects can be used to divide objects under them in the shape of the top object, like a cookie cutter

- When a filled, open path is divided, each dip in the path is converted to an individual object with the same fill and stroke color as the original path.

- New path layers are created in the Layers palette for the resulting divided objects.

To divide an object:

1. Assemble the objects to be divided. They don't have to be selected.

   - Using the Layers palette, hide any object layers for objects you don't want to be included when the command is applied.

2. Draw a new path or select an existing path to be used as the dividing object and position it over the objects to be divided.

   - When the Divide Objects Below command is applied to the dividing object, it is applied to *all* selected paths, so make sure no other paths are selected in your artwork except the one you want to use as the cutting pattern.

3. Choose **Object ➪ Path ➪ Divide Objects Below**.

   - The path or object used to divide the underlying objects into separate paths is deleted automatically.

fyi To keep an object that's under a dividing object from being affected by the Divide Objects Below command, hide it or lock it using the menu command or the Layers palette.

activity 9.13

1. Create a new document: Letter size, CMYK color mode.

2. Draw a rectangle. Apply a 1 pt black stroke and 80% yellow fill.

3. Draw a circle. Apply a 6 pt red stroke and a blue fill. Position it so it overlaps the bottom right side of the rectangle.

4. Draw a star. Remove the stroke and apply a green fill. Position it so it overlaps the bottom left side of the rectangle and the left side of the circle, but make sure some of the yellow rectangle is visible.

5. Draw a round corner rectangle and apply a 2 pt black stroke and a 100% cyan fill. Position it so it overlaps the other shapes. Send it backward in the stacking order until it is stacked between the yellow rectangle and the blue circle (as shown).

6. Display the Layers palette and expand the top-level layer so you can see the object layers. Hide the layer containing the cyan rounded corner rectangle.

7. Draw a polygon that's about half the size of the other shapes. Hold the spacebar down before you release the mouse and drag it to position it over the center of the other objects you've drawn. Don't deselect the polygon.

   ■ It doesn't matter what the fill and stroke attributes are.

8. Choose Object ⇨ Path ⇨ Divide Objects Below.

9. With the Selection tool, drag the pieces apart.

   ■ Notice that the individual pieces have the same attributes as their original shapes. It's like a jigsaw puzzle.

10. In the Layers palette, show the cyan rectangle layer.

    ■ It wasn't cut because it was hidden.

11. With the Pen tool, draw a wavy line. Apply a 4 pt dark blue stroke and a red fill.

12. With the Line Segment tool, draw a straight segment and place it diagonally somewhere on the wavy line.

13. With the line still selected, choose Object ⇨ Path ⇨ Divide Objects Below.

    ■ The wavy line wasn't just sliced where the straight line was lying across it, it was converted to several individual pieces.

14. Drag the separate pieces apart.

15. Close this document without saving it to a file.

Offset a Copy of a Path

Use the Offset Copy command (**Object ➪ Path ➪ Offset Path**) to place a copy of the original path around the outside or the inside of it by a specified amount. The copy of the path is reshaped automatically to be a larger or smaller version of the original path.

 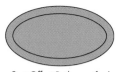

Object copy scaled to 75% and center points aligned. Spacing between the two shapes is uneven.

-9 pt Offset Path specified. Spacing between the two shapes is even.

You can apply the Offset Path command to an open or closed path, but the resulting path after the Offset Path command is applied is always a closed path. This means that an open path will end up with an offset path on both sides of it.

When an irregularly shaped path is scaled, larger or smaller, it probably won't align perfectly with the original path. Using the Offset Path, the second path aligns perfectly with the original path.

To offset a copy of a path:

1. Select the path (or paths) you want to offset. In most cases you'll want to have the Selection tool in the Toolbox active rather than the Direct-Selection tool to be sure the entire path is selected.

2. Display the Offset Path dialog box:

    ■ Choose **Object ➪ Path ➪ Offset Path**.

3. **Offset** — Enter a positive number in the field to place a copy of the path that distance around the *outside* of the original path. Enter a negative number to place the copy that distance *inside* the original path. All sides of the new copy are an equal distance in all directions from the original path. The value in the offset field should be larger or smaller than the size of the stroke weight that is applied to the path so they don't overlap one another.

    ■ Offset paths that are larger than the original path are placed *behind* the original path. Offset paths that are smaller than the original path are placed *in front of* the original path.

4. **Joins** — Click the arrows to display the drop-down menu and make your choice from the three options for the type of corner you want the new offset path to have. They're the same options that are available in the Stroke palette.

Type characters can be offset after they're converted to outlines.

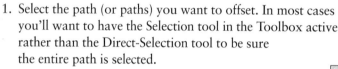

Specify how far to offset a path, the type of join you want it to have, and its miter limit in the Offset Path dialog box

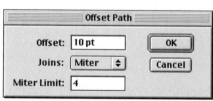

Options in the pop-up menu for the types of joins are the same as those available in the Stroke palette

- Sometimes the offset path has funky corners where paths overlap. You can fix the shape by applying the Merge command from the Pathfinder palette. This command is discussed later in this chapter.

5. **Miter Limit** — When Miter is the Join type selected, enter a high Miter Limit value if you want long pointed corners. A low Miter Limit value creates a bevel join.

6. Click OK or press *return/enter*.

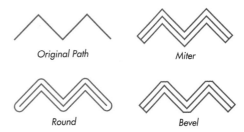

Original Path   *Miter*

Round   *Bevel*

Examples of the types of joins available when offsetting a path

activity 9.14

1. Create a new document: Letter size, CMYK color mode. Save it into your Practice Folder as an .eps file named Offset Path Practice.eps.

2. Draw a 1½"×1" round-corner rectangle, with a 0.167 corner radius. Apply a white fill and a 6 pt red stroke.

3. With the object still selected, choose Object ⇨ Path ⇨ Offset Path. Enter 6 pt in the Offset field of the Offset Path dialog box that displays.

   - Entering an offset that's the same width as the stroke produces abutting paths.

4. Color the new stroke a dark blue.

5. Select the red stroke, then double-click the Scale tool in the Toolbox to display the Scale dialog box and enter 110 in the Scale field in the Uniform section.

6. Click the Preview box to see how enlarging the stroke compares to creating an Offset path.

   - The red stroked object that was scaled to 110% matched the width of the blue stroked object, but the corners don't match up and the height of the object is off a little.

7. Click OK or press *return/enter*.

8. Move to a clear spot on your document page and display the grid.

9. With the Pen tool, draw a path similar to the one shown here (CMB). Apply a 3 pt black stroke, no fill.

10. With the path selected, choose Object ⇨ Path ⇨ Offset Path and enter 6 pt in the Offset field. Click OK or press *return/enter*.

11. Deselect the path. With the Selection tool, select the original path (stroke), leaving the outside path deselected.

12. Change the stroke to 3 pt 100% yellow.

13. With the Direct Selection tool, select the outside path (the offset path). Change the stroke to None and the fill to 95% cyan, 75% magenta, 0% yellow, 0% black.

14. Deselect the shape.

15. Save your file and close the document.

Convert a Stroke Into an Object

Illustrator has provided two commands for changing a stroke into an object. The Outline Stroke command in the Object menu allows you to convert a stroke applied to a path into an object. Fill and stroke attributes applied to the stroke are applied to the newly-created stroke object, including join and endcap settings. You can apply different fill, stroke, effects, and so on, to this new object the same as any other object you create. Dashed stroke patterns can't be converted to objects, though.

When a stroke is converted to an object, it becomes a compound path that's separate from the original object. You end up with two separate objects, the fill object and the stroke object. Compound paths are discussed later in this chapter.

Unfortunately, once you've converted a stroke to an object, you can't change it back to a regular stroke without using the Undo command. This, of course, eliminates any functions you've performed since the Outline Stroke command was used. When you click in the fill of the original object, the path line follows the path line of the original stroke.

12 pt Stroke
applied to object

Stroke converted
to an object

Outlining a Stroke

To convert a stroke to an object using the Outline Stroke command:

1. Select the path with the Selection tool or the Lasso tool.

2. Choose **Object** ⇨ **Path** ⇨ **Outline Stroke**.

Expanding a Stroke

To convert a stroke to an object using the Expand command:

1. Select the path with the Selection tool or the Lasso tool.

2. Choose **Object** ⇨ **Expand** to display the Expand dialog box.

3. In the Expand section of the dialog box, click everything off except the Stroke checkbox. Click OK or press *return/enter*.

activity 9.15

1. Create a new document: Letter size, CMYK color mode. Name it Button.eps and save it into your Practice Folder as an .eps file.

2. On the document page, draw a 1½" circle. Apply a 12 pt black stroke, any fill color. Leave the object selected.

3. Create a Linear gradient that is 100% Cyan, 50% Magenta, 0% Yellow, and 0% Black on the lefthand Gradient Slider and 50% Cyan, 0% Magenta, 0% Yellow, and 0% Black on the righthand Gradient Slider. The angle is 0.

4. Create a gradient swatch for this gradient.

   ■ Drag the Gradient Fill box and drop it in the Swatches palette. Name it Button gradient.

5. Convert the stroke into an object by choosing Object ⇨ Path ⇨ Outline Stroke.

6. Apply the same gradient swatch to the stroke object, except, in the Gradient palette, change the angle to 180°.

7. On a clean place on your page, draw a 1½" square. Apply the same Button gradient.

8. Draw a 1" circle and place it inside the square. Align the center points.

9. Apply the Button gradient and change the angle to 180°.

10. Select both objects and blend them by choosing Object ⇨ Blend ⇨ Make.

11. Change angle values in the Gradient palette to alter the appearance of the buttons.

12. Save the file and close the document.

Average and Join Anchor Points

Illustrator provides two commands in the Object menu for aligning and joining selected anchor points, the Average command and the Join command.

Averaging Anchor Points

The Average command can be applied to two or more anchor points or endpoints on the same path or on different paths. Illustrator calculates the average of selected points along the horizontal or vertical axes, or both, and realigns all selected points that are the average of their current location.

To average anchor points:

1. With the Direct Selection tool or the Direct Select Lasso tool, marquee or *Shift*-click to select the points you want to realign.

2. Display the Average dialog box:

   ■ Choose **Object ⇨ Path ⇨ Average**

   or

   ■ Press ⌥ ⌘ j

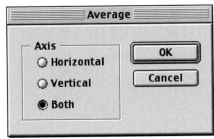

Average two or more anchor points along the horizontal axis, the vertical axis, or along both axes

or

■ Display the context-sensitive menu and choose **Average**.
  - *Macintosh:* ⌃-click
  - *Windows:* Right-click

3. Click one of the three radio buttons:
   - ■ **Horizontal** — Aligns selected anchor points horizontally (*x* axis).
   - ■ **Vertical** — Aligns selected anchor points vertically (*y* axis).
   - ■ **Both** — Moves selected anchor points and segments and positions them one on top of the other. This is the program default.
     - ▪ This can be accomplished by using the Join command (see below) to join the anchor points, also.

4. Click OK or press *return/enter*.

Joining Anchor Points

In Step 4, *The Pen & Pencil Tools*, you learned to join anchor points using the Pen tool. The Join command in the Object menu performs the same function. You can join two endpoints of an open path to create a larger open path or a closed path. Unless the endpoints are precisely on top of one another, a straight segment connects the two anchor points.

To connect the endpoints of an open path:

1. With the Direct Selection tool or the Direct Select Lasso tool, select the endpoints of an open path.

2. Choose **Object** ⇨ **Path** ⇨ **Join**

   or

   Press ⌘ j

   or

   Display the context-sensitive menu and choose Join.
   - *Macintosh:* ⌃-click
   - *Windows:* Right-click

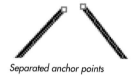

Separated anchor points

Anchor points lying one on top of the other after Average command is applied

To join, you must select two open endpoints. If they are not on the same path, they cannot be on text paths nor inside graphs, and if both of them are grouped, they must be in the same group.

OK

If you attempt to join two endpoints in a graph or in different groups, this warning box displays

Close an Open Path Without Adding a Segment To join two selected endpoints without creating a new straight segment, the endpoints must be *precisely* on top of one another. You can let Illustrator determine the resulting shape by performing the Average command (**Object** ⇨ **Path** ⇨ **Average**) to place the endpoints on top of one another in the middle between the two points. Or you can determine the final shape of the object by dragging the anchor points as close as you can (enlarge the view as large as possible), perform the Average command, then the perform Join command.

If two endpoints are coincident (one on top of the other) when the Join command is performed, the Join dialog box displays.

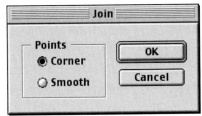

Choose the type of anchor point you want to end up with when you join two anchor points into one

- Click the Corner radio button to join corner points into a single corner point.

- Click the Smooth radio button to join two smooth points into a single smooth point with direction lines.

- Click OK or press *return/enter* to exit the dialog box.

1. Create a new document: Letter size, CMYK color mode.

2. Draw a 1" circle on the document page with a fill of white, 1 pt black stroke.

   - All anchor points should be selected.

3. Choose Object ➪ Path ➪ Average ➪ Both.

   - Your circle should look like the one shown here because all the anchor points are now on top of each other in the center of the shape.

4. Draw a triangle on the page, starting at the top of the shape and ending back at the top, but don't join the last segments.

5. Deselect the path.

6. Zoom in close, choose the Direct Lasso tool, and circle the top two anchor points to select them.

7. Choose Object ➪ Path ➪ Average and verify that the Both button is selected.

   - This action puts the two anchor points on top of each other.

8. Choose Object ➪ Path ➪ Join and verify that the Corner button is selected.

   - Converts the two anchors points into one anchor point, closing the path.

9. Press ⌘z twice to undo the Join and Average commands, ending with the original open path.

10. Deselect the path.

11. With the Direct Lasso tool, circle the top two anchor points again, then press ⇧ ⌥ ⌘ j (jay).

   - This action joins the two anchor points and converts them to one anchor point all in one action.

12. Close the document without saving changes.

413

Compound Paths

A compound path is two or more separate paths combined into one object. You can combine as many paths as you want into a compound path. Where objects in a compound path overlap, a transparent hole is created so you can see what's behind them. The auto shown here is an example of the use of the Compound Path command.

The compound path command was applied to the windows and tires of the car so the background would show through

Some of the functions you perform create compound paths automatically, such as outlining strokes, which was discussed previously in this chapter. But you can create your own compound paths, too. Compound paths can be created using open or closed paths.

Individual paths in a compound path are called subpaths. Subpaths can be manipulated as you would a regular path by selecting them with the Direct Selection tool. To select the entire compound path, select it with the Selection tool or ⌥-click it with the Direct Selection tool.

Only one fill or stroke color or stroke weight can be applied to a compound path. Once you apply the Compound Path command, all objects assume the fill attributes of the backmost object in the stacking order. Changing the fill or stroke of one subpath in a compound path applies the same changes to all the other subpaths, too. Converting a compound path back into it's individual components does not reapply an object's original fill attributes.

- A compound path is designated in the Layers palette as **\<Compound Path\>**. Subpaths are all placed on the frontmost object's layer (because Illustrator thinks it's a single path).

Creating a Compound Path

To convert two or more objects into a compound path:

1. With the Selection tool, marquee or *Shift*-click to select all the objects you want to convert into a single compound path.

   - Place smaller objects in front of larger objects in the stacking order.

2. Choose **Object ⇨ Compound Path ⇨ Make**

   or

   Press ⌘8

   or

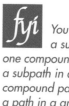

read this!

Printing errors can occur if an illustration has too many compound paths or if a compound path is composed of complex subpaths.

fyi You can't join a subpath in one compound path to a subpath in another compound path or to a path in a group. You must release the compound path and ungroup the grouped paths first.

If the objects aren't grouped, you can choose **Make Compound Path** from the context-sensitive menu.

- *Macintosh:* ⋏-click
- *Windows:* Right-click

■ You can't create a compound path with two individual objects belonging to two different compound paths or two different groups. If you attempt it, a warning box displays.

Adding Paths to an Existing Compound Path

To add objects to an existing compound path, select the compound path and the objects you want to add to it with the Selection tool (marquee or *Shift*-click). Then use one of the methods described above to create a new compound path.

You can also cut (⌘x) objects and paste them in front of (**Edit ⇨ Paste in Front,** or ⌘f) or in back of (**Edit ⇨ Paste in Back,** or ⌘b) a selected subpath in the compound path, making them part of the compound path. If the entire compound path is selected when you paste objects in front or in back, the pasted objects *do not* become part of the compound path.

Changing the Direction of the Subpath

To create the transparent "holes" in a compound path, Illustrator assigns a direction to the paths, either clockwise or counterclockwise. When paths are combined into a compound path, Illustrator assigns a clockwise direction to the backmost path. All subpaths are assigned a counterclockwise direction.

If you have only two paths combining into a compound path, the command works every time. But when you have more than one subpath, problems can arise. The transparent "holes" may not be where you want them. You can fix the problem by changing the direction of the compound path or its subpaths. To change the direction of subpaths in a compound path:

1. Deselect everything.
   - ■ Press ⇧⌘a

   or

   - ■ Choose **Select ⇨ Deselect.**

2. Display the Attributes palette (Figure 9.8).
   - ■ Choose **Window ⇨ Attributes**

   or

   - ■ Click on the Attributes folder tab in a palette.

3. With the Direct Selection tool, select the individual subpath in the compound path for which you want to change direction. *Shift*-click to select more than one subpath, but don't select the whole compound path.

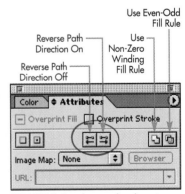

FIGURE 9.8 Change the direction of a subpath by clicking a button in the Attributes palette.

415

4. Click the Reverse Path Direction button that isn't highlighted.

■ If neither of the buttons is active, the entire compound path is probably selected.

Releasing a Compound Path

When subpaths in a compound path are converted back into their original separate paths, which you can do at any time, the attributes of the compound path are applied to all separate subpaths. In the Layers palette, the objects are all displayed on object layers in the top-level layer or sublayer that originally contained the compound path.

To release the subpaths in a compound path, select the compound path with the Selection tool, and

■ Choose **Object** ⇨ **Compound Path** ⇨ **Release**

or

■ Press ⌘ ⌥ 8

or

■ If the objects aren't grouped, you can choose Release Compound Path from the context-sensitive menu.

▪ *Macintosh:* ⌃-click
▪ *Windows:* Right-click

Remove a Single Path from a Compound Path

You can remove a single subpath from a compound path without releasing the whole compound path:

1. Select the subpath with the Direct Selection tool.

2. Press the *Delete* key (*Windows* users can also press *Backspace*)

or

Press ⌘ x to cut the path.

■ If you want to save the path that you cut from the compound path, paste it back into the document (⌘ v).

 When type characters having an interior shape, such as the letters a, b, e, p, and others, are converted to outlines, they become compound paths automatically. If you release these compound paths, the fill and stroke attributes of the interior shape (called a counter) become the same as the outer portion of the character.

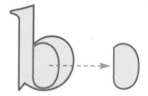

 *activity 9.17*

1. Create a new document: Letter size, CMYK color mode. Save it as an .eps file into your Practice Folder named Cheese.eps.

2. Draw a 4½" × 2½" oval on the page. Apply a fill of cyan 100%, 82% magenta, 30% yellow, 0% black. No stroke.

3. Drag the color box in the Color palette to the Swatches palette and change it to a global process color.

4. Choose Object ⇨ Path ⇨ Offset Path and enter –2p6 in the Offset field. Click OK or press *return/enter.*

Continued

5. Change the color of this interior oval to 60% of the swatch you just created.

6. On a clear spot on the page near the circles, draw a 3½" × 1½" rectangle. Fill it with 20% magenta, 60% yellow. No stroke.

7. Deselect the object. Then reselect it with the Direct Selection tool so that all anchor points are hollow.

8. Select the upper right anchor point and drag it to the left (as shown).

9. Select the object with the Selection tool. Choose the Free Transform tool in the Toolbox.

10. Start to drag the upper left corner slightly, then hold down the ⌘ key and continue dragging to reshape the object, as shown.

11. Choose the Rotate tool in the Toolbox and rotate from the center about 20°.

   ■ Check the Info palette to verify the rotation angle.

12. Drag the yellow object and place it on the blue object, as shown.

13. With the Pencil tool, draw several randomly sized and shaped roundish objects on the yellow rectangle.

14. Select the yellow rectangle and all the random circles you just drew, choose Object ➪ Compound Path ➪ Make.

15. Draw a 6½" × 4" rectangle. Fill with the Jungle Stripe pattern swatch.

16. Send to the back of the stack and position behind the swiss cheese on the plate.

17. Save the file but don't close the document.

18. With the Selection tool, select the cheese. Choose Object ➪ Compound Path ➪ Release.

   ■ The "holes" in the cheese disappear, leaving only the paths of the circles.

19. Close the document without saving changes to the file.

The Knife Tool

Use the Knife tool (hidden under the Scissors tool (✂) in the Toolbox) to slice an object in the shape of the freeform path you draw with the tool. It's similar to using the Divide Objects Below command, except underlying objects are cut as you draw a path with the Knife tool. It works on filled open and closed paths, but not on an open path with a fill of None.

A major difference between using the Knife tool and using the Divide Objects Below command to cut objects is that if a path is selected when it's cut with the Knife tool, all other paths are left alone and only the selected

Knife tool icon in the Toolbox palette

417

path is cut. If no paths are selected, when the Knife tool cuts through them, all paths the Knife moves over are cut.

- If you draw a path with the Knife tool that's completely inside another object, the resulting shape becomes a compound path.

- Stroke and fill attributes applied to the objects being cut are applied to the new "pieces" that are cut off.

- When a filled, open path is cut with the Knife tool, each dip in the path is converted to an individual object with the same fill and stroke color as the original path.

To cut an object with the Knife tool:

1. Select a path or a grouped object if you only want the selected items to be cut.

2. Choose the Knife tool in the Toolbox (⌴).

3. Draw a cutting path where you want the cut (or cuts) to be made.

   - To cut in a straight line, hold down the ⌥ key as you drag.

   - To keep the cut horizontal, vertical, or at a 45° angle, hold the *Shift* keys down.

   - To keep the cut straight and horizontal, vertical, or at a 45° angle, hold the *Shift* and ⌥ keys down.

4. Deselect the objects, then select the knifed object with the Selection tool and move or delete it.

activity 9.18

1. Open the file named Cheese.eps that you created in Activity 9.17.

2. Zoom in so you can see the cheese easily.

3. Select the slice of cheese.

4. Choose the Knife tool in the Toolbox and slice off, in an oval shape, some of the edges of the cheese, as shown.

   - Make sure the path of the Knife tool begins and ends outside the edge of the cheese.

5. Deselect all.

6. With the Selection or Direct Selection tool, select the knifed sections and drag them off the object to the scratch area of the artboard, or delete them.

7. Use the Save As command to rename the file Knife Tool Practice.eps and save it into your Practice folder.

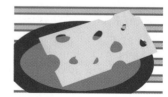

8. Close the artwork window.

The Pathfinder Palette

The commands in the Pathfinder palette (choose **Window** ➪ **Pathfinder** or press ⇧ *F9*) contains commands for combining multiple objects into a single compound shape. Most of the resulting shapes could be created using other Illustrator tools, but the commands in this palette make it much easier to accomplish.

- Commands in the Pathfinder palette cannot be applied to mesh objects.
- Complex objects, such as gradients and blends, combined by using commands in the Pathfinder palette can use a lot of memory.

The Pathfinder palette (Figure 9.9) consists of two sections: Shape Modes and Pathfinders. When Shape Mode commands are applied to overlapping selected objects, a compound shape is produced that can be modified. Pathlines of the objects used to create the shape are visible when the object is selected.

Commands found in the Pathfinder palette can also be applied to objects by choosing the corresponding command in the Effect menu (**Effect** ➪ **Pathfinder** ➪ **[command]**). The difference is that applying the commands from the Pathfinder palette actually changes the objects, but when the commands are applied from the Effect menu, the original paths are not affected — only the appearance of the paths is changed, and paths can be restored easily to their original state. The Effect command function in Illustrator is discussed in Step 11, *Filters & Filter Effects*.

Pathfinder Options

Settings in the Pathfinder Options dialog box apply to all Pathfinder commands. To display the Pathfinder Options dialog box, display the Pathfinder palette Options menu and choose Pathfinder Options.

- **Precision** — Determines how precisely Illustrator calculates the effects of the Pathfinder commands. A higher number causes Illustrator to draw the resulting object more accurately, but it also slows down processing time, sometimes considerably.

- **Remove Redundant Points** — Removes all duplicate anchor points in the same location (one anchor point on top of another anchor point) when a Pathfinder command is applied to selected objects. It's a good idea to have this box checked because I can't think of a reason for ever needing to have overlapping anchor points.

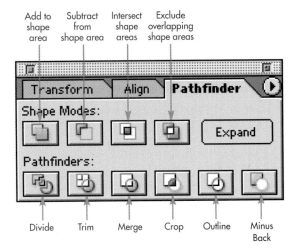

FIGURE 9.9 The Pathfinder palette contains options for combining two or more selected objects into compound paths.

- **Divide and Outline Will Remove Unpainted Artwork** — Any *non*overlapping areas of the original objects that have a fill of None will be deleted if this box is checked when the Divide or Outline command is applied to selected objects. Check this box so you don't have to remove paths that are filled or stroked with None.

Options selected in the Pathfinder Options dialog box control how commands in the Pathfinder palette are applied to objects

Shape Mode Options

Shape Mode commands in the Pathfinder palette can be applied to two or more individual objects, text (editable text and outlines), blends, groups, compound paths, warp, and so on. You can't apply a Shape Mode command to objects that are grouped, but you can apply it to a group and an individual object that isn't in the group. When text is combined with objects, the Shape Mode commands can be applied without converting the characters to outlines.

In the Layers palette, the original objects are displayed as object layers within a Compound Shape layer (<Compound Shape>). Objects on individual object layers can be moved, modified, and restacked, which updates the compound shape automatically. It isn't necessary to release or expand the object first.

Add to Shape Area (▣*)* (Figure 9.10A) Creates a shape using only the outside edges of the selected overlapping shapes. Interior edges of the objects are ignored. Any "holes" between overlapping objects are reversed out of the compound shape. Fill and stroke attributes applied to the frontmost object are applied to the resulting compound shape.

- *Non*-overlapping objects become part of the compound shape and assume the fill and stroke attributes of the topmost object.

- Illustrator automatically closes open paths before joining the selected objects.

Subtract from Shape Area (▣*)* (Figure 9.10B) All objects in front of the backmost object are removed from the backmost object, joining all the outside edges of the objects. The resulting compound shape retains the fill and stroke attributes of the backmost object.

Intersect Shape Areas (▣*)* (Figure 9.10C) Only overlapping portions of selected shapes are retained. Non-overlapping portions of the shape are clipped. Fill and stroke attributes applied to the topmost object are applied to the resulting compound shape.

read this!

If the compound shape commands don't work on selected objects, check to make sure the objects aren't grouped. Grouped objects can't be used in compound shapes.

Exclude Overlapping Shape Areas () (Figure 9.10D)

Overlapping portions of selected shapes become transparent. Fill and stroke attributes applied to the topmost object are applied to the resulting compound shape. Even though it looks like a compound path, you can't change the path direction like you can with a compound path you created using the Make Compound Path command in the Object menu.

Expand Compound Shapes

When you expand a compound shape that was created with a Shape mode command, the pathlines of the original objects are removed, creating a single path. It's the same function as flattening the object. If the compound shape has "holes," a compound path is created. To expand a compound shape:

1. Select the entire shape.

2. Click the Expand button on the Pathfinder palette

   or

   Display the Pathfinder palette Options menu and choose **Expand Compound Shape**.

timesaver
To apply the last command used in the Pathfinder palette again, press ⌘ 4. You can display the Pathfinder palette Options menu and choose Repeat [command name], too, but it's not a timesaver.

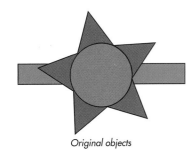

Original objects

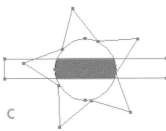

A

Add to shape area — Outside edges of objects combined to create shape

B

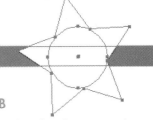

Subtract from shape area — Objects in front of the backmost object are subtracted from the shape and become transparent

C

Intersect shape areas — Only the portion of the objects that overlap is preserved

D

Exclude overlapping shape areas — Portions of objects that overlap become transparent

FIGURE 9.10 Examples of objects after Shape Mode commands have been applied.

Step 9 — RESHAPE, COMBINE, & DISTORT OBJECTS

421

Release Compound Shapes

Releasing a compound shape that was created with a Shape mode command restores the individual objects into their original appearance. To release a compound shape:

1. Select the entire shape.

2. Display the Pathfinder palette Options menu and choose Release Compound Shape.

Pathfinder Commands

When the Pathfinder commands in the Pathfinder palette are applied to two or more selected objects, the resulting shape is a compound path. A compound path differs from a compound shape in that the individual objects that created the compound path can't be modified after it's created. When working with Pathfinder commands in the Pathfinder palette, it's a good idea to work on a copy of the objects in the event you want to start over.

Pathfinder commands in the Pathfinder palette can be applied to brushstrokes, objects filled with gradients or patterns, and objects that have effects applied to them. But unlike compound shapes, type characters must be converted to outlines to be included in the resulting compound path. If they aren't converted to outlines, they're ignored.

■ Unlike compound shapes created using the Shape Mode commands, objects combined using commands from the Pathfinders section of the Pathfinder palette retain their original fill and stroke characteristics.

Divide (⬚) Overlapping objects are cut into separate non-overlapping objects that keep their original fill and stroke attributes. It's like creating a jigsaw puzzle of all the intersecting paths. After deselecting the object, you can select individual paths with the Direct Selection tool or the Direct Lasso tool and move them or change their attributes.

■ To make part of the object transparent (see-through), select a path and apply a fill of None or press the *delete* key to eliminate the path.

Trim (⬚) Overlapping objects behind the frontmost object are deleted. Strokes are removed. All paths are separated where they intersect with the frontmost object, even if they're the same fill color.

timesaver
To change a Shape Mode command into a Pathfinder command, hold down the ⌥ key when clicking the Shape Mode button in the Pathfinder palette.

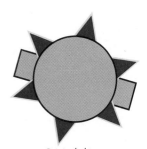

Original objects

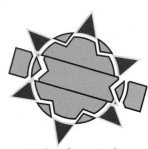

Divide Paths are cut where they intersect, creating a jigsaw puzzle-like object

Merge (▣) Overlapping objects behind the frontmost object are deleted. Strokes are removed. Objects having the same fill color and shade become part of the frontmost object. All other paths are separated where they intersect with the frontmost object.

Crop (▣) "Cookie-cutter" command. The topmost object is used as a pattern to delete overlapping objects extending beyond its boundaries. Strokes are removed; the backmost object keeps its original fill color. The topmost object is deleted. Portions of any objects that extend beyond the edges of the topmost object are deleted. Only the portions of the overlapping paths or objects behind the frontmost object are kept. The original top object is deleted. Fill color of the backmost object is applied to resulting object and strokes are removed.

Outline (▣) Objects become separate line segments where paths intersect. The fill is removed and a stroke with a weight of 0 is applied to each segment. Stroke color for each segment becomes the fill color of the original object. You can specify a different stroke weight to these paths. In fact, if you want the paths to print, you must specify a stroke weight.

- Any transparency settings applied to the objects are retained.

Minus Back (▣) The backmost object is cut out of the frontmost object and the resulting shape has the fill and stroke attributes that were applied to the frontmost object.

- To cut the backmost object out of two or more selected *non*overlapping paths that are in front of it in the stacking order, make them a compound path. Then Illustrator treats them as a single path and will cut the backmost object out of all objects.

- If selected objects don't overlap, the backmost object is deleted.

Trim Objects behind and that overlap the frontmost object are deleted. Strokes are removed. Objects with the same fill color remain separate objects.

Merge Functions the same as the Trim command except that overlapping objects with the same fill color as the frontmost object merge to become part of the frontmost object

Crop "Cookie-cutter" command. Topmost object is used as pattern to delete overlapping objects extending beyond its boundaries. Strokes are removed; backmost object keeps its original fill color. Topmost object is deleted.

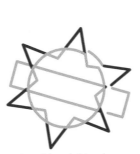

Outline Selected objects become line segments the same color as the fill color of the original object. Segments are broken where paths overlap.

Minus Back Backmost object deletes all objects overlapping topmost object and all portions extending beyond the outside edge of topmost object

423

 activity 9.19

1. Open the file you saved in your practice folder as My Posie.eps. Save it save back into your Practice folder as an .eps file named Pathfinder Practice.eps.

2. With the Selection tool, marquee to select all the objects that make up the posie.

3. *Shift*-click the center circle to deselect it.

4. Display the Pathfinder palette and click the Merge button in the Pathfinders section.

   ■ Interior paths of all the circles that make up the pink part of the posie are converted to one object without altering its original shape.

5. Undo the last command to return the posie to its original state.

6. Select all the paths, including the center circle, and click the Exclude Overlapping Shape Areas button. Deselect the object.

   ■ All objects are now the color of the frontmost object (the center circle) and are separate paths.

7. With the Direct Selection tool or the Lasso Direct Select tool, select some of the paths and move them around.

8. Use the Revert command (press *F12* or choose File ⇨ Revert) to return the file to its last-saved version.

9. Again, select all the circles except the center one.

10. Click the Merge button in the Pathfinders section of the Pathfinder palette to combine these paths into one object.

11. Select all the paths of the object.

12. Display the grid (View ⇨ Show Grid).

13. Choose Object ⇨ Compound Path ⇨ Make to create a compound path.

   ■ The center is now transparent and grid lines are visible through the center circle.

14. Close the document without saving the changes.

15. Open the file you saved into your Practice folder as Rotate Practice.eps.

16. Select all the paths in the object shown here.

17. Click each of the Pathfinder buttons, then click off so you can see the results of the command. Between each button, press the Undo command until you get back to the original file, or choose the Revert command in the File menu.

   ■ Move some of the individual paths around or delete some to create a different design. Recolor some of the paths. In general, play around with the design.

18. Unless you want to save the object, close the file without saving changes.

19. Create a new document: Letter size, CMYK color mode.

20. Draw three or four overlapping shapes and apply different fill and stroke attributes to each.

21. Experiment with the different commands in the Pathfinder palette.

22. Save the practice file into your Practice folder or close it without saving the changes.

Align and Distribute Objects

When you have multiple objects that need to be lined up in a row or a column (align) or objects that need to be evenly spaced (distribute), use the commands available in the Align palette (**Window** ⇨ **Align**). To show the Distribute Spacing panel, display the Align palette Options menu and choose Show Options (Figure 9.11).

■ You can apply several Align or Distribute commands to the same objects to achieve different results.

■ Aligning and Distributing objects does not affect their stacking order.

Align Objects

Click one of the six buttons in the Align Objects section of the palette to align two or more objects. Click one of the Horizontal buttons to align the left edges, center points, or right edges of objects. The Vertical buttons align the top edges, the center points, or the bottom edges of all selected objects. The icons in the palette represent graphically the results of applying a particular command.

Objects that are aligned horizontally don't change their vertical positions. For example, if you select several objects and click the Horizontal Align Left button, if they overlap vertically, they'll just pile up at the left margin.

Key Object The object that determines where the other objects are positioned is called the Key object. The Key object varies, depending upon the command being used. When you click the Horizontal Align Left button, the leftmost object is the Key object and remains stationary and the left edges of the other selected objects align with the left edge of it. When you click the Horizontal Align Right button, the rightmost object is the Key object. When you click Horizontal Align Center, though, the center points of all selected objects are aligned with the horizontal center of the bounding box that surrounds all the objects. There is no real Key object in that case.

You don't have to always use the default Key object. As long as Align to

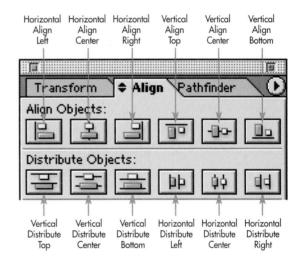

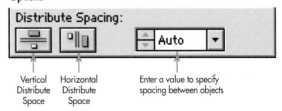

FIGURE 9.11 Line up two or more objects in different ways using the Align palette. By displaying the palette options menu, you can space objects evenly.

Artboard in the Align palette Options menu is unchecked, you can specify a different object as the Key object that the other selected objects align with:

1. With the Selection tool, select all the objects you want to line up or distribute.

2. Click an object other than the default Key object for the alignment button you're going to use.

3. Click the alignment button you want.

To revert back to the default Key object, display the Align palette Options menu and choose Cancel Key Object.

Use Preview Bounds Illustrator normally aligns objects by the path line of the object. If a stroke is applied, the visual edge of the object is the outer edge of the stroke. Because the stroke is centered on the path line, that means half the width of the stroke weight is outside the path line. To align objects at the edge of the stroke rather than the path line, display the Align palette Options menu and choose Use Preview Bounds.

Distribute Objects

The buttons in the Distribute Objects section of the palette adjust the position of objects so the edges or the center points of the objects are an equal distance apart. You must have at least three objects selected for these commands to work. Choose a Horizontal button to specify a side-to-side relationship between objects, a Vertical button to specify an up-and-down relationship.

That doesn't mean, necessarily, that the objects will have an equal amount of "white" space between them. When you specify to distribute objects, for example, by clicking the Horizontal distribute center button, the center points of the objects are an equal distance apart. If the objects are different widths, the visual "white" space between them can vary considerably. The Distribute Spacing buttons can fix the problem (see the following page).

Align to Artboard

When the Align to Artboard option is checked in the Align palette Options menu, selected objects align at the top, bottom, right edge, or left edge of the artboard, rather than to a Key Object. Display the Align palette Options menu and choose Align to Artboard, then click one of the Align or Distribute buttons to determine how the objects are aligned. For example, to distribute objects vertically and align to the artboard, the topmost of the selected objects aligns with the top of the artboard, the bottommost object aligns with the bottom of the artboard, and the other objects are positioned between them.

Distribute Spacing

Display the Align palette Options menu and click Show Options to expand the palette to show the two Distribute Spacing options and field. When Auto is the selection in the field, the two objects that are the farthest apart, either horizontally or vertically, depending upon which button you click, remain in place. The location of the other objects is adjusted so that equal space is between each object. The relative vertical and horizontal positions don't change, just the spacing between them.

To specify an exact distance between selected objects:

1. Select all objects.

2. With the Selection tool, click on one object to designate it as the Key object.

   ■ The designated Key object determines the starting point for adjusting the spacing of the objects.

   ■ If you forget to designate a Key object, a warning box displays.

3. Enter a value in the field.

4. Click one of the Distribute Spacing buttons.

   ■ Click Vertical Distribute Space to put an equal amount of "white" space between the top and bottom edges of all objects.

   ■ Click Horizontal Distribute Space to put and equal amount of "white" space between the right and left edges of all objects.

   ■ All objects, even the outermost objects, will probably move to achieve equal spacing between all objects.

1. Create a new document: Letter size, CMYK color mode.

2. Draw five shapes on your page, all with a white fill: one circle with no stroke, one square with a 2 pt blue stroke, one star with a 6 pt red stroke, one polygon with an 8 pt purple stroke, and one rectangle with a 12 pt yellow stroke. Scatter them randomly on your page.

3. Select all the objects, display the Align palette (Window ⇨ Align), and click the Horizontal Align Center button.

   ■ The center points of all the objects are lined up.

   ■ Notice that the stacking order of the objects hasn't changed.

4. With the objects still selected, click the Vertical Align Center button.

   ■ All the objects are placed one on top of the other because their center points are aligned horizontally and vertically.

5. Undo the last command.

Continued

6. Display the Align palette Options menu and click Align to Artboard.

7. Click the Horizontal Align Right button.

   - The path lines of the right edges of all objects aligned to the right edge of the artboard (not the edge of the page).

   - Notice that the strokes of the different paths hang out past the artboard by half the weight of the stroke.

8. Display the Align palette Options menu and check Use Preview Bounds. Then click the Horizontal Align Right button again.

   - Notice that now the actual edge of the object, not the path line, is aligned with the right edge of the artboard.

9. Click the Vertical Distribute Top button.

   - Because Align to Artboard and Use Preview Bounds are still checked in the Options menu, the topmost and bottommost objects aligned with the top and bottom of the artboard and the other objects are spaces equally between them.

   - If you measure them, you'll find that in each case the top of one object is the same distance from the top of the object above or below it. That's why some objects may overlap.

10. Display the Align palette Options menu and uncheck Align to Artboard.

    - I leave Use Preview Bounds checked because I want objects to line up visually. It's up

to you whether to uncheck it or leave it checked.

11. Select each object individually and scatter them on the page again.

12. Select all the objects and click the Horizontal distribute center button.

    - The left most object (in my example, the yellow rectangle) and the right most object (in my example, the blue square) didn't move, and the left edges of all the other objects are spaced equally between them.

13. Make sure the Selection tool is selected in the Toolbox, and click one of the objects to designate it as the Key object from which the spacing is calculated.

14. Enter .25" in the Distribute Spacing field, and click the Horizontal distribute space button.

    - All objects have ¼" of white space between them.

15. With all the objects still selected, click the Vertical Align Center button to make it easier to see that there is, indeed, ¼" of white space between all the objects.

16. Continue manipulating the location of objects by clicking the different Align, Distribute, and Distribute Spacing buttons.

17. Close the document without saving it to a file.

The Liquify Tools

Illustrator 10 provides 7 new tools, called the Liquify tools (Illustrator spells the word with an *i* instead of an *e*), for distorting a selected object's shape (Figure 9.12). They're under the Warp tool in the Toolbox and only the Warp tool has a keyboard command: ⇧r. The other tools are Twirl, Pucker, Bloat, Scallop, Crystalize, and Wrinkle, and their names are descriptive of the distortion created when the tool is used.

With a liquify tool selected, hold the mouse in one spot or drag the mouse over one or more objects or a group of objects (except graphs, symbols, or text objects). Objects can contain effects, brushstrokes, styles, and appearances, and text characters must be converted to outlines (**Type ⇨ Create Outlines**). Objects don't have to be selected, but if objects are selected, other objects won't be affected by the liquify tool if you move the brush across them.

- ▪ To apply a Liquify tool to a pattern fill, expand the fill first (**Object ⇨ Expand**).

- ▪ To apply a Liquify tool to a symbol set or symbol instance, it must be unlinked from the original symbol. See Step 10, *Brushes, Patterns, & Symbols* for information about symbols.

When a Liquify tool in the Toolbox is active, the cursor changes to a round "brush." As you drag the "brush" over an object, its shape is altered and anchor points are added or removed from the paths, depending upon which tool is selected. You can adjust the size and shape of this "brush" in the Tool Options dialog box.

To affect an object, the edge of the brush must intersect an edge of the path when you click to start the drag. The brush can't be fully inside or fully outside the object. The center of the brush can be outside the object to be distorted, but an edge of the brush must be at least touching an edge of the object.

Liquify Tool Options

Display the Tool Options dialog box by double-clicking a Liquify tool in the Toolbox. The top section of the dialog box contains settings that apply to all the

fyi Warp effects can also be applied using the Effects menu (refer to Step 11, Filters & Filter Effects, for more information) and by using an envelope and the Make with Warp command in the Object menu (discussed later in this chapter).

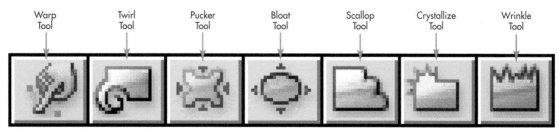

FIGURE 9.12 The Liquify tools.

tools (Global Brush Dimensions). When you change these options, they apply to all the Liquify tools. The bottom section contains settings that apply only to the selected tool.

- Reset the tool options to the default by clicking the Reset button.

- Some tools have hints pertaining to that tool at the bottom of its Options dialog box.

Global Brush Dimensions In addition to adjusting the size of the tool's "brush," Angle and Intensity values in this section of the Options dialog box control the effect of the distortion as it's applied to the object. Global brush dimensions remain in effect until they're changed for another tool or until default preferences for the Illustrator program are deleted and restored.

You can enter a value in the field, display the pop-up submenu by clicking the arrow on the right side of the field and choose a preset value, or click the up/down arrows on the left side of the field to increase or decrease the value. If a fractional value is present in the field, the first click rounds the value up or down to a whole number or to the next value divisible by 10. Subsequent clicks or *Shift*-clicks are by the whole values.

- **Width/Height** — Values control the size and shape of the "brush" and they can be entered in any unit of measure.
  - Preset values in the pop-up submenu on the right side of the field are always in points, no matter what unit of measurement is set for the document.
  - Values entered by clicking the arrows on the left side of the field vary depending upon the unit of measure entered:

	Click	*Shift*-click	Min.–Max.
Points —	1 pt	6 pt	1 pt–1000 pts
Picas —	3 pt	12 pt	p1–83p4
Inches —	⅛"	1"	0.02"–13.88"
Millimeters —	1 mm	10 mm	0.36 mm–352.77 mm
Centimeters —	0.1 cm	1 cm	0.04 cm–35.27 cm
Pixels —	1 pixel	10 pixels	1 pixel–1000 pixels

- **Angle** — This value specifies the tilt of the "brush" when its shape is an oval rather than a circle, measured counterclockwise from the vertical axis.
  - Clicking the arrows on the left side of the field increases or decreases the value by 1. To increase or decrease the value in increments of 10, *Shift*-click an arrow.

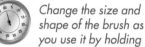

timesaver
Change the size and shape of the brush as you use it by holding down the ⬝ key and dragging toward the center of the brush shape or away from it. To change only the size of the brush without altering its shape, hold down the Shift key, too. The Global Brush Dimensions section of the Options dialog boxes reflect the changes made to the brush size and shape and apply to all tools until changed. The Undo command won't restore the brush size, either.

Brush size and shape changed — Width: 60 pt; Height: 100 pt; Angle: –25°

- **Intensity** — This value (from 1%–100%) specifies how fast and how much change is made to the shape. A lower value causes only a little change; a higher value causes greater change. For example, a value of 100% causes the distortion to follow exactly as you drag the cursor or hold it in one spot over an object. If more distortion is created than you want, lower the value.

    - Clicking the arrows on the left side of the field increases or decreases the value by 1. To increase or decrease the value in increments of 10, *Shift*-click an arrow.

- **Use Pressure Pen** — This option is available only if a pen or graphics tablet is attached to the computer. Check this option to have the pen or graphics table control the intensity of the tool.

Options Available for All Tools Some options are available for every tool and, although they appear on most of the Options dialog boxes, these options affect only the currently selected tool. Some tools have additional options and those options are explained with the discussion of the individual tool.

- **Detail** — This option is available for all Liquify tools. Enter a value in the field or move the slider (1–10) to control the spacing of anchor points that are added when the shape is distorted. A higher value places more anchor points closer together. When the Detail option is unchecked, no new anchor points are added and only the anchor points in the original shape are used.

- **Simplify** — This option is available for only the Warp, Twirl, Pucker, and Bloat tools. Enter a value in the field or move the slider (0.2–100) to eliminate unnecessary anchor points, which makes for smoother curves. The higher the value, the smoother the curves. When the Simplify option is unchecked, the resulting shape will have more anchor points than are necessary.

- **Show Brush Size** — When checked, the size and shape of the brush is visible when a Liquify tool is active.

timesaver
Increase or decrease the value in a highlighted field of a tool Option dialog box by pressing the arrows on the keyboard. Hold down the Shift key to increase the increment value by the same amount as when clicking the arrows to the left of the field.

Detail = 2, Simplify = Unchecked. Original object was a straight line segment with only two endpoints.

Detail = 8, Simplify = Unchecked. Object is too complex, with numerous unnecessary anchor points.

Detail = 8, Simplify = 50. Unnecessary anchor points were removed.

Warp Tool

The Warp tool (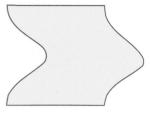) distorts paths of objects by pushing or pulling them in the direction the mouse is moved, stretching and molding them like clay.

- Leave the Detail and Simplify options checked and change values as necessary to control the smoothness of the curves.

- No additional options are available for the Warp tool.

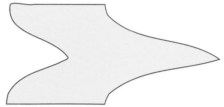

The Warp tool, using default specifications, was dragged from left to right across the center of the square

The Warp tool, with Intensity value increased to 70%, dragged in the same motion as the example above. Distortion is exaggerated.

Twirl Tool

Use the Twirl tool (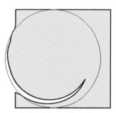) to swirl the edge of an object from the center of the brush. How far the center point of the brush is from the edge of the object determines how much swirl effect is created. If the edge of the brush is barely touching the edge of the object, the narrower the swirl path is. If the center point of the brush is on the pathline of the object, the swirl path is wider.

- The Twirl tool differs from the Twist tool (discussed previously) in that the Twist tool rotates an entire object, while the Twirl tool twirls only the portion of the object that's under the brush.

Twirl Tool Options In addition to the Detail and Simplify options, one more option is added for this tool: Twirl Rate. Enter a value in the field or move the slider (from −180° to 180°) to control the speed and amount of twirl created. A positive value produces a counterclockwise twirl; a negative value produces a clockwise twirl.

- To switch the direction of the Twirl after you've started creating it, hold down the ⌥ key. Release the mouse before releasing the ⌥ key.

Brush for the Twirl tool positioned so that only a small portion extends beyond the edge of the object. Small swirls are created.

The center point of the Twirl Tool brush was positioned on the edge of the path. Larger swirls are created.

Step 9 — RESHAPE, COMBINE, & DISTORT OBJECTS

Pucker Tool

The Pucker tool (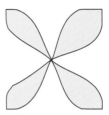) pulls the edges of the path toward the center of the brush. The closer the path gets to the center of the brush, the more it moves, until it reaches the center of the brush, where it stops.

Pucker Tool Options No additional options are available for the Pucker tool.

- Leave the Detail and Simplify options checked and change values as necessary to control the smoothness of curves.

Square was distorted by the Pucker tool

Bloat Tool

Distorting an object with the Bloat tool (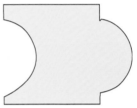) moves the object's path that's inside the cursor toward the outside edge of the brush. If the center point of the cursor is inside the object, the path is moved outward until it reaches the outside edge of the brush (plumps the path out). If the center point of the cursor is outside the object, the path is moved inward to the outside edge of the brush (takes a bite out of the object).

- You don't have to move the brush to apply the distortion effect. Just click and hold.

Distortion on the left was produced by positioning the Bloat brush slightly outside the left edge of the square. Distortion on the right was produced by positioning the Bloat brush slightly inside the right edge of the square.

Bloat Tool Options No additional options are available for the Bloat tool.

- Leave the Detail and Simplify options checked and change values as necessary to control the smoothness of curves.

Scallop Tool

The Scallop tool () creates curves or spikes along the path of an object. The path is distorted in the direction of the drag, or if the brush is held in one spot, the path moves toward the center of the brush.

Scalloped edges created by dragging edge of brush quickly around all four sides of square

Crystallize Tool

This tool ()) produces pointed arcs in the direction you drag the tool. If the brush is held in one spot, the arcs move outward from the center of the brush. So to create arcs into the interior of the object, position the center point of the brush outside the edge of the object.

Distortion created by dragging edge of Crystallize brush around all four sides of square

433

Scallop Tool and Crystallize Tool Options In addition to the Detail option, the Scallop tool Options dialog box and the Crystallize tool Options dialog box contain several more options. The Simplify option is not present for these tools.

- **Complexity** — Controls how many scallops are added to the portion of the path that's under the brush. The value ranges from 0–15; a high value creates lots of bumps or spikes that are close together. It works in conjunction with the Detail value. A high detail value together with a high Complexity value can really slow down the computer.

- **Brush Affects Anchor Points, Brush Affects In Tangent Handles, Brush Affects Out Tangent Handles** — Only one or two of these three options can be checked at one time. When Brush Affects Anchor Points is checked, the distorted paths are more pointed than round. Different combinations of the three options produce varying results. But checking or unchecking the Brush Affects In Tangent Handles and Brush Affects Out Tangent Handles appears to have little effect on the distortion as far as I could tell.

Wrinkle Tool

This tool (⊞) produces bumps and spikes along the path of an object. The amount of distortion is determined by the settings in the Wrinkle Tool Options dialog box. The longer the brush is held over an edge, the more distortion is achieved. You can drag the brush along an edge numerous times, too, to apply more wrinkle effect. This tool makes a path look like it was handdrawn.

Wrinkle Tool Options The options available for the Scallop and Crystallize tool are also present in the Wrinkle Tool Options dialog box. The only difference is that Brush Affects Anchor Points, Brush Affects In Tangent Handles, and Brush Affects Out Tangent Handles can all be checked at the same time.

In addition, Horizontal and Vertical options have been added to the dialog box to control how far apart the control points are placed. Enter values in the field, or click the up/down arrows to increase or decrease the value, or click the arrow on the right side of the field to display preset values and choose one.

- If the value in the Horizontal field is 0 and a value is entered in the Vertical field, only the Vertical field can be wrinkled. And vice versa.

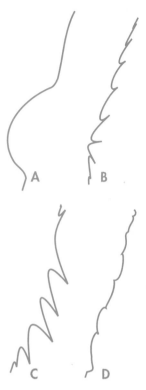

Liquify tools applied to straight line segments — A: Bloat, B: Scallop, C: Crystallize, D: Wrinkle

Distortion created by clicking and holding in each corner of square with the Wrinkle tool

activity 9.21

1. Create a new document: Letter size, CMYK color mode. Save it into your Practice folder as an .eps file named Liquify Tools.eps.

2. Draw a large star in the middle of the artwork page. Fill it with 90% cyan and 25% yellow, 1pt black stroke. Save the file.

3. Display the Warp Tool Options dialog box and click the Reset button (just in case the default settings have been changed). Click OK or press *return/enter*.

4. Drag the Warp tool over the star to distort its shape. Experiment with the tool until you're familiar with how it performs. You can press ⌘ z to undo changes and start over if you want to.

5. Revert to the last version saved (press *F12*).

6. Apply the other Liquify tools to the star, experimenting with different movements until you're familiar with the tool's operation. Between each tool selected, revert to the last version saved so you start with the original star.

7. Revert to the last saved version, which is the original star.

8. Double-click the Twirl tool in the Toolbox to display the Twirl Tool Options dialog box. Change the size of the brush to 50 pt wide and 90 pt high, with a −20% angle and 50% Intensity. Click OK or press *return/enter*.
   - Notice that the brush is now an oval and it's tilted at an angle.

9. Place the center point of the brush over an end point of the star. Click and hold until several spirals are created. Before releasing the mouse, press the ⌥ key to reverse the spiral.

10. Return to the original star, by using the Revert command *(F12)* or the Undo command *(⌘ z)*.

11. If the size of the brush is larger than the star, reduce it's size so it's smaller than the star.

12. Position the brush inside the star so it's fully enclosed by the star, then click and hold.
    - Nothing happens because the brush must be touching a path before it can distort it.

13. Release the mouse, hold down the ⌥ key, then click the mouse and move it up and down to change the size of the brush.
    - You have to press the ⌥ key before clicking the mouse to change the size of the brush.

14. Double-click the Wrinkle tool in the Toolbox to display its Options dialog box. Specify a 90 pt round brush, 0°, 50% Intensity. Click OK or press *return/enter*.

15. Drag along both sides of one point of the star.

16. Display the Wrinkle Tool Options dialog box again and change the Intensity value to 90%. Click OK or press *return/enter*.

17. Drag along both sides of a different points of the star at about the same speed as you dragged around the first star point.
    - Notice the difference in the amount of distortion between the two points of the star.

18. Draw a circle, any color, any stroke. Position it so that it doesn't overlap the star.

19. Draw a polygon, any color, any stroke. Position it so it overlaps the circle, but so that both shapes are visible.

20. With the polygon still selected, choose the Crystallize tool in the Toolbox, and drag the brush over the star.
    - The shape isn't distorted because an object in the document is selected.

21. Drag the brush over the polygon and circle.
    - Only the polygon is affected by the tool because it's selected.
    - If nothing in the document is selected, the liquify tools affect any object that is under the brush's area when you click to start the drag.

22. Experiment with the brushes, changing the values in the Tool Options dialog boxes for each tool, until you're familiar with how they work.

23. You can choose to save the file or not, then close the artwork window.

435

Envelopes

In addition to the many other ways to distort paths, Illustrator 10 provides a new feature called Envelopes that you can use to distort entire objects at the same time (Figure 9.13). An envelope is used to distort or reshape one or more selected objects. You can (a) define the shape of an envelope using an object or path you draw, (b) use predefined Warp styles, (c) create a mesh object to use as the envelope, or (d) apply Warp effects from the Effect menu.

Envelopes can be used on almost all objects created or placed in Illustrator, including linked or embedded TIFF, GIF, and JPEG images, clipping masks, type, symbol instances, and objects that have styles, effects, brushstrokes, and so on, applied to them. Objects that can't be used with envelopes include graphs, guides, and linked images except those listed in the preceding paragraph.

Objects distorted using envelopes created by using predefined styles, user-drawn shapes, and mesh objects can be edited, deleted, expanded, or released. Envelopes created using the Warp commands in the Effect menu cannot be edited by adjusting anchor points or path segments. These envelopes can be altered only by changing values in the Warp Options dialog box.

Distorting mesh objects using envelopes is discussed in Step 12, Meshes, Masks, Blends, & Transparency.

- An envelope is displayed in the Layers palette as <Envelope>. Objects in an envelope are not displayed on individual object layers until they're expanded, at which time they're listed as a <Group>.

- The more objects there are and the more complex the objects are, the longer it takes to complete the distortion.

- Scatter brush objects are not distorted when included in an envelope. Only the path to which they're applied is distorted.

To specify the type of envelope you want to use:

1. Select one or more objects to be distorted.

2. Choose **Object** ⇨ **Envelope Distort** ⇨ [choose one of the following commands]:
   - **Make with Warp,** or press ⌥⌘w
     - Creates an envelope using a preset style
   - **Make with Mesh,** or press ⌥⌘m
     - Creates an envelope from a mesh object
   - **Make with Top Object,** or press ⌥⌘c
     - Creates an envelope from a shape you draw.

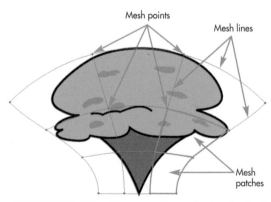

FIGURE 9.13 This object was distorted using the Shell Upper predefined Warp envelope.

Creating a Warp Envelope

The easiest way to produce an envelope distortion is to start by choosing a predefined shape supplied by Illustrator. Later in this chapter, you'll learn how to edit the envelope to customize it. You can change the predefined envelope shape to another predefined shape, too.

1. With the Selection tool, select one or more objects or a group of objects.

2. Display the Warp Options dialog box (Figure 9.14) and choose **Object ⇨ Envelope Distort ⇨ Make with Warp**

   or

   press ⌥⌘w

3. Choose options and enter values in the fields:

   ■ **Preview** — Click this checkbox to see the results of your actions as soon as you choose options.

     • A grid displays on the object being distorted.

   ■ **Style** — Choose one of the 15 predefined styles from the pop-up submenu.

   ■ **Horizontal/Vertical** — Click one of the radio buttons to determine the orientation of the predefined style.

   ■ **Bend** — Enter a value in the field, from –100 to 100, or move the slider to control the amount of distortion applied to the envelope.

     • A negative number reflects the envelope across the horizontal or vertical axis, depending upon whether the Horizontal or the Vertical radio button is chosen.

   ■ **Distortion** — Enter values in the fields, from –100 to 100, or move the sliders to apply additional distortion to the predefined envelope style.

4. Click OK or press *return/enter* to apply the distortion to the object.

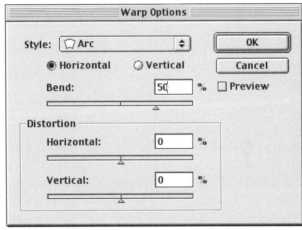

FIGURE 9.14 Changes you make in the Warp Options dialog box control the shape of the warp envelope.

Predefined warp envelope styles in the Warp Options dialog box

Step 9 — RESHAPE, COMBINE, & DISTORT OBJECTS

437

Change an Existing Warp Style To change the Warp style of an existing Warp envelope or to revert back to the original warp shape for a warp style that you've made changes to:

1. With the Selection tool, select the distorted object.

2. Choose **Object** ⇨ **Envelope Distort** ⇨ **Reset with Warp**

   or

   Press ⌥⌘w

   ■ The Warp Options dialog box displays.

3. Display the Style pop-up menu and choose a different warp style.

   ■ Values in the other fields are still applied.

4. Change the other options, if desired.

5. Click OK or press *return/enter.*

Creating a Mesh Envelope

Another way to distort an object or objects is to create a grid (mesh) having a specified number of rows and columns to use as the envelope. Envelopes created in this manner can be edited, expanded, or released the same as other envelopes. To create a mesh envelope:

1. Select one or more objects or a group of objects.

2. Display the Envelope Mesh dialog box:

   ■ Choose **Object** ⇨ **Envelope Distort** ⇨ **Make with Mesh**

   or

   ■ Press ⌥⌘m

3. Click the Preview checkbox to see the effects of your changes before exiting the dialog box.

4. Change the values in the Rows (horizontal) and Columns (vertical) fields to specify how many of each the grid contains.

   ■ Enter a value in the fields.

   or

   ■ Click the up/down arrows to change the increment by 1 for each click.

   or

   ■ *Shift*-click the up/down arrows to change the increment by 10 for each click.

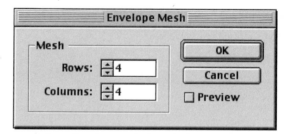

Specify the number of rows and columns for the mesh envelope in the Envelope Mesh dialog box

5. Click OK or press *return/enter*.

   ■ The shape of the mesh is the same as the bounding box of the selected objects or group.

Editing an Envelope

This section discusses how to change an envelope shape. To learn how to edit the objects inside an envelope, refer to the next section.

1. Select the envelope:

   ■ Select the object with the Selection tool

   or

   ■ Display the Layers palette and click the Target (◎) on the <Envelope> layer.

2. Make one or more of the following changes:

   ■ Move mesh lines and mesh points by selecting them with the Direct Selection tool or the Mesh tool ([⊞]) and dragging them.

      ▪ When you click inside a mesh patch, all the mesh points that create the mesh patch are selected (solid).

   ■ Add or delete anchor points to mesh lines with the Add Anchor Point ([⊞]) and Delete Anchor Point ([⊞]) tools.

   ■ Convert anchor points from smooth to corner or combination, and vice versa, with the Convert Anchor Point tool ([⊠]) or by holding down the ⌥ key and clicking on them with the Pen tool.

   ■ Select mesh points with the Direct Selection tool and apply transform commands.

   ■ Change mesh lines or points using any of the liquify tools (warp, twirl, pucker, bloat, scallop, crystallize, or wrinkle).

   ■ Delete mesh lines and mesh points by holding down the ⌥ key and clicking on a mesh line with the Mesh tool ([⊞]) in the Toolbox selected.

Revert to Original Envelope Shape To reset an envelope to its original shape before it was modified:

1. Choose **Object** ⇨ **Envelope Distort** ⇨ **Reset with Warp** or press ⌥⌘w. When the Warp Options dialog box displays, click OK or press *return/enter*.

   or

read this!

If an <Envelope> layer is targeted in the Layers palette, any appearances applied are applied to the envelope, not the objects inside the envelope.

fyi Turn on Smart Guides when editing envelopes so you can see the envelope and anchor points even when it's not selected.

2. Choose **Object** ⇨ **Envelope Distort** ⇨ **Reset with Mesh** or press ⌥⌘m

   ■ Check *Maintain Envelope Shape* to change mesh points inside the envelope without changing the overall shape of the envelope. When unchecked, the entire envelope changes to a rectangularly-shaped mesh.

   ■ Change the value in the rows and columns fields, if desired.

   ■ Click OK or press *return/enter.*

fyi If you think you may want to change the envelope shape or edit the objects inside the envelope, save a copy before expanding the envelope.

Editing Objects in an Envelope

You can edit the objects in an envelope without changing the shape of the envelope itself.

1. Select an envelope.

2. Choose **Object** ⇨ **Envelope Distort** ⇨ **Edit Contents**

   or

   Press ⇧⌘v

   ■ The envelope layer in the Layers palette can now be expanded, displaying object layers or group layers for the objects inside the envelope.

3. Click the Target (◎) of any object layer in the envelope layer or sublayer to select it for editing.

4. Edit the objects as you would any object not in an envelope.

5. Choose **Object** ⇨ **Envelope Distort** ⇨ **Edit Envelope** when you're finished modifying objects in the envelope

   or

   Press ⇧⌘v

 *activity 9.22*

1. Create a new document: Letter size, CMYK color mode.

2. Draw a 2½" circle and fill it with 100% cyan, 80% magenta.

3. Draw a 3½" wide, ½" high oval and fill it with 80% cyan, 80% magenta, and 80% yellow. Position it so the bottom of the oval is about ¼" above the top of the circle and so the center-points of both shapes are lined up vertically.

   ■ Snap the centerpoint of the oval to the centerpoint of the circle, then hold down

the *Shift* key and drag the oval up until it's about ¼" above the circle.

4. Marquee with the Selection tool to select both objects.

5. Choose Object ⇨ Envelope Distort ⇨ Make with Warp to display the Warp Options dialog box.

6. Click the Preview checkbox so you can see what happens to the objects without exiting the dialog box.

Continued

7. Adjust the objects on the screen and/or the Warp Options dialog box so all of them are visible.
   - Notice the mesh lines and points in the envelope shape.

8. Choose different styles from the Style pop-up submenu and adjust the settings of the other options to create different distortions. Click the Preview checkbox to turn it off to revert back to the undistorted objects, then click it again to turn it back on after changing the options in the dialog box.
   - Pay attention to how the mesh lines and points move when you choose different styles and change the various settings.

9. When you're through experimenting with the various styles and settings, specify the following settings, then click OK or press *return/enter:*
   - Style: Bulge
   - Horizontal
   - Bend: 80%
   - Distortion, Horizontal: 60%
   - Distortion, Vertical: 0%

10. Press ⇧⌘a to deselect all.

11. Display the Layers palette, locate the Envelope layer, and click the Target to select the Envelope.

12. Choose the Add Anchor Point tool in the Toolbox, then click in the middle of both of the vertical mesh lines in the middle of the envelope.

13. Deselect all.

14. With the Direct Selection tool, click on one of the anchor points you just added to the mesh line, and move it around to reshape the object.

15. Using the same method, reshape the other anchor point you just added.

16. Choose the Delete Anchor Point tool and click on one of the anchor points you added to delete it.

17. Choose Object ➪ Envelope Distort ➪ Edit Contents.
   - The pathlines of the original objects display.
   - In the Layers palette, the Expand Layer arrow displays to the left of the Envelope name.

18. Click the Expand Layer arrow to display the object layers for the objects in the envelope.

19. With the Selection tool in the Toolbox selected, drag the original objects up and release the mouse.
   - Notice that the distorted shape moves, too.

20. With the Direct Select Lasso tool in the Toolbox selected, circle the leftmost anchor point of the circle to select it without selecting any of the other anchor points of the shape.

21. Choose the Direct Selection tool, click on the selected anchor point, and drag it to the left and down a little.
   - Notice that the distortion of the shape adjusts to the new location of the anchor point.

22. Choose Object ➪ Envelope Distort ➪ Edit Envelope.
   - The pathlines of the original objects disappear.
   - In the Layers palette, the Expand Layer arrow disappears so you can't select the objects in the envelope.

23. Choose Object ➪ Envelope Distort ➪ Reset with Warp.
   - The Warp Options dialog box displays so you can make changes to the envelope shape.

24. Click the Cancel button or press *esc* on the keyboard.

25. Choose Object ➪ Envelope Distort ➪ Reset with Mesh.
   - The Envelope Mesh dialog box displays.

26. Click the Preview checkbox to turn the feature on.

27. Click the Maintain Envelope Shape checkbox to uncheck it.
   - Notice that the outside mesh lines of the envelope revert to the rectangular shape of the imaginary bounding box surrounding the objects.

28. Change the number of rows to 4 and the number of columns to 5, then click the Preview checkbox off and then back on again.
   - The number of mesh lines in the envelope matches the values entered in the dialog box.
   - Sometimes it's necessary to add mesh lines to achieve the distortion you want.

29. Click OK or press *return/enter.*

30. Close the artwork window without saving changes.
   - The features demonstrated in this activity apply to all envelopes, regardless how they're created.

Specifying Envelope Options

Choices you make in the Envelope Options dialog box (Figure 9.15) control how the contents of objects are distorted in an envelope and what happens to the object's contents when the envelope is expanded. Expanding an envelope is discussed later in this chapter.

1. Display the Envelope Options dialog box by choosing **Object** ⇨**Envelope Distort** ⇨ **Envelope Options**.

    - Change the settings for only an existing envelope by having it selected before displaying the Envelope Options dialog box.

    or

    - Change settings for all envelopes created after the changes are made by not having any envelopes or objects selected when the Envelope Options dialog box is displayed.

2. Change the option settings.

    - **Preview** — Click this checkbox to see the results of your actions as soon as you choose options.

    - **Anti-Alias** — Check the Anti-Alias checkbox to smooth the edges of linked or placed raster images or images rasterized in Illustrator.

    - Distortion may take longer when this option is checked.

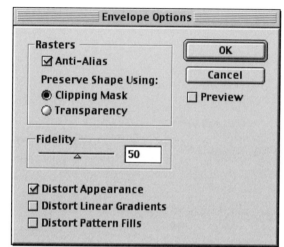

FIGURE 9.15 Settings in the Envelope Options dialog box control the distortion of the contents of objects in an envelope.

    - **Preserve Shape Using** — Determines how the shape of raster images are expanded after being distorted by envelopes:

      - **Clipping Mask** — Places an expanded raster image in a clipping mask.
      - **Transparency** — Makes the background of an expanded raster image transparent.

    - **Fidelity** — This value, from 0–100, determines how closely objects in the envelope conform to the envelope shape. Anchor points may be added to the object paths to make them fit the envelope shape. A higher value adds more anchor points, and the object more closely fits the shape of the envelope, but it may take more time to complete the distortion.

    - **Distort Appearance** — When checked (default), appearances such as styles, live effects, and so on, are distorted. When expanded, any appearances applied to the objects are expanded and they are displayed on the Layers palette on separate layers.

- When unchecked, objects are distorted, but any appearances applied to them are not distorted. When expanded, objects are displayed as a single object layer.

- **Distort Linear Gradients** — (Becomes available only when Distort Appearance is checked.) When checked, any linear gradient applied to objects in the envelope are distorted. If unchecked, linear gradients are unaffected by the envelope distortion.

  - When checked and the envelope is expanded, the linear gradient is displayed in the Layers palette as a mesh nested within nested groups.

  - When unchecked and the envelope is expanded, the linear gradient is not displayed separately from the object in the Layers palette.

- **Distort Pattern Fills** — (Becomes available only when Distort Appearance is checked.) When checked, any pattern fill applied to objects in the envelope is distorted. If unchecked, pattern fills are unaffected by the envelope distortion.

  - When checked and the envelope is expanded, the components of the pattern fill are displayed in the Layers palette as nested groups.

  - When unchecked and the envelope is expanded, the pattern fill is not displayed separately from the object in the Layers palette.

3. Click OK or press *return/enter*.

Expanding an Envelope

To expand a selected envelope, choose **Object ⇨ Envelope Distort ⇨ Expand**. The envelope disappears and leaves the distorted objects grouped. The only way to get the envelope back is to apply the Undo command ($\mathcal{H}$z).

- Type in an expanded envelope is converted to outlines.

- Brushstrokes and symbol instances in an expanded envelope are converted to regular paths.

  - Symbol sets remain intact when an envelope is expanded.

- Gradient mesh objects in an expanded envelope are unaffected.

Releasing an Envelope

Releasing an envelope restores objects inside the envelope to their original state, including effects, appearances, fill and stroke attributes, and so on. The envelope becomes a separate mesh object on top of the other objects in the stacking order.

Release a selected envelope by choosing **Object ⇨ Envelope Distort ⇨ Release**. In the Layers palette, objects are displayed as individual object layers (<Path>), and the mesh object is displayed as <Mesh>. If the envelope has been modified, you can save the mesh object to use as a user-defined envelope.

activity 9.23

1. Create a new document: Letter size, CMYK color mode.

2. Draw a cloud shape that's about 4" wide and 2" high. The object shown here was filled with the Ink and Wash texture (Illustrator Application CD ⇨ Illustrator Extras ⇨ Pattern & Texture Libraries ⇨ Nature).

3. With the object selected, choose Object ⇨ Envelope Distort ⇨ Make with Mesh to display the Envelope Mesh dialog box.

4. Click the Preview checkbox to turn it on, then change the Rows value to 2 and the Columns value to 3, and click OK or press *return/enter*.

   ■ Notice the mesh envelope containing mesh lines and mesh points that displays in front of the cloud.

5. Press ⇧ ⌘ a to deselect all.

6. Choose the Direct Selection tool and click on the object to display the mesh envelope.

   ■ The mesh points are hollow except those that create the mesh patch you clicked in.

7. Click in the top center mesh patch and drag it up to reshape the cloud.

8. With the Direct Selection tool, click on one of the anchor points at the bottom of the mesh envelope to select only that mesh point. Drag it down.

9. Experiment with reshaping your cloud object by selecting mesh patches and mesh points.

10. When you're finished experimenting with moving mesh lines, patches, and points, marquee to select the cloud shape and delete it.

11. In the middle of the document page, hold down the *Shift* key and draw a straight line from one side of the page to the other side with the Line Segment tool.

12. Apply a 60 pt black stroke.

13. Choose Object ⇨ Path ⇨ Outline Stroke to make the stroke an object.

14. Fill the object with the Rainbow gradient from the Swatches palette.

15. Display the Gradient palette. Display the Gradient palette Options menu and choose Show Options.

16. Change the Angle to 90° and press *return/enter*.

17. Display the Symbols palette and click on the Sequoia swatch.

18. Spray several of the sequoia under the rainbow.

19. Display the Brushes palette and click on the Radiant Star swatch.

20. With the Paintbrush tool, draw a slightly wavy path horizontally along the middle of the rainbow.

21. Choose Object ⇨ Envelope Distort ⇨ Envelope Options to display the Envelope Options dialog box. Uncheck the Distort Appearance checkbox and click OK or press *return/enter*.

22. Select all the objects, then choose Object ⇨ Envelope Distort ⇨ Make with Warp.

23. With Arc the selection in the Style pop-up sub-menu, Horizontal, 50% Bend, and 0% on both the Distortion sliders, click the Preview button so you can see what happens to the objects.

   ■ Notice that the rainbow rectangle became an arc, and the sequoias were distorted, too. The brushstroke was distorted, but the stars along the brushstroke weren't altered.

24. Click OK or press *return/enter*.

25. Choose Object ⇨ Envelope Distort ⇨ Envelope Options to display the Envelope Options dialog box.

26. Place a checkmark in the Distort Appearance checkbox, then click the Preview button to apply the change to the selected objects.

   ■ Notice that stars along the brushstroke are now distorted.

Continued

27. Place a checkmark in the Distort Linear Gradients checkbox, then click the Preview button to apply the change.

   ■ Notice that rainbow follows the shape of its object.

28. Click OK or press *return/enter*.

29. Choose Object ⇨ Envelope Distort ⇨ Expand to delete the envelope and leave the objects grouped.

30. Choose Object ⇨ Ungroup to ungroup the objects.

   ■ Display the layers in the Layers palette and notice that the symbol instances are grouped and the brushstroke and rainbow are on individual object layers.

31. Close this artwork window without saving changes.

Creating an Envelope From a Path You Draw

Any path you draw in Illustrator can be used as an envelope to distort objects behind it in the stacking order. Restack the objects using the Arrange commands in the Object menu or adjust the layers in the Layers palette if necessary.

   The object to be used as the envelope must be at the front of the stack. The object to be used as the envelope doesn't have to overlap the other objects. It doesn't even have to be touching them. It can be anywhere on the document page. When the envelope is created, all selected objects are sucked into the envelope.

   The path or object can be open or closed, but if it's an open path, it's closed automatically when it's made into an envelope. The path or object can have fill and stroke attributes applied to it; they're removed automatically when the envelope is created.

   Before a type character can be used as an envelope, it must be converted to outlines, released from its compound path and ungrouped (if the character has a counter). Only one character at a time can be used as an envelope for selected objects.

   To create an envelope from a path or object you've created:

1. In the Layers palette, check the stacking order of the objects, making sure the path or object to be used as the envelope is at the top of the stack. Restack if necessary.

2. Select all the objects, including the object to be used as the envelope.

3. Choose **Object ⇨ Envelope Distort ⇨ Make with Top Object**

   or

   Press ⌥⌘c

   ■ Objects are sucked into the envelope and reshaped to fit as closely as the Fidelity setting in the Envelope Options dialog box allows. If objects don't conform to the shape of the envelope, increase the Fidelity setting.

1. Open the ice cream cone you created and stored in your Practice Folder. Save it into your Practice folder as Envelope Distort Practice.eps.

2. Choose the Type tool, click on the left side of the page, and type the word CONE (all caps).

3. Make it 200 pt Benguiat Gothic Book, horizontal scaled to 65%.

   ■ This font is supplied by Adobe on the Illustrator 10 application CD-ROM. If, for some reason, it isn't available on your computer, substitute a different font.

4. With the Direct Selection tool, select the type and convert it to outlines.

5. Choose Object ⇨ Compound Path ⇨ Release.

6. With the Direct Selection tool, select the path of the counter in the letter O (the inside path).

   ■ Change to Outline mode if you can't find the counter to select it.

7. With the counter still selected, hold the *Shift* key down and marquee to select the entire ice cream cone.

8. Choose Object ⇨ Envelope Distort ⇨ Make with Top Object.

   ■ The ice cream cone is sucked into the counter of the letter.

9. Choose Object ⇨ Envelope Distort ⇨ Envelope Options to display the Envelope Options dialog box.

10. If it's unchecked, click the Preview checkbox.

11. Move the Fidelity slider to 100% to adjust the ice cream cone to fit into the shape better.

   ■ It doesn't change much, does it? This is a subtle change.

12. Move the Fidelity slider to back and forth from 100% to 0%, clicking the Preview feature off and on so you can see that there isn't much change from 0% to 100%. Click OK or press *return/enter*.

13. Display the Layers palette and expand the layer until you can see the Envelope layer.

14. Click the Envelope layer's target circle to select the envelope.

15. Choose Object ⇨ Envelope Distort ⇨ Reset with Mesh to display the Reset Envelope Mesh dialog box.

16. If the Preview checkbox is unchecked, click it to check it.

17. Click the Maintain Envelope Shape checkbox to turn it on.

   ■ Notice what happened to the ice cream cone. It reverted back to its original size and shape.

   ■ Notice the placement of the ice cream cone in the stacking order.

18. Click OK or press *return/enter*.

19. Save the file, print it, and close the artwork window.

PRACTICE ACTIVITY 9-1 — Playing Cards

1. Create a new document: Letter size, CMYK color mode. Save it into your Practice Folder as an .eps file named Playing Cards.eps.

2. *Heart:* Using the Pen tool, draw the left half of a heart shape. Fill it with 100% magenta, 100% yellow, no stroke.

3. Choose the Reflect tool in the Toolbox, then ⌥-click in the vertical center of the straight edge to establish the point of origin and display the Reflect dialog box.

4. Click the Vertical Axis button, then the Preview checkbox to make sure the heart will reflect like you want it to.

5. Click the Copy button to exit the dialog box and create a reflected copy of the original half.

6. With the Direct Lasso tool, circle the anchor points where the two paths intersect at the top of the heart.

   - If you placed the point of origin precisely on the vertical edge of the left half, the two anchor points will be too close together to select individually.

7. Choose Object ⇨ Path ⇨ Average ⇨ Both, or press ⌥⌘j (jay).

   - Using the Average command here ensures that the two points are *precisely* on top of each other. Otherwise, a very small segment (that you don't want) will be added between the two points.

8. Choose Object ⇨ Path ⇨ Join (Corner or Smooth), or press ⌘j (jay).

9. Repeat #6–8 to join the anchor points at the bottom of the heart shape.

   - The heart shape is now a single path.

10. *Spade:* Select the heart shape you just drew.

11. Choose the Reflect tool in the Toolbox and ⌥-click at the point at the bottom of the shape to display the Reflect Options dialog box.

12. Click the Horizontal button, then click the Copy button to reflect a copy of the heart. Drag it to a new location on the page away from the heart shape.

13. Change the fill to 100% black.

14. Draw a black .15" × .3" rectangle, then deselect it.

15. With the Direct Lasso tool, select the top two anchor points of the rectangle.

16. Choose Object ⇨ Path ⇨ Average ⇨ Both to bring the two anchor points to the center.

17. With the Convert Anchor Point tool, convert the bottom left anchor point to a smooth point by clicking on it and dragging diagonally toward the middle of the shape.

18. Select the Direct Selection tool and hold down the ⌥ key. Click on the direction line that controls the bottom of the shape. Move it up and to the right so the bottom of the shape is straight again.

Continued

19. Drag the upper direction point up and to the right to shape the curve of the stem.

20. Repeat #16–19 for the bottom right anchor point, except in #16, drag the anchor point down and to the right when converting it to a smooth point.

    ■ If the direction points are in approximately the same position, the shape of the curves are the same.

21. Position the shape at the bottom of the Spade shape, as shown.

22. Select all the paths and Merge them using the Pathfinder command.

23. Press ⌘ s to save your file.

24. *Diamond:* Display the grid and, with the Pen tool, draw the top left part of the diamond shape, making sure the line isn't straight but has a slight bow to it.

    ■ I applied a red stroke and a white fill temporarily so I can see what the shape looks like.

25. Choose the Reflect tool and ⌥-click the top anchor point to display the Reflect Options dialog box. Click the Vertical Axis button, verify that 90° is the value in the Angle field, then click the Copy button to reflect a copy of the path to the opposite side.

26. With the Direct Lasso tool, circle the anchor points at the top of the shape, then press ⇧ ⌥ ⌘ j to average and join the anchor points.

27. With the Selection tool, select the entire shape. Switch to the Reflect tool in the Toolbox and position the pointer exactly in the middle between the two bottom anchor points. Then ⌥-click to display the Reflect Options dialog box.

    ■ Use the grid to help you find the exact center.

28. Click the Horizontal Axis button to reflect a copy.

29. Circle the anchor points on the left side of the shape, then press ⇧ ⌥ ⌘ j to average and join the anchor points. Repeat this step for the anchor points on the right side of the shape.

30. Remove the stroke and fill the shape with 100% magenta, 100% yellow.

31. Hide the grid, then press ⌘ s to save your file.

32. *Club:* The Club card is a little more difficult. With the Pen tool, draw a shape similar to the one shown here and place a vertical ruler guide down its center. Color it black with no stroke.

33. Select the Rotate tool and ⌥-click toward the bottom of the shape (as shown in #31) to establish the point of origin and display the Rotate dialog box. Enter 110 in the Angle field and click the Copy button.

34. Drag a horizontal ruler guide and place it at the bottom of the shape.

35. With the Rotate tool still selected, ⌥-click the same point of origin. When the dialog box displays, enter 135 in the Angle field and click the Preview button to see where it will land. Adjust the value in the Angle field until the bottom of the new shape rests on the horizontal ruler guide.

36. When it's where you want it, click the Copy button.

    ■ If necessary, adjust the last shape so the vertical ruler guide is exactly in the center of the shapes.

37. With the Pen tool, draw the stem shape similar to the one shown here.

    ■ Use the vertical ruler guide to help draw the shape.

Continued

448

38. When the shape is like you want it, select all the paths, display the Pathfinder palette and click the Merge button to join all the pieces into one path.

39. Press ⌘ s to save your file.

40. With the Rounded Rectangle tool, create four boxes that are 2½" × 3½" with .125" corner radius. Apply a White fill and a 2 pt black stroke.

41. Scale the four shapes you created until they are approximately .65" (48 pts) high. Place them inside the rounded rectangles as shown in the examples at the beginning of this activity, drag-copying as many as you need of each shape.
    - Use the Measure tool to determine when the size is correct.
    - Use the Reflect tool to flip the shapes upside down.

42. Scale the smaller shapes to 40% of the larger size. Use ruler guides to help you align the shapes on each card so they're consistent from card to card.

43. Display the Character palette (⌘ t), choose the Type tool in the Toolbox, click on the document page, and type the number or letter (A) corresponding to the playing card you created.

44. Change the type size to 30 pt and the font to Lubalin Graph Book.

45. Apply the same fill color as the color of the card it will be placed on.

46. Drag it so it's positioned on the first card just above the small shape, as shown in the illustration on the first page of this activity.

47. With the character still selected, double-click the Rotate tool in the Toolbox to display the Rotate dialog box. Change the angle to 180°, then click the Copy button.
    - An upside-down copy of the character is created.

48. Drag the character and place it under the small shape on the opposite side of the card, as shown in the illustration on the first page of this activity.

49. Repeat #43–47 for the other three cards.

50. Press ⌘ s to save your file. Print the file and close your document.

EXERCISE 9-1 — Auto

Draw the automobile as shown. Make a compound path so the background shows through the windows and the tires.

Preview Mode

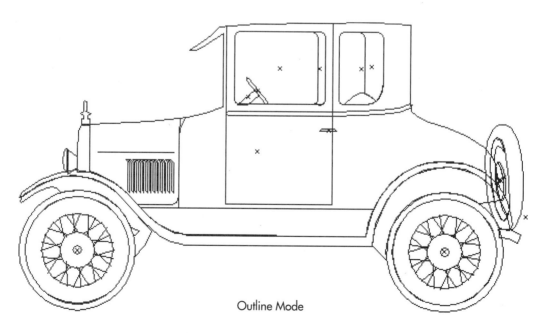

Outline Mode

Brushes, Patterns, & Symbols

Chapter Outline

- Brushes
- Brushes Palette
- Paintbrush Tool
- Create or Modify Brushes
- Create or Modify a Calligraphic Brush
- Create or Modify a Scatter Brush
- Colorization Options
- Create or Modify an Art Brush
- Create or Modify a Pattern Brush
- Edit Existing Scatter, Art, or Pattern Brushes
- Change Brushstrokes on a Selected Object
- Convert Brushstrokes into Separate Objects
- Pattern Fills
- Symbols
- Symbolism Tools

Brushes

When you draw a stroked path with the Pen tool or the Pencil tool, or when you apply a stroke to a path you've drawn with the predefined shape tools, the stroke is a solid line. Illustrator also provides a palette full of brush-stroke patterns that you can use when drawing paths. You can draw paths that look like actual brushstrokes, or you can scatter art along a path, or draw lines that are thick in some places and thin in others. You can also apply brush patterns to existing paths.

The Brushes palette contains the default brush patterns provided by Illustrator, but you can create your own custom brushes and store them in the Brushes palette. You can import brushes from the Brushes folder stored inside the Presets folder that's in the Adobe Illustrator 10 folder on your hard drive, too. Or, you can use one of the many brushes stored in the Brush Libraries folder that's in the Illustrator Extras folder on the Illustrator 10 CD-ROM.

Paths to which a brush from the Brushes palette has been applied can be reshaped, transformed, or modified the same as any other path created with another of the path-creation tools. You can add, delete, average anchor points, erase, smooth, reshape, scale, rotate, reflect, move paths, and so on. Brush objects adjust, as necessary, to the new shape.

There are four types of brushes available in Illustrator (see Figure 10.1):

- **Calligraphic** — Creates brushstrokes that vary in thickness, much like when you draw with a calligraphic pen. There are settings to control the size of the stroke, the angle of the tip, and the roundness of the brush. The Calligraphic brush is ideal for use with a pressure-sensitive tablet.

- **Scatter** — Randomly disperses a single object or group of objects along the selected path or along a path as you draw it with the Paintbrush tool. Controls are provided for adjusting the size of the objects, their spacing along the path, and how far from the path line the objects are allowed to stray, as well as the rotation angle of the object. The Scatter brush can be used with a pressure-sensitive tablet.

- **Art** — Stretches an object or group of objects evenly along the length of a selected path. Options available allow you to control the direction the artwork flows along the path, the width of the artwork, and whether or not you want the artwork to flip across the path.

- **Pattern** — Repeats a specified pattern along the selected path or as you draw a path with the Paintbrush tool. You can control the appearance of the beginning and ending of the path and the inner and outer corners of the pattern as it follows the path. A Pattern brush differs from the Scatter brush in that the artwork follows the path exactly and artwork in the Scatter brush does not.

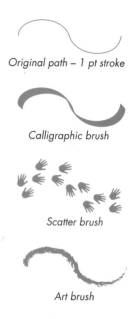

Original path – 1 pt stroke

Calligraphic brush

Scatter brush

Art brush

Pattern brush

FIGURE 10.1 Samples of the types of brushes available in Illustrator 10.

Brushes Palette

The Brushes palette is similar to the Swatches palette (see Step 7, *Add Color to Artwork*). Display the Brushes palette (see Figure 10.2) by choosing **Window ⇨ Brushes** or click its folder tab if it's in a palette group that's already displayed. Many of the features and options for managing thumbnails in the Brushes palette are the same as in the Swatches palette. Brush designs and patterns are stored as thumbnails (or swatches) on the palette and you can display, move, delete, and add thumbnails to the palette.

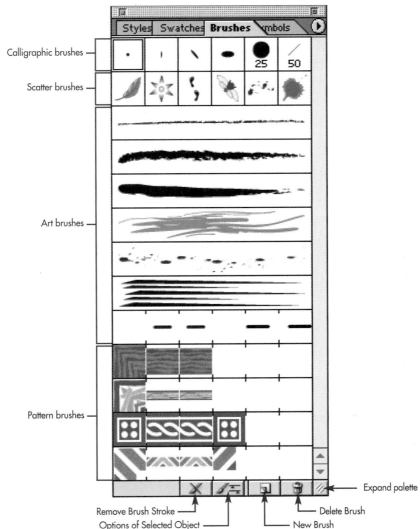

Calligraphic brushes

Scatter brushes

Art brushes

Pattern brushes

FIGURE 10.2
The default
Brushes palette.

Remove Brush Stroke
Options of Selected Object
New Brush
Delete Brush
Expand palette

Managing Brushes in the Brushes Palette

Displaying Brushes To display all the brushes available
in the Brushes palette, click and drag the Expand Palette
icon at the bottom right corner of the palette.

You don't have to display all the default and custom
brushes in the brushes palette. In the Brushes palette
Options menu, you can choose the types of brushes you
want displayed in the document's Brushes palette. If a
checkmark displays to the left of the option, those brushes
are displayed in the palette. If there is no checkmark,
they are hidden.

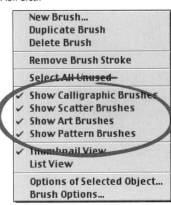

Options available in the Brushes palette
Options menu

Displaying Brushes by Name As with swatches in the Swatches palette, brushes in the Brushes palette can be displayed as thumbnail representations or by their names. When List View is checked in the Brushes palette Options menu, a small thumbnail displays on the left side of the palette, followed by its name and, on the right side of the palette, the icon for the brush type displays.

- ▪ 〰 — Calligraphic brush icon
- ▪ ⋯ — Scatter brush icon
- ▪ ▭ — Art brush icon
- ▪ ⌐ — Pattern brush icon

●	25 pt Round	〰
/	50 pt Flat	〰
◢	Banana Leaf	⋯

Examples of brush icons in the Brushes palette

Moving Brushes in the Brushes Palette You can reposition brushes *within its category* in the Brushes palette by selecting and dragging it to a new spot. Release the mouse to drop the thumbnail when a dark line displays where you want the thumbnail to be placed.

- ▪ To select a series of thumbnails, click the first one, then *Shift*-click the last one to select all thumbnails between the clicks.

- ▪ To select random thumbnails, ⌘-click them.

A dark line displays between two brushes where a new brush will be placed in the Brushes palette

Delete a Brush from the Brushes Palette To remove a brush from the Brushes palette:

1. Select the brush you want to delete.
   - ▪ Click to select a single thumbnail.
   - ▪ ⌘-click to select random thumbnails.
   - ▪ Click the first thumbnail in a series, then *Shift*-click to select the last in a series of thumbnails.
   - ▪ Choose Select All Unused in the Brushes palette Options menu to select all brushes that were not used in the current document.

2. Delete the brush thumbnail.
   - ▪ Drag the selected brush thumbnails over the Delete Brush button (🗑) at the bottom of the Brushes palette.

   or

   - ▪ Click the Delete Brush button (🗑) at the bottom of the Brushes palette. An alert dialog box displays asking if you're sure you want to delete the Brush.
     - ▪ To leave the brush in the Brushes palette, click the No button or press the *esc* key on the keyboard.

read this!

If a style that's applied to an object uses a brush, you can't delete that brush until the style is removed from the object. An alert displays if you attempt it.

- To delete the brush, click the Yes button or press *return/enter*.

or

■ Choose Delete Brush from the Brushes palette Options menu.

■ ⌥-click the Delete Brush button (🗑) at the bottom of the Brushes palette to delete the brush without displaying the warning dialog box.

If you attempt to delete a brush thumbnail that has been applied to a path in the current document, an alert dialog box displays offering three options:

■ Click the Cancel button or press the *esc* key on the keyboard to leave the brush untouched.

■ Click the Remove Strokes button to remove the brushstroke attributes from the path and remove the thumbnail from the Brushes palette.

■ Clicking the Expand Strokes button removes the brush thumbnail from the Brushes palette and converts the objects used to create the brush into individual selected objects on any paths to which the brush was applied.

> ⚠ **One or more of the brushes are in use and cannot be deleted until their strokes are expanded or removed.**
>
> [Expand Strokes] [Remove Strokes] [Cancel]

Alert dialog box that displays if you attempt to delete a brush that's applied to a path in the document

Add Brushes from Brush Libraries Illustrator has provided brush libraries containing additional brushes for your use. You can create your own custom brush library, too. In addition, new brushes you create can be added to your Custom Startup file (see Step 6, *Rulers, Grids, & Guides* for information about creating a Custom Startup file). To add a brush to the current document's Brushes palette:

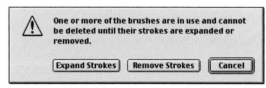

Animal Sample
Arrow Sample
Artistic Sample
Border Sample
Calligraphic
Default_CMYK
Default_RGB
Floral Sample
Object Sample

Other Library...

You can create your own brushes to add to this list of default brushes supplied with Illustrator 10

1. Deselect all objects in your document.

2. Display the list of available brush libraries by choosing **Window** ⇨ **Brush Libraries** and choose the one you want.

   or

   Choose **Window** ⇨ **Brush Libraries** ⇨ **Other Library**, locate a custom library from the Brushes folder inside the Presets folder in the Adobe Illustrator 10 folder on your hard drive. Double-click its name or highlight it and click Open.

3. Click a brush in the opened library and drag it onto an object in your document to apply it to that object. A thumbnail appears automatically in the Brushes palette. The object doesn't have to be selected.

   or

   Click a brush in the Library palette. Its thumbnail appears in the Brushes palette automatically.

4. Close the Library palette by clicking its Close box. If you've dragged the Library palette's folder tab into another palette group, drag it out of the palette group before clicking it's Close box.

- Dragging a Library palette into another palette group is temporary. When you exit the Illustrator program, the palette group reverts to its default state.
- To make a Library palette open each time Illustrator is launched, display the palette, then choose Persistent from the palette's Options menu.

Duplicate a Brush You can use an existing brush as a starting point for creating a new brush by creating a duplicate of it first. The word "copy" is added to the end of the Brush name.

1. In the Brushes palette, click the brush you want to duplicate.

2. Display the Brushes palette Options menu and choose Duplicate Brush.

   or

   Drag the selected brush over the New Brush button at the bottom of the palette.

3. Double-click the duplicate brush to display the Brush Options dialog box and rename it.

Create a Custom Brush Library To create a custom brush library that displays in the Brush Libraries submenu in the Window menu:

1. Create a custom brush in the current document (see the discussion about creating brushes later in this chapter).

2. Save the file into the Brush Libraries folder that's located in the Brushes folder inside the Presets folder in the Adobe Illustrator 10 folder on your hard drive (**Adobe Illustrator 10** ➪ **Presets** ➪ **Brushes**).

   or

   Save the file anywhere on your hard drive, then drag it into the Brushes folder inside the Presets folder in the Adobe Illustrator 10 folder on your hard drive (**Adobe Illustrator 10** ➪ **Presets** ➪ **Brushes**)

3. Close the document, exit Illustrator, then re-launch the program.

- The name of the file displays in the Brush Libraries submenu.

 To restore the default brushes to a file, choose Window ➪ Brush Libraries ➪ Default CMYK or Default RGB, depending upon the color mode of the current document. Then add the brush thumbnails to the current document's Brushes palette.

456

Paintbrush Tool

The Paintbrush tool functions just like the Pencil tool except that it applies a brushstroke as you draw freeform paths. Illustrator automatically places anchor points along the path when you release the mouse. You can adjust them, if necessary, the same way you adjust anchor points and segments of any other path created in Illustrator.

Paintbrush tool icon in the Toolbox palette

Drawing with the Paintbrush Tool

1. Choose the Paintbrush tool in the Toolbox.

2. Click on the document page and move the mouse to draw the path.

   ■ The 3 pt Round Calligraphic brush is the default that is used when you draw with the Paintbrush tool.

3. To close the path, hold down the ⌥ key before you release the mouse. Release the mouse before releasing the ⌥ key.

fyi The keyboard command for selecting the Paintbrush tool is the letter b on the keyboard.

With all the brushes except Pattern brushes and some scatter brushes, the stroke color displayed in the Color palette or in the Toolbox determines the color of the brushstroke. Pattern brush colors and some scatter brush colors are set when the patterns or objects are created.

Reshape a Brushstroked Path To reshape a path to which a brushstroke has been applied, whether it was drawn with the Paintbrush tool or whether a brushstroke was applied to an existing path:

1. With the Selection tool, select the path you want to modify.

2. Choose the Paintbrush tool (▨) in the Toolbox.

3. Set Preferences for the Paintbrush tool. (See the following section).

4. Position the Paintbrush pointer on the path line of the path, then click and drag the path in a new direction.

   ■ Be sure the Paintbrush pointer is on the path line or you'll create a new path rather than editing the existing path.

   ■ To add to an open brushstroked path with the Paintbrush tool, position the Paintbrush pointer on an endpoint, then click and drag.

   ■ Press the Caps Lock key on the keyboard to change the Paintbrush pointer into a Crosshair pointer. Press the Caps Lock key again to revert back to the regular pointer.

timesaver To select all paths in the current document to which a brushstroke has been applied, choose Select ⇨ Object ⇨ Brush Strokes.

Refer to Step 4, *The Pen & Pencil Tools,* for more information about reshaping paths with the Pencil tool. You reshape a path with the Paintbrush the same as you do with the Pencil tool.

Setting Paintbrush Tool Preferences

The Paintbrush tool has the same Preference options as the Pencil tool, with one additional checkbox: Fill new brushstrokes. Display the Paintbrush Tool Preferences dialog box by double-clicking the Paintbrush tool or by selecting the Paintbrush tool in the Toolbox and pressing *return/enter.*

The following points are a quick review of the options:

 *Changes in tool preferences affect only brushstrokes you draw after the change is made, not those already drawn.*

- **Fidelity** — The value in this field determines how many pixels away from the path Illustrator can stray to produce smooth curves. You can enter a value from 0.5–20.

  - The lower the value, the closer the path mirrors the movement of the mouse. More anchor points are placed in the path.

  - A higher setting produces a smoother path, but it has fewer anchor points so the resulting path isn't followed as closely as the original path you drew.

- **Smoothness** — Enter a value from 0% to 100% to control the smoothness of curves as you draw.

  - The higher the value, the smoother the curve.

- **Fill new brushstrokes** — This is the option that isn't found in the Pencil Preferences dialog box (Figure 10.3). When the box is checked, which is the default setting, paths are filled with the current fill color displayed in the Color palette. When unchecked, paths are not filled.

- **Keep Selected** — When this box is checked, paths remain selected after you've finished drawing them with the Paintbrush tool.

- **Edit Selected Paths** — The value entered in the Within field determines how close you have to be to a path to edit it with the Paintbrush tool. When the box is unchecked, you can't edit a path with the Paintbrush tool.

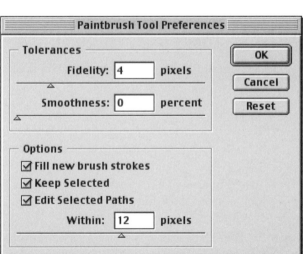

FIGURE 10.3 Change options in the Paintbrush Tool Preferences dialog box to control how the Paintbrush tool functions.

Applying a Brushstroke to an Existing Path

Apply a brushstroke to an existing path much like applying color with a swatch in the Swatches palette. You can even apply a brushstroke to type characters without converting them to outlines. You can't, though, use an object with a brushstroke applied to it to create a compound path or a blend. You have to create the compound path first, then apply the brushstroke.

To apply a brushstroke to an existing path:

1. If the Brushes palette isn't visible, display it by choosing **Window ⇨ Show Brushes** or clicking its folder tab in a palette group.

2. Select a path, any kind of path, then click on a brush in the Brushes palette.

   or

   Click on a brush in the Brushes palette and drag it onto the path. The object doesn't have to be selected.

   - If the object has a fill of None, you must drop the brush on its path line. If it has a fill color, even white, you can drop it anywhere inside the object.

Removing a Brushstroke

When you apply a brushstroke to a path or draw a path with the Paintbrush tool, that brush remains attached to any creation tool you use to draw a path (Pen, Pencil) from that point on unless you remove the brushstroke. Or, you may want to remove the brushstroke from an existing path because you don't want it any more or you want to change it. The original path remains after the brushstroke has been removed.

To remove a brushstroke from an existing path, select the path, then:

- Click the Remove Brush Stroke button (![×]) at the bottom of the Brushes palette.

or

- Display the Brushes palette Options menu and choose Remove Brush Stroke.

or

- Click the stroke box in the Color palette or on the Toolbox, then click the None button.

Paths drawn with the 6 pt flat calligraphic brush

Banana leaf scatter brush applied to a path

Flying beetles scatter brush applied to a path

Type, converted to outlines, with the Charcoal art brush applied to it

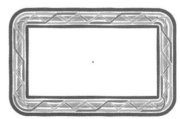

Rectangle with Polynesian pattern brush applied to it

459

activity 10.1

1. Create a new document: Letter size, CMYK color mode.

2. By clicking and dragging the icon at the bottom left corner of the Brushes palette, extend the palette until you can see all the default brushes.

3. Display the Brushes palette Options menu and choose List View.

   ■ A checkmark displays to the left of the menu option.

   ■ Note the different icons in the palette showing the brush type.

4. Display the Brushes palette Options menu again and choose Thumbnail View.

5. Display the Animal Sample Brush library (Window ➪ Brush Libraries ➪ Animal Sample), and click on the Butterfly 1 thumbnail.

   ■ The thumbnail is automatically placed in the current document's Brushes palette.

6. Close the Animal Sample Brush library.

7. In the Brushes palette, click on the Butterfly 1 thumbnail and drag it over the Human Feet thumbnail until the dark line appears on its right side. Release the mouse to reposition Butterfly 1 between the Human Feet and Flying Beetle thumbnails.

8. Using the Pencil tool, draw a curvy path from one side of the document page to the other.

9. Because the Butterfly 1 brush is still selected in the Brushes palette, it's applied to the path you drew.

10. Deselect the path.

11. Click on the Human Feet thumbnail in the Brushes palette, then select the Paintbrush tool in the Toolbox.

12. Draw another curvy path with the Paintbrush.

   ■ Notice that the footprints on this path are more consistent than the butterflies applied to the previous path. That's because of different options that were chosen when the brush was created.

13. With the last curvy path still selected, click on the 12 pt Oval Calligraphic brush.

   ■ Notice how the stroke is thicker in some sections and thinner in others.

14. With the Calligraphic path still selected, click on the Dry Ink art brush.

15. Drag the Charcoal thumbnail over the path line that has Butterfly 1 applied to it, and drop it.

   ■ Even though it wasn't selected, the Charcoal brush is applied to the path.

16. Zoom in so you can see the path easily.

17. Select the path and verify that the Paintbrush tool is selected in the Toolbox. Click on or near the path and drag in a different direction.

   ■ The path is reshaped to follow the new path.

18. With the Rectangle tool, draw a square on the document page. With the Paintbrush tool, click on or near the path and drag in a different direction.

   ■ The path is split and the brushstroke pattern is adjusted to follow the new path.

19. Deselect the object, then click on the path line with the Direct Selection tool, so that all anchor points are hollow.

20. Click on the endpoint where the path was split and drag it away so you can readily see that the path is split.

21. Select the Dry Ink path again, display the Brushes palette Options menu, and choose Remove Brush Stroke.

   ■ The path reverts to its original stroke weight and color.

22. Draw shapes and apply different brushes. Display various brush libraries so you're familiar with all the brushes available.

23. Close the document without saving changes.

Create or Modify Brushes

Even though Illustrator provides a lot of brushes for you to use, you may find you want to create your own custom brushes or you may want to change an existing brush. To create a new brush, you have to choose the type of brush you want to create. You can't create a new brush by modifying an existing brush, renaming it, and saving it into the Brushes palette. If you do that you lose the original brush.

To create a new brush, display the New Brush dialog box and:

1. Click the New Brush button (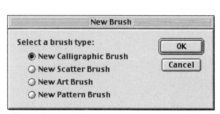) at the bottom of the Brushes palette.

   or

   Display the Brushes palette Options menu and choose New Brush.

   or

   Drag selected objects onto the Brushes palette.

Choose the type of brush you want to create in the New Brush dialog box

2. Click the radio button for the new brush you want to create and click OK or press *return/enter*.

To modify an existing brush, display the Brush Options dialog box for that brush type:

1. Double-click the brush in the Brushes palette.

   or

   Display the Brushes palette Options menu and choose Brush Options.

2. Make the appropriate changes in the options in the dialog box, then click OK or press *return/enter*.

   ■ If you enter values in the fields of a dialog box, the change doesn't register on any paths in the current document until you click in a different field or check and uncheck the Preview box to turn it off and on.

   ■ If you use the sliders to enter values in the fields and the Preview checkbox is checked, changes are applied as soon as you release the slider.

If you modify an existing brush that has been applied to objects in the current document, an alert displays and you must decide what you want to do.

   ■ **Apply to Strokes** — Click this button to apply the modified brush to existing paths that have the original brush applied to them.

   ■ **Leave Strokes** — Click this button to leave existing paths untouched. A new brush thumbnail displays in the Brushes palette.

   ■ **Cancel** — Click this button or press *esc* to cancel the changes made to the brush.

Determine what action to take when deleting a brush that's been applied to paths in the document

Create or Modify a Calligraphic Brush

Strokes created with Calligraphic brushes vary in thickness as you draw them or as they wrap around existing paths. You can change the angle, roundness, and diameter of calligraphic brushstrokes. When modifying an existing brush, if you want to keep the original brush intact, duplicate the brush first and alter the copy.

All calligraphic brushes are created in black. The stroke color in the document determines the color of the brushstroke.

To create or modify a calligraphic brush:

1. To create a new Calligraphic brush, choose New Calligraphic Brush in the New Brush dialog box to display the Calligraphic Brush Options dialog box. To modify an existing brush, double-click the brush to display the Calligraphic Brush Options dialog box (Figure 10.4).

2. Enter a new name or change the existing name in the Name field. You can enter up to 30 characters.

3. The Preview window shows how the brushstroke is affected by changes you make to the options.

   - The black center image in the Preview window shows the shape of the brushstroke without any Variation value applied.

   - The gray image on the left shows the shape of the brushstroke when the minimum Variation values are applied to it.

   - The gray image on the right shows the shape of the brushstroke when the maximum Variation values are applied.

   - When you modify an existing Calligraphic brush, a Preview checkbox displays in the Options dialog box. When checked, paths to which the brushstroke has been applied are updated

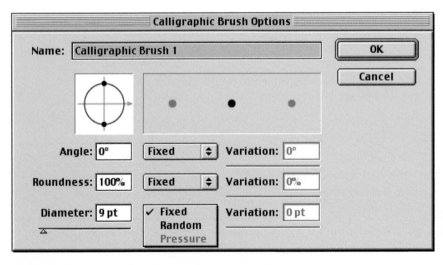

FIGURE 10.4
Calligraphic Brush Options dialog box.

immediately when you make changes in the dialog box. Uncheck it if you don't want to see changes to brushstrokes in the document as you make them.

4. Each of the three options, Angle, Roundness, Diameter, has a pop-up menu containing the same three options.

   - **Fixed** — The attribute (angle, roundness, diameter) is always the same throughout the stroke.
     - The Variation slider and field are unavailable.
     - If you're using a pressure-sensitive tablet, applying more pressure (or less) won't have any effect.

   - **Random** — The attribute can vary; the amount of variation is set by the value in the Variation field. You can use the slider to enter the value or type it in.
     - For example, an Angle value of 45° with a Random Variation value of 15 means the Angle of the brushstroke will vary anywhere between 30° and 60°.
     - There is no setting to specify *where* the stroke will vary when it's applied to a path. Illustrator decides that.

   - **Pressure** — This option is available only when you're using a pressure-sensitive drawing tablet. The value in the Variation field determines how much or how little the attribute will vary based on how hard you press the tablet.

5. Enter a value in the Angle field or click in the lefthand preview window to control how thick or thin the brushstroke gets on vertical or horizontal paths.

   - The gray arrow snaps to the point you click. Or you can drag the arrow around to set the value in the Angle field.
   - A 0° angle produces a thin stroke on a horizontal path and a thick stroke on a vertical path.
   - A 90° angle produces a thick stroke on a horizontal path and a thin stroke on a vertical path.

6. Enter a value from 0–1296 in the Roundness field or click and drag one of the bullets in the image in the lefthand preview window. Then enter a value in the Variation field (or drag the slider) to set the minimum and maximum amount the brushstroke can change shape as it flows along a path.

7. The Diameter option controls how thick the brushstroke is before any Variation value is applied. Enter a value in the field or drag the slider.

8. Click OK or press *return/enter*.

   - The new Calligraphic brushstroke is added to the Brushes palette after the last Calligraphic brush. A new row is added to the section, if necessary.

activity 10.2

1. Create a new document: Letter size, CMYK color mode. Name it New Calligraphic Brush.eps and save it into your Practice Folder as an .eps file.

2. With the Paintbrush tool, draw a very curvy path on the document page. Apply a stroke color.

   - The 3 pt Round Calligraphic brush is applied to the path because it's the default brush.

3. In the Brushes palette, click on the 6 pt Flat thumbnail, display the Brushes palette Options menu, and choose Duplicate Brush.

   - A second 6 pt Flat thumbnail is placed in the Brushes palette at the end of the row.

4. Double-click the new 6 pt Flat thumbnail to display the Calligraphic brush Options dialog box. Position the dialog box so you can see at least part of the path you drew.

5. Enter the name My Calligraphic Brush in the Name field.

6. If the Preview checkbox isn't checked, click it to turn it on so you can see how the changes you make affect the path on the document page.

7. Because you're not using a pressure-sensitive tablet, change the Diameter pop-up menu to Fixed.

8. Move the Diameter slider back and forth several times, releasing the mouse between new positions. Notice what happens to the path on the document page as well as the three images in the Preview window of the dialog box. End up with 36 as the value in the Diameter field.

   - Notice that the three the images in the palette are the same height (width of the stroke) because the pop-up menu selection is Fixed.

9. Change the selection in the Diameter pop-up menu to Random, enter 18 in the Variation field. Turn off the Preview, then back on again to apply the change to the path in the document.

   - The three images in the Preview window show the width of the path at its original size (middle), the smallest it's allowed to be (left), and the largest it's allowed to be (right).

10. Enter 40% in the Roundness field, change the Roundness pop-up menu to Random, and, using the slider, change Roundness Variation to 25%. Uncheck and check the Preview checkbox.

11. Change the Angle pop-up menu to Random, enter 40° in the Angle field and, using the slider, change Angle Variation to 20°.

    - Notice the changes to the images in the Preview window of the dialog box, as well as the change it made to the path on the document page.

12. Play around a little with various settings until you become familiar with how different settings affect the brushstroke.

13. Click OK or press return/enter to exit the dialog box and save your changes to the brush in the Brushes palette.

    - Choose Apply to Strokes when the Alert box displays.

14. Remove the brushstroke from the path on the document page, so you're left with a plain stroked path.

    - Click the Remove Brush Stroke button at the bottom of the Brushes palette or choose Remove Brush Stroke in the Brushes palette Options menu.

15. Display the Brushes palette Options menu and choose New Brush. Verify that New Calligraphic Brush is the selection in the New Brush dialog box that displays. Click OK or press return/enter to display the Calligraphic brush Options dialog box.

16. Create a new Calligraphic brush from scratch by changing the default values.

    - There is no Preview checkbox so you can't see how your changes look when applied to a stroke.

17. When you're finished making changes to the options in the dialog box, name it and store your new brush in the Brushes palette by clicking OK or pressing return/enter.

18. Apply your new brush to the path, then modify it to be exactly the brush you want by following the steps you learned earlier in this activity.

19. Save the file and close the document.

Create or Modify a Scatter Brush

An object(s) must be selected to make a Scatter brush out of it. You can make a Scatter brush from open or closed paths, compound paths, blend objects, text objects, or text that's been converted to outlines. You cannot make a Scatter brush out of a bitmap image or a vector object containing a pattern fill, a gradient, or a gradient mesh.

A Scatter brush is used when you want multiple copies of objects to follow a path in a random pattern. Using the options in the Scatter Brush Options dialog box, you can set the size of the objects, the rotation, and spacing of the objects as they're applied to a path. To move from one field to the next or to apply changes you've made in the fields, press the *tab* key or click in a different field. You can also click the Preview checkbox off and on to apply changes to a selected path.

fyi Scatter brushes provided by Illustrator in the Brushes libraries (Window ⇨ Brush Libraries) include Animal Sample, Arrow Sample, Floral Sample, and Object sample.

1. To create a new Scatter brush, select the object or objects with the Selection tool, display the New Brush dialog box (described previously), and choose New Scatter Brush to display the Scatter Brush Options dialog box (Figure 10.5).

   To modify an existing Scatter brush, deselect all paths and double-click the brush to display the Scatter Brush Options dialog box

   or

   ■ Click the brush in the Brushes palette and choose Brush Options from the Brushes palette Options menu.

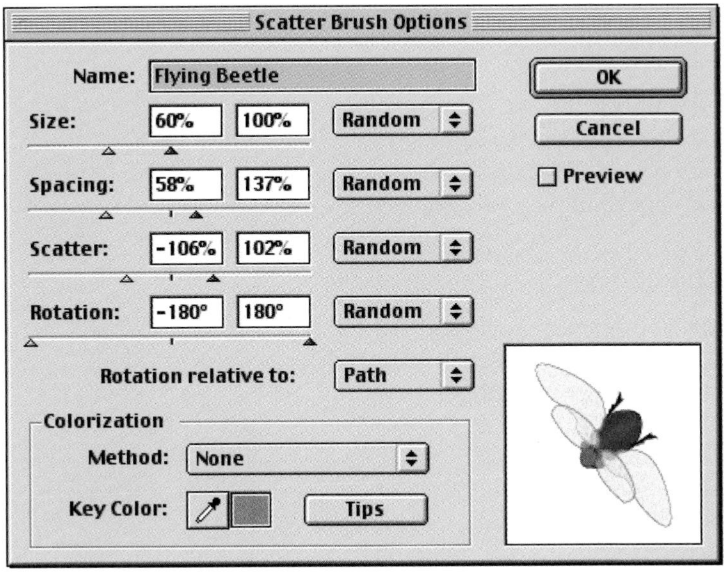

FIGURE 10.5
Scatter Brush Options dialog box.

465

2. When the Scatter Brush Options dialog box displays, enter the desired changes:

   ■ In the Name field, enter a new name or change the existing name. You can enter as many as 30 characters.

   ■ When modifying an existing brush, check the Preview checkbox if you want to see the effects of your changes on any paths in the current document to which that brush was applied.

      ▪ You can see the results of your changes to the original object in the Preview window as you make them.

   ■ Each of the four options, Size, Spacing, Scatter, and Rotation, has a pop-up menu containing the same three options.

      ▪ **Fixed** — The attribute (size, spacing, scatter, rotation) is always the same throughout the stroke.

         ▪ The second field for each attribute is unavailable.

      ▪ **Random** — Allows the values of the specific attribute to vary.

         ▪ Both fields for each attribute become available and two slider triangles appear on the slider bar.

   ■ **Pressure** — This option is available only when you're using a pressure-sensitive drawing tablet. Light pressure equates to the value in the left field and heavy pressure to the value in the right field.

3. **Size** — Controls the size of the objects in the brushstroke in random fashion in relation to the size of the original object that created the brush. You can enter any percentage from 1% to 1000%. 100% is the size of the original object, so a value smaller than 100% specifies that some objects smaller than the original are displayed on the path. A value larger than 100% allows objects larger than the original to display on the path.

   ■ Stroke weight also affects the size of brushstroke objects. For example, a 1 pt stroke weight displays objects the same size as the size specified in the Fixed Size field. A .5 pt stroke weight displays objects 50% of the size entered in the Fixed Size field.

4. **Spacing** — Determines how close together the objects are spaced on the path. Enter a value from 1% to 1000%.

   ■ If Random is the selection in the pop-up menu, one field determines the minimum distance between objects, the other field determines the maximum distance between objects.

timesaver
To move both sliders at the same time and maintain their spacing, Shift-drag a slider. To move sliders apart by the same distance, ⬊ -drag a slider.

5. **Scatter** — Specifies how far from the pathline objects can stray.

   ■ When the selection in the pop-up menu is Fixed, a positive value in the field aligns all objects above a horizontal path or to the right of a vertical path. Conversely, a negative value places all objects below a horizontal path or to the left of a vertical path.

   ■ The higher the value, the more objects stray from the path and the less distinct the path becomes.

6. **Rotation** — Rotate the objects along the path by the value specified.

   ■ If Fixed is the selection in the pop-up menu, all objects are rotated to the angle specified in the field.

   ■ If Random is the pop-up menu selection, objects are randomly rotated to the minimum and maximum angles specified in the fields. Enter positive numbers to rotate the objects counterclockwise, enter negative numbers to rotate the objects clockwise. Enter a negative number in one field and a positive number in the other field to randomly rotate objects both ways.

7. **Rotation relative to** — Using the two options available in the pop-up menu, determine whether the rotation values are calculated from the bottom of the page (Page) or from the orientation of the path (Path).

8. **Colorization** — The Colorization section of the dialog box controls how the Scatter brush is affected by changes in stroke color. The options are the same for Scatter, Art, and Pattern brushes. Refer to Colorization Options in the next section.

9. Click OK or press *return/enter*.

   ■ The new Scatter brush is added to the Brushes palette after the last scatter brush. A new row is added to the section, if necessary.

activity 10.3

1. Create a new document: Letter size, CMYK color mode. Save it into your Practice folder as an .eps file named Leaf Scatter Brush.eps.

2. Locate and open the file in your Practice folder that you created and named Leaf.eps.

3. Copy one of the leaves, including its "veins," and paste it into the file you just created.

   ■ It doesn't matter what color the leaf is.

4. Close the Leaf.eps file without saving changes.

5. With the Selection tool, select the entire leaf and move it up to a corner of the page or onto the scratch area so it's out of the way.

6. Display the Brushes palette and click the New Brush button at the bottom. Choose New Scatter Brush when the New Brush dialog box displays.

7. When the Scatter Brush Options dialog box displays, name it Leaf Scatter Brush, and change the Size, Spacing, and Scatter fields from Fixed to Random.

8. Click OK or press *return/enter*, then deselect the leaf.

   ■ A thumbnail of the new brush displays in the Brushes palette.

9. With the Pencil tool, draw a path on the page with a fill of None and a 1 pt black stroke.

10. Apply the Leaf Scatter Brush you just created. Leave the path selected.

11. Double-click the thumbnail of the Leaf Scatter Brush in the Brushes palette to display the Scatter Brush Options dialog box. Move it so you can see the dialog box and the path you drew on the page.

    ■ The Preview box is now present in the dialog box because a path is selected on the document page.

12. Make the following changes to the designated fields:

    ■ Size: 20% – 60%

    ■ Spacing: 20% – 40%

    ■ Scatter: –20% – 20%

- Notice that because the Preview box was checked, as soon as you entered a value in a different field, your previous changes were applied immediately to the active path on the document page.

- Notice that because the option in the Rotation pop-up menu remains Fixed, the leaves are all in the same orientation as the original leaf, that is, straight up and down with the edges of the page.

13. Change the Rotation Relative To pop-up menu to Path.

    ■ Notice that now the leaves tilt to orient themselves to follow the direction of the path.

14. Change the Rotation pop-up menu to Random and enter –20 and 20 in the two fields.

    ■ The rotation of the leaves become even more varied as they follow the path.

15. Click OK or press *return/enter* to exit the dialog box.

    ■ When the Alert box displays, click Apply to Strokes.

16. With the Pencil tool or the Pen tool, draw another path on the page.

    ■ The brushstroke is applied automatically because the Remove Brushstroke command has not been applied to remove it.

17. Double-click the Leaf Scatter Brush thumbnail to display the Brush Options dialog box. Experiment by making different combinations of changes in the various fields to customize your new brush to your liking. Then save it into the Brushes palette.

    ■ Use the sliders to adjust the values. To move values apart by the same amount, ⬚-drag a slider.

18. Display a Brush library (Window ➪ Brush Libraries) and modify one of the Scatter brushes provided by Illustrator.

19. Save the file and close the document.

Colorization Options

The Colorization section in the Brush Options dialog box is the same for Scatter, Art, and Pattern brushes, but is not available for Calligraphic brushes. This section allows you to choose how color is applied to a brushstroke, regardless of the color of the original object used to create the brush. You can even change the color of the brush itself, not just the brushstroke that's applied to a path.

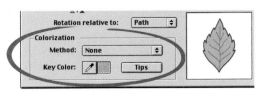

Determine how color is applied to scatter, art, and pattern brushes in the Colorization section of the Brush Options dialog boxes

The examples section at the bottom of the Colorization Tips dialog box (Figure 10.6) shows examples of the results of applying the options in the Method pop-up menu.

- **Method** — This pop-up menu offers four ways to color Scatter brush objects after they've been applied to a path.

  - **None** — Color of the original brush object is used, regardless of stroke color in Color palette.

  - **Tints** — Use for black and white, grayscale, or spot color brushes. Black areas in brushstroke objects are changed to 100% of the current stroke color in the Color palette. White areas remain white. Non-black and non-white areas become tints of the stroke color. You can change stroke color in the Color palette or Toolbox to change the brush color on a path.

  - **Tints and Shades** — Use for black and white and grayscale brushes. The darkest color in the brush object is converted to 100% black; white areas remain white. Other areas become shades of the stroke color in the Color palette.

  - **Hue Shift** — Use for process color brushes or multi-colored spot colors. Applies the stroke color in the Color palette to the areas of the brush object that are designated as the Key Color. Other colors, if any, become colors that are related to the stroke color. Black, white, and gray colors are unchanged.

- **Key Color** — The most prominent color in the brush object. The Key Color for the brush object displays in the Key Color box next to the eyedropper.

  - **Change Key Color** — You can change the Key Color to a different color in the object:

    1. Click the Key Color eyedropper.

    2. In the Preview window, sample the desired color in the brush object to select it and display it in the Key Color box.

✓ None
   Tints
   Tints and Shades
   Hue Shift

Options available in the Method pop-up submenu in the Colorization section of the Brush Options dialog boxes

Because black is added to brushstroke objects when the Tints & Shades method is used, you can't use this option for a 1-color project, unless the color is black.

3. Deselect the eyedropper by clicking it again.

■ **Tips** — Click the Tips button to display a box displaying examples of what happens to colors when the different options are selected in the Methods pop-up menu (Figure 10.6).

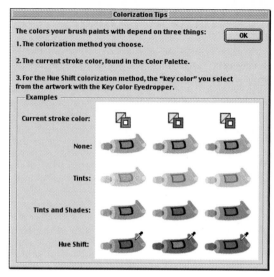

FIGURE 10.6
Colorization tips.

 *activity 10.4*

1. Open the file you saved into your Practice folder in Activity 10.3, named Leaf Scatter Brush.eps.

2. Select the brushstroke to which the Leaf Scatter Brush has been applied.

3. In the Color palette, change the stroke color to 85% cyan, 0% magenta, 50% yellow, 0% black.

4. Double-click the Leaf Scatter Brush in the Brushes palette to display the Scatter Brush Options dialog box. Verify that the Preview box is checked.

5. In the Colorization section, change the Method pop-up menu to Tints.

■ Notice what happens to the color of the brushstroke objects. The outlining stroke is 100% of the stroke color as displayed in the Color palette and the interior color is a tint of that color.

6. In the Colorization section, change the Method pop-up menu to Tints and Shades.

■ The outlining stroke is changed to black and the interior color is a tint of the stroke color as displayed in the Color palette.

7. Change the Method pop-up menu to Hue Shift.

■ The outlining stroke and the veins remain black, as they were in the original object, and the interior of the leaf becomes the stroke color that's in the Color palette.

8. Click OK or press *return/enter* to exit the dialog box. In the alert box that displays, choose Apply to Strokes. then deselect all paths.

9. Display the Floral Sample Brush library (choose Window ➪ Brush Libraries ➪ Floral Sample).

10. Click the Pansy Art brush in the Brush library so it displays in the current document's Brushes palette, then close the Floral Brush library.

11. Select the Pansy art brush then, with the Paintbrush tool, draw a sweeping curve on the document page.

12. Double-click the Pansy Art brush to display the Art brush Options dialog box.

13. Verify that the Preview box is checked. In the Colorization section, change the pop-up menu selection to Hue Shift.

■ Notice what happened to the color of the pansy on the path.

14. Click the Preview button off and on a couple of times. Then click OK or press *return/enter*.

■ Make the appropriate response when the Alert box displays.

15. Save the document and close the file.

Create or Modify an Art Brush

Artwork containing one or more objects or compound paths can be used to create art brushes. You can't use objects containing gradients, gradient meshes, or clipping masks. An art brush stretches along a path and has a front and a back. You can change the size and direction of the object, or flip it across the path.

To create an art brush:

1. With the Selection tool, select the object or objects to be used as an art brush.

2. To create a new art brush, display the Art Brush Options dialog box (Figure 10.7).

   ■ Drag the selected object(s) onto the Brushes palette.

   or

   ■ Click the New Brush button at the bottom of the Brushes palette to display the New Brush dialog box. Click the New Art Brush button, then click OK or press *return/enter*.

   or

 Illustrator provides art brushes in the Animal Sample, Arrow Sample, Artistic Sample, Floral Sample, and Object Sample libraries. Choose Window ⇨ Brush Libraries to display these brush libraries.

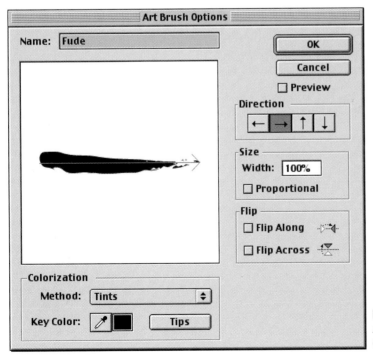

FIGURE 10.7
Art Brush Options dialog box.

Step 10 — BRUSHES, PATTERNS, & SYMBOLS

471

- Display the Brushes palette Options menu and choose New Brush to display the New Brush dialog box. Click the New Art Brush button, then click OK or press *return/enter*.

or

- To modify an existing art brush, double-click its thumbnail in the Brushes palette.

3. Enter a new name in the Name field, or leave the existing name to replace an existing brush. Enter as many as 30 characters.

4. If you're modifying an existing brush, the Preview box appears in the dialog box. When checked, any paths to which the art brush has been applied update immediately as you make changes, even if they aren't selected.

5. Choose Direction, Size, and Flip options to create a custom brush.

- **Direction** — Controls the direction the art is drawn when you drag the paintbrush. The artwork flows along the path in the direction the arrow points.

  - Specifying a vertical arrow to a horizontal piece of artwork causes the width of the object to stretch along the path — and may distort the path into something unrecognizable. And vice versa with a horizontal arrow on a vertical piece of artwork.

- **Size** — Sets the thickness of the artwork on the path. Click the Proportional checkbox to scale the artwork uniformly.

- **Flip** — Click the Flip Along checkbox to reverse the direction of the brush object along its axis. Click the Flip Across checkbox to flip the object across the axis of the path.

6. Apply the desired Colorization options. Refer to the previous section that explains Colorization Options.

7. Click OK or press *return/enter*.

fyi To control where the end of an art brush or pattern brush is placed on a closed path, split the path with the Scissors tool. If it still doesn't look like you want it to, select the endpoints with the Lasso tool and join the endpoints (Object ⇨ Path ⇨ Join), so you have a closed path again. Then split the path in a different place.

![mouse graphic] *activity 10.5*

1. Create a new document: Letter size, CMYK color mode. Name it Arrow Art Brush.eps and save it into your Practice folder as an .eps file.

2. Draw a custom arrow:
   - Display the grid.
   - Change the fill to None and the stroke to 1 pt blue.
   - With the Pen tool, click at the intersection of two gridlines. Move up two cells and, with the *Shift* key held down, click.
   - Move to the left 6 cells and down 3 cells, click.
   - Move to the right 6 cells and down 3 cells, click.
   - Move up 2 cells and, with the *Shift* key down, click.
   - Move to the right about 20 cells and, with the *Shift* key down, click.
   - Move up 1 cell and to the left 2 cells, click.
   - Move up 1 cell and to the right 2 cells, click.
   - Move to the left to the first anchor point you created and, when the loop displays on the Pen tool pointer, click to close the shape.
   - Deselect the shape, then reselect it with the Direct Selection tool so that all anchor points are hollow. Click on the top anchor point of the arrowhead and drag it back 1 cell. Drag the bottom anchor point back one cell.
   - Remove the stroke and apply a blue fill.

3. Hide the grid and save the file.

4. With the Selection tool, select the object and drag the shape onto the Brushes palette to display the New Brush dialog box. Choose New Art Brush and click OK or press *return/enter* to display the Art Brush Options dialog box.

5. Enter the name Arrow Art Brush in the Name field. Click OK or press *return/enter*.
   - The Preview checkbox is not available when creating a new brush.

6. Draw a rectangle with a None fill, and apply the new brush.

7. Double-click your new Arrow Art Brush thumbnail to redisplay the Art Brush Options dialog box.

8. Position the dialog box and the rectangle so you can see both on your screen.

9. Make changes in the dialog box and notice how each change affects the brushstroke on the rectangle.

10. Click OK or press *return/enter* when you like how the arrow looks on the path.
    - Click Apply to Strokes when the Alert box displays.

11. Select the original arrow object. Change the fill color to yellow and the stroke to 2 pt purple.

12. Drag the yellow arrow onto the Brushes palette and click the New Art Brush button. Then click OK or press *return/enter* to display the Art Brush Options dialog box.

13. Enter the name Yellow Arrow Art Brush in the Name field then click OK or press *return/enter*.

14. Select the rectangle and apply the yellow arrow art brush.

15. Double-click Yellow Arrow Art Brush to display it's Art Brush Options dialog box.

16. Make changes in the Colorization options and notice how the changes affect the color of the brushstroke on the rectangle.

17. Click OK or press *return/enter* when you've finished experimenting.
    - Click Leave Strokes when the Alert box displays.

18. Save the file and close the document.

Create or Modify a Pattern Brush

Pattern brushes were devised by Illustrator so brushes applied to shapes with square corners, such as rectangles, triangles, and so on, flow smoothly around the corners. When you create a pattern brush, you first create "tiles" that make up the pattern, then you designate them as a Pattern brush.

It may require as many as five tiles to create a smoothly flowing pattern when it's applied to a square-cornered closed path. The most confusing part about constructing a pattern tile is getting the corners right (see Figure 10.8).

- **Side** () — defines the sides of the path.
- **Outer corner** () — defines the outer edge of corners in the path.
  - Corner pattern starts at the bottom of the bounding box and ends at the right edge of the bounding box (turns left).
- **Inner corner** () — defines the inner edge of corners in the path.
  - Corner pattern starts at the right side of the bounding box and ends at the bottom of the bounding box (turns right).
- **Start** () — defines the beginning of the path.
- **End** () — defines the end of the path.

Not all pattern brushes require 5 tiles. For example, a brush that will be applied only to curved paths doesn't need tiles for the inner and outer corners. Some patterns may not require start and end tiles.

Once pattern tiles have been drawn, store them in the Swatches palette.

1. With the Selection tool, select the artwork for the tile and drag onto the Swatches palette.
2. Double-click the pattern swatch to display the Swatch Options dialog box.
3. Enter a name for the swatch in the Swatch Name field.
   - To help you remember where the tile goes in the pattern, include a description in the name, such as *side*, *start*, *end*, and so on.
4. Click OK or press *return/enter*.
5. Deselect the tile objects on the document page.
6. Follow the instructions on Defining the Pattern Brush later in this chapter.

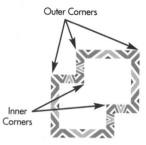

FIGURE 10.8 Square-cornered path having outside and inside corners. Notice the difference between the outer corner and inner corner design.

Side   Outer   Inner   Start   End

fyi Pattern brush samples can be found in the Border Sample library (Window ⇨ Brush Libraries ⇨ Border Sample). Additional pattern brushes can be found in the Brushes Libraries folder inside the Illustrator Extras folder that's in the Adobe Illustrator 10 folder on your hard drive or on the Illustrator 10 CD-ROM.

Guidelines for Creating the Pattern Tiles

Draw artwork for pattern tiles the same way you draw other objects in Illustrator. You can use any of the creation and reshaping tools. Some guidelines for creating pattern tiles are:

- Separate shapes may need to be drawn for corner, side, start, and end tiles.
- Draw tiles large enough to work with easily. Tiles can be scaled later in the Pattern Options dialog box.
- Side tiles should be horizontally rectangular in shape. Rotate vertical rectangular shapes to a horizontal position, if necessary.
- Corner tiles should be square, *exactly* the same height as the side tile.
  - Corner tiles are rotated automatically for each corner (of the same type) in the path, that is, all outer corners or all inner corners.
- Tiles must align precisely. A rectangle with a fill and stroke of None can be used to aid in fitting the tiles together.
  - A boundary-defining rectangle doesn't actually crop the shape as it does when creating a pattern fill (later in this chapter).
- If you apply global process color swatches to pattern tiles, colors can be changed easily by modifying the global process color.

Defining the Pattern Brush

Once you have created the pattern tiles and stored them in the Swatches palette, you can use them to define the pattern for the pattern brush:

1. Display the New Brush dialog box and click the New Pattern Brush button to display the Pattern Brush Options dialog box (see Figure 10.9).

2. Enter a name for the new brush in the Name field.

3. Click one of the tile buttons at the top of the dialog box to select the part of the pattern to define.
   - The small white square shows which part of the pattern the tile pertains to. For example, the leftmost tile button has the white square on a side segment, indicating that the tile button is defining a side element.

4. Click the name of a pattern swatch that's stored in the Swatches palette.
   - All pattern swatches currently stored in the Swatches palette are displayed by name in the Scroll window.

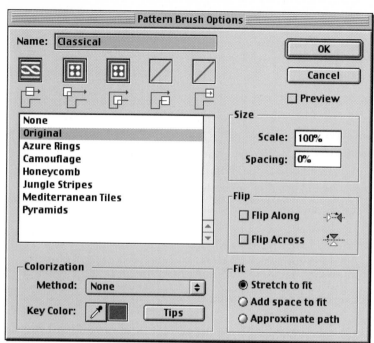

FIGURE 10.9
Pattern Brush Options
dialog box.

5. Repeat #3 and #4 above until all necessary tiles for the pattern are defined.

- If a tile isn't required for the pattern you're defining, click None in the Scroll window.

- For a pattern that will be applied only to a curved closed path, only the Side tile needs to be defined.

6. Click OK or press *return/enter*.

- The Pattern Brush Options dialog box doesn't display the Preview checkbox when a new pattern brush is being defined. It's easier to specify other options in a pattern design using the preview function, so follow the instructions in the Modifying a Pattern Brush to tweak your design.

- Individual tiles are arranged in a pattern brush row in the Brushes palette in the following order, from left to right: Outer corner, side, inner corner, start, and end.

Modifying a Pattern Brush

To change an existing pattern brush:

1. Select an existing path in the document, or draw a new one.

2. Display the Pattern Brush Options dialog box.

- Double-click the pattern brush you want to change.
  or

476

 You may notice that very thin lines sometimes appear between tiles. Most of the time these lines don't print, but you should enlarge the pattern and print it to verify that they aren't going to print. If they do print, continue tweaking where paths intersect the edges of the tiles. They must be aligned precisely with the edge.

- Display the Brushes palette Options menu and choose Brush Options.

3. Check the Preview checkbox to turn it on.
    - Changes are updated immediately on brushes applied to paths in the current document. If a path in the document isn't selected, the Preview box doesn't display in the dialog box.

4. Click a tile button to replace the current tile with another, then choose a new tile from the list in the scroll window.
    - To remove a pattern from a selected tile, click None in the list.
    - To return a selected tile to the state it was in when the dialog box was opened, click Original in the list.

5. Specify settings for the following options:
    - **Size: Scale** — Determines the size of the tiles. 100% is the size of the original object. A lower number reduces the size of the tiles; a higher number enlarges the size of the tiles.

      Spacing — Adds space between tiles.
    - **Flip Along** — Reverses the direction of pattern tiles.
    - **Flip Across** — Flips pattern tiles across the path's axis. That is, what was on the bottom of a horizontal path is now on the top, or what was on the left side of a vertical path is now on the right side.
    - **Fit:** Provides three options for fitting tiles to the selected path.
      - **Stretch to fit** — Shorten or lengthen pattern tiles, where necessary, to fit on the path.
      - **Add space to fit** — Space is added between tiles, where necessary, so the pattern fits on the path.
      - **Approximate path** — Adjust position of the tiles on the path (slightly inside or slightly outside the pathline) to fit the tiles on the path without changing their shape or spacing.
    - To return a selected tile to the state it was in when the dialog box was opened, click Original in the list.

6. Specify the appropriate changes in the Colorization section. For information, refer to the Colorization Options section previously discussed in this chapter.

7. Click OK or press *return/enter*.
    - If the pattern brush is applied to a path in the current document, an alert dialog box displays.
      - Click Apply to Strokes to apply the new pattern to brushstrokes in the current document.
      - Click Leave Strokes to leave brushstrokes in the current document unchanged.

 If you reshape a path with a pattern brushstroke applied, the pattern adjusts along the new path shape. Corner, side, or end tiles are added or eliminated automatically as needed.

activity **10.6**

1. Create a new document: Letter size, CMYK color mode. Name it New Pattern Brush.eps and save it into your Practice folder as an .eps file.

2. Verify that Snap to Point is turned on.

3. With the rectangle tool, draw a 1" square shape. Apply a fill color of 24% cyan, 92% magenta, 84% yellow, 11% black, no stroke.

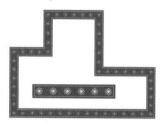

4. Create ¾" square, no fill, 3 pt white stroke. Position it inside the first square so the center points align.

5. In the Units & Undo Preferences dialog box, change the General Unit of Measurement to Points.

6. Draw an oval that's 9 pt wide and 18 pt high. No fill, 2 pt white stroke. Snap it's bottom anchor point to the center point of the square.

7. Deselect the objects, then, with the Selection tool, reselect only the oval.

8. Choose the Rotate tool in the Toolbox. ⌥-click the bottom anchor point of the oval to establish that point as the point of rotation. When the Rotate dialog box displays, enter 45° in the Angle field, and click the Copy button to create a copy that's rotated at a 45° angle.

   - Zoom in as much as necessary to make sure you click precisely on the anchor point.

9. Press ⌘d 6 times to rotate copies around the point to complete the shape.

10. This is the basic design of the pattern tile. Now it has to be converted into a start, end, side, and corner tiles. So drag-copy three more of the tiles so you have a total of four tiles.

11. Start tile:
   - With the Selection tool, select the square with the 3 pt white stroke.
   - Choose the Scissors tool in the Toolbox and click on the top right anchor point to split the path there.
   - With the Scissors tool, click on the bottom right anchor point to split the path there, too.
   - Select the vertical path that you just split away from the rest of the square and delete it.
   - Enlarge the view to 6400%.
   - With the Direct Selection tool, select the 3-sided path. Click on the top right endpoint of the horizontal path to select it and press the right-pointing arrow key repeatedly until the edge of the stroke is aligned exactly with the right edge of the tile. Repeat for the bottom right endpoint.
     - The number of times you have to press the arrow key depends upon the setting in the Keyboard Increment field in the General Preferences dialog box.

12. End tile:
   - Follow the instructions as given for creating the Start tile, except perform them on the left side of the tile instead of the right side.

13. Side tile:
   - Follow the instructions as given for creating the Start tile, except remove both vertical paths and extend the white paths to the edge on both sides.

Continued

478

14. Corner tile (this is the tricky one):

- Select the white-stroked square in this pattern tile and, with the Scissors tool, click on the top right anchor point to split the path. But don't delete any paths.

- With the Scissors tool, click on the bottom left anchor point to split the path. But don't delete any paths.

- With the Scissors tool, click on the bottom right anchor point to split the path. But don't delete any paths.

- With the Direct Selection tool, click on the top horizontal white line, select the righthand endpoint, and drag it to the right until it aligns precisely with the right edge of the tile.

- With the Direct Selection tool, click on the left vertical white line, select the bottom endpoint, and drag it down until it aligns precisely with the bottom edge of the tile.

- With the Direct Selection tool, select the bottom horizontal path, and click on the right endpoint to select it. Using the right-pointing arrow key move the endpoint to the right until it is aligned with the right edge of the tile.

- With the Direct Selection tool, select the bottom horizontal path, and click on the left endpoint to select it. Using the right-pointing arrow key move the endpoint to the right until it is aligned (or close) with the white vertical stroke.

- With the Direct Selection tool, select the right vertical path, and click on the bottom endpoint to select it. Using the down-pointing arrow key move the endpoint down until it is aligned with the bottom of the tile.

- With the Direct Selection tool, select the right vertical path, and click on the top endpoint to select it. Using the down-pointing arrow key move the endpoint down until it is aligned with the top of the white horizontal stroke.

15. In each instance, the white stroke must align *precisely* with the edge of the tile. If it extends beyond the tile by even a fraction, a space will appear between tiles when they're applied to a path. If it doesn't extend close enough to the edge so that part of the tile is visible, it will be visible when the brush is applied to a path, too. To avoid this problem, change the Keyboard Increment value in General Preferences to .001 pt. Enlarge the view to 6400% and, using the arrow keys, move the endpoints back into the tile until you can see a tiny part of the edge of the tile. Then move the endpoint back out until that tiny part of the edge of the tile disappears.

16. When you've finished tweaking the tiles, convert them into a pattern brush. With the Selection tool, select the entire Start tile and drag it to the Swatches palette. Deselect the tile. Double-click the pattern swatch in the Swatches palette and enter a descriptive name in the Name field when the New Swatch dialog box displays.

17. Repeat #16 for the side, end, and corner tiles.

18. In the Brushes palette, display the Brushes palette Options menu and choose New Pattern Brush. Click OK or press *return/enter*.

19. When the Pattern Brush Options dialog box displays, enter a name for this pattern brush in the Name field.

20. Click the Side icon (the first one in the row) then locate the name of your side tile in the scroll window and click on it to assign to the Side tile icon.

21. Repeat #19 for the corner, start, and end tiles. Use the same corner tile for both the inner corner and outer corner tiles.

- Even though the inner corner and outer corner tiles are the same, you must assign it to both icons.

22. Change the value in the Scale field to 10%

- Because we made the pattern tiles so large, you may want to scale them down before creating a pattern brush. Then you have more flexibility with size in the scale field in this dialog box. Use the Transform Scale command to change the size of the tiles in the document, though. Don't drag a corner

Continued

handle or use the Scale tool, because the tiles must be *precisely* the same size.

23. Click OK or press *return/enter*.

24. On the document page, draw a shape similar to the one shown at the beginning of this activity and apply the new pattern brush.

25. If you can see gaps or tile edges, go back to your original tiles and tweak them, then remake the brush.

- I had to remake my brush about three times when I created it for this book.

- Sometimes you'll see gaps and marks on your screen, but when you print a page containing the brushstroke they don't show up.

26. Save the file.

27. When you're satisfied with your brush, print it, and close the document.

Edit Existing Scatter, Art, or Pattern Brushes

In addition to making changes to a Scatter, Art, or Pattern brush in its Options dialog box, you can change the shape or color of the original object.

1. Drag the brush onto the document page or the artboard to display the original object that created the brush.

2. Select the objects or parts of the objects using the same selection tools you would use for any other object drawn in Illustrator, including selecting it in the Layers palette. Make the desired changes to the object, then save it as a new brush.

3. To replace an existing Scatter or Art brush:

   - With the Selection tool, select the object(s), then drag to the Brushes palette until it's over the thumbnail for the original object. Hold down the ⌥ key until a thumbnail displays a solid black border, then release the mouse. When the Brush Options dialog box displays, enter a new name or leave it as is.

4. To replace an existing Pattern brush:

   - Drag modified pattern tiles onto the Swatches palette and change its name in the Swatch Options dialog box.

   - Double-click the original Pattern brush in the Brushes palette and redefine the pattern tiles. Click OK or press *return/enter*.

   or

   - Drag the new pattern tile over the tile it's replacing in the Brushes palette. Hold down the ⌥ key before you release the mouse to drop the tile.

     - The Pattern Brush Options dialog box displays with the new tile replacing the original tile.

     - Click OK or press *return/enter* to exit the dialog box.

5. If the brush is applied to a path in the current document, an alert dialog box displays.

   - Click Apply to Strokes to apply the new pattern to brushstrokes in the current document.

   - Click Leave Strokes to leave brushstrokes in the current document unchanged.

Change Brushstrokes on a Selected Object

You can change a brushstroke that's been applied to a path, without affecting other paths to which that brush has been applied and without changing the brush itself. To change only the color of most brushstrokes that have been applied to a path is simple. Just highlight the path and change the stroke color. Some brushes, such as Flying Beetle and the Banana Leaf, though, are not affected by the color of the stroke.

To change brushstroke options (other than color) on a single path:

1. Select a single path or multiple paths having the same brushstroke applied.

2. Click the Options of Selected Object button () at the bottom of the Brushes palette to display the Stroke Options dialog box for the *type* of brush being changed.

   - The dialog box that displays is similar to the Brush Options dialog box that displays when you modify a brush.

3. Make the desired changes in the dialog box.

   - Refer to the information earlier in this chapter regarding the options found in the dialog boxes for the specific brush type being changed.

4. Click OK or press *return/enter*.

   - Only the brushstroke on the selected path is changed. The original brush in the Brushes palette is not affected.

   - If you decide you want to remove the changes you made and go back to the original brushstroke, click a different brush on the Brushes palette, then click the original brush again.

fyi If you've customized an art brushstroke using the Options of Selected Object button on the Brushes palette, you can apply a different brush using those same options by ⌥-clicking a different brush.

Convert Brushstrokes into Separate Objects

You can convert a brushstroke on a path into its individual objects by selecting the brushstroked path and choosing **Object ⇨ Expand Appearance.** You can edit the paths, but you can't edit the original brush and reapply it to the path to change its appearance. The separate objects are no longer a brushstroke.

fyi *When releasing a layer or group containing a scatter brush, the brush object remains on its own object layer. If you select a scatter brush object and select Release to Layers, each path in the brush object is moved to a separate layer, without changing the original scatter brush path.*

activity 10.7

1. Create a new document: Letter size, CMYK color mode.

2. Drag the Banana Leaf scatter brush thumbnail onto the document page. Apply a .5 pt black stroke to all paths in the shape, except the rectangle that surrounds the leaf.

   ■ The default brush has a 0.44 pt dark green stroke.

3. Drag the modified banana leaf over the original banana leaf and, before releasing the mouse, press the ⬚ key. When the solid black border displays around the original banana leaf, release the mouse to replace the original leaf with the modified one.

   ■ The Scatter Brush Options dialog box displays.

4. Click OK or press *return/enter* without making any changes.

5. Draw a circle on the page and apply the new Banana Leaf brush.

6. With the Pencil tool, draw two paths on the document page and apply the Ink Spatter Scatter brush to both of them.

7. Select both paths and change the color by changing the stroke color in the Color palette.

8. Deselect one of the paths.

9. Click the Options of Selected Object button at the bottom of the Brushes palette.

   ■ The Stroke Options dialog box displays.

10. Change the Size fields to 60% and 150%, Spacing fields to 40% and 130%, and Scatter fields to −160% and 160%.

11. Click the Preview button off and on to toggle between the original specifications and the new ones.

   ■ The deselected path is unaffected by the changes made to the scatter objects in the other path.

12. Click OK or press *return/enter*.

13. With the path still selected, apply the Polynesian Pattern brush.

14. Choose Object ⇨ Expand Appearance.

   ■ The objects in the brush are converted to the individual objects that created the pattern. You can select and modify the paths like you would any other path in Illustrator. You just can't treat it like a brushstroke any longer.

15. Close the document without saving it to a file.

Pattern Fills

In addition to filling paths with colors and gradients, you can fill them with patterns. A pattern fill is a design created in Illustrator that repeats over and over to fill an object. When a design is designated as a pattern fill, it's called a pattern tile. Unlike a brush pattern, which can have up to five tiles in one pattern, only one tile makes up a pattern fill.

You can fill an object with a pattern

The Illustrator Extras folder on the Adobe Illustrator 10 CD-ROM includes a folder named Pattern & Texture Libraries that contains pattern and texture libraries for your use. Or you can create your own patterns. Open the libraries and display the pattern swatches the same way you do brushes in the Brushes palette. When you define a design as a pattern, it must be stored as a swatch in the Swatches palette or in a library palette.

- All paths you create in Illustrator, except paths in a graph, can be used as a pattern, including compound paths, brushstrokes, and type converted to outlines.

- Placed images or bitmap images cannot be converted for use as a pattern.

- Fill attributes must be a solid color fill, including white, or no fill.

- You cannot define an object as a pattern fill that is filled with a gradient, a blend, a gradient mesh, or a different pattern fill.

 read this!

If Illustrator won't let you drag selected items onto the Swatches palette to create a Pattern Swatch, one of the objects is probably filled with a gradient, a blend, a gradient mesh, or a pattern.

Applying Pattern Fills to a Path

Apply a pattern fill to a path by clicking its swatch in the palette in which it's stored. When a pattern fill is applied to a path, the pattern tile fills the path (repeats) from left to right and from the bottom to the top according to the placement of the Ruler Origin (see the section on changing the Ruler Origin in Step 6, *Rulers, Grids, & Guides*. Unless the Ruler Origin has been changed in the document, the first pattern tile is placed at the bottom left corner of the path.

- If the Ruler Origin has been moved from its default position, pattern tiles in an object adjust according to the new position of the Ruler Origin.

Move the Pattern Within the Path If you don't like how the pattern is positioned in the path to which it's applied and you don't want to change the Ruler Origin:

- Hold down the ~ key and press the arrow key corresponding to the direction you want to move the pattern.

or

- Hold down the ~ key and, with the Selection tool selected in the Toolbox, drag inside the object.

  - The object can be selected or deselected.

  - The bounding box of the object filled with the pattern appears to move when you drag with the mouse, but it doesn't really move. Just the pattern inside the object moves the distance you dragged with the mouse.

  - It isn't as easy to control the movement of the pattern with this method as it is using the ~ and arrow keys.

Creating a Pattern Fill

It's a simple process to create a fill pattern, but there are a few things you should be aware of.

Guidelines for Creating Pattern Fills

- Complex patterns can choke a printer. A document may take an extraordinarily long time to print or not print at all. So keep pattern fill designs simple.

- The size of a pattern tile should be ½" to 1" square.

  - Use the Info palette to verify the size of the objects.

  - Zoom in and make sure there are no flaws in your design before you designate it as a pattern tile.

  - The smaller the objects are that create a pattern tile, the more copies are needed to generate the pattern. A simple pattern can be placed into a pattern tile multiple times so fewer pattern tiles are required to fill an object.

- Objects aligned in a straight horizontal or vertical manner tend to be boring.

- A pattern tile should be designed in such a way that you can't see the individual pattern tiles.

- A pattern fill can't be enlarged or reduced once it's been applied to a path. You must create a new pattern swatch with the pattern elements at the proper size.

To create a pattern fill and place its swatch into the Swatches palette:

1. Draw, position, and scale one or more objects that you want to define as a pattern fill.

2. Select all the objects.

   - Marquee with the Selection tool.

   - The overall bounding box of the objects defines the boundaries of the pattern tile.

fyi Holding down the ~ key and the ⬚ key at the same time distorts the image in the pattern, creating some interesting effects.

Sample Patterns in Pattern & Texture Libraries

*Basic Graphics ⬡
Grads_2 ⬡
Undulating dots-coarse*

*Cartographic ⬡
Trees ⬡
Topographic Trees 2*

3. To create a pattern swatch and place it into the Swatches palette:

- Choose **Edit ➪ Define Pattern**.
  - The New Swatch dialog box displays automatically. Enter a name for the new pattern swatch and click OK or press *return/enter*.

or

- Drag the selected items onto a blank area of the Swatches palette.
  - A new pattern swatch is created automatically. Double-click the new swatch to display the Swatch Options dialog box and rename it. Then click OK or press *return/enter*.

4. Deselect all the objects.

- If you don't deselect the objects before double-clicking the swatch to display the Swatch Options dialog to name it, the pattern fill is applied to the path of the pattern object.

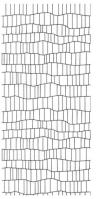

Lithologic ➪ Litho_1 ➪ Lava flows-basic

Define the Boundaries of Your Pattern Fill You don't have to accept the overall bounding box of the objects as the boundary of your pattern tile. You can draw your own boundaries and thus control how much white space appears around pattern objects. Or, using the same procedure, you can eliminate parts of your illustration so they don't appear in the pattern tile.

1. Draw a ½" to 1" rectangle (or drag an existing rectangle) around the objects or the portions of the objects you want to designate as a pattern tile.

- The rectangle defines the boundaries of the pattern tile. Objects extending beyond its boundaries are not part of the pattern tile.
- To eliminate any white space around the pattern object, position the rectangle so it's tight against the object paths. Zoom in so you can position the rectangle accurately.

2. Apply a fill and stroke of None.

3. Send the rectangle to the back of the stack (**Object ➪ Arrange ➪ Send to Back**).

Nature ➪ Environments ➪ Falling Snow

4. If you want a background color behind the pattern, draw another rectangle that's slightly larger than the boundary rectangle and apply a fill color (not a gradient). Then arrange this colored rectangle in the stacking order to fall just in front of the boundary rectangle.

- Send the colored rectangle to the back, then select the boundary rectangle by clicking on its path line and send it to the back.

5. Then select all the objects, including the rectangle, and create a pattern swatch by performing the Define Pattern command (**Edit ➪ Define Pattern**) or by dragging the objects onto a blank area of the Swatches palette.

Classic ➪ Ornament ➪ Medieval diamonds

1. Create a new document: Letter size, CMYK color mode. Name it Patterns Practice.eps and save it into your Practice Folder.

2. Draw a star on the page:
   - Radius 1: 1"
   - Radius 2: .5"
   - Points: 5

3. Color it blue using the Blue (C = 100 M = 50) swatch in the Swatches palette, no stroke.

4. Draw a 1" circle. Color it with the Red (M = 100 Y = 100) swatch in the Swatches palette, no stroke.

5. Position the circle in the center of the star.

6. With the Selection tool, select both objects and drag them to a blank spot in the Swatches palette.

7. Deselect the object.

8. Double-click the swatch to display the Swatch Options dialog box and name the new swatch Star-circle Pattern.

9. Move the objects that created the pattern to the pasteboard so they're out of the way.

10. Draw a fairly large closed path on your page. It can be a polygon, rectangle, or a freehand shape you draw with the Pen tool. Fill the shape with the pattern swatch you just created.

   - Because the bounding box of the star shape was used to define the size of the tile, the stars in the pattern touch each other.

11. Drag the objects that created the pattern onto a blank spot on the document page.

12. Deselect them, then draw a rectangle so it leaves some of the points of the star outside its boundaries. Apply a fill and stroke of None.

13. Send the rectangle to the back of the stack (Object ⇨ Arrange ⇨ Send to Back).

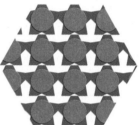

14. Select all three objects, choose Edit ⇨ Define Pattern. When the New Swatch dialog box displays, name the new swatch Star-circle Pattern 2.

15. Select the object you drew in #10 and fill it with this new pattern swatch (Star-circle Pattern 2).

   - Notice the points of the star are chopped off where the rectangle was drawn around the circle.

16. With the shape still selected, hold down the ~ key and press the arrow keys to move the pattern around in the object. Release the ~ key when you're satisfied with its position in the object.

17. With the Selection tool selected in the Toolbox, hold down the ~ key and click and drag the shape to reposition the pattern fill.

   - The object itself looks like it's going to move, but then it snaps back into its original position and only the pattern fill moved.

18. Pay close attention to the position of the pattern fill in your object. Click on the Ruler Origin box in the top left corner of the document window, drag the Ruler Origin about 3" down and 3" to the right, and drop it.

   - Notice that the pattern fill in your object moved, too.

19. Restore the Ruler Origin to its original default position by clicking in the Ruler Origin box.

20. Locate and select the original objects that created the pattern again.

Continued

21. Delete the current rectangle and draw a new one that's about ⅛" outside the boundaries of the points of the star. Apply a fill and stroke of None and send it to the back of the stack.

22. Select all three objects and drag them to the Swatches palette and name it Star-circle Pattern 3.

23. Fill your shape with this new pattern.
    - Notice the difference in the pattern between this one and the first one you used. This one

has space between the stars because you enlarged the size of the pattern tile.

24. Delete the objects that you used to create the pattern.

25. Save the file then close the document.

Creating Uniformly Spaced Patterns

A good pattern fill is one that repeats itself seamlessly, that is, you can't tell where the tiles begin and end. To do this accurately, the object should be in the center of the rectangle and a copy of the object must be in precisely the same relative position in each corner. That is, each copy in the corners of the rectangle must be the same distance from original object and at the same relative angle.

1. Create an object for your pattern that's about ½" high.
    - The object can be a type character or a shape you draw with the Pen tool, the Pencil tool, or one of the defined-shape creation tools (ellipse, rectangle, star, and so on).

2. Verify that Snap to Point is checked in the View menu and turn on Smart Guides.

3. Draw a rectangle around your object to set the size of your pattern tile. Apply a fill and stroke of None, and send it to the back of the stack.
    - Align the center points of the rectangle and your object.
        - If the object doesn't have a center point, display the Attributes palette and click the Show Center button (▣).
    - When Smart Guides is turned on, you're able to see the rectangle when you pass the cursor over it even if it has a None fill and stroke.
    - Or you can apply a .1 black stroke to the rectangle so you can see it when you're working with it. Then remove it before defining the object as a pattern fill. This is what I usually do.

4. ⤵-drag the object to make a copy of it and position it in the upper left corner of the rectangle so the center point of the object snaps to the upper left anchor point.
    - If the pattern consists of multiple objects, align with the center point of the overall bounding box.

Uniform pattern fill

487

5. Drag-copy or copy-and-paste the original object and align one in each of the other three corners of the rectangle.

6. Deselect all paths.

7. If you want a background color behind the objects, draw a rectangle that's slightly larger than the boundary-defining rectangle and apply a fill color. Place it in the stacking order just in front of the boundary-defining rectangle.

8. Select all the objects and drag them to the Swatches palette to create a pattern swatch.

9. Display the Swatch Options dialog box and name the new pattern swatch.

activity 10.9

1. Create a new document: Letter size, CMYK color mode. Name it Spade Pattern.eps and save it into your Practice Folder.

2. Open the document named Playing Cards.eps that you created in Step 9, *Reshape, Combine, & Distort Objects*.

3. Copy the spade you drew (⌘c) then close the document without saving changes.

4. Verify that Snap to Point and Smart Guides are checked in the View menu.

5. Paste your spade into the Spade Pattern.eps document.

6. If the spade object doesn't have a center point, display the Attributes palette and click the Show Center button.

7. Draw a rectangle with no fill or stroke and send it to the back of the stack. Align the center points of the spade and the rectangle.

8. ⟵-drag the spade to make a copy of it and drag it to snap the center point of the spade to the anchor point in the upper left corner of the rectangle.

9. Drag-copy three more spades and position them in the other three corners of the rectangle, aligning the center points of the spade with the corner anchor points.

10. Let's add a colored background behind the spades. Draw a rectangle that's slightly larger than the original boundary rectangle. Apply a 60% yellow fill and send it to the back of the stack.

11. Select the boundary-defining rectangle by clicking on its pathline, then send it to the back.

12. With the Selection tool, select all the shapes and drag them to a blank spot on the Swatches palette.

13. Deselect the shapes, then double-click the new swatch to display the Swatch Options dialog box. Name the new pattern swatch Black Spades.

   ■ If you don't deselect the shapes before you double-click on the swatch to display the Swatch Options dialog box, all the shapes that you used to create the pattern are filled with the new pattern swatch.

14. Draw a large shape and fill it with the Black Spades pattern.

15. Save the file and close the document.

Step 10 — BRUSHES, PATTERNS, & SYMBOLS

Creating Irregular Pattern Fills

To create an irregular pattern tile that repeats so you can't tell where the tile begins and ends can be tricky. To assure that the individual tiles can't be seen, some of the elements must extend beyond the borders of the boundary rectangle into the tile that's next to it.

1. Make sure the Snap to Point and Smart Guides options are checked in the View menu.

2. Draw a boundary-defining rectangle around your object, apply a fill and stroke of None, and send it to the back of the stack.

   ▪ When Smart Guides is turned on, you're able to see the rectangle when you pass the cursor over it even if it has a None fill and stroke.

   ▪ Or you can apply a .1 black stroke to the rectangle so you can see it when you're working with it. Then remove it before defining the object as a pattern fill. This is what I usually do.

3. Draw the paths of your pattern so they intersect the left side of the boundary rectangle, with part of each element extending beyond its border. Assign fill and stroke attributes to the paths.

   ▪ Vary how far the shapes extend outside the boundary rectangle.

4. With the Selection tool, select all paths, including the rectangle.

5. Click the lower left anchor point of the rectangle, drag to the right, hold down the ⬚ key, and snap it to the lower right anchor point. Release the mouse before releasing the ⬚ key.

6. Deselect all paths, then delete the rightmost rectangle.

7. Draw and position paths of the pattern so they intersect only the top side of the rectangle. Pay careful attention to the corners, keeping in mind that the top corner paths have to mesh with the bottom corner paths.

8. With the Selection tool, select only the paths that intersect the rectangle and the rectangle itself.

9. Click the upper left anchor point of the rectangle, drag downward, hold down the ⬚ key, and snap it to the lower left anchor point. Release the mouse before releasing the ⬚ key.

10. Deselect all paths, then select and delete the bottom rectangle.

11. Fill in the rectangle with the pattern element, varying the size, shape, rotation, and so on.

12. Select all elements with the Selection tool and drag onto the Swatches palette to create a new pattern swatch.

13. Assign a name to the new pattern.

activity 10.10

1. Create a new document: Letter size, CMYK color mode. Name it Star Pattern.eps and save it into your Practice Folder as an .eps file.

2. Make sure Snap to Point and Smart Guides are checked in the View menu.

3. Draw a boundary-defining rectangle about 1" square with a fill of None and .1 black stroke.

4. Draw several different sized stars and apply a fill of 50% cyan, 90% magenta, 0% yellow, 0% black to each, no stroke. Rotate them to different angles.

5. Position them along the left edge of the rectangle, varying the distance they extend beyond the edge of the rectangle (Illus. #1).

1

6. With the Selection tool, select all paths, including the rectangle.

7. Click the lower left anchor point of the rectangle, drag to the right, hold down the ⌥ key, and snap it to the lower right anchor point. Release the mouse before releasing the ⌥ key (Illus. #2).

2

8. Deselect all paths, then delete the rightmost rectangle.

9. Draw more different sized stars and rotated stars. Position them so they intersect only the top side of the rectangle (Illus #3).

3

■ Pay careful attention to the corners, keeping in mind that the top corner paths have to mesh with the bottom corners.

10. With the Selection tool, select only the rectangle and the stars that intersect the top side of the rectangle.

11. Click the upper left anchor point of the rectangle, drag downward, hold down the ⌥ key, and snap it to the lower left anchor point. Release the mouse before releasing the ⌥ key (Illus. #4).

4

12. Deselect all paths, then select and delete the bottom rectangle.

13. Fill in the center area of the rectangle with more stars of varying sizes and angles (Illus. #5).

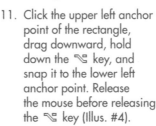

5

14. Deselect all paths.

15. Select the boundary-defining rectangle and apply a stroke of None.

16. With the Selection tool, select all stars and the boundary rectangle. Drag it onto the Swatches palette and drop it in a blank area. Name it Stars Pattern.

17. In a blank spot on your page, draw a large shape on your document page and fill it with your new pattern.

■ Can you see the pattern tiles? If so, read the next section about Modifying Pattern Fills, and adjust your pattern fill until the pattern is seamless.

18. Save the file and close the document.

Modifying Pattern Fills

Pattern fills, including those supplied by Illustrator, can be changed easily.

1. Drag a pattern swatch onto a blank area of your document page.

   - The objects that created the pattern fill become a group with the bounding rectangle that defines the pattern tile behind them.

2. Make any changes to the objects.

   - Use the Direct Selection tool to select individual objects.

   or

   - Use the Layers palette to select individual items. Refer to the information about layers in Step 8, *Layers & Links*, if necessary.

3. With the Selection tool, select all the objects that create the pattern, then drag them back onto the Swatches palette.

   - Drag the objects to a blank area on the palette to create a new swatch, leaving the original swatch unchanged.

     • Objects filled with the original swatch pattern are not changed to the new pattern.

   - To replace the original swatch, ⬎-drag the selected pattern objects over the original swatch until it displays a dark border, then drop it.

     • Any objects filled with the original pattern will update automatically to the new pattern.

Transform Pattern Fills Once a pattern fill has been applied to an object, you can change its appearance by applying the transform tools and commands — Move, Scale, Rotate, Shear and Reflect. The dialog boxes associated with these commands have checkboxes that control whether the transformation is applied to the object, the pattern fill applied to the object, or both at the same time.

   - To transform the pattern fill applied to an object without changing the object, check the Patterns checkbox.

   - To transform the pattern fill applied to an object and the object, too, check both checkboxes.

   or

   - You can transform the pattern fill and the object when you apply the command using a transform tool by checking the Transform Pattern Tiles checkbox in General Preferences (**Edit** ⇨ **Preferences** ⇨ **General** ⇨ **Transform Pattern Tiles**).

Classic ⇨ Ornament ⇨ Medieval diamonds — Color was changed by dragging the swatch to the document page, recoloring it, and returning it to the Swatches palette. The pattern was rotated 90° using the Object ⇨ Transform ⇨ Rotate command.

activity 10.11

1. Open the document named Patterns Practice.eps that you saved into your Practice Folder.

2. Drag the Star-circle Pattern 3 swatch in the Swatches palette onto a blank spot on the document page.

   ■ All the objects that made up the pattern, including the boundary-defining rectangle display as a group with all the paths selected.

3. Draw a white star with no stroke the size of the circle. Position it so it fits entirely within the red circle.

4. With the Selection tool, select all the objects, including the rectangle, and ⤡-drag them over the Star-circle Pattern 3 swatch in the Swatches palette to replace the old one with the new pattern.

   ■ The shape on your document page that contained the old pattern fill updates automatically to the new pattern, even though it wasn't selected.

5. Delete the objects you used to create the pattern fill.

6. Select the shape that's filled with the new pattern.

7. Double-click the Rotate tool in the Toolbox to display the Rotate dialog box. If there isn't a Rotate value in the field, enter 35°. If the Preview box isn't checked, check it.

8. In the Options section, uncheck the Objects checkbox and check the Patterns checkbox.

   ■ The object didn't rotate, but the pattern inside the object did. Don't exit the dialog box.

9. Click the Objects checkbox to turn it on and leave the Patterns checkbox checked, too.

   ■ This time the object and the pattern inside the object rotated. Click Cancel to exit the dialog box without applying the changes.

10. Double-click the Scale tool in the Toolbox. If the Preview checkbox isn't checked, check it then enter 50% in the Uniform field and uncheck the Objects checkbox in the Options section.

   ■ The pattern fill inside the object shrank to 50% of its original size without affecting the size of the object.

   ■ The same procedure works on the Shear and Reflect tools and the Move command.

11. Save the file and close the document.

Convert a Pattern Fill Into Individual Objects You can make changes to elements of a pattern fill after it's been applied to an object. The Expand command in the Object menu converts the elements of a pattern fill into individual paths.

1. Select an object that contains a pattern fill.

2. Choose **Object ⇨ Expand**.

   ■ The Expand dialog box displays.

3. Verify that the Fill and Stroke checkboxes are checked (if the object has a fill and stroke applied to it).

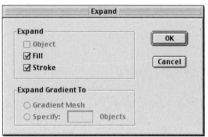

Click the Fill and Stroke checkboxes to convert elements of a pattern fill into individual paths.

4. Click OK or press *return/enter*.

   ■ The pattern fill is converted to its original shapes and becomes a group inside a clipping mask. See Step 12, *Meshes, Masks, Blends, & Transparency*, for information about clipping masks.

   ■ Strokes become compound paths.

This works well if you want to change one element in the pattern fill, for instance, to a different color, but you don't want to change all the duplicates of that element to the new color. Perform the Expand command then select the individual object with the Direct Selection tool and make the appropriate changes.

   ■ Once an object containing a pattern fill has been expanded, it can't be "unexpanded". That is, the pattern can't be manipulated like a regular pattern fill.

You can change the Fill and/or Stroke color/weight of a single element in a pattern fill by expanding its Fill and Stroke using the Expand dialog box

activity 10.12

1. Open the document named Spade Pattern.eps that you saved into your Practice Folder.

2. Select the shape filled with the Black Spades pattern.

3. Choose Object ⇨ Expand to break up the pattern into its individual paths.

4. With the Direct Selection tool, click in the yellow background in the center of the shape to display a pattern tile. Select the spade that's in the center of that tile. Apply a fill of 0% cyan, 0% magenta, 100% yellow, 0% black to the spade.

5. Save the document into your practice folder as Expanded Pattern.eps. Close the document.

Symbols

Each time a path is created in an Illustrator document, the size of the digital file increases. A symbol, in Illustrator, is artwork that can be used many times in a document but it's stored in the file only once, which keeps the file size smaller. File size can be critical when creating artwork for use on the Web because it's important to keep download time as short as possible. For example, you can spray a sky full of stars, but only the original artwork is "counted" in the size of the file.

Banana leaf symbol instances with drop shadow applied. Drop shadows are discussed in Step 11, Filters & Filter Effects.

Symbols can be created from almost any artwork you can create in Illustrator, including gradient meshes, compound paths, type, and embedded raster images. You can't make linked images or graphs into symbols, though. You can't select or edit individual paths in symbol instances placed on a document page. You have to edit the original symbol artwork. When you change the original artwork of a symbol, all instances placed in the document are updated automatically.

Each time a symbol is placed on the document page, it's called an *instance*, and it's linked to the original in the Symbols palette. A *symbol set* consists of multiple symbol instances, connected by a bounding box, that are treated as a single object. You can alter symbol instances or symbol sets without affecting the original artwork by dragging its bounding box handles, applying Transform commands, changing its opacity or blending mode, or applying styles or effects to it.

- Symbol instances placed on the page one at a time and symbol instances sprayed on the page, creating a symbol set, are displayed in the Layers palette as a single object.

Symbols Palette

Symbols are stored on the Symbols palette (Figure 10.10) in the same way that swatches, brushes, and patterns are stored on their respective palettes. Display the Symbols palette by choosing **Window** ➪ **Symbols**. They're saved with the document so when you reopen the document, they'll still be there.

Change Palette Display Change the way symbols are displayed in the Symbols palette by displaying the Symbols palette Options menu and choosing:

- **Thumbnail View** — Displays symbols as swatches.
- **Small List View** — Displays small swatches and the symbol name.
- **Large List View** — Displays large swatches and the symbol name.
- **Sort by Name** — Sorts symbols alphabetically by name.

494

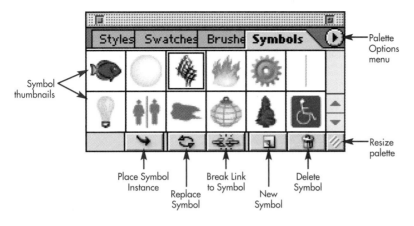

Symbol thumbnails →

Palette Options menu →

Place Symbol Instance

Replace Symbol

Break Link to Symbol

New Symbol

Delete Symbol

→ Resize palette

FIGURE 10.10 Default Symbols palette.

New Symbol...
Redefine Symbol
Duplicate Symbol
Delete Symbol

Place Symbol Instance
Replace Symbol
Break Link to Symbol

Select All Unused
Select All Instances

Sort by Name

✓ Thumbnail View
Small List View
Large List View

Symbol Options...

Symbols palette Options menu

Rearrange Symbols in the Symbols Palette Symbol swatches can be repositioned in the Symbols palette. Drag the symbol to a new place in the palette and release the mouse to drop the thumbnail when a dark line displays between two swatches. The swatch is placed following the dark line.

- To select a series of thumbnails, click the first one, then *Shift*-click the last one to select all thumbnails between the clicks.

- To select random thumbnails, ⌘ -click them.

A dark line displays between two symbols where the moved symbol will be placed

Rename a Symbol You can change the name of any symbol in the Symbols palette. You cannot change the name of a symbol in a Symbol library palette, though, until you place it into the current document's Symbols palette. See the section on Symbol libraries later in this chapter.

1. Display the Symbol Options dialog box:
   - Double-click a symbol on the Symbols palette

   or

   - Click on a symbol in the Symbols palette to select it, display the Symbols palette Options menu, and choose Symbol Options.

2. In the Name field, enter a new name or change the existing name.

3. Click OK or press *return/enter*.

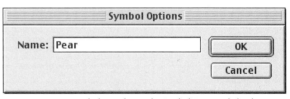

Name or rename symbol swatches in the Symbol Options dialog box

Duplicate a Symbol When you create a new symbol, you may want to start with an existing symbol. Or when redefining an existing symbol, you may not want to destroy the original symbol. In that event, you can duplicate the symbol in the Symbols palette. Duplicate symbols appear in the Symbols palette after the last symbol shown (on a new line, if necessary).

- Drag and drop a symbol swatch on the New Symbol button ( ) at the bottom of the palette.

or

- Click a symbol swatch to select it, display the Symbols palette Options menu, and choose Duplicate Symbol.

or

- Drag one symbol over another symbol, then hold down the key and drop it. The first symbol is copied and the second symbol is deleted.
  - A dark line appears around the second symbol when it's going to be replaced with another symbol.

Select Unused Symbols You can select all symbols in the Symbols palette that aren't used in the document by displaying the Symbols palette Options menu and choosing Select All Unused.

Delete a Symbol You can delete symbols in the Symbols palette.

- Drag and drop a symbol swatch on the Delete Symbol button ( ) at the bottom of the palette.

or

- Click a symbol swatch to select it, then click the Delete Symbol button ( ) at the bottom of the palette.

or

- Click a symbol swatch to select it, display the Symbols palette Options menu, and choose Delete Symbol.

An alert displays so you can be certain you really want to delete the symbols. If you attempt to delete a symbol that's linked to symbol instances in the document, an alert displays with three options:

- Expand Instances — Converts instances into regular objects whose paths can be edited.

- Delete Instances — Deletes all linked instances existing in the document.

- Cancel — Forgets you mentioned it.

If you try to delete a symbol from the Symbols palette that is linked to a symbol instance in the document, this alert displays

Symbol Libraries

More symbols are available than just those shown in the Symbols palette. Display the Symbol Libraries menu (**Window ⇨ Symbol Libraries**) to choose a library.

- Click a symbol in the library palette to add it to the current document's Symbols palette.

or

- Drag a symbol from a library palette onto the document page to add it to the document's Symbols palette.

Default symbol libraries (Window ⇨ Symbol Libraries)

Create Custom Libraries   You can create your own Symbol library by placing symbols in a document and saving it as a native Illustrator document in the Symbols folder inside the Presets folder in the Adobe Illustrator 10 folder on your hard drive (**Adobe Illustrator 10 ⇨ Presets ⇨ Symbols**). Choose your custom library the same way you choose other Illustrator default libraries. Your new custom library won't appear in the Symbols Libraries menu until you quit and relaunch Illustrator 10.

Placing Symbols in a Document

You can place symbols onto a document page one at a time from the Symbols palette or by spraying them with the Symbol Sprayer (discussed later in this chapter). To place them one at a time:

- Drag a symbol from the Symbols palette onto the document page.

or

- Click to select a symbol in the Symbols palette, then click the Place Symbol Instance button ( ) at the bottom of the palette.
  - The symbol is placed in the middle of the artwork window.

The instance is linked to the original symbol in the Symbols palette. Add as many separate instances of the symbol as you want in the document. Or you can select an instance in the document and drag-copy it (⌥-drag) to create additional instances.

When you place symbol instances on a document page one at a time, you can't add symbol instances to them to make a symbol set. Symbol sets can only be created or added to by spraying with the Symbol Sprayer tool.

Select Symbol Instances   You can select all instances of a symbol in a document at one time:

1. Click a symbol thumbnail in the Symbols palette to select it.

2. Display the Symbols palette Options menu and choose Select All Instances.

Charts
Default_CMYK
Default_RGB
Maps
Nature
Objects
Other Library...

fyi *When you select multiple thumbnails in a symbol library, you have to drag them to the document's Symbols palette. Otherwise, only the first symbol is transferred to the Symbols palette.*

Replace a Symbol You can replace a selected symbol instance in a document with a different symbol. Any changes made to the instance, such as transformations, transparency, effects, are applied to the new symbol instance.

1. With the Selection tool, select an instance in your document.

    ■ A black border displays around the Symbol swatch in the Symbols palette.

2. Click a different symbol swatch in the Symbols palette.

3. Click the Replace Symbol button (⎙) at the bottom of the palette.

    or

    Display the Symbols palette Options menu and choose Replace Symbol.

Break the Link of a Symbol Instance to Its Original Symbol You can break the link of a symbol instance to its original symbol in the Symbols palette so it won't be affected by any modifications made to the original symbol:

1. Select an instance of the symbol in the document.

2. Click the Break Link to Symbol button (⎙) at the bottom of the Symbols palette.

    or

    Display the Symbols palette Options menu and choose Break Link to Symbol.

    ■ The paths of the unlinked object are selected in the document.

Creating a New Symbol

Almost any object you create in Illustrator can become a symbol. The exceptions are linked images and graphs. If you're going to spray a lot of them in a single document, it's best to keep the object simple. To create a symbol:

1. Draw a new object and scale it to the desired size. Leave it selected.

    or

    With the Selection tool, select an existing object in your document.

2. With the Selection tool active, drag the selected object on to a blank area of the Symbols palette.

    ■ Rename the new symbol.

    or

    Click the New Symbol button (⎙) at the bottom of the Symbols palette.

    ■ Rename the new symbol.

    or

    Display the Symbols palette Options menu and choose New Symbol.

    ■ When the Symbol Options dialog box displays, type a new name for the symbol in the Name field.

Redefining a Symbol

You can change an existing symbol and change all instances of that symbol in the document or you can create a new symbol without changing any instances in the document. It's a good idea to work on a duplicate of a symbol in the event you decide you want to keep the original, too. If you decide you don't want to keep the original symbol, you can always delete it.

1. In the Symbols palette, make a duplicate of the symbol you're going to edit. If necessary, refer to the instructions for duplicating a symbol earlier in this chapter.

2. In the document, select a symbol instance. Drag one to the document page if necessary.

3. Break the link of the symbol instance with its original symbol in the Symbols palette. Refer to the instructions on breaking the link discussed earlier in this chapter.

4. Edit the object the same way you would any object created in Illustrator.

5. To redefine an existing symbol, thus changing any instances of that object that exist in the document, ⍑-drag the object over its original symbol in the Symbols palette. Release the mouse when the dark line displays around the symbol.

    or

    Click the original symbol on the Symbols palette, display the Symbols palette Options menu, and choose Redefine Symbol.

    ■ Any effects, transformations, etc., applied to symbol instances in the document before the symbol was redefined remain applied to the symbol instances after the original object is redefined.

fyi You can drop the object on any symbol in the Symbols palette, or click any symbol to redefine it with the selected object. It doesn't have to be the original object that created the symbol instance.

Expanding a Symbol Instance or Symbol Set

The Expand command in the Object menu (**Object ⇨ Expand**) can be applied to a symbol set to disconnect the symbols from the set, making them individual instances. These individual instances are still linked to the original object in the Symbols palette. The symbol set becomes a group and, in the Layers palette, individual instances are nested under the <Group> layer. The instances can be ungrouped using the Ungroup command the same as any other group created in Illustrator.

1. Select a single instance, multiple instances, or a symbol set.

2. Choose **Object ⇨ Expand** to display the Expand dialog box.

3. Check the Object checkbox or the Fill checkbox, or both.

4. Click OK or press *return/enter*.

When the Expand command is applied to a single symbol instance, the link to the original symbol is broken. The paths become a group, and the individual paths of the symbol are displayed in the Layers palette as individual object layers nested under the <Group> layer. Select these individual object layers in the Layers palette to modify paths in the group.

- Live appearances contained in the original artwork are editable after a symbol instance has been expanded using the Expand Appearance command in the Object menu (**Object ⇨ Expand Appearance**). Appearances are discussed in Step 11, *Filters & Filter Effects*.

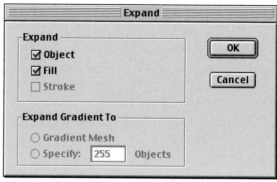

When expanding symbol instances, Object and Fill should be checked in the Expand dialog box

 *activity 10.13*

1. Create a new document: Letter size, CMYK color mode. Save it into your Practice folder as an .eps file named Symbols Practice.eps.

2. Locate and open the file named Pear.eps that you created in Step 4 and saved into your Practice folder.

3. Marquee to select the entire object, then press ⌘c to copy it. Close the artwork window.

4. Press ⌘v to paste the pear artwork into the new document you created.

5. Save the file.

6. Reduce it's size until it's about 1" high.
   - (a) Hold down the *Shift* key and drag the object's bounding box diagonally, (b) use the Scale tool, or (c) use the Scale transform command.

7. Drag the object onto a blank area of the Symbols palette to create a new symbol.

8. Double-click the new symbol to display the Symbol Options dialog box. Name the symbol Pear.

9. Display the Symbols palette Options menu and choose Place Symbol Instance.
   - A symbol instance of the pear is placed in the middle of the artwork window.

10. Drag three or four more pear symbols onto the document page. Don't deselect the last one.

11. Click the Break Link to Symbol button at the bottom of the Symbols palette.
    - The paths of the Pear symbol instance become selected. It's listed as a group in the Layers palette, with its individual components shown as nested <Path> layers

12. Choose Window ⇨ Symbol Libraries and choose Nature.
    - A new Symbols palette displays.
    - Notice that there are no buttons at the bottom of the library palette because you can't alter symbols when they're in a library palette. You must put them in the document's symbols palette before you can use them.

Continued

13. Choose Window ➪ Symbol Libraries again, and choose Objects.

- The second library is displayed in the same palette with a new folder tab.

14. Click the Nature folder tab to display the Nature symbol thumbnails, and click the Grass symbol.

- The Grass thumbnail appears in the document's Symbols palette.

15. In the Symbols palette, drag the Grass thumbnail and drop it so it appears before the Paper Lantern thumbnail.

16. Press the ⌘ key, then select the Grass, Sequoia, and Flames thumbnails. Release the ⌘ key and drag the selected thumbnails over the New Symbol button at the bottom of the Symbols palette. Release the mouse to drop them.

- All three symbols are duplicated in the Symbols palette.

17. Select the duplicated symbols and drag-and-drop them on the Delete Symbol button at the bottom of the Symbols palette.

- These symbols are removed from the palette.

18. One at a time, select the Blue Tang, Gear, and Paint Dab symbols and place them on the document page.

19. Display the Symbols palette Options menu and choose Select All Unused.

- Notice that in the Symbols palette only symbol thumbnails that have not been placed in the document are selected.

20. Click the Delete Symbol button at the bottom of the Symbols palette. Click Yes when the alert box displays.

- All symbols that haven't been placed on the document page are deleted from the Symbols palette.

21. Select the Pear symbol in the Symbols palette, then display the Symbols palette Options menu and choose Select All Instances.

- Notice that in the document all instances of the Pear symbol are selected except the one whose

link was broken in #11 of this activity and the original object used to create the symbol.

22. Place three or four instances of the Paint Dab symbol onto the document page.

23. Make sure the last instance is still selected, then click the Break Link to Symbol button at the bottom of the Symbols palette.

24. Change the color of the object to a dark blue.

25. ⬔-drag the blue paint dab over the original Paint Dab symbol in the Symbols palette and drop it when the dark line appears around the symbol.

- The blue Paint Dab symbol replaces the original gray Paint Dab symbol and all the paint dabs in the document become blue.

26. Choose Window ➪ Symbol Libraries and choose Default_CMYK from the pop-up submenu.

27. When the symbols display in the library palette, select the first symbol, then *Shift*-click the last symbol in the palette.

- All symbol thumbnails between the two clicks are selected.

28. Drag the thumbnails to the document's Symbols palette.

- Now there are two Paint Dab symbols — one gray and one blue.

29. With the Selection tool, click on the Blue Tang (fish) symbol you placed on the page in #18 of this activity.

30. Choose Object ➪ Transform ➪ Reflect to display the Reflect dialog box and reflect the symbol 90° Vertical.

31. Scale it 150%, then drag it into the Symbols palette (don't replace the original symbol). Name it Big Fish.

32. Save the file, then close the artwork window.

Symbolism Tools

There are eight Symbolism tools in the Toolbox that you can use to manipulate symbol instances or symbol sets on a document page: change size, location, rotation, stacking order, and more. Each Symbolism tool applies different characteristics to a symbol instance or a symbol set. A predefined round circle "brush" displays when applying characteristics of a Symbolism tool to a selected symbol instance or symbol set. You can adjust the size and shape of this "brush" in the Symbol Tool Options dialog box.

Except for the Symbol Sprayer tool, symbolism tools are used to change the position (Scruncher and Shifter), stacking order (Shifter), size (Sizer), orientation (Spinner), colorization (Stainer), transparency (Screener), and applied styles (Styler). The transparency features in Illustrator 10 are discussed in Step 12, *Meshes, Masks, Blends & Transparency*, and styles are discussed in Step 11, *Filters & Filter Effects*.

If a symbol set contains more than one kind of symbol instance, changes made with a symbolism tool affect only the symbol instances whose thumbnail is selected in the Symbols palette. If you want the symbolism tool to apply to all the different kinds of symbol instances in the symbol set, click in a blank section of the Symbols palette to deselect all symbol thumbnails.

Symbol Tool Options

The Symbolism Tool Options dialog box (Figure 10.11) is displayed by double-clicking a Symbolism tool in the Toolbox. The top section of the dialog box contains settings that apply to all the tools (global settings). The bottom section contains settings that apply only to the selected tool.

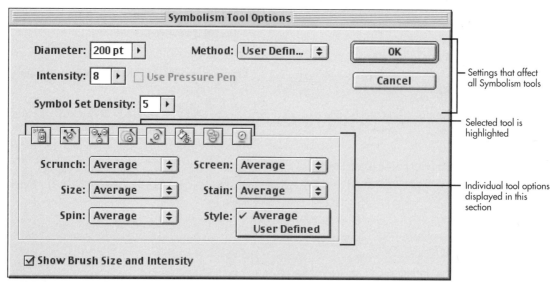

FIGURE 10.11 Symbolism Tool Options dialog box. Change settings to affect characteristics of individual symbol instances or symbol sets on a document page.

The selected tool is highlighted in the row of tools icons in the middle of the dialog box. Some tools have hints pertaining to that tool at the bottom of the dialog box.

Global Settings That Affect All Symbolism Tools

A symbol instance or symbol set doesn't have to be selected when changing options in the Symbolism Tool Options dialog box but it must be selected to apply a Symbolism tool to it. If a symbol instance or symbol set isn't selected when you attempt to apply a Symbolism tool, a warning box displays.

- **Diameter** — Sets the size of the active area covered by the "brush", from 1 to 999 points or .02 to 13.87 inches, etc., depending upon the document's current unit of measurement. You can use any unit of measurement. Click the arrow to display a slider you can drag to change the value.
  - A small brush affects a smaller number of instances; a large brush affects a larger number of instances.

- **Intensity** — Adjusts the rate at which symbol instances are changed, from 1 to 10. The higher the Intensity, the faster a characteristic is applied. When adjusting the Intensity of the Symbol Sprayer tool, a higher Intensity value causes more instances to be sprayed in a given amount of time.
  - Click the arrow to display a slider you can drag to change the value.
  - You can change the intensity of an existing symbol set.

- **Use Pressure Pen** — Check this checkbox to control the intensity with a drawing tablet when one is connected to your computer.

- **Symbol Set Density** — Controls how close together symbol instances in a symbol set are to each other. The value can range from 1 to 10. The higher the value, the closer instances are to each other.
  - Click the arrow to display a slider you can drag to change the value.
  - You can change the density of an existing symbol set.

- **Show Brush Size and Intensity** — When this checkbox is checked, the circle delineating the size of the "brush" is visible. The Intensity value is shown by the shade of the tool's icon: High intensity is black, medium intensity is gray, and low intensity is light gray.
  - I find that trying to ascertain intensity by looking at the tool icon in the center of the brush isn't very accurate.

Click OK or press *return/enter* when you're finished changing values.

timesaver

- Press [to decrease the diameter or] to increase the diameter of the "brush" while applying it to a symbol instance or symbol set.

- Press ⇧ [to increase or ⇧] to decrease intensity as you apply a tool to a symbol instance or symbol set.

fyi The effect of a symbolism tool is strongest in the center of the brush and decreases toward the outer edge of the brush.

Options in the Symbolism Tool Options dialog box that apply to individual tools are discussed with that tool in the following sections.

Symbol Sprayer

Use the Symbol Sprayer tool to spray multiple symbol instances on a document page. To place a single symbol instance on the page, click once. Drag across the page to spread symbol instances as you move the mouse. If you click and hold the mouse in one spot, symbol instances pile up.

Symbol Sprayer tool icon in the Toolbox palette

Add Symbol Instances to an Existing Symbol Set
You can add symbol instances to an existing symbol set by selecting the existing set and spraying a symbol with the Symbol Sprayer. And it doesn't have to be the same symbol; you can add as many different symbols as you want. They all become part of the same symbol set.

Delete Symbol Instances from an Existing Symbol Set
Symbol instances in a symbol set can't be selected with a selection tool, which means they can't be deleted the same way you delete an ordinary object. They can be deleted, though, using the Symbol Sprayer tool.

To delete several different types of symbol instances in a symbol set, make sure no symbols in the Symbols palette are selected.

Symbol instances sprayed with the Symbol Sprayer are enclosed within a bounding box

1. Select the symbol set.

2. Choose the Symbol Sprayer tool in the Toolbox.

3. Select the symbol in the Symbols palette that matches the symbol instance you want to delete or make sure no symbols in the Symbols palette are selected.

4. Hold down the ⌥ key, position the icon over the symbol instance you want to delete, and click to remove a single symbol instance. Click and hold to eliminate several symbol instances, or click and drag over symbol instances to select the symbol instances to delete.

Specific Symbol Sprayer Tool Options
Options for the Symbol Sprayer tool determine how the other tools, except Symbol Shifter, behave when sprayed. Each tool has a pop-up menu from which you can choose Average or User-Defined (see Figure 10.11).

When Average is selected, symbol instances are added to a new or existing symbol set based on the average value of existing symbol instances within the brush circle. For example, if the colorization of the Blue Tang (fish) symbol has been changed until it's green, spraying more symbol instances near it when Average is chosen in the pop-up menu causes the newly sprayed fishes to be green also.

When User-Defined is selected in a tools' pop-up menu, symbol instances are added to a new or existing symbol set based on specific preset values, as follows:

- **Scrunch** — (Density) Based on the size of the original symbol.

- **Size** — Based on the size of the original symbol.

- **Spin** — Based on the direction the mouse moves.

- **Screen** — Based on 100% opacity.

- **Stain** — Based on 100% of the current fill color.

- **Styler** — Based on the style currently selected in the Styles palette.

Symbol Shifter

This tool adjusts the location of symbol instances within a symbol set and you can use it to change the stacking order of symbol instances.

Symbol Shifter tool icon in the Toolbox palette

1. Select a symbol set in the document with a Selection tool.

2. Choose the Symbol Shifter tool in the Toolbox.

3. Position the brush over the symbol instances you want to move, then click and drag in the direction you want the symbol instances to move.

Change Stacking Order of Symbol Instances With the Symbol Shifter tool in the Toolbox selected:

- *Shift*-click on a symbol instance to bring it in front of other symbol instances in the symbol set.

or

Symbol instances sprayed with the Symbol Sprayer tool

- Hold down the ⌥ key and *Shift*-click on a symbol instance to send it behind other symbol instances in the symbol set.

Specific Symbol Shifter Tool Options Double-click the Symbol Sprayer icon in the Toolbox to display the Symbolism Tool Options dialog box with specific options for this tool.

- **Diameter** — Determines how big the brush circle is.

- **Intensity** — Determines how much the spacing of symbol instances is adjusted. A higher value creates more movement of symbol instances.

Stacking of symbol instances rearranged using the Symbol Shifter tool

- **Symbol Set Density** — Specifies how closely packed the symbol instances remain.

- Click OK or press *return/enter* to exit the dialog box.

Method Choices

For the remaining six tools, the Method pop-up menu options are available.

- **Average** — Applies changes uniformly.
- **User Defined** — Applies the effects of the specific tool according to the options specified for that tool.
- **Random** — Applies the effects of the specific tool randomly to symbol instances.

Symbol Scruncher

The Symbol Scruncher tool draws symbol instances together or pushes them apart.

1. Select a symbol set in the document with a Selection tool.

2. Choose the Symbol Scruncher tool in the Toolbox.

3. To draw symbol instances closer together, click and hold in one spot or click and drag the brush inside the symbol set.

   or

   To push symbol instances apart, hold the ⌥ key down while you click and hold or click and drag.

Symbol Scruncher tool icon in the Toolbox palette

Symbol Sizer

Use the Symbol Sizer tool to reduce or enlarge symbol instances in a symbol set. To reduce or enlarge one symbol instance at a time, reduce the diameter of the brush so it covers only a single symbol.

1. Select a symbol set in the document with a Selection tool.

2. Choose the Symbol Sizer tool in the Toolbox.

3. Click or drag over symbol instances to make them larger.

   or

   ⌥-click or ⌥-drag over symbol instances to make them smaller.

   - To achieve a wide range of sizes, choose Random in the Method pop-up menu.

Symbol Sizer tool icon in the Toolbox palette

Specific Symbol Sizer Tool Options Double-click the Symbol Sizer tool in the Toolbox to display the Symbolism Tool Options dialog box containing specific options for the Symbol Sizer tool.

- **Proportional Resizing** — When checked, symbol instances are resized uniformly. When unchecked, symbol instances are distorted according to how you move the mouse.

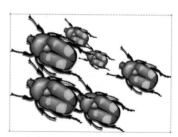

Symbol instances resized using the Random Method

- **Resizing Affects Density** — When checked, symbol instances move apart proportionally when enlarged and move closer together when symbol instances are reduced. When this option is unchecked, instances don't move, which may cause overlapping.

Symbol Spinner

The Symbol Spinner tool rotates symbol instances within a symbol set. Rotate an individual symbol instance by reducing the diameter of the brush so it covers only a single symbol.

Symbol Spinner tool icon in the Toolbox palette

1. Select a symbol set in the document with a Selection tool.

2. Choose the Symbol Spinner tool in the Toolbox.

3. Drag over symbol instances to rotate them in the direction you move the mouse.

   - Clicking on individual symbol instances doesn't have any effect.

   - An arrow displays on affected symbol instances to tell you the direction they're moving. If the arrows are hard to see, change the layer selection color in the Layers palette.

Directional arrows

Arrows display on symbol instances when Symbol Spinner tool is dragged over them

Symbol Stainer

The Symbol Stainer tool functions like the colorization method of tinting brushes; that is, varied tints of the current fill color are applied. It applies tints of the current fill color to solid fill colors, but its gradients and patterns are unaffected. Black and white symbol instances don't change when the Symbol Stainer tool is applied to them.

Symbol Stainer tool icon in the Toolbox palette

1. Select a symbol set in the document with a Selection tool.

2. Choose the Symbol Stainer tool in the Toolbox.

3. Click on a single symbol instance (small brush size) to apply a tint of the current fill color. Additional clicks with the Symbol Stainer tool increases the tinting.

   or

   Drag across multiple symbol instances to apply the tint to of them that fall within the brush circle. Keep in mind that the effect is more intense under the point of the click and decreases as it extends outward to the edge of the brush. Drag across the symbols again to increase the effect.

   - To decrease the amount of colorization, hold down the ⌥ key when you click or you drag across symbol instances.

fyi Using the Symbol Stainer tool increases file size and decreases performance, so avoid its use when file size is a concern.

- To apply the Symbol Stainer tool to only those symbol instances that have already been "stained" without affecting those symbol instances that haven't been stained, hold the *Shift* key down while clicking or dragging.

Individual trees in a grove stained to various shades using the Symbol Stainer tool

Symbol Screener

The Symbol Screener tool changes the opacity of symbol instances; that is, it makes them look more transparent.

1. Select a symbol set in the document with a Selection tool.

2. Choose the Symbol Screener tool in the Toolbox.

Symbol Screener tool icon in the Toolbox palette

The Symbol Screener tool was used on the butterfly to make its wings more transparent, which lets the grass below show through

3. Click or drag over symbol instances to make them more transparent.

   or

   ⌥-click or ⌥-drag over symbol instances to make them more opaque (nontransparent).

   - To achieve a wide range of opacity in multiple symbol instances, choose *Random* in the *Method* pop-up menu.

Symbol Styler

The Symbol Styler tool applies a style selected in the Styles palette to symbol instances in the symbol set. You can apply more than one style to symbol instances to change their appearance. Use the same tool to remove styling from a symbol instance.

Styles and the Styles palette are discussed in the next chapter, Step 11, *Filters & Filter Effects*. For now, though, display the Styles palette (**Window ⇨ Styles**) and click on a thumbnail to select it.

Symbol Styler tool icon in the Toolbox palette

1. Select a symbol set in the document with a Selection tool.

2. Choose the Symbol Styler tool in the Toolbox.

3. Display the Styles palette and click on a thumbnail to select it.

4. Click-and-hold or drag over symbol instances to apply the selected style to symbol instances. The longer the Symbol Styler tool is over a symbol instance the more the intensity of the style is applied.

- Sometimes it takes a while for the screen to refresh after a style has been applied, so be patient.

or

3. ⟋-click or ⟋-drag over symbol instances to remove the effect of the style. The longer you pause over a symbol instance, the more the intensity of the style is lessened.

4. *Shift*-click or *Shift*-drag over symbol instances to apply the selected style to those symbol instances that already have the style applied to them, leaving any unstyled symbol instances in the symbol set unchanged.

activity 10.14

1. Create a new document: Letter size, CMYK color mode. Save it into your Practice folder as an .eps file named Symbolism Practice.eps.

2. Type the words Butterfly Sanctuary in two lines. Format it to 72 pt Garamond Book, flush left, 60 pt leading. Kern between letters until the letters are evenly spaced.
   - Notice that the *f* and *l* in butterfly are touching.

3. Display the Nature symbol library (Window ⇨ Symbol Libraries) and drag the Butterfly and the Fern swatches it into your Symbols palette.

4. In the Symbols palette, select the Fern swatch, and drag it onto the document page to place only one instance of the fern.

5. Adjust its size and angle to suit you, and position it on the right side of the name. Send to the back of the stack.
   - With a single symbol instance, you can use the Symbolism tools to adjust size (Symbol Sizer), angle (Symbol Spinner), and position (Symbol Shifter), or you can use its bounding box.

6. Deselect the symbol instance.

7. Select the Butterfly symbol in the Symbols palette, choose the Symbol Sprayer tool (⬚) in the Toolbox, and spray five or six butterflies on top of the type.

8. Choose the Symbol Sizer tool (⬚) and make the butterflies random sizes.
   - Double-click the tool in the Toolbox and change the Diameter value to 50 pt to reduce the size of the brush so it's small enough to isolate a single butterfly.
   - Hold down the ⟋ key to reduce the size of a symbol instance.

9. Choose the Symbol Shifter tool (⬚) and drag individual butterflies to position them around the characters.

10. Choose the Symbol Spinner tool (⬚) and drag to rotate the butterflies to random angles.

11. Save the file, print it, then close the artwork window.

PRACTICE ACTIVITY 10-1 — Art Brush

1. Create a new document: Letter size, CMYK color mode. Name it Name Art Brush.eps and save it into your Practice Folder as an .eps file.

2. With the Type tool, type your first and last name on the page. Don't enter a middle name or middle initial. Change the size to 24 pt and the font to Myriad Bold. Apply 100% black fill, no stroke.

   ■ If you don't have Myriad, use a different typeface, such as Arial.

3. Convert the type to Outlines (Type ⇨ Create Outlines).

4. With the Selection tool, select all the paths and drag them into the Brushes palette. When the New Brush dialog box displays, choose Art Brush.

5. When the Art Brush Options dialog box displays, enter your name as the name for the brush, then click OK or press *return/enter*.

6. Deselect the paths that created the art brush and change the fill color in the Color palette to white.

7. With your new art brush selected in the Brushes palette, choose the Paintbrush tool in the Toolbox. Draw a wavy path on the page.

8. Change the stroke color in the Color palette (or Toolbox) to 100% cyan, 0% magenta, 50% yellow, 0% black.

9. Double-click your name brush to display its Art Brush Options dialog box. Verify that the Preview box is checked. In the Colorization section, change the Colorization Method to Tints.

   ■ The color of the brushstroked path changed to the stroke color.

10. Click OK or press *return/enter* and choose Apply to Strokes when the Alert box displays.

11. Change the stroke color to a different color.

    ■ The color of the brushstroked path changed to the new stroke color.

12. Change the stroke width to 18 pt.

    ■ Depending upon the shape of your path, you could have something pretty funky.

13. Change the stroke width back to 1 pt.

14. Choose the Rectangle tool, and on a clear area of your page, click and drag down and to the right to draw a rectangle about 5" × 3". Don't click and specify values in the Rectangle Options dialog box.

    ■ Because the brush was still selected and you haven't removed the brushstroke, the brush is automatically applied.

    ■ Notice how the type is placed on the path.

15. Draw another rectangle by clicking and dragging up and to the left.

    ■ Notice that the type flows along the path differently.

16. Make separate art brushes for your first name and your last name. Change the Colorization Method to Tints so you can change the color by changing the stroke color. Name the paths First Name and Last Name, respectively.

Continued

17. Draw a 3" circle on your page using the Ellipse Options dialog box. Fill with white and apply the brush that is your first and last name.

18. Rotate the path until your first name is centered at the top of the circle.

    ■ Your last name is upside down.

19. Drag down a horizontal ruler guide and position it across the circle in the middle of the first character of your first name.

20. With the Scissors tool, split the path on both sides of the circle where the ruler guide intersects it.

    ■ Now you have two separate paths that have your first and last name applied to them.

21. Apply the First Name brush to the upper path and the Last Name brush to the lower path.

    ■ Your last name is still upside down.

22. With the lower path still selected, click the Options of Selected Object button at the bottom of the Brushes palette to display the Art Brush Options dialog box for that path only.

23. Click the Flip Along and the Flip Across checkboxes to turn them on. Click OK or press *return/enter.*

24. Now your last name is right-side up, but there's no space between your first and last name. So, drag another horizontal ruler guide down and position it about ½" below the other ruler guide. Split the path on both sides where the ruler guide intersects it.

    ■ Now you have two short paths, each containing your last name.

25. Select both of the short paths (*Shift*-click), then display the Brushes palette Options menu and choose Remove Brush Stroke.

    ■ You're left with plain colored strokes on the paths.

26. Apply a stroke of None to these two short paths.

    ■ You have a circular path containing your name.

    ■ If you know in advance that you don't want a visible line on the path, you can remove the brushstroke and the stroke path in one step by applying a stroke color of None.

27. Save your file, then print the document and close the document window.

EXERCISE 10-1 — Ceramic Teapot

- Draw a teapot and flower design similar to those shown here.

- Draw separate paths for the spout, handle, and top of the teapot.

- Don't align the pattern straight up and down by using a single flower as the pattern. Follow the instructions in the chapter for creating a uniformly spaced pattern.

- Move the design around to align the flower design on the top of the teapot to the flower design on the body of the teapot so it appears as one single design.

- Use the Transform command to reduce the size of the pattern in the handle and the spout.

EXERCISE 10-2 — Tatonka Park

- Create three types of buffalo as shown here.
    1. One with front feet "walking"
    2. One with head down eating.
    3. One with front feet standing.
- Create a gradient fill and apply to the buffalo.

- Use the Transform Each command to create additional buffalo of each type. Change the sizes.

- Create a tree symbol and spray them at the top of the hill. Vary the sizes and colors using the Symbol Sizer tool and Symbol Stainer tool. Change stacking order using the Symbol Shifter tool.

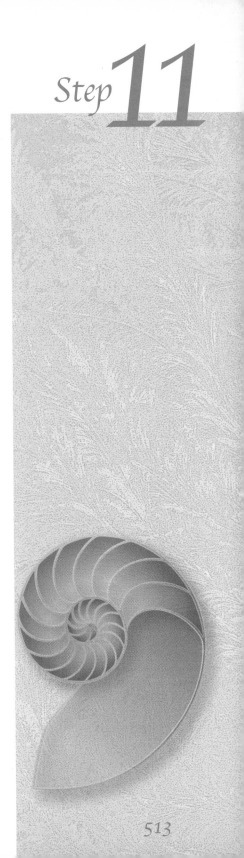

Filters & Filter Effects

What are Filters and Filter Effects?

In Illustrator, filters and filter effects (called simply "effects") allow you to change the appearance of objects, sometimes in interesting ways. While some filter commands are also present in the Effect menu, there is a significant difference between filters and filter effects.

Filters permanently alter the paths to which they're applied. You can remove them only by applying the Undo command.

Effect commands change only the appearance of paths to which they're applied, without affecting the original shape at all. This means you can change the settings in its dialog box, or remove the effect completely at any time. When an object is selected that has an effect applied to it, the path of the original shape displays.

Some of the filters and effects available in these two menus perform the same function as other commands discussed previously in the book. You have a choice as to whether to use the filter or effect command or the commands in other menus. We won't go over those duplicated commands here.

Filters and Filter Effects with Bitmap Images

When importing bitmap images on which to apply filters and filter effects, embed the images rather than linking them. Filters and effects don't work on linked images.

Some bitmap images require a lot of memory to process filters or effects that are applied to them. Make sure your computer has enough memory available for the task.

Which Filters or Filter Effects Work on Which Type of Image

Even though they're listed in the bottom part of the menus, not all filters or filter effects work with every type of raster image. And not all filters or filter effects on the top half of the menus work on all vector objects.

- The Photo Crosshatch (in the Pen & Ink submenu) can't be applied to vector images, only to photographs.

- The following filters and filter effects don't work on CMYK raster images: Artistic, Brush Strokes, Distort, Sketch, Stylize, Texture, and Video. All the filters and filter effects work on RGB and grayscale bitmap images.

- The commands on the bottom half of the menus can't be applied to 1-bit (black and white) images.

fyi *Plug-in filters and filter effects from other Adobe products, such as Photoshop, as well as some third-party plug-ins, can also be used in Illustrator. If there is an installer with the plug-in, use it to install it into Illustrator. If not, just drag the plug-in into the Plug-Ins folder inside the Adobe Illustrator 10 folder on your hard drive.*

Rasterize Vector Objects

You can convert vector objects into bitmap images using the Rasterize command in the Object menu (**Object ⇨ Rasterize**) or in the Effect menu. The Object menu command is permanent and cannot be reversed except by the Undo command. The Effect menu Rasterize command can be changed or removed using the Appearance palette. Refer to the Appearances section later in this chapter for more information about the Appearance palette.

In the Rasterize dialog box you can specify color mode and resolution, determine whether the background is white or transparent, determine whether or not to apply anti-aliasing or create a clipping mask, and determine the amount of space around an object. To rasterize a vector object:

1. Choose **Effect ⇨ Rasterize** or **Object ⇨ Rasterize** to display the dialog box (Figure 11.1).

2. Set the following options:
   - **Color Model** — Choose one of the three available in the pop-up submenu, depending upon the color mode of the document:
     - **CMYK** — Use when the artwork is to be printed. Only the Blur, Pixelate, and Sharpen raster filters and filter effects are available.
     - **RGB** — Use when the artwork is to be displayed on a screen, for example, on the web. All the raster filters and filter effects are available.
     - **Grayscale**— Generates shades of gray. All the raster filters and filter effects are available.

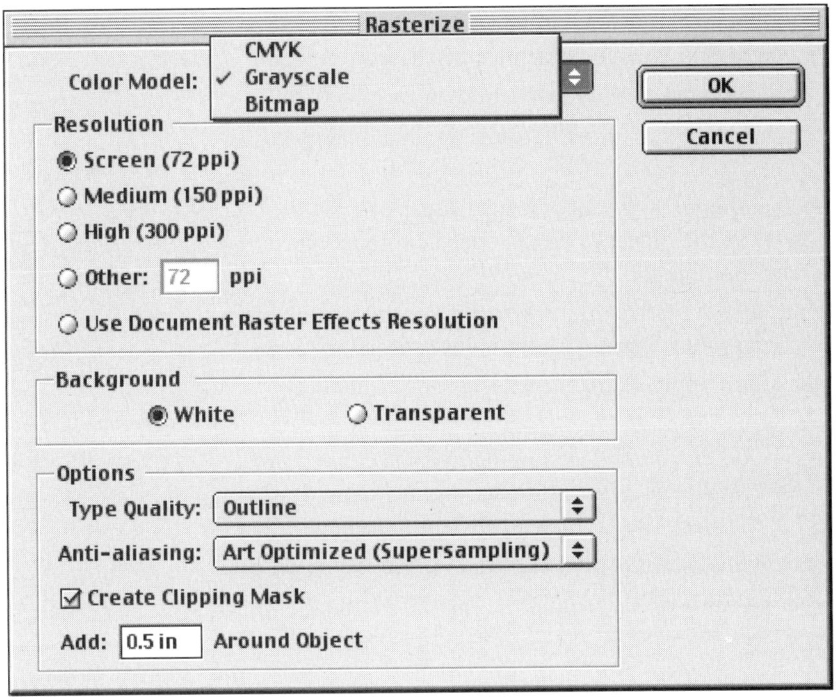

FIGURE 11.1 Use the Rasterize command in the Object menu or the Effect menu to convert a vector object into a bitmap image, making raster filters and filter effects available.

- **Bitmap**— Generates 1-bit (bi-level) image (line art). Raster filters and filter effects are not available.

■ **Resolution** — Sets the resolution (ppi, pixels per inch) for the rasterized image.

- **Screen (72 dpi)** — For images to be displayed only on a screen.
- **Medium (150 ppi)** — For images to be printed on low-resolution printers.
- **High (300 ppi)** — For images to be printed on high-resolution printers.
- **Other** — Enter a custom value.
- **Use Document Raster Effects Resolution** — Uses the settings specified in the **Effect ➪ Document Raster Effects Settings** dialog box.

■ **Background** — Choose to make the background white (opaque) or transparent.

- A raster image is always defined by a rectangular bounding box, so when it's rasterized in Illustrator, you can choose Transparent to eliminate the white area that extends from the edge of the image to the edge of its rectangular bounding box.

read this!

If you're attempting to apply a raster filter or filter effect to an image and it isn't working, check the color mode. Some filters work only on RGB images.

515

- **Type Quality** — When type is rasterized:
  - **Streamline** — Type weight isn't changed when it's rasterized.
  - **Outline** — Type weight becomes slightly heavier when its rasterized.
- **Anti-aliasing** — Determines whether anti-aliasing is applied during rasterization.
  - **Art Optimized (Supersampling)** — Reduces jagged edges of artwork. Don't use this option when the object to be rasterized contains type because characters may look blurry.
  - **Type Optimized (Hinted)** — Use this option when the rasterized object contains type to keep edges more crisp without being jagged.
  - **None** — No anti-aliasing is applied and curved shapes will likely be jagged.
- **Create Clipping Mask** — When checked, a clipping mask is created that makes the background of the image appear transparent. Clipping masks are discussed in Step 12, *Meshes, Masks, Blends, & Transparency.*
  - You don't need to check this box if the background option is Transparent.
- **Add [#] Around Object** — Adds pixels around the rasterized image.

3. Click OK or press *return/enter.*

Raster Effects Settings

When you apply a filter or filter effect to an image (bitmap or vector), Illustrator uses the settings in the Document Raster Effects Settings dialog box (**Effect ⇨ Document Raster Effects Settings**) to determine how the filters are applied. This dialog box has the same options as the Rasterize dialog box. Refer to the previous section for an explanation of those options.

Applying Filters and Filter Effects

To apply a filter or filter effect,

1. In the document, select an object.

   or

   In the Layers palette, target a layer, sublayer, group, or object layer. A more complete discussion about targeting layers can be found in the Appearances section later in this chapter.

2. Display the Filter or Effect menu, and choose an option to display the submenu containing the individual filter or effect.

3. Most commands display a dialog box containing settings or options for controlling the way the filter or filter effect is applied to the layer, group, or object. Enter the desired values and select options.

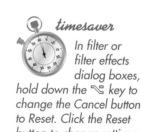

timesaver

In filter or filter effects dialog boxes, hold down the ⌥ key to change the Cancel button to Reset. Click the Reset button to change settings back to what they were when the dialog box was opened.

- To apply settings to the selected object without exiting the dialog box, click the Preview checkbox (if one is present).
  - After making changes in the dialog box, press the Tab key to update the preview.

or

Choose one of the two commands at the top of the menu:

- **Apply [name of last filter used]** — Applies the last filter or effect used to currently selected objects.
  - **Filter:** Press ⌘ e
  - **Effect:** Press ⇧ ⌘ e
- **[Name of Filter or Effect]** — Displays the dialog box for the last filter or effect that was used.
  - **Filter:** Press ⌥ ⌘ e
  - **Effect:** Press ⇧ ⌥ ⌘ e

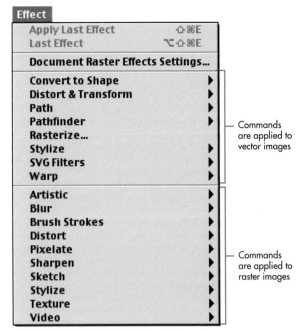

Effects on the Effect menu (shown) and filters on the Filter menu are divided into two types

- The dialog boxes of many of the filters and filter effects contain a preview window so you can see the results of your changes before exiting the dialog box, which saves time.
  - Click and drag in the preview window to move the image around and preview different sections of it.
  - Click the buttons below the preview window to enlarge (⊞) or reduce (⊟) the size of the image in the Preview window.

4. Click OK or press *return/enter* to apply the filter.

 To remove an effect, click the Clear Appearance button (⊘) at the bottom of the Appearance palette. For more information, review the section on Appearances later in this chapter.

Filters

The only filters that aren't available as filter effects are Object Mosaic and the Pen and Ink filters. They're described briefly here and the rest of the filters are described in the Filter Effects section later in this chapter. Commands in the Colors option in both the Filter and the Effect menu were discussed in Step 7, *Add Color to Artwork*.

Object Mosaic

The Object Mosaic filter, which is not available as a filter effect, creates a grid of little tiles from a embedded bitmap (RGB or grayscale) image that was saved in TIFF format. Or you can rasterize it using the Rasterize command in the Effect menu. Resulting tiles are vector objects.

Tiles are filled with shades of the color in the image. In the Object Mosaic dialog box, you can specify how many tiles are used to create the mosaic pattern and how much space is between each tile. The more tiles you ask for, the more detail that's retained in the finished mosaic.

The placed image doesn't have to be high-resolution. A low-resolution image mosaic looks just as good as one with a high resolution. And the lower the resolution, the faster it processes and prints.

The stacking order of the tiles created with the Object Mosaic filter are from the top-left corner to the bottom right-corner. The top left tile is at the back of the stack, and the bottom right tile is in the front. Check the Layers palette to see the relative order of each tile.

To create a mosaic:

1. Select an embedded bitmap image or rasterized vector object.

2. Choose **Filter** ⇨ **Create** ⇨ **Object Mosaic** to display the Object Mosaic dialog box (Figure 11.2).

   ■ The size of the image is displayed in the Current Size section, using the current unit of measurement specified for the document.

3. Change any options necessary to achieve the desired effect.

   ■ **New Size** — Change the Width and Height values if you want the finished mosaic larger or smaller than the original image. To change the size by specifying a percentage of the original size, check the Resize using Percentages checkbox at the bottom of the dialog box.

   • To ensure that the image keeps its same proportions, enter a value in one field (either Width or Height), then click the Use Ratio button to have Illustrator calculate the other value.

   ■ **Tile Spacing** — Enter a value in the Width and Height fields

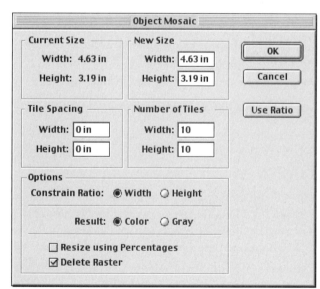

FIGURE 11.2 Control the size of the mosaic tiles and the space between them, as well as other options, by settings entered in the Object Mosaic dialog box.

518

to specify how much space you want between the tiles. The value can be 0.

- **Number of Tiles** — Enter a value in the Width and Height fields to specify how many tiles the mosaic should have, which determines how large each tile will be.

  - Enter a value in one field (either Width or Height), then click the Use Ratio button to have Illustrator calculate the other value.

  - If the number of tiles you specify requires more memory than you have allocated to Illustrator, some tiles may be omitted.

- **Options** — When the Use Ratio button is used to calculate values, choose to restrict the Width to the size of the original image and let Illustrator calculate the Height value, or vice versa.

- **Result** — Choose Color or Gray for the resulting mosaic image.

- **Delete Raster** — When applied to a bitmap image, a copy of the original image is created and the filter is applied to the copy rather than the original image. If you want to delete the original image, check this option.

fyi You can apply other filters and filter effects to the object mosaic image, as well as many of the transform, reshape, and distort tools and commands (refer to Step 9, Reshape, Combine, & Distort Objects).

 *activity 11.1*

1. Create a new document: Letter size, CMYK color mode. Save it into your Practice folder as an .eps file named Object Mosaic Practice.eps.

2. Choose File ⇨ Place.

3. In the Student Files folder on the CD-ROM that accompanies this book, locate the file named Lucy.tif and embed it into your document.

4. With the embedded file still selected, choose Filter ⇨ Create ⇨ Object Mosaic to display the Object Mosaic dialog box.

5. Enter 60 in the Width field of the Number of Tiles section.

6. Enter 1 pt in the both the Width and Height fields of the Tile Spacing section.

7. Click the Use Ratio button to let Illustrator calculate the number of tiles for the Height in the Number of Tiles section.

8. Check the Delete Raster checkbox.

9. Click OK or press *return/enter*.
   - The mosaic grid displays.

10. Deselect everything to see the final result.

11. Experiment with the Object Mosaic command by applying varying settings to the image.

12. When you're finished, save the file, print it, and close the artwork window.

519

Pen & Ink Filters

The Pen & Ink filters are available only as filters, not as filter effects, which means objects and images are permanently altered. The only way to remove these effects is to apply the Undo command. For that reason, it's a good idea to work on a copy of the image.

Be cautious when applying hatch effects to vector objects or photo crosshatch patterns to bitmap images. These features consume a lot of memory and may take a long time to print or refuse to print at all. If your artwork doesn't print:

1. With the problem file open, choose **File ⇨ Document Setup** to display the Document Setup dialog box.

2. Choose Printing & Export from the pop-up submenu at the top of the dialog box.

3. Enter a lower value (100–9600) in the Output Resolution field.
   - Use the highest resolution that will print the document without jagged edges.

Hatch Effects

Hatch effects are patterns of lines that are applied to vector objects (not bitmap images). Illustrator provides 26 preset line styles for you to use. You can modify the preset patterns or create your own custom patterns.

Apply a Pen & Ink Filter To apply a hatch filter to a vector object:

1. Select an object.

2. Choose **Filter ⇨ Pen & Ink ⇨ Hatch Effects** to display the Hatch Effects dialog box (Figure 11.3).
   - **Preview** — When checked, the preview displays only in the preview window in the dialog box, not on the object in the document.
   - **Hatch Effect** — Choose a predefined hatch effect from those listed in the Hatch Effect pop-up submenu.
   - **Hatch** — Choose another hatch pattern to add to the effect from the the pop-up submenu.
   - **Match Object's Color** — Check this box to make the hatch objects match the fill color of the object.
   - **Keep Object's Fill Color** — Check this box to keep the fill color of the object and make the hatch objects black.

Hatch effects were applied to the automobile

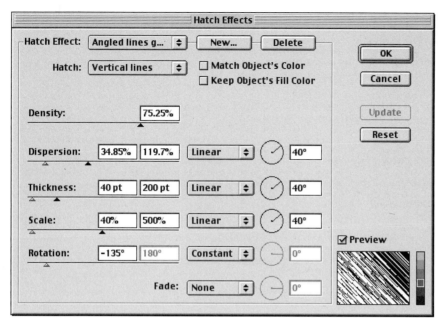

FIGURE 11.3 Change the settings in the Hatch Effects dialog box to control the pattern of lines applied to objects.

- **Density** — Adjust the number of shapes in the fill by (a) moving the slider, (b) entering a value in the field, or (c) click in the grayscale bar to the right of the preview window at the bottom of the dialog box.

- **Dispersion** — Specifies the spacing between hatch objects.

- **Thickness** — Control the thickness of lines in hatch styles made up of line segments.

- **Scale** — Determines the size of hatch objects.

- **Rotation** — Sets the angle of hatch objects.

- **Fade** — If you want the hatch effect to fade across the shape, choose To White or To Black from the pop-up submenu. If hatch objects contain a gradient, choose Use Gradient to apply the gradient to hatch objects.

3. If desired, click one of the following buttons, then click OK or press *return/enter*:

   - **New** — Saves the new settings as a custom Hatch Effect. Enter a name in the Name field, and click OK or press *return/enter*.

   - **Delete** — Deletes the the current Hatch Effect. When the Warning box displays, click Yes.

     - Be absolutely certain you want to do this, because you can't undo it, not even by clicking the Cancel button.

   - **Reset** — Removes any changes you've made to the current Hatch Effect and restores the default settings.

 fyi Definitions of options in the Hatch Effects pop-up menu for Dispersion, Thickness, Scale, and Rotation options:

Constant: Effect stays the same across the entire object.

Linear: Effect intensifies as it progresses from one side of the object to the other.

Reflect: Effect varies beginning in the center of the object, moving out to the edge.

Symmetric: Similar to Linear, except progression is more uniform.

Random: Effect is not in any regular pattern.

521

Create a New Hatch Pattern
To create the pattern tile that's used when applying Pen & Ink filters:

1. Draw a small object or multiple objects as the hatch pattern. You can't use brushstrokes, gradients, meshes, or pattern fills as a hatch object.

2. With the object selected, choose **Filter** ⇨ **Pen & Ink** ⇨ **New Hatch**.

3. Choose a style from the Hatch pop-up submenu.

4. Click the New button, then enter a name in Name field of the dialog box that displays, and click OK or press *return/enter*.

5. Click OK or press *return/enter* to save the new hatch style into the hatch library that's currently open.

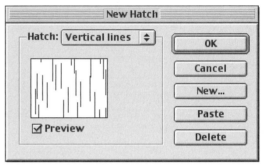

In the New Hatch dialog box, choose a hatch type, verify in the Preview window that it's what you want, then click New.

Modify a Hatch Pattern
To change an existing hatch pattern:

1. Deselect all objects in the document and move to a blank spot on the page.

2. Choose **Filter** ⇨ **Pen & Ink** ⇨ **New Hatch** to display the New Hatch dialog box and choose a hatch pattern from the Hatch pop-up submenu.

3. Click the Paste button. The objects that created the pattern are pasted into the document and remain selected.

4. Click OK or press *return/enter*.

5. Change the hatch pattern like you want it, then reselect the objects.

6. Choose **Filter** ⇨ **Pen & Ink** ⇨ **New Hatch**, click the New button, and type a name for the new pattern. Click OK or press *return/enter*.

   - If you don't specify a new name, Illustrator assigns Hatch [#].

   - Illustrator won't let you save a new hatch pattern with the same name as an existing pattern.

   - To delete an existing hatch pattern, click the Delete button. This action cannot be reversed, so be certain you want to do it.

7. Click OK or press *return/enter* again to exit the New Hatch dialog box.

   - The new hatch pattern is saved in the open hatch library.

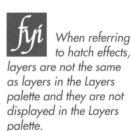

When referring to hatch effects, layers are not the same as layers in the Layers palette and they are not displayed in the Layers palette.

Open a Hatch Library To open a different hatch library, choose **Filter ➪ Pen & Ink ➪ Library Open**. Locate the Pen And Ink folder (**Adobe Illustrator 10 ➪ Plug-ins ➪ Illustrator Filters ➪ Pen and Ink ➪ Hatch Sets**), and click Open.

Save a Hatch Library Save the custom hatch patterns you create into a separate hatch library by choosing **Filter ➪ Pen & Ink ➪ Library Save As**. Enter a name for the new library and save it into the Pen And Ink folder on your hard drive (**Adobe Illustrator 10 ➪ Plug-ins ➪ Illustrator Filters ➪ Pen And Ink**).

Photo Crosshatch

This filter applies a crosshatch pattern to bitmap images (not vector objects), making the image look like a sketch. By setting options in the dialog box, you can control the Density (number of lines), Dispersion Noise (spacing between hatch segments), Thickness (weight of line segments), Max. Line Length (length of line segments), Rotation Noise (random rotation of the hatch lines on each layer), Rotation Variance (rotation of each layer relative to the previous layer), Top Angle (the angle of the top hatch layer), and Hatch Layers (number of hatch layers controls levels of shading).

Original photograph

- Images must be embedded, not linked.
- The filter doesn't work on an EPS image.
- Flatten a Photoshop image before applying the Photo Crosshatch filter.
- Adjust the appearance of shading by selecting specific anchor points of some of the line segments with the Direct Select Lasso tool and changing the stroke weight.

Photo Crosshatch: Density, 3 pt; Dispersion Noise, 0%; Thickness, .4 pt; Max Line Length, 24 pt; Rotation Noise, 0; Rotation Variance, 100%; Top Angle, 40; Hatch Layers, 5.

activity 11.2

1. Create a new document: Letter size, CMYK color mode. Save it into your Practice folder as an .eps file named Hatch Effects Practice.eps.

2. Choose the Type tool and type the word HATCH centered at the top of the document page. Format it to be 72 pt Bookman Bold.

3. In the Character palette, specify 200 as the tracking value.

4. Convert the word to outlines.

5. With the Direct Selection tool, select the first character.

6. Choose Filter ➪ Pen & Ink ➪ Hatch Effects to display the Hatch Effects dialog box.

7. Click the Preview checkbox, then click OK or press *return/enter* to apply the default hatch effect to the first character.

8. Select each character and apply a different hatch effect to each of them.

9. Experiment with the different options available for changing the effects.

10. When you've finished, save the file, print it, and close the artwork window.

Original image

Colored Pencil
Pencil Width = 1   Stroke Pressure = 15   Paper Brightness = 45

Cutout
No. of Levels = 6   Edge Simplicity = 2   Edge Fidelity = 1

Dry Brush
Brush Size = 5   Brush Detail = 8   Texture = 2

Film Grain
Grain = 10   Highlight Area = 8   Intensity = 4

Fresco
Brush Size = 2   Brush Detail = 2   Texture = 3

Neon Glow   Size = 14   Brightness = 20
Color: Hue Angle = 251   Saturation = 97   Value = 100

Paint Daubs
Brush Size = 12   Sharpness = 16   Brush Type = Dark Rough

524

RASTER FILTERS — Artistic

Palette Knife
Stroke Size = 9   Stroke Detail = 3   Softness = 0

Plastic Wrap
Highlight Strength = 14   Detail = 8   Smoothness = 8

Poster Edges
Edge Thickness = 8   Edge Intensity = 8   Posterization = 6

Rough Pastels   Stroke Length = 20   Scaling = 100%
Stroke Detail = 2   Relief = 10   Light Direction = Bottom

Smudge Stick
Stroke Length = 4   Highlight Area = 4   Intensity = 2

Sponge
Brush Size = 1   Definition = 7   Smoothness = 3

Underpainting   Brush Size = 4   Scaling = 100%
Texture Coverage = 9   Texture = Canvas   Relief = 9   Light Direction = Bottom

Water Color
Brush Detail = 4   Shadow Intensity = 1   Texture = 3

RASTER FILTERS — Blur

Gaussian Blur
Radius = 10 pixels

Radial Blur
Blur Method: Zoom   Amount = 16

RASTER FILTERS — Stylize

Glowing Edges
Edge Width = 2   Edge Brightness = 7   Smoothness = 3

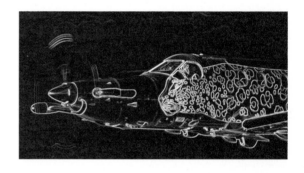

RASTER FILTERS — Brush Strokes

Accented Edges
Edge Width = 2   Edge Brightness = 5   Smoothness = 9

Angled Strokes
Direction Balance = 50   Stroke Length = 13   Sharpness = 2

RASTER FILTERS — Brush Strokes

Crosshatch
Stroke Length = 8   Sharpness = 8   Strength = 3

Dark Strokes
Balance = 2   Black Density = 2   White Density = 2

Ink Outlines
Stroke Length = 3   Dark Intensity = 10   Light Intensity = 10

Spatter
Spray Radius = 10   Smoothness = 10

Sprayed Stroke   Stroke Length = 12
Spray Radius = 7   Stroke Direction = Right Diagonal

Sumi-E
Stroke Width = 3   Stroke Pressure = 3   Contrast = 5

RASTER FILTERS — Distort

Diffuse Glow
Graininess = 3   Glow Amount = 6   Clear Amount = 18

Glass   Texture = Frosted
Smoothness = 6   Distortion = 6   Scaling = 100%

Ocean Ripple
Ripple Size = 7   Ripple Magnitude = 7

RASTER FILTERS — Pixelate

Color Halftone   Defaults

Crystallize   Cell Size = 10

Pointillize   Cell Size = 3

Mezzotint   Type = Fine Dots

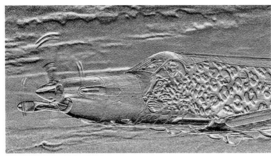

Bas Relief
Detail = 15   Smoothness = 2   Light Direction = Bottom

Chalk & Charcoal
Charcoal Area = 1   Chalk Area = 8   Stroke Pressure = 1

Charcoal
Charcoal Thickness = 1   Detail = 5   Light/Dark Balance = 90

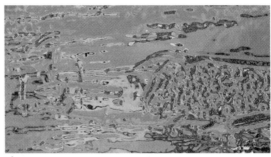

Chrome
Detail = 10   Smoothness = 4

Conte Crayon   Foreground Level = 11 Background Level = 7
Texture = Canvas   Scaling = 100%   Relief = 4   Light Direction = Top

Graphic Pen   Stroke Length = 13
Light/Dark Balance = 35   Stroke Direction = Right Diagonal

Halftone Pattern
Size = 1   Contrast = 7   Pattern Type = Dot

Note Paper
Image Balance = 25   Graininess = 5   Relief = 14

529

Photocopy
Detail = 15   Darkness = 13

Plaster
Image Balance = 20   Smoothness = 1   Light Position = Top

Reticulation
Density = 10   Black Level = 15   White Level = 40

Stamp
Light/Dark Balance = 25   Smoothness = 6

Torn Edges
Image Balance = 23   Smoothness = 14   Contrast = 2

Water Paper
Fiber Length = 10   Brightness = 70   Contrast = 70

Craquelure
Crack Spacing = 15   Crack Depth = 6   Crack Brightness = 9

Grain
Intensity = 70   Contrast = 50   Grain Type = Clumped

Mosaic Tiles
Tile Size = 12   Grout Width = 3   Lighten Grout = 9

Patchwork
Square Size = 2   Relief = 6

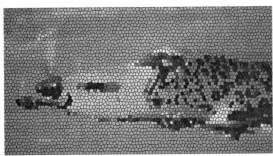

Stained Glass
Cell Size = 5   Border Thickness = 2   Light Intensity = 1

Texturizer   Texture = Burlap
Scaling = 125%   Relief = 10   Light Direction = Top

Filter Effects

Applying filter effects to objects can become time consuming — not because of long processing times, but because it's so much fun that time can get away from you. A brief description of each filter effect that you can apply to vector objects is included in this section. But the best way to become familiar with the commands is to experiment with them.

Some filter effects, such as the Path, Pathfinder, and Warp commands in the Effect menu, have corresponding commands elsewhere in the program. The difference is that when they're applied using an Effect command, the object isn't changed, just its appearance, making it an appearance attribute.

Filter effects, because they're appearance attributes, can be changed or removed after they're applied to objects. Instructions for editing filter effects can be found in the Appearances section later in this chapter.

Some of the filters and filter effects have options for choosing blending modes and specifying opacity values. Information about these features can be found in Step 12, *Meshes, Masks, Blends, & Transparency*.

Drop shadow applied to Leaves symbol

When selected, most filter effects display a dialog box so you can control how the effect is applied. For the most part, the options are self-explanatory. Two options that appear frequently that may be unclear, however, are Absolute and Relative. These options usually refer to the size of an object, the size of the effect that's applied to the object, or the amount of change to be applied.

- **Absolute** — Enter specific values in the fields. For example, enter a definite size. If you know exactly the values you want, use this option.

- **Relative** — Value in the fields may vary, depending upon other options selected, or may be percentages of original values. If you want Illustrator to calculate values, choose this option.

Unlike filters, when a filter effect is applied to selected objects, the settings may "stick" and may be applied to the next object you draw, too. If that happens, display the Appearance palette and verify that the leftmost button at the bottom of the palette has a gray background. If Tool Tips are turned on, the button should read New Art Has Basic Appearance. If it doesn't, click the button.

Convert to Shape

The Convert to Shape commands make objects *appear* to be the shape of the command, as implied by its name: Rectangle, Rounded Rectangle, or Ellipse. The Shape dialog box displays:

- **Shape** — Choose one of the three shapes for the object's appearance.

- **Absolute** — Enter Width and Height values for the size of the final shape.

- **Relative** — Enter values in the **Extra Width** and **Extra Height** fields to increase or decrease the size of the final shape. A positive value increases the size of the shape; a negative value makes the final shape smaller than its original size.
- **Corner Radius** — Available only when Rounded Rectangle is the shape selected. Specify the corner radius for the object's final shape.
  - You can also apply the Round Corners effect in the Stylize submenu to add round corners to objects.

 *activity 11.3*

1. Open the illustration of the pear that you drew in Step 4, *The Pen & Pencil Tools,* and saved into your Practice folder.

2. Marquee to select all the paths of the artwork.

3. Choose Effect ⇨ Convert to Shape ⇨ Rectangle to display the Shape dialog box. Choose Relative and enter 0 in both fields. Click OK or press *return/enter.*
   - Rectangles having the same fill colors are created around each closed path. They're the same height and width of the original path.

- Notice that you can still see the paths in the pear artwork.

4. Press ⌘z to undo the applied effect.

5. Experiment with these commands, applying varying options, until you're familiar with the results achieved with different values.

6. Close the artwork window without saving changes.

Distort & Transform

The Filter menu lists these filters in a menu called simply Distort. Transform is added to the name in the Effect menu because the Transform command is only a filter effect. The other filters are the same.

Free Distort Allows you to change the selected object's shape. When the Preview checkbox is checked, an outline of the object displays in the dialog box's preview window. Grab the corners of the bounding box and drag to change the shape of the object. Click the Reset button to restore the object to its original shape.

Pucker & Bloat Move the slider toward Pucker to move the object's existing anchor points outward into sharp points; curve segments move inward. Move the slider toward Bloat to create drag the object's existing anchor points toward the center; curve segments move outward.

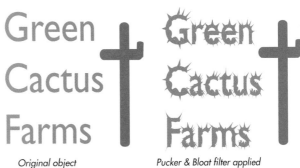

Original object   *Pucker & Bloat filter applied*

Roughen Anchor points are added to the selected object to cause the edges of the path to become jagged. In the dialog box, the Size value specifies the amount of change applied to the path and Detail controls the number of anchor points added. Choose to add Smooth anchor points or Corner anchor points.

■ To prevent the addition of anchor points, set the Detail slider to zero.

Original object

Scribble & Tweak Paths in the selected object are distorted by moving anchor points away from the original path, horizontally, vertically, or both. In the Modify section of the dialog box, check Anchor Points to move the anchor points in the object; check "In" Control Points to move control points that lead into anchor points on the path; check "Out" Control Points to move control points that lead out of anchor points on the path.

Roughen filter applied:
Size 1%, Detail 50%

■ Each time you apply the Scribble & Tweak filter or filter effect, random changes result. Just keep checking and unchecking the Preview checkbox until you get the shape you want.

Original object

Both sliders set at 28% and all three Modify checkboxes are checked

Transform This command displays the Transform Effect dialog box, which has the same options as the Transform Each dialog box in the Transform submenu of the Object menu (**Object ⇨ Transform ⇨ Transform Each**). When applied to an object as an effect, the changes aren't permanent. Refer to the section later in this chapter about appearances. See the instructions regarding this dialog box in Step 9, *Reshape, Combine, & Distort Objects*.

Twist This filter and filter effect achieves the same result as using the Twist tool, except you can specify the angle of the distortion and it isn't a permanent change. The underlying object is unchanged and the angle can be changed using the Appearance palette.

Original object

Zig Zag Objects are distorted in a uniform pattern of back-and-forth distortions. In the Zig Zag dialog box, Size determines how far the path can vary from its original position, Ridges per Segment specifies how many zigs and zags are created, and Points can be Smooth or Corner points.

Feather twisted 50°

activity 11.4

1. Create a new document: Letter size, CMYK color mode. Save it into your Practice folder as an .eps file named Starburst.eps.

2. Display the Appearance palette, and verify that the leftmost button at the bottom of the palette has a gray background (Tool Tip reads New Art Has Basic Appearance).

3. Choose the Star tool in the Toolbox, click on the document page to display the Star Options dialog box. Enter the following specifications, then click OK or press *return/enter*.
   - Radius 1: 2"
   - Radius 2: 1.35 in.
   - Points: 30

4. With the star selected, choose Effect ➪ Distort & Transform ➪ Roughen to display the Roughen dialog box.

5. Change the Size slider to 5 and the Detail slider to 1, and click the Corner Points option. Then click OK or press *return/enter*.

   - The points of the star are no longer uniform.

6. Apply a fill color of 20% cyan, 60% magenta.

7. To make a starburst that's even more uneven, create a Star with 2" in both Radius fields and 30 points. Then, in the Roughen dialog box, change the Size to 25 and the Detail to 30, with Corner Points. Click OK or press *return/enter*.

8. With any of the selection tools, try to select points of the star.
   - You can't select them because they're just appearances. The actual shape isn't changed.

9. Draw other shapes and apply the rest of the Distort & Transform commands. Try several shapes with varying specifications for each tool until you're familiar with how they change objects.

10. Save the file, print it, then close the artwork window.

Path

Offset Path This command functions similarly to the command in the Object menu (**Object ➪ Path ➪ Offset Path**), except (a) it doesn't permanently change the path, (b) a second object isn't created, and (c) it can be changed using the Appearance palette. See the discussion on the Offset Path command in Step 9, *Reshape, Combine, & Distort Objects*.

Outline Object Generates a stroke with a value of None around selected objects. Sometimes objects with a drop shadow applied are clipped off before the full fade effect is printed. That's because there isn't enough space around the object to allow for the applied effect. If that happens, applying a stroke of None around the object forces Illustrator to give it the space it needs to print the entire effect.

Outline Stroke This command functions the same as the command in the Object menu (**Object ➪ Path ➪ Outline Stroke**), except it doesn't permanently change the path and can be changed using the Appearance palette. See the discussion on the Outline Stroke command in Step 9, *Reshape, Combine, & Distort Objects*.

Pathfinder

Most of the Pathfinder effects commands are also available in the Pathfinder palette. See Step 9, *Reshape, Combine, & Distort Objects*, for information about the Pathfinder palette and Pathfinder commands. Again, the difference between the two commands is that Pathfinder effects change only the appearance of an object without changing its actual path.

Pathfinder appearance attributes can be changed or removed in the Appearance palette (discussed later in this chapter). Before applying a Pathfinder effect to objects, all the objects to which you want to apply the command must be on the same layer, sublayer, or group. Then target that layer, sublayer, or group. Targeting layers is discussed in the Appearance Palette section of this chapter, too.

Compound paths are not created when Pathfinder effects commands are applied to objects.

Add Creates the appearance of a shape using the outside edges of targeted overlapping objects. Fill and stroke attributes of the frontmost object are applied to the object.

Intersect All portions of targeted objects that don't overlap appear to be removed. Fill and stroke attributes of the frontmost object are applied to the object.

Exclude Overlapping areas of targeted objects become transparent. Opaque portions assume the fill color of the frontmost object.

Subtract Overlapping portions of objects in front of the backmost object appear to be removed from the backmost object (like a cookie cutter). The color of the backmost object is retained in the final shape.

Minus Back The backmost object appears to be cut out of the frontmost object. Fill and stroke attributes of the frontmost object are applied to the final object.

Divide Overlapping objects appear to be cut into separate nonoverlapping objects that keep their original fill and stroke attributes. Overlapping areas of the objects are not divided into separate objects that you can move around or change color.

Original artwork

Pathfinder Hard Mix filter effect applied

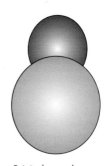

Original artwork

Pathfinder Intersect filter effect applied

Trim This command hides objects behind the front object and removes stroke attributes. Fill attributes remain intact.

Merge Deletes portions of objects behind the topmost object, removes stroke attributes, and merges overlapping objects that have the same fill color. Objects are not separated into individual objects.

Crop Any portion of objects extending beyond the boundaries of the frontmost object are deleted. The original frontmost object is removed. Objects retain their original fill color, but strokes are removed. This command is comparable to the Crop command in the Pathfinder palette.

Outline Fill color is removed and a stroke with a weight of 0 and the fill color of the original object is applied to the shapes. Objects are not separated into open paths that can be manipulated independently.

Hard Mix Overlapping colors of targeted objects are combined, using the highest C, M, Y, K or R, G, B values (depending upon the color mode of the document) of each of the objects. Strokes are removed.

Soft Mix Pathfinder Options dialog box displays when this effect is selected. Set the mixing rate to determine how transparent objects in front will become. Strokes are removed. Values higher than 50% darken the frontmost object; a value lower than 50% lightens the color of the frontmost object.

- **Expand Appearance** — Apply the Expand Appearance command to objects to which the Hard Mix or Soft Mix commands have been applied to separate overlapping areas into separate objects having the color of the overlapping areas.

- Global process colors and spot colors are converted to non-global process colors in the current document color mode when the Hard Mix or Soft Mix effect command is applied to objects. This means you can't use these commands in a project using only spot colors.

Trap Creates a trapping effect. Information about trapping can be found in Appendix A, *Output: Printing & Exporting Files.*

Original artwork

Pathfinder Trim filter effect applied

Original artwork

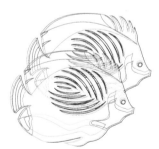

Pathfinder Outline filter effect applied; stroke weight changed from 0 to .4 pt because a stroke weight of 0 won't print — even though it displays on your screen and displays when printed to a laser printer

Stylize

The commands in the Stylize submenu add enhancements to paths and objects. Only three of these filter effects are also available as filters: Add Arrowheads, Drop Shadow, and Round Corners. The other three are available only as filter effects in the Effect menu.

Add Arrowheads Illustrator provides 27 predefined arrowhead shapes that you can add to one or both ends of an open path. In the dialog box, click the arrows beneath each window to scroll through the available arrowheads. The size of the arrowhead is based on the width of the segment's stroke, but you can enter a value in the Scale field, from 1% to 1000%, to alter the default size.

- If arrowheads are added as a filter, you can edit them the same as any other object, but they aren't attached to the line to which they're applied, so they don't move when the line is moved. If they're added as a filter effect, they're attached to the line segments to which they're applied and move when the line is moved, but they can't be edited by moving anchor points.

- When applied as a filter effect, arrowheads adjust automatically to changes in the width of the line to which they're attached, without affecting its Scale value.

- To customize the appearance of arrows, apply other filters and filter effects.

Drop Shadow Adds a soft shadow enhancement to selected objects to make them appear three-dimensional. In the dialog box that displays, you can specify how far and in which direction the shadow is offset from the original object (X Offset or Y Offset), determine the blending mode, how blurry it is, what color the shadow is, and how dark a black shadow is.

- To change the shadow color, click the Color button, then click the color box to the right of the button to display the Color Picker box. Click in the color field to choose a different color, then click OK or press *return/enter*.

In the Effect menu, the vector filter effects are in the top section of the menu. The Stylize commands in the bottom section of the menu can be applied only to bitmap RGB images.

Paths are brushstrokes using the Charcoal swatch with #4 arrowhead applied at 27% of the original size, and a drop shadow applied. The trees are the Sequoia symbol swatch.

Feather This command softens the edges of a selected object, from dark to transparent, by the amount specified in the Feather Radius field of the dialog box that displays.

Inner Glow and Outer Glow These two filter effects apply a feathery glowing appearance to selected objects. In the dialog boxes for both commands, you can specify the color of the glow by clicking in the color box next to the Mode pop-up menu, its blending mode in the Mode pop-up submenu, its opacity value, and the amount of blur.

In addition, the Inner Glow dialog box allows you to determine whether to start the glow from the center of the object and fade outward to the edge, or to start the glow at the edge of the object and fade toward the center.

Round Corners Convert any corner anchor point on an open or closed path to a rounded corner by applying this filter or filter effect. Specify the radius for the corner in the dialog box that displays. A larger number creates a bigger curve.

- Don't try to change the corner radius of a rounded rectangle shape by applying this command. It's doesn't work.

SVG Filters

The standard SVG filters are provided by Illustrator for application to artwork saved as scalable vector graphics that will be displayed in a web browser. These filter effects are applied to the object in the browser, not in the Illustrator file. For that reason, SVG filters must be the last effect applied to an object (if more than one effect is used). If it isn't at the bottom of the Appearance palette (above the Transparency listing), the object is rasterized rather than its appearance changed.

You can use the standard set of filters provided in the Effect menu, you can edit the code to create new SVG effects, or you can create your own SVG filter effects.

Warp

The filter effect options displayed in the Warp submenu are the same as those in the Style pop-up submenu in the Warp Options dialog box (**Object ⇨ Envelope Distort ⇨ Make with Warp**). Both the Warp filter effect and the Make with Warp commands display the same dialog box for controlling the

Original arrow

Feather command applied — .13 in radius

The Free Distort effect command applied to the first two lines, with Outer Glow applied

shape. Refer to the section discussing envelopes in Step 9, *Reshape, Combine, & Distort Objects*, for information about the Make with Warp command.

When a path is distorted using the commands in the Object menu, an envelope mesh is produced that can be edited. Warp filter effects applied to a selected object or objects affect only the appearance of the selection. Because warp filter effects create an appearance attribute, it can be modified or removed using the Appearance palette, discussed next.

 *activity 11.5*

1. Create a new document: Letter size, CMYK color mode. Save it into your Practice folder as an .eps file named Stylize Filters Practice.eps.

2. Draw a horizontal wavy line segment, apply a 6 pt green stroke.

3. With the line segment still selected, choose Filter ⇨ Stylize ⇨ Add Arrowheads to display the Add Arrowheads dialog box.

4. Leave the Start field set at None (window is empty). Click the arrows under the End window until 2 of 27 displays and the arrowhead style displays in the window. Scale value, 100%. Then click OK or press *return/enter*.

   ■ The arrowhead is placed at the end of the path. The direction the path is drawn determines which end the arrowhead is placed on.

5. Display the Layers palette and expand the top-level layer. The object is displayed as a group with two object layers.

6. Deselect the object, then with the Direct Selection tool, click on the arrowhead. Choose the Selection tool to display its bounding box, then move the pointer until the rotate arrows (↵↗) display. Drag a corner handle to rotate the arrowhead independently of the stroke.

7. With the Direct Selection tool, click on the stroke to display the direction lines. Drag the direction point of the direction handle closest to the arrowhead and reshape the path.

   ■ The angle of the arrowhead doesn't adjust to follow the direction of the end of the path.

8. On a blank spot on the page, draw a similar horizontal wavy line segment.

9. Choose Effect ⇨ Stylize ⇨ Add Arrowheads to display the Add Arrowheads dialog box. Choose the same arrowhead and size, then click OK or press *return/enter*.

   ■ Notice in the Layers palette that the arrowhead and line segment is a single object layer.

   ■ Notice that there isn't a pathline around the arrowhead. That's because it's an appearance and isn't really an object.

10. Deselect the path, then reselect it with the Direct Selection tool so that the endpoints are hollow. Click on the endpoint with the arrowhead so its direction lines display.

11. Drag the direction handle around.

   ■ Notice that the direction the arrowhead points adjusts to the direction of the line segment.

12. Click on the endpoint with the arrowhead and drag it to a new location.

   ■ The arrowhead moves with the endpoint.

13. With the object selected, choose Effect ⇨ Stylize ⇨ Drop Shadow to display the Drop Shadow dialog box. Enter the following specifications, then click OK or press *return/enter*.

   ■ Mode: Multiply   ■ Y Offset: 0.01 in
   ■ Opacity: 75%   ■ Blur: 0.07 in
   ■ X Offset: 0.01 in   ■ Darkness: 50%

14. Experiment with the other Stylize filter effects. Draw various shapes and apply combinations of the commands.

15. When you're finished, save your file, then print it and close the artwork window.

Appearances

In Illustrator, *appearances* are attributes that have been applied to objects, groups, or layers that determine how they look. Any attribute that's applied to objects, groups, or layers, other than the basic fill and stroke attributes, is called an *appearance attribute*. Appearance attributes can be fill and stroke color, stroke weight, blending modes, brushstrokes, transparency settings, and effects.

Appearance attributes don't permanently change an object's shape, color, and so on — just how they look. When an object that has appearance attributes applied is selected, the path of the original object displays. When appearance attributes are removed, the object reverts to the way it was originally created, with only basic fill and stroke attributes applied.

Using the Appearance palette, you can add, remove, restack, or change attributes that are applied to objects, groups, or layers. Even after saving, closing, and reopening an artwork file, you can still change appearance attributes applied to objects in the document.

fyi Filters actually change an object's basic paths so they are not listed in the Appearance palette.

Appearances and Layers

The Layers palette and the Appearance palette work together to apply appearance attributes to selected layers, groups, or objects. Using the Layers palette, you can apply appearance attributes to entire layers, sublayers, or groups all at once. Just click the target (○) in the Layers palette; the icon changes to a double circle (◎) when the layer is targeted. The target icon changes to gray (◉) when appearances are applied. When targeted in the Layers palette, all objects in that layer or group become selected and appearance attributes are applied to all objects in the layer, sublayer, or group.

The name that displays in the Layers palette (Path, Mesh, Group, Envelope, Type, etc.) is the same identifying name that displays in the Appearance palette. If a targeted object is nested within a layer or group to which appearance attributes have been applied, the layer or group name is also displayed in the Appearance palette above the the name of the targeted object (see Figure 11.4).

- To display the attributes in the Appearance palette for a layer, group, or object, click on the gray target circle.

- When the targeted item is a layer or group having attributes applied to nested objects, *Contents* displays in the Appearance palette. Double-click it to display the appearance attributes of objects.

- To select a layer but not target it, click the Selection area. The Selection box (■) displays on the right side of the layer row.

- To deselect a targeted top-level layer, sublayer, group layer, or object layer, *Shift*-click the gray target circle in the Layers palette.

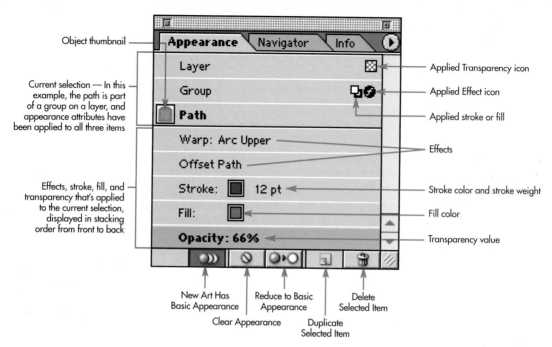

Object thumbnail — **Appearance** Navigator Info

Layer — Applied Transparency icon

Current selection — In this example, the path is part of a group on a layer, and appearance attributes have been applied to all three items

Group — Applied Effect icon

Path — Applied stroke or fill

Warp: Arc Upper — Effects

Offset Path

Effects, stroke, fill, and transparency that's applied to the current selection, displayed in stacking order from front to back

Stroke: ▮ 12 pt — Stroke color and stroke weight

Fill: ▮ — Fill color

Opacity: 66% — Transparency value

New Art Has Basic Appearance — Reduce to Basic Appearance — Delete Selected Item

Clear Appearance — Duplicate Selected Item

FIGURE 11.4 Appearance attributes applied to selected objects, groups, or layers are managed in the Appearance palette.

- When appearance attributes are applied to individual object layers, *Mixed Appearances* displays in the Appearance palette rather than a list of applied appearance attributes.

The Appearance Palette

Appearance attributes are displayed as a list in the Appearance palette (Figure 11.4). Display the Appearance palette by choosing **Window** ⇨ **Appearance**. If nothing in the document is selected, *No Selection* displays in the top section, and the current Fill and Stroke attributes are listed.

- A thumbnail of the contents of a path layer displays to the left of the Path listing. To hide this thumbnail, display the Appearance palette Options menu and choose Hide Thumbnail.

Applying Appearance Attributes Using the Appearance Palette To apply new appearance attributes or to modify existing attributes, display the Appearance palette (**Window** ⇨ **Appearance** or click the Appearance tab in an existing palette set).

1. Select an object or group in the document

   or

timesaver
You can apply appearance attributes to an object on the artboard by dragging the thumbnail in the Appearance palette and dropping it onto the object. The object doesn't have to be selected.

Target a layer, group, or object in the Layers palette

or

To modify an existing attribute, click its listing at the top of the Appearance palette.

2. Click an item listed in the Appearance palette. Attributes are applied immediately to selected objects.

Indicates that transparency is applied to the entire layer or group

- **Stroke** — Selects the Stroke box in the Color palette so you can change the stroke color. When this listing is selected, you can also change the stroke weight in the Stroke palette.
  - Stroke weight displays to the right of the stroke attribute.
  - If a brush is applied to a stroke, the brush name displays to the right of the stroke attribute.
  - If a transparency attribute or an effect is applied to a stroke, a listing for it is nested under Stroke. Click the Expand arrow (▶) to display it.

Indicates that an Effect is applied to the entire layer or group

- **Fill** — Selects the Fill box in the Color palette so you can change the fill color.
  - Fills can be colors, gradients, or patterns and you can select them from the Swatches palette.
  - If a transparency attribute or an effect is applied only to the fill of an object, a listing for it is nested under Fill. Click the Expand arrow (▶) to display it.

Indicates that a stroke or fill attribute is applied to the entire layer or group

- **Transparency (default or applied)** — Displays the Transparency palette so you can change the opacity value or the blending mode, or both.

- **Effects** — Display the Effect menu (not Filters) and choose the effect you want to apply. If a dialog box is associated with the command, it displays so you can change settings to control the appearance of the effect. Click OK or press *return/enter* to exit the dialog box.
  - Double-click an existing effect appearance attribute to display its dialog box to change settings.

Applying Multiple Fill or Stroke Attributes You aren't limited to applying only one fill or stroke attribute to selected layers, groups, or objects. Multiple appearance attributes can be applied to fills and strokes.

It's important, though, to pay attention to the stacking order of multiple fills or strokes. For example, in the Appearance palette, the listing for a narrow stroke should be above the listing for a wider stroke. Otherwise you won't see the narrow stroke because it will be hidden by the wider stroke. You can rearrange them using the methods described in *Rearranging Appearance Attributes,* discussed next.

To apply multiple stroke or fill attributes:

1. In the Layers palette, target a layer, group, or object.

2. In the Appearance palette, click on the attribute you want to add.

3. Display the Appearance palette Options menu and choose Add New Fill or Add New Stroke.

   ■ A new Stroke or Fill attribute is displayed above the original listing.

   or

   Duplicate an existing Fill or Stroke attribute using one of the methods described later in this chapter, then change its appearance attributes.

   ■ A copy of the Stroke or Fill attribute is displayed below the original listing.

4. Change its appearance attributes.

Rearranging Appearance Attributes You can change the order that appearance attributes are displayed in the Appearance palette, which also changes the order in which they're applied to targeted objects, thereby affecting their appearance. Just click on the listing in the Appearance palette and drag up or down. When the double black line displays (the same as in the Layers palette), release the mouse to drop the attribute.

Appearance attributes can be rearranged only within their respective sections. Fill and Stroke attributes can only be rearranged with other fill and stroke attributes; Effect attributes can only be rearranged with other Effect attributes, and so on.

Duplicating Appearance Attributes Using the Appearance Palette
It's sometimes quicker to edit an existing appearance attribute than it is to create a new one. To make a copy of an appearance attribute so you can make changes to it without changing the original attribute:

1. In the Layers palette, target a layer, group, or object.

2. In the Appearance palette, click on the attribute you want to copy.

3. Click the Duplicate Selected Item button ([⬚]) at the bottom of the palette.

   or

   Drag the attribute listing down and drop it on the Duplicate Selected Item button ([⬚]) at the bottom of the palette.

   or

   Display the Appearance palette Options menu and choose Duplicate Item.

Duplicating Appearance Attributes Using the Layers Palette

To copy appearance attributes from one layer to another in the Layers palette, ⬚-drag the target circle (⬤) on the layer having the appearances you want to copy and drop it on the target circle of another layer, group, or object.

- It may take a few seconds for the appearances to copy and display on the selected objects in the document.

Moving Appearance Attributes Using the Layers Palette

You can move appearance attributes from one layer, group, or object to another one by dragging the target circle (⬤) on one layer to the target circle on another layer. The appearance attributes are removed from the original layer, group, or object and transferred to the new one. You can move the attributes from a path to a layer, from a layer to a group, from a group to an individual path, etc.

Removing Appearance Attributes

You can easily remove individual appearance attributes that have been applied to layers, groups, or objects.

1. In the Layers palette, target a layer, group, or object.

2. In the Appearance palette, click on the attribute in that layer or group that you want to remove.

3. Click the Delete Selected Item button (🗑) at the bottom of the palette.

   or

   Drag the attribute listing down and drop it on the Delete Selected Item button (🗑) at the bottom of the palette.

   or

   Display the Appearance palette Options menu and choose Remove Item.

   To apply a stroke color of None, including strokes that have brushstrokes applied, click the Stroke attribute listing, then click the Delete Selected Item button (🗑) at the bottom of the Appearance palette.

   To remove all appearance attributes, including changing fill and stroke attributes to None:

- Click the Clear Appearance button (🚫) at the bottom of the Appearance palette

or

- Display the Appearance palette Options menu and choose Clear Appearance.

fyi Appearance attributes can be copied from one object to another using the Eyedropper and Paint Bucket. Refer to Step 7, Add Color to Artwork, for more information about using these tools.

read this! If you attempt to remove the basic fill and stroke attributes using one of the methods described here, None becomes the fill or stroke attribute.

fyi To apply the Clear Appearance command or the Reduce to Basic Appearance command to paths nested in a layer or group, don't target the top-level layer or group layer. Target the object layer.

To remove all appearance attributes, but leave the bottommost fill and stroke attribute in the Appearance palette applied:

- Click the **Reduce to Basic Appearance** button () at the bottom of the Appearance palette

or

- Display the Appearance palette Options menu and choose **Reduce to Basic Appearance.**

Specifying Appearance Attributes for New Objects You can control the appearance attributes of new objects you create. You can (a) specify that all new objects have basic fill and stroke attributes and default transparency, or (b) you can specify that new objects have the appearance attributes currently listed in the Appearance palette.

- To apply a single fill and a single stroke attribute to new objects:
  - Click the **New Art Has Basic Appearance** button (▭) at the bottom of the Appearance palette.

    or

  - Display the Appearance palette Options menu and choose **New Art Has Basic Appearance.**

- To apply the appearance attributes currently listed in the Appearance palette to new objects:
  - Click the **New Art Has Basic Appearance** button (▭) at the bottom of the Appearance palette to deselect it. The Tool Tip display changes to read **New Art Maintains Appearance.**

    or

  - Display the Appearance palette Options menu and choose **New Art Has Basic Appearance** to deselect it. The **New Art Has Basic Appearance** button at the bottom of the Appearance palette also deselects.

fyi When the button (▭) at the bottom of the Appearance palette is selected, the option is New Art Has Basic Appearance. If the button is deselected, the option is New Art Maintains Appearance.

activity 11.6

1. Open the file named Appearances Practice.eps that's in the Student Files folder on the CD-ROM that accompanies this book. Save it into your Practice folder with the same name.

2. In the Layers palette, expand both layers so you can see their object layers.

3. In the document, click on the star to select it.

4. In the Appearance palette, click on the Stroke attribute listing.

   ■ The Stroke box in the Color palette becomes active.

5. Change the stroke color to white and, in the Stroke palette, change the stroke weight to 3 pt.

   ■ Notice that the attributes in the Appearance palette reflect the changes.

Continued

6. In the Appearances palette, click the Path listing.

7. Display the Effect menu, click on Distort & Transform to display the submenu, and choose Pucker & Bloat. When the dialog box displays, move the slider to 80% Bloat, then click OK or press *return/enter*.

   ▪ In the Layers palette, notice that the target circle is gray (because appearance attribute has been applied to an object on that layer).

8. Display the Effect menu again, display the Distort & Transform submenu again, and choose Twist. When the dialog box displays, change the angle to 35°, then click OK or press *return/enter*.

   ▪ In the Appearance palette, notice the order of the listings.

9. In the Appearance palette, click on Pucker & Bloat and drag-and-drop it under Twist.

   ▪ Notice the effect changing the order in which appearance attributes are applied has on the targeted object.

10. In the Layers palette, target Layer 1 to select the type in the document.

    ▪ In the Appearance palette, notice that *Contents* is displayed instead of the fill and stroke attributes.

11. Double-click *Contents*.

    ▪ The layer name is replaced by *Type* and, in the Layers palette, the *Heading* object layer becomes targeted.

12. Apply a fill color of 50% yellow.

13. Display the Effect menu, display the Stylize submenu, and choose Outer Glow. When the dialog box displays, choose Exclusion from the Mode pop-up submenu, specify 75% opacity, and 0p7 Blur value. Click OK or press *return/enter*.

14. Display the Transparency palette and change the opacity value to 90%. Press *return/enter*.

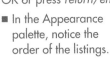
Keeping Up Appearances

15. In the Layers palette, target the group in Layer 2. Apply the Azure Rings pattern fill (Swatches palette). Then change the Opacity setting in the Transparency palette to 65%.

    ▪ All the circles were filled with the pattern and the transparency setting is applied to all the objects.

16. Press ⌘ z to undo the last action and deselect all.

    ▪ In the Layers palette, notice the the object layers are highlighted but not targeted.

    ▪ Notice that in the Appearance palette, the Fill, Stroke, and Opacity attributes are displayed.

17. In the Layers palette, *Shift*-click the target circle of each object layer to target them.

18. In the Appearance palette, click the Fill appearance attribute, then change the Opacity setting in the Transparency palette to 25%.

    ▪ Notice that only the pattern fill in the circles became more transparent, but the stroke didn't change.

19. In the Layers palette, target Layer 2.

20. Display the Effect menu, display the Distort & Transform submenu, and choose Roughen. When the dialog box displays, change Size to 3%, Relative, 5 Detail, Smooth Points. Click OK or press *return/enter*.

    ▪ All paths on that layer were modified by the Roughen command, but the heading was unaffected because it's on a different layer.

21. Target the Group layer again and double-click the listing for Contents to display Stroke information.

22. In the Appearance palette, click on the Stroke attribute, display the Appearance palette Options menu, and choose Add New Stroke.

    ▪ A new Stroke listing displays above the existing Stroke attribute listing in the Appearance palette.

Continued

23. Click on the new Stroke appearance attribute, and change it to 6 pt with a fill color of 20% cyan, 100% magenta.

24. You can't see the original purple stroke, because it's covered up by the 3 pt pink stroke. So drag the Purple Stroke appearance attribute and drop it above the pink Stroke attribute.

   ■ Now the pink stroke is behind the Purple stroke and you can see both of them.

25. Press ⌘ s to save the file.

26. Target the Heading layer in Layer 1.

27. In the Appearance palette, display the Appearance palette Options menu and choose Reduce to Basic Appearance.

   ■ All effects were removed and the text reverted to its original appearance.

28. Save the file, print the page, and close the artwork window.

Styles

In Illustrator, styles are sets of multiple attributes that can be applied to single objects, groups, or entire layers at one time. Virtually any attribute that can be defined can be combined into a style — for example, fill and stroke colors, stroke weight, transparency settings, filters, and effects.

Styles applied to objects affect how an object looks, without changing the actual path that created it. Styles can be applied, removed, or edited without changing the original object. If you edit a style that's been applied to an object in the document, the object is updated automatically.

Styles are saved onto the Styles palette as thumbnail swatches just as color, gradient, and pattern swatches are saved onto the Swatches palette. This means that the same set of attributes can be applied to multiple objects, guaranteeing consistency. A style's individual appearance attributes are displayed in the Appearance palette, which is used to create new style or modify existing ones. (See the preceding section in this chapter for information about the Appearance palette.)

Styles are saved with the document, so if you close a document containing styles applied to objects and reopen it, the styles are still applied to the objects. Newly created styles saved onto the Styles palette also save with the document.

The default Styles palette contains swatches of sets of Styles supplied by Illustrator, but you can create your own styles and save them onto the Styles palette. Styles you create also can be stored in your custom startup file. Refer to Step 6, *Rulers, Grids, & Guides* for information about custom startup files.

fyi Only one style at a time can be applied to a layer, group, or object.

The Styles Palette

Many of the functions in the Styles (Figure 11.5) palette are the same as other palettes in Illustrator. Refer to instructions on using the Swatches palette in Step 7, *Add Color to Artwork*, or for using the Brushes palette in Step 10, *Brushes, Patterns, & Symbols* if you need a refresher.

- Choose the way Styles are viewed in the Styles palette by choosing one of three options available in the Styles palette Options menu:
    - **Thumbnail View** — Displays only a thumbnail representation of the style.
    - **Small List View** — Displays a small thumbnail as well as style names.
    - **Large List View** — Displays a large thumbnail as well as style names.
- Select multiple styles in the Styles palette by *Shift*-clicking to select all the swatches between the clicks, or ⌘-clicking to select random swatches.
- Sort styles in the Styles palette alphabetically by name by choosing Sort by Name from the Styles palette Options menu.
- Rearrange swatches by dragging and dropping.
- Remove styles that aren't used in a document by choosing Select All Unused from the Styles palette Options menu and clicking the Delete Style button (🗑) at the bottom of the Styles palette.
- Display other Style libraries available in Illustrator by choosing **Window ⇨ Style Libraries** and selecting one from the pop-up submenu.
- Add a style from another Style library to the current document's Styles palette by clicking a swatch in the other library

    or

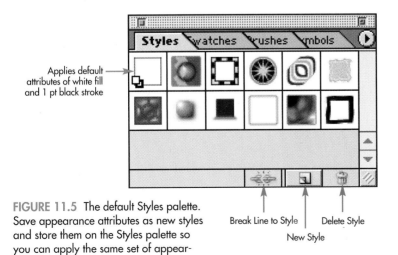

Applies default attributes of white fill and 1 pt black stroke

Break Line to Style

New Style

Delete Style

New Style...
Duplicate Style
Merge Styles
Delete Style

Break Link to Style

Select All Unused

Sort by Name

✓ Thumbnail View
Small List View
Large List View

✓ Override Character Color
Style Options...

Styles palette Options menu

FIGURE 11.5 The default Styles palette. Save appearance attributes as new styles and store them on the Styles palette so you can apply the same set of appearances to other objects.

by applying a style from another library to an object in the current document.

or

by dragging a style from another library onto the current document's Style palette.

■ Create your own Style library by creating new styles, applying them to objects in a document, then saving the document into the Styles folder inside the Presets folder in the Adobe Illustrator 10 folder on your hard drive (**Adobe Illustrator 10** ⇨ **Presets** ⇨ **Styles**). When you quit Illustrator and relaunch it, your new Style library will be listed in the Style Libraries pop-up submenu.

▪ If you delete a default swatch from the Styles palette and then want it back, you can restore it by displaying the Style Libraries submenu in the Windows menu and choosing Default_CMYK or Default_RGB, depending upon the color mode of your current document.

Applying Styles to Objects

Styles can be applied to individual objects or to all the objects on a layer, sublayer, or group. The name of the applied style is displayed at the top of the Appearance palette.

1. In the document, select the object or objects.

   or

   In the Layers palette, target an object layer. To apply a style to an entire layer, sublayer, or group, click their target circles.

2. In the Styles palette, click a style swatch.

   or

   Drag a style swatch and drop it on object(s) or group in the document.

   ■ The object or group doesn't have to be selected to apply a style to it.

Create a New Style

In addition to the styles on the default Styles palette and the styles available in Style libraries supplied by Illustrator, you can create and save your own styles. You can start from scratch and build a set of appearances or you can start with a set of appearances from an existing style. If you want to create a new style from an existing style, it's a good idea to copy it first so you keep the original style intact.

1. In the document, select an object or create a new one.

2. Build a new set of appearance attributes or apply an existing style to start with some appearances already applied to the object.

3. In the Styles palette, click the New Style button () at the bottom of the Styles palette.

or

In the Appearances palette, drag the object thumbnail onto the Styles palette.

- The thumbnail for the new style is placed at the bottom of the Styles palette.

4. Double-click the new Style swatch to display the Style Options dialog box. Type a name for the new style, then click OK or press *return/enter*.

Managing Your Styles

Styles can be duplicated, renamed, changed, unlinked from the object it's applied to, combined with other styles, or deleted.

Duplicate a Style If you want to alter a style but you also want to keep the original style in the Style palette, make a copy of it and change one of them.

1. In the Styles palette, click on the style you want to copy to select it.

2. Click on the New Style button () at the bottom of the Styles palette.

or

Drag the style and drop it on the New Style button () at the bottom of the Styles palette.

or

Display the Styles palette Options menu and choose Duplicate Style.

The copied style's swatch is placed at the end of the existing styles (row or list) in the Styles palette and has the same name as the original style with a 1 added to it. You can rename the style, though (see below).

Rename a Style To rename an existing style:

- In the Styles palette, double-click the style swatch (or listing) to display the Style Options dialog box, enter a new name in the Style Name field, then click OK or press *return/enter*.

or

- In the Styles palette, click a swatch (or listing) to select it, display the Styles palette Options menu, and choose Style Options to display the Style Options dialog box. Enter a new name in the Style Name field and click OK or press *return/enter*.

Edit a Style You can change the appearances of an existing style. Any objects in the document that have the style applied to them will be updated automatically unless you unlink the objects first (see

read this!

If you edit a style attribute on an object to which the style has been applied, rather than editing the style itself, the link between the selected object and the style is broken. Therefore, if you then edit the style, that object won't be affected by the change in the style.

below). You can also copy the style and make the changes on the copy (see *Duplicate a Style* discussed previously) to avoid changing objects that have the original style applied to them.

1. Create an object in the document and apply the style you want to edit (or a copy of it); otherwise you won't be able to see what you're doing.

2. In the Appearance palette, change the appearance attributes for the style. You can change, restack, add, or remove attributes to change the style.

3. In the Appearance palette, display the Appearance palette Options menu and choose Redefine Style "[name of style]".

   or

   In the Appearance palette, drag the object thumbnail over the style swatch (the one you're changing) in the Styles palette.

Unlink a Style from Objects   You can break the link between a style in the Styles palette and objects in the document to which it's been applied. Then you can change the style without affecting objects that already have the style applied to them.

1. Select the object(s) in the document.

   or

   In the Layers palette, target the layer, group, or object.

   - You can target a layer or group only if the style was applied to the entire layer or group.

2. Click the Break Link to Style button (⬚) at the bottom of the Styles palette.

   or

   Display the Styles palette Options menu and choose Break Link to Style.

   or

   In the document, change an appearance attribute for the selected object.

   - The name of the style for that object is no longer displayed in the Appearance palette (because it's not a style now, just a set of appearances).

Merge Styles   You can combine two selected styles and make a new style without changing either of the original styles. The new merged style thumbnail swatch is displayed at the bottom of the Styles palette.

The order in which the selected swatches are displayed in the Styles palette determines the order in which their appearance attributes are applied to objects. The attributes for the style swatch (or listing) closest to the top of the palette are listed above the attributes for the style swatch below it in the Styles palette. This means that attributes in the topmost style may cover up attributes in the other style, making them invisible. To fix the situation, remove attributes you don't need or move them in the Appearance palette.

1. In the Styles palette, select two swatches (or two listings) by *Shift*-clicking to select two swatches that are beside each other or by ⌘-clicking two random swatches.

2. Display the Styles palette Options menu and choose Merge Styles.

3. Enter a descriptive name for the new style, then click OK or press *return/enter*.

Delete Styles   When you delete a Style from the Styles palette, any layers, groups, or objects to which the style was applied keep the style's appearance attributes, but they're no longer linked to a style swatch in the Styles palette (because it's no longer there).

1. In the Styles palette, click on a Style swatch or listing to select it.

2. Click the Delete Style button ([🗑]) at the bottom of the Styles palette.

   or

   Drag a style and drop it on the Delete Style button ([🗑]) at the bottom of the Styles palette.

   or

   Display the Styles palette Options menu and choose Delete Style.

3. Click Yes or press *return/enter*.

Expand an Object's Appearance

When you expand the appearance attributes of a style applied to an object, the objects that created the style are selected in the document and displayed in the Layers palette as a group or a series of groups. The style is unlinked from the style in the Styles palette. If you want to, you can target the layer, groups, or objects, apply new appearance attributes, and define it as a new style.

activity 11.7

1. Create a new document: Letter size, CMYK color mode. Save it into your Practice folder as an .eps file named Styles Practice.eps.

2. In the document, draw a rectangle and leave it selected.

3. Click the Raindrop CMYK style to apply it to the rectangle.

4. In the Styles palette, click the Silver Ribbon style swatch to apply it to the rectangle.

   ■ The Raindrop CMYK style was replaced by the Silver Ribbon style because only one style at a time can be applied to an object.

5. Open the file you saved into your Practice folder as Appearances Practice.eps.

6. Click on the shape that was originally a star before the Twist and Pucker & Bloat effects were applied.

   ■ Notice that the path for the original shape displays.

7. In the Appearance palette, delete the Pucker & Bloat appearance.

8. Delete the Twist appearance to get back to the original star shape.

Continued

- All the effects applied to the star have been deleted so why isn't it back to its original shape?

9. In the Layers palette, the target circle is gray, indicating that an appearance has been applied to all the objects in that layer. Click the gray target circle for that layer. In the Appearance palette, delete the Roughen effect.

  - Now the star is back to its original shape.

10. Deselect all and reselect only the star. Display the Effect menu, then display the Warp submenu. Choose Shell Upper and enter the following specifications, then click OK or press *return/enter*:

  - Horizontal   ■ Distortion, Horizontal: 0%
  - Bend: 50%   ■ Distortion, Vertical: 0%

11. Apply a Drop Shadow (Stylize):
  - Mode: Multiply   ■ Y Offset: 0p7
  - Opacity: 75%   ■ Blur: 0p8
  - X Offset: 0p7   ■ Darkness: 50%

12. Apply Inner Glow (Stylize):
  - Mode: Screen
  - Opacity: 75%
  - Blur: 3p
  - Center

13. In the Appearance palette, click the object thumbnail and drag-and-drop it into the Styles palette.

14. Double-click the new swatch and, when the Style Options dialog box displays, name the Style Warped. Click OK or press *return/enter*.

15. Press ⌘c to copy the star.

16. Save this file into your Practice folder. Name it Appearances Practice 2.eps.

17. In the document you created named Styles Practice.eps, press ⌘v to paste the star you copied in the other document.

  - Notice that the style associated with the star is now present in this document's Styles palette.

18. Delete the star.

  - The style in the Styles palette is left behind.

19. Select the rectangle in the document and apply the Warped style to it.

  - Notice that the appearance attributes are displayed in the Appearance palette.

20. In the Appearance palette, click on the Fill listing. Change the fill color to the Jungle Stripes pattern (from the Swatches palette).

21. In the Appearance palette, double-click Inner Glow to display the dialog box for the Inner Glow effect. Change the Blur value to 6p. Click OK or press *return/enter*.

  - Notice that the style swatch in the Styles palette hasn't changed.

22. Draw another rectangle on the page and apply the Warped style to it.

  - It's still the same blue warp shape.

23. Click on the first rectangle, the one with the Jungle Stripes. It's appearance attributes are displayed in the Appearance palette.

24. Drag the object thumbnail from the Appearance palette and drop it into the Styles palette. Rename the swatch Warped Stripes.

25. Drag the Warped Stripes style swatch over the blue warped rectangle and drop it.

  - It changes to warped jungle stripes even though it wasn't selected.

26. Deselect all.

27. Hold down the ⌘ key and click the Rustic Pen style swatch and the Warped Stripes swatch.

28. Display the Styles palette Options menu and choose Merge Styles. Name the new style swatch Merged Stripes.

  - In the Appearance palette, notice the listings of appearance attributes. Enlarge the palette if necessary to see all of them.

29. Select one of the rectangles and apply the new, merged style (Merged Stripes).

  - You can't see the white stroke, even though it's still listed in the Appearance palette because a wider black stroke is listed above it.

Continued

30. In the Appearance palette, drag the listing for the white stroke above the listing for the black stroke.

- Now you can see the white stroke. I don't like it there, but at least you can see it.

31. In the Appearance palette, delete the white stroke attribute.

32. In the Styles palette, delete the swatch named Merged Stripes.

33. Drag the object thumbnail from the Appearance palette onto the Styles palette and rename it Merged Stripes.

34. Experiment with creating, applying, and editing, styles. It's a lot of fun.

35. When you're finished, save and print the file, then close the artwork window.

PRACTICE ACTIVITY 11-1 — DIA

1. Draw a stylized representation of Denver International Airport as shown on the right. Save it into your Practice folder as an .eps file named DIA.eps.

2. Place each of the three sections on a separate layer.

3. To the backmost (largest) section, apply a fill of 40% cyan. Apply a fill of C 80%, M 80%, Y 0%, K 0%, and a 1 pt black stroke to the accent bars.

4. Choose Effects ⇨ Stylize ⇨ Inner Glow and enter the following specifications:
- Mode: Normal
- Opacity: 75%
- Blur: .25"
- Center
- Color preview box: Default (C 5%, M 2%, Y 24%, K 0%)

5. To the middle section, also apply a fill of 40% cyan.

6. Choose Effects ⇨ Stylize ⇨ Inner Glow and enter the following specifications:
- Mode: Normal
- Opacity: 75%
- Blur: .13"
- Center
- Color preview box: Default (C 5%, M 2%, Y 24%, K 0%)

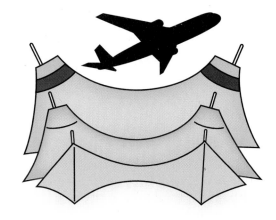

7. To the smallest section, apply a fill of 30% cyan.

8. Choose Effects ⇨ Stylize ⇨ Outer Glow and enter the following specifications:
- Mode: Normal
- Opacity: 75%
- Blur: .13"
- Color preview box: C 5%, M 15%, Y 55%, K 0%

9. Draw an airplane similar to the one shown here, apply a black fill, and position as shown.

10. Save the file, print it, then close the artwork window.

EXERCISE 11-1 — Opera House Poster

The photograph shown below is named Sydney Opera House.tif and is in the Student Files folder on the CD-ROM that accompanies this book.

Using the photograph and the type below, create a small poster announcing the upcoming opera season.

Sail away with us for an evening of symphonic splendor.
Be a part of the Sydney Symphony Orchestra as it launches its 2002–2003 season.
Sydney Opera House
October 1, 2002

For the type, choose a typeface, size, style, apply filters, etc. You can change the capitalization of words, if desired. Crop the photo, apply filters, create a mask, and so on. Be creative.

Enlarge the photo as necessary, regardless of the final resolution. Pretend it was scanned at the desired resolution.

Meshes, Masks, Blends, & Transparency

Chapter Outline

- Meshes
- Masks
- Blend Shapes and Colors
- Transparency

Meshes

The Mesh tool and Gradient Mesh command create objects, called *mesh* objects, with colors blending in various directions (see Figure 12.1). Applying a gradient mesh to an object can make it look more like a photograph. Adding shading can make a flat object look lumpy.

A mesh is just what it implies: a criss-crossing of mesh *lines* connected by mesh *points*, that create mesh *patches*, which you can manipulate to control color in an object. Mesh objects can be created from vector objects you draw in Illustrator and from bitmap images you embed into an Illustrator document. Compound paths, text objects, brush-stroked paths, and linked images cannot be mesh objects.

After a mesh object is created, you apply colors to mesh points and mesh patches, which you can move around to create the desired effect.

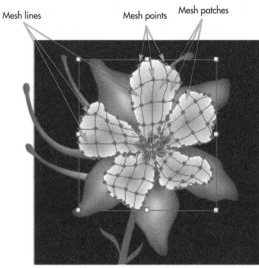

Mesh lines   Mesh points   Mesh patches

Mesh object   Mesh lines displayed

FIGURE 12.1 The columbine on the left is a mesh object and the figure on the right shows the mesh that was used to create it.

- Once a mesh object has been created, it cannot be converted back to a standard object except by applying the Undo command.

- When changing complex objects to mesh objects, use the Create Gradient Mesh command (**Object ⇨ Create Gradient Mesh**) rather than the Mesh tool (▨) in the Toolbox.

- Open paths are automatically closed when an object is converted to a mesh object.

- The Gradient Mesh command creates more consistently spaced lines and points than does the Mesh tool.

- The Gradient Mesh feature consumes large amounts of memory, and complex meshes can slow down the performance of your computer. It's better to have a few smaller, simpler mesh objects than one large, complex one. Printing errors are less likely to occur.

fyi *Make a copy of the object before converting it to a mesh object in the event you need it again.*

Elements of a Mesh Object

The elements of a mesh object are mesh points, mesh lines, and mesh patches.

- **Mesh line** — Lines that crisscross the object. Move and edit points on the mesh line to manipulate color in the object.

- **Mesh point** — Intersection of two mesh lines. Mesh points display as diamonds and can be added, deleted, or moved, and color can be applied to them. Mesh points control the placement of color.

- Anchor points also can be added to (Add Anchor Point tool — ✑₊) or deleted from (Delete Anchor Point tool — ✑₋) mesh lines. They're square rather than diamond-shaped so you can tell which is which. Anchor points can be manipulated the same as you would any other anchor point in an object. These anchor points can be used to reshape the overall mesh object or to reshape a mesh line, but color can't be applied to them.

- **Mesh patch** — The area between the meshlines. The color in mesh patches can be manipulated to achieve the desired effect.

Creating a Mesh Object

There are three ways to convert a standard object to a mesh object. You can use the Mesh tool in the Toolbox, choose the Create Gradient Mesh command in the Object menu, or choose the Expand command in the Object menu to convert a gradient object into a mesh object.

Mesh Tool Choose the Mesh tool in the Toolbox, then click a filled object to convert it to a mesh object with the minimum number of mesh lines that radiate out from the point of the click. Continue clicking in different areas to create additional sets of mesh lines.

When the Mesh tool is over a path on the document page, the mouse pointer changes to ⊞. When the the pointer is over a mesh point, it changes to ⊞.

Mesh tool in the Toolbox palette

- The object cannot have a fill of None applied. If ⊘ displays when you move the mouse pointer over an object, the object has a None fill.

- Any brushstroke applied to the object is removed.

- An alert box displays if an object contains too many anchor points. Remove unnecessary anchor points using the Delete Anchor Point tool (▣) or the Smooth tool (▨).

Create Gradient Mesh Command The Create Gradient Mesh command (**Object ⇨ Create Gradient Mesh**) allows you to specify how many rows and columns are used to create the mesh.

1. Select the object that you want to convert into a mesh object.

   - The object can have a fill of None.

2. Choose **Object ⇨ Create Gradient Mesh** to display the Create Gradient Mesh dialog box.

   - Any brushstroke applied to the object is removed when the command is applied.

Create Gradient Mesh	
Rows: 4	OK
Columns: 4	Cancel
Appearance: Flat ⬍	☐ Preview
Highlight: 100 %	

Display the Create Gradient Mesh dialog box by choosing Object ⇨ Create Gradient Mesh. Change values in the fields to convert an ordinary object into a mesh object.

3. Enter specifications for the mesh.

- **Preview** — Click the Preview box to turn it on.

- **Rows** — Enter a value to specify how many horizontal rows the mesh will have.

- **Columns** — Enter a value to specify how many vertical columns the mesh will have.

  - The values in the Columns field doesn't have to be the same as the value in the Rows field. You can have more of one than you have of the other.

  - The more rows and columns you have, the more complex the mesh is.

- **Appearance** — Make a selection from this pop-up menu to control the direction of the highlight:

  - **Flat** — The original color is spread evenly across the object; no highlight.

  - **To Center** — Creates a highlight in the center of the object.

  - **To Edge** — Creates a highlight around the edges of the object.

Flat   To Center   To Edge

- **Highlight** — This option has an effect on the selected object only when To Center or To Edge is selected in the Appearance pop-up menu. Enter a value to specify the intensity of the white highlight.

  - A value of 100% is the maximum; a value of 0% applies no white highlight.

Highlight: 100%   Highlight: 50%

4. Click OK or press *return/enter*.

Expand Command Use this command to convert an object containing a linear or radial gradient into a gradient mesh object.

1. Select the object, then choose **Object** ⇨ **Expand**.

- The Expand dialog box displays.

2. In the Expand Gradient To section, click the Gradient Mesh button.

3. Click OK or press *return/enter*.

- The mesh object that's created takes the shape of the gradient.

Add or Change the Color of a Mesh Object

The color added to elements of a mesh object is the fill color currently displayed in the Color palette. Apply the color to selected mesh elements the same way you add it to other objects drawn with Illustrator tools; that is, by dragging and dropping, applying a color swatch, or using the Paint Bucket tool (■).

■ Color that's applied to a mesh point also colors the surrounding area.

■ When you apply color to a mesh patch, all four mesh points that created the patch are colored the same color.

■ You can control the way the color is displayed by editing mesh lines, mesh points, and anchor points. See Reshape a Mesh Object later in this chapter.

To apply color to a mesh object:

1. Turn on Smart Guides so you can see the object even with a fill and stroke of None or white.

2. Deselect the mesh object.

3. With the Direct Selection tool or the Mesh tool (■), click on a mesh point and apply a fill color.

   or

   With the Direct Selection tool, select the mesh object and drag and drop a color from the Color palette or Swatches palette onto a mesh point or a mesh patch.

   or

   With the Direct Selection tool, click a mesh patch, choose the Mesh tool (■) in the Toolbox, and click inside the mesh patch.

   ■ A new mesh point with connecting mesh lines is created inside the original mesh patch and the color is applied.

   or

   With the Direct Selection tool, select a mesh point or a mesh patch, then choose the Eyedropper tool. *Shift*-click an existing color in the mesh object. The sampled color is applied to the active point or patch.

4. To change the color of mesh points and mesh patches having the same color, with the Direct Selection tool, select a mesh point having that color, then choose **Select** ⇨ **Same** ⇨ **Fill Color**.

5. To make a color area smaller, add mesh lines and apply a different color.

6. To make a mesh patch larger, delete mesh points. Or you can apply the same color to areas next to the patch you want to make larger.

fyi To keep file size from getting out of hand, try to create several smaller mesh objects rather than one large one.

Add Mesh Points and Lines

Mesh points and lines can be added by clicking inside the mesh object with the Mesh tool (). The current fill color is applied to the new mesh point.

- To add a mesh point without applying the current fill color, *Shift-*click a mesh line with the Mesh tool.

- To add a new mesh line perpendicular to an existing mesh line, click it with the Mesh tool.

Delete a Mesh Point

When you delete a mesh point from a mesh object, any mesh lines that are attached to that point also are deleted. To delete a mesh point (and its mesh lines) from a mesh object:

1. Choose the Mesh tool ( ) in the Toolbox.

2. -click on the point you want to delete. A minus sign displays on the tool pointer icon ( ).

Reshape a Mesh Object

To reshape the mesh of a mesh object, you can move the mesh lines, add anchor points, delete anchor points, convert anchor points from one type to another (smooth to corner, and so on). When you move mesh lines or mesh points, the color associated with them is adjusted, too. You can even move mesh lines and points outside the object boundaries.

With the Direct Selection tool, select mesh points and mesh lines, then reshape them like any other path object drawn in Illustrator.

- Drag a mesh point or mesh patch. You can even drag it outside the object, if necessary.

- Rotate, lengthen, or shorten the direction lines associated with an anchor point.

- Convert a mesh point into a corner point with independent direction lines by clicking it with the Convert Anchor Point tool ( ) (press ⇧ c).

Reposition a Mesh Point along a Mesh Line To move a mesh point on a mesh line without changing the line itself:

1. Choose the Mesh tool ( ) in the Toolbox.

2. *Shift-*drag a mesh point along an existing mesh line.

fyi If the printer is having trouble printing a document containing mesh objects, rasterizing it may solve the problem.

Step 12 — MESHES, MASKS, BLENDS, AND TRANSPARENCY

![Computer mouse illustration] *activity 12.1*

1. Open the document named Pear.eps that you created in Step 4, *The Pen & Pencil Tools*, and saved into your Practice folder.

2. So that we're all working with the same colors, change the body of the pear to C50%, M0%, Y100%, and K0%; and change the leaf to C85%, M0%, Y100%, K0%.

3. Click in the body of the pear object, then choose Object ⇨ Create Gradient Mesh to display the Create Gradient Mesh dialog box.

4. Click the Preview checkbox to turn it on, then enter the following values:
   Rows: 4
   Columns: 4
   Appearance: To Center
   Highlight: 80%

5. Click OK or press *return/enter*.
   - A mesh displays in the selected object.
   - Notice that the mesh is contoured to the shape of the pear.

6. Deselect the object, then, with the Direct Selection tool, click at the top or bottom of the pear body, so the center mesh points are hollow. Don't click near the center of the shape because I don't want you to select a mesh patch connected to the center mesh point.

7. Click on the center mesh point and drag it to the left slightly (as shown here). Deselect.

8. Still with the Direct Selection tool selected, *Shift*-click the top three mesh points of the Pear body to select all of them.

9. Change the color of those three anchor points to C50%, M20%, Y100%, and K0%.

10. Select the bottom three mesh points and change them to the same color as the three top mesh points.
    - This adds a little realistic shading.

11. With the Direct Selection tool, click on the leaf.

12. Choose Object ⇨ Create Gradient Mesh to display the Create Gradient Mesh dialog box.

13. Change values to:
    Rows: 4
    Columns: 4
    Appearance: To Center
    Highlight: 15%

14. Click OK or press *return/enter*.

15. Deselect the object, then, with the Direct Selection tool, click somewhere on the right side of the leaf so the mesh points on the left side of the leaf are hollow.

16. To add shading to the leaf, change the colors of some of the mesh points. Your leaf may be a different shape than mine, so you may want to change different mesh points than I do. Experiment until the shading looks natural.

   a. Click on the mesh point shown here and change its color to C64%, M45%, Y23%, K0%.

   b. Select the mesh point above it on the same mesh line and apply a color of C63%, M18%, Y75%, K0%.

   c. *Shift*-click to select the top three interior mesh points and one in the center mesh line. Change the color to C63%, M0%, Y65%, K0%.

   d. *Shift*-click to select the bottom two interior mesh points. Change the color to C80%, M0%, Y75%, K0%.

   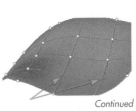

   Continued

e. Click the mesh point at the tip of the leaf. Change the color to C85%, M34%, Y100%, K0%.

f. Click the next mesh point down on the same mesh line. Change the color to C85%, M19%, Y100%, K0%.

g. Click the next mesh point down on the same mesh line. Change the color to C85%, M17%, Y100%, K0%.

17. Adjust mesh points in your Pear artwork until you're satisfied with it's "natural" appearance.

18. Save the file, print it, then close the artwork window.

Masks

A *clipping mask* is an object or group of objects that hides (clips) objects that extend outside its boundaries so only objects inside its borders are visible. It's kind of like opening the drapes of a window. You can see only what's behind the window. The whole tree is there, but you may be able to see only one limb. The rest of the tree is masked from view.

Objects in clipping masks can be manipulated by moving them manually on the page or by using features in the Layers palette. You can move objects in a clipping mask, change their stacking order, or reshape and recolor them.

- The frontmost object in a layer or group becomes the clipping path for everything behind it.

- A clipping mask and the objects it's masking must be in the same Layer or group in the Layers palette, but the clipping mask cannot be a top-level layer.

- Any fill or stroke attributes applied to an object are removed when it's used as a masking object.

- The masking object can be an open or closed path, even a brushstroke or type characters.

  - Type characters don't have to be converted to outlines to use them as a masking object.

- Objects, including the masking object, are grouped automatically when a clipping mask is created with the Make Clipping Mask command. When a clipping mask is created using the Layers palette, objects are not grouped.

- Convert multiple objects to a compound path before using them as a masking object, keeping in mind that the shape of the outer edge of the masking object is used to mask the objects beneath it.

- Objects outside the boundaries of the clipping path are still counted when calculating the size of the file, so crop unnecessary portions of images to reduce file size.

Creating Clipping Masks

Objects can be masked using the Make Clipping Mask command in the Object menu or by using the commands in the Layers palette. The Make Clipping Mask command results in all the objects being grouped. The clipping path is shown on the Layers palette as part of a group. A clipping mask created in the Layers palette leaves the clipping path loose on its layer.

Use the Make Clipping Mask Command To create a clipping mask using the command in the object menu:

1. Assemble all the objects and position them like you want them.

2. Make sure the masking object is at the front of the stack.

3. With the Selection tool, select all the objects, including the masking object.

4. Choose **Object ⇨ Clipping Mask ⇨ Make**

   or

   Press ⌘7

   - Objects are grouped and are selected.

   - If objects were created on different layers, they're assembled into a group in the Layers palette in the clipping path's top-level layer.

   - The masking object's layer in the Layers palette will display the name <u>\<Clipping Path\></u> and it will be underlined, unless the masking object is text. In the case of text characters as masking objects, the text characters will display and will be underlined.

Create a Layer Mask   Clipping masks created using the Layers palette, called Layer Masks, mask all objects on that top-level layer, regardless where they are in the stacking order. The masking object must be the frontmost object in the layer. Refer to Step 8, *Layers & Links* for information about manipulating layers in the Layers palette.

   To create a Layer mask:

1. Assemble the objects you want to mask onto one layer in the Layers palette.

2. Move the masking object to the front of the stack (the top of the list in that layer).

3. Highlight the layer.

   - The objects don't need to be selected on the document page.

4. Click the Make/Release Clipping Mask button ( ) at the bottom of the Layers palette.

   or

   Display the Layers palette Options menu and choose Make Clipping Mask.

   - Everything on that layer that is outside the boundaries of the masking object is no longer visible on the document. Make sure that only the objects on the same layer as the masking object are the objects you want masked.

Releasing a Clipping Mask

There are a couple of ways to convert a clipping mask back to its original objects.

1. With the Selection tool, click on any part of the group that is the clipping mask.

   or

fyi   If you move a clipping path into a different top-level layer, it loses its status as a clipping mask and won't clip objects in the new layer. It becomes a regular path with a fill and stroke of None.

fyi   In the Layers palette, if you release a layer or sublayer containing a clipping path, objects within the sublayer are still clipped.

In the Layers palette, click in the Selection area of the layer containing the clipping path.

2. Choose **Object** ➪ **Clipping Mask** ➪ **Release**

or

Press ⌥⌘7

or

In the Layers palette, click the Make/Release Clipping Mask button ( ) at the bottom of the palette.

- If the clipping mask object is filled with a pattern or a gradient, this method of releasing the mask may cause the clipping path to become solid black. If this happens, Undo the command and use one of the other methods instead.

- Because a clipping path is converted to an object with a fill and stroke of None, you may have to turn on Smart Guides to find it. It's visible in Outline view, too.

Adding an Object to an Existing Clipping Mask

You can add new objects to an existing clipping mask.

Standard Clipping Mask With the Selection tool, select the object to be added to the mask. Then move the object to the desired position in the mask and drop it there. Then, using the Layers palette, drag its object layer into the group layer.

Layer Mask In the Layers palette, drag object layers into the clipping mask's top-level layer. You can change its stacking order by moving the object layers around within the top-level layer.

Applying Color to the Masking Object

You can add a fill color behind the masked objects and add a stroke to the masking object after the clipping mask has been created. Just select the masking object with the Direct Selection tool or by clicking in its object layer's Selection area in the Layers palette. Then apply a fill color, including gradient or pattern, and specify a stroke width and stroke color the same way as any other path in Illustrator.

- The fill color displays behind the masked objects. The stroke displays in front of them.

fyi Objects in clipping masks can be copied, moved, deleted, and so on, in the Layers palette the same as any other objects. Refer to Step 8, Layers & Links, for information.

Step 12 — MESHES, MASKS, BLENDS, AND TRANSPARENCY

567

1. Create a new document: Letter size, CMYK color mode. Save it into your Practice Folder as an .eps file named Clipping Mask Practice.

2. Draw a star, a polygon, a circle, and a rectangle on the document page so they overlap each other. Apply a different color to each object. Make sure the rectangle is the frontmost object.

3. With the Selection tool (v), select all the objects.

4. Choose Object ⇨ Clipping Mask ⇨ Make.

   ■ Only the portions of the star, circle, and polygon that are inside the boundary of the rectangle are visible.

   ■ The rectangle is still part of the group, but it has a fill and stroke of None so you can't see it.

5. Expand the layer in the Layers palette so you can see the object layers.

   ■ Notice that the objects are a group in the top-level layer in the Layers palette.

6. Turn on Smart Guides and locate the masking rectangle and select it with the Direct Selection tool.

7. Apply a 100% yellow fill and a 2 pt 100% Magenta stroke.

   ■ Notice that the fill appears behind the objects and the stroke is in front.

8. In the Layers palette, create a new layer.

9. Draw a 4" × 1" rectangle. Fill it with the Azure Rings pattern from the Swatches palette, no stroke.

10. With the Type tool, type the word MASK in 72 pt Bookman Bold, all caps, and position it in the center of the rectangle.

   ■ If you don't have Bookman Bold on your computer, use any typeface you have that has thick strokes.

11. In the Layers palette, target the layer containing the rectangle and the type to select the objects. Expand the top-level layer so you can see its object layers.

12. Click the Make/Release Clipping Mask button at the bottom of the Layers palette.

   ■ Notice that the word MASK is underlined in the Layers palette, indicating that it's a masking object.

13. In the Layers palette, click the type object layer to select the type, then apply a 1 pt dark blue stroke to the characters.

14. Select the type and drag it down so it's out of the mask area.

15. Verify that the Color box is active in the Color palette and apply the Camouflage pattern to the rectangle.

   ■ The characters are now filled with the new masking pattern.

16. With the Direct Selection tool, click on the word MASK and drag it back up so it's over the masking rectangle.

   ■ The characters are now filled with both patterns.

17. Save the file, print it, then close the artwork window.

Blend Shapes and Colors

The Make Blend command in the Object menu and the Blend tool in the Toolbox () enable you to morph the color *and* shape of two or more selected objects; that is, one shape changes into the other shape (see Figure 12.2). The objects can be open or closed paths, part of a group, or part of a compound path. Objects can be filled with differing fill colors, grayscale, gradients, or patterns. They can have differing stroke colors, stroke weights, and differing endcaps, joins, or dash patterns.

Spacing: Smooth color
Orientation: Align to page

FIGURE 12.2 Swan is morphed to the shape of a fish. Notice the shape of the intermediate object.

- When an individual path in a group or in a compound path is selected, the entire group or compound path is included in the blend.

- If the original objects are filled with different patterns (see Step 10, *Brushes, Patterns, & Symbols*), transition objects are filled automatically with the pattern that fills the topmost object in the stack.

The objects created between the original object and the final object in a blend are called *transition steps*. Each clone of the original shape and color is changed slightly, with the degree of change dependent upon the number of steps used. Objects are grouped automatically. In the Layers palette, they display on one layer (not a grouped sublayer) and are named <Blend>.

Stroke colors as well as fill colors are affected by the Make Blend command. For example, when you blend from an object with a stroke to an object without a stroke, the stroke weight of the transition objects decreases on each step.

If you move any of the original shapes that made up the morphed object (not the transition objects), the overall shape is updated automatically. You can even add and delete anchor points in the original two objects to reshape them, change fill color, or change stroke color and weight.

Objects are blended according to their stacking order. The object on the top of the stack is the first object in the blend, and the object on the bottom of the stack is the last object in the blend. Transition objects are stacked between the top and the bottom, one in back of another.

read this!
If one of the blended objects is filled with a process color and another is filled with a spot color, or if objects are filled with more than one spot color (not a tint of the same color), the intermediate objects are filled with process colors.

Using the Make Blend Command

The Make Blend command in the Object menu (**Object ⇨ Blend ⇨ Make**) creates a blend between two or more objects automatically, depending upon the options chosen in the Blend Options dialog box. Illustrator analyzes the paths and produces the smoothest possible blend between them. To create a blend using the Make Blend command:

1. Draw two or more objects (closed paths, open paths, or groups). Specify fill and stroke colors and stroke weights to each.

   ■ A stroke applied to the original objects is applied to "in between" objects. Stroke weight is decreased or increased when blended from an object with no stroke to one with a stroke and vice versa.

2. Position the objects to allow enough room for the transition shapes that will be created.

3. Select all objects using the Selection tool or the Lasso tool.

4. Choose **Object ⇨ Blend ⇨ Make** or press ⌥⌘b (see Figure 12.3).

5. The blend is created automatically using the Smooth Color spacing method and follows a straight line from the center point of the first object to the center point of the last object (called the *spine*). Read the information in the Modifying Existing Blends section later in this chapter to learn how to change a blend once it has been created.

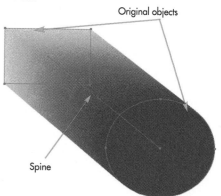

FIGURE 12.3 Blend created between a rectangle and a circle using the Make Blend command in the Object menu.

Blend Options

The Blend Options dialog box contains spacing and orientation settings for the currently selected blend (Figure 12.4). They also affect any new blends you create. Changes are updated automatically to all selected blends and you can see the effects of your changes before exiting the dialog box by clicking the Preview button.

To display the Blend Options dialog box:

■ Choose **Object ⇨ Blend ⇨ Blend Options**

or

■ Select a blend and double-click the Blend tool (🔲) in the Toolbox

or

■ Hold down the ⌥ key as you click on a path with the Blend tool.

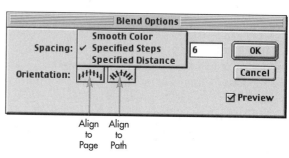

FIGURE 12.4 Blend Options dialog box.

Spacing The Spacing pop-up menu gives three options for how transition steps are placed in a blend.

- **Smooth Colors** — This is the program default, used when Illustrator calculates the optimum number of steps to achieve the best blend of colors.

- **Specified Steps** — Choose this option and enter a value in the field to specify an exact number of transition objects from the original object to the final object. Be aware, though, that banding may occur if an incorrect number of steps is specified.

- **Specified Distance** — Choose this option and enter a value in the field to specify an exact distance from one transition object to the next, measured from the edge of one object to the same edge on the next object. Changing the Specified Distance value doesn't change the length of the blend because the original object and the final object don't move.

Orientation You can choose to align blend objects perpendicular to the bottom of the page (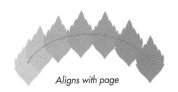) or to align blend objects to the path they're placed on (). The program default is set to align blend objects with the bottom of the page.

Remove a Blend

To delete the transition steps in a blended object and return objects to their original state, choose **Object ➪ Blend ➪ Release**. If the blend was placed on a path (spine), the path remains and you have to delete it separately. You can also apply the Undo command (⌘z).

Using the Blend Tool

The Blend tool in the Toolbox allows you to determine which points in the two objects are used to calculate the blend. If you select only one anchor point, Illustrator selects the other anchor point for you automatically.

To create blends using the Blend tool:

1. Draw two or more objects (closed paths, open paths, or groups). Apply a fill color (even a gradient) and stroke color and weight to each object.

2. Position the objects to allow enough room for the transition shapes that will be created.

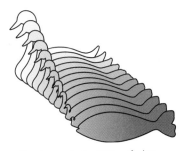

Blend created using 10 Specified Steps.

Aligns with page

Aligns with path

The same objects that were used in Figure 12.2 except orientation was changed to Align to Path. Notice the shape of the transition object.

Blend tool icon in the Toolbox palette

571

3. Select both objects using the Selection tool or the Lasso tool.

4. Choose the Blend tool in the Toolbox (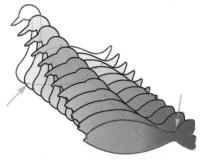).

5. Click in the fill of the first object — but don't click on its center point — then click in the fill of the second object. Illustrator decides which anchor points will create the smoothest blend.

   or

   Click on an anchor point of the first object, then click on an anchor point in the second object.

   Anchor points that were chosen to use in the blend are indicated by the arrows. Notice the difference in the shape of the transition objects from those in Figure 12.5.

   ■ If selected objects are open paths, you must select an endpoint of each path.

   ■ Clicking similar anchor points in the two paths creates smoother blends. For example, click the top left anchor point of each object.

   ■ Blending objects containing the same number of anchor points creates smoother blends. Add anchor points to an object if necessary.

   ■ Selecting different anchor points on the objects allows you to create a rotating effect between the objects and colors in the objects.

6. The blend displays automatically. To change the number of steps created or the spacing of the steps, display the Blend Options dialog box. See the Blend Options section discussed previously in this chapter for an explanation of the options available.

7. Continue clicking the fill area or anchor points of any additional objects you want to include in the blend.

Modifying Existing Blends

Once you apply a blend to objects, you're not stuck with it. You can change blend colors, add or delete anchor points, change stacking order of the objects, change the position of the objects, place the blend along a path (spine), and even change the way it follows the shape of the path. You can even apply a command that allows you to select and edit the transition steps individually. When changes are made to objects in a blend, Illustrator updates all selected blend objects automatically.

Change Color of Blend Objects

You can change the color of all the objects in a blend using the Adjust Colors command in the Filter menu (**Filter** ⇨ **Colors** ⇨ **Adjust Colors**). In addition, you can change blend colors by changing the color of one of the original blend objects — the first object or the final object — but you can't change the color of transition objects individually. You can also change the stroke weight of the original blend objects. The stroke weight on transition objects changes accordingly.

To change the color or stroke weight of one or both of the original blend objects:

1. Deselect all blend objects.

2. With the Direct Selection tool, select either the first or last object in the blend.

3. Apply a different fill or stroke color from the color palette or apply a color swatch from the Swatches palette. Change the stroke weight in the Stroke palette.

Color of swan is changed after blend was created. Other objects in the blend adjust accordingly.

Change Shape of Blend by Moving Blend Objects

You can change the shape of a blend by moving the original objects. Select the first or last object in a blend with the Direct Selection tool and drag to a new position. The transition objects adjust automatically to the new shape. These transition objects cannot be moved while grouped in a blend. See the section called Select and Edit Transition Steps of a Blend later in this chapter.

Add, Delete, or Move Anchor Points

The shape of a blend can be changed by adding, deleting, or moving selected anchor points in the original objects. The shape of the blend updates automatically.

The fish object was moved after the blend was created. The transition object adjusted its position accordingly.

- Add anchor points — using the Add Anchor Point tool (🖉) — to paths of the original objects, then move them to a new position to reshape the path.

- Delete anchor points by selecting them with the Direct Selection tool and pressing the *Delete* key.

- Move anchor points by selecting them with the Direct Selection tool and dragging them to a new position.

You can also add, delete, and move anchor points on the spine of a path to change the shape of the blend, even the spine of a blend created with the Make Blend command.

Anchor points in the swan's tail were deleted after the blend was created. Notice what happens to the transition object.

Reverse the Stacking Order of Objects When a blend is created, the object on the front of the stack (the last of the blended objects drawn) blends into the object at the back of the stack (the first of the blended objects drawn). To reverse the stacking order, select the blend and choose **Object** ⇨ **Blend** ⇨ **Reverse Front to Back**. Applying this command doesn't change the actual position of the transition steps in the blend, just how they're stacked from front to back.

Reverse the Position of Objects Switch the positions of blended objects by selecting the blend and choosing **Object** ⇨ **Blend** ⇨ **Reverse Spine**. All objects in the blend, including the two original objects, switch places (X/Y location), but their stacking order is not affected.

Apply an Existing Blend to a Path Once a blend has been created using either the Make Blend command or the Blend tool, you can make the blended objects follow an open or closed path.

1. Draw a path or select an existing path along which you want the blend to flow.

2. Using the Selection tool or the Lasso tool, select both the path and the blend objects.

3. Display the **Object** menu and choose **Blend** ⇨ **Replace Spine**.

   ■ Blends applied to closed paths follow the path as closely as possible. See the section on Blend Options to specify whether blend objects remain perpendicular to the page or adjust to follow the curve of the path.

Select and Edit Transition Steps of a Blend Transition steps between the original object and the final object cannot be selected unless you apply the Expand Blends command. Select the blended objects, and choose **Object** ⇨ **Blend** ⇨ **Expand**. This command enables you to select and edit the transition steps, but objects become ungrouped and can no longer be edited as a blend.

Reverse Front to Back command is applied after blend is created

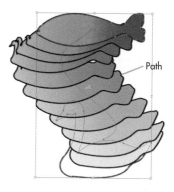

Path

The swan/fish blend was applied to an open path created with the Pen tool

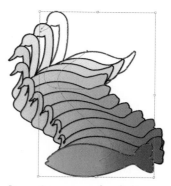

Reverse Spine command applied to blend objects in the illustration above

![mouse icon] *activity 12.3*

1. Create a new document: Letter size, CMYK color mode. Name it Blends Practice.eps, and save it into your Practice Folder as an .eps file.

2. Draw a 1" square, color it red with no stroke. Draw a 2" circle, color it yellow with no stroke, and position it so it's about 1" away from the square, with their center points aligned horizontally (as close as possible).

3. Double-click the Blend tool (![blend tool icon]) in the Toolbox to display the Blend Options dialog box. If the setting in the Spacing pop-up menu isn't Smooth Color, display the pop-up menu and select Smooth Color. Click OK or press *return/enter* to exit the dialog box.

4. Select both objects.

5. Choose Object ⇨ Blend ⇨ Make to blend the two shapes and colors together.

6. Deselect the objects.

7. With the Direct Selection tool, select the circle, move it up and to the right a little bit, then drop it.

   ■ Notice that the blend is recalculated according to the new position of one of the original objects.

8. Draw another 2" circle, color it green, no stroke, and place it below and to the right of the original circle.

9. Select all the objects and blend all the shapes.

10. With the Direct Selection tool, select the lower left anchor point of the square and drag it up and to the left a little bit.

■ Notice that the blend adjusted to the new shape of one of its original objects.

11. Select the Blend object, then choose Object ⇨ Blend ⇨ Reverse Spine.

12. On a clean spot on your page draw a vertical straight segment about an inch high. Apply a 9 pt 100% cyan stroke.

13. Hold down the *Shift* and ![key icon] keys and drag-copy another straight segment. Drop the object about 3 inches to the right of the original segment.

14. Select both segments and double-click the Blend tool to display the Blend dialog box. Change the Spacing selection to Specified Steps and enter 6 in the field. Click OK or press *return/enter*.

15. Choose Object ⇨ Blend ⇨ Make to create 6 more segments evenly spaced between the original objects.

   ■ You don't always have to change the shape of a blend. Just blend two objects with the same shape to create duplicates equally spaced between the two original objects.

16. Just below the vertical segments, draw a curved path that's about the same width. Don't apply a stroke or fill.

17. Select the blend object and the path you just drew. Choose Object ⇨ Blend ⇨ Replace Spine.

   ■ The objects in the blend now follow the curve of the path, and their bottoms are aligned with the bottom of the page.

Continued

575

18. With the blend objects still selected, double-click the Blend tool in the Toolbox to display the Blend Options dialog box. Click the Align to Path button in the Orientation section. Click OK or press *return/enter*.

   ■ The objects in the blend still follow the curve of the path, but they are slanted according to the shape of the path.

19. Create more shapes, even draw illustrations, and practice blending them with the Make Blend command and by choosing anchor points with the Blend tool to create a blend.

20. Save the file and close the document.

21. Create a new document: Letter size, CMYK color mode. Save it into your Practice folder as an .eps file named Stylized Starburst.eps.

22. With the Star tool, draw a star:
   ■ Radius 1: 2"   ■ Radius 2: 1.25"
   ■ Points: 27

23. Apply a fill of 85% cyan, 30% yellow, no stroke.

24. With the star selected, choose Filter ➪ Distort ➪ Roughen. Change the Size slider to 5 and the Detail slider to 0, with Corner Points selected.

25. Drag-copy another starburst and move it to a blank spot on the page and apply a white fill. Then scale it to 20%.

26. Drag it inside the first starburst and align the center points.

   ■ If the center points aren't visible, display the Attributes palette and select the Show Center button.

   ■ Drag ruler guides on the center point of the large star to snap to if you have trouble snapping the center points. Then in the Layers palette, delete the guide layers.

27. Select both stars, then choose Object ➪ Blend ➪ Make.

   ■ Illustrator chooses the anchor points to use to create the blend.

   ■ You can create the same effect by selecting corresponding anchor points with the Blend tool.

28. Undo the Blend command, but don't deselect the two objects.

29. Choose the Blend tool in the Toolbox, click on an anchor point in the smaller starburst. Then, in the larger starburst, move five anchor points clockwise and click that anchor point.

   ■ The two anchor points you selected are used to create the blend, giving it a different look.

30. Deselect both objects. With the Direct Selection tool, click on the smaller star and change it's color to 85% cyan, 30% yellow. Click on the larger star and change its color to white.

   ■ The blend updates automatically.

31. Save the file, then close the artwork window.

Transparency

Transparency is the ability to see through an object and see any objects stacked behind it. An object with a fill of None is a transparent object because objects behind it in the stacking order are visible. *Opacity* is the degree of transparency or darkness, from 0% (transparent) to 100% (opaque, or maximum darkness).

When you target a layer, group, or sublayer in the Layers palette, you can apply transparency settings to all the objects in that layer, group, or sublayer. If you add objects to that layer, group, or sublayer, those objects assume the applied transparency.

Transparency values applied to objects are additive. If you apply transparency to an individual object in a group or layer to which transparency has been applied to the entire group or layer, the value of the object's transparency is added to the value of the group's or layer's transparency.

The Transparency Palette

Using the settings and options in the Transparency palette (Figure 12.5), you can change the degree of opacity of any selected or targeted object, including type and placed images. Values are applied to selected or targeted objects as soon as they're specified in the palette. You can choose a blending mode and specify the degree of transparency.

By choosing the checkboxes in the Transparency palette Options menu, you can tell Illustrator to apply the opacity setting only to objects in the selected group or layer, whether objects in a group or layer show through where they overlap, and control how much effect the opacity mask has on other objects in the group or layer.

Blending Modes

Choosing a blending mode, other than Normal, from the pop-up submenu in the Transparency palette, changes the way the colors of overlapping objects blend with the colors of objects stacked behind them. The top object can completely hide objects behind it or the colors of the two objects can be blended. Illustrator uses the following terms when describing blending modes:

- *Base color* is the color of the backmost object in the artwork.
- *Object color* is the color of the selected or targeted layer, sublayer, group, or object.

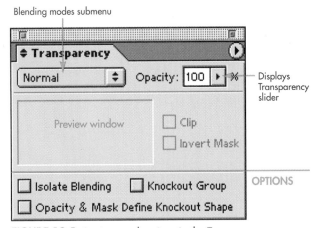

FIGURE 12.5 Settings and options in the Transparency palette controls the transparency of selected objects.

- *Resulting color* is the color that results after the colors are blended.
- *Hue* is the color of the object.
- *Saturation* is the intensity of the color.
- *Brightness* is the amount of black in the color.

Normal No blending is applied. (This is the program default).

Multiply The base color and the object color are multiplied, which always results in a darker color unless the base color is white. In that event, colors are unchanged. If one of the colors is black, the resulting color is black.

Screen Produces the opposite effect of Multiply (above). The resulting color is always lighter than the original colors, unless one of the objects has a fill color of black. In that event, the colors are unaffected. If one of the colors is white, the resulting color is white.

Overlay If the base color is dark, it becomes darker; if it's light, it becomes lighter. Black and white areas are unchanged.

Soft Light A light object color lightens the base color; a dark object color darkens the base color. It's like shining a soft light on an object.

Hard Light The base color is darkened if the object color is dark; the base color is lightened if the object color is light. More contrast results in blended areas; it's not as subtle as Soft Light (above).

Color Dodge The base color is lightened if the object color is light. If the object color is dark, the base color is tinted slightly. No change results if one of the colors is black.

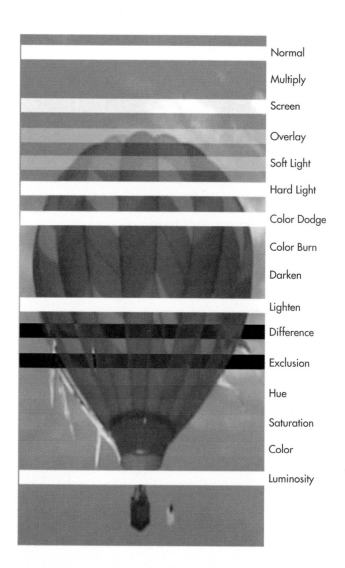

Normal
Multiply
Screen
Overlay
Soft Light
Hard Light
Color Dodge
Color Burn
Darken
Lighten
Difference
Exclusion
Hue
Saturation
Color
Luminosity

Color Burn The base color is darkened if the object color is dark. If the object color is light, the base color is tinted slightly. No change results if one of the colors is white.

Darken Base colors that are lighter than the object color are replaced with the object color. Base colors that are darker than the object color are unchanged.

Lighten Base colors that are darker than the object color are replaced with the object color. Base colors that are lighter than the object color are unchanged.

Difference Subtracts the object color from the base color or the base color from the object color, depending upon which is brighter. Blending with white inverts the color values of the base color; no change results when blending with black.

Exclusion Creates an effect similar to Difference (above), but produces less contrast. Blending with white inverts the color values of the base color; no change results when blending with black.

Hue Blends the saturation and brightness (luminosity) values of the base color and the hue of the object color.

Saturation Blends the hue and brightness (luminosity) values of the base color and the saturation value of the object color.

Color Blends the saturation and hue of the object color and ignores the brightness values of the base color.

Luminosity Blends the hue and saturation values of the base color and the brightness values of the object color.

Applying Transparency to Objects

To change the transparency of selected or targeted objects:

1. Select the objects in the document, including type objects.

   or

   In the Layers palette, target the layer, sublayer, group, or object layer.

   or

   With the Type tool, select one or more characters.

   or

   To change the opacity or blending mode of an object's fill or stroke, independently of each other, click the Fill or Stroke listing displayed on the Appearance palette. (The Appearance palette was discussed in Step 11, *Filters & Filter Effects*.)

   ■ By default, transparency commands are applied to an object's fill and stroke.

read this!

The Difference, Exclusion, Hue, Saturation, Color, and Luminosity blending modes don't work on spot colors.

2. Choose **Window** ➪ **Transparency** to display the Transparency palette (Figure 12.5).

   ■ A thumbnail of the selected or targeted object displays in the Preview window.

3. To control how an object blends with objects behind it in the stacking order, select one of the 16 blending modes from the pop-up submenu.

4. To set the degree of opacity, enter a value in the Opacity field or display the pop-up submenu and move the slider.

   ■ 100% is opaque; 0% is completely transparent.

Values are applied to selected or targeted objects immediately.

Apply Transparency to Only the Fill or Only the Stroke Using the Appearance palette, you can make the fill opacity value of selected objects different from the stroke opacity value.

1. Select the object or type object.

2. Display the Appearance palette, then display the Appearance palette Options menu and choose Add New Fill (or Add New Stroke).

3. In the Appearance palette, click on the Fill listing (or the new Stroke listing) to highlight it, then apply a new color.

4. In the Color palette, change the fill (or stroke) color to None.

5. Click on the Fill (or Stroke) listing in the Appearance palette and, in the Transparency palette, specify a different blending mode or change the opacity value.

 *activity 12.4*

1. Create a new document: Letter size, CMYK color mode.

2. Choose the Line Segment tool and click in the middle of the document page to display the Line Segment dialog box. Specify a line 3.5" long at 0°. Click OK or press *return/enter*.

3. Apply a 36 pt stroke, color it 100% M, 100% Y.

4. Choose Object ➪ Transform ➪ Move. Enter 0 in the Horizontal field and −42 pt in the Vertical field. Click the Copy button.

5. Press ⌘ d to duplicate the last command.

6. Select all the line segments and choose Object ➪ Path ➪ Outline Stroke.

7. With the Star tool, draw a star that has a Radius 1 value of 110 pt, a Radius 2 value of 55 pt, with 5 points. Position it so the center point of the star snaps the center point of the middle line segment.

   ■ If the center point isn't visible, click the Show Center button in the Attributes palette.

Continued

- Because a star, by default, is drawn from its center, click on the center point of the line segment with the Star tool selected and the star is automatically drawn with its center point lined up with the center point of the line segment.

8. Fill the star with the Azure Rings pattern swatch (Swatches palette), no stroke.

9. In the Layers palette, create a new layer.

10. With the Type tool, type the word TYPE. Format it to 66 pt Bookman Demi, fill it with 75% Y, and apply a 3 pt 100%C, 100%M stroke. Position it so it's precisely centered horizontally and vertically on the middle red bar.

   - Bookman Demi is available in the Fonts folder on the Adobe Illustrator 10 application CD. If you don't have Bookman Demi installed, use any heavy serif typeface you have.

11. Deselect all paths.

12. In the Layers palette, target Layer 1.

13. In the Transparency palette, change the opacity value to 60%.

   - Notice that all the objects on Layer 1 were lightened, but the type on Layer 2 was unchanged.
   - Notice in the Appearance palette that the Opacity value was changed to 60%.

14. In the Transparency palette, change the opacity slider back to 100%.

15. In the Layers palette, target Layer 2 to select the type.

16. In the Transparency palette, move the Opacity slider to 75% and change the blending mode to Multiply.

   - Notice what happens to the color of the type.

17. Choose each option in the blending mode pop-up submenu and notice what happens to the type. Read the explanation for how each blending mode is applied (pages 583 and 584) and try to anticipate what will happen to the colors.

18. When you've applied each blending mode, return the blending mode to Normal and the Opacity setting to 100%.

19. Target Layer 2.

20. In the Appearance palette, display the Appearance palette Options menu and choose Add New Fill. Display it again and choose Add New Stroke.

21. In the Appearance palette, click on the Fill listing and apply a fill of 75% Y.

22. In the Appearance palette, click on the new Stroke listing and apply a fill of 100% C and 100% M. In the Stroke palette, change the weight to 3 pt.

23. With the Type tool, select all the characters.

24. In the Color palette, change the fill and stroke colors to None.

   - Now the remaining fill and stroke colors are appearance attributes.

25. Make sure Layer 2 is still targeted, then in the Appearance palette, click on the Fill listing.

26. In the Transparency palette, change the Opacity setting to 65%.

   - Notice that the opacity of the fill color changed, but the stroke remained unaffected.

27. Change the Opacity setting back to 100%, then click the Stroke listing in the Appearance palette.

28. In the Transparency palette, change the Opacity setting to 65%.

   - Notice that the opacity of the stroke color changed, but the fill color remained unaffected.

29. Continue experimenting with opacity settings and blending modes until you're familiar with the results when varying combinations are applied to objects.

30. When you're finished, save the file as an .eps file named Transparency Practice.eps, and close the artwork window.

Using the Transparency Grid

When working with transparent or semi-transparent objects, it's sometimes difficult to tell if an object has a light fill applied to it or whether its opacity is reduced. To make it easier to tell the difference, you can display a checkerboard grid behind all the objects. If you can see the grid behind objects, they are transparent or semi-transparent; if you can't see the grid, the object's opacity is 100%.

■ Choose **View ⇨ Show Transparency Grid**

or

Press ⇧⌘d

  ▪ The command is a toggle. To hide the grid, repeat one of the above actions.

Set Transparency Grid Preferences You can change the size of the checkerboard blocks and change its color to make it easier to see if its colors blend too much with the colors of your artwork:

1. Choose **File ⇨ Document Setup**.

2. Display the pop-up submenu at the top of the dialog box and choose Transparency to display its dialog box.

3. Choose a different checkerboard size by displaying the Grid Size pop-up menu and choosing Small, Medium, or Large.

  ■ A representation of the grid displays in the Preview window.

4. Choose the grid colors from the preset colors in the Grid Colors pop-up submenu.

  or

Specify custom colors:

  a. Click the top color box. When the Color Picker displays, choose a color for the background of the transparency grid.

    ■ When the transparency grid is hidden, the artboard remains this color. The default is a white background.

Display the transparency grid to see the difference between light-colored opaque objects and transparent or semi-transparent objects

Sets the color of the background. The color in this box is used when Simulate Paper is checked.

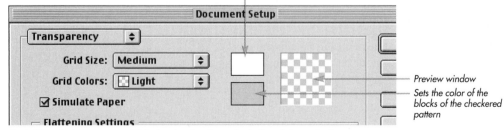

Preview window

Sets the color of the blocks of the checkered pattern

Control how the transparency grid displays by choosing a checkerboard size and color

b. Click the bottom color box and choose a color in the Color Picker to set the color of the checkered pattern.

5. Check the **Simulate Paper** checkbox to see how the objects might appear when they're printed on colored paper. The colors of the objects in the document blend with the color in the top color box in the dialog box to simulate the way they would appear when printed.

   ▪ You have to hide the transparency grid to see this effect.

6. Click **OK** or press *return/enter*.

Applying Transparency Knockouts

When an opacity value of less than 100% is applied to targeted objects in a group or layer, the selected objects blend with each other as well as the objects behind it in the stacking order. Using the Knockout Group option in the Transparency palette, you can specify whether or not selected objects show through each other or only the objects behind them in the stacking order.

This option also works on fills and strokes applied via the Appearance palette. For example, you can determine whether a stroke completely covers up the fill color, or if the fill color blends with the stroke color up to its pathline.

The Knockout Group option in the Transparency palette:

1. In the Layers palette, target a group or layer that has one or more blending modes applied to objects.

2. Display the Transparency palette Options menu and choose **Show Options**.

3. Click the **Knockout Group** checkbox until a checkmark displays.

   ▪ When a dash displays in the checkbox (*Windows:* checkmark is gray), it's called *neutral*. That means if the Knockout Group command is applied to a group of objects nested within a larger group, the setting for the nested group is independent of the Knockout Group setting for the larger group.

4. To turn off the **Knockout Group** option, click the checkbox until it's blank.

Knockout Group unchecked (off). Ovals blend with each other as well as the object behind them.

Knockout Group checked (on). Ovals no longer blend with each other, just the object behind them.

Knockout Group unchecked (off). The stroke is transparent to the character's fill. *Knockout Group checked (on). The stroke knocks out the fill.*

583

Isolating Blending Modes

When changes in blending mode are made to objects in a group or on selected layers, the effects of the blending mode selected is visible on any objects in the stacking order that's behind the group or layer, as well as the objects within the group or layer. You can restrict the application of the changes so they affect only the objects in the group or layer and not affect any objects behind them. This option is effective only when applied to objects that have a blending mode applied to them.

1. In the Layers palette, target a group or layer that has one or more blending modes applied to objects.

2. Display the Transparency palette Options menu and choose Show Options.

3. Click the Isolate Blending checkbox.

   ▪ Objects on the group or layer will blend with each other, but won't blend with objects behind them in the stacking order.

fyi *If the Knockout Group and the Isolate Blending checkboxes are checked, objects to which they're both applied appear as if they have a blending mode of Normal, regardless of the blending mode that's actually applied.*

 *activity 12.5*

1. Create a new document: Letter size, CMYK color mode. Save it into your Practice Folder as an .eps file named Knockout Practice.eps.

2. With the Ellipse tool, draw a vertical oval 1" wide and 2" high. Fill it with C 100%, M 0%, Y 0%, K 0%; 1 pt stroke that's C 100%, M 100%, Y 0%, K 0%.

3. Display the Transparency palette and change the opacity value to 50%.

4. Choose the Rotate tool in the Toolbox and ⌥-click on the bottom anchor point to display the Rotate dialog box. Enter 36 in the Angle field and click the Copy button.

5. Press ⌘ d eight times to complete the circle.

6. Select all the ovals, then press ⌘ g to group them.

7. Draw a 3" wide by 5" high rectangle. Apply the Rainbow pattern fill from the Swatches palette, 100% opacity, no stroke. Send it to the back of the stack.

8. Select all the ovals position them so their center point is aligned on the right vertical edge of the rectangle.

   ▪ Notice how the ovals blend with each other and with the rectangle.

9. In the Layers palette, target the group containing the ovals.

Continued

10. Display the Transparency palette Options menu and choose Show Options.

11. Click the Knockout Group checkbox twice.

- The first time you click the checkbox is Neutral. The second time you click it, the Knockout Group command is applied.

- Notice that now the ovals blend with the Rainbow colors in the rectangle, but they don't blend with each other.

12. Save the file, print it, then close the artwork window.

Creating Opacity Masks

An opacity mask is an object in front of all other selected objects that produces a transparent shape on the selected objects behind it in the stacking order. An opacity masking object can be any object or collection of objects created in Illustrator, including type and linked or embedded images, and they can be filled with anything, including gradients, meshes, patterns, etc.

The fill of the masking object controls the transparency effect of the objects behind it. If the fill of the masking object is a bright color, the masked objects are more opaque. The darker the color masking objects are, the more transparent the objects it masks become. You can change the appearance of the fill color, though, and make lighter fill colors have more effect.

To create an opacity mask:

1. Select all the objects to be masked and the masking objects.

2. Display the Transparency palette Options menu and choose Make Opacity Mask.

- A thumbnail of the masking object(s) displays in the righthand preview window of the Transparency palette. A thumbnail of the object(s) being masked displays in the lefthand preview window of the Transparency palette. A linking icon (⌗) displays between the preview windows, indicating that the masking object is linked to the other objects.

  - If the thumbnails aren't visible in the preview windows, display the Transparency palette Options menu and choose Show Thumbnails.

- If only two objects are selected (one as the object to be masked and one as the masking object, they're combined into one object.

- If more than two objects are used, they're combined into a group. In the Layers palette, the name displays with a dashed underline, which indicates that an opacity mask has been applied.

- If objects in different groups or on different layers are selected, they are moved automatically to the lowest selected object's group or layer.

- If an effect, such as a drop shadow, is targeted on the layer of the lowest object, all objects affected by the opacity mask assume that effect.

- If an object is moved from one layer to the lowest object's layer, any appearance attributes applied to the original layer, and thus to the object being moved, are not moved with the object to its new layer.

- Any effect, such as a drop shadow, is removed when it's applied to the layer containing the opacity masking objects. If the effect is applied directly to the masking object, it becomes part of the opacity mask.

- Appearance attributes, effects, styles, etc., can be applied to the object-mask combination just like you would apply them to any other object.

Clip You can make an opacity mask that clips all portions of the underlying objects that extend beyond its boundaries:

1. In the Layers palette, select the masking object layer.

2. In the Transparency palette, check the Clip checkbox.

   - If you want any new opacity masks to be clipped by default, display the Transparency palette Options menu and choose New Opacity Masks Are Clipping. When this command is turned on, a checkmark displays beside it.

Invert Mask To reverse the way fill color values of the masking object affect the underlying objects, that is, causing a lighter object to make the underlying objects more transparent:

1. In the Layers palette, select the masking object layer.

2. In the Transparency palette, check the Invert Mask checkbox.

   - If you want any new opacity masks to be inverted by default, display the Transparency palette Options menu and choose New Opacity Masks Are Inverted. When this command is turned on, a checkmark displays beside it.

Release an Opacity Mask When an opacity mask is released, all the objects that were linked become separate objects. Any appearances applied to the objects or changes made to the masking object(s) are still retained.

1. In the Layers palette, select the opacity mask object.

read this!

Black type used as a masking object isn't visible when the Clip option is turned on (checked). To make the type visible, apply a different fill color to the type or uncheck the Clip checkbox.

2. Display the Transparency palette Options menu and choose Release Opacity Mask.

   ■ The right thumbnail disappears from the preview window in the Transparency palette. Both disappear if you deselect everything.

Disable an Opacity Mask Temporarily   To deactivate an opacity mask without releasing it:

1. In the Layers palette, select the opacity mask object.

2. In the Transparency palette, *Shift*-click the mask thumbnail in its preview window (the window on the right).

   or

   Display the Transparency palette Options menu and choose Disable Opacity Mask.

   ■ A red X displays over the preview window.

3. To reactivate the opacity mask, *Shift*-click the mask thumbnail in its preview window (the window on the right) again.

   or

   Display the Transparency palette Options menu and choose Enable Opacity Mask.

Changing an Opacity Mask

You can edit the opacity masking object(s) or its underlying object(s), including reshaping the paths of the objects, changing fill colors or patterns, changing opacity values, applying effects or styles.

1. In the Layers palette, select the <Group> layer containing the opacity mask (the name of the layer has a dashed underline).

   ■ Thumbnails of the masking object and the masked object(s) display in the Transparency palette preview windows.

2. To edit the masking object, click the mask thumbnail in the Transparency palette (the right preview window).

3. Make your changes to the masking object.

   ■ To hide the underlying objects and display only the opacity masking object, ⌥-click the opacity mask thumbnail (the right preview window). ⌥-click again to display the entire illustration.

   ■ Changes made to the masking object are updated immediately in the preview window of the Transparency palette.

   ■ When you're in the mask-editing mode, the Layers palette displays <Opacity Mask>.

4. To exit mask-editing mode, click the masked objects thumbnail in the Transparency palette (the preview window on the left).

   ■ If you don't click the left preview window, you stay in mask-editing mode.

Reposition Masking Objects By unlinking the masking object from its underlying objects, you can move the masking object or the masked objects around. Then relink the objects.

1. Select the opacity masking object.

2. In the Transparency palette, click the link icon (⧉) between the two preview windows.

   or

   Display the Transparency palette Options menu and choose Unlink Opacity Mask.

3. Click the masked objects thumbnail (left preview window) or the masking object thumbnail (right preview window).

4. In the document, move either the masking object or the masked objects to a new position.

5. To relink the opacity mask, click the masked object thumbnail (left preview window) to make sure it's selected, then click the link icon between the two preview windows.

Defining the Knockout Shape

If a layer or group containing an opacity mask has the Knockout Group option turned on, the Knockout Group command keeps objects from showing through transparent areas in the opacity mask. You can make objects behind the opacity mask visible using the Opacity & Mask Define Knockout Shape command in the Transparency palette.

1. In the Layers palette, target the sublayer or group with the opacity masking object and the masked objects.

   ■ Make sure the Knockout Group checkbox is checked.

2. In the Layers palette, target the opacity masking object.

3. In the Transparency palette, click the Opacity & Mask Define Knockout Shape checkbox to turn it on.

Saving Artwork Containing Transparent Objects

When files are saved or printed, Illustrator automatically *flattens* the artwork, which may affect the appearance of applied transparency. What this means is that the areas where transparent objects overlap other objects are separated into individual pieces. Illustrator analyzes each chunk to determine whether the best results will be achieved using its vector data or by rasterizing the artwork into pixels.

Using the settings in the Document Setup dialog box (**File** ⇨ **Document Setup** ⇨ **Transparency**), you can control how all artwork in the document is flattened. Or you can apply flattening only to selected objects by choosing the Flattening Transparency command in the Object menu (**Object** ⇨ **Flatten Transparency**). That's the command we'll discuss here.

In addition to dividing areas where selected paths overlap into non-overlapping objects, strokes are converted into non-overlapping objects and the transparency of an object's fill is permanent and can't be changed. For that reason, it's a good idea to apply the Flatten Transparency command to a copy of your artwork. Then if you want to make changes, you have an editable copy to work on.

  ■ Changing values and options in the Flatten Transparency dialog box does not update those settings in the Transparency panel of the Document Setup dialog box.

To flatten objects and keep the appearance of transparency:

1. With the Selection tool, select the transparent objects and any underlying objects.

2. Choose **Object** ⇨ **Flatten Transparency**.

3. Click the Preview checkbox to turn it on so you can see how the changes you make in the dialog box affect the artwork in the document.

4. Move the Raster/Vector Balance slider to tell Illustrator how much of the artwork should be preserved as vector art and how much should be rasterized to keep the appearance of transparency.

  ■ The lower the number in the field (the closer the slider is to the left side), the more rasterization occurs; the higher the number the more vector information is used.

  ■ When the slider is in the far right position (100%), no rasterization occurs; when the slider is in the far left position, all objects are rasterized, whether or not transparency has been applied to them.

5. Enter a value in the Rasterization Resolution field to specify the resolution at which rasterized artwork will be printed.

  ■ For artwork that is to be printed, the recommendation is that the output resolution should be double the screen resolution. For example, artwork that is to be printed at 133 lpi (lines per inch screen resolution), the rasterization resolution should be 266 dpi.

fyi *If artwork is to be saved to an older version of Illustrator that doesn't support transparency or if it's to be exported to a program that doesn't support transparency, use the Flatten Transparency command to control how transparent objects are flattened.*

- For artwork that is to be displayed on the Web, 72 dpi is a high enough resolution value because most monitors display images at 72 dpi. Some newer monitors display 100 dpi, but 72 dpi rasterization resolution is still adequate.

6. Depending upon where the Raster/Vector Resolution slider is positioned, the commands at the bottom of the dialog box are available:

   - **Convert All Strokes to Outlines** — When checked, all strokes are converted to filled objects, which keeps all the strokes in the selected objects consistent. Small type, though, may get thicker.

   - **Clip Complex Regions** — Available only when some rasterization is specified. When checked, this command applies clipping masks to areas of the artwork that's rasterized. Applying this command may slow down output times significantly.

   - **Preserve Overprints When Possible** — Illustrator automatically eliminates overprint settings when a file is flattened. Checking this option keeps the overprint settings for objects not affected by transparency.

7. Click OK or press *return/enter*.

 *activity 12.6*

1. With Illustrator launched, choose File ⇨ Open and locate the file named Koala.tif in the Student Files folder on the CD-ROM that accompanies this book.

2. Open the file as an Illustrator document. Save it into your Practice folder as an .eps file named Koala.eps.

   - If you get an error message regarding color profiles, click OK or press *return/enter* to discard the color profile associated with the photograph.

   - Opening a TIFF file with Illustrator automatically places the photograph in the center of a new Illustrator document page.

3. Make sure rulers are visible (press ⌘ r if they're not).

4. In the Layers palette, create a new layer and name it Koala.

5. Drag a vertical ruler guide and place it on the left edge of the photograph. Drag another one and place it on the right edge of the photograph so you have margins for aligning the type.

6. With the Type tool, type KOALA. Change it to Bauhaus Heavy, all caps. Size it until both sides are flush with the vertical ruler guides.

   - Bauhaus Heavy is in the Fonts folder on the Adobe Illustrator 10 application CD.

   - Line up the left edge of the K with the left ruler guide, then display the Character palette, and click the top arrow on the left side of the Size field until the right edge of the A lines up with the right ruler guide. It should be about 94 points.

Continued

- If you don't have Bauhaus Heavy installed on your computer, use any heavy typeface.

7. Position the type above and away from the photo.

8. In the Layers palette, select Layer 1. Type COUNTRY, also in Bauhaus Heavy, and size it so it also is flush with the vertical ruler guides. Fill it with C 100%, M 100%, Y 0%, K 0%.

- If necessary, add or reduce tracking until it fits precisely between the ruler guides.

9. Position it so the top of the characters butts up to the bottom of the photograph.

10. In the Layers palette, select the Koala layer and draw a rectangle slightly larger than the word KOALA. Fill it with C 100%, M 0%, Y 35%, and K 0%. Send it to the back and position it behind KOALA so KOALA is centered horizontally and vertically.

11. Fill KOALA with white, no stroke.

12. To create an opacity mask, Select the KOALA type and the rectangle.

13. Display the Transparency palette Options menu and choose Show Options.

14. Display the Transparency palette Options menu again and choose Make Opacity Mask.
    - The word KOALA is now the color of the rectangle that was behind it and the rectangle is gone.

15. Position KOALA so the bottom of it aligns with the bottom of the photo.

16. Select the photograph, zoom in to the right side, and, using the bounding box, adjust the size of photograph so the type is precisely on the edge. Check the left side alignment, too.

17. Select the mask, then, in the Transparency palette, reduce the opacity to 60%.

18. Save the file and print it.

19. Continue experimenting with opacity masks. Apply some filter effects, apply varying blending modes.

20. When you're finished experimenting, close the artwork window.

591

PRACTICE ACTIVITY 12-1 — Medical: Arteries

1. Create a new document: Letter size, CMYK color mode. Name it Veins.eps and save it into your Practice Folder as an .eps file.

2. Using the Pen tool, draw the outline of the arteries, as shown here.

   ■ Your final shape should be about 5" square. Place ruler guides and use the Measure tool to measure your shape. Adjust its size using the Scale command in the Transform pop-up menu in the Object menu.

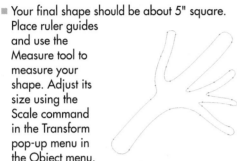

3. Select the object (if it's deselected), and choose Object ➪ Path ➪ Offset Path and enter −4 pt in the Offset field when the Offset Path dialog box displays.

4. Deselect the interior path, so the only path that's selected is the outside path. Apply a fill of C 10%, M 95%, Y 95%, K 28%, no stroke.

5. Deselect the outside path and select the interior path. Assign a fill of C 5%, M 90%, Y 95%, K 0%, no stroke.

6. If there are unnecessary anchor points on the interior path, especially at the ends of the arteries, delete them and conform the interior shape to the outside shape, trying to use the same number of anchor points in corresponding positions.

7. With the Selection tool, select both paths.

8. Choose the Blend tool. Click on an anchor point in the outside path (the square in the pointer turns black when its over an anchor point), then click on the corresponding anchor point in the interior path.

   ■ Blending the two paths adds contour to the object.

   ■ If you have an end that's not blended very well, it probably has too many anchor points.

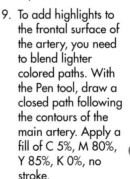

9. To add highlights to the frontal surface of the artery, you need to blend lighter colored paths. With the Pen tool, draw a closed path following the contours of the main artery. Apply a fill of C 5%, M 80%, Y 85%, K 0%, no stroke.

   ■ There are now three colors to blend. The complexity of the paths will determine if blending can be accomplished sequentially.

10. With the Selection tool, select all three paths, then choose Object ⇨ Blend ⇨ Make.

    ▪ Obviously, that won't work.

11. Undo the last command.

12. Select the path you just drew and apply the same fill as the interior of the original path: C 5%, M 90%, Y 95%, K 0%.

13. With the path still selected, choose Object ⇨ Path ⇨ Offset Path. Enter −4 pt in the Offset field. Apply a fill of C 5%, M 70%, Y 75%,K 0%, no stroke, to the new path.

14. Select these two new paths, and choose Object ⇨ Blend ⇨ Make.

15. To add further dimension to the arteries, create a cross-section by drawing an oval to fit the bottom end of the main artery. Rotate, shape, and scale it to fit.

16. Apply a fill of C 5%, M 57%, Y 60%, K 0%, no stroke.

17. Offset a new path by entering −3 pt in the Offset Path dialog box.

18. Apply a linear gradient to the new path as follows: Left Slider: C 62%, M 77%, Y 37%, K 0%; Right Slider: C 5%, M 90%, Y 95%, K 0%; Midpoint Diamond: 43%, Angle: −120°.

19. Save the file, print it, then close the document.

PRACTICE ACTIVITY 12-2 — Wavy Line Border

1. Create a new document: Letter size, CMYK color mode. Save it into your Practice folder as an .eps file named Wavy Line Border.eps.

2. At the top center of the page, draw a 36 pt square and rotate it 45°. Apply a fill of C 75%, M 0%, Y 25%, K 0%, no stroke.

3. Display the Move dialog box and enter 0 in the Horizontal field and −8" in the Vertical field. Click the Copy button to place another diamond 8" below the original diamond.

4. Choose Object ⇨ Blend ⇨ Blend Options to display the Blend Options dialog box. Enter the following specifications, then click OK or press *return/enter*.
   - Spacing: Specified Steps = 20
   - Align to Page

5. Select all the diamonds, then choose Object ⇨ Blend ⇨ Make.

6. With the blend object selected, choose Object ⇨ Blend ⇨ Expand.

7. With the objects still selected, display the Pathfinder palette, and click the Merge button (bottom row).

8. Apply a 3 pt stroke: C 100%, M 100%, Y 0%, K 0%.

9. Choose Filter ⇨ Stylize ⇨ Round Corners and, when the Round Corners dialog box displays, enter 6 pt in the Radius field. Click OK or press *return/enter*.

10. Choose the Scissors tool in the Toolbox and split the path at the top and at the bottom.

11. Deselect all.

12. With the Selection tool, select the left half of the split shape and delete it.

13. With the Pen tool, click on the top endpoint and extend the path in a straight line to the dotted line that defines the page imageable area at the left edge of the page, then straight down to align horizontally with the bottom of the wavy line, then join it to the endpoint at the bottom of the wavy line.

14. Deselect all.

15. With the Pen tool, draw a rectangle that overlaps the wavy line object on the left side and extends to the dotted line at the right edge of the page. Apply a fill of 50% yellow, no stroke.

16. Choose Object ⇨ Arrange ⇨ Send to Back.

17. Save your file, print it, then close the artwork window.

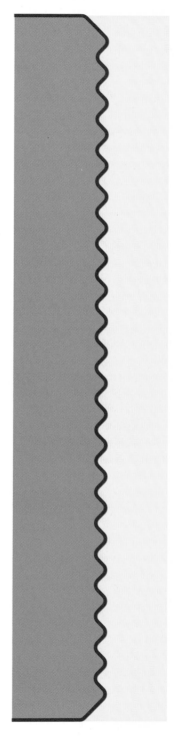

PRACTICE ACTIVITY 12-3 — Mountain Lake

1. Create a new document: Letter size, CMYK color mode. Save it into your Practice folder as an .eps file named Mountain Lake.eps.

    ■ You're going to use this artwork in Exercise 12-1.

2. With the Pen tool or the Pencil tool, draw a mountain range.

3. With the path selected, choose Object ⇨ Path ⇨ Join or press ⌘ j to join the two endpoints. Adjust the endpoints until the path joining the endpoints is horizontal.

4. Select the path, remove the stroke and apply a vertical linear gradient of C 100%, M 23%, Y 40%, K 60% at the bottom of the mountain range up to the peak of the mountains at C 50%, M28%, Y 26%, K10%.

5. Draw irregular closed paths to simulate snowfields. Apply a linear gradient of C 0%, M 0%, Y 0%, K 0% at the bottom to C 10%, M 0%, Y 0%, K15% at the top of each snowfield.

6. To create the reflection:

    a. Marquee to select the mountain range and snow fields. Choose the Reflect tool in the Toolbox and ⌥-click precisely at a point midway along the bottom of the mountain range.

    b. When the Reflect dialog box displays, select the Horizontal axis (0°) and click Copy.

    c. Highlight the reflected copy (with its snowfields) and choose the Scale tool in the Toolbox. ⌥-click to display the Scale dialog box and change the value in the Vertical field to 80%, leaving the horizontal field at 100%. Click OK or press *return/enter*. If necessary, reposition the reflection so it's aligned along the bottom of the mountains.

7. Draw a lake with a linear gradient fill of C 100%, M 44%, Y 46%, K 2% at the bottom edge to C 100%, M 57%, Y 31%, K 3% at the top edge.

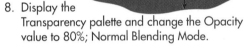

8. Display the Transparency palette and change the Opacity value to 80%; Normal Blending Mode.

9. Draw a shoreline and fill with a vertical linear gradient of C 100%, M 40%, Y 40%, K 28% at the bottom to C 90%, M 44%, Y 84%, K 22% at the top.

10. Position it between the mountain range and the lake.

11. Draw a tree and fill it with C 100%, M 40%, Y 90%, K 30%.

12. Select the tree and drag it into the Symbols palette.

13. With the new symbol selected, choose the Symbol Sprayer tool in the Toolbox and spray the trees along the shoreline

14. Using the Symbol Sizer, Symbol Screener tools, make the trees random sizes and shades of green. Use the Symbol Shifter to reposition them.

15. Finish the scene by adding more pine trees in various sizes and shades of green, placing them in the foreground and sides of the lake (see the finished illustration at the top of the page).

EXERCISE 12-1 — Regional Map

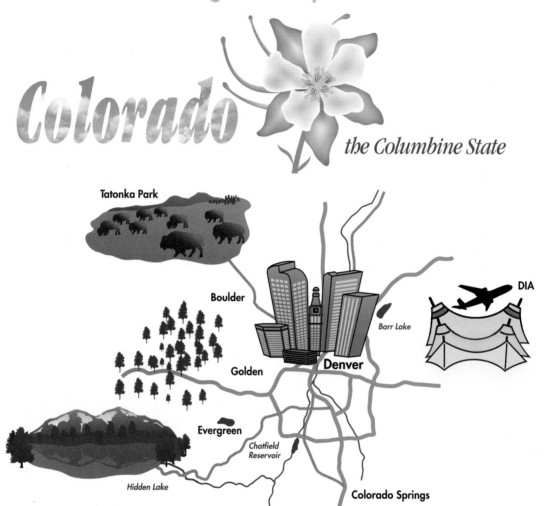

Colorado

the Columbine State

Tatonka Park

Boulder

Golden

Denver

Barr Lake

DIA

Evergreen

Chatfield
Reservoir

Hidden Lake

Colorado Springs

Draw a map similar to the one shown here.

1. Draw a columbine and create a mesh object to achieve the color gradations.

2. You drew Hidden Lake in Activity 12.3. Scale it to the correct size and place it in position.

3. Tatonka Park was drawn in Exercise 10.2.

4. DIA was drawn in Exercise 11.1.

5. The name "Colorado" is a clipping mask.

Additional Exercise:

Choose a section of a different map and draw pictographs of surrounding areas.

596

Graphs

Chapter Outline

- What is a Graph?
- General Steps for Creating a Graph
- The Graph Data Window
- Graph Data
- Graph Types
- Modify an Existing Graph
- Select Parts of a Graph
- Design Your Graph
- Jazz Up Your Graph
- Use Artwork to Display Graph Data

What is a Graph?

A graph is a pictorial representation of data, usually numbers, that shows a relationship between two or more items using dots, lines, bars, and curves. When you're deciding which kind of graph to draw, you should consider the amount and type of data you want to display and how often the data will change. A complex graph may make it difficult to update when new information becomes available.

Most graphs need two types of data: category (what is it) and value (how much, how long, etc.). A Pie graph, however, requires only a single value (how much, how long, etc.) because the Pie itself is the category. Each of the other types of graphs displays the information along two axes: the horizontal axis (*x*) and vertical axis (*y*). You can't mix the data in each axis; all categories must appear on the same axis and all values must be on the other axis.

In Illustrator, graphs are created as grouped objects. You can select parts of a graph with the Direct Selection tool or the Group Selection tool, providing the means by which you can modify attributes of graph elements. When you ungroup a graph, the connection between the graph data and the graph itself is lost and you can't modify it by changing its graph type or by changing its data.

What Kind of Graph Should You Draw?

The first step in creating a graph is to determine what type of graph you want to draw. Evaluate the information to be graphed and decide which type of graph will produce the most understandable, easily read graph. A section describing each type of graph available in Illustrator and how to create it is included later in this chapter.

General Steps for Creating a Graph

When you've decided the type of graph that best displays your data, perform the following steps to create your graph.

Types of graphs you can create in Illustrator

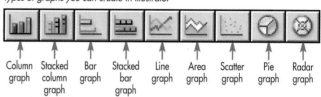

Column graph | Stacked column graph | Bar graph | Stacked bar graph | Line graph | Area graph | Scatter graph | Pie graph | Radar graph

1. Select the graph tool that matches the type of graph you want to create.

   ■ Choose a graph tool from the Toolbox.

      • The Column Graph tool (▥) is the default graph tool and displays in the Toolbox. Display the hidden tools and scroll to select the appropriate graph tool.

      • The currently selected Graph tool displays in the Toolbox and remains displayed until a new graph tool is selected or until Illustrator is closed and relaunched.

   or

   ■ Double-click the Graph tool in the Toolbox to display the Graph Type dialog box (Figure 13.1). Click on the appropriate button in the Type section and click OK or press *return/enter*.

   or

   ■ Choose **Object** ➪ **Graph** ➪ **Type** to display the Graph Type dialog box. Click on the appropriate button in the Type section and click OK or press *return/enter*.

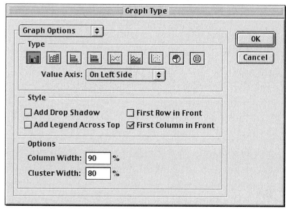

FIGURE 13.1 Graph Type dialog box

2. Determine the size of your graph. When you define the size of your graph, you're deciding how large its graphic elements will be — columns, lines, and so on, excluding the labels (text) and the legend. Graph size can be changed after the graph is drawn by using the Scale tool. See Modify an Existing Graph later in this chapter.

- Click and drag with the selected Graph tool, starting from the top left corner — just like any shape you draw with the predefined creation tools (ellipse, rectangle, star, etc.).
  - Keep track of the size of the graph by viewing its measurements in the Info palette as you drag.
  - ⌥-drag to draw from the center rather than the top left corner.
  - *Shift*-drag to draw a perfect square.

or

- With a Graph tool selected in the Toolbox, click on the document page to display the Graph dialog box. Enter values in the Width and Height fields and click OK or press *return/enter*.
  - By default the graph is drawn from the upper left corner at the point of the click.
  - ⌥-click on the page to draw the graph from the center.
  - Illustrator remembers the size of the last graph that was drawn and its specifications remain in the Graph dialog box when it's displayed.
  - Dimensions are displayed in the current unit of measure specified for the document in the Units & Undo Preferences dialog box.

read this!

Previous changes made to options for the same type of graph are retained until Illustrator is closed and relaunched. To avoid problems when creating a new graph, display the menus and restore them to their default state. Figures 13.1, 13.12, and 13.13 display default values for these dialog boxes.

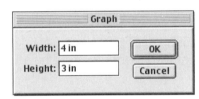

Specify the size of your graph by entering values in the Graph dialog box

3. Enter or import the data you want to graph. After you establish the size of your graph by one of the methods in #2 above, the Graph Data window displays and a basic graph with one element of that graph type is drawn. See the sections on Entering Data Manually and Importing Data from Another Application later in this chapter for instructions on entering data in the Graph Data window. A graph must be selected before you can enter or change its data — the whole graph, not just a portion, must be selected.

There is no OK or Cancel button because this is a palette, not a dialog box. It has a close box in the upper left corner (*Windows:* upper right corner) and a resize box in the lower right corner. But it doesn't have a folder tab, so you can't place it into another palette window and you can't display it using the Window menu because it isn't listed there.

4. When data have been entered and arranged like you want them, click the Apply button in the Graph Data window or press *return/enter* to see your graph.

Apply button

5. Make any changes necessary to get the graph the way you want it. By default, graphs are displayed in shades of gray, but you can change stroke and fill attributes and assign a design to the columns or markers. See the section on Modify an Existing Graph later in this chapter.

6. To update the graph on the document page after data have been entered or changes to the data have been made:

   ■ Click the Apply button (☑) to apply the data to the selected graph but leave the Graph Data window open.

   ■ Click the window's Close box to apply the data to the selected graph and close the Graph Data window.

   ■ ⌥-click the *Enter* key on the numeric keypad to apply the data to the graph but leave the Graph Data window open.

The Graph Data Window

When you release the mouse after dragging to define the size of a graph, the Graph Data window (Figure 13.2) automatically pops up on the screen. You can also display the Graph Data window when a graph is selected by choosing

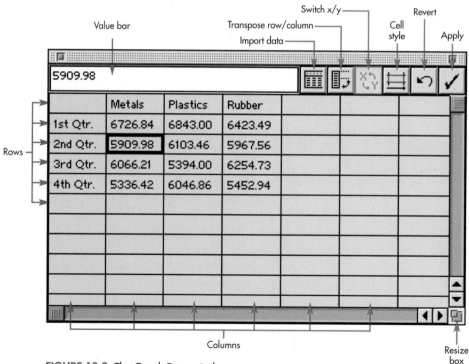

FIGURE 13.2 The Graph Data window.

Object ⇨ Graph ⇨ Data or by displaying the context-sensitive menu and choosing **Data**. If a graph isn't selected, the data window isn't available.

- *Macintosh:* ⌃-click
- *Windows:* Right-click

Information you enter or import into the window is what gets graphed. The Graph Data window looks much like a standard spreadsheet matrix. You can enter data in as many as 32,767 rows and 32,767 columns if you have enough memory in your computer. The "boxes" in the rows and columns are called *cells*.

Unlike a standard spreadsheet program, Illustrator can't calculate information, such as adding, multiplying, figuring percentages, and so on. Nor can it insert, delete, or sort cells. So you should have your data planned and organized before entering it into the data window.

Changing the Width of the Cells

Sometimes data you enter into the cells is too long for the width of the cell and it isn't visible. It's still there, but you can't see it. Or, if the information in the cells is short, you may want to make the cells narrower so you can see more cells in the window. These changes affect only the appearance of the Graph Data window. They have no effect on the graph itself.

Change the Width of All Cells To change the width of all the cells in the Graph Data window, click the **Cell style** button in the window to display the Cell Style dialog box.

Cell Style button

- **Number of Decimals** — In this field, enter the number of digits, from 0 to 10, that you want to appear after a decimal point. The default is 2 decimals in a 7-digit column.

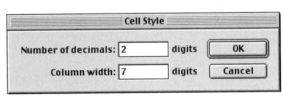

The Cell Style dialog box enables you to change the width of the cells in the Graph Data window

- **Column Width** — In this field, determine how wide cells are by entering the number of characters that will fit in the cell. The default is 7 characters. To make a cell wider, enter a larger number; to make a cell narrower, enter a smaller number.

- Click OK or press *return/enter* to exit the dialog box and apply the values to the Graph Data window.

Change the Width of Individual Columns You can drag the column dividers to widen only cells in certain columns rather than cells in every column. Position the crosshair pointer over a column divider until the ⊞ icon displays, then click and drag the column divider to its new position.

- When you widen one column, the column next to it isn't shortened. It's just moved over and keeps its same width.

activity 13.1

1. Create a new document: Letter size, CMYK color mode.

2. Choose the graph tool in the Toolbox (it doesn't matter which one), then click and drag about a 4" square on the document page.

   ■ The Graph Data window displays and a basic graph with one element of that graph type is drawn on the document page.

3. Click the Cell Style button (▦) at the top of the window to display the Cell Style dialog box.

4. Enter 12 in the Column Width field. Click OK or press *return/enter*.

   ■ The width of every cell in the data window is widened.

5. Position the crosshair cursor over one of the vertical lines in the data window until the ⊞ icon displays. Then click and drag the line left or right to widen or shorten the column.

   ■ Notice that the width of the column next to the one you moved isn't affected, it's just moved over to accommodate the wider column.

6. Close the document without saving it to a file.

Graph Data

A set of data used to plot a graph is called a *series*, and it includes any text for the legend. Most graphs compare multiple series of data. Data for a series may be entered into the Graph Data window in a different order for different kinds of graphs. Data can be entered manually or by importing a text file that was created in a different program.

Entering Data Manually

Data are entered in the field at the top of the Graph Data window called the Value Bar, then they are transferred to the cell that's highlighted — displays a dark border around it — in one of the following ways.

■ Press the *return/enter* key to accept the data and move down one cell in the same column.

■ Press one of the Arrow keys to accept the data and move one cell in the direction of the arrow you pressed.

■ Press the *Tab* key to accept the data and move to the cell in the next column to the right.

■ Press the Enter key on the numeric keypad to accept the data and apply it to the graph.

■ Click in another cell to accept the data and move to the cell you clicked.

Step 13 — GRAPHS

If you enter characters other than numbers (such as letters, $, %, and so on) in non-label cells, Illustrator won't graph the data. You must stick with numbers and the + and – signs in those cells. Letters can be entered to create labels, but only in cells designated as label cells (see the section on Graph Labels and Legends later in this chapter).

Importing Data from Another Application

Data that were created in other programs can be imported into the Graph Data window. Data created in a spreadsheet program (such as Microsoft Excel® or Lotus 1-2-3®) can be imported into the Graph Data window if it is saved as a tab-delineated file (tabs between values) and if each row is separated by a paragraph return. Data created in a word processing program such as Microsoft Word® or WordPerfect® or a page layout program such as QuarkXPress™ can also be imported into the Graph Data window by inserting tabs between the values and paragraph returns between the rows, then saving the file as a text-only (ASCII) document.

To import data from a spreadsheet or word processing file:

1. Create a new graph or open an existing one.

   ■ Make sure the graph is selected.

2. Display the Graph Data window (**Object** ⇨ **Graph** ⇨ **Data**).

3. Click the cell where you want the imported data to start.

4. Click the Import data button to display the Import Graph Data dialog box. This dialog box functions the same as the Open dialog box — navigate to locate the file you want to import and double-click on it or click the Import button.

Import data button

   ■ Data in the text file are placed into the cells according to the tabs and paragraph returns stored in the text file.

   ■ Any data already entered into the cells are replaced by the new imported data.

   ■ Nonnumerical characters, such as commas or = signs, must be removed or the data won't be plotted.

   ■ Click the Show Preview button to display a preview of the selected file (if one is available) on the right side of the dialog box.

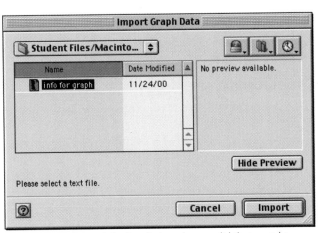

The Import Graph Data dialog box displays when you click the Import data button in the Graph Data window.

Copying and Pasting Data Data copied in another application and placed onto the Clipboard can be pasted into the cells in the Graph Data window. Make sure the first cell that will hold the start of the copied data is highlighted in the Graph Data window. Just remember that if nonnumerical characters are pasted into cells that are intended only for numerical values, the information won't be graphed.

Fixing Data Errors To change data for an existing graph, display the Graph Data window, highlight the appropriate cell, enter new data, then click the Apply button.

   If you find you've made an error when entering graph data, but it hasn't yet been applied to the graph, you can fix your mistake in a couple of ways:

- Apply the Undo command (press ⌘z).

or

- Click on another object in the artwork window. An alert box displays asking you if you want to save your changes. If you don't want to save them, press *d* or click the Don't Save button; if you do want to save them, press *return/enter* or click Save.

or

- Click the Graph Data window's Close box. The alert box displays asking you if you want to save your changes. If you don't want to save them, press *d* or click the Don't Save button; if you do want to save them, press *return/enter* or click Save.

or

- Click the Revert button. The data that were last applied to the graph are restored.

If you've already applied changes in graph data to the graph, you can

- Apply the Undo command (⌘z)

or

- Close the document without saving changes and start over.

or

- Use the Revert command (choose **File** ➪ **Revert** — *Windows:* press *F12*).

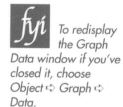

fyi To redisplay the Graph Data window if you've closed it, choose Object ➪ Graph ➪ Data.

Revert button

Graph Labels and Legends

For most graphs, legend text is entered in the top row of the Graph Data window, leaving the first column empty. Text for category labels that are to appear along the bottom of a column graph are entered in the left-hand (first) column. Delete data from the first cell in the first column and move to another cell, leaving the first cell in the first column empty. See Figure 13.3.

   If numbers are entered into cells in the top row or down the first column, Illustrator graphs them. So, if you don't want to create a legend for your graph, enter numbers in those cells. To create labels that include numbers, such as 1990, enclose the numbers in the straight quotes (*Shift*-quote key). If the label contains both numbers and letter characters, is isn't necessary to enclose the numbers in quotes.

Special Characters Some characters have special functions and can't be used in labels or legends (or in data cells, either).

- **Quotation marks** — To use numbers as a legend or label, enclose them with quotes (") (press the *Shift*-quote key). To actually have quotes appear in the labels, use the "curly" quotes rather than the straight quotes.

- **Vertical Line character** (|) — If you want the text of a label to have more than one line, enter a vertical line (| = *Shift-backslash*) where you want the line to break.

fyi To create "curly" open quotes ("):

Macintosh: press ⌥[

Windows: hold down the ⌥ key and press 0147 on the keypad

To create "curly" close quotes ("):

Macintosh: press ⇧⌥[

Windows: hold down the ⌥ key and press 0148 on the keypad

Types of Graphs

Column Graphs

A Column graph (Figure 13.3) usually shows change in one or more categories over a period of time. Data are displayed with vertical columns (rectangles) above the names of the categories. The height of a column corresponds to the value entered in the Graph Data window.

Column Graph tool

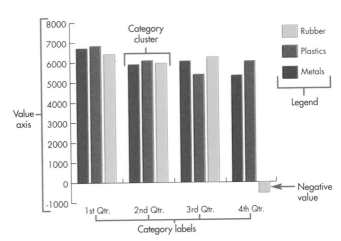

Graph Data window for Column graph sample below

When more than one set of data, called a series, is represented for each category, corresponding columns are clustered together above the name of the category. Columns for the same series of data in each category cluster are filled with the same color or pattern and a legend is generated to depict what each column represents.

Data with negative values can be entered and displayed in Column graphs. Negative values display as columns below the horizontal axis (or zero point) of the graph.

FIGURE 13.3 Sample of a Column graph. Column Width value was changed to 80%.

605

Data Format for Labels and Legend Enter text for labels that will appear under the columns into cells down the first column in the Graph Data window. Enter text for the legend across the top row in the Graph Data window. Leave the first cell empty.

Options for Column Graphs Two options are available at the bottom of the Graph Type dialog box for setting the width of individual columns and the space between category clusters.

- **Column Width** — A value of 100% aligns columns flush against each other. A value higher than 100% causes the columns to overlap. The default value is 90%, which gives a small space between columns. If you want more space between columns, perhaps to allow for label text, enter a smaller percentage value in the field.

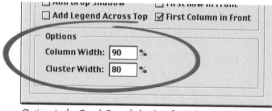

Options in the Graph Type dialog box for Column graphs

- **Cluster Width** — The cluster width value is the total width of all columns in a category. A value of 100% aligns clusters flush against the cluster next to it. A value higher than 100% causes the clusters to overlap. The default cluster width is 80%, which gives a slightly larger space between clusters than that between individual columns in a cluster. Enter a smaller percentage value to put more space between clusters.

Stacked Column Graphs

Use a Stacked Column graph (Figure 13.4) to display more than one series of data. They're similar to Column graphs except that series values for each category are placed on top of each other rather than side by side in a cluster. Values in each series are added together, which generates a total value for the category. Use a Stacked Column graph when you want to show what portion of a total value each data series represents.

Stacked Column Graph tool

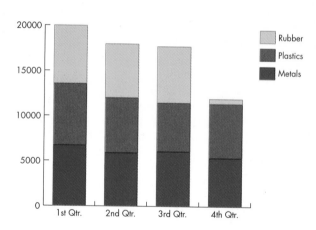

FIGURE 13.4 Sample of a Stacked Column graph. The same values were used for this graph that were used for the Column graph except the negative 4th Qtr value was changed to a positive value. Notice how you can instantly see how the totals of the three items measured for each quarter compare to each other.

All values in the Graph Data window must be either positive or negative. You can't mix them in the same graph. An error message displays if you attempt to mix positive and negative values.

Data Format for Labels and Legend Enter text for labels that will appear under the columns into cells down the first column in the Graph Data window (except the first cell). Enter text for the legend across the top row in the Graph Data window. Leave the first cell empty.

Options for Stacked Column Graphs Options for Column Width and Cluster Width are exactly the same as for Column Graphs.

Bar Graphs

A Bar graph (Figure 13.5) displays the same type of information as a Column graph, except it's in a horizontal rather than vertical format. It's ideal for timeline data, such as months, days, years, and so on. When more than one set of data is represented for each category, corresponding bars are clustered together beside the name of the category. In a Bar graph, negative values display to the left of the vertical axis (zero point).

Bar Graph tool

Data Format for Labels and Legend Enter text for labels that will appear beside the bars into cells down the first column (except the first cell) in the Graph Data window. Enter text for the legend across the top row in the Graph Data window. Leave the first cell empty.

Options for Bar Graphs Options for Bar Width and Cluster Width are exactly the same as for Column Graphs, except the field is titled Bar Width instead of Column Width.

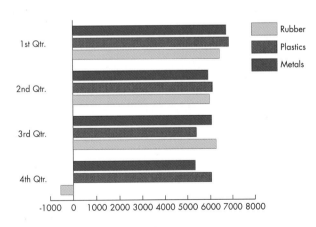

FIGURE 13.5 The same values were used for this sample of a Bar graph that were used for the Column graph.

Stacked Bar Graphs

If you want to graph more than one series of data, create a Stacked Bar graph (Figure 13.6). Stacked Bar graphs are similar to Bar graphs except that series values for each category are placed end to end. Values in each series are added together, which generates a total value for the category. For that reason, all values must be either positive or negative; you can't mix them in one graph. Use a stacked bar graph when you want to show what portion of a total value each data series represents.

Stacked Bar
Graph tool

Data Format for Labels and Legend Enter text for labels that will appear beside the bars into cells down the first column in the Graph Data window (except first cell). Enter text for the legend across the top row in the Graph Data window. Leave the first cell empty.

Options for Stacked Bar Graphs Bar Width and Cluster Width options are exactly the same as for Column Graphs, except the field is titled Bar Width instead of Column Width.

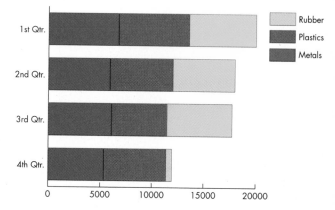

FIGURE 13.6 Sample of a Stacked Bar graph. The same values were used for this graph that were used for the Stacked Column graph. Notice how you can instantly see how the totals of the three items measured for each quarter compare to each other.

Line Graphs

Use a Line graph (Figure 13.7) when you want to show changes in data over a period of time. Data points (x, y coordinates) are displayed as symbols and are connected by a straight segment. Each series of data is represented by a different line color, shade, or type (solid, dotted, etc.). This type of graph is ideal for showing trends in data. Negative as well as positive data can be displayed in a Line graph.

Data Format for Labels and Legend Enter text for labels that will appear under the graph into cells down the first

read this!

Be careful not to have the lines on a Line graph cross each other too many times. It becomes difficult to read and can be confusing.

	Metals	Plastics	Rubber				
1st Qtr.	3726.84	6843.00	5123.49				
2nd Qtr.	5909.98	2103.46	4967.56				
3rd Qtr.	4066.21	1394.00	5254.73				
4th Qtr.	5336.42	6046.86	547.23				

Data window for the Line graph shown on the next page

Line Graph
tool

column in the Graph Data window (except first cell). Enter text for the legend into cells across the top row. Leave the first cell blank. Each column of numbers generates a single line in the graph. If you're plotting data over a period of time, enter the values representing time along the *x* axis (horizontally in the rows), not down a column.

Options for Line Graphs

Line graphs display four checkboxes at the bottom of the Graph Type dialog box.

- **Mark Data Points** — Click this box to place square markers at each data point. This is the program default. If you uncheck this box, no markers display at data points. You can apply stroke and fill attributes to markers.

- **Connect Data Points** — When this checkbox is checked (this is the program default), a straight segment connects data points. If the checkbox is unchecked, only data point markers display. If you uncheck both the Mark Data Points and Connect Data Points checkboxes, data for that particular series won't be plotted in the graph. Stroke weight and color can be applied to the segments.

- **Edge-to-Edge Lines** — The program default is to center the value marker between the label tick marks. Checking this box aligns the first marker with the left edge of the graph and the last marker with the right edge of the graph. Markers falling between the first and last marker are spaced evenly between them and are not necessarily aligned with the labels at the bottom of the graph.

- **Draw Filled Lines** — When the Connect Data Points box is checked, this option becomes available. When you check this box, enter a value in the Line Width field to specify the width of the straight segments that connect data points. You can apply stroke and fill attributes to the segments.

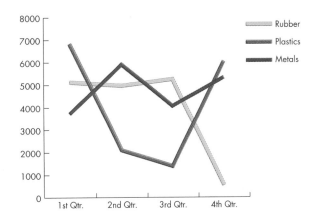

FIGURE 13.7 Sample of a Line graph, with Mark Data Points unchecked, Connect Data Points checked, and Draw Filled Lines checked and 3 pt entered in the Line Width field. This is not the same data that were used for the first four graphs.

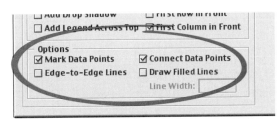

Options in the Graph Type dialog box for Line graphs

 A tick mark is a horizontal or vertical line that separates categories or shows units of measurement. It can be short or it can extend the full width or height of the graph.

Area Graphs

Create an Area graph (Figure 13.8) when you want to compare at least two sets of data with the total of all data. Data from each series are added together to provide a cumulative analysis of the data. Values in each column are added to the values in the previous column. Areas representing each data series are filled with a different color or pattern and stacked on top of each other. Values must be either all positive or all negative; you can't mix them in the same graph.

Area Graph tool

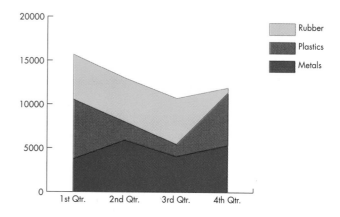

FIGURE 13.8 The same values were used for this Area graph as were used for the Line graph.

Data Format for Labels and Legend Enter text for labels that will appear under the columns into cells down the first column in the Graph Data window (except the first cell). Enter text for the legend across the top row in the Graph Data window. Leave the first cell empty.

Options for Area Graphs There are no options available for Area graphs.

Scatter Graphs

A Scatter graph (Figure 13.9) is similar to a line chart (plots data points on the horizontal and vertical axes and connects them with straight segments), except vertical data for each series aren't lined up with predetermined x-axis data points. Each series of data can have varying numbers of data points. This kind of graph is useful for displaying a large number of data points.

Data Format for Labels and Legend You can't enter text category labels in a scatter graph, and each series requires a value for the y axis and a value for the x axis. Values in

Scatter Graph tool

Sheryl		Patricia				
34.00	17.00	45.00	12.00			
58.00	25.00	81.00	22.00			
94.00	37.00	82.00	31.00			
76.00	46.00	47.00	43.00			
66.00	56.00	36.00	59.00			
91.00	63.00	87.00	67.00			

Data window for the Scatter graph shown in Figure 13.9

the first column display on the *y* axis (vertically) and data in the second column display on the *x* axis (horizontally). Enter text for the legend at the top of the first column, third column, fifth column, and so on. Don't leave the first cell blank.

Options for Scatter Graphs
Three of the options for the Line graph are available for the Scatter graph: Mark Data Points, Connect Data Points, and Draw Filled Lines. The Edge-to-Edge Lines checkbox is not available. These options function the same way they do for a Line graph.

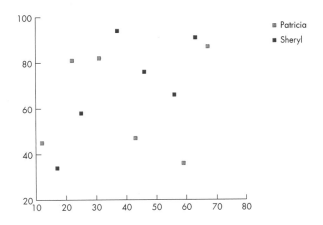

FIGURE 13.9 Sample of a Scatter graph using the values in the Data Window shown on the previous page. The Connect Data Points option is unchecked.

Pie Graphs

Only one data series can be displayed in a Pie graph (Figure 13.10). Data values are represented as wedge-shaped "slices" of a 360° circle (pie). Each value in the series represents a percentage of the whole pie. If you want to graph more than one category with a Pie graph, two pies are created, one for each category. Values must be all negative or all positive; you can't mix them in a pie graph.

Pie Graph tool

Data Format for Labels and Legend
Each pie graph has a single row of data. If more than one row of data is entered, a separate pie graph is displayed for each row. Enter the text for the legend across the first row, leaving the first cell empty. Text for the Pie graph's label that displays beneath the pie is entered in the first cell in its row.

	Cardiov...	Others	Cancer	Accidents	COPD
Leading ...	41.00	27.00	23.30	4.10	4.60
Leading ...	44.40	20.40	26.70	4.60	3.90

Leading Causes of Death|Women

Data window for the Pie graphs shown below and on the following page. Notice that even though text is invisible in the cell, it displayed in the graph.

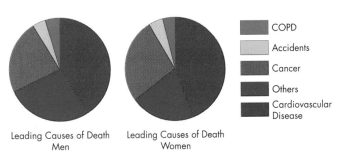

Leading Causes of Death
Men

Leading Causes of Death
Women

COPD
Accidents
Cancer
Others
Cardiovascular Disease

FIGURE 13.10 Sample Pie graphs. Notice the two-line labels. In the data window (shown above) notice the | character where the line breaks.

Options for Pie Graphs Pie graph options consist of three pop-up menus in the Options section at the bottom of the Graph Type dialog box.

- **Legend** — The three options in this pop-up menu affect the placement of the labels.

  - **No Legend** — Eliminates the legend altogether.

  - **Standard Legend** — Legend text is placed outside the Pie graph as with other types of graphs. This is the program default.

  - **Legends in Wedges** — Places legend text as labels inside the wedges of the Pie. If a legend isn't visible because the wedge is a dark color, change the color of the wedge or change the color of the type.

- **Sort** — These choices determine the order in which the wedges are arranged, with "12 o'clock" being the starting position of the first wedge. Pies are arranged clockwise, depending upon which Sort option is selected.

  - **All** — Wedges are displayed from the largest to the smallest value. Each pie in a graph containing multiple pies could display a different wedge in the starting position.

  - **First** — Arrangement of wedges of all pies in the graph is determined by the largest wedge in the first pie, with the rest of the wedges arranged by size from largest to smallest. All other pies in the graph are arranged in the same order, regardless of the size of the wedges.

  - **None** — Wedges are arranged in the order values are arranged in the Graph Data window.

- **Position** — The choices in this pop-up menu control the size of the pie graph(s) when multiple pies are displayed.

  - **Ratio** — Pies are proportional according to the total value of the pie's data, from the smallest total of a row to the largest.

  - **Even** — All Pies are the same size, regardless of their total values.

  - **Stacked** — Pies are sized proportionally and are stacked on top of each other, aligned at their center points.

All Sets of the Following Pie Graphs Use the Same Data

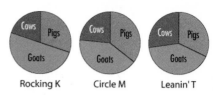

Pie graphs with a Sort of None (first column in Graph Data window is shown in the 12:00 position, clockwise); Position option is Even, so all 3 graphs are the same size

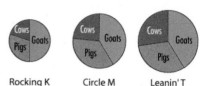

Pie graphs with a Sort of All (column with largest total values are shown in the 12:00 position, then to smallest value, clockwise); position option is Ratio, so graphs are arranged proportionally according to the total value of their data, from smallest to largest

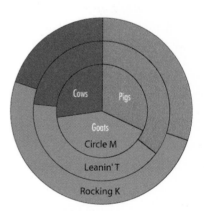

Position of Pie graphs is Stacked, with a Sort of None, so they're arranged as they were entered in Graph Data window

fyi To display graphed values in the wedges along with the legend text, enter it after the legend text, separated by a vertical line character (Shift-backslash). The second line of the legend is the graphed values.

Radar Graph

A Radar graph (Figure 13.11) isn't used much in the U.S., probably because it's so confusing. Data in a Radar chart is plotted as the distance from the center of the circle, with each series connected by a different type of line. Radar graphs are used in other countries for scientific or engineering data.

Data Format for Labels and Legend Text for each label entered in the first vertical column generates a separate axis. Each number entered in the row is plotted on its axis and is connected to the others with a straight segment if the Connect Data Points option is checked. The resulting graphic resembles a spider web. Enter text for the legend into cells across the top row. Leave the first cell blank.

Options for Radar Graphs Radar graphs have the same four options as Line graphs and they perform the same functions.

Radar Graph tool

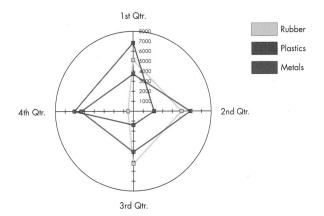

Data window for the Radar graph shown below

FIGURE 13.11 Sample of a Radar graph using the values in the Data Window shown above. Mark Data Points and Connect Data Points options are turned on.

Modify an Existing Graph

Changing Graph Type

If, after you have created a graph, you decide that a different type of graph will display the information more effectively, you can change it easily.

1. With the Selection tool, select the entire graph.

2. Display the Graph Type dialog box.

   ■ Double-click the Graph tool

   or

   ■ Choose **Object** ➪ **Graph** ➪ **Type**.

3. Choose Graph Options from the pop-up menu at the top of the dialog box.

4. Click the appropriate graph button for the type of graph you want.

   ■ Options for the type of graph you chose are displayed in the Options section at the bottom of the dialog box.

5. Click OK or press *return/enter*.

   ■ The new graph is plotted according to the values entered into the Graph Data window.

Editing Graph Data

You can update the data in an existing graph, then save it as a new file or overwrite the existing file.

1. With the Selection tool, select the graph you want to change.

2. Display the Graph Data window.

   ■ Choose **Object** ➪ **Graph** ➪ **Data**

   or

   ■ Display the context-sensitive menu and choose Data.

3. Click in a cell to highlight it.

   ■ The information in the highlighted cell displays in the Value bar.

4. In the Value bar, type new information for the cell or press the *delete* key to remove the information from the cell.

5. Highlight another cell to change it or apply changes to the graph using one of the methods described earlier.

fyi To avoid possible unpleasant results when changing the graph type of a graph that has had a gradient fill applied to its elements, change the fill to a solid color. When the changes are complete, reapply the gradient fill.

Copy Data in Cells To copy the data in a cell and move it to another cell, use the standard Edit commands (choose **Edit** ⇨ **Copy** or press ⌘ c). To paste them into new cells, use the standard Paste commands (choose **Edit** ⇨ **Paste** or press ⌘ v).

- *Shift*-click to select more than one cell.
- To select a series of cells:
  - Click the first cell in the series and drag to the last one.
  - Click the first cell in the series and *Shift*-click the last one in the series.
  - Click the first cell in the series, then press an arrow key until you reach the last one in the series.
- To paste information that was copied from multiple cells, highlight the first cell where you want the information to start, then press ⌘ v to paste the data.

Transpose Rows and Columns When you click the Transpose row/column button at the top of the Graph Data window, all data in the window switches places. What was previously displayed in a column is now displayed in a row, and vice versa, including label and legend text. This command affects every cell in the Graph Data window, not just highlighted cells.

Transpose row/column button

Switch X and Y Axes Each plotted point on a Scatter graph requires two columns of data, one for the *x* axis and for the *y* axis. To swap columns, making the data in the *y* column become the data in the *x* column, and vice versa, click the Switch x/y button at the top of the Graph Data window. Column 1 switches with column 2, column 3 switches with column 4, and so on.

Switch x/y button

activity 13.2

1. Create a new document: Letter size, CMYK color mode. Name it Practice Graphs.eps and save it into your Practice folder as an .eps file.

2. Display the Info palette.

3. Double-click the Column Graph tool in the Toolbox to display the Graph Type dialog box. Using Figures 13.1, 13.12, and 13.13 in this chapter, verify that all options display default values.

4. Choose the Column Graph tool in the Toolbox, then click on the document page and enter 4" in both the Height and Width fields in the dialog box.

5. In the Graph Data window that displays when you release the mouse after drawing the graph, delete the 1 that displays in the Value bar. Then

click the top cell in the second column to select it. Leave the first cell in the top row blank.

6. Type John in the Value bar and move to the next cell to the right.
   - Press the right arrow key (→)
   or
   - Press the *Tab* key
   or
   - Click in the next cell.

7. Enter Marsha in the third cell on the top row, then move to the fourth cell on the top row and enter Patricia.

8. Select the first cell in the second row and enter June 12, 2001. Enter 160 in the cell under John in that row, 210 under Marsha, and 170 under Patricia.

Continued

615

9. Select the first cell in the third row and enter June 19, 2001. In the same row, enter 140 under John, 180 under Marsha, and 150 under Patricia.

10. Select the first cell in the fourth row and enter June 26, 2001. In the same row, enter 170 under John, 220 under Marsha, and 190 under Patricia.

11. Click in a blank cell so the last entry in the Value bar is transferred to its cell.

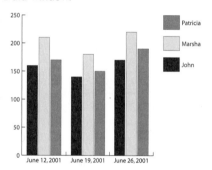

12. Click the Apply button at the top of the Graph Data window to apply the data to the graph.

   ■ Notice where the labels and legend are placed in relation to their entries in the Graph Data window.

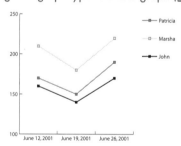

   ■ Notice the clusters in relation to their entries in the Graph Data window.

   ■ Notice how close together the columns are.

   ■ If the graph isn't centered on the page, select it with the Selection tool and drag it so it's centered.

13. With the entire graph selected, not just part of it, double-click the Graph tool in the Toolbox to display the Graph Type dialog box. Change the value in the Column Width field to 70%, then click OK or press *return/enter*.

   ■ Notice that now the individual columns have more space between them. And the space between the clusters adjusted slightly, even

though you didn't change the cluster width value.

14. Display the Graph Type dialog box again and click the Stacked Column graph button (▣). Click OK or press *return/enter*.

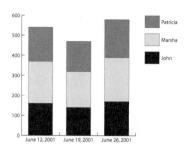

   ■ Your graph immediately changes to a Stacked Column graph and you can see how the totals for the three weeks compare.

15. Change the graph type to a Bar graph (▤) and a Stacked Bar graph (▥) to see how they compare with the Column and Stacked Column graphs.

   ■ They're the same, except the Bar Graph and Stacked Bar graph displays the information horizontally rather than vertically.

16. Change the graph type to a Line graph (▨)

17. Display the Graph Type dialog box again and change the options in the Options section. Click OK or press *return/enter* so you can see how your changes affect the graph.

18. Repeat #16 until you've displayed the graph using all the options and combinations of options.

19. Change the graph type to the Scatter, Area, Pie, and Radar graphs. Change their options, too, so you see how the graphs are affected.

20. When you've finished creating the different kinds of graphs, save your file and close the document.

Select Parts of a Graph

You can apply the options in the Graph Type dialog box to an entire graph or to only selected portions of it. When a graph is created, information in each column in the Graph Data window is grouped together. When you select any part of a graph with the Selection tool, the entire graph is selected, including the Legend. To assign fill and stroke attributes, send to front, send to back, and so on, you need to select the entire series of information that's grouped together, that is, all the information in one column. You can use the Group Selection tool to select elements in a graph, or the Direct Selection tool.

Selecting Parts of a Graph Using the Group Selection Tool

To select a series of grouped elements in a graph using the Group Selection tool:

1. Choose the Group Selection tool (▓) in the Toolbox.

2. Double-click the legend for the columns you want to select.

   - All columns grouped with that legend are selected.

   - Another click selects all columns and legend elements.

   - Different types of graphs require different numbers of clicks to select a group of elements. Keep track of what's being selected as you click.

   - To select the type in a graph, click once on the baseline of the type you want to change, that is, the category labels, legend labels, value axis labels, and so on. A second click selects the rest of the type in that element. A third click selects all the elements in the graph.

     - If you want to select other type element sets without selecting all the graph elements— for example, only the value axis labels and the category labels — you have to click on the sets individually.

Selecting Parts of a Graph Using the Direct Selection Tool

To select a series in a graph using the Direct Selection tool:

1. Choose the Direct Selection tool in the Toolbox.

2. ⌥-double-click one of the columns (or lines, and so on) in the series to select all the columns. One more ⌥-click selects the Legend element for that series.

   - If you click the Legend element first, the second ⌥-click selects all the columns for that legend item.

   - A third ⌥-click selects all columns and legend elements in the graph.

   - Different types of graphs require different numbers of ⌥-clicks to select a group of elements. Keep track of what's being selected as you ⌥-click.

   - To select the type in a graph, ⌥-click once on the baseline of the type you want to change, that is, the category labels, legend labels, value axis labels, etc. A second ⌥-click selects the rest of the type in that element. A third ⌥-click selects the all the elements in the graph.

- If you want to select other type element sets without selecting the whole graph — for example, only the legend and the category labels — you have to ⌥-click the sets individually.

Deselecting Parts of a Selected Group

Deselect individual elements that have been selected and are part of a series, hold the *Shift* key down and click on the object with the Direct Selection tool or the Group Selection tool. This is the same way you deselect an individual object from multiple selected objects when drawing other Illustrator objects.

Design Your Graph

Once you have entered all the data in the Graph Data window that you want displayed as a graph and applied them to create a graph, you can add color, reflect, shear, rotate, or scale it like any other object you create in Illustrator. You can change its typefaces and type styles, change the way tick marks are displayed, and so on. Or you can apply changes to only selected objects in the graph. You can even create illustrations to use in your graph.

Adjusting the Value Axis

In a graph, the Value axis is the column of numbers that displays the value of what is being graphed. In a default graph, the Value Axis is on the left side and starts at zero on the bottom (at the horizontal axis) and extends upward to one increment beyond the largest value in the graph. Increments are indicated by tick marks and you can specify the value of the increments (see the following section on Controlling Axis Tick Marks).

You can also position the Value axis on the right side of the graph, or on both sides. To specify the position of the Value axis of a selected graph:

1. Display the Graph Type dialog box and click on the button in the Type section for the kind of graph you are creating.

2. Choose one of the options from the Value Axis pop-up menu:

   - **On Left Side, On Right Side,** or **On Both Sides** for Column, Stacked Column, Line, and Area graphs.

If more than one graph is created during a working session, many options selected for a previous graph are still selected in the Graph Type dialog box. Verify all options carefully.

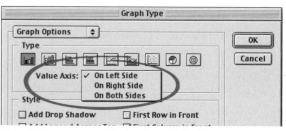

Value Axis pop-up menu in the Graph Type dialog box

- If you choose On Both Sides without specifying different data for each Value axis, the axis information will be the same on both sides of the graph.

■ **On Top Side, On Bottom Side,** or **On Both Sides** for Bar and Stacked Bar graphs.

■ Scatter graphs have only two choices, **On Left Side** (default) and **On Both Sides.**

■ Pie graphs don't have a value axis, so when the Pie Graph button is clicked in the Graph Type dialog box, the Value Axis pop-up menu is gray.

■ Radar graphs have only one Value Axis position, **On All Sides,** so you can't change it.

Controlling Axis Tick Marks

Illustrator automatically adds tick marks to the Value axis and the Category axis. In the Graph Type dialog box, you can change the number of tick marks that appear between value labels or category labels and you can determine whether they're short or the full width or height of the graph.

Value Axis   To change tick marks in the Value axis:

1. Display the Graph Type dialog box by double-clicking the graph tool in the Toolbox.

2. If the selection in the Value Axis pop-up menu below the Graph Type buttons is On Left Side or On Right Side, choose Value Axis in the pop-up menu at the top left side of the dialog box (Figure 13.12). If On Both Sides is selected in the Value Axis pop-up menu below the Graph Type buttons, choose the axis you want to change (Left Axis or Right Axis).

3. Click the Override Calculated Values checkbox in the Tick Values section to make the fields that control placement of the tick marks on the Value axis available.

   ■ **Min** — Enter the lowest number you want displayed — appears at the junction of the vertical axis with the horizontal axis.

   ■ **Max** — Enter the highest number you want displayed on the Value axis.

     - By default, Illustrator displays one increment above the largest value in the graph data.

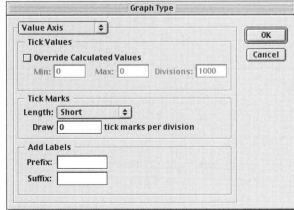

FIGURE 13.12 Value Axis dialog box

■ **Divisions** — Enter a number in this field to specify how many increments you want displayed.

4. In the Tick Marks section of the dialog box, you can specify how long the tick marks are or if you don't want any at all.

   ■ **Length** — Choose Short (the default), Full Width, which extends from one edge of the graph to the other, or None to remove the tick marks altogether.

   • Choosing None doesn't remove the labels, it just removes the tick marks.

   ■ **Draw [#] tick marks per division** — Enter a value in the field to specify how many tick marks you want between labels.

   • By default, Illustrator places a tick mark at each division as specified in the Division field of the Tick Values section. If you want one tick mark between each label, enter 2. If you want two tick marks between each label, enter 3, and so on. Even though the default value in the field is 0, Illustrator still puts a tick mark at the division mark.

5. Click OK or press *return/enter*.

Category Axis To change tick marks in the Category axis of a selected graph:

1. Display the Graph Type dialog box by double-clicking the graph tool in the Toolbox.

2. Choose Category Axis in the pop-up menu at the top left corner of the dialog box to display its dialog box (Figure 13.13).

   ■ If your graph is a Scatter graph, this option isn't available. An option called Bottom Axis is there instead and contains the same options as the Value Axis (above).

   ■ For a Radar Graph, this option isn't available at all.

3. Choose options in the Tick Marks section.

   ■ **Length** — Choose Short (the default), Full Width, which extends from one edge of the graph to the other, or None to remove the tick marks altogether.

   • Choosing None doesn't remove the labels. It just removes the tick mark.

   ■ **Draw [#] tick marks per division** — Enter a value to specify how many tick marks you want between labels.

   • By default, Illustrator places a tick mark at each division as

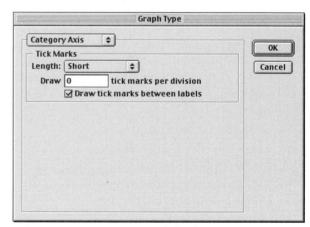

FIGURE 13.13 Category Axis dialog box.

specified in the Division field of the Tick Values section. If you want one tick mark between each label, enter 2. If you want two tick marks between each label, enter 3, and so on. Even though the default value in the field is 0, Illustrator still puts a tick mark at the division mark.

- **Draw tick marks between labels** — By default, this box is checked and tick marks display between labels. If you uncheck this box, each tick mark is centered above its label.

4. Click OK or press *return/enter.*

Setting Label Options

You can add text to the labels in the Value axis of a selected graph.

1. Display the Graph Type dialog box by double-clicking the graph tool in the Toolbox.

2. In the pop-up menu at the top left corner of the dialog box, choose Value Axis to display its dialog box.

3. To add text before the numbers, such as $, in the Value axis, enter the characters in the Prefix field of the Add Labels section of the dialog box. To add text after the number, such as °F, enter the characters in the Suffix field.

4. Click OK or press *return/enter* when you're finished.

activity 13.3

1. Open the file named Practice Graphs.eps that you saved into your Practice folder.

2. Select the graph with the Selection tool and, if it's not already, change it to a Column graph.

3. Display the Graph Type dialog box and choose On Both Sides in the Value Axis pop-up menu that's below the Type buttons. Click OK or press *return/enter*.

   ■ A value axis displays on both sides of the graph. and it probably crashes into the legend on the right side.

4. With the graph still selected, display the Graph Type dialog box again and choose On Right Side.

   ■ The value axis displays on the right side of the graph rather than the left side.

5. Return the Value Axis pop-up menu option to On Left Side, then display the Value Axis dialog box by choosing that option in the pop-up menu at the top left corner of the Graph Type dialog box.

6. Make the following changes in the dialog box:

   ■ Check the Override Calculated Values checkbox, then enter 50 in the Min field, enter 225 in the Max field, and enter 2 in the Division field.

   ■ Change the Length selection to Full Width, and enter 2 in the Draw tick marks per division field.

   ■ Type $ in the Prefix field.

7. Click OK or press *return/enter*.

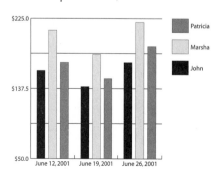

8. With the graph still selected, display the Graph Type dialog box and convert the graph to a Line graph. Uncheck the Mark Data Points checkbox if it's checked and make sure Connect Data Points is still checked.

9. Choose Category Axis from the pop-up menu in the top left corner.

10. Make the following changes:

    ■ In the Length pop-up menu, choose Full Width.

    ■ Uncheck Draw tick marks between labels.

11. Click OK or press *return/enter*.

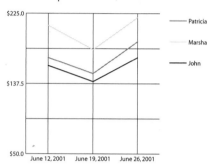

12. To mark where the data point is on the vertical tick mark, drag a horizontal ruler guide down and position it where one of the data lines intersects the June 12 tick mark. Repeat for the other lines.

13. Select the graph with the Selection tool, then display the Graph Type dialog box. Check the Edge-to-Edge Lines checkbox and the Mark Data Points checkbox. Click OK or press *return/enter*.

    ■ Notice that the data points aren't centered on the labels or the tick marks, making it difficult to accurately read the graph.

14. Continue making tick mark and label changes to different types of graphs. When you're finished, close the document without saving changes.

Specifying a Different Scale for Each Value Axis

You can design a graph that displays data using two different scales. For example, you can show values in dollars and British pounds at the same time. When entering the data for the graph in the Graph Data window, you must have at least one series of data using each value scale. For example, you must have a data series as dollars and a data series as pounds.

1. Draw a new graph or select an existing graph containing the data.

2. Display the Graph Type dialog box.

   ■ Double-click the graph tool in the Toolbox

   or

   ■ Choose **Object** ⇨ **Graph** ⇨ **Type**.

3. Choose On Both Sides from the Value Axis pop-up menu.

4. In the Graph Options pop-up menu, choose Left Axis, and make the appropriate changes for one of the value scales.

5. In the Graph Options pop-up menu, choose Right Axis, and make the appropriate changes for the other value scale.

6. Click OK or press *return/enter*.

7. Deselect the graph.

8. Using the Direct Selection tool or the Group Selection tool, select the series of data, including its legend box or legend line, for the second value scale.

9. Display the Graph Type dialog box again and choose On Right Side from the Value Axis pop-up menu.

10. Choose Value Axis from the Graph Options pop-up menu. The values you entered previously in the Right Axis dialog box should still be there, but if they aren't, re-enter them. Then click OK or press *return/enter*.

The graph now shows all values in both scales.

read this!

Once you've specified separate information for the right and left axes of a graph, you can't make changes to the axis values. You have to convert the graph back to having only a left-side value axis, then start over.

activity 13.4

1. Create a new document: Letter size, CMYK color mode. Name it Dollars & Pounds Graph.eps and save it into your Practice folder.

2. Draw a new column graph that's about 7" wide and 5" high.

3. Using Figures 13.1, 13.12, and 13.13 in this chapter, verify that all options in the Graph Type dialog box display default values.

4. Enter the following data in the Graph Data window and apply it to the graph:

	ABC Co	DEF Co	GHI Co
"1998"	303.00	485.00	260.00
"1999"	471.00	642.00	400.00
"2000"	650.00	739.00	412.00

   - Data for ABC Company and DEF Company was entered in dollars. Data for GHI Company is entered in British pounds.

5. Double-click the Graph tool to display the Graph Type dialog box.
   - Choose On Both Sides from the Value Axis pop-up menu.
   - In the Style section, check the Add Legend Across Top and the First Column in Front checkboxes.
   - In the Options section:
     • Column Width: 90%
     • Cluster Width: 80%

6. Choose Left Axis from the Graph Options pop-up menu and click the Override Calculated Values checkbox so the fields are available. Enter:
   - 0 in the Min field.
   - 1000 in the Max field.
   - 4 in the Divisions field.

7. Change the option in the Tick Marks pop-up menu to Full Width. Leave 0 in the "Draw [#] tick marks per division" field.

8. Enter $ in the Prefix field of the Add Labels section. Leave the Suffix field blank.

9. Choose Right Axis in the pop-up menu at the top of the dialog box (Graph Options). Click the Override Calculated Values checkbox so the fields are available and enter:
   - 0 in the Min field.
   - 673.4 in the Max field (the current exchange rate for British pounds (673.4 British pounds equals 1000 U.S. dollars)
   - 4 in the Divisions field.

10. Change the option in the Tick Marks pop-up menu to None.

11. Enter £ in the Prefix field of the Add Labels section. Leave the Suffix field blank.
    - The keyboard command for the £ character on a Macintosh is ⌥3.
    - The keyboard command for the £ on Windows is ⌥0163 on the numeric keypad.

12. Click OK or press *return/enter*.

13. Deselect the graph.

14. Select the series of data for GHI Company, including its legend.

15. Double-click the Graph tool to open the Graph Type dialog box and choose On Right Side from the Value Axis pop-up menu.

16. Choose Value Axis from the Graph Options pop-up menu and verify that the specifications you entered earlier are still there. If not, re-enter them.

17. Click OK or press *return/enter*.

18. Select and move the legend to the bottom of the graph. Position it so it's evenly spaced in a single line across the bottom of the graph. Your graph should look like the one below.

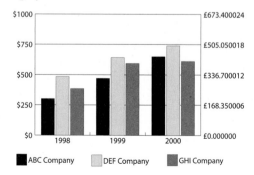

19. Save the file, print it, and close the document.

Combining Different Graph Types into One Graph

In addition to specifying a different value axis to each side of a graph, you can combine two types of graph in one graph. For instance, you can display some of the data as a column graph and some data as a stacked column graph. One value axis can measure one type of graph while the other value axis measures the other type of graph.

You must know ahead of time which sets of data are going to be applied to the different types of graphs so you can enter the values into the Graph Data window correctly. It may take some experimenting before you get it right.

To combine two different types of graphs in one graph:

1. Enter the data for both types of graphs into the Graph Data window.

   ■ It doesn't matter which type of graph you choose to draw so the Graph Data window displays. You can change it to the type you want after you have entered the data.

2. Using the Direct Selection tool, select a set of data, including its legend box or legend line.

3. Display the Graph Type dialog box.

   ■ Double-click the graph tool in the Toolbox

   or

   ■ Choose **Object** ⇨ **Graph** ⇨ **Type**.

4. Click the button for the desired graph type and check the appropriate options for this set of data.

5. Choose On Left Side from the Value Axis pop-up menu.

6. Choose Value Axis from the Graph Options pop-up menu and make the appropriate changes. Click OK or press *return/enter*.

7. Deselect the graph.

8. Using the Direct Selection tool or the Direct Selection tool, select a different set of data, including its legend box or legend line.

9. Display the Graph Type dialog box again and click a different graph type and check the appropriate options for the selected data.

10. Choose On Right Side from the Value Axis pop-up menu.

11. Choose Value Axis from the Graph Options pop-up menu and make the appropriate changes. Click OK or press *return/enter*.

activity 13.5

1. Create a new document: Letters size, CMYK color mode. Name it Combination Graph.eps and save it into your Practice folder.

2. Double-click the Column Graph tool in the Toolbox to display the Graph Type dialog box. Using Figures 13.1, 13.12, and 13.13 in this chapter, verify that all options display default values.

3. Draw a new Column graph that's about 7" wide and 5" high.

4. Enter the following data in the Graph Data window and apply it to the graph:
   - Widen the cells so you can see all the text.

	Company 1	Company 2	Qtr Totals
1st Qtr	244.00	133.00	377.00
2nd Qtr	257.00	253.00	510.00
3rd Qtr	243.00	162.00	405.00
4th Qtr	376.00	393.00	769.00
1st Qtr	174.00	189.00	363.00
2nd Qtr	205.00	221.00	426.00
3rd Qtr	273.00	251.00	524.00
4th Qtr	224.00	264.00	488.00

   - Data in the Qtr Totals column are the totals of each row for Company 1 and Company 2.

5. Double-click the Graph tool to display the Graph Type dialog box.
   - Choose On Both Sides from the Value Axis pop-up menu.
   - In the Style section, verify that First Column in Front is the only box checked.
   - In the Options section:
     - Column Width: 90%
     - Cluster Width: 80%

6. Choose Left Axis from the Graph Options pop-up menu and click the Override Calculated Values checkbox so the fields are available. Enter:
   - 0 in the Min field.
   - 1000 in the Max field.
   - 8 in the Divisions field.

7. Choose Short in pop-up menu in the Tick Marks section; 0 tick marks per division.

8. Enter $ in the Prefix field of the Add Labels section. Leave the Suffix Field blank.

9. Choose Right Axis in the pop-up menu at the top of the dialog box (Graph Options). Click the Override Calculated Values checkbox so the fields are available and enter:
   - 0 in the Min field.
   - 1000 in the Max field.
   - 4 in the Divisions field.

10. Choose Short in pop-up menu in the Tick Marks section; 0 tick marks per division.

11. Enter $ in the Prefix field of the Add Labels section. Leave the Suffix field blank.

12. Click OK or press *return/enter*.

13. Deselect the graph.

14. Select the Qtr Totals series of data, including its legend.

15. Double-click the Graph tool to open the Graph Type dialog box, click the Line graph button, and choose On Right Side from the Value Axis pop-up menu.

16. Choose Value Axis from the Graph Options pop-up menu and verify that the specifications you entered for the Right Axis (#9) are still there. If not, re-enter them.

17. Click OK or press *return/enter*.

18. With the Direct Selection tool, select all the type in the graph and change it to 17 pt.

19. Select the legends for Company 1 and Company 2 and position them under the graph. Select the legend for Qtr Totals and position it under the graph as shown on the following page.

Continued

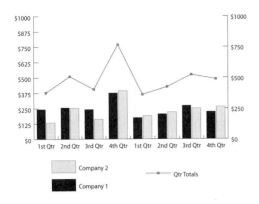

20. Save the file, print it, and close the document.

Jazz Up Your Graph

In the Style section of the Graph Type dialog box, there are four check-boxes for changing a graph's appearance. In addition, you can select columns and apply fill and stroke attributes, including gradients, you can change the typeface and point size of type used in the graph, and you can apply fill and stroke attributes to the type.

Setting Options in the Graph Type Dialog Box

In the Style section, choose any, or all, of the four options available:

- **Add Drop Shadow** — When this checkbox is checked, a black drop shadow is placed behind selected elements in the graph.

  - You can select the drop shadows with the Direct-Selection tool and reposition them, apply a different color, add a stroke, and so on. If you're going to move the drop shadows, be certain all anchor points are selected (solid) before you begin the drag to move the objects.

- **First Row in Front** — Check this box to arrange the stacking order of columns, or lines, and so on, in descending order so the elements representing the first *row* of data in the Data Window are in front and the elements for the last *row* of data are in back.

  - In a column or bar graph in which you've specified a Column Width or Cluster Width greater than 100%, you can control which elements appear in front.

  - Use this feature to control which lines are in front of other lines in a line graph in which lines overlap.

- **First Column in Front** — Check this option to arrange stacking order of columns, lines, and so on, in descending order so the elements representing the first *column* of data in the Data Window are in front and the elements for the last *column* of data are in back.

  - Use this feature to control which lines are in front of other lines in a line graph in which lines overlap.

  - In a column or bar graph in which you've specified a Column Width or Cluster Width greater than 100%, you can control which elements appear in front.

- **Add Legend Across Top** — When checked, the legend is repositioned horizontally across the top of the graph.

Adding Color, Reshaping, Etc.

Add fill and stroke attributes, reshape elements, add drop shadows using the Effects menu, and so on, like you do any other object you draw with the other creation tools. By default, a graph is created with fills in varying shades of gray with varying shades of gray strokes. You can fill the elements, such as columns, markers, and so on, with solid colors, gradients, patterns, change stroke weights, and so on. Change the typeface of labels and the legend, change the color of the type, and so on.

You can use the transform tools in the Toolbox, the transform commands in the Object menu, or the commands in the Transform palette to reshape, move, and rotate your graph. There are any number of ways to make your graph interesting.

There are, however, a few things to remember when modifying your graph.

- Don't ungroup elements in your graph. If you do, you can't make changes to the data in the Graph Data window and replot the graph.

- If you make changes in the type in a graph with the Type tool rather than making changes in the Graph Data window, then later have to edit data and replot the graph, those changes you made with the Type tool are lost. The text that is entered in the Graph Data window is restored.

- Size and font changes to type may be lost if you make changes in the Graph Data window and redraw the graph.

 To display a graph's data values in or around a column or marker, see the instructions in the section on Displaying Data Values in the Graph later in this chapter.

activity 13.6

1. Create a new document: Letter size, CMYK color mode. Name it My Graph.eps and save it into your Practice folder as an .eps file.

2. Double-click the Column Graph tool in the Toolbox to display the Graph Type dialog box. Using Figures 13.1, 13.12, and 13.13 in this chapter, verify that all options display default values.

3. Using the Graph tool, draw a 4" square Column graph in the center of the page.

4. In the Graph Data window, widen the cells to 10 digits.

5. Delete the text in the first cell and leave it blank, then import the text file named My Graph data.txt that's in the Student Files folder on the CD-ROM that accompanies this book.

6. Click the Apply button to create the graph, then close the Graph Data window so it's out of your way.

7. With the entire graph selected, display the Graph Type dialog box. With Graph Options selected in the pop-up menu at the top of the dialog box, choose the following options:

   ■ Choose On Left Side in the Value Axis pop-up menu.

   ■ Verify that the only box checked in the Style section is First Column in Front.

   ■ Set the Column Width to 120% and leave the Cluster Width value at 80%.

   ■ In the pop-up menu at the top of the dialog box, display the Value Axis dialog box and change the Length of the Tick Marks to Full Width; draw 0 tick marks per division.

   ■ Enter °F into the Suffix Label field; Prefix field blank.
     • Macintosh: Degree sign = ⇧⌥8
     • Windows: Degree sign = ⌥0176

8. Click OK or press return/enter.

   ■ The columns in each cluster overlap. And the Value Axis labels display °F.

9. With the entire graph selected, display the Graph Type dialog box, and uncheck First Column in Front and check the First Row in Front checkbox.

10. Set the Column Width to 80% and click OK or press return/enter.

    ■ The columns for each series are clustered together with space between the clusters.

11. Deselect the graph, then with the Direct Selection tool, ⌥-triple-click the darkest set of columns to select them, including the legend. Change the color to C 10%, M 100%, Y 0%, K 0%, and the stroke to .5 wide and 60% black.

12. Create a new linear gradient, using any colors you choose, and apply it to the lightest set of columns. Change the stroke color to 60% black. Leave the stroke width at .5.

13. Choose a pattern from the Swatches palette and apply it to the third set of columns. Apply the same stroke attributes as the other two series.

14. With the Direct Selection tool, select the right-most vertical tick mark on the horizontal axis. Select the topmost anchor point and Shift-drag it up until it overlaps the top horizontal full width tick mark, forming a perfect corner.

15. With the Rectangle tool, draw a box covering the columns, starting in the top left corner and ending at the bottom right corner. Fill it with 14% Yellow, no stroke.

    ■ You could fill it with a pattern, a gradient, or any other fill attribute.

16. Send it to the back of the stack.

17. Select the graph with the Selection tool, display the Graph Type dialog box, and check Add Legend Across Top. Click OK or press return/enter.

18. With the Direct Selection tool, select the type in the legend and change its size to 10 point.

19. With the Direct Selection tool, select only the three legend swatches in the legend. Choose the Scale tool in the Toolbox, and drag to make the legend swatches smaller.

20. Select the legend swatch and the type for each set in the legend and reposition them so they're evenly spaced.

    ■ Hold the Shift key down as you drag the selection so the baseline doesn't shift.

Continued

21. ⌘-click twice on a label in the Value Axis to select all the labels in the Value Axis. Change the type size to 12 point.

22. ⌘-click twice on a label in the Category Axis to select all the labels in the Category Axis. Change the type size to 12 point.

23. Save your file, print it, but don't close the document.

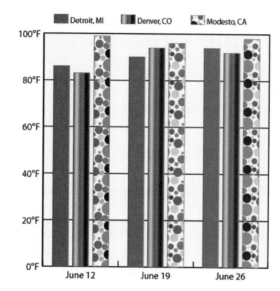

The column graph you created shows how temperatures for the three cities compare to each other for each date. If you want to display the temperature trend (is it going up or is it going down), you should use a Line graph.

24. Select the graph with the Selection tool, display the Graph Type dialog box, and change the graph type to a Line graph.

   ■ Displaying the information with a Line graph, is easier to see whether the temperature is going up over time or going down.

   ■ Notice that the fill and stroke attributes applied to the column graph were lost when the graph was converted to a Line graph.

25. With the Selection tool, select the graph. Display the Graph Type dialog box and make the following changes:

   ■ Change the length of the tick marks in the Category Axis to Full Width and uncheck the Draw tick marks between labels checkbox.

■ Add tick marks to the Value Axis.

   • If you want labels on the tick marks, change the value in the Division field of the Tick Values section of the dialog box to 4. This is my choice.

   • If you don't want labels on the tick marks, change the value in the Draw [#] tick marks per division field of the Tick Marks section of the dialog box to 5.

   ■ In Graph Options, uncheck Mark Data Points.

   ■ Check Draw Filled Lines and enter 4 pt in the Line Width field.

   ■ Check the First Column in Front checkbox.

26. Click OK or press return/enter.

   ■ Notice that the fill and stroke attributes reappeared because the lines were filled.

   ■ Notice which line is in front in the graph. Is it Denver or Detroit?

27. Using the Scale tool, enlarge the legend swatches so they're square (or close). Reposition type and swatches so they're evenly spaced.

28. With the Selection tool, select the entire graph and display the Graph Type dialog box. Uncheck First Column in Front and leave First Row in Front checked.

   ■ They switched places in the stacking order.

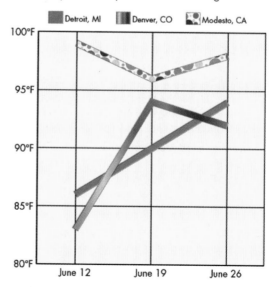

29. Save the file as My Graph2.eps, print it, and close the document.

Use Artwork to Display Graph Data

To add interest to a graph, you can draw an illustration, save it as a graph design, then use it to display the data you enter into the Graph Data window. Creating a graph design is similar to creating a pattern fill (Step 10, *Brushes, Patterns, & Symbols*). You can apply graph designs to column, bar, line, and scatter graphs.

A graph design is saved in the file in which it's created. To use that design in another file, copy and paste the graph to the new document page, then delete it. The design stays with the new file even though the graph is no longer in the document.

Creating a Design for Column, Stacked Column, Bar, and Stacked Bar Graphs

To create a graph design to display columns or bars as artwork:

1. Draw a rectangle with no fill and a .1 black stroke.

   ■ To accurately determine what size the rectangle should be, copy and paste the smallest column in your graph to use as the boundary-defining rectangle.

2. Create a new design or copy and paste an existing design and position it in front of the boundary-defining rectangle.

   ■ If a design extends beyond the boundary of the rectangle, it extends beyond the column boundary in the graph. For example, if the design overlaps the bottom of the rectangle, it hangs out below the bottom of the horizontal axis of the graph.

   ■ Unless you have a specific reason for doing otherwise, the vertical sides of the graph should be within the boundaries of the rectangle.

   ■ The position of the rectangle with respect to the bottom of the design determines where the design sits on the baseline of the graph when the Vertically Scaled and Uniformly Scaled options are selected. For best results, place the bottom of the rectangle on the pathline of the bottom of the design.

      • When the rectangle is below the bottom of the design, the bottom of the design may fall below the horizontal axis line of the graph.

      • When the rectangle is above the bottom of the design, the bottom of the design may sit above the horizontal axis line of the graph.

3. If the graph design is to be stretched or compressed to represent the value of the data, you need to tell Illustrator where to stretch the design. This step is not required if the design is to be Vertically Scaled, Uniformly Scaled, or is a Repeating Design.

   ■ Make sure Lock Guides is unchecked in the View menu. Refer to Step 6, *Rulers, Grids, & Guides*, for more information.

Incorrect placement of rectangle

Correct placement of rectangle

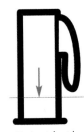

Horizontal guide

631

- Using the Pen tool, draw a straight horizontal line that's slightly wider than the graph design at the spot at which you want the stretching to occur. You can reposition the line, if necessary.

- Convert the line into a guide by choosing **View** ⇨ **Guides** ⇨ **Make Guides**.

  - The line is solid or dotted, depending on the setting in the Guides Style pop-up menu in the Guides & Grid Preferences dialog box.

4. Using the Direct Selection tool, select the boundary-defining rectangle and remove the stroke.

5. Send the rectangle to the back (just in case it isn't already) (**Object** ⇨ **Arrange** ⇨ **Send to Back**).

6. Using the Selection tool, select all the objects making up the graph design, including the rectangle and the horizontal guide.

7. Choose **Object** ⇨ **Graph** ⇨ **Design** to display the Graph Design dialog box.

8. Click the New Design button to add the design to the list in the scroll window.

   - A representation of the design is displayed in the Preview window as it fits inside the boundary-defining rectangle.

   - If Illustrator won't let you create a new design, make sure the boundary-defining rectangle is at the back of the stack in the design. Click the Cancel button or press *esc* to exit the dialog box and correct the problem.

9. Click the Rename button and type a name for your design.

10. Click OK or press *return/enter*.

Applying a Design to Column, Stacked Column, Bar, and Stacked Bar Graphs

To apply a new or existing design to a Column, Stacked Column, Bar, or Stacked Bar graph:

1. Select the columns you want to fill with the design.

   - With the Direct Selection tool, ⬧-click on a set of columns or bars until the entire series is selected, including the legend.

   or

   - With the Group Selection tool, click on a series of columns or bars until entire series is selected, including the legend.

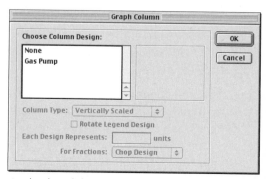

Graph Column dialog box

2. Choose **Object** ⇨ **Graph** ⇨ **Column** to display the Graph Column dialog box.

3. In the Choose Column Design window, select the name of the design you want to apply to the columns.

   ■ A thumbnail representation of the design displays in the preview area of the dialog box.

4. To control how Illustrator stretches or repeats the graph design, choose one of the options in the Column Type pop-up menu.

   ■ **Vertically Scaled** — Stretches the graph design vertically to represent data values.

   ■ **Uniformly Scaled** — Scales the graph design proportionally to represent data values.

   ▪ This option works best when data values are similar. Large differences between data values can generate unappealing differences in the size of the design in the columns.

   ■ **Repeating** — Stacks individual copies of the graph design on top of each other until the column is filled. When this option is selected, the Each Design Represents field becomes available.

   ▪ **Each Design Represents** — Enter a value in the field to assign the value that each individual graph design represents as it's stacked in the column. For example, if the data value for the column is 35 and you assign a value of 10 in the Each Design Represents field, three full images of the design display in the column, plus one that's only a partial image, in the example described here, half of the design. You can, however, choose Scale in the For Fractions pop-up menu to scale the final design image to fit.

   ▪ **For Fractions** — The two options in this pop-up menu control how Illustrator treats the design element when it can't display a whole image. Choose Chop Design to lop off the portion that doesn't fit. Choose Scale Design to scale the last image to fit in the space available.

   ■ **Sliding** — Stretches or compresses the graph design at the spot determined by the position of the horizontal guideline placed when the graph was drawn.

5. Check the **Rotate Legend Design** checkbox to display the graph design on its side in the legend. If unchecked, the graph design displays upright the way it was designed.

6. Click OK or press *return/enter*

✓ **Vertically Scaled**
Uniformly Scaled
Repeating
Sliding

Options in the Column Type pop-up menu

✓ **Chop Design**
Scale Design

Options in the For Fractions dialog box

activity 13.7

1. Create a new document: Letter size, CMYK color mode. Name it Gas Pump Graph.eps and save it into your practice folder as an .eps file.

2. In a corner of the document page, draw a very simple gas pump, similar to the one shown here.

   - Use round corner joins and round endcaps.

   - You can draw it large, then scale it down to the size you need.

3. Select the object with the Selection tool, hold down the *Shift* key, and drag a corner of the bounding box so the object is scaled proportionally to about 1" high.

4. Draw a boundary-defining rectangle around the object, no fill, no stroke, and send it to the back of the stack.

5. With the Pen tool, about a third of the way up from the bottom of the object, click just outside the left edge of the rectangle, then *Shift*-click just outside the right edge of the rectangle to draw a straight horizontal line.

6. Check to make sure that Lock Guides is unchecked (View ⇨ Guides ⇨ Lock Guides).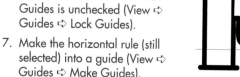

7. Make the horizontal rule (still selected) into a guide (View ⇨ Guides ⇨ Make Guides).

8. With the Selection tool, select all the objects, including the horizontal rule, then display the Graph Design dialog box (Object ⇨ Graph ⇨ Design).

9. Click the New Design button, then click the Rename button, and type Gas Pump to name the design.

10. In the center of the document page, draw a 5" × 4" Column graph.

11. Double-click the Column Graph tool in the Toolbox to display the Graph Type dialog box. Using Figures 13.1, 13.12, and 13.13 in this chapter, verify that all options display default values.

12. Enter the following data into the Graph Data window, then click the Apply button:

	Price l Per l Gallon
"1960"	.30
"1970"	.65
"1980"	1.10
"1990"	1.25
"2000"	1.65

    - You must add the quotes around the years so Illustrator uses them as a label rather than plotting them in the graph.

    - A vertical line (*Shift-backslash*) is between the words in the legend text instead of a space.

13. Close the Graph Data window or move it out of the way. Deselect the graph.

14. With the Direct Selection tool or the Group Selection tool, select the data series, including the legend, then choose Object ⇨ Graph ⇨ Column to display the Graph Column dialog box.

15. Choose Vertically in the Column Type pop-up menu. Leave the Rotate Legend Design checkbox checked. Click OK or press *return/enter*.

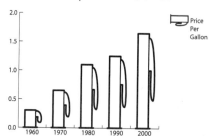

    - That's not bad, but look what happened to the gas pump on the legend.

16. If you deselected the graph, select the columns again, then display the Graph Column dialog box. Choose Uniformly Scaled, and uncheck the Rotate Legend Design checkbox. Click OK or press *return/enter*.

Continued

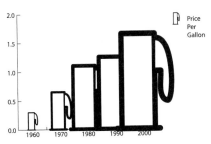

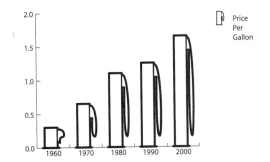

■ Definitely isn't going to work.

17. If you deselected the graph, select the columns again, and display the Graph Column dialog box. Choose Repeating, enter .25 in the Each Design Represents field, and choose Scale Design in the For Fractions dialog box. Click OK or press *return/enter*.

   ■ That's not bad either.

18. If you deselected the graph, select the columns again, and display the Graph Column dialog box. Change the option in the For Fractions dialog box to Chop Design. Click OK or press *return/enter*.

   ■ I tend to like Chop Design better, because it's easier to tell the size of the partial amount.

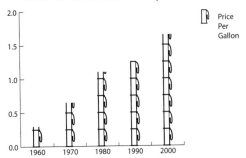

   ■ This option isn't really appropriate for this design, though.

19. If you deselected the graph, select the columns again and display the Graph Column dialog box. Choose Sliding. Click OK or press *return/enter*.

   ■ The graph (at the top of the next column) looks a little weird. There's really no good place to stretch with this design.

20. Change the Column Type to Vertically scaled columns in the Graph Column dialog box.

21. With the Direct Selection tool, drag the legend design onto the scratch area so it won't display when you import the graph into a page layout program.

   ■ Illustrator won't let you eliminate parts of a graph without ungrouping it, thereby destroying the link between the graph and its data.

22. With the Selection tool, select the entire graph. Double-click the Graph tool in the Toolbox to display the Graph Type dialog box.

23. Choose Value Axis in the Graph Options pop-up menu. Enter $ in the Prefix Label field and a 0 (zero) in the Suffix Label field. Click OK or press *return/enter*.

24. Drag the legend type to the left side of the graph. Position it so it's centered vertically on the Value Axis.

25. You could leave it like that or, with the Type tool, delete the returns between the lines replace them with a space. Then rotate the line 90° and re-center it on the Value Axis.

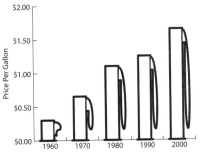

26. Save the file, print it, and close the document.

Creating a Marker Design For Line or Scatter Graphs

To create a design for the marker that displays in a Line or Scatter graph:

1. Draw a boundary-defining rectangle for the design with a fill and stroke of None. It must be the backmost object in the design.

   - The shape must actually be square, because that's the shape of the graph marker. Because it's drawn with the rectangle tool, it's called a rectangle.

   - I usually apply a .1 black stroke on the rectangle until I'm finished with my design. Otherwise, you can't see it.

   - When the design is applied to a graph, the rectangle that you draw (and its associated artwork) is scaled to the size and shape of the markers in the graph.

2. Draw the artwork you want to display as markers in the graph.

   - For the marker design to be readily visible, I've found that the artwork should be 3–4 times the size of the marker rectangle. You can draw it larger, then scale it to the correct size.

3. With the Selection tool, select all the paths in the design, including the rectangle, then choose **Object** ➪ **Graph** ➪ **Design** to display the Graph Design dialog box.

4. If a design is highlighted in the scrolling window, clicking the New Design button replaces the existing design with the new design. To add the new artwork rather than replacing a design that's already there, click in the dialog box window to deselect the existing design, then click the New Design button.

5. Click the Rename button to display the Rename dialog box. Enter a name for the new design in the field, then click OK or press *return/enter*.

6. Click OK or press *return/enter*.

   - The new graph design is stored with the document file.

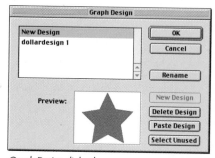

Graph Design dialog box

Applying a Marker Design to a Line or Scatter Graph

To apply a new or existing marker design to a Line or Scatter graph:

1. Select the markers to which you want to apply a graph design.

   - With the Direct Selection tool, ✇-click on a set of markers until all the markers for that series, including the legend, are selected.

   or

   - With the Group Selection tool, click on a set of markers until all the markers for that series, including the legend, are selected.

2. Choose **Object** ➪ **Graph** ➪ **Marker** to display the Graph Marker dialog box.

3. In the Choose Marker Design window, click on the name of the design you want to apply to the markers in the graph.

   - A thumbnail representation of the design displays in the preview area of the dialog box.

4. Click OK or press *return/enter*.

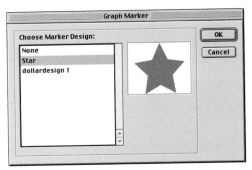

Graph Marker dialog box

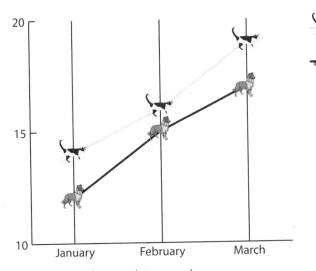 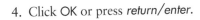

Graph displaying data using designs as markers

Size of rectangle as compared to size of design used to create the line graph

Displaying Data Values in the Graph

You can display a column's data values in a graph automatically.

1. Create the graph design.

   - If graph elements — columns, bars, and so on — are to have only fill and stroke attributes applied, copy the smallest column, apply the desired fill and stroke attributes, then draw the boundary-defining rectangle the same size and send it to the back.

2. Using the Type tool in the Toolbox, click on or near the graph design where you want the value to appear.

   - You can position the type above, below, or beside the design (right or left).

3. To control how the data are displayed, type a percent sign (%) then two numbers (from 0 to 9).

   - The first number determines how many digits display before the decimal point.
   - The second number determines how many digits display after the decimal point.
     - Values are rounded up or down to accommodate settings you choose.
     - Zeroes are added as necessary.
   - If your data don't include decimals, enter a 0 so only whole numbers are displayed.

4. If desired, change type attributes, including alignment, the same way you do any other type created in Illustrator.

   - Type size is relative to the size of the rectangle. If you drew a small rectangle, you may have to enlarge the type size considerably for it to be read easily.
   - To align decimals, choose Right Alignment in the Paragraph dialog box.

5. Using the Selection tool, select the whole design, including any type.

6. Choose **Object** ⇨ **Graph** ⇨ **Design** and click the New Design button. Click the Rename button and rename the design, if desired. Click OK or press *return/enter*.

7. Click OK or press *return/enter*.

fyi *Examples of settings to display data values graph designs:*

Typing	Results in
%20	43
%21	43.3
%22	43.35
%23	43.345

and so on.

Managing Graph Designs

In addition to the New Design and Rename buttons, the Graph Design dialog box contains three more buttons to help you manage your graph designs.

- **Delete Design** — Deletes designs highlighted in the Choose Marker Design window.

- **Paste Design** — Pastes a copy of the original objects that created a design into the open document — providing the graph design has been applied to a graph. This feature allows you to edit a graph design even when you can't find the original design.
  - Apply the graph design to a column of a "dummy" graph, if necessary, so you can paste a copy of the original design onto the document page.
- **Select Unused Design** — Highlights all the designs that aren't applied to graphs in any open documents. Click the Delete Design button to delete the unused designs.

Click OK or press *return/enter* when you're finished managing your graph designs.

activity 13.8

1. Create a new document: Letter size, CMYK color mode. Name it Practice Scatter Graph.eps and save it into your Practice folder as an .eps file.

2. Draw a 6" × 4" Scatter graph in the center of the page.

3. Double-click the Scatter Graph tool in the Toolbox to display the Graph Type dialog box. Using Figures 13.1, 13.12, and 13.13 in this chapter, verify that all options display default values.

4. Enter the following data in the Graph Data window:

Company A		Company B	
23.62	1.50	5.27	1.90
22.12	2.96	6.38	3.27
20.87	4.21	8.23	5.11
19.32	5.36	10.57	6.75
17.95	6.92	13.07	7.82
16.52	8.12	18.43	9.91
14.97	9.35	15.59	11.17
11.76	10.74	17.54	14.67
13.52	12.64	19.77	18.48
14.01	14.82	21.33	20.69
15.97	16.51	22.12	22.60
16.73	18.35	23.46	24.00
18.41	20.37		
18.97	22.48		
19.12	24.00		

- Each set of data requires two columns in the Graph Data window. The first column determines where the marker is placed vertically.

The second column determines where the marker is placed horizontally.

5. Widen the columns containing the Company name so the entire name is visible in the column.

6. Apply the data to the graph and close the Graph Data window.

7. Display the Graph Type dialog box and uncheck the Connect Data Points checkbox.

8. Display the Value Axis dialog box, check the Override Calculated Values checkbox, and enter 0 in the Min field, 25 in the Max field, and 5 in the Divisions field.

9. Display the Bottom Axis dialog box, check the Override Calculated Values checkbox, and enter 0 in the Min field, 24 in the Max field, and 8 in the Divisions field.

10. Click OK or press *return/enter* to exit the dialog box.

11. In a blank area of the page or in the scratch area, draw two simple designs about 1½" in diameter. I chose to draw a circle with a star in the center and a star with a circle in the center.

12. Apply colors to the shapes.

13. Draw two ½" rectangles, apply fill and stroke attributes of None. Position one of the rectangles in the center of each of the designs, aligning its center points.

Continued

14. One at a time, send both rectangles to the back.

15. With the Type tool, click just below one of the designs. Type %22.
    - Each data value has two whole numbers and two decimal points.

16. Change the typeface to Times Bold Italic and the type size to 54 pt.

17. Add the same type to the other design.

18. With the Selection tool, select all the paths for one of the designs, including the type.

19. Choose Object ⇨ Graph ⇨ Design to display the Graph Design dialog box. Click the New Design button, then the Rename button. Enter a name for the design in the field. Click OK or press *return/enter* then click OK or press *return/enter* again to exit the Graph Design dialog box.

20. Designate the other object as a graph design by performing the steps in #17 and #18 above.

21. With the Group Selection tool or the Direct Selection tool, select one set of graph data, including the legend.

22. Choose Object ⇨ Graph ⇨ Marker and choose one of the designs from the list. Click OK or press *return/enter*.

23. Repeat #20 and #21 above for the second set of data.

24. If your designs look too large for the graph, scale the designs (not the type) down, then designate the new size as a graph design (#17 and #18 above) and reapply it to the markers (#20 and #21 above).

25. With the Direct Selection tool or the Group Selection tool, select the type along the vertical and horizontal axes and the legend. Change it to 14 pt.

26. With the Direct Selection tool, select the values that display below the legend design and, one at a time, drag them into the scratch area.
    - Illustrator won't let you delete these elements without ungrouping the graph.

27. With the Direct Selection tool, select the legend (design and type) and reposition it on one line below the graph, showing Company A first.
    - Your graph should look similar to the one shown below.

28. Save the file and close the document.

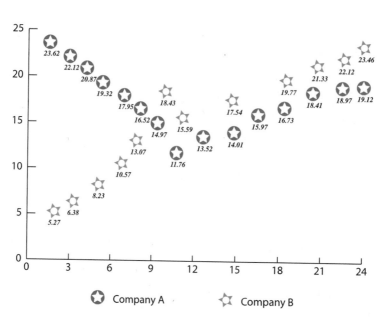

PRACTICE ACTIVITY 13-1 — Line Graph

1. Create a new document: Letter size, CMYK color mode. Name it Bowling Scores Graph.eps and save it into your practice folder as an .eps file.

*Draw Graph Design —
Bowling Pin & Ball*
*Draw Graph Design —
Bowling Pin & Ball*

2. Drag a vertical ruler guide onto the center of the document page.

3. With the Pen tool, draw one side of the bowling pin with the first and last anchor points on the ruler guide to set the halfway point. Make it about 2¾" high. Apply a 2 pt black stroke.

4. With the shape selected, choose the Reflect tool in the Toolbox. -click at the bottom of the shape near the anchor point on the ruler guide to display the Reflect dialog box. Click the Vertical Axis radio button, then click the Copy button.

5. With the Direct Lasso tool, circle the two center anchor points at the top of the shape. Choose Object ⇨ Path ⇨ Average ⇨ Both, then choose Object ⇨ Path ⇨ Join ⇨ Smooth. Click OK or press *return/enter*.

6. Repeat #5 for the bottom center anchor points to make the object a closed path, except select Corner in the Join dialog box. Apply a White fill.

7. With the Line Segment tool, hold the *Shift* key down and draw two the stripes. Choose Object ⇨ Path ⇨ Outline Stroke and adjust to fit the curve of the bowling pin. Color them red.

8. To draw the bowling ball, draw a circle about half the size of the bowling pin and fill it with 100% black. Draw three small white ovals and position them for the finger holes, as shown.

9. Group the paths that created the bowling ball, then move them into position next to the bowling pin, as shown.

10. Select all the paths in the design and move the design to the scratch area outside the page.

11. Save your file.

Create the Graph

12. Draw a 7" × 6" Line graph in the center of the page. Makes sure values in Axis dialog boxes are default values.

13. Enter the following data in the Graph Data window:

	Don	Vivian	Elaine	Joe	Mike
Oct 12	208.00	154.00	98.00	120.00	177.00
Oct 19	214.00	158.00	84.00	122.00	182.00
Oct 26	202.00	172.00	94.00	140.00	226.00
Nov 2	182.00	160.00	96.00	134.00	212.00
Nov 9	198.00	176.00	88.00	112.00	220.00
Nov 16	220.00	157.00	92.00	114.00	188.00

14. Click the Apply button, then close the Graph Data window or move it out of the way so you can see the graph easily.

15. With the Direct Selection tool, select the legend, design and text, and drag them to the right so they're away from the right axis.

16. Select the graph, then double-click the graph tool in the Toolbox to display the Graph Type dialog box. In the Style Section, only the First Column in Front checkbox should be checked. In the Options section, all checkboxes should be checked except Edge-to-Edge Lines. Enter 3 in the Line Width field.

17. With the Group Selection tool, select each set of data, including the legend, and apply a different color to each set of data.

18. With the Selection tool, select the entire graph.

19. In the Value Axis pop-up menu, change the selection to Both Sides.

20. Choose Left Axis in the Graph Options pop-up menu and click the Override Calculated Values checkbox to make the options available.

21. Enter 0 in the Min field, 300 in the Max field, and 6 in the Divisions field. Leave the Length pop-up menu on Short, and enter 5 in the Draw [ ] tick marks per division field.

22. Without clicking the OK button display the Category Axis dialog box, and change the Length option to Full Width. *Continued*

23. Click OK or press *return/enter*.

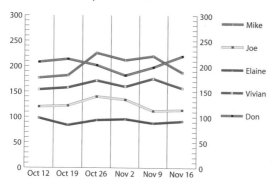

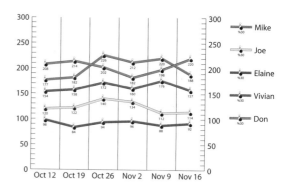

24. Save your file.

25. Near the bowling pin and ball design that you drew earlier, draw a ½" square. Change the fill and stroke attributes to None.

26. Scale the design down until it's about 3 times the size of the rectangle. Then position its center point over the rectangle.

27. Send the rectangle to the back of the stack.

28. Choose the Type tool in the Toolbox. Click below the design and type %30.

29. Change the size of the type to 48 point.

30. With the Selection tool, select all the objects, including the rectangle and the type.

31. Choose Object ➪ Graph ➪ Design to display the Graph Design dialog box. Click the New Design button, then click the Rename button. Type the name, Bowling ball/pin, in the Rename field and click OK or press *return/enter*.

32. Click OK or press *return/enter* to exit the Graph Design dialog box.

33. With the Selection tool, select the entire graph. Choose Object ➪ Graph ➪ Marker to display the Graph Marker dialog box.

34. Highlight the Bowling ball/pin design in the window and click OK or press *return/enter*.

35. With the Direct Selection too, *Shift*-click the interior vertical tick marks and change them to 50% black.

36. Using the Direct Selection tool, select all the type except the type on the markers. Change the size of the type to 18 pt.

37. Because the type was reduced in size, the labels aren't exactly centered on their tick marks. Using the Direct Selection tool, select the type on both value axes and move it up slightly.

   ■ Hold down the *Shift* key when you move the type so it is constrained to move vertically, or press the Up arrow key (↑).

38. With the Direct Selection tool, select the tick mark on the left Value Axis for the 300 value. Hold the *Shift* key down to keep the movement horizontal, and align the left end of the tick mark with the vertical rule so it's perfectly square. Then, still with the *Shift* key down, drag the right end across the graph to the vertical rule that is the right axis. A short tick mark is already there, so just cover it up.

39. Select the short tick mark that you covered up and drag it away from the graph so it won't print.

   ■ You can't delete it without ungrouping the graph.

40. Drag the other tick marks that correspond with a label across to the right axis. Apply a 50% black color to the interior tick marks but not to the lines for 0 or 300 (leave them 100%). Then drag off the short tick marks that are no longer necessary.

Continued

41. With the Direct Selection tool, select the legend (text and design), and position them below the graph (see the graph below).

42. With the Direct Selection tool, select the %30 below the design in the each legend and move it off the page so it won't print.

- Your graph should look like the one shown below.

43. Save the file, print it, and close the document.

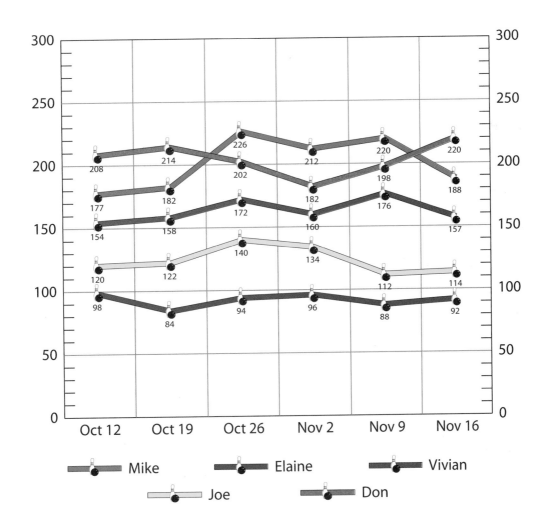

EXERCISE 13-1 — 3-Dimensional Pie Graph

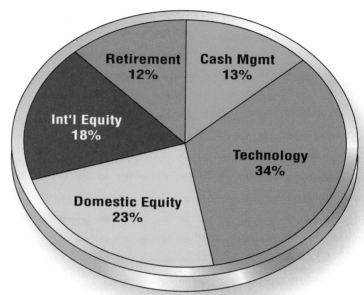

Draw a 3-D pie graph with drop shadow similar to the one shown here. Choose your own fill colors for the wedges. Use the following data.

Retirement   18%
Cash Management   11%
Technology   38%
Domestic Equity   21%
International Equity   12%

EXERCISE 13-2 — Monthly Expenses

Use the following data to prepare a graph showing how expenses compare to each other, and prepare a graph showing the trend of the expenses throughout the year.

Monthly Expenses

	Jan	Feb	Mar	Apr	May	June	July	Aug	Sept	Oct	Nov	Dec
Housing	$1016	$1016	$1016	$1016	$1016	$1016	$1016	$980	$980	$980	$980	$1080
Groceries	316	282	345	367	378	392	404	388	367	389	401	414
Utilities	282	276	245	174	101	74	64	69	112	143	148	179
Transportation	96	86	94	101	97	106	244	174	113	121	99	87
Entertainment	66	73	86	79	93	118	465	329	74	96	53	358
Miscellaneous	214	206	215	194	183	235	402	383	191	247	238	973
TOTAL	$1990	$1939	$2001	$1931	$1868	$1941	$2595	$2323	$1837	$1976	$1919	$3091

Web Graphics

Chapter Outline

- File Format
- File Size
- Color
- Working with Bitmap Images
- Save for Web Window
- JPEG Images
- GIF Images

- PNG Images
- SVG Images
- SWF Images (Flash)
- Slicing for Web Images

Illustrator 10 has expanded features for creating and preparing graphic images for use in Web browsers. A discussion solely of Web-based graphics would require an entire separate volume. Here, we'll provide the basics you need to know before creating graphics for use on the Web.

Web graphic images have different requirements than those for print. You are limited with Web-based graphics because their display is dependent on Web browsers as well as the limited resolution of a computer screen. File format, file size, and color are important characteristics to consider when you are creating graphics for Web use.

File Format

The most common file formats used are pixel-based, bitmap images — JPEG, GIF, and, to a lesser extent, PNG. Some older Web browser versions do not support PNG, however. Web browsers can also display artwork you create and save in vector formats such as SVG and SWF (SWF is a format developed by Macromedia® Flash™).

Bitmap images generally have mediocre resolution and more time is required to download an image when compared to vector-based artwork, such as SVG and SWF. Also, a Web user can magnify vector-based artwork without losing sharpness or detail.

- Learn more about JPEG, GIF, and PNG, SVG graphics, and SWF graphics later in this chapter.

SVG can be used only with XML Web publishing tools.

File Size

The time required to download Web pages, including its graphic images, depends upon the total size of the file. The larger the file size, the longer it takes to download. And long download times frustrate users.

- Download time is calculated from the image size and the download rate. Choose a download rate in the Preview Menu. Image size depends upon a variety of factors you select from the file format settings.

Color

Most computer screens display about 72 dots per inch (dpi) and *every* computer screen displays color differently. The way a color appears on one screen will look slightly different on another screen. You can create graphics with RGB (16 million colors), although some computers may additionally alter the color. To be "safe," you can specify Web-safe colors from Illustrator's color palette.

Working with Bitmap Images

When artwork you create is for display on the Web, create them as you normally would, except create them in RGB color mode rather than CMYK. Then export them as GIF, JPEG, or PNG, using the Save for Web feature in Illustrator. Illustrator can output artwork in many file formats, so we'll discuss only the most common and currently used formats on the Web.

Before we get started, there are some common features or tools you should know about when creating Web graphics, regardless of file format.

- **Dithering** — Mixing two palette colors to create a third, somewhere in between the two original colors. The purpose of dithering is to make an image appear to have a wider range of colors and shades, which is great for photographs or continuous-tone images. Creating a third color not only increases file size, but it can make the image look "grainy," especially when you have a continuous-tone image.

- **Color depth** — Making colors appear duller in bitmap graphics to reduce file size and ultimately, download time. Reducing color depth also may dither hard edges. Before reducing the color depth, evaluate the resulting image by previewing it at 100%.

- **Optimization** — A software process that manipulates file format, colors used, and file size to reduce the sum total of the file and decrease download time.

- **Compression** — A software process to reduce and compact a file to reduce the file size. GIF, JPEG, and PNG file formats use different methods of compression.

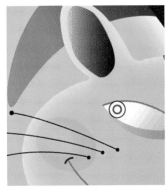

Pixel preview off

- **Anti-aliasing** — Blending the edge of a darker object with that of its background to smooth the transition between the colors or shapes. For a black line that is anti-aliased against a white background, progressively colorized pixels (gray, in this case) are added along the edge of the black line, creating a "halo" to reduce the jagged appearance of the line.

- **Web-safe colors** — The 216 colors used by all Web browsers. If it's important that all Web browsers display a color in an image in only *one way*, and *not* with inconsistent variations in that color. Be sure to use Illustrator's Web-safe color palette.

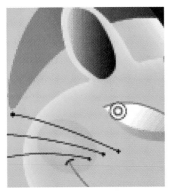

Pixel preview on

While you're creating artwork in Illustrator that will become part of a Web site, you can get a fair idea of how the artwork will display. Open your artwork file and choose **View ➪ Pixel Preview**. Illustrator *rasterizes* the image (turns lines into pixels) and snaps it to a 72 dpi grid. You can see how converting to a pixel view anti-aliases the edges of the artwork. You may see edges that you want to adjust, and you can move the image or parts of the image to improve its appearance.

Save For Web Window

Once you create artwork in Illustrator, you can convert the artwork to a file format that is compatible with Web browsers. After creating your artwork, choose **File ➪ Save For Web**. The preview area of the dialog box displays the image to convert, plus the active tools to manipulate the image for Web use (Figure 14.1).

- **Preview menu** — The Preview menu lets you change the download rate of the image (download rates are modem rate settings). Illustrator uses these

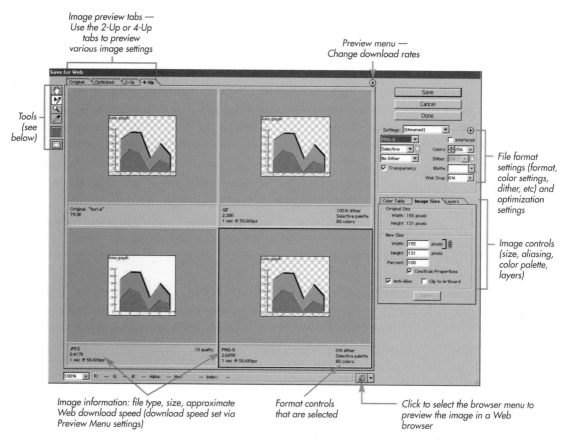

FIGURE 14.1 Manipulate an image for web use in the Save For Web window.

settings to calculate the time required to download an image. Most Web users now have modems that are 56k (56.6 Kbps) or faster.

- **Image preview tabs** — You can display only the original image, a single optimized image, the original image and one copy (2-up), or the original image and three copies (4-up). By having the image displayed four times you can compare various settings applied to the image.

- **Image information** — In the lower left corner of each Save For Web preview window, Illustrator displays current information for the image: image file type (GIF, JPEG, etc.) file size, and download time and rate.

- **Format controls selected** — In the lower right corner of each Save For Web image window, Illustrator displays the format controls you have selected for the image.

- **Select browser menu** — If a Web browser is installed on your computer, you can preview the image you've created.

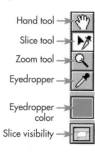

Hand tool
Slice tool
Zoom tool
Eyedropper
Eyedropper color
Slice visibility

Tools available in the Save for Web dialog box

File Format Settings

You control various output formats of the files you create. These settings include file format (GIF, JPEG, etc.), color controls, transparency, matte, dither, and other file-specific controls. Different file types display different settings in this control section (Figure 14.2). See File Format and Image Control settings for GIF, JPEG, PNG, and SVG later in this chapter.

You can also "capture" custom file format settings that you want to use over and over (Figure 14.3):

1. Create your custom settings.

2. Click on the Settings button and select "Unnamed".

3. Click on the Optimize Menu and select Save Settings.

4. Save the settings with a unique setting file name. The settings and name are saved and you can get them again by choosing the Settings button and selecting the settings file you just created.

Image Controls

In the image control section, you can change the color table used, image size, and layers you want to use. See File Format and Image Control settings for GIF, JPEG, PNG, and SVG later in this chapter.

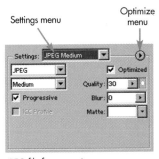

JPEG file format settings

GIF file format settings (PNG settings are the same as GIF control settings)

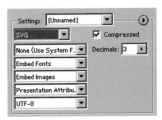

SVG file format settings

FIGURE 14.2 File format settings.

1. Create custom settings to use again, then select "Unnamed."

2. Click on the Optimize Menu button and select Save Settings.

3. Save settings with a unique setting name. The setting name is then available to use again without re-creating custom settings.

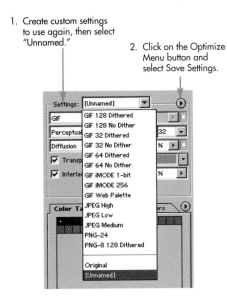

FIGURE 14.3 Custom file format settings.

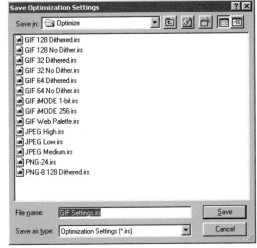

JPEG Images

JPEG (Joint Photographic Experts Group) is probably the most popular format currently used on the Web. It is a high-compression format and images can display with up to 16 million colors (24 bit). JPEG compression is *lossy* — when you compress a JPEG file, image data is lost because the format creates "blocks" of similar, surrounding colors or unneeded colors, or reduces detail to achieve high compression. Each time a JPEG image is opened, it's compressed. Eventually, the image quality is degraded and it appears fuzzy. It's recommended that you work with the image in a lossless format (AI, TIFF, PSD, etc.) while you are making changes or modifications, and when you're finished, save it as a JPEG file.

JPEG may not be the best choice for high-detail images with large areas of solid color and sharp lines, flat-color images, or type. Generally speaking, use the JPEG format if your image has continuous tones or if the original image is a digital photograph.

JPEG File Format Settings

With JPEG file settings, you control the quality of the image and *optimize* the file with regard to file size, image quality, and other settings (Figure 14.4). You can select the settings you desire and then save the settings with a setting name you choose. This can be very useful if you are creating a large number of files and want to reuse settings rather than remembering how to re-create them.

- **Settings menu** — Select a file type and format (low, medium, etc.). The file type displays in the "file type selected and quality" menu.

- **File type selected and quality** — Displays the format and the JPEG compression "quality" of the file: low = low compression (higher-quality image, larger file size) to maximum compression (lower-quality image, smaller file size).

- **Progressive** — The image displays progressively in the Web browser. Rather than Web users waiting until the entire image downloads, they see a low-resolution image progressively display while the image is downloading.

- **ICC Profile** — This setting is not available unless you are working with an image with an ICC profile for color management (some Web browsers use ICC profiles for color correction).

- **Display Optimize menu** — From the Optimize menu, you can save settings (quality, blur, matte, etc.) or delete settings that you've saved, or you can optimize the file to a specific size.

- **Quality** — The Quality setting works in conjunction with the JPEG quality compression setting. When the Quality setting is High, the JPEG compression algorithm saves image detail (and does not reduce file size). When the Quality setting is Low, image detail and file size are reduced.

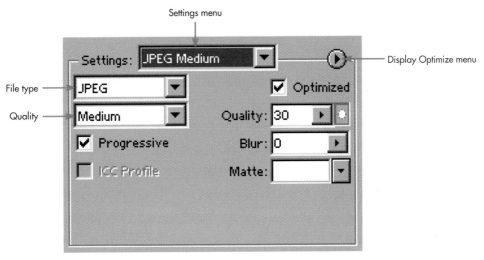

FIGURE 14.4 JPEG file format settings.

- **Blur** — This setting applies Gaussian blur to the image. Using a setting greater than 0.5 is not recommended.

- **Matte** — You can select a fill color for pixels in the original image that are transparent. You can choose none, black, white, a color selected using the eye-dropper, or a custom color from the Color Picker.

JPEG Image Control Settings

JPEG does not have a color table available because it is a continuous tone image. You can, however, change settings for the image size and the layers produced.

Image Size The image size window displays the current image size. You can change the image size.

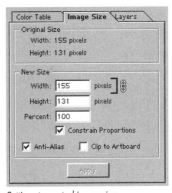

Settings to control image size

- **Constrain Proportions** — When selected and you change the width, height, or percent, the image increases proportionally in the other dimension. When deselected, the image does not change proportionally in the other dimensions.

- **Anti-Alias** — Use anti-alias to add or remove jagged or blurry edges from an image.

- **Clip to Artboard** — The clipping boundary is set to the artboard dimensions and exports the entire artboard. Any artwork outside the boundaries of the artboard are clipped off.

Settings to control layers

651

Layers A CSS (cascading style sheet) layer is an HTML (Hypertext Markup Language) element that has an absolute position and it can overlap other elements of a Web page. You can generate CSS layers from your image to put in a resulting HTML file. Selecting Visible creates a visible layer, Hidden hides the layer, and Do Not Export prevents the layer from being exported to an HTML file.

GIF Images

GIF (CompuServe's Graphics Interchange Format) is another high-compression image file format. It contains no more than 256 colors, but it's still a good choice for images that contain type or images that have large areas of consistent colors or gradients. Also, it's easy to create and preserve transparent areas or color in an image.

When you create images with Illustrator, you frequently use a variety of all available colors to produce the most appealing image. However, when you create images that will end up as GIF files, you should consider the relatively limited colors available for this format. You can use the Color Table to choose a color reduction to the 256-color format of GIF or to convert custom colors to Web-safe colors. If you use colors that are not in the 256-color range, the GIF format dithers them to intermix color pixels to simulate an approximate color.

To prevent unwanted dithering, use Illustrator's optimization feature or Web-Snap, which "snaps" a color to the closest approximate Web-safe color.

GIF and PNG-8 File Format Settings

Although GIF and PNG-8 files formats are different, the settings are the same, primarily because both are good formats that can successfully reduce the number of colors in a file while maintaining image quality. For information on PNG-24 format settings, see PNG-24 File Format Settings later in this chapter.

With the GIF and PNG-8 file settings (Figure 14.5), you control the quality of the image and *optimize* the file with regard to file size, image quality, and other settings. You can select the settings you desire and then save the settings with a setting name you choose. This can be very useful if you are creating a large number of files and want to reuse settings rather than remembering how to re-create them.

- **Settings menu** — GIF has several settings for 128-, 64-, and 32-bit color including dithering and no dithering. You can also select iMODE 1-bit and the 256 GIF color settings. PNG-8 has only a 128-color dithered pattern. For GIF, choose a dithered format if you have colors that might not be available in the Web-safe palette (dithering simulates unavailable colors). Also, note that dithered images usually have a larger file size.

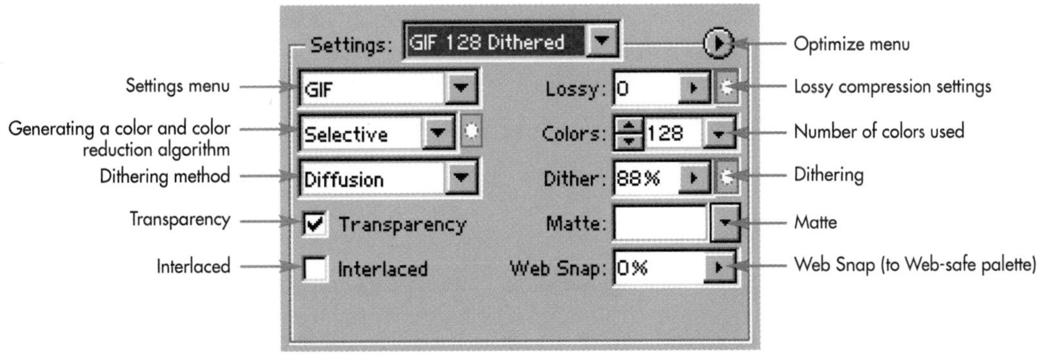
Settings: GIF 128 Dithered
Optimize menu
Settings menu
GIF
Lossy: 0
Lossy compression settings
Generating a color and color reduction algorithm
Selective
Colors: 128
Number of colors used
Dithering method
Diffusion
Dither: 88%
Dithering
Transparency
Transparency
Matte:
Matte
Interlaced
Interlaced
Web Snap: 0%
Web Snap (to Web-safe palette)

FIGURE 14.5 GIF and PNG-8 file format settings.

- **Generating a color reduction table and algorithms** — Illustrator generates a color table for images based on color options you choose for optimization. The color tables available are:
  - **Perceptual** — Creates a custom color table based on colors used in the image. It also gives priority to the color perception of the eye.
  - **Selective** — Similar to the perceptual table, but favors Web-safe colors.
  - **Adaptive** — Builds a custom color table by sampling colors used in the image.
  - **Web** — Determines the number of colors in the color table based on the frequency of colors in the image.
- **Dithering method** — If you have images with continuous-tone color and color gradient, you may need dithering to prevent color banding. Choose No Dither or select one of the following options from the Dithering Method menu:
  - **Diffusion** — Applies a random pattern that is usually less visible than Pattern dither. Dither effects are diffused across adjacent image pixels.
  - **Pattern** — Applies a halftone-like square pattern to simulate any colors not in the color table.
  - **Noise** — Applies a random pattern similar to the Diffusion dither method, but without diffusing the pattern across adjacent pixels (no seams appear with the Noise dither method).
- **Transparency** — If your original image has a transparent color, you can save this or change it for your Web-based bitmap image. If you have an image with "hard" edges, select Transparency, then select None on the Matte submenu. Doing so will reduce or eliminate the pixelation of the hard edge against a transparent color.

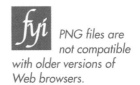

fyi *PNG files are not compatible with older versions of Web browsers.*

- **Interlaced** — Select Interlaced if you want the image to display in successive detail as the image downloads. If you do not want successive detail displayed during the download, the Web user has to wait for the entire image to download before it displays.

- **Optimize menu** — From the Optimize menu, you can save settings (color reduction, transparency, compressions settings, etc.), delete settings you've saved, or optimize the file to a specific size.

- **Lossy compression settings** — Moving the slider changes the compression algorithm to eliminate pixels from the image, which further reduces file size. The Lossy option does not work with the Interlaced, Noise, or Pattern Dither algorithms.

- **Colors used** — Manually reduce the number of colors (128, 64, etc.) and dither or undither the image.

- **Dither** — Percentage of dithering, add noise or a pattern.

- **Matte** — Set the Matte background to the color of the Web page, the color in the eyedropper, or a custom color.

- **Web Snap** — Shift image colors to the nearest color in the Web-safe palette (a higher number increases the number of colors shifted).

GIF and PNG-8 Image Controls

Decreasing colors for GIF images affects optimization including the download time and image appearance. You have several color table options (reduction algorithms) to help you make the best choices for GIF output.

Color Table Palette Menu You can choose precise colors or other color palettes with the Color Table palette menu. You can also "lock" the colors so they are not altered by changes to file format settings. To open the menu, click on the Color Table Palette Menu button (⊙). You have the following options:

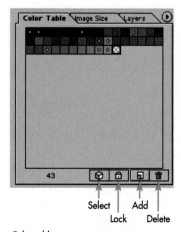

Color table

- Choose not to sort the color table at all, or choose to sort the color table by hue, luminance, or popularity.

- Add new colors using the eyedropper tool, select only Web-safe colors or non-Web safe colors, and lock or unlock the colors. If you already have 256 colors in the color table, you cannot add colors.

- Save the current color table as a file that you can access later or use a different color table.

- You can also edit a color: double-click on a color in the color table to display the Color Picker.

654

Image Size The image size window displays the current image size. You can change the image size.

- **Constrain Proportions** — When selected and you change the width, height, or percentage, the image increases proportionally in the other dimension. When deselected, the image does not change in the other dimensions.

- **Anti-Alias** — Use anti-alias to add or remove jagged or blurry edges from an image.

- **Clip to Artboard** — Sets the clipping boundary to the artboard and exports the entire artboard. Any artwork outside the artboard boundaries is clipped off.

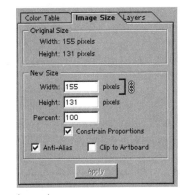

Image size

CSS Layer A CSS (cascading style sheet) layer is an HTML element that has an absolute position and it can overlap other elements of a Web page. You can generate CSS layers from your image to put in a resulting HTML file. Selecting Visible creates a visible layer, Hidden hides the layer, and Do Not Export prevents the layer from being exported to an HTML file.

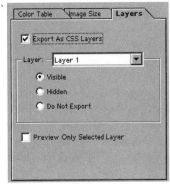

Layers

PNG Images

PNG (Portable Network Graphics) combines the advantages of GIF and JPEG — small file size, excellent compression, up to 36-bit color and clean background transparency, but currently has one disadvantage in that it is not currently supported by all versions of Web browsers.

There are two PNG file types: PNG-8 and PNG-24. PNG-8 files are smaller and you can adjust color output, dithering, and matte settings. PNG-24 files provide a high-quality image, but the file size is larger than PNG-8 and is usually larger than JPEG. Also, they can save up to 256 transparency levels. See GIF and PNG-8 File Format Settings earlier in this chapter, for information on PNG-8 options.

PNG-24 File Format Settings

The PNG-24 file format works well for compressing continuous-tone images, similar to the JPEG file format. The file size of PNG-24 images is usually larger than JPEG images, though. PNG-24 can preserve up to 256 levels of transparency in an image.

- **Transparency** — If you want to produce a multi-level transparency, select this checkbox and None from the Matte menu.

- **Optimize Menu** — From the Optimize menu, you can save settings (color reduction, transparency, compressions settings, etc.), or delete settings you've saved, or optimize the file to a specific size.

- **Interlaced** — Select Interlaced if you want the image to display in successive detail as the image downloads. If you do not want successive detail displayed during the download, you have to wait for the entire image to download before it displays.

- **Matte** — Set the Matte background to the color of the Web page, the color in the eyedropper, or a custom color.

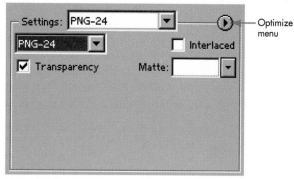

PNG-24 file format settings

PNG-24 Image Control Settings

PNG-24 does not have a color table available because it is a continuous tone image, similar to the JPEG file format. You can change settings for the image size and layers produced.

Image Size The image size window displays the current image size. You can also change the image size.

- **Constrain Proportions** — When selected and you change the width, height, or percentage, the image increases proportionally in the other dimension. When deselected, the image does not change proportionally in the other dimensions.

- **Anti-Alias** — Use anti-alias to add or remove jagged or blurry edges from an image.

- **Clip to Artboard** — Sets the clipping boundary to the artboard and exports the entire artboard. Any artwork outside the artboard boundaries is clipped off.

Settings to control image size

Layers A CSS (cascading style sheet) layer is an HTML element that has an absolute position, and it can overlap other elements of a Web page. You can generate CSS layers from your image to put in a resulting HTML file. Selecting Visible creates a visible layer, Hidden hides the layer, and Do Not Export prevents the layer from being exported to an HTML file.

Settings to control layers

656

SVG Images

SVG (Scalable Vector Graphics) is a vector graphic file that is becoming more common now that Web browsers are capable of viewing this type of file. With Illustrator 10, SVG is a "native" file format and Illustrator can open and save SVG files.

A Web user can zoom-in on an SVG image without losing image quality, clarity, or color appearance. Zooming-in would be useful for Web users with limited vision, to show greater detail of a product, or to help the Web user visualize a complex process or procedure.

Older Web browsers may not have the software installed to view SVG files and the Web user may have to download a program for viewing them. In the future, SVG software will likely be included in all Web browsers. SVG can be used only in XML-based Web documents (technically, SVG files *are* XML documents), with JavaScript files, and cascading style sheets (CSS).

Illustrator can also create SVGZ files — a compressed SVG file. SVGZ files are typically half the size of SVG files, but you can't edit these files with an XML text editor.

SVG Considerations

Before you create an SVG image with Illustrator, consider the following:

- If you use Illustrator filter effects such as rasterize, artistic, blur, etc., in the original Illustrator image, they will become rasterized in the SVG output and they cannot be edited like other SVG elements. Use SVG filter effects (**Effect ➪ SVG Filters**) for such effects to avoid undesired rasterization.

- Use only one transparency setting for each object.

- You can import a bitmap image in an SVG image. Imported images that do not have an alpha channel convert to JPEG; images with an alpha channel convert to PNG.

- Image layers become grouped elements, nested layers become nested group elements, and hidden layers are saved with the SVG styling property called "display:none".

- Mesh objects created in Illustrator are rasterized.

Optimizing SVG Images

SVG files are, in essence, XML-based documents and therefore, the output options are different than bitmap graphic output options. Use the Document Raster Effect Settings (**Effects ➪ Document Raster Effects**) if you want to alter the image resolution (72 dpi and higher). See Figure 14.6 for settings to optimize SVG images.

- **Select SVG** — SVG is not set from the Settings Menu; select SVG from the menu just below the Settings menu.

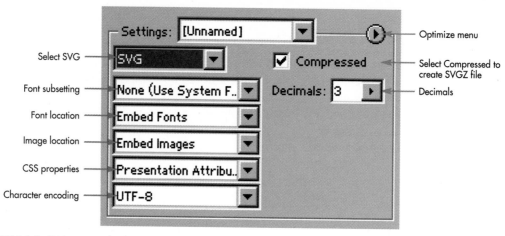

FIGURE 14.6 SVG settings for optimizing images.

■ **Font Subsetting** — Choices are basically None (use computer's fonts), Use glyphs (include glyphs used in the image), or allow for dynamic text content such as server-garnered text or user-interactive text (common English, Roman, other glyphs). Use Select All Glyphs to include the entire font set with the image. While this increases file size, the Web user will see the image type as you created it.

· Use None if your Web user's computer has the same font used in the image.

■ **Font location** — Selecting Embed Fonts increases file size but ensures that the Web user will see the image as you created it. Use Link Fonts if you have other SVG image files that share the same fonts — you will only have to link to the fonts rather than including them in the image file.

■ **Image location** — Embedding the image within the file increases file size or links to an image in another location or to an SVG image file.

■ **CSS properties** — Sets style attributes in the SVG code. Presentation Attributes applies properties at the highest point in the hierarchy; Style Attributes creates the most "readable file" but increases file size; Entity References make file transfer faster and reduces file size; Style Element is used for HTML shared files.

■ **Character encoding** — Choose how characters are encoded in the SVG file. UTF is used by all XML processors. UTF-8 and UTF-16 are 8- and 16-bit formats, respectively. If you are concerned with metadata, do not use ISO 8859-1 or UTF-16.

■ **Decimal** — Reduces the vector quality to reduce file size.

■ **Optimize menu** — From the Optimize menu, you can save settings (color reduction, transparency, compressions settings, etc.), delete settings you've saved, or optimize the file to a specific size.

Apply an SVG Filter to an Image

Use the SVG filter to apply filter effects to an object.

1. Select an object or part of an object, then select **Effect** ➪ **SVG Filters** ➪ **Apply SVG Filter**.

2. The Apply SVG Filter dialog box displays (Figure 14.7) and you can select from the available filters. Check the Preview checkbox to see the filter effect on the image.

3. Select a filter and click OK. If you want to see the results, click the Preview checkbox.

You can add or edit the SVG filters. Check the Internet for downloadable filters, or if you wish to edit filters, see the *Adobe Illustrator 10 User's Guide*. You should be familiar with the JavaScript programming language if you want to create or edit SVG filters.

Saving Illustrator Images in SVG Format

1. Open an Illustrator image. If you desire, apply any SVG filters (**Effect** ➪ **SVG Filters**) to the image.

2. Select **File** ➪ **Save As Web**. Under the Settings menu, select SVG.

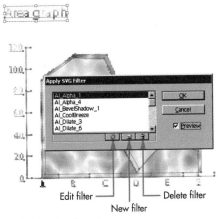

Edit filter — New filter — Delete filter

Apply SVG Filter dialog box

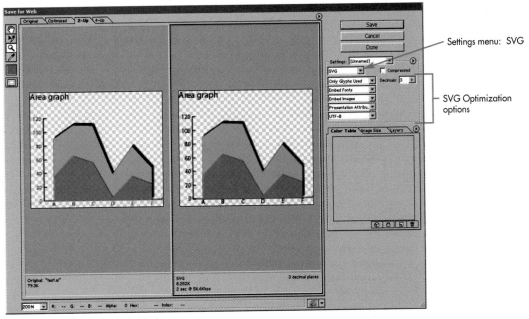

Settings menu: SVG

SVG Optimization options

FIGURE 14.7 SVG filter dialog box.

SWF Images (Flash)

If you create animation frames with Illustrator, you can save and export the layers for use with Macromedia's Flash program that uses the extension SWF (ShockWave format). SWF, like SVG, is a vector-based format that provides better clarity and scalability. Also, if you make each animation frame a Symbol, so that each Symbol is contained only one time in the SWF file, you can reduce the size of the animation file.

SWF Considerations

- Flatten the transparency before exporting to SWF to maintain the effect (blending modes and opacity masks cannot be exported).

- Place each animation frame on a separate layer, and select **AI Layers to SWF Frames** when exporting.

- Gradients with fewer than eight stops are exported as gradients. Mesh objects and gradients with more than eight stops are rasterized and will appear as bitmap-filled shapes.

- Patterns are rasterized into small images and retain the size of the pattern art. The patterns are tiled to fill the art.

- Fonts with beveled or square caps and joins are converted to round caps when they are exported to SWF.

- Some font information (leading, kerning, and tracking) is broken up into SWF records to simulate the look of leading. To export text as paths, convert the text to outlines before exporting (**Type ➪ Create Outlines**).

To create SWF files, you *export* the series of images as SWF rather than using the Save for Web feature.

1. Open the image or images you want to convert to SWF.

2. Select **File ➪ Export**, and select SWF as the file type. The SWF Format Options dialog box displays.

Export Options (Figure 14.8)

- **Export As** —The pop-up submenu offers three options for exporting the artwork:
  - **AI File to SWF File** — Export to one frame; this preserves layer clipping masks.
  - **AI Layers to SWF Frames** — Export each layer to a separate SWF *frame*, This creates an animated SWF.
  - **AI Layers to SWF Files** — Export each layer to a separate SWF *file*. This creates multiple SWF files, each containing a single frame with the artwork from a single Illustrator layer.

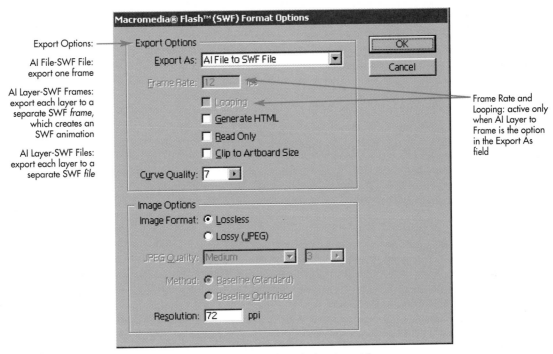

Export Options:

AI File-SWF File:
export one frame

AI Layer-SWF Frames:
export each layer to a
separate SWF *frame*,
which creates an
SWF animation

AI Layer-SWF Files:
export each layer to a
separate SWF *file*

Frame Rate and
Looping: active only
when AI Layer to
Frame is the option
in the Export As
field

FIGURE 14.8 Options for exporting artwork in Macromedia® Flash™ (SWF) format.

- **Frame Rate** — Frame Rate is active only when you select **AI Layers to SWF Frames**. This option specifies the animation player's animation rate.

- **Looping** — Looping is active only when you select **AI Layers to SWF Frames**. The animation will loop continuously.

- **Generate HTML** — Generates HTML code for the SWF file. This option includes the SWF file in a Web page, and the generated HTML file is saved to the same location as the SWF file.

- **Read Only** — Prevents the Web user from modifying the SWF file.

- **Clip to Artboard Size** — Exports the entire artboard and any artwork within its borders to the SWF file (artwork outside the artboard boundaries is clipped).

- **Curve Quality** — Determines Bézier curve accuracy. This also affects the output file size (a low number reduces quality and file size).

Image Options

- **Image Format** — Sets the image compression. Lossless results in high image quality and a larger file size. Lossy (JPEG) compression makes the resulting SWF file smaller but creates image artifacts.

fyi *Use Lossless if you have more work to do on the file(s) in Macromedia Flash; if you're done modifying the image, select Lossy.*

661

- **JPEG Quality** — Compression settings are low to maximum and these JPEG settings are available only if you select Lossy compression. This retains the accuracy of detail in the image. Higher quality has a better resulting image and a larger file size.

- **Method** — Available only if you select Lossy compression. Specifies the JPEG compression standard (high, medium, low, maximum).

- **Resolution** — Sets bitmap screen resolution for bitmap images (72 to 2400 ppi). High resolution means better image quality and large file sizes.

3. Set additional options, and click OK.

activity 14.1

1. Open the Flower.ai located in the Sample Art folder inside the Sample Files folder in the Adobe Illustrator 10 folder on your hard drive. Or open a file you've created in Illustrator and saved into your Practice folder.

2. Choose File ➪ Save for Web to display the Save for Web dialog box.

3. Click the 4 Up tab at the top of the window.

   - We'll apply different formats and settings for each of the four windows so you can see how changes in the settings affect the different formats.

4. Using the Hand tool, select the image in the upper right corner. In the Settings pop-up submenu, select GIF 64 No Dither from the file formats.

5. Select the image in the lower left corner. In the Settings pop-up submenu, choose JPEG Medium from the file formats.

6. Select the image in the lower right corner. In the Settings pop-up submenu, select PNG-8 from the file formats.

   - In the image information area of the file format section of each image window notice the file size and the download rates for each image.

   - The GIF image has the smallest file size, the shortest download time and the PNG-8 is the largest file size and the longest download time.

While the image quality is similar between all images, the GIF file will download faster than the other images.

7. Change the GIF image setting to GIF 128 No Dither and check the image information area.

   - Note that the file size increased and the download time increased. While you will have a better image quality, the Web user will have to wait longer for it to download.

8. Select the Preview Menu button and change it to the 1.5 Mbps (Mbps is megabits per second) and check the image information area of all images.

   - Note how much the download time decreases. If all of your Web users have such a download rate, the images will appear very quickly (this download rate is comparable to DSL or T1 line capabilities). Currently, most Web users are connected to the Internet with a standard telephone line and a 56 K modem. Your best estimate of their Web experience will be selecting the 56.6 Kbps download rate.

9. Select the Interlaced checkbox and notice that the Settings name goes from GIF 128 No Dither to "Unnamed".

   - It is unnamed because "interlaced" is not the standard setting provided by Illustrator for GIF 128 No Dither format. But if you have to

Continued

convert many Illustrator images, in this example as GIF 128 No Dither with interlacing, you can save this setting, give it a name, and then have that setting name available for all the other images you may need to make. This is also true if for all the other file formats (JPEG, PNG, etc.).

10. Select the Image Size tab (under the file format settings).

11. Under New Size, change the percent reading to 50% and click *Apply*.

   ■ Again, note that the file size changes (it gets smaller) and the download time decreases. Also note that when you change the Percent value, all images in the Save for Web window are affected.

12. With the hand tool, click on the JPEG format image.

13. Click on the Select Browser button at the bottom of the window.

   ■ This starts your Web browser and the JPEG image appears in the browser.

   ■ If you have light and dark interfaces in the image, note if they appear jagged.

14. Go back to the JPEG image in the Save for Web window.

15. Under New Size, make sure the Anti-Alias box is checked, then click Apply.

   ■ You may notice that anti-aliasing softens the dark/light interfaces in the image.

16. Click on the Select Browser button. This "loads" the image in the Web browser again. Check the light/dark interface areas and note how the anti-aliasing has softened the light/dark interfaces.

17. Return to the Save for Web window. Select the image in the upper right corner and apply the JPEG High format to it; in the lower left image, apply the JPEG Medium format; in the lower right image, apply the JPEG Low format.

   ■ Compare the three images (you may need to magnify the image with the Zoom tool). The JPEG High format has better image quality and larger file size than the JPEG Low format.

By using the Save for Web 4-Up you can decide which image best balances the image quality and file size.

18. Use the Hand tool to select the upper right image. Change the format to GIF 128 Dithered.

19. Click on the Color Table tab below the image format settings.

   ■ Note the number of colors available in the color table.

20. In the image format area, change the file format to GIF 32 Dithered and note the Color Table.

   ■ Because the GIF 32 Dithered is a lower quality image, you have fewer colors available (and also a smaller file size).

21. Click on the Web Snap button and move the slider (default is 0%) to 50% and watch the image.

   ■ As you change the number of colors to snap to the Web-safe palette, the image quality, available colors in the Color Table, and file size changes. Here, you can balance image quality and file size.

22. Double click on one of the colors in the Color Table and the Color Picker displays.

   ■ Here is where you can edit or change a color used in the output image. Note that this will not alter your original Illustrator image, only the resulting output image file.

23. If the Transparency checkbox is checked, click in it to have "no transparency".

24. Click on the Matte button and play with the background Matte. Choose, white, black, and also the Eyedropper Color.

25. Alter the Eyedropper color by double-clicking on the Eyedropper Palette (tools on left side of the screen). The color picker displays and you can change the Eyedropper color and then apply it to the image Matte.

26. Experiment with various settings until you're familiar with the commands. When you're finished, click the Cancel button in the Save for Web dialog box, then close the artwork window without saving changes.

Slicing for Web Images

Some images you create may consist of vectors, text, and an imported bitmap image. You can "slice" areas of an image, text, or layer, and save them as elements of a Web page. A slice can therefore be imagined as a way to section elements of an image that are separate from the rest of the image, which you can export in different file formats and optimization settings for a Web image. A separate file is exported for each slice and if you like, you can edit slices in Adobe Photoshop or Adobe ImageReady.

fyi   *Illustrator generates automatic slices as an HTML table when you save the slices to a Web page.*

You can view the slices in the regular artboard as well as in the Save for Web dialog box. The slices are numbered from the upper left to the lower right of the screen (Figure 14.9). You can change the arrangement of the slices and if you add or update slices, Illustrator automatically reflects the new quantity or order.

Creating a Slice

To create a slice in Illustrator:

1. Select a graphic element in the document.

2. Choose **Object** ⇨ **Slice** ⇨ **Make** to slice a bounded area in your image, which can include a vector element or a text object.

   or

   Choose **Object** ⇨ **Slice** ⇨ **Create from Selection/Create from Guides** to slice dimensions that are separate from the

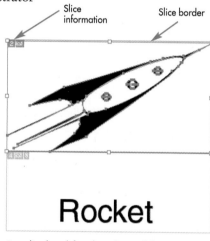

Slice information   Slice border

Bounding box defines boundaries of slice

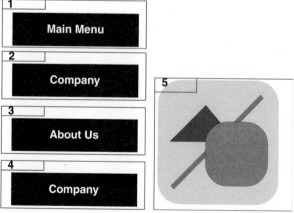

Create images and text areas, then create slices

- You can slice several parts of an image and then export each slice as a Web page
- You can slice an entire image and export it as a Web page

FIGURE 14.9 Options for exporting artwork in Macromedia® Flash™ (SWF) format.

underlying artwork. Slicing with the Slice tool creates layers that you can edit in the Layers palette.

or

Select the Slice tool and drag it over the area you want to slice.

3. To select text as a slice, select the text element, then select **Object** ⇨ **Slice** ⇨ **Make**: slice borders and slice information appear around the text element selected.

4. To use the slice tool, select this tool from the tool palette and drag the tool over the area you want as a slice.

Bounding box of text object define boundaries of slide

5. To select a slice, select the Slice Select tool from the Toolbox palette. With the Slice Select tool you can select slices, then:

- Resize the slice area or move the slice (click and drag).

- Duplicate the slice (choose **Object** ⇨ **Slice** ⇨ **Duplicate Slice**) and copy and paste the slice into the current artwork or new artwork.

- Select multiple slices (*Shift*-click) and choose **Object** ⇨ **Slice** ⇨ **Combine**) to combine them into a single slice.

- Align slices (choose **Window** ⇨ **Align** to display the Align palette).

- Divide into smaller slices (choose **Object** ⇨ **Slice** ⇨ **Divide Slices**).

- Stack or restack slices (choose **Object** ⇨ **Arrange**).

- Lock/Unlock slices (**View** ⇨ **Lock Slices**).

- Remove slicing from objects (**Object** ⇨ **Slice** ⇨ **Release**).

- Delete slices (press the *delete* key or choose **Object** ⇨ **Slice** ⇨ **Delete All**).

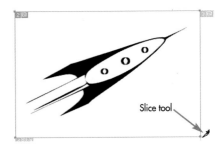

Drag around an object with the Slice tool to define boundaries for the slice

read this!

When you delete an object slice, the objects in the slice are deleted, too.

Slice Select tool icon in the Toolbox palette

fyi The tool that's hidden under the Slice tool in the Toolbox is called the Slice Select tool on the Macintosh, but on the Windows platform, it's called the Slice Selection tool. Use them interchangeably.

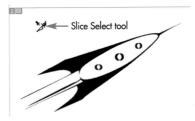

Select a slice with the Slice Select tool

Slice Options

You can save a slice and modify the options before saving it as a Web-based image.

1. Select the slice.

2. Choose **Object** ⇨ **Slice** ⇨ **Slice Options**.

   ■ Use HTML Text to capture text and simple formatting characteristics of the slice. You then enter HTML formatting tags for Web use. You cannot view the HTML content you enter in the Illustrator window — use a Web browser to view the results.

     ▪ Use **Object** ⇨ **Slice** ⇨ **Make** to create HTML text.

   ■ Image makes the sliced artwork a linked image in the Web page output.

   ■ No Image is for solid colors or text that you want to appear on a Web page. You can modify the HTML text options in the Text Displayed dialog box. To view the content, you must save it for the Web and then view it in a Web browser.

Optimizing Slices

If you're creating multiple slices, you must specify which slices you want to optimize. Link the slices to apply the same settings. GIF and PNG-8 slices share a color palette and dither so that seams do not appear between the slices. To link slices:

1. From your image, select Save for Web and select the Slice Select tool, then click on the slice (you can *Shift*-click or *Shift*-drag) to include several slices).

2. To link slices, select the one to link, then select Link Slices from the Optimize pop-up submenu. To unlink slices, select Unlink Slice from the Optimize pop-up submenu.

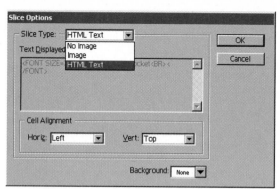

HTML Text slice type: enter standard HTML formatting tags, alignment, color. HTML code displays in window.

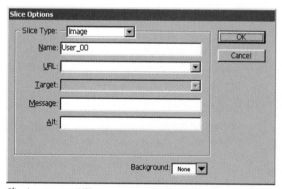

Slice image: enter URL, target, message or ALT text

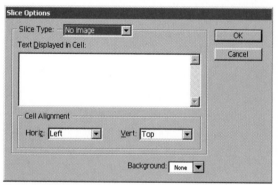

No slice image: for slice areas with text or a solid color

activity 14.2

1. Create a new document: Letter size, CMYK color mode. Name it Slices Practice.eps and save it into your Practice folder as an .eps file.

2. With the Rectangle tool, draw a rectangle that's 4" long and ¼" high. Fill it with C 100%, M 40%, Y 0%, K 0%, no stroke.

3. Choose Object ➪ Transform ➪ Move to display the Move dialog box. Enter 0 in the Horizontal field and −30pt in the Vertical field. Click the Copy button.

4. Press ⌘d five times to create a total of seven blue bars.

5. Select the middle bar. Choose the Star tool and click on the center point of the middle blue bar. When the Star dialog box displays, enter 144 pt in the Radius 1 field, 72 pt in the Radius 2 field, and 9 in the Points field. Click OK or press *return/enter*. Rotate the star until one of its points is straight up. Fill it with C 90%, M 0%, Y 50%, K 0%, no stroke.

6. With the Ellipse tool in the Toolbox selected, ⌥-click in the middle of the star. When the Ellipse dialog box displays, enter 144 pt in both fields. Click OK or press *return/enter*.

7. Apply a fill of 50% Yellow, no stroke. Position the circle in the center of the star.

8. With the Type tool, type the word SLICE. Format it to 48 pt Bauhaus Heavy and apply a fill of C 100%, M 100%, Y 0%, K 0%. Center it vertically and horizontally inside the yellow circle.

9. Save your file.

10. Select the star, then choose Object ➪ Slice ➪ Make.

   ■ The bounding box of the star is used for the boundaries of the slice.

■ A number displays in the upper left corner of each slice to identify its position in the sequence of slices.

■ A small icon also displays to the right of the sequence number that identifies what kind of slice it is (object or text).

■ If any portion of the other objects fall outside the bounding box of the star, they are divided into rectangular *automatic* slices. An automatic slice can't be selected or edited.

Automatic slice

11. Select the yellow circle, then choose Object ➪ Slice ➪ Make to create another slice.

   ■ The objects are divided into separate objects wherever paths intersect, creating many small objects.

12. Select the type, then choose Object ➪ Slice ➪ Make to make a separate slice for the type. Leave the slice selected.

13. Choose Object ➪ Slice ➪ Slice Options to display the Slice Options dialog box and choose HTML Text in the Slice Type pop-up submenu.

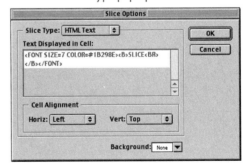

■ Notice the HTML coding that displays in the Text Displayed in Cell window. Click OK.

■ Notice that the Information box in the upper left corner of the slice changed to reflect that the slice is now a text slice. *Continued*

14. With the Selection tool, click on the star to select it. Then drag the upper left corner handle down and to the right to resize the star.

   - The size of the slice adjusts to the new size of the bounding box.

15. Press ⌘ a to select all the objects. With the Selection tool, *Shift*-click on the yellow circle to deselect it.

16. Choose View ➪ Lock Slices.

17. Choose the Slice tool in the Toolbox and move it over the object.

   - You can't create a user-defined slice if slices are locked. The ⊘ icon displays.

18. Choose View ➪ Lock Slices again to unlock them.

19. Choose Object ➪ Slice ➪ Release to remove all the slices from the objects.

20. With the Slice tool in the Toolbox still selected, create two user slices from the top two blue bars that extend to the left of the point of the star.

21. Choose the Slice Select tool in the Toolbox and click the top slice to select it. Position the pointer (🖋) over the top left corner until the reshape arrows (↖) display. Then click and drag down and to the right to resize the slice.

   - The object doesn't change, just the size of the slice you made.

22. With the Selection tool, select the top blue bar. Drag the upper left corner of the bounding box down and to the right to resize the bar.

   - Notice that the size of the slice didn't change. User-defined slices don't resize automatically when the size of the underlying object is changed.

23. With the Slice Select tool in the Toolbox, *Shift*-click to select the two slices you created.

24. Choose Object ➪ Slice ➪ Combine Slices.

   - The two slices became a single slice.

25. Choose Object ➪ Slice ➪ Divide Slices to display the Divide Slices dialog box. Enter 3 in the Divide Horizontally into [?] slices down, evenly spaced field. Then click the Preview checkbox.

26. Enter 3 in the Divide Vertically into [?] slices across, evenly spaced field. Then click the Preview checkbox. Click OK or press *return/enter*.

   - The two slices are divided into 9 evenly divided slices.

27. Experiment with the Slice tool and the Slice Select tool until you're familiar with how they function. When you're finished, close the artwork window without saving changes.

There are no Practice Activities or Exercises for this chapter.

Actions & Keyboard Shortcuts

Chapter Outline

- Actions
- Keyboard Shortcuts

Actions

An *action* is a series of recorded menu commands, tool functions, selections, and so on. When you play an action, all recorded tasks are performed for you automatically. A few default actions are included in Illustrator 10 and they can be found in the Actions palette (**Window ⇨ Actions**). Use actions for sequences you do repeatedly that are always exactly the same, such as creating a logo that appears on every piece of artwork for a client.

You can record, play, edit, save, and delete the prerecorded actions as well as any new ones you create. In addition, you can reorganize actions, move them out of one set and into another one, or copy them. You can even record a path in an action so that when you play back the action, the path is reproduced as part of the action.

To display the Actions palette, choose **Window ⇨ Actions**. Actions can be displayed in the palette as a list (Figure 15-1A) or as a set of buttons (Figure 15-1B). The command to change the palette mode is a toggle in the Actions palette Options menu. The absence

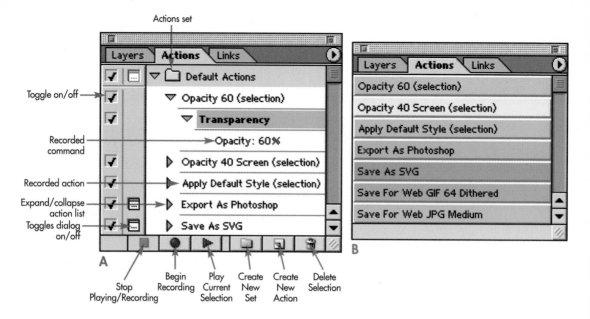

FIGURE 15.1 The Actions palette. (A) List mode, (B) Button mode.

of a checkmark to the left of Button Mode indicates that the palette is in List mode. If the option has a checkmark, the palette is in Button mode.

- When the palette is displayed in Button mode, the only thing you can do with actions stored in the palette is to play them.

- When the palette is displayed in List mode, sets can be expanded to show the individual commands. Use this mode to record, edit, play, save, and load actions.

- Groups of actions are organized in sets, indicated by folder icons on the Actions palette.

- Saved actions sets can be used in other Illustrator documents.

- Keyboard shortcuts can be assigned to actions. See the next section in this chapter, Keyboard Shortcuts, for information about creating custom keyboard shortcuts.

Playing an Action

When you play an action, the series of commands is played back in the exact order in which they were recorded. You can play a complete set of actions, begin playing the action at a specific command, or play a single command in an actions set. You can even stop the playing of an action while you perform a manual operation, then have it resume the commands in the actions set automatically.

Play an Action in List Mode

1. Open a file.

2. If appropriate, select an object or objects in the document.

3. Specify what you want to play:
   - Make sure the checkmark displays in the leftmost column of the Actions palette. If the box is unchecked, the action won't play.
   - To play an entire set of actions, highlight the set name (folder icon).
   - To play a single command in an action, highlight the individual action name.
   - To play only part of an actions set, highlight the first command in the set you want to play. Commands in the set listed after the highlighted command play.

   or

   Click the leftmost column in the Actions palette to remove the checkmark, which turns off that action.

4. Click the Play Current Selection button (▶) at the bottom of the Actions palette

   or

   Display the Actions palette Options menu and choose Play.

   or

   Hold down the ⌘ key, and double-click the action command in the list.

Play an Action in Button Mode

1. Open a file.

2. If appropriate, select an object or objects in the document.

3. Click the button or press the shortcut key(s) for the action you want to play.

Loading Actions Sets Into a Document

To display and be able to use custom actions sets in a document:

1. Display the Actions palette, then display the palette Options menu and choose Load Actions.

2. Navigate until you locate the actions set you want to load.

3. Click Open to display the actions set on the current document's Actions palette.

activity 15.1

1. Create a new document: Letter size, CMYK color mode.

2. Display the Actions palette (Window ⇨ Actions).

3. Display the Actions palette Options menu and choose Load Actions.

4. Locate the Star logo.aia actions file that's stored in the Student Files folder on the CD-ROM that accompanies this book.

5. Select it and click Open or press *return/enter*.
   - The Star logo actions set name displays in the list of actions in the Actions palette.

6. Click on the Star logo name to select it, then click the Play button (▶) at the bottom of the Actions palette.
   - The actions recorded in that actions set play and draw the logo.

7. Close the document without saving changes.

Creating a New Actions Set

New actions can be inserted into existing actions sets, or a new actions set can be created to contain them. To create a new actions set:

1. Display the Actions palette (choose **Window ⇨ Show Actions**).

2. Click the Create New Set button (▭) at the bottom of the Actions palette

   or

   Display the Actions palette Options menu and choose New Set.

3. In the New Set dialog box that displays, enter a descriptive name in the Set Name field.

4. Click OK or press *return/enter*.
   - A new folder icon and set name displays on the Actions palette.

Recording a New Action

The first thing you need to know is that not all commands can be recorded. The menu commands that *aren't* recordable are most of the commands in the View menu, commands in the Effect menu, and the gradient mesh commands. The only tools that *are* recordable are the shape creation tools (rectangle, rounded rectangle, ellipse, star, polygon, spiral, the Rotate, Scale, Shear, and Reflect transform tools, and the Twirl tool. In addition, fill and stroke attributes can be recorded as actions.

To record an action:

1. Create a new file or open an existing one.

2. Display the Actions palette (**Window ⇨ Show Actions**). Create a new set (see previous section) or click on an existing set in the palette to add the new action to an existing set.

read this!

It is strongly recommended that you create actions on a copy of a file. Then you can play the action on the original file when you're certain it's correct.

3. Display the New Action dialog box.

  ■ Click the Create New Action button (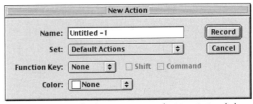) at the bottom of the Actions palette

  or

  ■ Display the Actions palette Options menu and choose New Action.

4. Enter a descriptive name for the action in the Name field.

5. The Set into which your action will be placed is displayed in the Set pop-up menu. To change it, choose another set from those listed.

6. If you want a keyboard shortcut for the action, assign it to a Function key by choosing one in the Function Key pop-up menu. Click the Shift or Command checkboxes, or both, to include those keys in the shortcut command.

  ■ If you assign a shortcut that's currently used for a menu command, the shortcut you assign in the action will apply, not the menu command.

  ■ Shortcut keystrokes display on that action's button when the Actions palette displays in Button mode.

7. From the Color pop-up menu, choose a color for the action name when displayed in Button mode.

8. Click Record or press *return/enter*.

  ■ The Begin Recording button (●) at the bottom of the Actions palette is red until you click the Stop Recording button (■) to stop recording an action.

  or

  Display the Actions palette Options menu and choose Begin Recording.

9. Create or edit object in the document as usual.

  ■ Recordable tool and menu commands appear on the list in the Actions palette as you use them when recording an action.

  ■ To ensure that you're working on a copy of an object, include the Save a Copy command at the beginning of the action.

  ■ Unless you assign fill and stroke attributes in your action, the current attributes in the Color palette at the time you play the action is applied to objects created in the action, if any.

  ■ Styles, symbols, and swatches from libraries must be present in their respective palettes to be used in an action. For example, in a new document, if a style used in an action isn't present in the Styles palette, that part of the action is ignored.

Set the parameters for the new action in the New Action dialog box

timesaver

⌥-click the Create New Set button at the bottom of the Actions palette to automatically create a new action (named Untitled) and begin recording. Follow the instructions for editing an action to assign a name.

✓ None
  Red
  Orange
  Yellow
  Green
  Blue
  Violet
  Gray

Colors that can be chosen for buttons when the Actions palette is displayed in Button mode

- If you use a command that opens a dialog box, clicking the OK button when you're finished records the command. If you click the Cancel button, the command isn't recorded.

10. Click the Stop Recording button (　■　) at the bottom of the Actions palette to end the recording session.

11. If you want to keep this actions set for future use in the current document or in other documents, save the actions set.

Save Your Actions Sets

To make new actions sets or changes to the default set available for use with other Illustrator files, you should save them to a file. The most logical place to save them is in the Actions folder inside the Presets folder in the Adobe Illustrator 10 folder on your hard drive (**Adobe Illustrator 10** ➪ **Presets** ➪ **Actions**). To save an actions set:

1. In the Actions palette, click on the *actions set* (not the individual action) you want to save.

2. Display the Actions palette Options menu and choose **Save Actions**.

    - The Save Set To dialog box displays. It's similar to the Save dialog box.

3. If you want to, you can change the name of the Actions set in the Name field.

4. Click the New Folder button (　**New**　) if you want to store the actions set inside a new folder.

    - **Windows:** The .aia extension is automatically added to the name.

5. Click Save or press *return/enter*.

Editing Actions

After an action or actions set has been recorded, you may find you want to modify it. There are several things you can do to change an action once it's been created. Before you change an existing action, though, make sure the original action has been saved. Then you can create a new actions set using the original as a basis or you can overwrite the original action.

Options for editing actions are in the Actions palette Options menu. The Actions palette must be in List mode (Button mode unchecked in Options menu) to edit actions.

Insert Menu Items into Existing Action List   If you want to add a menu command to an action's list of commands:

1. Expand the actions list to display the individual actions and commands.

2. In the list, click the command before the spot you want the new command inserted.

fyi   *When you draw an object in an action using one of the predefined shape tools, Illustrator remembers the x/y position where the object was created. When the action is played, the object is drawn in the same x/y location on the page where it was created.*

| New Action... |
| New Set... |
| Duplicate |
| Delete |
| Play |
| Start Recording |
| Record Again... |
| Insert Menu Item... |
| Insert Stop... |
| Insert Select Path |
| Select Object... |
| Action Options... |
| Playback Options... |
| Clear Actions |
| Reset Actions |
| Load Actions... |
| Replace Actions... |
| Save Actions... |
| Button Mode |
| Batch... |

Selections available in the Actions palette Options menu

3. Display the Actions palette Options menu and choose Insert Menu Item.

   ■ The Insert Menu Item dialog box displays.

4. Using the menus in the Menu bar, select the desired menu command.

   or

   Type the command name or a partial command name in the Find field, and click the Find button.

5. Using the menus in the Menu bar, select the desired menu command. If a dialog box displays for the menu command, click OK or press *return/enter* to exit the dialog box without changing any options.

Insert Menu Item

Menu Item: **Offset Path**

Find: | Offset Path |

OK

Cancel

To record a menu item, select a menu item using the mouse, or type a partial name and press the Find button.

Identify the menu command you want to insert into an action in the Insert Menu Item dialog box

---

6. The menu command is inserted into the list of actions in the Actions palette.

   ■ When you play the action, the dialog box displays and stays open until you click it's OK button, it's Cancel button, or press *return/enter*. Then the rest of the actions in the actions list resume playing.

To Play or Not to Play The leftmost column of a listing in the Actions palette is a toggle command that determines whether an actions set, an action, or an individual command is off or on. A checkmark in the box indicates the element will play. A blank checkbox indicates the action or command is disabled and it won't play.

Uncheck this box in the Actions palette to prevent an action from playing

   ■ ⌥-click a set, action, or command to turn all other sets, actions, or commands off (or on) *except* the one selected.

Add Recordable Commands into an Existing Action If you find you want to add more recordable commands into an existing action:

1. In List mode, select the command you want the new command to follow.

2. Begin recording:

   ■ Click the Begin Recording button (●) at the bottom of the Actions palette

   or

   ■ Display the Actions palette Options menu and choose Begin Recording.

3. Perform the actions you want recorded.

4. Click the Stop Recording button (■) at the bottom of the Actions palette.

   ■ The actions you record are inserted after the command you highlighted in the list of actions.

Record Paths as Part of an Action Freeform paths drawn with the Pen, Pencil, or Paintbrush tool cannot be recorded like paths created with the predefined shape tools (Ellipse, Rectangle, etc.) can. But they can be inserted into an action:

1. In List mode, begin recording an action by clicking the Begin Recording button.
   - ■ To insert a path into an existing action, select the command after which you want the path to appear.
2. Display the Actions palette Options menu and choose Insert Select Path.
   - ■ A listing displays in the Actions palette named "Set Work Path".
     - ▪ You can't rename this action.
   - ■ You can draw as many as 10 paths.
   - ■ Paths cannot be a blend, a compound path, a clipping mask, or part of a group.
   - ■ Fill and stroke attributes for the paths must be recorded in separate action steps.
3. When you're finished recording the action, click the Stop Recording button (▢) at the bottom of the Actions palette.

Stop an Action in the Middle of Its Play Inserting a Stop into an action sequence causes the action to pause during playback, allowing you to perform a manual operation, such as entering type. When the manual operation is completed, the action sequence resumes playing.

1. With the Actions palette in List mode, begin recording an action.
2. At the spot in the sequence where you want the action to stop so you can perform a manual operation, display the Actions palette Options menu and choose Insert Stop.
   - ■ To insert a Stop message in an existing action, select the command after which you want the Stop inserted, then display the Actions palette Options menu and choose Insert Stop.

Insert an instructional message in the Record Stop dialog box

3. In the Message window of the Record Stop dialog box that displays, type an explanation of what manual operation needs to be done. At the end of the message, remind the user to resume playing the action.
   - ■ To allow the user to bypass the stop, click the Allow Continue checkbox.
4. Click OK or press *return/enter.*
5. Record the rest of the commands for this action.
6. Click the Stop Recording button at the bottom of the Actions palette.

When a Stop action is encountered while an action is playing, an alert box displays containing your instructions.

- Click OK, perform the operations given in the instructions, then click the Play Current Selection button (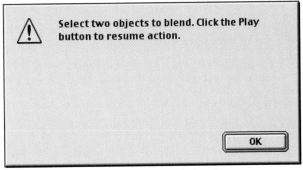) at the bottom of the Actions palette to resume playing the action.

When a Stop is placed in an action, an alert displays the instructions you inserted

Select a Path When Playing an Action If the action you're performing requires that you select a path or display a palette while the action is playing:

1. Display the Attributes palette, then display the Attributes palette Options menu and choose Show Note to display the Note window.

2. Type a descriptive name for the path that will be selected.

   - It doesn't matter what the note says, but it should be something that is associated with the path so you remember it's tagged to that particular path.

   - As soon as you press *return/enter*, a listing named Attribute Setting displays in the Actions palette.

3. Select the path in the document that you want to select in the action.

4. Click the Create New Action button at the bottom of the Actions palette or choose New Action in the Actions palette Options menu to start recording a new action.

5. Enter a name for the action and change any other options in the New Action dialog box that displays.

6. At the point in your action where you want to select the path, display the Actions palette Options menu and choose Select Object. In the Set Selection dialog box that displays, type the path name *exactly* as it is in the Attributes palette.

Type a descriptive message in the Note window of the Attributes palette to identify a path that's to be selected during the play of an action

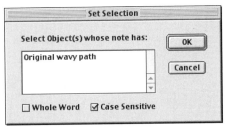

Type the exact message in the Set Selection dialog box that you entered in the Note window of the Attributes palette

■ **Whole Word** — To select object(s) when checked, whole words in this window must match *exactly* every word in the Note window in the Attributes palette.

■ **Case Sensitive** — Uppercase and lowercase words in the window must match Note text in the Attributes palette *exactly* to select objects.

7. Click OK or press *return/enter*, then continue recording the action.

Pause to Make Changes in a Dialog Box If a recorded action contains a command or tool with a dialog box, the action is played with the values that were entered into the dialog box when you recorded the action (the dialog box doesn't display). But you can insert a *modal control* (▭) to pause the action, display the dialog box, and allow you to make changes to options in the dialog box, and then continue the action.

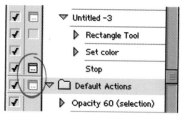

A red modal control icon in the Actions palette indicates that a modal control is present in the command or actions set

With the Actions palette in List mode, you can toggle the modal control off and on by clicking the second checkbox in the row. When the modal control is on, its icon displays in the checkbox, indicating that the dialog box will display when the action is played.

■ All modal controls require you to press *return/enter* to apply its effect.

■ A red modal control icon (▭) in the Actions palette indicates that a command in that actions set or in that action contains a modal control. All modal controls for commands in an action or actions set can be turned off (or on) by clicking the red modal control icon.

Include an Action from a Different Action You can combine actions from different actions sets by inserting a Play Action command as you're recording an action or by inserting a Play Action command in a prerecorded command.

1. Begin recording an action.

■ To insert a Play Action command into a prerecorded action, click the command after which you want the action to play.

2. Select the existing action you want to play, then click the Play button and allow the action to play until it's finished.

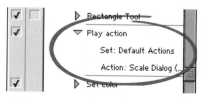

A Play action inserted into an actions set in the Actions palette

3. Finish recording the action.

■ If you're inserting a Play Action command into an existing prerecorded action, click the Stop Recording button (▭).

- The command is named Play Action and, when expanded, displays the original set name and action name.
- If an action that is included and another action is moved, an alert box displays warning that the the moved action is not available.

Adjust the Speed at Which an Action Plays Actions play at a rapid rate. If you need to slow down the playback so you can watch each command to discover where a problem occurs, display the Actions palette Options menu and choose Playback Options. Three options for controlling the speed of the playback of an action are offered in the Playback Options dialog box:

- **Accelerated** — This is the default speed at which the actions normally play.
- **Step by Step** — This option tells Illustrator to complete each action before beginning the next one. There's still not much time between actions.
- **Pause for [ ] seconds** — Click this button, then enter a value in the field to specify the length of time to pause between each step in the action.
- Click OK or press *return/enter*.

Adjust the speed an action plays in the Playback Options dialog box

Move a Command With the Actions palette in List mode, and the expansion arrows closed, click on the action command you want to move, then drag it upward or downward in the list, much like moving a layer in the Layers palette. Drop the action command when the insertion indicator (double lines) displays between two commands to insert the command you're moving at that position in the list.

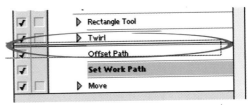

The insertion indicator displays between two actions when an action is to be inserted

- If you move a command from one actions set into another, the command is placed at the bottom of the destination actions set. Then you can move it to its proper position in the list.

Copy a Command Make sure the Actions palette is in List mode, click on the command you want to copy, then:

- Drag and drop the command name onto the Create New Action button ([▫]) at the bottom of the Actions palette, then move it to the correct position in the list. Follow the instructions for Moving a Command (above).

or

- ⌥-drag the command to a new position in the list. Release the mouse before releasing the ⌥ key.

  - The original command remains where it was and a copy is moved to a new place in the list.

or

- Display the Actions palette Options menu and choose Duplicate.

Follow the instructions later in this chapter to assign a different name to a copied command than that of the original command.

Delete an Action or Command With the Actions palette in List mode, select the Actions set, the Action, or the command you want to delete, then:

- Click the Delete button (🗑) at the bottom of the palette.

  - An alert box displays. Click Yes or press *return/enter*.

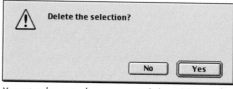

You get a chance to change your mind about deleting an actions set, action, or command

or

- Display the Actions palette Options menu and choose Delete.

  - An alert box displays. Click Yes or press *return/enter*.

or

- Drag and drop the selection on the Delete button (🗑) at the bottom of the palette.

or

- ⌥-click the Delete button (🗑) at the bottom of the palette.

Managing Actions Sets

You can rename actions sets, delete all actions sets from the Actions palette (including the Default Actions set), replace all the actions in the Actions palette with a new actions set, or reset the Actions palette so that only the Default Actions set is displayed. If you don't save the current actions sets before using the following commands to delete, reset, or replace actions, they're lost.

Rename an Actions Set To rename an actions set, including the Default Actions set:

1. In List mode, display the Set Options dialog box:

   - Double-click the name of the set.

   or

   - Display the Actions palette Options menu and choose Set Options.

2. Enter a new name in the Set Name field.

Delete All Actions All actions can be deleted from the Actions palette when actions are displayed in the Button mode or the List mode. Display the Actions palette Options menu and choose Clear Actions. Click Yes when the alert displays.

Reset Actions to the Default Actions Set If you've deleted or replaced the Default Actions set, you can get it back easily. You can delete all the actions currently in the Actions palette and replace them with the Default Actions set or you can add the Default Actions set to the actions currently listed.

1. Display the Actions palette Options menu and choose Reset Actions.

2. When the alert displays:
   ■ Click Append to add the Default Actions set to the current actions in the Actions palette.

   or

   ■ Click OK to replace the actions currently in the Actions palette with the Default Actions set.

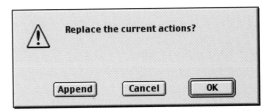

Click OK to replace the current actions or click Append to add the Default Actions set to the actions currently listed in the Actions palette

Replace All Actions with New Set of Actions All actions currently in the Actions palette can be replaced with a different set of actions.

1. Display the Actions palette Options menu and choose Replace Actions.
   ■ A dialog box named Load Set From displays that's similar to the Open dialog box.

2. Locate the file containing the actions file you want to load.

3. Select the file, then click Open, or double-click the file name.

Batch Processing

Batch processing means to apply a command to multiple files at the same time — in this case, actions. For example, if you want to run actions to prepare files for sending to an output provider, you can do it all at once, even when the files aren't open and even if they're in subfolders.

1. Display the Batch dialog box by displaying the Actions palette Options menu and choosing Batch at the bottom of the menu list.

2. From the Set pop-up menu, choose the actions set you want to be applied to all files.

3. Choose the desired Action.

4. Click the Choose button in the Source area to select the files to which you want the action applied.

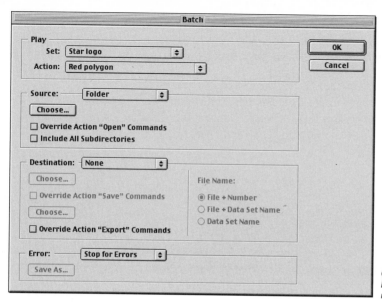

Change values in the Batch dialog box to set parameters for playing multiple actions, one after the other

- ■ If you recorded an Open command in the action, click the Override Action "Open" Commands checkbox.

- ■ If some of the files to which you want the action to be applied are stored in subfolders within the original folder, click the Include All Subdirectories checkbox.

5. Choose an option from the Destination pop-up menu to specify where the processed files should be saved:

- ■ **None** — Leaves files open without saving changes, unless you recorded a Save command in the action.

  - ▪ If you want to save the modified files in a different format than the original file, record the Save As command or Save a Copy command, followed by the Close command, in the action. Then specify the Destination as None.

- ■ **Save and Close** — Overwrites the current files, and closes the document.

- ■ **Folder** — Saves files in a different location. Click the Choose button to specify the new location.

  - ▪ If Save As or Save a Copy commands are recorded in the action, click the Override Action "Save In" Commands checkbox so files are saved to the destination specified when the Choose button was clicked. Don't click this checkbox if you want to save the file in a different format than the original file.

  - ▪ If an Export command is recorded in the action, click the Override Action "Export" Command checkbox so files are saved to the destination specified when the Choose button was clicked. Don't click this checkbox if you want to save the file in a different format than the original file.

Choose one of these options to specify where processed files are saved

682

6. Specify how you want errors handled if any are found during processing by choosing an option in the pop-up menu.

- **Stop for Errors** — Stops the processing procedure if errors are encountered.
- **Log Errors to File** — If errors are found during processing, a text file is created listing the errors, without stopping the batch process.
    - An alert displays to let you know that errors were encountered. Click Save As to name and save the file.

Choose one of these options for handling errors during batch processing of actions

 activity 15.2

1. Create a new document: Letter size, CMYK color mode.

2. With the Rectangle tool, draw about a 1" rectangle on your screen. Zoom in so you can easily see any changes you make.

3. Display the Actions palette (Window ⇨ Actions).

4. If the Default Actions list isn't expanded, click the Expand arrow to the left of the set name.

5. Enlarge the palette or scroll down until you find the Shear Dialog (selection) action. Highlight the action name.

6. With the rectangle you just drew still selected, click the Play Current Selection button (▶) at the bottom of the Actions palette.
    - The Shear dialog box displays.

7. Click OK or press *return/enter* to exit the dialog box and apply the value to the selected object.
    - You can change the values in the dialog box before exiting to apply a different shear amount.

8. Double-click the Shear Dialog (selection) name in the Actions palette to display the Action Options dialog box.

9. Display the Function Key pop-up submenu and choose F9. Click the Shift and Command checkboxes. Click OK or press *return/enter*.

10. Draw another rectangle on the page, then press ⇧ ⌘ F9.
    - The Shear dialog box displays.

11. Accept or change the values in the fields, then click OK or press *return/enter*.

- If you use the same shear value frequently, you could set up an action with those values and a function key assigned to it. To apply those values to an object, all you'd have to do is press the function key combination and press *return/enter*.

12. Move to a blank area on your document page.

13. Display the Actions palette Options menu and choose New Set. Enter Star in the Name field to identify your new actions set.

14. Display the Actions palette Options menu and choose New Action. Name the action Draw Star, display the Function Key pop-up submenu and choose F9, then click the Shift and Command checkboxes. Click Record or press *return/enter*.

15. Click the default Fill and Stroke button (⬚) at the bottom of the Toolbox palette, then choose the Star tool in the Toolbox and click on the document page to display the Star Options dialog box.

16. Enter the following values, then click OK or press *return/enter*.
    Radius 1: 35 pt   Radius 2: 15 pt   Points: 5

17. Click the Stop Playing/Recording button (■) at the bottom of the Actions palette.

18. Display the New Action dialog box, name this action Drop Shadow, and click Record or press *return/enter*.

19. Display the Filter menu, choose Stylize, then select Drop Shadow from the pop-up submenu.

Continued

20. When the dialog box opens, change the Opacity value to 50%, and click OK or press *return/enter*. Click the Stop Playing/Recording button at the bottom of the Actions palette.

21. Display the Style Libraries menu (Window ➪ Style Libraries), and choose Fills.

22. Display the New Action dialog box, name this action Back Shadow, and click Record or press *return/enter*.

23. Click the Back Shadow style icon (■) on the Fills library palette, then click the Stop Playing/Recording button (■) at the bottom of the Actions palette.

24. Select the Star actions set and click the Play Current Selection button (▶) at the bottom of the Actions palette to play the action.

   ■ A star is drawn on the page in the same x/y position where you clicked to create it in the action.

   ■ The drop shadow and the Back Shadow style are applied automatically to the star.

25. In the Actions palette, click the Star actions set name, then display the Actions palette Options menu, and choose Save Actions to display the Save Set To dialog box.

26. Locate your Practice folder, create a new folder named My Actions, and save this new action into it, leaving the name Star as the name of the action.

27. In the Actions palette, locate the Scale Dialog (selection) action in the Default Actions set. Highlight it and drag and drop it on the Create New Action button at the bottom of the palette.

   ■ A copy of the action is placed beneath the original action in the list.

28. Close all the actions in the Star actions set so only the action names are visible, then drag the Scale Dialog (selection) copy down and drop it between Draw Star and Back Shadow.

29. Press *d* to change to the default fill and stroke colors.

30. Move to a blank area of the document page and draw another rectangle.

31. In the Actions palette, click the Toggle Item On/Off checkmark for the action named Draw Star to disable it.

32. With the rectangle selected, click on the Star actions set in the Actions palette, then click the Play Current Selection button at the bottom of the palette. When the Scale dialog box displays, enter 90 in the Uniform Scale field, and click OK or press *return/enter*

   ■ The Drop Shadow and the Back Shadow style were applied to the rectangle.

33. Save the new actions set into your My Actions folder in your Practice folder. Name it Star 2.

34. Close the file without saving changes.

Keyboard Shortcuts

When Adobe Illustrator 10 is installed, default keyboard shortcuts for commands and tools, called Illustrator Factory Defaults, are installed with the basic program. These are the keyboard commands you've been using throughout this book. But Illustrator 10 also gives you the ability to assign your own keyboard shortcuts to tools and commands.

Keysets

A group of keyboard shortcuts is called a *keyset*. Changes to keysets are made in the Keyboard Shortcuts dialog box (Figure 15.2). To display a keyset:

■ Choose **Edit ➪ Keyboard Shortcuts**

or

■ Press ⇧ ⌥ ⌘ k

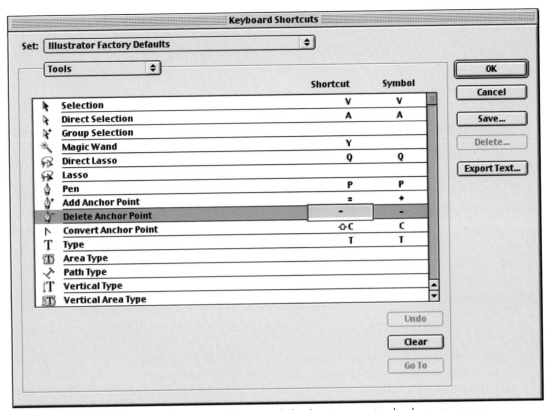

FIGURE 15.2 Make changes in the Keyboard Shortcuts dialog box to customize the shortcuts you use.

A list of custom keysets displays in the Set pop-up submenu at the top of the palette after they've been created and named. See the next section, called Defining New Shortcuts and Keysets. In the dialog box, you can choose to display keyboard shortcuts for Tools or for Menu Commands by making a selection in the pop-up submenu beneath the Set pop-up submenu.

You can use the default keyset supplied by Illustrator, you can create an entirely new keyset, or you can change shortcuts in an existing keyset. In addition, you can switch between keysets. Keep track of keyboard shortcuts by printing the keyset list.

Defining New Shortcuts and Keysets

1. Display the Keyboard Shortcuts dialog box (choose **Edit** ⇨ **Keyboard Shortcuts** or press ⇧ ⌥ ⌘ k). (See Figure 15.2.)

2. Choose a keyset name from the Set pop-up menu.

   ■ You can't make changes to the Illustrator Factory Defaults or the Adobe Illustrator 6 keysets. You can use them to make changes to commands, but you're required to create a new keyset to save new the new shortcuts.

3. Choose Tools or Menu Commands from the pop-up menu at the top of the scroll window.

  ■ All tool names and menu commands are listed and the current keyboard shortcuts are displayed.

4. Locate and highlight the tool name or command in the scroll window. A highlighted field is displayed in the Shortcut column.

  ■ Expand the list, if necessary, by clicking the triangle at the left side of the entry.

5. Enter the new shortcut characters you want to use.

  ■ Don't use a combination of characters that you may press accidentally when working in a document. Try to choose a combination that you are unlikely to press at any time.

  ■ As soon as you make a shortcut change, the selection in the Set pop-up menu changes to Custom.

  ■ Shortcuts for tools can be a single letter, number, or punctuation mark. They can be modified only with the *Shift* key.

    ▪ An alert displays at the bottom of the dialog box if you attempt to create a tool shortcut using the ⌘ or ⌥ modifier.

  ■ Shortcuts for menu commands must contain the ⌘ modifier to a letter, number, punctuation, or *F1–F12* key. In addition to the ⌘ modifier, you can add the *Shift* and ⌥ keys.

    ▪ *Macintosh:* You cannot use the ⌃ (*control*) key.

    ▪ Some of the *F1* and *F4* combinations are reserved and cannot be changed.

  ■ If you assign a shortcut that is already assigned to another tool or menu command, an alert displays at the bottom of the dialog box warning you that the shortcut will be removed from the other command or tool. The Go To button also becomes available. Click it to go immediately to the tool for which you just removed its shortcut so you can assign a new one.

  ■ If you change your mind after assigning a keyboard shortcut, click the Undo button to reassign the keyboard shortcut to its original tool or command.

6. If desired, enter a new keyboard symbol in the Symbol column to assign a different symbol that displays on the menu or on the tool tip for the menu command or tool.

  ■ Almost all tools and commands use, by default, the same character as that used for the shortcut, but you can change it if you want to.

7. Click OK or press *return/enter* when you're finished assigning keyboard shortcuts.

  ■ If you're changing the default keyset, the Save Keyset File dialog box displays in which you can enter a new name for the keyset. Enter the name, then press OK or press *return/enter* to return to the Keyboard Shortcuts dialog box, then again to exit the Keyboard Shortcuts dialog box.

- The name of the custom keyset displays in the Set pop-up menu.

Name your new keyset when you save it

Managing Keysets

You can use the keyset supplied by Illustrator, you can create an entirely new keyset, or you can change shortcuts in an existing keyset. In addition, you can switch between keysets.

Print Keyset Lists To help you remember keyboard shortcuts, you can print them as a text file. Then you can post them near your computer for easy reference.

1. Display the Keyboard Shortcuts dialog box.

2. Choose the keyset name from the Set pop-up menu.

3. Click the Export Text button to display the Save Key Set File As dialog box. Enter a name for the keyset and click the Save button.

   ■ Click the New Folder button to create a new folder to save the text file in.

4. Import the text file into any application that has the ability to import a text file, such as QuarkXPress and SimpleText on the Macintosh or Microsoft Word and Notepad on the Windows platform. Then print it.

Delete Keyboard Shortcuts To remove an individual keyboard shortcut from a command or tool:

1. Select the keyset in the Set pop-up menu.

2. Locate and select the command name or tool name in the scroll list.

3. Click Clear.

4. Click OK or press *return/enter.*

Delete Keysets To delete an entire set of keyboard commands:

1. Select the keyset in the Set pop-up menu.

   ■ The default keyset supplied by Illustrator cannot be deleted.

2. Click the Delete button.

3. Click OK or press *return/enter.*

Move Keysets to Another Computer Additional keysets you create are saved by Illustrator as .kys files in a Keyboard Shortcuts folder inside the Presets folder in the Adobe Illustrator 10 folder on your hard drive. To move custom keysets, copy the file from one machine and drag it into the Keyboard Shortcuts folder on a different machine. When you launch Illustrator after the file is placed in the folder, the keyset becomes available for use.

activity 15.3

1. Create a new document: Letter size, CMYK color mode. Save it into your Practice Folder as an .eps file named New Shortcuts.eps.

2. Choose Edit ➪ Keyboard Shortcuts to display the Keyboard Shortcuts dialog box.

3. Verify that Tools is the selection in the pop-up menu.

4. Scroll down until all the Symbolism tools are visible in the list.

5. Click the Symbol Shifter tool name and enter *Shift-~* in the field.

6. No, I don't want that for the keyboard shortcut, so deselect it, and click the Clear button.

7. Select the Symbol Shifter tool again and press *Shift-2*.

8. Change the rest of the Symbolism tools:
   Symbol Scruncher: *Shift-3*
   Symbol Sizer: *Shift-4*
   Symbol Spinner: *Shift-5*
   Symbol Stainer: *Shift-6*
   Symbol Screener: *Shift-7*
   Symbol Styler: *Shift-8*

9. Change the pop-up menu selection to Menu Commands. Click the expansion arrow at the left of the listing for Object, then scroll down and click the arrow beside Path to display the commands.

10. Click Outline Stroke and change the keyboard command to ⇧ ⌘ F11.

11. Click OK or press *return/enter*.

12. When the Save Keyset File dialog box displays, enter the name Practice Keyset in the field and click OK or press *return/enter*.
    - Practice Keyset displays in the Set pop-up menu and the Keyboard Shortcuts dialog box disappears.

13. Draw a rectangle on the keyboard and apply a 6 pt stroke (any color). Press ⇧ ⌘ F11.
    - The stroke is converted to a filled path.

14. Press ⇧2.
    - The Symbol Shifter tool (⬛) in the Toolbox is selected.

15. Check the other keyboard shortcuts you created to verify that they work.

16. Display the Keyboard Shortcuts dialog box again and click the Export Text button. When the Save Keyset As File dialog box displays, navigate to save the file into your Practice folder. Create a new folder named Keysets to store it in.

17. Click Save or press *return/enter*.

18. If a word processing program, such as Microsoft Word, or a page layout program such as QuarkXPress or InDesign is available to you, import the text file and print it so you have a list of your new shortcuts.

19. Close the artwork window without saving changes.

There are no Practice Activities or Exercises for this chapter.

Output: Printing & Exporting Files

When you create images with Illustrator, you may print proof-copies or final designs of your work in-house, send them to an offset printing company, or export them for use in another printed or Web document. Exporting artwork from Illustrator to another application may require a format different from the native Illustrator format (.ai), such as bitmap or EPS.

Before you deliver your artwork to a printing company or before you make image files for an electronic image delivery such as the Web, it's always wise to check with your end-user and make sure that your "output" matches the "input" expectations and needs.

Printing

Some printing concepts with which you should become familiar are:

- **Bleed** — An image that runs off or "bleeds" off the edge of the printed area. Many brochures, for example, have colors that bleed off the edges of the final printed product.
- **Color separation** — A printing process that divides colors into four "plates." Each of the plates prints varying color tones of cyan, magenta, yellow, and black on a sheet of paper to create a full-color printed image.

The separations are grayscale images with a maximum possible color depth of 256 color levels. Informally, color separations sometimes are called "color seps" or "seps."

- **Composites** — A printed image that contains all color separations.
- **Halftone** — A gradation from light-to-dark or dark-to-light tones created by increasing or decreasing dot size and density. Black-and-white newspaper photographs are examples of "halftones." Some people interchange the terms *halftone* and *screen*.
- **Knockout** — An overlapping color that blocks out a color it overlaps.
- **Overprint** — One color over the top of another color, which creates a third color (a blend of the two colors).
- **PostScript®** — A page language description program developed by Adobe, describing vector shapes — images, outlines, and fonts — and also filled shapes, colors, and line style. Vector images retain print quality without the pixelization (jagged edges on images) that occurs with bitmap images. Most computers and printers have a PPD (PostScript Printer Driver) file so a computer and a printer can communicate in the PostScript language.

- **Registration Marks** — "Star targets" to ensure precise alignment of the color printing plates so the plates do not shift in the printing process. If the plates aren't precisely aligned, colors are shifted out of the proper position and the printed image looks blurry.

- **Trapping** — Controlling the adjacent colors of two objects so white space does not appear between the adjacent colors. Trapping allows a lighter-colored ink to spread under a darker-colored ink to eliminate white space.

Printing a Document

Printing with in-house laser printers or ink jet printers is a great way to produce proofs (prints of the composite image. Printing options vary between Windows and Macintosh platforms and between different printers. You may have more options when printing from Macintosh, though the basic printing is straightforward.

Laser Printing

The procedure for printing a page to a black-and-white laser, a color laser, or a color inkjet printer is as follows:

1. With the Illustrator image open, select **File** ➪ **Print**.

2. Select the printer you wish to use, the number of copies, and page range, if needed.

    - If the image size is larger than the paper you have in the printer, select **File** ➪ **Document Setup** and select *Tile Imageable Areas* (use the Page tool to drag the tiling grid as desired), then click OK or press *return/enter*. If you change this setting, you have to return to the Print menu.

3. Click OK or press *return/enter*.

Printing to File

When your project is ready to be printed, you often "print" the image to a file and give the file to an output provider. To create a "print file," you use a software printer driver to convert the file to another format — .prn (**Windows**) or .ps (**Macintosh**). Output providers have software to read the file, which they use to make printing plates or film. A number of other printing options — separations, crop marks, etc. — can be considered before actually taking the project to an output provider, but the basic procedure is as follows:

1. Select **File** ➪ **Print**. The Print dialog box displays.

2. Click the Print to File checkbox, then click in the Printer Name drop-down menu. Choose a PostScript printer driver. A PostScript printer driver may be called "xxx.PPD" or

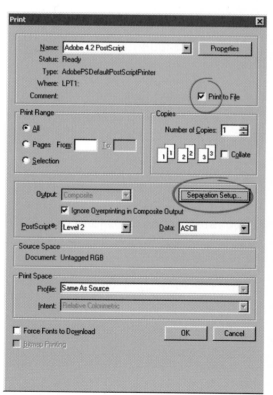

The Print dialog box

"Adobe x.x PostScript," or something similar.

3. If you have not printed to a file before, you'll need to choose (open) a PPD. Click on the Separations Setup button to display the Separations Setup dialog box.

    Illustrator has sample PPDs installed with the program. The location of these files varies, depending on your computer's operating system version.

    ■ *Windows*: **Program Files** ⇨ **Adobe** ⇨ **Illustrator 10** ⇨ **Utilities** ⇨ **Sample PPDs**.

    ■ *Macintosh*: **Adobe Illustrator 10** ⇨ **Utilities** ⇨ **Sample PPDs**.

4. Click OK or press *return/enter* to display the Print to File dialog box. You can now print an electronic file, (.prn or .ps) and you are asked to give the file a name and a location to store the .prn file.

When finished, you can make a PDF file from the .prn (or .ps) file or you can take the .prn (or .ps) file to your output provider.

Print Dialog Box Options

Output Composite prints a composited color image; Separate prints a color separated image. The Separate option is available only after you select options in the Separations Setup dialog box.

PostScript Select PostScript 2, or Language Level 3 for optimized printing of complex gradients, gradient mesh objects, or other highly-designed images.

Data and Bitmap Printing Data is for Macintosh systems, and Bitmap is for Windows systems. Under Data, select ASCII for a wide range of printers and Binary to decrease the amount of data (and also reduce printing time). Select Bitmap if you are printing complex documents or documents on a low-resolution printer.

Force Fonts to Download This option downloads fonts (temporarily) from your computer to the printer. Using fonts downloaded from your computer will be lower quality than using fonts stored on the printer.

Color Separation

Color separation is the process of creating four separate transparencies that will be used to create a grayscale printing plate or film (much like a photographic negative) for each of the four process colors (cyan, magenta, yellow, black). The printing function of Illustrator is used to create the transparencies as negatives or positives.

    Another separation that you can make is for spot colors or spot varnishes to enhance one area of an image. This separation is outside the normal four-color process, so you will have to create an extra transparency so the printer can build a plate to print the spot color or spot varnish.

    Not all four-color printing requires you to use all four colors. In fact, you can save time, effort, and money by creating an image that requires only two colors (duotone) or three colors (tritone). Fewer colors to be printed means that the image will require fewer "trips" through the printing equipment and, hence, fewer separations and plates, less ink, and lower costs.

    Before sending your artwork to an output provider:

    ■ Make proofs of your work before sending it to the output provider.

    ■ Include registration marks in your artwork so it can be accurately reproduced on the printing press.

    ■ Use crop or trim marks where necessary so your artwork can be trimmed to the proper size and shape.

- Check with your output provider before setting traps, knockouts, or overprinting.

Color Separations Dialog Box

Settings that control the separation of colors in your artwork are in the Separations Setup dialog box (Figure A.1). To display the Separations Setup dialog box:

1. Select Print to File from the Print dialog box and choose a PostScript printer.

2. Select a PPD to use.

3. Click on the Separations Setup button.

Preview of Image The preview shows you current settings for crop marks and the entire artboard. You can click and drag the crop marks or the image to different positions. If you drag the crop mark box, you'll notice that it appears to be a double box. The space between the two boxes represents the bleed area, and the outer box is the printing bounding box.

Printer Marks These print the star targets, registrations and crop marks, progressive color bars, gradient, separation labels, and overprint.

Margin Settings for Printer You can change the settings numerically, or you can drag the settings in the preview window. The button marked "Revert" changes the setting to the last saved setting in the file.

Page Settings The page size and orientation are not the same as those in the Page Setup dialog box. Change these settings to correspond to the film or paper or plate.

Emulsion Film has an *emulsion* side, which appears shiny, and a *non-emulsion* side, which appears dull. "Up" is *right reading*. The film image looks "normal," text goes left-to-right, and images appear as you have created them. The emulsion side faces you. "Down" means that the shiny side faces away from you.

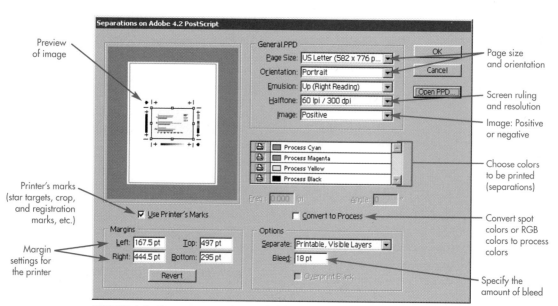

FIGURE A.1 The Separations Setup dialog box.

Halftone Halftone settings are set by the PPD. You can choose higher or lower line screen settings (lpi = lines per inch). Check with the output provider for the proper setting for your project.

Image: Positive or Negative This option is for printing a positive of a negative image, similar to photographic film, for the plates. Check with your output provider.

Choose Colors for Separations This is used to list all colors you used to create the image, including spot colors or varnish. To print only one of the colors to create a separation, deselect the small printer icon next to all of the undesired colors and only the selected color prints. Also, you can change color lpi and dot angle.

Convert to Process All colors including spot colors, are converted to CMYK process colors,

Separate, Bleed, Overprint Black

- Choose Separate to decide which image layers to include for printing: Printable, Visible Layers, Visible Layers Only, or All Layers.
- Bleed determines how far printed colors extend beyond the edge of the page (beyond the crop marks).
- Overprint Black helps reduce trapping because black prints over all other colors. This does not apply to color areas that, when blended, appear black.

Registration Colors

To print one color on all plates in the printing process, you can convert it into a registration color. Typically, you print the registration color, crop marks, and trim marks all in the same color, and this color appears on all separations. This way, the printer can align all printing plates with greater accuracy.

To choose a registration color:

1. Select an object in the image to apply registration color.

2. Select **Window** ⇨ **Swatches** to display the Swatches palette. Click on the Registration swatch palette.

3. In the Swatches palette, click the Registration color swatch (⊕), and the selected objects are converted into registration color objects.

4. Use the Color palette to change the on-screen appearance of the registration color to something other than black (black is the default color).

The color you choose is used for showing registration-colored objects on the screen. It always prints gray on composites and as an equal tint in all separations.

Trapping

In the printing press, paper stretches and plates can shift, which results in gaps between colored objects that are butted up against one another. For CYMK, this isn't much of a problem, but for spot colors, it can result in misregistration and shift. Trapping normally is done by the output provider or they can tell you how much trap to include.

In trapping, you have to look at the image. Objects in the image are usually *foreground* and *background* and one of them may be darker or lighter than the other. The two types of trapping (Figure A.2) are:

- **Choke** — A lighter background overlaps a darker foreground object and the background seems to squeeze or "choke" the foreground object.

fyi You can trap Illustrator images only if you are working in CMYK documents.

Choke: A lighter and larger background "chokes" a smaller, darker foreground object

Spread: A lighter and larger foreground object "spreads" into a smaller, darker background object

FIGURE A.2 Trapping: Choke versus spread.

- **Spread** — A darker background overlaps a lighter foreground object and the foreground object "spreads" into the background.

You can manipulate trap using the Pathfinder menu to change an object's stroke width, height, and tint reduction. You basically select the foreground object and change the Stroke to the same color as the fill and alter the Stroke thickness.

You also can create traps for process and spot colors (traps the lighter color to overprint the darker color) and set reverse traps (traps darker colors into light colors).

Saving and Exporting

You create images in Illustrator and save them as an Illustrator file in formats such as .ai, PDF, SVG, SVGZ, or EPS. When you've finished creating or manipulating an image in Illustrator, you can *export* the image to a *non-native* Illustrator format, or to an earlier version of Illustrator. Saving or exporting Illustrator files consists of:

- Exporting the image to non-native Illustrator formats such as JPEG, PICT, CGM, TIFF, text, AutoCad, Photoshop, or Flash (SWF) formats

- Saving an image for Web use (**File ⇨ Save For Web**) and controlling the file size, displayed colors, and image quality.

- Copying an image or object to the Clipboard for use in other applications, such as Photoshop or drag-and-drop an object into another application. Copying images to other applications converts the images to that application's native file format and preserves many of the features (transparency, layers, and some others).

Exporting to Bitmap File Formats

Illustrator's export function contains many similar options regardless of export format type. We'll cover the most widely used file format exports: Photoshop, JPEG, and TIFF.

The process is simple: Select **File ⇨ Export**, and choose from the options (Figure A.3).

Photoshop

Exporting to Photoshop preserves transparency effects you create, such as raster/vector balance, output resolutions, and text-to-outlines. You

694

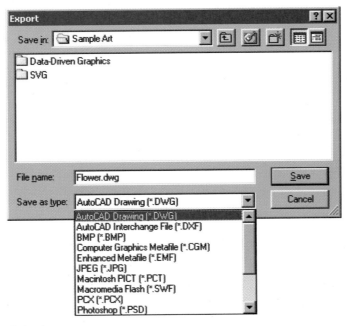

FIGURE A.3 Export dialog box.

also can specify resolution setting for screen or print use and control layer output. Keeping layers intact allows you to access them with Photoshop filters.

To export an Illustrator file to Photoshop (.psd), select **File ⇨ Export**, and select Photoshop format (Figure A.4).

- Choose the color model desired, CMYK, RGB, or grayscale. For images used only on a computer, choose RGB; for print, choose CMYK or grayscale.

- Select an output resolution, 72 dpi or higher.

- Turn anti-aliasing on or off.

- If you have layers, use Write Layers to export stacked layers and preserve the stacked appearance and groups nested within a layer. You also can save compound shapes and save text so it can be edited in Photoshop (the

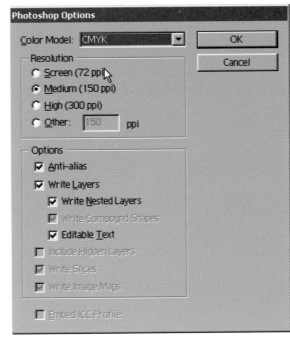

FIGURE A.4 Photoshop Options dialog box.

compound shapes and text must be a top-level layer). If you don't export the layers, they will be flattened into one layer in Photoshop.

- You also can save hidden layers and create editable slices.

JPEG

Exporting to JPEG (Figure A.5) will compress the file you are exporting in which you may have placed a continuous-tone bitmap image or gradient-filled object.

- Set image quality (and the resulting compression) and color model (RGB, CMYK, or Grayscale) in the Image area of the dialog box. Again, greater compression will result in a smaller file size with lower image quality.

- Under Format Method, you can choose Baseline, Baseline Optimized (adjust color quality), or Progressive (progressive means that the image slowly displays rather than waiting for the entire image to download before displaying).

- Resolution changes the image dpi. For print, choose a high resolution, for Web images, choose Screen (72 dpi).

- Under Options, you can create anti-aliasing. Use Imagemap if you have a URL-linked object in your file. Server-side saves the file for use with a Web server, and client-side saves the file with an accompanying HTML file and the HTML file contains link information.

TIFF

TIFF (Tagged Image File Format) is supported by almost all desktop publishing programs as well as image-editing programs such as Photoshop and Paint Shop Pro. With TIFF (Figure A.6), you can save in RGB, CYMK, and grayscale, and it follows LZW compression standards for lossless image (JPEG and GIF are lossy images). TIFF is not supported for Web browsers.

- Color mode sets the file for CMYK, RGB, or Grayscale.

- Resolution changes the image dpi. For print, choose a high resolution, for Web images, choose Screen (72 dpi).

- Turn anti-aliasing on or off.

- Turn LZW compression on or off. LZW compression enables lossless compression (recommended).

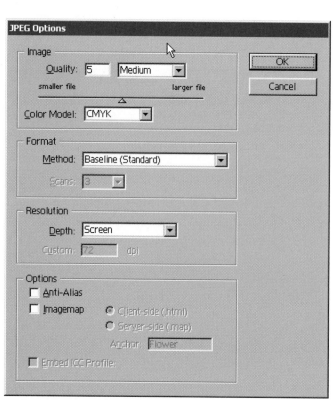

FIGURE A.5 Exporting to JPEG dialog box.

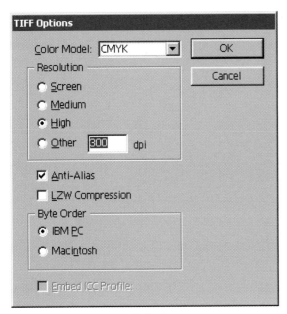

FIGURE A.6 TIFF Export dialog box.

■ With Byte Order, you choose the operating system (Macintosh or PC) where the file will be used.

Saving to Vector Format

Vector formats are native to Illustrator. These formats include Illustrator, PDF, and EPS. For information about saving SVG or SVGZ, see Step 14, *Web Graphics*.

Save as PDF

Use Illustrator's Save As feature to create PDF files. Saving your artwork as a PDF file might come in handy if you want to send a composite to someone who has Acrobat or Acrobat Reader but does not have Illustrator or any other program capable of viewing your artwork. You also could link a Web site to a PDF file and allow the Web user to view the PDF version of the artwork.

To create a PDF file select **File ➪ Save As** and select PDF (Figure A.7).

■ Default saves the image "as is." Use Screen Optimized for images that you use on the Web. This optimized setting reduces file size and converts the image to RGB. You can further enhance the compression by selecting the lower drop-down menu and choosing Compression instead of General.

■ Under File Compatibility, select Acrobat 4.0 or Acrobat 5.0 (note that Acrobat 4 won't open a file saved in Acrobat 5). If you want to edit the PDF file with Illustrator, select Preserve Illustrator Editing Capabilities. Note that you can open most older PDF files with Illustrator, but if you want to prevent editing, deselect this option.

■ Embedding fonts includes the font information in the PDF file. If users don't have the font, they either will get an error message or their computer will attempt to subset (replace) the font.

■ Subset fonts allows Illustrator to embed fonts or not, based on the percentage of a specific font's use within the document.

■ Select Generate Thumbnails to create a set of Acrobat thumbnails that will appear in the PDF file.

Save to EPS Format

EPS (Encapsulated PostScript) can be used in almost every desktop publishing program as well as by most printing companies (Figure A.8).

■ Compatibility is for saving as an Illustrator version the same as your current version or an earlier version. Version 9 and higher preserves transparency, spot colors, and text if you place it in a another application such as Adobe InDesign or QuarkXPress. Saving in earlier versions converts text to outlines, converts spot colors to process

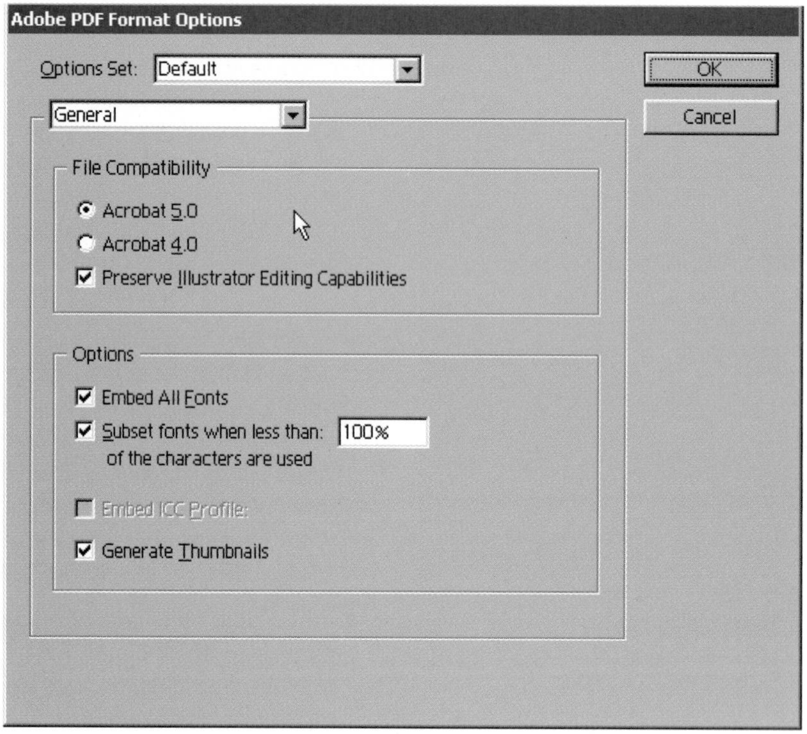

FIGURE A.7 PDF Export dialog box.

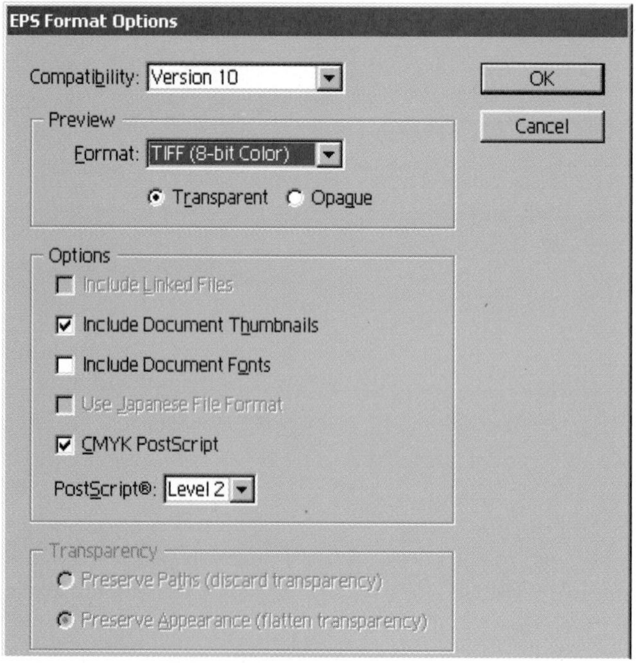

FIGURE A.8 Saving to EPS dialog box.

colors, and alters transparencies (they will be flattened or removed).

- Choose EPS preview to see what the image looks like when it's imported into a document in a desktop publishing program. For programs that cannot display an EPS file, e.g., some versions of UNIX, you can select how it can be previewed: TIFF, 8-bit color, black and white, none, and transparent, or opaque. If the EPS file will be used in any Microsoft Office application (e.g. Word, Power Point, etc.), select opaque.

- Options: If you have files or fonts linked to the image, you can include or embed them in the file. CMYK PostScript allows you to print RGB images from application programs that do not support RGB output. PostScript determines the PostScript version used to save the image.

- Transparency is available if you select an output for Illustrator version 9 or below. Transparency determines the outcome of transparent objects. **Preserve Paths** discards transparency effect and resets transparent objects to 100% opacity. **Preserve Appearance** keeps the original transparency appearance and flattens transparent areas in the image.

Save Images to the Clipboard

The Clipboard (copy and paste) can be used to transfer parts of an image to another Adobe application such as Adobe Photoshop, Premiere, and others. If you are creating a path in Illustrator, you can copy the path to the Clipboard and save its properties because the paths can be copied as PostScript language descriptions.

When you want to copy something from Illustrator, first set the Files and Clipboard Preferences by selecting **Edit ⇨ Preferences ⇨ Files & Clipboard**. When you copy an object to the Clipboard, it is copied in PICT format. Depending on the option you choose, PDF or AICB (an Adobe format that is similar to EPS), the object can be pasted into another Adobe application.

- Selecting PDF preserves transparency and blending modes for Photoshop and InDesign.

- AICB does not preserve transparency but you can choose to preserve the path or the appearance of the object.

Character Sets & Utilities

Key Caps *(Macintosh Only)*

What Is It?

The Key Caps feature is an application installed with your Mac OS System. It allows you to determine the location of all characters in any typeface currently loaded on your computer. It resides in the Apple menu.

How to Use Key Caps

Pull down the Apple menu and highlight Key Caps to display the dialog box on the screen (Figure B.1).

1. Click on the Key Caps menu (across the top of the screen) and a menu will display showing all the typefaces currently loaded on your computer.

2. Select the typeface for which you want to determine the location of a character. That font will load into the Key Caps dialog box.

3. Press ⇧, or ⌥, or ⇧ ⌥ to display the characters available with each of those selections.

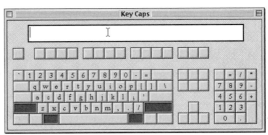

FIGURE B.1 Key Caps dialog box.

4. Press the key displaying the character you want. That character will then display in the dialog box window.

5. You can copy (⌘c) the character and paste (⌘p) it into your document. The character will be pasted in the typeface currently selected in your document (but it tells you which character it is). Highlight it and change the typeface to the one you selected in Key Caps.

Macintosh Standard Character Set

	`	1	2	3	4	5	6	7	8	9	0	-	=
Unshift	`	1	2	3	4	5	6	7	8	9	0	-	=
Shift	~	!	@	#	$	%	^	&	*	(	)	_	+
Option	`	¡	™	£	¢	∞	§	¶	•	a	o	–	≠
Shift Option	`	/	¤	‹	›	fi	fl	‡	°	·		,	—	±
KEY	`	1	2	3	4	5	6	7	8	9	0	-	=

	a	b	c	d	e	f	g	h	i	j	k	l	m
Unshift	a	b	c	d	e	f	g	h	i	j	k	l	m
Shift	A	B	C	D	E	F	G	H	I	J	K	L	M
Option	å	∫	ç	∂	´	ƒ	©	˙	^	Δ	°	¬	µ
Shift Option	Å	ı	Ç	Î	´	Ï	˝	Ó	ˆ	Ô		Ò	Â
KEY	A	B	C	D	E	F	G	H	I	J	K	L	M

	n	o	p	q	r	s	t	u	v	w	x	y	z
Unshift	n	o	p	q	r	s	t	u	v	w	x	y	z
Shift	N	O	P	Q	R	S	T	U	V	W	X	Y	Z
Option	~	ø	π	œ	®	ß	†	¨	√	Σ	≈	¥	Ω
Shift Option	~	Ø	∏	Œ	‰	Í	ˇ	¨	◊	„	‚	Á	˛
KEY	N	O	P	Q	R	S	T	U	V	W	X	Y	Z

	[	]	\	;	'	,	.	/
Unshift	[	]	\	;	'	,	.	/
Shift	{	}	|	:	"	<	>	?
Option	"	'	«	…	æ	≤	≥	÷
Shift Option	"	'	»	Ú	Æ	¯	˘	¿
KEY	[	]	\	;	'	,	.	/

Zapf Dingbats — Macintosh

Unshift	❁	☞	➔	✓	✔	✗	✘	✕	✖	✚	✎	✍	†
Shift	〞	✂	✠	✄	✀	☎	✿	✆	☛	✈	✉	❀	☞
Option	❁	②	♥	⚬	⚫	⑤	♥	❧	☞	❻	❼	❼	②
Shift Option	❁	➚	→	➜	→	➡	➥	➦	ℊ	➡	➢	❽	❻
KEY	`	1	2	3	4	5	6	7	8	9	0	-	=
Unshift	❁	✺	✳	❄	❅	❆	✳	✴	✳	✻	✽	●	◯
Shift	✡	✛	✜	✢	✣	✦	✧	★	☆	✪	✫	✬	✯
Option	{	❺	}	❶	♠	⑤	♦	➘	➹	⑦	➙	③	❿
Shift Option	)	➛	(	⇦	♠	⇨	➤	⇨	➹	⇨		⇨	➡
KEY	A	B	C	D	E	F	G	H	I	J	K	L	M
Unshift	◼	❑	❐	❏	❒	▲	▼	◆	❖	◗	│	❘	❙
Shift	✩	✮	✫	✱	✲	✳	✴	✵	✶	✷	✸	✹	✺
Option	➴	❿	❹	❻	♣	❧		①	④	❷	⑥	⑨	❽
Shift Option	➴	④	❸	❺	➤	⇨		①	↕	➢	⇒	❙	➤
KEY	N	O	P	Q	R	S	T	U	V	W	X	Y	Z
Unshift	✳	✴	✳	✚	❂	✌	✎	✏					
Shift	❛	❝	❜	✚	✄	✜	✝	✞					
Option	❾	→	⑧	❿	❾	⑦	⑧	↔					
Shift Option	❿	→	⑨	⮌	③	➤	➹	①					
KEY	[	]	\	;	'	,	.	/					

Appendix B — CHARACTER SETS & UTILITIES

Symbol — Macintosh

	`	1	2	3	4	5	6	7	8	9	0	-	=
Unshift	‾	1	2	3	4	5	6	7	8	9	0	–	=
Shift	~	!	≅	#	∃	%	⊥	&	*	(	)	_	+
Option	‾	ℑ	♠	≤	′	°	/	f	∞	≈	…	∠	↑
Shift Option	‾	∨	⇔	⇐	⇑	⇒	⇓	◊	ϒ	〈	®	∇	±
KEY	`	1	2	3	4	5	6	7	8	9	0	-	=

	A	B	C	D	E	F	G	H	I	J	K	L	M
Unshift	α	β	χ	δ	ε	φ	γ	η	ι	φ	κ	λ	μ
Shift	Α	Β	Χ	Δ	Ε	Φ	Γ	Η	Ι	ϑ	Κ	Λ	Μ
Option		≡		∂	↔	⊗	♥		∣	⟩	∅	⌋	ℜ	∝
Shift Option		∫		⌊	↔	⌈	{	⌊	⟩	∣			〉	Σ
KEY	A	B	C	D	E	F	G	H	I	J	K	L	M

	N	O	P	Q	R	S	T	U	V	W	X	Y	Z
Unshift	ν	ο	π	θ	ρ	σ	τ	υ	ϖ	ω	ξ	ψ	ζ
Shift	Ν	Ο	Π	Θ	Ρ	Σ	Τ	Υ	ς	Ω	Ξ	Ψ	Ζ
Option	∣	↵	≠	∉	♦	♣		←	℘	•	⊕	×	∣
Shift Option	∣	↓	÷	∈	™	∣		←	·	©	⌡	∣	∣
KEY	N	O	P	Q	R	S	T	U	V	W	X	Y	Z

	[	]	\	;	'	,	.	/
Unshift	[	]	∴	;	∍	,	.	/
Shift	{	}	∣	:	∀	<	>	?
Option	®	™	∩	⊃	—	″	≥	√
Shift Option	©	∏	∪	∫	→	⌉	⌉	ℵ
KEY	[	]	\	;	'	,	.	/

Wingdings — Macintosh

	`	1	2	3	4	5	6	7	8	9	0	-	=
Unshift	♊	📁	📄	📄	📑	▯	⌛	⌨	🖱	🖲	📁	📫	💾
Shift	”	✎	✐	✂	✁	🔔	♈	📖	✉	☎	☏	♉	⌷
Option	♊	🕐	✦	◉	◯	⊕	⊙	◯	◎	🕙	🕚	♋	✳
Shift Option	♊	▽	◖	◗	◓	◒	←	→	◯	↑	↓	♌	⊕
KEY	`	1	2	3	4	5	6	7	8	9	0	-	=

	A	B	C	D	E	F	G	H	I	J	K	L	M
Unshift	♋	♌	♍	♎	♏	♐	♑	♒	♓	℞	&	●	○
Shift	✌	👌	👍	👎	☜	☞	👆	👇	✋	☺	😐	☹	💣
Option	❶	🕐	❷	☆	★	⤵	▲	▫	⬈	⬊	✘	🕑	✪
Shift Option	①	⬃	②	◤	★	⬈	⊠	⬂	⬀	⬅	⇨	⇧	⬋
KEY	A	B	C	D	E	F	G	H	I	J	K	L	M

	N	O	P	Q	R	S	T	U	V	W	X	Y	Z
Unshift	■	□	□	□	▢	♦	◆	◆	❖	◆	⊠	△	⌘
Shift	☠	⚐	⚑	✈	☼	⬤	❄	✝	✞	☥	✠	✡	☾
Option	⬀	🕓	🕕	♋	□	◾	·	★	⬃	🕖	⬅	◈	🕘
Shift Option	⬀	✳	🕗	♋	⬈	↓	⊞	★	◄	◤	☑	←	✓
KEY	N	O	P	Q	R	S	T	U	V	W	X	Y	Z

	[	]	\	;	'	,	.	/
Unshift	☯	☸	ॐ	▭	♋	📪	📫	📬
Shift	❀	"	✿	💻	♋	💾	💿	✍
Option	♋	♋	⬑	⬐	🕙	✧	⌑	⌧
Shift Option	♋	⊠	⬏	⬇	✴	⬂	▫	🕙
KEY	[	]	\	;	'	,	.	/

Character Map (Windows Only)

The Windows utility for entering special characters into text in a document can be found in System Tools in the Accessories menu. To add a special character:

1. Display the **Character Map** (**Start** ⇨ **Programs** ⇨ **Accessories** ⇨ **System Tools** ⇨ **Character Map**).

2. Find the font you're using in the Font pop-up menu in the dialog box and select it.

3. Locate the special character you need in the table of characters.

4. Click in the box containing the character you want; click the Select button to place it in the Characters to copy field.

   or

   To place the character in the Characters to copy field, double-click in the box containing the character you want; click the Copy button.

5. Return to your document and Paste (⌘v) the character where you want it.

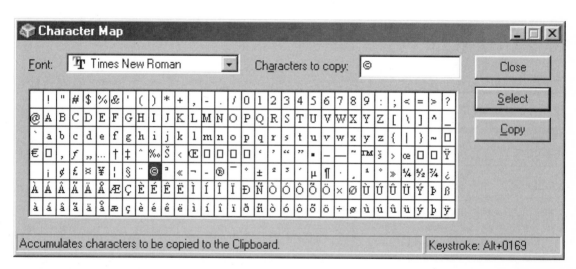

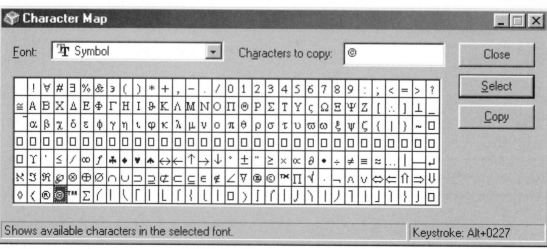

Windows ANSI Code Set

Numerical Code	Times New Roman	Symbol	Wingdings
0001–0007	No characters		
0008	backspace	backspace	
0009	tab	tab	tab
0010–0012	No characters		
0013	return	return	
0014–0031	No characters		
0032	space	space	
0033	!	!	
0034	”		❾
0035	#	#	
0036	$	∃	
0037	%	%	
0038	&	&	
0039	'		❼
0040	(	(	☎
0041	)	)	
0042	*	*	✉
0043	+	+	
0044	,	,	
0045	-	—	
0046	.	.	
0047	/	/	
0048	0	0	
0049	1	1	
0050	2	2	
0051	3	3	
0052	4	4	
0053	5	5	
0054	6	6	⌛
0055	7	7	

Numerical Code	Times New Roman	Symbol	Wingdings
0056	8	8	
0057	9	9	
0058	:	:	
0059	;	;	
0060	<	<	
0061	=	=	
0062	>	>	
0063	?	?	
0064	@	≅	
0065	A	A	
0066	B	B	
0067	C	X	
0068	D	Δ	
0069	E	E	
0070	F	Φ	
0071	G	Γ	
0072	H	H	
0073	I	I	
0074	J	ϑ	☺
0075	K	K	
0076	L	Λ	☹
0077	M	M	
0078	N	N	☠
0079	O	O	
0080	P	Π	
0081	Q	Θ	✈
0082	R	P	☼
0083	S	Σ	
0084	T	T	❄
0085	U	Y	✚

Numerical Code	Times New Roman	Symbol	Wingdings
0086	V	ς	✝
0087	W	Ω	✠
0088	X	Ξ	✶
0089	Y	Ψ	✡
0090	Z	Z	☪
0091	[	[	☯
0092	\	∴	ॐ
0093	]	]	☸
0094	^	⊥	♈
0095	_	_	♉
0096	`		♊
0097	a	α	♋
0098	b	β	♌
0099	c	χ	♍
0100	d	δ	♎
0101	e	ε	♏
0102	f	φ	♐
0103	g	γ	♑
0104	h	η	♒
0105	i	ι	♓
0106	j	φ	er
0107	k	κ	&;
0108	l	λ	●
0109	m	μ	○
0110	n	ν	■
0111	o	o	□
0112	p	π	□
0113	q	θ	□
0114	r	ρ	□
0115	s	σ	◆
0116	t	τ	◆
0117	u	υ	◆

Numerical Code	Times New Roman	Symbol	Wingdings
0118	v	ϖ	❖
0119	w	ω	◆
0120	x	ξ	⊠
0121	y	ψ	▢
0122	z	ζ	⌘
0123	{	{	❀
0124	|	|	✿
0125	}	}	"
0126	~	~	"
0127	delete		
0128	€		⓪
0129			①
0130	,		②
0131	f		③
0132	„		④
0133	…		⑤
0134	†		⑥
0135	‡		⑦
0136	^		⑧
0137	‰		⑨
0138	š		⑩
0139	‹		❶
0140	Œ		❶
0141			❷
0142			❸
0143			❹
0144			❺
0145	'		❻
0146	'		❼
0147	"		❽
0148	"		❾
0149	•		❿

Numerical Code	Times New Roman	Symbol	Wingdings
0150	–		
0151	—		
0152	~		
0153	TM		
0154	š		
0155	›		
0156	œ		
0157			
0158			•
0159	Ÿ		●
0160	en space		
0161	¡	Υ	○
0162	¢	′	
0163	£	$\leq$	
0164	¤	/	
0165	¥	∞	
0166	¦	f	
0167	§	♣	
0168	¨	♦	
0169	©	♥	
0170	ª	♠	
0171	«	$\leftrightarrow$	
0172	¬	$\leftarrow$	
0173	-	$\uparrow$	
0174	®	$\rightarrow$	
0175	¯	$\downarrow$	
0176	°	°	
0177	±	±	
0178	²	″	
0179	³	$\geq$	
0180	è	×	
0181	µ	$\propto$	

Numerical Code	Times New Roman	Symbol	Wingdings
0182	¶	∂	☆
0183	·	•	
0184	¸	$\div$	
0185	¹	$\neq$	
0186	º	$\equiv$	
0187	»	$\approx$	
0188	¼	…	
0189	½	$\mid$	
0190	¾	—	
0191	¿	$\hookleftarrow$	
0192	À	$\aleph$	
0193	Á	$\Im$	
0194	Â	$\Re$	
0195	Ã	$\wp$	
0196	Ä	$\otimes$	
0197	Å	$\oplus$	
0198	Æ	$\varnothing$	
0199	Ç	$\cap$	
0200	È	$\cup$	
0201	É	$\supset$	
0202	Ê	$\supseteq$	
0203	Ë	$\not\subset$	
0204	Ì	$\subset$	
0205	Í	$\subseteq$	
0206	Î	$\in$	
0207	Ï	$\notin$	
0208	Ð	$\angle$	
0209	Ñ	∇	
0210	Ò	®	
0211	Ó	©	
0212	Ô	TM	
0213	Õ	Π	

Numerical Code	Times New Roman	Symbol	Wingdings
0214	Ö	√	⊠
0215	×	·	◄
0216	Ø	¬	►
0217	Ù	∧	▲
0218	Ú	∨	▼
0219	Û	⇔	☊
0220	Ü	⇐	☋
0221	Ý	⇑	☊
0222	þ	⇒	☋
0223	ß	⇓	←
0224	à	◊	→
0225	á	⟨	↑
0226	â	®	↓
0227	ã	©	↖
0228	ä	™	↗
0229	å	Σ	↙
0230	æ	⌠	↘
0231	ç	⎮	←
0232	è	⌡	→
0233	é	⌈	↑
0234	ê	⎮	↓

Numerical Code	Times New Roman	Symbol	Wingdings
0235	ë	⌊	↖
0236	ì	⌈	↗
0237	í	{	↙
0238	î	⌊	↘
0239	ï	⎮	⇐
0240	∂		⇒
0241	ñ	⟩	⇑
0242	ò	∫	⇓
0243	ó	⌠	⇔
0244	ô	⎮	⇕
0245	õ	⌡	↘
0246	ö	)	↗
0247	÷	⎮	↗
0248	ø	)	↘
0249	ù	⌉	□
0250	ú	⎮	□
0251	û	⌋	✗
0252	ü	)	✓
0253	ý	}	☒
0254	þ	⌋	☑
0255	ÿ		⊞

Glossary

A

Acrobat Reader Application required to view PDF files.

Action Series of recorded menu commands, tool functions, selections, etc. When an action is played, tasks recorded in the action sequence are performed for you.

Additive color Colors projected by a light source. A combination of all additive colors is seen as white. The more you add intensity to the three primary colors (red, green, blue), the lighter the resulting color becomes.

Alignment In text, the positioning of lines of type — left, right, centered, or justified.

Anchor point Corner point or smooth point that connects two segments of a path.

Anti-aliasing Blends the edge of a darker object with that of its background, which smooths the transition between the colors or shapes.

Appearance attributes Any attribute, other than the basic fill and stroke attributes, that can be applied to objects, layers, or groups.

Arc Curved segment.

Area text Type in Illustrator that is enclosed in a text container. Any vector object can be used as a text container.

Artboard Area upon which an illustration is created, outlined onscreen by a black rectangle.

Ascender That part of a lowercase letter that extends above the x-height of the character — b, d, f, h, k, and l.

Artwork window Window that displays when a new document is created or opened.

B

Banding Visible changes from one color to another onscreen or in print that disrupts smooth transition from one color to another.

Baseline An imaginary line along the bottom of most letters and numbers; for example, lowercase g, j, p, q, and y in most fonts drop below the baseline.

Baseline shift In typography, the term for the movement of type characters above or below the baseline.

Bézier path Mathematically-defined path consisting of anchor points and line segments.

Bilevel image 1-bit image; consists only of black and white pixels.

Bit depth In a bitmap image, the number of color or shades of color in each pixel.

Bitmap (1) When referring to color, images that consist of only black and white pixels; 1-bit color. (2) raster image consisting of pixels.

Bleed Any portion of an image that extends beyond the crop marks. Most commercial printers require a minimum bleed distance of $\frac{1}{8}$".

Blend Combining two or more objects smoothly.

Bold Thicker, heavier version of characters in a font family.

Bounding box Non-printing box surrounding selected items with handles that can be used to manipulate the objects.

Brightness Intensity of hue determined by how much black is added to a color.

Brushstroke Path drawn by the Paintbrush tool or a path to which a calligraphic, scatter, art, or pattern brush has been applied.

Butt cap Blunt end of a path to which a stroke has been applied that stops even with the endpoint.

C

Cap height Height of most capital letters in a font, measured from the baseline to the top of a capital letter; varies with each font.

Category axis That part of a graph that displays *what* is being graphed.

Center point Non-editable point that appears in the center of a vector object. It can be displayed or hidden using commands in the Attributes palette.

Character Individual letter, number, or symbol.

Choke In *trapping*, to extend the surrounding light color onto an enclosed dark color.

Clicking Pressing and releasing the mouse button quickly.

Click and drag Pressing the mouse button and, without releasing, moving the mouse. Release the mouse when the move is complete.

Clipboard Temporary storage area in the computer's memory.

Clipping mask Object or group of objects that hides other objects outside its boundaries so only object inside its borders are visible.

Clipping path Path used to create a clipping mask.

Closed path Path with no beginning and no end, such as a circle or square.

Cluster In graphing, a group of bars that correspond to a single row of data in the Graph Data window.

CMYK Cyan (C), magenta (M), yellow (Y), black (K). The four process colors used in commercial printing.

Color model A specific, defined color space, such as CMYK, RGB, or HSB.

Color separations Process wherein each color in a document is divided into its own plate, with each plate containing varying tones of that color.

Color space Range of colors that can be displayed or printed; color gamut.

Color stop Point in a gradient at which a new color is introduced.

Color swatch Small thumbnails (square) filled with color stored in the Swatches palette.

Combination point Anchor point that has the attributes of both a smooth point and a corner point.

Compound path Two or more objects combined into a single object with transparent sections where objects overlap.

Composite (in printing) Printed page with all colors in the document visible.

Compound path two or more overlapping individual paths that have transparent interior spaces, such as a doughnut.

Compression Compaction of file information to reduce file size.

Concentric Circles having a common center point, as in a target.

Constrain Restrict.

Context-sensitive menus Temporary menu containing commonly-used options pertaining to the document or to a selection in the document.

Corner point Anchor point that connects straight segments.

Corner radius Amount of curve at the corners of a rounded rectangle.

Crop marks Marks or lines indicating where a document is to be trimmed to its final size and shape.

Cursor Icon (pointer) on your screen indicating the position of your mouse.

Custom startup file File created by the user that contains custom settings, and custom swatches, styles, symbols, and so on.

D

Dash Visible portion of a stroke.

Decay value In a spiral, tightening of the coil.

Descender That part of a lowercase letter that extends below the baseline, such as g, j, q, and y.

Dingbats/wingdings Special characters, usually decorative.

Direction point Point at the end of a direction handle attached to smooth anchor points that can be manipulated to determine the shape of a curved segment of a path.

Direction handle Attached to smooth points that you can manipulate to control the shape of a curved segment of a path.

Display font Typeface designed for use at large sizes.

Dithering Process that mixes two colors together to simulate a third color that's somewhere between the original two colors.

Docking Hooking two or more palettes together.

Dots per inch (dpi) Refers to the resolution of an output device; the number of dots printed in one square inch.

Double-click Press and release the mouse button rapidly two times.

Downsampling The average color of the pixels in an area of the image is determined by Illustrator and those pixels are replaced by a larger single pixel of the average color.

Drag Click the mouse and move it, releasing when the move is complete.

Drag and drop Process of copying items between applications or open windows by dragging selected items from one to the other.

Drag copy Process of duplicating selected objects by holding down the ⌥ key while dragging, then releasing the mouse before releasing the ⌥ key.

Drop cap First letter of a paragraph that's set larger than the text and aligned at the top.

Duotone Image or illustration having only two colors.

E

Ellipsis Three periods in a row, indicating that one or more words are missing, usually from a quotation.

Em space In typography, standard unit of measure that's the square of it's point size. For example, an em space in 8 point type is 8 points wide.

Em dash Long dash; dash that's the width of an em space.

Endcap Shape of the end of a stroked path.

Endpoint Anchor point at the end of an open path.

EPS Encapsulated PostScript; standard cross-platform image format based on the PostScript printer language.

F

Fill Interior area of an open or closed path; it can be filled with a color or be transparent.

Filter Modification applied to paths that permanently change its shape or how it looks.

Filter effect Modification applied to paths that affects only the appearance of a path, without changing the underlying path, that can be edited or removed using the Appearance palette.

Font Typeface; set of letters, numbers, and standard symbols. Some fonts may contain only special characters.

G

Gamma Brightness of midtone values; gamma adjustment compensates for tonal reproduction of output devices such as computer monitors.

Gamut Range of colors that can be displayed or printed; color space. A color that's out of gamut is out of the color range available for that color model.

Gap Transparent part of a stroke.

Global process colors Process colors that can be adjusted by moving a single slider.

Glyph Special characters, such as arrows, bullets, and so on.

Gradient Gradual blending of two or more shades of the same color or two or more colors.

Graph Pictorial representation of data, usually numbers, that shows a relationship between two or more items using dots, lines, bars, and curves.

Graph data Information to be graphed.

Grayscale Various shades of black ink, normally expressed as 8-bit color, which results in 256 possible shades of gray.

Greeking Gray bars representing type that's too small to be displayed on the screen. The size at which type is greeked is controled in the Type & Auto Tracing Preferences dialog box.

Grid Nonprinting set of lines or dots that displays on your document like a piece of graph paper that you can use to measure and align objects.

Group Collection of objects can be selected and manipulated as a single object.

Group Selection tool Tool used for selecting groups.

Guides Nonprinting vertical and horizontal lines that are dragged from the horizontal and vertical rulers that can be used to align objects.

Gutter In type, the space between columns.

H

Halftone Gradation from light-to-dark or dark-to-light tones created by increasing or decreasing dot size and density. Some people interchange the terms *halftone* and *screen*.

Hanging indent All lines of a block of text are indented except the first one.

Hanging punctuation Punctuation that extends beyond the margin of a block of text.

Hinting (fonts) Information built in to most Type 1 fonts that allows type at small sizes to print correctly.

Hue Pure color.

I

Imageable area Portion of a document page that prints on the installed printer. Artwork that extends beyond the imageable area is clipped off and doesn't print.

Indent Line of text or block of text moved inward from the edge of the text block. Indent value is the distance text is moved.

Interlacing In Web browsers, the process of increasing resolution and detail of an image as it appears.

Italic Slanted version of a font, generally used for emphasis in body text.

J

Jaggies Visible pixels on the edge of a curve, creating a stair-step appearance.

Joins Intersection of two segments.

JPEG (Joint Photographic Experts Group) Compression program; most commonly used for image display on the Web.

Justification The left and right edges of a text block are aligned evenly.

K

Kerning Process of adding or removing spacing between two adjacent characters.

Keyset Group of keyboard shortcuts.

Knockout One color or object prints on top of another color, preventing the color or object on the bottom from printing.

L

Landscape Page orientation that is wider than it is tall.

Layers Independent, self-contained levels of the same artwork page.

Leading (pronounced *ledding*) In typography, space between lines of text, measured from baseline to baseline.

Letter spacing In type, space between adjacent characters.

Ligature The joining of two serif characters, such as fl or fi, into a single character.

Line screen Printing term referring to the number of dots per inch.

Linked file External raster file attached to an image in an Illustrator document.

Lpi (lines per inch) Refers to line screen frequency.

M

Misregistration Slight misalignment of colors on a printed page; may be caused by shifting of the printing plates, stretching of the paper.

Miter The extrusion of the stroke weight at a sharp change in direction.

Modifier keys Shift, ⌥, ⌘, and ⌃ keys on the keyboard.

Multiple Master PostScript Type 1 fonts developed by Adobe Systems that can be customized for size, weight, width, and style.

N

Nesting Files, folders, layers, etc., inside other files, folders, layers, etc.

Non-global process colors Process colors that can't be altered by moving a single slider.

Nudge Moving a selection using the arrow keys on the keyboard.

O

Object Any path or piece of artwork in an Illustrator document.

1-bit Raster image that contains only black and white pixels.

Opaque Nontransparent; dark; solid.

Opacity Degree of transparency or darkness, from 0% (transparent) to 100% (opaque, or maximum darkness).

Opacity mask Object in front of all other selected objects that produces a transparent shape on the selected objects behind it in the stacking order.

Open path Path that has two unconnected endpoints.

Optimization In web graphics, the process that manipulates file format, and colors used, to reduce the size of the file and speeding download time.

Out of gamut Color that cannot be reproduced in CMYK color space.

Outline format View of artwork paths with no attributes visible.

Overprinting One color prints on top of another color, which creates a third color.

P

Paste Command used to insert cut or copied objects into a document from the clipboard.

Pasteboard Scratch area of the artboard.

Path Vector object that determines the shape of objects. In finished artwork, paths can be visible (stroked) or invisible (unstroked). They can be closed (continuous) or open (unconnected).

Pattern, brush Design created in illustrator that can be applied to brushstrokes.

Pattern, fill Design created in illustrator that repeats over and over to fill a path.

Path type Text applied to an open path.

PDF (Portable Document File) Cross-platform file format.

Pentagon Five-sided object.

Pica In printing, one-sixth of an inch, or 12 points. Sometimes erroneously interchanged with em.

Pixel (Picture element). Colored square defining the color in an image. Bitmap images are made up of pixels.

Pixels per inch (ppi) Refers to the resolution of a bitmapped image; the number of pixels in one square inch of a bitmap image; sometimes expressed erroneously as dpi.

Pixelated Individual pixels are visible.

Place Importing an image or art into an Illustrator document by embedding or linking.

Plug-in Extension or addition that adds functionality to an application.

Point 1/72 of an inch.

Point of origin Point on an object or grouped objects from which calculations are made when using the Transform tools.

Point text In Illustrator, type attached to a single anchor point.

Point size Measurement of a character from its lowest descender to its highest ascender.

Polygon Shape having a specified number of sides of equal length with all sides an equal distance from the center of the shape.

Pop-up menus Many palettes and dialog boxes have pop-up menus. To access a pop-up menu, click the option that is showing, and additional choices are made available.

Portrait Orientation of a page that's taller than it is wide.

PostScript® Programming language developed by Adobe Systems for printing and page layout.

PPD (PostScript Printer Description) File that supplies all the variables for a PostScript printer or imagesetter.

Preflight Checking of all aspects of a document to ensure proper construction to avoid problems when printing.

Print area Image area of a page that prints on the installed output device, based on information in the current printer's PostScript Printer Description file (PPD).

Printer resolution Number of dots in a specified area, usually expressed in dots per inch (dpi).

Printer's marks Crop marks, trim marks, registration marks, and so on.

Process color Four standard colors of ink (cyan, magenta, yellow, and black) that are combined to reproduce the widest possible range of colors for printing.

Projecting cap End of a stroked path that extends beyond the endpoint.

R

Raster image Image made up of pixels.

Reflect Flip; create a mirror image.

Registration In printing, the alignment of printing plates to ensure that colors are placed exactly in relationship to each other.

Resolution In a bitmap image, the number of pixels in a specified distance, usually expressed as pixels per inch (ppi) and sometimes as dots per inch (dpi).

RGB (red, green, blue) Additive color mode.

RIP (Raster Image Processor) Hardware, and sometimes software, used to output files to an imagesetter or other output device.

Rotate Turn an object on an angle.

Round cap Shape of the end of a stroked path that is curved and extends beyond the end of the path half the width of the stroke.

Ruler Guide across the top and down the left side of an Illustrator document that you can turn on and off to aid in sizing and aligning objects.

Ruler guides Straight lines, either horizontal or vertical, solid or dotted, along which you can align paths.

Ruler origin Zero point of the rulers from which measurement is calculated.

S

Sample "Read" attributes of an object.

Saturation How much hue you see. The greater the saturation, the more intense the color.

Scale Resize, when referring to scaling an object. When referring to type, to increase or decrease the size of a font.

Scratch area Blank area on both sides of the artboard.

Script Series of commands, including commands in other programs, that you set up to tell your computer to perform specific functions.

Segment Straight or curved line between two anchor points.

Separations Individual color plates for printing.

Serif Typeface having tiny projections at the end of the stroke of a character.

Sans serif Typeface with no projections at the end of the strokes of a character.

Shear Skew; slant.

Small caps In type, smaller versions of the uppercase characters, usually used to substitute for lowercase letters.

Smart quotes Sometimes called *curly quotes*. Open quotes and closed quotes are different, the "tails" of both pointing toward the adjacent character.

Smooth point Anchor point connecting curved segments.

Snapping tolerance How close an object must be before it snaps to a guide, snaps to another object (smart guides), or snaps to a grid.

Spine In a blend, an imaginary line from the center point of the first object to the center point of the last object.

Spot color Premixed ink color; in multi-color printing, a spot color separates to its own plate.

Spread In trapping, the process of extending a light color into the surrounding dark color.

Stacking order Relationship of objects according to the order in which they're created, with the first object created at the back and subsequent objects in front of it.

Stray point Single anchor point without a segment attached to it.

Stroke Color or pattern applied to a path.

Stroke weight Thickness of the color or pattern applied to a path.

Styles In Illustrator, sets of multiple attributes that can be applied to objects, layers, or groups.

Sublayer Layer nested inside another layer.

Subtractive colors Opaque colors (cyan, magenta, yellow that filter out different colors of light (red, green, blue), so your eye sees what's left over.

Superscript characters Reduced-sized characters raised above the baseline.

Subscript Reduced-sized characters dropped below the baseline.

Swatch A small square containing a predefined color or pattern used for selecting a color that can be applied to a path.

T

Tabloid Standard size sheet of paper; 11" × 17".

Thumbnail Small representation of an image or object.

Tick mark Vertical or horizontal lines in a graph that separate categories or show units of measurement.

TIFF (Tagged Image File Format) Standard raster image file format.

Toggle Click on an option once to turn it on; click again to turn it off. Click once again to turn it back on, and so on.

Toolbox Palette containing all the tools in Illustrator.

Tracking In typography, the term for adding or removing space between a series of characters.

Transition steps In a blend, the objects that are created by Illustrator between the original object and the final object.

Transparency The ability to see through an object and see any objects stacked behind it; measured in percent of opacity and controlled through the Transparency palette.

Trapping The process of slightly overlapping adjacent colors to ensure that no unwanted white space appears between them because of misregistration on press.

Trim marks Crop marks.

Typeface Specific set of characters, numbers, and symbols designed to be used together; font.

U

Undo (⌘z) Reversing the application of a command or function as though it were never performed.

V

Value axis The part of a graph that displays the *value* of what is being graphed.

Vector objects Mathematically defined paths.

W

Web-safe colors Refers to the 216 colors that can be viewed accurately on both Windows and Macintosh computers using only the systems' native color palettes.

Word spacing Space between words.

X

x-Height Distance from the bottom of a font's lowercase x to its top.

Z

Zoom Screen magnification; enlarging or reducing the contents of an Illustrator document without affecting the actual size of the artwork.

Index

INDEX

INDEX

INDEX

Join two selected endpoints . . . . ⌘ j
Average two selected endpoints. . . . . ⌥ ⌘ j
Average and Join two selected endpoints. . . ⇧ ⌥ ⌘ j
Close path while drawing with Pencil
    or Paintbrush tool . . . . Drag, then ⌥-release
Cut in a straight line with Knife tool . . . . . ⌥-drag
Cut in 45° increment with
    Knife tool. . . . . ⇧ ⌥-drag

Restackng (keyboard)

Bring To Front . . . . ⇧ ⌘]
Send To Back . . . . ⇧ ⌘ [
Bring Forward . . . . ⌘]
Send Backward . . . . ⌘ [

Combine Paths

Compound Path ➪ Make . . . . ⌘ 8
Compound Path ➪ Release . . . . ⌥ ⌘ 8
Repeat last-used Pathfinder command . . . . ⌘ 4

Transform

Transform tool dialog/set origin (any
    transform tool except Free Transform) . ⌥-click
Transform object along multiple of 45°
    (Shear, Reflect, Rotate tool) . . . . ⇧-drag
Scale object uniformly (Scale, Free
    Transform tools). . . . . ⇧-drag
Transform Again. . . . . ⌘ d
Transform pattern fill, not object
    (any transform tool) . . . . ~ drag
Transform copy of object (any
    transform tool) . . . . Start dragging, then ⌥-drag
Transform copy of object (Transform
    palette) . . . . . . Change value, then press ⌥-Enter
Scale object uniformly (Transform
    palette) . . . Change W or H value, then p⌘ss -
    Enter
Transform Each dialog box . . . . ⇧ ⌥ ⌘ d

Warps

Envelope Distort ➪ Make with warp . . . . . ⌥ ⌘ w
Envelope Distort ➪ Make with mesh . . . . . ⌥ ⌘ m
Envelope Distort ➪ Make with top object . . ⌥ ⌘ c
Envelope Distort ➪ Edit contents . . . . ⇧ ⌘ v

Blends

Blend ➪ Make . . . . ⌥ ⌘ b
Blend ➪ Release. . . . . ⇧ ⌥ ⌘ b

Free Transform tool

Transform from center. . . . . ⌥-drag a handle
Distort . . Start dragging corner handle, then ⌘ -drag
Skew. . . . . Start dragging side handle, then ⌘ -drag
Make Perspective . . . . Start dragging corner handle,
    then ⇧ ⌥ ⌘ -drag

Grouping

Group . . . . ⌘ g
Ungroup . . . . ⇧ ⌘ g

Lock/unlock (keyboard)

Lock selection . . . . ⌘ 2
Lock all unselected objects . . . . ⇧ ⌥ ⌘ 2
Unlock all. . . . . ⌥ ⌘ 2

LAYERS PALETTE

Select

Select layer, sublayer, group,
    or object . . . . Click selection square
                       or ⌥-click name
Add to selection. . . . . ⇧-click selection square
Copy selection to new layer,
    sublayer, group . . . . ⌥-drag selection square

Views

Hide/show all other layers . . . . ⌥-click 👁
View a layer in Outline/Preview view . . ⌘-click 👁
View all other layers in
    Outline/Preview view . . . . ⌥ ⌘-click 👁
Lock/unlock all other
    layers . . . . . ⌥-click blank box in second column

Create top-level layers

Create layer above currently selected layer . . ⌘ l (el)
Create layer at top of list . ⌘-click New Layer button
Create layer below currently
    selected layer- . . . . . ⌥ ⌘-click New Layer button

TYPE

Hard Return . . . . Enter
Soft Return . . . . ⇧-Enter
Highlight font field on Character palette . ⇧ ⌥ ⌘ m
Discretionary hyphen . . . . ⇧ ⌘ - (hyphen)
Create Outlines . . . . ⇧ ⌘ o

Type tools

Use Area Type tool (Type tool selected,
    over open path) . . . . ⌥
Use Path Type tool (Type tool selected,
    over closed path) . . . . ⌥
Switch to vertical/horizontal
    type tool . . . . ⇧ with any type tool
Switch to Type tool when selecting
    type block . . . . Double-click with any selection tool

Selecting type

Select a word . . . . Double-click word
Select a paragraph . . . . Triple-click word
Select all the type in a block . . . . ⌘ a
Move insertion pointer left/right one word ⌘ ←, →
Select next character. ⇧→

Select previous character . . . . ⇧←
Select next line . . . . ⇧↓
Select previous line . . . . ⇧↑
Select next word . . . . ⇧⌘→
Select previous word . . . . ⇧⌘←
Select next paragraph . . . . ⇧⌘↓
Select previous paragraph . . . . ⇧⌘↑

Alignment

Align left . . . . ⇧⌘l (el)
Align center . . . . ⇧⌘c
Align right . . . . ⇧⌘r
Justify . . . . ⇧⌘j
Force-justify last line . . . . ⇧⌘f

Point size

Increase point size . . . . ⇧⌘>
Decrease point size . . . . ⇧⌘<

Leading

Increase leading . . . . ⌥↓
Decrease leading . . . . ⌥↑
Set leading to the same as current
  font size . . . . Double-click leading button
                               on Character palette (A/IA)

Horizontal scale

Reset horizontal scale to 100% . . . . ⇧⌘x

Kerning/tracking

Increase kerning/tracking (spread) . . . . ⌥→
Decrease kerning/tracking (squeeze) . . . . ⌥←
Increase kerning/tracking 5x (spread) . . . . ⌥⌘→
Decrease kerning/tracking 5x (squeeze) . . . . . . ⌥⌘←
Reset kerning/tracking to 0 . . . . ⇧⌘q

Baseline

Increase baseline . . . . ⇧⌥↑
Decrease baseline . . . . ⇧⌥↓
Increase baseline 5x . . . . ⇧⌥⌘↑
Decrease baseline 5x . . . . ⇧⌥⌘↓

Curly quotes —	Mac	Windows
' Open single quote	⌥]	⌥-0145
' Apostrophe (close single quote)	⇧⌥]	⌥-0146
" Open double quote	⌥[	⌥-0147
" Close double quote	⇧⌥[	⌥-0148

MESH

Reapply last-used gradient . . . . (period)
Reset gradient palette
  to black and white . . . . ⌘-click thumbnail
Duplicate color stop . . . . ⌥-drag
Apply swatch color to active
  color stop . . . . ⌥-click swatch

Move mesh point along one
  of its lines . . . . ⇧-drag with Mesh tool
Add mesh point using adjacent
  mesh color . . . . ⇧-click with Mesh tool
Remove mesh point . . . . ⌥-click with Mesh tool

CLIPPING MASKS

Clipping Mask ⇨ Make . . . . ⌘7
Clipping Mask ⇨ Release . . . . ⌥⌘7

EFFECTS

Apply Last Effect . . . . ⇧⌘e
Last Effect (reopen last effect dialog box) . . . . ⇧⌥⌘e

FILTERS

Apply Last Filter . . . . ⌘e
Last Filter (reopen last filter dialog box) . . . . . . ⌥⌘e

APPEARANCES

Add new fill . . . . ⌘/
Add new stroke . . . . ⌥⌘/
Sample style and append appearance
  of selected object . . . . . . ⇧⌥-click with Eyedropper

RULERS/GRIDS/GUIDES

Show/Hide Rulers . . . . ⌘r
Show/Hide Guides . . . . ⌘;
Make Guides . . . . ⌘5
Release Guides . . . . Click selection square
                        on Layers palette, ⌘⌥-5
Release a guide . . . . ⇧⌘5
Convert guide between horizontal/vertical
  orientation . . . . ⌥-drag new guide
Lock/Unlock Guides . . . . ⌥⌘;
Show/Hide Grid . . . . ⌘"
SnapTo Grid . . . . ⇧⌘"
Snap To Point (Pixel Preview off);
  Snap To Pixel (Pixel Preview on) . . . . ⌥⌘"
Smart Guides . . . . ⌘u
Constrain Measure tool
  to multiple of 45° . . . . ⇧-drag with tool

PRINT/EXPORT

Page Setup/Print Setup dialog box . . . . ⇧⌘p
Print dialog box . . . . ⌘p
Save for Web . . . . ⇧⌥⌘s

MISCELLANEOUS

General Preferences dialog box . . . . ⌘k
Keyboard Shortcuts dialog box . . . . ⇧⌥⌘k